BIOLA BOOKSTORE
LA MIRADA, CAL

NORMAL FAMILY PROCESSES
BY WALSH 0898620511
LIST PRICE: $26.95
YOU PAY: $26.95

Walsh

AUTHOR

Normal Family
Processes

TITLE

| DATE DUE | BORROWER'S NAME |
|----------|-----------------|
|          |                 |
|          |                 |
|          |                 |
|          |                 |
|          |                 |
|          |                 |
|          |                 |
|          |                 |
|          |                 |
|          |                 |
|          |                 |
|          |                 |
|          |                 |
|          |                 |

# NORMAL FAMILY PROCESSES

# NORMAL FAMILY PROCESSES

EDITED BY

**FROMA WALSH**

Center for Family Studies/
The Family Institute of Chicago
Northwestern University Medical School

FOREWORD BY ROY R. GRINKER, SR.

**THE GUILFORD PRESS**

New York    London

©1982 The Guilford Press, New York
A Division of Guilford Publications, Inc.
200 Park Avenue South, New York, N.Y. 10003

Printed in the United States of America

*Fourth printing, April 1984*

LIBRARY OF CONGRESS CATALOGING IN PUBLICATION DATA
Main entry under title:

Normal family processes.

(The Guilford family therapy series)
Includes bibliographies and indexes.
1. Family research. I. Walsh, Froma.
II. Series.
HQ728.N83      306.8      81-7197
ISBN 0-89862-051-1      AACR2

This book is dedicated
to
**GREGORY BATESON**
for his appreciation of the patterns which connect.

# CONTRIBUTORS

Manhal Al-Khayyal, PhD, Department of Psychiatry, University of Rochester, Rochester, New York

Carol Anderson, PhD, Department of Psychiatry, School of Medicine, University of Pittsburgh, Pittsburgh, Pennsylvania

Lawrence M. Baldwin, PhD, Butler Hospital and Section of Psychiatry and Human Behavior, Brown University, Providence, Rhode Island

W. Robert Beavers, MD, Clinical Faculty, Department of Psychiatry, University of Texas Health Science Center, Dallas, Texas

Duane S. Bishop, MD, Butler Hospital and Section of Psychiatry and Human Behavior, Brown University, Providence, Rhode Island

Elizabeth A. Carter, ACSW, Faculty, Family Institute of Westchester

Bertram J. Cohler, PhD, The Committee on Human Development, The Department of Behavioral Sciences, The University of Chicago, Chicago, Illinois

Nathan B. Epstein, MD, Butler Hospital and Section of Psychiatry and Human Behavior, Brown University, Providence, Rhode Island

Larry B. Feldman, MD, Center for Family Studies/The Family Institute of Chicago, Institute of Psychiatry, Northwestern Memorial Hospital and Northwestern University Medical School, Chicago, Illinois

Scott Geyer, MA, The Committee on Human Development, The Department of Behavioral Sciences, The University of Chicago, Chicago, Illinois

Jean Goldsmith, PhD, Center for Family Studies/The Family Institute of Chicago, Institute of Psychiatry, Northwestern Memorial Hospital and Northwestern University Medical School, Chicago, Illinois

Tamara K. Hareven, PhD, Department of History, Clark University, Worcester, Massachusetts, and Center for Population Studies, Harvard University, Cambridge, Massachusetts

James E. Jones, PhD, Department of Psychiatry, University of Rochester, Rochester, New York

Monica McGoldrick, ACSW, Family Training, College of Medicine and Dentistry of New Jersey–Rutgers Medical School, Community Mental Health Center, Piscataway, New Jersey, and Faculty, Family Institute of Westchester

Jill Metcoff, MA, Consultant in Videotape Observation and Intervention in Family Interaction, Chicago, Illinois

Braulio Montalvo, MA, Philadelphia Child Guidance Clinic, Philadelphia, Pennsylvania; Bryn Mawr College, Graduate School of Social Research and Social Work, Bryn Mawr, Pennsylvania; and Aspira Research Project, Philadelphia, Pennsylvania

Mary Ellen Oliveri, PhD, Center for Family Research and Department of Psychiatry and Behavioral Sciences, George Washington University School of Medicine, Washington, D.C.

Betty B. Paul, ACSW, Social Work Staff, Arlington, Massachusetts, Public Schools; Wheelock College Center for Parenting Studies, Boston, Massachusetts; New England Center for the Study of the Family, Newton, Massachusetts; and private practice of family therapy

Norman L. Paul, MD, Department of Neurology, Boston University School of Medicine, Boston, Massachusetts; Department of Psychiatry, Harvard Medical School, Boston, Massachusetts; and New England Center for the Study of the Family, Newton, Massachusetts

David Reiss, MD, Center for Family Research and Department of Psychiatry and Behavioral Sciences, George Washington School of Medicine, Washington, D.C.

Jules Riskin, MD, Mental Research Institute, Palo Alto, California

John Schwartzman, PhD, Center for Family Studies/The Family Institute of Chicago, Institute of Psychiatry, Northwestern Memorial Hospital and Northwestern University Medical School, Chicago, Illinois

Emily B. Visher, PhD, Stepfamily Association of America, Inc., and private practice, Palo Alto, California

John S. Visher, MD, Clinical Faculty, Department of Psychiatry, Stanford University, Stanford, California, and Adult Services, San Mateo County Mental Health Services, Daly City, California

Froma Walsh, PhD, Center for Family Studies/The Family Institute of Chicago, Institute of Psychiatry, Northwestern Memorial Hospital and Northwestern University Medical School, Chicago, Illinois

Carl A. Whitaker, MD, Department of Psychiatry, University of Wisconsin Medical School, Madison, Wisconsin

Lyman C. Wynne, MD, PhD, Department of Psychiatry, University of Rochester, Rochester, New York

# ACKNOWLEDGMENTS

I would like to express my deep appreciation to Mary Zaglifa for her able editorial assistance in the preparation of this volume. I am grateful also to Alan Gurman and to my colleagues at the Family Institute of Chicago for their ideas and comments. Thanks are also due to our librarian, Berenice O'Brien, for her helpfulness in my review of the literature, and to Guy Whitney for his support and encouragement. Finally, I am grateful to the "normal" families who participated in my research for sensitizing me to the richness and complexity of normal family processes.

FW

# FOREWORD

Froma Walsh and her collaborators have made a unique contribution to the clinical literature in directing attention to the normal transactional processes in well-functioning family systems. This volume's orientation to normality from a systems perspective represents an important conceptual shift from psychiatry's traditional focus on mental illness and the individual, rooted in the medical model.

In the past three decades, profound changes have taken place in the field of psychiatry, with the development of the mental health movement and conceptualizations of normality and health. It has become increasingly clear that "normal" and "abnormal" are not discrete entities, that both are value systems within our unfixed surround, and that they represent a wide range of functioning and dysfunction. With the application of general systems theory to human systems has come an appreciation of mankind as a biopsychosocial system composed of several smaller systems, all regulated and interrelated.

We are moving toward a unified concept of behavior, recognizing that variables from biological, psychological, and social fields all contribute to human functioning over time. The family system plays a central mediating role in transaction with all other parts of the human system and in their integration through family coping processes. This volume makes a valuable contribution to our knowledge in identifying critical variables and dimensions in the coping processes of normal families.

This is the first volume designed to acquaint mental health professionals with major conceptualizations of and research on normal family processes. It is imperative for clinicians, regardless of their particular discipline or treatment orientation, to become more knowledgeable about the functioning of normal families and to consider ramifications for clinical theory and practice.

The volume is well organized to provide a broad overview of normal family processes. Walsh has clearly delineated important issues for consideration. She has invited distinguished authors who are at the forefront of conceptualization and investigation to address specific aspects of normal family functioning and to present various points of view on the subject. This volume represents the state of the art and does so admirably.

Roy R. Grinker, Sr., MD

# PREFACE

This volume is an inquiry into the processes that characterize normal family functioning. Leading theorists and investigators present current conceptualizations of and research on normal family processes. This inquiry is grounded in a family systems orientation, examining the family as an interactional unit that operates in social and temporal contexts.

In addressing normal family processes, the book meets a pressing need in the clinical literature and clinical training programs. The mental health profession, in its concentration on psychopathology, has given insufficient attention to normality. Although important developments in family systems theory and family therapy have taken place, clinical emphasis has been primarily on dysfunctional family patterns. At the same time, assumptions about normal families explicitly and implicitly influence clinical assessment, treatment goals, therapeutic approaches, and research instruments. Where knowledge about normal family processes is limited, inferences tend to be derived from pathology-based models, prevalent social norms, and personal family experience. Moreover, concepts of "normality" and "health" are often confounded, and myths of "the normal family" abound.

The need to develop models for family coping and competence is especially urgent at the present time of social and economic upheaval in our society. Questions about the breakdown of the family are raised as families are undergoing transformations in structure, functions, and resources. The stress and confusion accompanying these attempts at adaptation make it at once more difficult and more imperative to identify crucial processes that distinguish well-functioning families.

Increasing recognition of the importance of this topic for mental health professionals of all disciplines is currently leading to a new thrust in clinical training programs toward formal instruction on normal family processes. This volume is designed to serve as a comprehensive sourcebook that will enable students, practitioners, and researchers to compare and critically assess the most current research on and conceptualizations of normal families and their potential utility for clinical assessment and treatment.

This volume represents the rapidly advancing state of the art of knowledge about normal family processes. Clinically oriented theorists and investigators who are at the forefront of theory building and research were invited to contribute original chapters. Each chapter addresses various critical aspects of normality with attention to clinical implications. The selection of contributors reflects a diversity of orientations and thus offers different perspectives and specific emphases on normal families. The multi-authored format and multidisciplinary scope of the volume are intended to bridge the gap among clinicians, researchers, and theorists.

The format of the book was designed to present an organized conceptual whole including a theoretical overview; major research contributions; and an examination of important temporal, structural, and sociocultural variables in normal family functioning.

My introductory chapter presents an overview of conceptualizations of normal family functioning, with particular attention to family-systems-based models and contributions from the social sciences. In Section II, five major research projects are presented: Investigators describe their research priorities, strategies, and findings to date. Multiple aspects of family functioning, such as problem-solving styles and communication patterns, are addressed in the various studies. Different methodological approaches are utilized, including laboratory-experimental and naturalistic observation models; microscopic and macroscopic analyses; and longitudinal and cross-sectional perspectives. Thus, readers are given the opportunity to compare the various study approaches, to assess what is currently known and how it was learned, and to consider new research directions and clinical applications. Additionally, practitioners will find several family assessment tools of potential utility in clinical evaluation.

Sections III, IV, and V examine temporal, structural, and sociocultural dimensions of the family that must be taken into account in understanding normal family functioning and dysfunction. Whereas most normal family research (largely due to methodological constraints) has concentrated on intact nuclear families, at only one point in the life cycle, and in the dominant, middle-class culture, considerable diversity exists among normal families in different temporal and social contexts. Chapters in Section III examine the temporal dimension: how normal families pattern themselves and vary over time, and how normal transitions can pose both problems in adaptation and opportunities for therapeutic intervention and growth. Chapter 7 highlights the salient issues and potential complications typical of each developmental stage from a multigenerational perspective. Other chapters consider more specific issues of autonomy and interdependence; death, bereavement, and sexual functioning; and a microscopic view of sequential communication patterns.

Section IV addresses common structural variations from the traditional intact nuclear family model. Chapters discuss the normal processes and typical adjustment complications in disrupted families; in divorced family systems and the coparenting relationship; in remarried stepparent families; and in families with nontraditional sex roles.

Finally, Section V considers normal family processes in sociocultural context. Chapter 15 places questions of normality and dysfunction within a cross-cultural perspective. Chapter 16 describes ethnic variations among normal families and their responses to therapy. The importance of social networks to family functioning is then considered in Chapter 17. In conclusion, normal family patterns are examined in Chapter 18 from a broad sociohistorical perspective, with implications for future trends.

Like many other contributors to this volume, my professional interest in nonclinical families emerged from the study of a so-called "normal control group" for purposes of comparison to families of schizophrenics. In attempting to determine selection criteria for the normal sample, I struggled with the question of how to define a normal family. A review of the literature and consultation with other investigators revealed this to be a common dilemma. With so little direct investigation of normal family processes at that time, it was unwise to impose criteria of normality that lacked empirical validation. Therefore, I chose, as most other investigators had, to limit selection criteria to a negative, or conservative, definition of normality: absence of severe psychiatric symptoms of any nuclear family member. In my contact with the normal control group families, I became increasingly aware of the diversity of patterns in nonsymptomatic families, such that any singular concept of a homogeneous normal control group had to be called into question. Moreover, my observations raised questions about the validity of many commonly held clinical assumptions regarding distinctions between well-functioning and symptomatic families.

Because the purpose of the investigation was to test hypotheses related to schizophrenia, results for the normal control group were limited to *negative* findings—that is, as a group they displayed a significantly lesser degree of particular dysfunctional patterns under study. At this point I directed my attention toward the development of a *positive* conceptualization of normal families. I became interested in delineating the typical processes, positive strengths, and diversity that characterize normal families. Several investigations of normal family processes were under way at that time. So that investigators might have the opportunity to share preliminary findings, I organized a panel on normal family processes for the 1978 Annual Meeting on the American Orthopsychiatric Association. The enthusiastic response led to an invitation to hold a second panel on normal family research the following year. The interest generated by these discussions led directly to the development of this volume. We have been unusually fortunate in having many of the leaders in the field contribute to this project.

In sum, this volume is unique in assembling leading research on and conceptualizations of normal family processes with relevance to a broad range of mental health professionals. The field has now matured to a point that a thorough scrutiny of concepts and premises is timely. While it is not intended, at this early stage of knowledge building, to provide a definitive analysis or synthesis of normal family processes, this text introduces clinicians to important advances and identifies major dimensions and variables that must be taken into account. I have chosen not to comment in editorial notes, but rather to encourage readers to consider each point of view in relation to the ideas and findings of other authors in this volume.

Finally, the normal family perspective offers a valuable framework to clinicians for assessment, intervention, and outcome. It provides clinicians with an appreciation of patterns that characterize normal families, their orientations and modes of response to treatment, and their constructions of the meaning of health and illness. Furthermore, it offers important implications for preventive work with families confronting normal adaptational challenges.

FW

# CONTENTS

## I. OVERVIEW

## II. RESEARCH ON NORMAL FAMILY PROCESSES

# IV. NORMAL FAMILY STRUCTURAL VARIATIONS

## V. NORMAL FAMILIES IN SOCIOCULTURAL CONTEXT

# I

# OVERVIEW

# 1

# CONCEPTUALIZATIONS OF NORMAL FAMILY FUNCTIONING

## FROMA WALSH

All happy families are alike; every unhappy family is unhappy in its own way. —TOLSTOY

All happy families are more or less dissimilar; all unhappy ones are more or less alike. —NABOKOV

What is a normal family? Are normal families essentially alike, or do they vary in structure and functioning? This overview chapter seeks to clarify our understanding of normal family processes by examining conceptualizations of family normality that have an impact on the understanding and treatment of dysfunction. First, the problem of defining family normality is addressed. Next, recent changes in family forms are surveyed. Then, an overview of clinical and social science theories of normal family functioning is presented, with emphasis on family systems models and family coping theory. In conclusion, issues of special relevance for clinicians are discussed.

## DEFINITIONS OF FAMILY NORMALITY

To approach the question of normality in families we must first define what is meant by the term "normal." The label may be used to refer to quite different concepts of normality, depending on one's frame of reference. The term may mean one thing to a clinician, another to a researcher, and altogether something else to families who regard themselves as normal. One's personal experience and professional knowledge base, values, and expectations influence one's perspective on normality. To further confound

Froma Walsh. Center for Family Studies/The Family Institute of Chicago, Institute of Psychiatry, Northwestern Memorial Hospital and Northwestern University Medical School, Chicago, Illinois.

the issue, other terms, such as "healthy," "typical," and "adequate," are often used interchangeably with the label "normal." Clearer distinctions among terms and concepts are needed.

## Defining Normality

Offer and Sabshin (1966), in an overview of theoretical and clinical concepts of mental health, identified various definitions of normality from the clinical and social science literature. They synthesized these into four major perspectives on normality: (1) Normality as Health; (2) Normality as Utopia; (3) Normality as Average; and (4) Normality as Process. (The fourth category was relabeled "Normality as Transactional Systems" in the authors' 1974 revision.)

1. *Normality as Health.* This perspective, which includes the traditional medical–psychiatric approach, holds to a negative definition of normality as the absence of pathology. Attention is focused on definitions of pathology; all persons who are asymptomatic, manifesting no severe disturbance, are considered normal—that is, healthy.

2. *Normality as Utopia.* This approach, embodied in psychoanalytic and humanistic theories, conceives of normality as ideal or optimal functioning, or as "self-actualization" of potential. Offer and Sabshin comment that this perspective—often implicit in therapeutic goals—makes the normal person not only one to be admired, "but also one who is seldom, if ever, seen in flesh and blood" (p. 104).

3. *Normality as Average.* This perspective, commonly employed in sociological and behavioral studies, attends to the statistical norm, or average; it is based on the normal distribution, or bell-shaped curve, with the middle range as normal and both extremes as deviant.

4. *Normality as Process.* From this perspective normal behavior is viewed in the context of multiple circular processes in transactional systems. Unlike the other perspectives, which define normality cross-sectionally at a single point in time, this approach views normality as a process over time. Illustrative of this approach is Erikson's conceptualization (1959) of normal personality development as a lifelong process that involves mastery of sequential life stage tasks. General System Theory (Bertalanffy, 1968) views normal functioning in terms of a transactional system that operates over time, according to certain organizational principles governing interaction. Likewise, Grinker's thesis of a unified concept of behavior (1967) encompasses interacting variables from biological, psychological, and social fields, all contributing to the functioning of a viable system over time.

Offer and Sabshin also discuss coping and adaptation as complex concepts not adequately explained by any single theory or hypothesis. Building on their process concept of normality, Offer and Sabshin conclude that there are a number of possible adaptational routes and that each person, based on an interaction of biopsychosocial variables, develops a unique coping style. They postulate that healthier individuals have a larger variety of coping techniques, utilize the more adaptive and object-seeking strategies, and show more flexibility in dealing with internal and external life events.

## Defining Family Normality

In conceptualizing family normality, a confusing array of terms and definitions are used throughout the literature. (Moreover, the topic "normal" is rarely listed in text indexes, requiring readers to search for relevant discussion and indirect references in the literature.) Concepts can be grouped into four basic perspectives related to the Offer and Sabshin categories. Normal families can be defined in terms of asymptomatic functioning; optimal functioning; average functioning; and transactional processes.

1. *Asymptomatic family functioning.* From this clinical perspective, a family is considered normal if there are no recent symptoms of dysfunction or psychopathology in any family member. Absence of symptoms is equated with health. This negative, or conservative, concept has been utilized by family researchers for two purposes: in order to study normal families as a homogeneous group for comparison with families of emotionally disturbed patients; and in order not to impose other definitions or selective criteria that as yet lack empirical validation (Jacob, 1975; Riskin & Faunce, 1972). Riskin, for this latter reason, prefers the term, "nonclinical" or "nontherapy" families (Riskin, 1976).

2. *Optimal family functioning.* This approach to normality seeks to define a successful family in terms of positive or ideal characteristics. Optimally functioning families are viewed at the top of a continuum, with average or asymptomatic families in the midrange, and severely dysfunctional families at the low end. The term, "healthy family," generally refers to a successful or ideal family that fits a model based on the values of a particular conceptual paradigm. Most often, the judgment is based on outcome in terms of accomplishment of family tasks, particularly the successful development of offspring (Solnit, 1980). Empirically based models, such as those developed by the Timberlawn group (Lewis, Beavers, Gossett, & Phillips, 1976) and the McMaster team (Epstein, Bishop, & Levin, 1978), have begun to provide a more solid data base for evaluations of family competence.

3. *Average family functioning.* A family is viewed as normal from this perspective if it is average, or fits a pattern that is typical or prevalent in most families. This concept is used most often by sociologists with statistical measures of central tendency. A family is termed normal if it falls within the normal range; families outside that range are regarded as abnormal. From this standpoint, an optimally functioning family is as uncommon and therefore as deviant or abnormal as a severely dysfunctional family. Furthermore, by this definition, normal families are not necessarily asymptomatic. If most

families are found to have occasional problems, the presence of a problem does not in itself imply that a family is not normal. This perspective thus disengages the concepts of health, normality, and absence of symptoms.

4. *Transactional family processes.* From this perspective, normal families are conceptualized in terms of universal processes that are characteristic of all systems. Basic processes involve the integration, maintenance, and growth of the family unit, in relation to both individual and social systems. What is normal—either typical or optimal—is defined in temporal and social contexts, and it varies with the different internal and external demands that require adaptation over the course of the family life cycle.

### Functional and Normative

Two terms easily confounded with concepts of family normality should be clarified. "Functional" refers to a judgment about the utility of a structural or behavioral pattern in achieving objectives. It is contingent on the objectives and context: functional to what end, for whom, and in what situation. What may be functional at one level of analysis—individual, family, or society—may not necessarily be functional at the others (Price, 1979). A functional pattern at one stage in the family life cycle may be dysfunctional at another phase (Walsh, 1980).

"Norms" refer to ranges of conduct deemed permissible. Each family establishes its own rules that serve as norms to proscribe and regulate behavior (Jackson, 1965). Family norms are largely influenced by "normative" expectations, or value judgments prevailing in society or in an ethnic subculture. These standards of what is customary, or what ought to be done, are established through mores, laws, and folkways in each culture (Bott, 1957). These norms may or may not correspond to the statistical norm of a population or to the typical, average family pattern, and they often lag behind family and social changes.

### Changing Family Forms and Norms

Popular myths and idealized images of normal family life are transmitted in the folklore of every culture, both shaping and reflecting normative values and expectations. In contemporary society, the media—and television in particular—have a tremendous impact on family life, providing a common shared experience as well as parent and family models in domestic dramas, "soap operas," situation comedies, and commercials. Often these norms are unrealistic, as is the implicit assumption that most family problems can be solved in half an hour. Other questions have been raised by a televised series on the everyday life of an actual family, the Louds, who considered themselves successful in achieving the "American Dream." The dream image dissolved on camera as the parents ended their marriage and the eldest son announced his homosexuality. Was this process catalyzed by the observation? Was this family not, in fact, "normal" or was the American dream image revealed to be a myth? These are but a few of the issues regarding media and the family that are important for social science investigation.

The predominant image of the "normal American family"—as idealized in the 1950s television portrayal of *Father Knows Best*, a formative model for most adults today—is the self-reliant, intact nuclear family, with father as sole wage-earner, mother as full-time homemaker, and dependent children in the home. While this model remains a standard by which family normality is widely judged, in fact fewer than one in four American families currently fits this description.

Recent government population analyses (1979–1980) reveal that in the last two decades, American family structures have been changing dramatically and are likely to continue to change (Masnick & Bane, 1980). Family patterns have most significantly been altered by three trends: (1) the increase in divorce; (2) the increase in working mothers; and (3) the lower birth rate coupled with lengthened life expectancy.

### Divorced and Remarried Family Systems

The divorce rate in the United States has doubled since 1965. Currently, one-third of all first marriages are likely to end in divorce. Consequently, almost one in five families with children is maintained by one parent, usually the mother. As many as four children in ten born in the 1970s are expected to spend part of their childhood in a one-parent household. With most divorced parents remarrying, increasing numbers of blended stepfamily units are being created.

Despite the recent increase in divorce, the proportion of families undergoing dissolution and remarriage is not significantly greater than in earlier historical times, due to lower life expectancy and earlier widowhood in the past. In fact, more children than ever before are reared throughout childhood by at least one parent; fewer are now adopted or institutionalized (Bane, 1976; Hareven, 1977). Nonetheless, the situation of divorce does pose complicated transitional tasks and coparenting issues for divorced and remarried family systems to resolve (see Goldsmith, Chapter 12, and Visher & Visher, Chapter 13, this volume).

### Working Mothers

More than half of all mothers with school-age children—and over 40% of mothers with younger children—currently work outside the home, with most in full-time jobs. This pattern reflects not only changes in women's personal aspirations, but also, in most cases, a growing economic necessity. Two-parent families are finding two incomes increasingly essential to maintain a moderate standard of living and to rear children through college. Also, a large proportion of working women head one-parent households and have primary or sole support for their children. (Of note, women are less likely than men to remarry, and the likelihood of a woman remarrying is inversely related to the number of children she has [Bane, 1976].) In sum, the trend away from women's occupation in full-time childcare and homemaking is a reality requiring changes in the functional organization of the family system and coparental unit, more flexible work situations, and supportive child care services (Pleck, 1977).

### Population Shifts

Increasingly, young adults are electing to remain single, to delay marriage, to have fewer children, and to postpone or forego childrearing. At the same time, life expectancy in adulthood is lengthening. A combined impact of these trends is the declining birth rate and increasing proportion of older adults. Because we tend to conceptualize normal family life as centered on childrearing functions, we lack family models appropriate to childless adults and to families in the later phases of the life cycle (Walsh, 1980).

Other alternate family forms are becoming more common, including families headed by homosexuals and communal arrangements (Macklin, 1980). Many regard deviations from the traditional norm as symptomatic of the demise of the family and as inherently pathogenic in their impact on children. (The 1980 White House Conference of Families, for example, saw a battle waged between self-proclaimed "Profamily" advocates of the traditional family form and supporters of family options, who were labeled "Antifamily.") Others view changes in family forms as attempts toward adaptive transformation of the family in response to recent societal upheavals and changing family functions—from chiefly economic and educational requisites to primarily psychosocial needs (Bane, 1976; Mead, 1980; Skolnick & Skolnick, 1971). While research evidence is only beginning to emerge, one longitudinal study by Eiduson (1979) has found, to date, no significant difference among a variety of family forms in impact on early childhood cognitive and socioemotional development. Variance within each form was high; some families in each form were more effective than others, which suggests that each form holds the potential for successful adjustment. Family processes were found to be more important factors than family forms were.

Clearly, no single family form is a representative or appropriate model for most families in a pluralistic society with diverse family forms and with varying life stage demands, value orientations, ethnic styles, and economic resources (Kluckhohn, 1960; McGoldrick, Chapter 16, this volume; McQueen, 1979; Opler, 1980; Spiegel, 1971). Two tasks are foremost for social scientists and clinicians. First, we need to delineate the normal processes that are expectable, or typical, for different family forms and value orientations. Secondly, we need to study effective families and to develop models of optimal family functioning for a variety of family situations. The guiding question is that of how families, with variant forms and requisites, organize their resources and function to accomplish their objectives. Discussion now focuses on the interior processes of families, examining major clinical and sociological conceptualizations of normal family functioning and dysfunction.

# CLINICAL MODELS OF NORMAL FAMILY FUNCTIONING AND DYSFUNCTION

Concepts of normal family functioning and dysfunction by selected leading theorists representing major clinical models of the family are examined here in a review of the literature. This overview focuses on the theoretical models that have been most influential and that hold the greatest potential utility for clinicians and researchers seeking to understand functional family systems better and to treat families in distress.

Family systems theory, as a general framework underlying major clinical approaches to the family, is briefly summarized in terms of basic assumptions about the operation of normal family systems. The following clinical family models are then surveyed: the structural model; the strategic model; behavioral/social exchange models; psychodynamic/multigenerational models; the Bowen model; and experiential models.

## Family Systems Orientation

Family systems theorists conceptualize the family as an open system that functions in relation to its broader sociocultural context and that evolves over the life cycle. As an interactional system, normal families operate according to rules and principles that apply to all systems (Bertalanffy, 1968; Buckley, 1967).

1. *Circular causality.* A family system can be defined as a group of individuals interrelated so that a change in any one member affects other individuals and the group as a whole; this, in turn, affects the first individual in a circular chain of influence. Every action in this sequence is also a reaction. Causality is thus seen as circular rather than linear.

2. *Nonsummativity.* The family as a whole is greater than the sum of its parts, and it cannot be described simply by summing up characteristics of individual members. The family organization and interactional patterns involve an interlocking of the behavior of its members. It is necessary to attend to the *pattern* that connects (Bateson, 1979).

3. *Equifinality.* According to this principle, the same origin may lead to different outcomes, and the same outcome may result from different origins.

Watzlawick, Beavin, and Jackson (1967) refer to the error, or genetic fallacy, in confusing origin with significance in determining outcome. Rather, they assert, the influence of initial conditions or events will be outweighed by the impact of the family organization—its ongoing interactional patterns and responses to stress. Thus, one family may be disabled while another family rallies in response to the same crisis; or two well-functioning families may have evolved from quite different circumstances.

4. *Communication.* All behavior is regarded as communication, transmitting interpersonal messages. Every communication has two functions: a "content" (report) aspect, conveying factual information, opinions, or feelings; and a "relationship" (command) aspect, which, in conveying how the information is to be taken, defines the nature of the relationship (Ruesch & Bateson, 1951). In an ongoing relationship, this definition cannot be left unclear without pathological consequences. Family units, as ongoing relationships, stabilize the process of defining relationships through mutual agreements or family rules.

5. *Family rules.* Relationship rules, both explicit and implicit, organize family interaction and function to maintain a stable system by prescribing and limiting members' behavior. They provide expectations about roles, actions, and consequences that guide family life. Through the operation of a "redundancy principle," a family tends to interact in repetitious sequences, so that family operations are governed by a relatively small set of patterned and predictable rules. Family rules operate as *norms within* a family, by which behavior is measured and from which it varies in degree. Values, most often originating in extrafamilial influences, such as religion and culture, exert leverage on family relationships by enforcing or affirming family norms (Jackson, 1965). Families develop different life styles based on their family rules (Ford & Herrick, 1974).

6. *Homeostasis.* In order to maintain a steady, stable state in the ongoing interaction system, norms are delimited and enforced by homeostatic mechanisms. All family members contribute to the homeostatic balance through a mutually reinforcing feedback loop, such as in complementary or reciprocal behavior. Too great a deviation from the family norm may be counteracted in the negative feedback process in order to regulate tension and to restore the family equilibrium or homeostasis.

7. *Morphogenesis.* At the same time, flexibility is required for a family to adapt to internal and external change (Hoffman, 1971). Internally, the family must reorganize in response to new developmental imperatives as its members—and the family as a whole—evolve over the course of the life cycle. A shift of rules, or "second-order change," is required in transition from one developmental stage to the next, as new phase-appropriate needs and tasks demand new norms and options (Carter & McGoldrick, 1980). Crisis events, such as significant losses and changing circumstances in relation to the social world, stress the family and require adaptational shifts for the

continuity of the family and the adjustment of its members (see McGoldrick & Carter, Chapter 7, this volume).

From a systems vantage point, individual dysfunction is also seen as symptomatic of current family dysfunction. While an individual's functioning and development are impaired, the symptoms may be functional and adaptive to the family context. The individual's distress may function as a homestatic regulator, restoring family stability by expressing and deflecting family tension. Psychopathology is thus defined as a relationship problem (Haley, 1970). The individual's symptomatic behavior is seen as embedded in a dysfunctional interaction pattern.

Regardless of the origin of symptoms, given the circular nature of causality, the family's response to the individual's distress will be an important factor in the readjustment or recovery of the individual symptom-bearer. Dysfunctional family systems tend to maintain or reinforce the symptoms in ongoing interactional processes. Symptoms may shift from one member to others if the dysfunctional relationship pattern is not altered.

Having outlined universal characteristics of family systems and basic assumptions about individual and family dysfunction, we now examine more specific views of normal family functioning that are grounded in a systems orientation, each with a particular theoretical and clinical focus. The discussion will address the following questions: How is normal family functioning conceptualized in terms of the four perspectives on family normality defined above? What are thought to be essential characteristics distinguishing normal families from dysfunctional families? How do views of normal family processes influence therapeutic goals and approaches?

### Structural Model

Structural family therapy, developed by Minuchin and his colleagues (Minuchin, 1974; Minuchin, Montalvo, Guerney, Rosman, & Schumer, 1967), emphasizes the importance of family organization for the functioning of the family unit and the well-being of its members. Minuchin directly addresses the issue of normality, contending that a normal, or ordinary, family cannot be distinguished from an abnormal family by the absence of problems. He attacks the myth of "placid" normality—the prevailing idealized view of the normal family as nonstressful, living in constant harmony and cooperation, while coping with social input without upset. Such an image crumbles, contends Minuchin, whenever one looks at any family with ordinary problems.

Minuchin presents interviews with effectively functioning families from different cultures to illustrate the normal difficulties of family life that transcend cultural differences. He describes "an ordinary family; that is, the couple has many problems of relating to one another, bringing up children, dealing with in-laws, and coping with the outside world. Like all normal families, they are constantly struggling with these problems and negotiating the compromises that make a life in common possible" (1974, p. 16).

Assuming that problems are common to all families, Minuchin cautions therapists not to base judgments of family normality or abnormality on the presence or absence of problems. Instead, he proposes a conceptual schema of family functioning to guide therapists in family assessment. This model is based on the view of a family as a social system, operating within specific social contexts and having three components. First, the family structure is that of an open sociocultural system in transformation. Second, the family undergoes development over time, progressing through successive stages requiring restructuring. Third, the family adapts to changed circumstances in ways that allow it to maintain continuity and to further the psychosocial growth of its members.

The family structure common to all families is defined as the invisible set of functional demands organizing the ways in which family members interact. Transactional patterns defining relationships and regulating behavior are maintained by two constraints: universal rules governing family organization, especially the power hierarchy; and mutual expectations in particular families—explicit or implicit contracts that persist out of habit, mutual accommodation, and functional effectiveness. Each system thus maintains itself according to preferred patterns, resisting change beyond a certain accustomed range. At the same time, a functional family must be able to adapt to changing internal (developmental) and external (environmental) demands.

The family differentiates and carries out its functions through subsystems, formed by generation, sex, interest, or function. The boundaries of a subsystem—the rules defining who participates and how—function to protect the differentiation of the system. For proper family functioning, boundaries must be defined well enough for subsystem members to carry out their functions without undue interference, and at the same time must still permit contact with other subsystems. Minuchin stresses that the *clarity* of subsystem boundaries is far more important than the particular *composition* of subsystems. A parental subsystem that includes a grandparent or a parental child, for example, can function quite well as long as lines of authority and responsibility are clearly drawn.

The clarity of family boundaries is thus, for Minuchin, a useful parameter for the evaluation of family functioning. All family patterns are conceived as points on a continuum, with enmeshment, characterized by diffuse boundaries, at one extreme. In an enmeshed family pattern, differentiation among members is blurred, distance is decreased, and the sense of belonging interferes with autonomy, problem mastery, and cognitive–affective skills. Such a system may become overloaded and may lack resources to adapt and change under stress. At the other extreme, in a disengaged family pattern, rigid boundaries impede communication and the protective functions of the family, as individual members' autonomy is achieved at the expense of relatedness and of response to one another.

Patterns of enmeshment and disengagement are viewed as transactional styles or preferences for a type of interaction, and not as indications of qualitative differences between functional and dysfunctional families. Most families fall within the wide normal range on the continuum, with somewhat enmeshed or somewhat disengaged subsystems. Cultural norms vary; an enmeshed family style, for example, is typical and functional in many ethnic groups. Patterns may also vary with different requirements at various life cycle stages. For instance, the parent–child subsystem normally tends toward greater disengagement as the child develops and separates from the family. Extremely enmeshed or extremely disengaged patterns indicate areas of possible pathology. For example, a highly enmeshed parent–child subsystem that breaches generational boundaries undermines both the marital-parental unit and the child's autonomy, and appears to be an important factor in the development of symptoms (see Haley, 1967; Lidz, 1976; Walsh, 1979).

Minuchin emphasizes the importance of hierarchy to the effective functioning of the family system. First, the spouse subsystem must establish a boundary to protect it from interference by demands and needs of others, such as children and members of the extended family. Adults in a family must have their own psychosocial territory. The spouse subsystem requires complementarity and mutual accommodation to implement vital tasks. In this process, spouses may support the better characteristics and creative aspects of their partners. At other times, they may activate negative aspects of or undermine their partners in attempting to improve or rescue them. Such negative patterns, states Minuchin, may exist in average couples without necessarily implying malevolent motivation or severe pathology.

In an intact family, spouses must also establish a strong parental subsystem to perform child-rearing tasks. Minuchin asserts that parenting has become an increasingly difficult process in today's complex, rapidly changing world. The unquestioned authority of the traditional patriarchal model has been replaced by a concept of flexible, rational authority. Minuchin notes that the ideal family is often described as a democracy: "But they mistakenly assume that a democracy is leaderless, or that a family is a society of peers" (1974, p. 58). Rather, effective functioning requires the differentiated use of authority by the parental subsystem. To carry out their functions, parents must have the power to do so. Accordingly, structural family therapy holds as a primary objective the reorganization of a dysfunctional system in such a way that the parental subsystem and hierarchy are strengthened.

Minuchin further notes that therapists, in their concentration on pathology and related family dynamics, may not give sufficient attention to the process of continuity and change in a family's adaptation. All families must respond to internal pressures associated with developmental changes, as well as to external demands to accommodate to society and its institutions that have an impact on the family. Stresses of accommodation are inherent and may come from four sources: extrafamilial forces on a member, such as job pressure; extrafamilial forces on a whole family, such as economic recession or racial discrimination; transitional points in the family, such as the beginning of a new developmental phase; and idiosyncratic problems, such as illness or disability.

Each new situation stresses the family and requires reorganization. Transitional processes of adaptation carry the lack of differentiation and the anxiety that characterize all new processes and that may be misjudged or mislabeled as pathological. Minuchin urges therapists to focus on the family as a social system in transformation:

> With this orientation, many more families who enter therapy would be seen and treated as average families in transitional situations, suffering the pains of accommodation to new circumstances. The label of pathology would be reserved for families who in the face of stress increase the rigidity of their transactional patterns and boundaries, and avoid or resist any exploration of alternatives. In average families, the therapist relies on the motivation of family resources as a pathway to transformation. In pathological families, the therapist needs to become an actor in the family drama, entering into transitional coalitions in order to skew the system and develop a different level of homeostasis. (1974, p. 60)

In summary, from a structural perspective, no family style is inherently normal or abnormal, functional or dysfunctional. A particular family's differentiation is idiosyncratic, depending on its own composition, developmental stage, and subculture; any model is workable. Each family has a structure and a preference for certain transactional patterns that may meet ordinary demands. The strength of the system depends on its ability to mobilize alternative patterns when stressed by internal or external change. The boundaries of the system must be clear and firm; yet the system must be flexible enough for interchange between autonomy and interdependence, for promotion of psychosocial growth of members and maintenance of the integrity of the system, and for continuity and restructuring in response to stress.

In essence, Minuchin proposes an optimal model of normality, which is ultimately defined in terms of functional accomplishment. This model of an effectively functioning family underlies the structural approach to family therapy. Functional and dysfunctional are determined by the *fit* of a system's structural organization to its functional requirements in developmental and social contexts (Aponte & Van Deusen, 1981).

### Strategic Model

The strategic model is best represented by the Palo Alto group, the Milan team, and Haley's problem-solving approach. Strategic therapists in the

Palo Alto group (Watzlawick, Weakland, & Fisch, 1974; Weakland, Fisch, Watzlawick, & Bodin, 1974) are concerned primarily with the issue of how families attempt to handle or resolve normal problems in living. Based on the assumption that all families confront problems, the therapeutic focus is on how families *maintain* a problem by precisely the means they are using to handle the problem. The attempted solution thus becomes the problem requiring therapeutic change.

Strategic theorists contend that most families do what they do because they believe it is the right or best way to approach a problem or because it is the only tack they know to take. The therapeutic task, therefore, is to interrupt ways of handling the problem that do not work. It requires learning the language and conceptualization of each family in order to see the problem through its members' eyes, taking into account their values and expectations that determine their approach to handling the problem and their resistance to change (Sluzki & Ransom, 1976; Selvini Palazzoli, Boscolo, Cecchin, & Prata, 1978).

The Palo Alto group and the Milan team view normal families as extremely flexible, using a large repertoire of behaviors to cope with problems, in contrast to a pathological family, which demonstrates a rigidity and paucity of alternatives. Beyond this generalization, they believe that each family must define what is normal or healthy for itself. The responsibility of the therapist is limited to initiating change that will get a family "unstuck" from unworkable interactional patterns that maintain symptoms.

Haley has developed a strategic problem-solving approach to family therapy that integrates a communicational orientation derived from his early research with Palo Alto colleagues and structural principles formulated in his later collaboration with Minuchin. Like Minuchin, Haley stresses the importance of viewing the family in the context of its current ecosystem and stage in the life cycle. Symptoms are thought to arise when families are unable to adjust to life cycle transitions and become "stuck" within a phase. For example, the problem "mad young people" have in leaving home—which may be expressed in schizophrenic symptoms, substance abuse, or other behavior disorders—is seen as a family separation problem related to the crisis of transition to the next life phase (Haley, 1980). Accordingly, it makes more sense to Haley to view families in relation to their developmental passages than to try to define a family typology.

Haley, like other strategic family therapists, has been more concerned with developing a theory of therapeutic change than with developing a model of the family, and he makes a careful distinction between the two. In his view, clinicians have been hampered by theory that attempts to explain human experience and pathology but does not lead to problem solution. Haley, therefore, selectively focuses on certain family variables that he believes relevant to therapeutic change. Key variables involve power and organization within the family.

According to Haley (1978), if any generalization applies to humans and other animals, it is that all creatures able to learn must organize. People with a shared history and future follow patterned redundant ways of behavior with one another, and they relate in a hierarchy. Organization is necessarily hierarchical. The organization of the family, in terms of hierarchy, includes members of different generations and different levels of income, intelligence, and skills. The complex hierarchical lines are related to the many different functions of the family and are maintained by all participants. The most basic hierarchy involves the generation line: parents nurture and discipline children.

Depending on the composition of a family, three or even four generations may be involved, with different levels of power or status, related in part to cultural norms. Haley observes that in the traditional family, as still evidenced in Asia, the highest status and power resides with the eldest generation, with parents secondary, and children lowest. In Western society, especially at the present time, with nuclear family living arrangements and rapid social change, power resides more with parents; grandparents are removed to an advisory, or even a superfluous, position. In one-parent households, grandparents may function in more important capacities than they do in two-parent families. A variety of arrangements can be functional. The crucial matter is that, whatever the arrangement, every family must deal with the issue of organizing in a hierarchy and must establish clear rules to govern the power and status differential. Like Minuchin, Haley contends that individual symptoms occur when the hierarchical arrangement is confused.

Haley asserts that if there is a fundamental rule of social organization, it is that an organization becomes dysfunctional and members experience distress when coalitions occur across levels of a hierarchy, particularly when such coalitions are covert and when the transactional sequences become organized and repetitive. Basic rules of organization are violated when a member at one level consistently forms coalitions against a peer with a member at another level. Thus, a parent–child coalition against the other parent violates basic rules of organization and results in pathological distress. A symptom is seen as a communicative act, appearing when an individual is locked into a family pattern and cannot see a nonsymptomatic means of altering it. The degree of disturbance is seen as proportional to the number of malfunctioning hierarchies, or triangles, in which members are embedded.

In a malfunctioning hierarchy, parents are not relating as peers in an executive capacity. Their difficulties with each other and their attempts to protect each other interfere with their defining a clear family hierarchy. In diagnostic assessment, a therapist can map the family hierarchy by observing the interactional sequences that occur in the organization, with particular attention to triadic patterns or triangles. The therapeutic goal is to change the rigid repeating sequences by interrupting dysfunctional coalitions and encouraging parents to define a clearer hierarchy. Presenting symptoms are then expected to subside.

Haley emphasizes that these descriptions of family interactions are offered as a way of thinking for purposes of therapy—not as a model for what normal families *should* be like. When a clinician examines the context of a symptom and finds a confusion of hierarchical levels in a family, this does not necessarily imply that to raise normal children, a family should not have hierarchical confusion. Where there is a symptomatic child, a certain family organization can be described, but it is an error to deduce from that description a model for raising normal children.

From observations of more than 200 normal, or average, families in research, Haley found patterns so diverse that to talk about a "normal" family seems to him naive:

> How to raise children properly, as a normal family should, remains a mystery that awaits observational longitudinal studies with large samples. Thinking about the organization of a family to plan therapy is another issue. As an analogy, if a child breaks a leg, one can set it straight and put it in a plaster cast. But one should not conclude from such therapy that the way to bring about the normal development of children's legs is to place them in plaster casts. A clinical description that is used to plan for a change and a research description of ordinary situations are not synonymous. (1978, p. 108)

However, it seems that Haley ultimately sides with Minuchin in defining a healthy family as a functional system that accomplishes its tasks. Also, like Minuchin, Haley stresses the importance of hierarchy as necessary for adaptation in any complex system such as the family.

### Behavioral/Social Exchange Models

Behavioral approaches to family therapy, as advanced by Patterson, Reid, Jones, and Conger (1975), Liberman (1970), and Weiss (1978), have developed from behavior modification and social learning traditions in psychology. While the behavioral model differs in some ways from the family systems orientation, both emphasize the importance of family rules and patterned communication processes, as well as a functional approach to outcome. The behavior model emphasizes the interactional behaviors and conditions under which persons learn social behavior and influence or change the behavior of others. While giving little direct attention to the question of normality in families, the model implicitly defines a normal family in a functional sense. An assumption is made that all behavior is adaptive in terms of its functional relationship properties. Thus, behavior is not inherently good or bad, or even normal or sick; rather, it is a vehicle for achieving relationship outcomes in regard to intimacy and distance (Barton & Alexander, 1981; Ekeh, 1974).

Families are conceptualized as critical social learning contexts, which members create and to which they respond simultaneously. According to social exchange principles, in well-functioning families, participants exchange benefits that outweigh costs. Since family relationships involve behavioral exchange over a wide range of possibilities, there are many opportunities for rewarding exchanges likely to maintain the relationship. Relationship failure is explained by deficient reward exchanges, as when the reward system shifts from positive to coercive control (Patterson *et al.*, 1975). In addition to contingency control, relationships may become distressed due to communication deficits, when there is a discrepancy between the intended communication and the impact of the message on the receiver. The concept of reciprocity is important; short-term reciprocity is thought to be characteristic of distressed relationships, while long-term exchanges tend to characterize more functional relationships.

The importance of positive reward for desired behavior is stressed. In well-functioning families, not only is maladaptive behavior not reinforced, but also adaptive behavior is rewarded through attention, acknowledgment and approval. Adaptability is defined by Weiss as the capability of using diverse behaviors in different situations (1978, p. 174).

### Psychodynamic/Multigenerational Models

Several family theorists from a psychoanalytic background have attempted to bridge psychodynamic, object relations, and family systems constructs in the formulation of their views of family functioning. Whereas early psychoanalytic theory, beginning with Freud, was directed primarily toward dyadic influences of parents on individual personality development, more recently attention has shifted to the family as a social unit with its own characteristic dynamic properties. Ackerman (1958) began direct observation of family interaction in an attempt to understand unconscious dynamics in the conscious organization of experience, the total integrative patterns of personality, and the prevailing interpersonal realities. The symptomatic family member was seen as serving as a scapegoat for unresolved family conflicts.

In Meissner's conceptualization of marriage and family dynamics (1978), family interaction is considered in terms of object relations, related internalizations, and introjection and projection processes. The goal of a normal family is to promote the development of well-differentiated and individuated identity in offspring. The parents, individually and in the marital and parental relationships they construct, are regarded as crucial determinants of healthy or pathological family functioning and development of individual members. It is assumed that the capacity of an indidivual to function as a spouse and a parent is largely a consequence of childhood relationships in the family of origin. The relative success of developmental tasks and the manner in which these tasks are accomplished are thought to be determined largely by residues of internalized objects and the organization of introjects contributing to identity integration. The extent to which spouses are unsuccessful in forming a productive shared marital experience depends largely on the extent to which that relationship is contaminated by pathogenic introjects rather than being organized in terms of a successfully differentiated and individuated sense of self.

Complementary need patterns are thought to influence mate choice as well as marital and parent–child relationship patterns. Boszormenyi-Nagy and Spark (1973) describe the implicit agreement among family members to relate on the basis of unfulfilled needs. Such reciprocal relationship bargains are presumed to occur in all families. Dysfunctional families are distinguished by a greater degree of unconscious unresolved conflict or loss that interferes with current family interaction and with realistic appraisal of and response to other family members (Paul & Paul, 1975).

Accordingly, Framo (1970) views symptoms as resulting primarily from unconscious attempts by parents to reenact, externalize, or master intrapsychic conflicts originating in their families of origin. Current life situations are interpreted in light of the parents' inner object world, and active (unconscious) attempts are made to modify close relationships to fit internal role models. The symptomatic member expresses the irrational role assignment, or projective transference distortion, which is reinforced by family myths and ritualized into the family's structural pattern. Stierlin (1974) identifies centripetal and centrifugal family patterns that can result in adolescent separation problems. Similar to Minuchin's concepts of enmeshment and disengagement, these are family pressures either to bind together or to expel members.

The contextual approach of Boszormenyi-Nagy (1981) emphasizes the ethical dimension of family relationships in terms of the multigenerational legacies of parental accountability and filial loyalty that guide members over the course of the life cycle. Families are thought to be strengthened by moves toward trustworthiness, based on consideration of members' welfare interests for survival, growth, and relatedness. Trustworthiness functions to enhance autonomy in problem solving. In well-functioning families, autonomy is permitted by the family legacy, and members are not bound by any real or imaginary "ledger" of unpaid debts. Autonomy is attained through efforts toward relational equitability. While imbalances of fairness are seen as inevitable, the criterion of functioning is flexibility.

Ideally, the family life cycle is characterized by open negotiation of transitions and changing loyalty commitments, with awareness of legacy expectations. Understanding and resolution of "ledger," loyalty, and legacy issues require active concern for the extended family; at the same time, relationships must neither prevent outside contact nor force outside contact as an escape.

While most psychoanalytically oriented family theorists do give recognition to systemic properties of families, Lidz (1963, 1976) has emphasized the family's structure and function as a mediating influence between the individual and society. Lidz notes that in every society, the family has been the primary agency to provide for the child's biological needs and development into an integrated person capable of living in society and of maintaining and transmitting its culture. Because families everywhere meet basic human needs, they have similarities in organization and function. Yet, within these limits, families must vary widely to fit into and assure the continuity of divergent societies.

Lidz conceptualizes three interrelated sets of cardinal functions that are served by the family for spouses, for children, and for society. First, in forming a marriage, the family completes and stabilizes the lives of husbands and wives. Second, the family provides nurturance for children and directs their personality development. Third, it fills a vital societal need through enculturation of its members, through assimilation of techniques of adaptation, and through transmission of language for communication and ego functioning. The family must have structure, rules, and leadership to fulfill its functions and to minimize devisive conflict. Foremost among these requisites, spouses must form a parental coalition, maintain generation boundaries, and model sex-linked roles.

1. *Parental coalition.* For Lidz, as for Minuchin and Haley, the stability of the family and the security of its members rest on the parents' ability to form a strong parental coalition. Lidz believes that for healthy development, a child requires two parents: a same-sex parent to identify with and model after; and an opposite-sex parent as basic love object, whose affections provide the child with a sense of worth. He does, however, believe that parents can form reasonably effective coalitions, despite marital disharmony and even separation, by maintaining agreement about how their children should be raised and by supporting spouses as worthwhile persons and good parents despite marital differences. (For support of this view in research of divorced families, see Goldsmith, Chapter 12, this volume.)

2. *Generation boundaries.* Again, like Minuchin and Haley, Lidz contends that the division of generations provides an essential structuring influence on the family. Parents, as the nurturant and educating generation, give to the children, provide adult models, and establish interactional patterns. Parents can and should be dependent on each other, but not on developing children, who need the security of dependency to use energies for their own development. The maintenance of generation boundaries also lessens role conflict and upholds different types of affectional relationships between spouses than those between parents and children. The boundary further assists the differentiation of children from parents, particularly in resolution of the mother–infant symbiotic attachment and the Oedipal situation, precluding arousal of incestuous interaction. When generation boundaries are confused, the ensuing role conflict distorts a child's cognitive and social development. (For empirical support of these contentions, see the

research comparing families of schizophrenic, disturbed nonschizophrenic, and normal young adults by Walsh, 1979.)

3. *Sex roles.* Lidz follows Parsons and Bales's structural–functional model of healthy family functioning (1955); this requires a division of sex-linked parental roles, with father as instrumental leader and mother as socioemotional caretaker. More recently, Lidz has adapted this model to refer primarily to a person's self-concept and self-esteem as a male or female, allowing that the sharing of parental tasks has become more necessary and acceptable in the contemporary family. Still, he contends that for a child's achievement of gender identity, some sex-linked role functions must be upheld, especially when fathers have major responsibility for financial support and mothers for affectional–affiliative tasks (Lidz, 1976).

In short, while a variety of relationships may be satisfying to couples, Lidz maintains that certain organizational requisites are essential to a well-functioning family for a child's ego development, integration, and adaptation in society. This optimal model emphasizes structural and functional aspects of the family, whereas other psychoanalytically oriented models concentrate on multigenerational dynamic processes.

From the psychodynamic perspective, family processes and psychopathology are primarily conceptualized in terms of the interlocking of parental individual dynamics, multigenerational loyalty issues, and transferences or unconscious role assignments from the past. More implicitly than explicitly, these theories hold a model of ideal or optimal functioning toward which therapeutic growth is encouraged. The ideal, however, is not well defined, and is generally described in terms of reduction of negative and unconscious dynamic processes in the family through insight, facilitation of more direct communication, and efforts toward relational equitability.

### Bowen Theory Model

The family systems theory of Bowen (1978) developed first out of his early research with families of schizophrenics, and subseqeuently from observations of a wide range of families—from the most impaired, to normal, to the best functioning families that could be found. He concluded from several impressionistic studies that schizophrenia and the psychoses are on the same continuum with neurotic problems, distinguished only by quantitative rather than qualitative differences; and that patterns originally thought to distinguish families of schizophrenics are present in varying degrees in all families some of the time and in some families most of the time.

Bowen accounted for the variability with the concepts of degree of anxiety and degree of differentiation in a family. According to Bowen, chronic or sustained anxiety largely determines differentiation of self. When anxiety is low, almost any organism can appear normal in the sense that it is symptom-free. When anxiety increases and remains chronic, the organism develops tension either within itself or in its relationship system, resulting in symptoms of dysfunction.

The characteristic of differentiation of self is thought to be so universal that it is used to categorize all people on a single continuum, according to the degree of fusion between emotional and intellectual functioning. (Bowen makes it clear that this continuum is a theoretical construct, not a scale for use as a measuring instrument.) At the low extreme, lives are dominated by automatic emotional processes and reactivity; people are easily stressed into dysfunction and have difficulty recovering. Toward the high end, intellectual functioning remains relatively autonomous under stress; individuals are more adaptable, flexible, and independent of surrounding emotionality, and they cope better with life stresses. The upper extreme is a theoretical ideal level of functioning, which is rarely, if ever, attained. Most people fall in the moderate range, with variable intellectual and emotional balance. Their overt feelings are intense, and their relationship orientations make them reactive to others out of needs for closeness and approval. Human problems and neurotic level symptoms erupt when the emotional system is unbalanced.

In the profile of "Moderate to Good Differentiation of Self," Bowen describes marriage as a functioning partnership in which spouses can enjoy the full range of emotional intimacy without losing their autonomy. They can permit their children to develop autonomous selves without undue anxiety or attempts to mold offspring in their own images. Parents and children are each responsible for themselves and do not credit others for their successes or blame others for failures. As situations require, they are able to function well alone or with others. Their lives are more orderly, they cope effectively with a broad range of human situations, and they are relatively free of human problems.

Bowen believes that each family has its own average level of differentiation around which members fluctuate. Variation in family and individual levels is related to several factors:

1. The "Nuclear Family Emotional System" is the pattern of emotional functioning in a single generation in a family. Certain basic patterns between mother, father, and children replicate those of past generations and can be expected to repeat themselves in future generations. Spouses begin marriage with levels of differentiation and lifestyle patterns developed in their families of origin, and they are thought to select partners at the same level of differentiation. Anxiety is present in all marriages to a varying degree, and is handled most commonly by emotional distance. Poor differentiation may also be manifested in marital conflict, illness or dysfunction of one spouse, or projection of problems to children.

2. The "Triangle," a three-person emotional configuration, is regarded as the basic building block of any emotional system and the smallest stable

relationship system. As anxiety increases, a two-person system tends to involve the most vulnerable third person to become a triangle. When tension can not be absorbed, a series of interlocking triangles may be formed, spreading to extended family and outsiders.

3. Through the "Family Projection Process," parental anxiety is focused on one or more children involved in a mother–father–child triangle. Bowen views the process as universal, present to some degree in all families and ranging from minimal to severely impairing. Most families use a combination of mechanisms, and the more a problem shifts from one area to another, the less likely it will be crippling in any one area. Almost every family has one child who is more triangled than the others and whose life adjustment is poorer. The intensity and the involvement of a particular child depends on a number of factors, such as the parents' levels of differentiation, the amount of anxiety at the time of conception and birth (Walsh, 1978), and sibling positions in the family (Toman, 1976).

4. "Emotional Cutoff" is a concept encompassing the ways in which people separate from their families of origin—isolation, withdrawal, running away, or denying the importance of the parental family. All people have some degree of unresolved emotional attachment; the lower the level of differentiation, the more intense it tends to be. Bowen asserts that the more a nuclear family maintains some kind of viable emotional contact with families of origin, the more orderly and asymptomatic the life processes will tend to be for each generation.

In summary, Bowen views "normality," neuroses, and schizophrenia as all located on one spectrum, from the highest level of functioning to the lowest. In his view, the conceptual schema based on differentiation of self eliminates the concept of "normality," which he believes psychiatry has never adequately defined simply in terms of freedom from emotional symptoms or of behavior in the normal range. The concept of differentiation is not directly connected with the presence or absence of symptoms. Even well-differentiated people can be stressed into dysfunction, but they tend to use a variety of coping mechanisms and to recover rapidly. Bowen thus presents a model of optimal functioning based on differentiation. Although he clearly states that this ideal is theoretical and probably not fully attainable, it does serve as a model toward which therapeutic progress is directed.

### Experiential Model

Two of the most influential family therapists, Satir and Whitaker, each with rather unique styles, pursue an experiential approach to family therapy that is highly intuitive and relatively atheoretical. Satir (1964, 1972) integrates communications and humanistic orientations in her views of family functioning. Drawing on her experience with optimally functioning families—defined as untroubled, vital, and nurturing—Satir describes a consistent pattern. The sense of self-worth in family members is high. Communication is direct, clear, specific, and honest. Family system rules for members are flexible, human, appropriate, and subject to alteration. The family linkage to society is open and hopeful.

In troubled families, in contrast, the sense of self-worth is low; communication is indirect, vague, and not honest; rules are rigid, inhuman, nonnegotiable, and everlasting; and the link to society is fearful, placating and blaming. Regardless of the specific problem or symptom that leads a family into treatment, Satir maintains that some way must be found to change those key factors for family pain to be relieved and family vitality to be enhanced.

Those four aspects of family life—self-worth, communication, rules and linking to society—are regarded by Satir as the basic forces operating in all families, whether it is an intact natural family, a one-parent family, a blended family, or an institutional family. She envisions that families in the future will have even greater variety and complexity of forms than families do at present, and she believes that these family ingredients for human growth will become even more essential.

Whitaker distinguishes the healthy or well-functioning family from a dysfunctional family on a number of dimensions (Whitaker & Keith, 1981). Foremost is the sense of the family as an integrated whole, characterized by separation of parent and child generations and by flexibility in power distribution, rules, and role structure. Normal families operate as open systems, relating to the extended family and the outside world while maintaining the primacy of the nuclear family unit.

A wide range of intimacy and separateness levels is found by Whitaker in healthy families, with increasing intimacy and separateness going together. The same linkage is seen between dependency and autonomy. "Passion and sexuality are the voltage in a family system. When the flow is free, things go well" (1981, p. 192); thus Whitaker states the value of expressing positive and negative feelings. At the same time, Whitaker notes that normal family process is largely covert and nonverbal. He stresses the importance of family play, or "as if" behavior, for creative, experimental process. Also, normal families are seen as able to regress *en masse* for the sake of growth.

The dimension of time is central in Whitaker's conception. Normal families have an evolutionary sense of time through which members progress over the course of the life cycle, with emphasis on the process of becoming. While a connection with past generations is experienced, introjects are brought up to date and modified. Family rituals are valued, and a guiding mythology evolves over time. In sum, family patterns are stable and yet can be altered as life changes are demanded. Finally, Whitaker believes that all families are essentially normal and only become abnormal in the process of pain caused by trying to be normal.

Experiential models direct therapeutic efforts beyond symptom reduction to individual and family growth, as do psychodynamic and Bowen models, according to their conceptions of healthy or optimal functioning. In contrast, less attention is given to the past and more to current, shared affective experience and to the totality of the family as an interactive, self-maintaining system (Napier & Whitaker, 1978).

### Clinical Models: Summary

The family models surveyed reflect somewhat different, and at times overlapping, definitions of family normality. The family systems orientation in general is clearly based on the perspective of normality as process, or as a transactional system operating over time. While grounded in this orientation, various family systems theorists and family therapy models differ in further elaboration of normality and dysfunction. Table 1-1 summarizes the views of normal family functioning, dysfunction, and therapeutic goals embodied in major clinical models.

The structural, strategic, and behavioral models view normality in functional terms; a normal family is primarily a family that does not maintain or reinforce symptoms in any member. While there is recognition of a family developmental process over time, the theoretical and clinical approaches are cross-sectional in the sense of focus on the current pattern, without attention to the historical course resulting in health or symptoms. Treatment goals reflect this view in that they are limited to reducing symptoms rather than promoting growth toward any ideal.

The insight-oriented family approaches—including psychodynamic and Bowen theory, and experiential models—view family normality in terms of particular ideal models of optimal functioning. Family and individual functioning are seen on a continuum, with an optimal level or ideal posited, at least theoretically, as the highest level. While there may be recognition that the optimal level is unattainable in most families, therapeutic goals nonetheless are directed toward growth and actualization of potential toward the ideal.

Conceptually, although the various family models differ in many ways in their definition of family normality and dysfunction, they are remarkably free in general from any major contradiction or inconsistency. There is considerable overlap among theorists in their views of what characterizes the functioning of nonclinical or average families; and those who posit a model of optimal functioning are not in disagreement about the distinguishing features of optimally functioning families.

Where differences among models appear, they reflect a more selective focus or emphasis on a particular aspect of family functioning: on structural patterns, communication processes, or relationship dynamics. For example,

TABLE 1-1.  MAJOR MODELS OF FAMILY THERAPY: NORMALITY, DYSFUNCTION, AND THERAPEUTIC GOALS

| Model of family therapy | View of normal family functioning | View of dysfunction/symptoms | Goals of therapy |
|---|---|---|---|
| *Structural*<br>Minuchin<br>Montalvo<br>Aponte | 1. Boundaries clear and firm.<br>2. Hierarchy with strong parental subsystem.<br>3. Flexibility of system for<br>  a. Autonomy and interdependence.<br>  b. Individual growth and system maintenance.<br>  c. Continuity, and adaptive restructuring in response to changing internal (developmental) and external (environmental) demands. | Symptoms result from current family structural imbalance:<br>  a. Malfunctioning hierarchical arrangement, boundaries.<br>  b. Maladaptive reaction to changing requirements (developmental, environmental). | Reorganize family structure:<br>  a. Shift members' relative positions to disrupt malfunctioning pattern and strengthen parental hierarchy.<br>  b. Create clear, flexible boundaries.<br>  c. Mobilize more adaptive alternative patterns. |
| *Strategic*<br>Haley<br>Milan team<br>Palo Alto group | 1. Flexibility.<br>2. Large behavioral repertoire for<br>  a. Problem resolution.<br>  b. Life cycle passage.<br>3. Clear rules governing hierarchy (Haley). | Multiple origins of problems; symptoms maintained by family's<br>  a. Unsuccessful problem-solving attempts.<br>  b. Inability to adjust to life cycle transitions (Haley).<br>  c. Malfunctioning hierarchy: triangle or coalition across hierarchy (Haley).<br>Symptom is a communicative act embedded in interaction pattern. | Resolve presenting problem only: specific behaviorally defined objectives. Interrupt rigid feedback cycle: change symptom-maintaining sequence to new outcome.<br>Define clearer hierarchy (Haley). |
| *Behavioral–social exchange*<br>Liberman<br>Patterson<br>Alexander | 1. Maladaptive behavior is not reinforced.<br>2. Adaptive behavior is rewarded.<br>3. Exchange of benefits outweighs costs.<br>4. Long-term reciprocity. | Maladaptive, symptomatic behavior reinforced by<br>  a. Family attention and reward.<br>  b. Deficient reward exchanges (e.g., coercive).<br>  c. Communication deficit. | Concrete, observable behavioral goals: change contingencies of social reinforcement (interpersonal consequences of behavior).<br>  a. Rewards for adaptive behavior.<br>  b. No rewards for maladaptive behavior. |

| | | | |
|---|---|---|---|
| *Psychodynamic*<br>Ackerman<br>Boszormenyi-Nagy<br>Framo<br>Lidz<br>Meissner<br>Paul<br>Stierlin | 1. Parental personalities and relationships well differentiated.<br>2. Relationship perceptions based on current realities, not projections from past.<br>Boszormenyi-Nagy: Relational equitability.<br>Lidz: Family task requisites:<br>  a. Parental coalition.<br>  b. Generation boundaries.<br>  c. Sex-linked parental roles. | Symptoms due to family projection process stemming from unresolved conflicts and losses in family of origin. | 1. Insight and resolution of family of origin conflict and losses.<br>2. Family projection processes.<br>3. Relationship reconstruction and reunion.<br>4. Individual and family growth. |
| *Family systems therapy*<br>Bowen | Differentiation of self.<br>Intellectual/emotional balance. | Functioning impaired by relationships with family of origin:<br>  a. Poor differentiation.<br>  b. Anxiety (reactivity).<br>  c. Family projection process.<br>  d. Triangulation. | 1. Differentiation.<br>2. ↑Cognitive functioning.<br>3. ↓Emotional reactivity.<br>4. Modification of relationships in family system:<br>  a. Detriangulation.<br>  b. Repair cutoffs. |
| *Experiential*<br>Satir<br>Whitaker | Satir:<br>1. Self-worth: high.<br>2. Communication: clear, specific, honest.<br>3. Family rules: flexible, human, appropriate.<br>4. Linkage to society: open, hopeful.<br>Whitaker: Multiple aspects of family structure and shared experience. | Symptoms are nonverbal messages in reaction to current communication dysfunction in system. | 1. Direct, clear communication.<br>2. Individual and family growth through immediate shared experience. |

Minuchin attends chiefly to organizational requisites of family functioning, while Satir focuses more on communication skills, and Meissner is concerned primarily with the intergenerational and marital dynamics that promote normal development. Treatment approaches tend to reflect those particular biases in therapeutic objectives and in change processes, or means of attaining those goals. Minuchin concentrates on restructuring the family to eliminate symptoms; Satir facilitates improved communication for growth; Meissner helps families to gain insight into and work through the dynamic processes thought to underlie symptoms.

Major features of functional families posited in one domain have their correlates in other domains. For example, while Bowen focuses on relationship patterns in his model of differentiation of self, the concept of differentiation has its structural and communicational correlates in terms of clear differentiation of generations in the organizational hierarchy and in clarity of communication.

No theorist states explicitly or implies that a variable deemed essential to a well-functioning family by another theorist either makes no difference to or is inversely related to normal functioning. For instance, no theorist claims that flexibility is unimportant or that it characterizes dysfunctional rather than well-functioning families. Unfortunately, clinical theorists too often ignore models other than their own. More dialogue among proponents of various clinical models would be useful in clarifying and relating concepts of family normality and dysfunction.

## CONCEPTUAL CONTRIBUTIONS FROM
## THE SOCIAL SCIENCES

In the social sciences, family theory has developed rapidly over the past three decades, with contributions from sociology, anthropology, social psychology, and social history. Conceptual frameworks most utilized in theory building and research have been identified in decade reviews by Hill and Hansen (1960), Broderick (1971), and Holman and Burr (1980). For comparison and integration of major sociological and clinical theories, readers are referred to Steinglass (1978) and Levant (1980).

Among the proliferation of family theories in the social sciences, several approaches are particularly useful frames of reference for considering normal family processes and dysfunction. Relevant models include systems theory, social exchange theory, behavioral theory, symbolic–interactionist theory, family developmental theory, and family coping theory. (The structural–functional model of Parsons and Bales [1955], once the predominant conceptual framework in the social sciences, has become less influential in recent theory and research.) The first three approaches are considered in the clinical theory section above. Symbolic–interactionist and family developmental models are now briefly summarized. Fuller attention is given to family stress and coping theory, which holds strong potential for contributing to our understanding of family adaptation processes.

## Symbolic–Interactionist Orientation

The symbolic–interactionist approach originated with Burgess (1926), who conceived of the family as a unity of interacting personalities. Two basic premises underlie this orientation: first, that humans respond to their environment in terms of the meaning the environment has for them; second, that such meanings are derived from—and modified in—the process of social interaction (Stryker, 1972). The importance of subjective perception and definition of events is emphasized. Individuals are viewed as active creators of their symbolic–social context, rather than as passive reactors. In the family, each member is assigned roles, according to the ascribed (e.g., sex) and achieved (e.g., marital status) positions they occupy. Roles are defined by normative expectations of reference groups and in accordance with an individual's self-concept. Normal family process is seen as involving the interactions of role-taking members, each viewing the world through a subjective frame of reference. Meanings, roles, and expectations are viewed as critical variables in family functioning (Turner, 1970).

Based on a study of nonclinical families, Hess and Handel (1959) identified four interactional dimensions of normal or nonpathological family processes: family efforts to attain a satisfactory pattern of separateness and connectedness; family efforts to achieve a satisfactory congruence of images, resulting in family interaction centered around particular themes; establishment of boundaries in the family's world of experience; and efforts to deal with significant biosocial issues of family life—particularly sex, generation, and birth order—and their definition in terms of feelings, rewards, and constraints. A well-functioning family is characterized by the successful accomplishment of these basic tasks. The conceptual overlap with family models proposed by Minuchin and Lidz is noteworthy.

## Family Developmental Orientation

The family developmental framework, advanced by Duvall (1977), Hill and Rogers (1964), and Aldous (1978), adds a temporal dimension to the interactionist perspective of the family as a unity of interacting personalities. It seeks to delineate the nature of interrelatedness of family members over the course of the life cycle. Role positions and reciprocal relationships, particularly relationships between parents and children, alter with the developmental changes of members.

The family life cycle is described in terms of developmental stages characterized by major family events—in particular, the addition and exiting of members. The concept of family developmental tasks, central to the theory, refers to changes in normative expectations for the family as a whole in terms of salient issues and of functions it is expected to fulfill for its members and society.

While various schemas punctuate the family life cycle passage somewhat differently in identification of major stages, most distinctions are based on individual developmental changes of offspring. Emphasis has been on early child-rearing phases of the family with less attention to family patterns in later life (Walsh, 1980).

The family developmental orientation has been increasingly well integrated with family systems theory, as evident in the discussion of clinical conceptualizations above. Carter and McGoldrick (1980) have expanded the developmental framework to include stages and transitions involved in divorce and remarriage processes. Their model, emphasizing a three-generational perspective, is summarized in Chapter 7 of this volume.

### Family Coping and Adaptation

Both interactional and family developmental frameworks have served as foundations for theory construction on family stress and coping processes. The most influential theory has been the ABCX (crisis) model first formulated by Hill (1949) to explain a "roller coaster course of adjustment" to war-induced separation and reunion. A set of variables and their relationship are outlined in a two-part framework. The first part regards the period of crisis: A, the *event* and related hardships, interacting with B, the family's crisis-meeting *resources*, and with C, the *definition* the family makes of the event, produce X, the crisis. The second part of the framework describes the process of family adjustment, involving a period of disorganization, an angle of recovery, and a new level of reorganization.

Hill's ABCX model has been modified by Burr (1973) to include concepts of family vulnerability and regenerative power. According to Burr, the stressor event (e.g., hospitalization of spouse), related family hardships (e.g., loss of family income and/or homemaker), and the family's vulnerability (e.g., diminution, absence, or paralysis of family resources) influences the amount of crisis experienced in the family system. The definition the family makes of the seriousness of the changes influences the family's vulnerability to crisis. The variation in a family system's ability to recover from the disruptiveness resulting from a stressor is explained by a family's regenerative power.

Recent investigators have concentrated efforts on definition, elaboration, and measurement of key variables in this process involving family stressors and adjustment. While the concept of family stress is widely used, its meaning is frequently unclear. "Stressors" are defined most often as those life events and related hardships that are of sufficient magnitude to bring about change in the family system. "Stress" and "crisis" are conceptualized not as inherent in the event, but rather as a function of the response by the distressed family, involving the emotional state of members, interpersonal conflict, and disorganization of the family system (Burr, 1973; Hill, 1949).

Attention to family stressors has focused on identification of stressful normative and nonnormative life events. "Normative," here, refers to scheduled events and transitions that most families can expect to occur at certain points in the life cycle. Transition periods are accompanied by family role-complex transformations that involve ambiguity in changing rules, expectations, and behaviors of family members (Boss, 1980). Rapoport (1962) has described the stressful transitions as points-of-no-return which lead either to resolution and growth or to maladaptation. Research on nonnormative family stressors has been concentrated in three areas: war-related separations and problems associated with reentry; natural and accidental disasters; and catastrophic illness and disability (McCubbin, Joy, Cauble, Comeau, Patterson, & Needle, 1980). The concurrence or clustering of stressors may be a significant factor increasing a family's vulnerability and reducing their regenerative ability. A family already struggling with one major life transition is likely to have difficulty coping with concurrent stressors (McCubbin et al., 1980; Walsh, 1978). Further research is needed to address the possible long-term complications as well as the immediate impact of stressors on family systems.

Family adjustment to stressors depends in large part on the family system's resources. Similar to Hill's conceptualization (1949) of the "crisis proof family" is Pratt's notion (1976) of an "energized family"—one endowed with a fluid internal organization characterized by flexible role relationships and shared power which promote personal growth and autonomy.

Problem-solving ability is seen as another of the family's basic resources. Several studies have sought to determine how families manage and resolve hardships (Aldous, Condon, Hill, Straus, & Tallman, 1971; Klein & Hill, 1979; Reiss & Oliveri, 1980). Family *adaptability* and *cohesiveness*, two of the fifteen family system resources in Burr's formulation (1973), are major axes in Olson's circumplex model of family functioning (Olson, Sprenkle, & Russell, 1979; this model is reviewed below in the discussion of integrative models).

The extended family, like the social network (see Anderson, Chapter 17, this volume), plays an important role in alleviating or mediating stress effects, particularly in certain ethnic groups. Caplan (1976) has cited the following supportive roles of a kin system that is functioning effectively as a modulator of stress: collector and disseminator of information; feedback guidance system; source of ideology; guide and mediator in problem solving; source of practical service and concrete aid; haven for rest and recuperation; reference and control group; source and validator of identity; contributor to

emotional mastery. Research has substantiated the fact that intergenerational patterns of reciprocal support continue throughout the life cycle (see
Cohler & Geyer, Chapter 8, this volume).

In the conceptualization of Hill and Burr, the family is viewed as a
*reactor* to stress and a manager of resources. More recent recognition has
been given to the *active* process of family adaptation involving family coping
strategies (e.g., Coelho, Hamburg, & Adams, 1974). A related shift has been
made away from the traditional view of stress as necessarily deleterious, in
contrast to smooth family functioning. Instead, stress is viewed as prevalent
and as holding potential not only for dysfunction but also for growth and
transformation in families. A major question that lies ahead for theory
building and research is this: Why are some families better able than others
to cope with stress, and why do some even become stronger through the
experience?

A study of my own, adapting the Holmes and Rahe stress inventory,
found that families in a normal control group had experienced as many
stresses in the past year, and while children were growing up, as had families
with a severely disturbed young adult child (Walsh, 1978). Moreover, many
parents in the normal group had experienced severe stresses in their own
childhood family of origin experience, but had managed to grow up, marry,
and raise children to adulthood without serious dysfunction in any family
member. Furthermore, these nonclinical families tended to report that their
life crises and hardships had strengthened them and their families. The
struggle to master, or necessity to find new solutions to, stressful family
situations may actually be an important training ground for the development
of creativity (Bateson, 1972).

The few family coping studies to date (McCubbin *et al.*, 1980) have
suggested four hypotheses: that coping behaviors decrease vulnerability;
strengthen family protective resources, such as organization, cohesion,
adaptability; reduce stressor events and hardships; and actively influence the
environment to change the social circumstances. Such studies have found
that family coping strategy is progressively modified over time. Because the
family is a system, coping involves the simultaneous management of various
dimensions of family life: maintaining organization; promoting member
independence and self-esteem; maintaining coherence and unity in family
bonds; developing and maintaining social supports; and controlling the
impact of the stressor and the amount of change in the family. Coping is thus
seen as a process of achieving a balance in the family system that facilitates
organization and unity while promoting individual growth and development.

Perception, including the meaning a family attaches to a stressful situation, appears to be a crucial factor determining the severity of impact of a
stressor and the fact of whether or not the family experiences a crisis
(McCubbin *et al.*, 1980). The difference between coping or dysfunction may

depend on the explanations families use to make sense of what happened, why it happened, and how the situation can be overcome. Shared social meaning can also render stressful situations more understandable and more acceptable in the context in which they are viewed. The degree of stress experienced also depends on whether the family perceives itself as "on time" or "off time" in regard to the normative schedule of expectable events in the family's social context and cohort reference group (Neugarten, 1970). Each family's particular history and association of events will also influence their response. For example, a father's retirement is likely to be more stressful for a family in which a grandfather had died immediately following a forced retirement (Walsh, 1980).

As attention shifts from the study of dysfunction to positive family coping and adaptation, McCubbin and his colleagues (1980) see the need to pursue knowledge about which coping strategies work or fail, under which conditions, and for which families. Reiss and Oliveri (1980) caution against judging certain strategies as better than others without considering them in relation to a particular family's historical and social context. They emphasize the extraordinary variety of coping strategies that families employ and the relationship of these strategies to each family's enduring structure of beliefs, convictions, and assumptions about its social world. Each family's own definition shapes the meaning of an event, the magnitude of stress, and the style of response (see Reiss & Oliveri, Chapter 4, this volume). The typology of family social environments proposed by Moos and Moos (1976) is one attempt to delineate such variables.

## TOWARD AN INTEGRATIVE MODEL
## OF NORMAL FAMILY FUNCTIONING

An important task lies ahead in further elaboration and integration of conceptualizations of normal family functioning. Integrative models combining constructs articulated in family systems theory have been proposed by Barnhill (1979), Fleck (1980), Kantor and Lehr (1975), and Olson et al. (1979). Barnhill has reviewed and attempted to synthesize concepts of the healthy family system as developed in the theoretical literature on family therapy. Eight dimensions of healthy family functioning are identified, grouped into four basic family themes, and integrated as a mutually causal system, termed "the family health cycle." The basic dimensions on which healthy and dysfunctional families are distinguished include the following:

1. Individuation versus enmeshment.
2. Mutuality versus isolation.
3. Flexibility versus rigidity.
4. Stability versus disorganization.

5. Clear versus unclear or distorted perceptions.
6. Clear versus unclear roles or role conflict.
7. Role reciprocity versus unclear or conflictual roles.
8. Clear versus diffuse or breached generation boundaries.

Because these variables are seen as interrelated and mutually reinforcing, an important implication is that a family, by improving its functioning
in one or a few areas, will likely improve functioning in other areas as well.

Fleck has expanded on the basic family tasks formulated by Lidz and
combined them with structural and communication constructs into a model
of family functioning and family pathology. Five family system parameters
and their functioning are posited:

1. *Leadership*: parental personalities, marital coalition, parental role com-
plementarities, and use of power (discipline).
2. *Family boundaries*: ego-boundary development, generation boundary,
and family–community boundary permeability.
3. *Affectivity*: interpersonal intimacy, equivalence of family triads, tolerance
for feelings, and unit emotionality.
4. *Communication*: responsiveness, verbal–nonverbal consistency, expres-
sivity, clarity in form and syntax, and abstract and metaphoric thinking.
5. *Task/goal performance*: nurturance, separation mastery and family triangles, behavior control and guidance, peer relationship and management,
leisure, crisis coping, emancipation, and post-nuclear-family adjustments.

These factors are assessed from the perspective of the biopsychosocial evolution of the family across the life cycle. The salience of tasks and the
appropriateness of organizational patterns vary with different developmental stages.

Based on this schema, Fleck has developed an interactional–historical
systems grid for clinical family evaluation of specific aspects of family
functioning and deficiency. The model has potential value in research and in
assessment of asymptomatic families for purposes of prevention and health
promotion.

Kantor and Lehr have developed a descriptive theory of family process,
dervied from certain elements of family systems theory, that seeks to answer
the basic question about family systems: A system of what? They were
concerned with basic, everyday issues confronting all families, believing that
for a model to be viable, it must be applicable to "healthy" or "normal" as
well as to pathological family processes. Naturalistic observation of family
life was used to identify basic components of family process. Their objective
was to describe how processes interrelate to regulate family members' behavior, particularly in regard to the actual and metaphorical distances each

family evolves in order to survive as a social entity. Their model postulates how families process information and develop strategies to regulate relational distance.

Three types of family systems are described, based on different homeostatic models, or ways that a family can maintain itself and achieve its purposes. In a "closed family system," stable structures (fixed living space, regular time, and steady energy) are relied upon as reference points for order and change. In an "open family system," order and change are expected to result from the interaction of relatively stable evolving family structures (movable space, variable time, and flexible energy). In a "random family system," unstable structures (dispersed space, irregular time, and fluctuating energy) are experimented with as reference points.

The three family types differ in core purposes and homeostatic ideals. Each establishes a different distance-regulation feedback plan for attaining that ideal. Stability is the core purpose of the closed-type family. The open type aims to create a system that is adaptive to the needs of the family and of individual members. The purpose of the random type is free exploration, with the exception being the norm.

Kantor and Lehr stress that one type is not inherently "healthier" than another. Moreover, typical families in the real world are not pure types but mixtures. It is a mistake to assume that a steady state, or harmonious equilibrium, is the homeostatic ideal for all families. Different families espouse different equilibrium–disequilibrium ideals; highly functioning families are found in each type, as are poorly functioning families. For example, a random-type family may be either highly creative or very chaotic. Unfortunately, Kantor and Lehr do not explain how differences between the two are accounted for.

Olson *et al.* (1979) have advanced a "circumplex model" to identify 16 types of marital and family systems based on the family dimensions of "cohesion" and "adaptability." The model proposes that a balanced level of both cohesion and adaptability is the most functional to marital and family development. It posits that too much cohesion, or closeness, results in enmeshed systems, while too little results in disengagement. In regard to adaptability, too much change leads to chaotic systems, while too little leads to rigidity. Thus, unlike Minuchin and Kantor and Lehr, Olson views enmeshment and disengagement, closed and random patterns, as dysfunctional rather than as variant styles.

Four balanced family organizational types representing more functional family systems are proposed by Olson: flexible separateness, flexible connectedness, structured connectedness, and structured separateness. These open systems are distinguished by the ability of individuals to experience and balance extremes of being independent and being connected to families. The model is dynamic in assuming that changes can occur in family types over the course of the life cycle; however, it fails to take into account varying homeostatic ideals and value orientations of particular families and subcultures.

It is apparent in reviewing these integrative models that, while there is a great deal of overlap, they are quite distinctive in many respects. It is also obvious that theorists bring their own selective interpretations to their readings of the literature in attempting to organize and synthesize variables thought to be crucial processes in family functioning. This is due, in part, to a looseness or lack of clarity in family theory, and in part to the failure of clinicians and social scientists to compare models and to combine them where fitting. More rigorous theory construction and empirical testing are needed to distill from various theories the critical concepts and variables related to normal family functioning and dysfunction. The research-based models presented in the second section of this volume, "Research on Normal Family Processes," take important strides in this direction.

## CLINICAL IMPLICATIONS

It has been said that a normal family is one that has not yet been clinically assessed. Clinicians are experts in diagnosing pathology and tend to focus on what they know best. Because clinical training is heavily concentrated on psychopathology, with little attention to normal processes, skewed perceptions of families tend to develop. We are set to look for evidence of family dysfunction; therefore, we may fail to see evidence of family strength or may erroneously assume that because a family is presenting a problem, the family form or style is pathogenic. In a clinical context, we expect to see a dysfunctional family and may not even recognize a normal—either a typical or a well-functioning—family.

Clinicians, moreover, bring certain values and assumptions about normal families into the treatment situation. Many of these are embedded— implicitly as well as explicitly—in each treatment model, as has been seen in this overview of the family therapy literature. It is important that these conceptualizations be made explicit in clinical training programs, since they influence assessment of families and setting of treatment goals. Other assumptions about normal family functioning are extrapolated from clinicians' experience with dysfunctional families; it is assumed that "healthy" families are at the other end of a continuum from the clinical families. A third source of values and assumptions comes from each clinician's own personal life experience, and most strongly and implicitly from one's family of origin. A normal family may be seen as one that is similar to or opposite from the therapist's own family, depending on how one's own family is perceived. In a recent survey I conducted on family therapists' views of normal families, almost half of the clinicians (48%; $n = 187$) reported that as children, they had perceived their own families as abnormal, in the sense of being atypical or unlike how they imagined most families to be. (Yet atypical did not necessarily imply dysfunctional: most clinicians rated their own families as moderately functional or only mildly dysfunctional.) As predicted, both their own family experiences and the family therapy models they used clinically were found to be associated with the family variables they listed and ranked as most important for a well-functioning family.

Family therapists' perceptions of normal family functioning have also been assessed by Fisher and Sprenkle (1978), who combined clinicians' rankings of specific aspects of the key family dimensions of cohesion, adaptability, and communication in Olson's circumplex model. Therapists were found to view a healthy family as one in which members feel valued, supported, and safe; in which they can express themselves openly and have opinions attended to empathically despite disagreement; and in which negotiation and change are possible. Rather similar therapist values were revealed in my own survey. Asked to list and rank five criteria that, in their opinion, are most important for family functioning, clinicians tended to value clear structure and communication, and such relational aspects as mutual caring, trust, and respect for differences. Humor, and the ability of a family to have fun together, were aspects noted by clinicians that deserve further attention in theory and research.

Singular idealized images, or myths of "the normal family" that are derived from professional and personal life experience, need to be carefully examined. Where these are based on pathological models, Beavers (1977) cautions mental health professionals that "We are not unlike energetic and enthusiastic missionaries who encourage others to be good Christians, but have knowledge only of sinners" (p. 123).

Clinicians need to recognize the abstract and subjective nature of any fantasy of health, or else, as Beavers warns, work with struggling clients will be discouraging. We need to guard against imposing a single standard on families with varying forms, functional requisites, and value orientations, so as not to set inappropriate treatment goals. Moreover, a fantasy of health, when combined with a therapist's rescue fantasy, may lead a clinician to set unrealistic treatment goals that a severely dysfunctional family is unlikely to attain. A vicious cycle of failure, unrealistic expectations, and repeated failure can ensue when families entering treatment with a sense of failure are encouraged to pursue unrealistic goals. As a result, both family and therapist experience frustration and failure. Such setting of unrealistic treatment goals is a major factor contributing to therapist burnout (Walsh, 1981a).

Finally, it is imperative for clinical training programs to keep abreast of current advancements in the theoretical and research literature on normal family processes. Equally important, more exposure to nonclinical families should be offered through live and videotape observations of family inter-action, and in assignments to assess nonclinical families on multiple systems dimensions. Naturalistic home observation can be combined with more structured, systematic family evaluation techniques. including, for example, a conjoint family task and a multigenerational family developmental history. Such training experiences will heighten sensitivity to the multiple dimensions of family functioning, to the crucial distinctions between well-functioning and dysfunctional families, and to the diversity that exists among normal families.

## REFERENCES

Ackerman, N. W. *The psychodynamics of family life.* New York: Basic Books, 1958.

Aldous, J. *Family careers: Developmental change in families.* New York: Wiley, 1978.

Aldous, J., Condon, T., Hill, R., Straus, M., & Tallman, I. *Family problem solving.* Hinsdale, Ill.: Dryden Press, 1971.

Aponte, H., & Van Deusen, J. Structural family therapy. In A. Gurman (Ed.), *Handbook of family therapy.* New York: Brunner/Mazel, 1981.

Bane, M. J. *Here to stay: American families in the twentieth century.* New York: Basic Books, 1976.

Barnhill, L. Healthy family systems. *Family Coordinator,* 1979, *28,* 94–100.

Barton, C., & Alexander, J. Functional family therapy. In A. Gurman (Ed.), *Handbook of family therapy.* New York: Brunner/Mazel, 1981.

Bateson, G. *Steps to an ecology of mind.* New York: Ballantine, 1972.

Bateson, G. *Mind and nature: A necessary unity.* New York: Dutton, 1979.

Beavers, W. R. *Psychotherapy and growth: A family systems perspective.* New York: Brunner/Mazel, 1977.

Bertalanffy, L. *General systems theory: Foundation, developments, applications.* New York: Braziller, 1968.

Boss, P. Normative family stress: Family boundary changes across the life-span. *Family Relations,* 1980, *29,* 445–450.

Boszormenyi-Nagy, I. Contextual family therapy. In A. Gurman (Ed.), *Handbook of family therapy.* New York: Brunner/Mazel, 1981.

Boszormenyi-Nagy, I., & Spark, G. *Invisible loyalties.* New York: Harper & Row, 1973.

Bott, E. *Family and social network: Roles, norms and external relationships in ordinary urban families.* London: Tavistock, 1957.

Bowen, M. Theory in the practice of psychotherapy. In *Family therapy in clinical practice.* New York: Aronson, 1978.

Broderick, C. B. Beyond the five conceptual frameworks: A decade of development in family theory. In C. B. Broderick (Ed.), *A decade of family research and acion, 1960–1969.* Minneapolis: National Council on Family Relations, 1971.

Buckley, W. *Sociology and modern systems theory.* Englewood Cliffs, N.J.: Prentice-Hall, 1967.

Burgess, E. W. The family as a unity of interacting personalities. *The Family,* 1926, *1,* 3–9.

Burr, W. R. *Theory construction and the sociology of the family.* New York: Wiley, 1973.

Burr, W. R., Hill, R., Nye, F. I., & Reiss, I. L. (Eds.). *Contemporary theories about the family* (Vol. 2). New York: Free Press, 1979.

Caplan, G. The family as a support system. In G. Caplan & M. Killilea (Eds.), *Support systems and mutual help.* New York: Grune & Stratton, 1976.

Carter, E., & McGoldrick, M. (Eds.). *The family life cycle.* New York: Gardner Press, 1980.

Coelho, G., Hamburg, D., & Adams, J. *Coping and adaptation.* New York: Basic Books, 1974.

Duvall, E. M. *Marriage and family development* (15th ed.). Philadelphia: Lippincott, 1977.

Eiduson, B. Emergent families of the 1970s: Values, practices, and impact on children. In D. Reiss & H. Hoffman (Eds.), *The American family: Dying or developing.* New York: Plenum Press, 1979.

Ekeh, R. *Social exchange theory.* Cambridge: Harvard University Press, 1974.

Epstein, N. B., Bishop, D. S., & Levin, S. The McMaster model of family functioning. *Journal of Marriage and Family Counseling,* 1978, *4,* 19-31.

Erikson, E. H. *Identity and the life cycle: Psychological issues.* New York: International Universities Press, 1959.

Falicov, C. Cultural variations in the family life cycle: The Mexican-American family. In E. Carter & M. McGoldrick (Eds.), *The family life cycle.* New York: Gardner Press, 1980.

Fisher, B., & Sprenkle, D. Therapists' perceptions of healthy family functioning. *International Journal of Family Counseling,* 1978, *6,* 9-18.

Fleck, S. Family functioning and family pathology. *Psychiatric Annals,* 1980, *10,* 46-57.

Ford, F. R., & Herrick, J. Family rules / Family life styles. *American Journal of Orthopsychiatry,* 1974, *44,* 61-69.

Framo, J. Symptoms from a family transactional viewpoint. In N. Ackerman (Ed.), *Family therapy in transition.* Boston: Little, Brown, 1970.

Grinker, R. R., Sr. Normality viewed as a system. *Archives of General Psychiatry,* 1967, *17,* 320-324.

Haley, J. *Uncommon therapy: The psychiatric techniques of Milton H. Erickson, M.D.* New York: Norton, 1973.

Haley, J. *Leaving home.* New York: McGraw-Hill, 1980.

Haley, J. *Problem-solving therapy: New strategies for effective family therapy.* San Francisco: Jossey-Bass, 1976.

Haley, J. Approaches to family therapy. *International Journal of Psychiatry,* 1970, *9,* 233-242.

Haley, J. Toward a theory of pathological systems. In I. Boszormenyi-Nagy & G. Zuk (Eds.), *Family therapy and disturbed families.* Palo Alto: Science & Behavior Books, 1967.

Hareven, T. Family time and historical time. *Daedalus,* 1977, *106,* 57-70.

Hersh, S. P. Children and their families in the U.S.A.: Three profiles of change with a commentary on stress, coping, and relative vulnerabilities. In E. J. Anthony & C. Chiland (Eds.), *The child in his family: Children and their parents in a changing world* (Vol. 5). New York: Wiley, 1978.

Hess, R., & Handel, G. *Family worlds: A psychological approach to family life.* Chicago: University of Chicago Press, 1959.

Hill, R. *Families under stress.* New York: Harper & Row, 1949.

Hill, R., & Hansen, D. A. The identification of conceptual frameworks utilized in family study. *Marriage and Family Living,* 1960, *22,* 299-311.

Hill, R., & Rogers, R. H. The developmental approach. In H. T. Christensen (Ed.), *Handbook of marriage and the family.* Chicago: Rand McNally, 1964.

Hoffman, L. Deviation-amplifying processes in natural groups. In J. Haley (Ed.), *Changing families.* New York: Grune & Stratton, 1971.

Holman, T. B., & Burr, W. R. Beyond the beyond: The growth of family theories in the 1970s. *Journal of Marriage and the Family,* 1980, *42,* 729-741.

Jackson, D. D. The study of the family. *Family Process,* 1965, *4,* 1-20.

Jacob, T. Family interaction in disturbed and normal families: A methodological and substantive review. *Psychological Bulletin,* 1975, *82,* 133-165.

Kantor, D., & Lehr, W. *Inside the family: Toward a theory of family process.* San Francisco: Jossey-Bass, 1975.

Klein, D., & Hill, R. Determinants of family problem-solving effectiveness. In W. R. Burr, R. Hill, F. Nye, & I. Reiss (Eds.), *Contemporary theories about the family* (Vol. 1). New York: Free Press, 1979.

Kluckhohn, F. Variations in the basic values of family systems. In N. Bell & E. Vogel (Eds.), *A modern introduction to the family*. Glencoe, Ill.: Free Press, 1960.

Kohn, M. The effects of social class on parental values and practices. In D. Reiss & H. Hoffman (Eds.), *The American family: Dying or developing*. New York: Plenum Press, 1979.

Levant, R. F. Sociological and clinical models of the family: An attempt to identify paradigms. *American Journal of Family Therapy*, 1980, *8*, 5–20.

Lewis, J. M., Beavers, W. R., Gossett, J. T., & Phillips, V. A. *No single thread: Psychological health in family systems*. New York: Brunner/Mazel, 1976.

Liberman, R. Behavioral approaches to family and couple therapy. *American Journal of Orthopsychiatry*, 1970, *40*, 106–118.

Lidz, T. *The person* (Rev. ed.). New York: Basic Books, 1976.

Lidz, T. *The family and human adaptation*. New York: International Universities Press, 1963.

Macklin, E. Nontraditional family forms: A decade of research. *Journal of Marriage and the Family*, 1980, *42*, 905–922.

Masnick, G., & Bane, M. J. *The nation's families: 1960–1990*. Cambridge, Mass.: Joint Center for Urban Studies, 1980.

McCubbin, H., Joy, C., Cauble, A., Comeau, J., Patterson, J., & Needle, R. Family stress and coping: A decade review. *Journal of Marriage and the Family*, 1980, *42*, 855–871.

McCubbin, H., McCubbin, M., Patterson, J., Cauble, A., Wilson, L., & Warwick, W. CHIP—Coping health inventory for parents: An assessment of parental coping patterns in the care of the chronically ill child. In H. McCubbin (Ed.), *Family stress, coping, and social support*. New York: Springer, 1981.

McQueen, A. The adaptation of urban Black families: Trends, problems, and issues. In D. Reiss & H. Hoffman (Eds.), *The American family: Dying or developing*. New York: Plenum Press, 1979.

Mead, M. Can the American family survive? In J. Henslin (Ed.), *Marriage and family in changing society*. New York: Free Press, 1980.

Meissner, W. W. The conceptualization of marital and family dynamics from a psychoanalytic perspective. In T. Paolino & B. McCrady (Eds.), *Marriage and marital therapy*. New York: Brunner/Mazel, 1978.

Minuchin, S. *Families and family therapy*. Cambridge: Harvard University Press, 1974.

Minuchin, S., Montalvo, B., Guerney, G., Rosman, B., & Schumer, F. *Families of the slums*. New York: Basic Books, 1967.

Moos, R. H., & Moos, B. S. A typology of family social environments. *Family Process*, 1976, *15*, 357–371.

Nabokov, V. *Ada*. New York: McGraw-Hill, 1969.

Napier, A., & Whitaker, C. *The family crucible*. New York: Harper & Row, 1978.

Neugarten, B. Dynamics of transition of middle age to old age: Adaptation and the life cycle. *Journal of Geriatric Psychiatry*, 1970, *4*, 71–78.

Offer, D., & Sabshin, M. *Normality: Theoretical and clinical concepts of mental health* (1st & 2nd eds.). New York: Basic Books, 1966, 1974.

Olson, D. H., Sprenkle, D. H., & Russel, C. Circumplex model of marital and family systems: I. Cohesion and adaptability dimensions, family type, and clinical applications. *Family Process*, 1979, *18*, 3–28.

Opler, M. Mental health and family life in urbanized America. *International Journal of Family Psychiatry*, 1980, *1*, 1–19.

Parsons, T., & Bales, R. F. *Family, socialization, and interaction process*. Glencoe, Ill.: Free Press, 1955.

Patterson, G. R., Reid, J. B., Jones, R. R., & Conger, R. E. *A social learning approach to family intervention*. Eugene, Ore.: Castalia, 1975.

Paul, N. L., & Paul, B. B. *A marital puzzle: Transgenerational analysis in marriage*. New York: Norton, 1975.

Pleck, J. The work-family role system. *Social Problems*, 1977, *24*, 417–427.

Pratt, L. *Family structure and effective health behavior: The energized family*. Boston: Houghton Mifflin, 1976.

Price, D. Normal, functional, and unhealthy? *Family Coordinator*, 1979, *28*, 109–114.

Rapoport, R. Normal crises, family structure, and mental health. *Family Process*, 1962, *2*, 68–79.

Reiss, D. Varieties of consensual experience: III. Contrast between families of normals, delinquents, and schizophrenics. *Journal of Nervous and Mental Diseases*, 1971, *152*, 73–95.

Reiss, D., & Oliveri, M. E. Family paradigm and family coping: A proposal for linking the family's intrinsic adaptive capacities to its responses to stress. *Family Relations*, 1980, *29*, 431–444.

Riskin, J. "Nonlabeled" family interaction: Preliminary repört on a prospective study. *Family Process*, 1976, *15*, 433–439.

Riskin, J., & Faunce, E. An evaluative review of family interaction research. *Family Process*, 1972, *11*, 365–455.

Ruesch, J., & Bateson, G. *Communication: The social matrix of psychiatry*. New York: Norton, 1951.

Satir, V. *Conjoint family therapy*. Palo Alto: Science & Behavior Books, 1964.

Satir, V. *Peoplemaking*. Palo Alto: Science & Behavior Books, 1972.

Selvini Palazzoli, M., Boscolo, L., Cecchin, G., & Prata, G. *Paradox and counterparadox*. New York: Aronson, 1978.

Skolnick, A., & Skolnick, J. *Families in transition: Rethinking marriage, sexuality, child rearing, and family organization*. Boston: Little, Brown, 1971.

Skynner, A. C. R. *Systems of family and marital psychotherapy*. New York: Brunner/Mazel, 1976.

Sluzki, C. E., & Ransom, D. C. (Eds.). *Double-bind: The foundation of the communicational approach to the family*. New York: Grune & Stratton, 1976.

Solnit, A. J. The appraisal of the individual in the family: Criteria for healthy psychological development in childhood. In C. Hofling & J. Lewis (Eds.), *The family: Evaluation and treatment*. New York: Brunner/Mazel, 1980.

Solomon, M. A. A developmental, conceptual premise for family therapy. *Family Process*, 1973, *12*, 179–188.

Spiegel, J. *Transactions: The interplay betwen individual, family, and society*. New York: Science House, 1971.

Steinglass, P. Marriage from a systems theory perspective. In T. Paolino & B. McCrady (Eds.), *Marriage and marital therapy*. New York: Brunner/Mazel, 1978.

Stierlin, H. *Separating parents and adolescents*. New York: Aronson, 1974.

Stryker, S. Symbolic interaction theory: A review and some suggestions for comparative family research. *Journal of Comparative Family Studies*, 1972, *3*, 17–32.

Tolstoy, L. *Anna Karenina*. New York: World, 1946.

Toman, W. *Family constellations* (Rev. ed.). New York: Springer, 1976.

Turner, R. *Family interaction*. New York: Wiley, 1970.

Vaillant, G. *Adaptation to life*. Boston: Little, Brown, 1977.

Visher, E., & Visher, J. *Stepfamilies: A guide to working with stepparents and stepchildren*. New York: Brunner/Mazel, 1979.

Walsh, F. Preventing burnout in therapeutic work with severely dysfunctional families. In A. Gurman (Ed.), *Questions and answers in the practice of family therapy*. New York: Brunner/Mazel, 1981. (a)

Walsh, F. Family therapy: A systemic orientation to treatment. In A. Rosenblatt & D. Waldfogel (Eds.), *Handbook of clinical social work*. San Francisco: Jossey-Bass, 1981. (b)

Walsh, F. The family in later life. In E. Carter & M. McGoldrick (Eds.), *The family life cycle: A framework for family therapy*. New York: Gardner Press, 1980.

Walsh, F. Breaching of family generation boundaries by schizophrenics, disturbed, and normals. *International Journal of Family Therapy*, 1979, *1*, 254–275.

Walsh, F. Concurrent grandparent death and birth of schizophrenic offspring: An intriguing finding. *Family Process*, 1978, *17*, 457–463.

Watzlawick, P., Weakland, J., & Fisch, R. *Change: Principles of problem formation and problem resolution.* New York: Norton, 1974.

Watzlawick, P., Beavin, J., & Jackson, D. *Pragmatics of human communication.* New York: Norton, 1967.

Weakland, J., Fisch, R., Watzlawick, P., & Bodin, A. Brief therapy: Focused problem resolution. *Family Process*, 1974, *13*, 141–168.

Weiss, R. L. The conceptualization of marriage from a behavioral perspective. In T. Paolino & B. McCrady (Eds.), *Marriage and marital therapy.* New York: Brunner/Mazel, 1978.

Wertheim, E. Family unit therapy and the science and typology of family systems. *Family Process*, 1973, *12*, 361–376.

Whitaker, C., & Keith, D. Functional family therapy. In A. Gurman (Ed.), *Handbook of family therapy.* New York: Brunner/Mazel, 1981.

# II

## RESEARCH ON
## NORMAL FAMILY PROCESSES

# 2

# HEALTHY, MIDRANGE, AND
# SEVERELY DYSFUNCTIONAL FAMILIES

## W. ROBERT BEAVERS

## INTRODUCTION

My interest in healthy family processes has evolved from 20 years of clinical work and research with both disturbed and healthy persons and families in a variety of settings. The psychological and social functioning of an individual has its roots in family experiences. Though biological factors are real and significant, identity emerges in large part from family interaction. Most mental health professionals become aware of the characteristics of communication and relationship patterns by observing families with identified patients. The Timberlawn study of healthy families (Lewis, Beavers, Gossett, & Phillips, 1976) provided a unique opportunity to understand the patterns of relating found in competent families. This research presented volunteer families containing no identified emotionally ill member with a series of tasks; the work was filmed, and raters were trained to rate the families with process-oriented, interactional rating scales. This group was selected to match as closely as possible a group of families who had an adolescent hospitalized in a private psychiatric hospital. These families were studied in a similar fashion. Thus a uniform research approach to families with widely varying competence produced significant findings of family processes correlated with family capabilities and the functioning capacity of offspring. I subsequently organized and expanded the findings from that study and delineated a spectrum of family patterns observable at various levels of functioning: "healthy," "midrange," and "severely dysfunctional" (Beavers, 1977).

W. Robert Beavers. Clinical Faculty, Department of Psychiatry, University of Texas Health Science Center, Dallas, Texas.

As two individuals become a couple, their expectations of each other are strongly influenced by the rule system in each person's family of origin. This couple tries to meet its own needs and then the needs of children as they are added to the unit, and it tries to do this within a broader framework of their community. Success in these efforts requires *negotiation*—negotiation about such fundamental and personal matters as living space, the use of time, expression of feelings, and value judgments. Only quite competent people are able to accomplish these negotiations well. The Timberlawn research, using process observations of healthy families, shed light on the processes evolved by couples who develop healthy families.

Offer and Sabshin describe four ways of defining "normality" or "health." One is a negative definition: if a family has an emotionally ill member, it is not healthy, and if no member of that family is so diagnosed (and usually such definitions are qualified by time limits, such as 2, 3, or 5 years), then it is healthy (Offer & Sabshin, 1976).

A second perspective on "health" is that of optimal functioning as determined by some theoretical approach. The Timberlawn research started with the first definition and proceeded to the second with a data based theoretical system.

A third definition of "normality" is statistical—the average. With this definition, families in the midrange of functioning would undoubtedly be closer to normal than the families to be described in this section. Optimal families are as deviant from the norm as are severely dysfunctional families at the opposite end of a scale of competence.

Offer and Sabshin's fourth definition of "normality" is that of health as a process, and of growth, adaptation, and change as integral parts of getting and staying healthy. Though the data are incomplete, follow-up reports from the Timberlawn study strongly suggest that families defined as optimal from a cross-sectional, process evaluation tend to remain healthy over several years. That is, competence at one point in a family's life is reasonably predictive of capability at a later date.

## OPTIMAL FAMILIES

Using these different definitions of health, our research group designated two subgroups of healthy families, the "optimal" and the "adequate." Optimal families demonstrate those skills that are crucial in dealing with the tensions between individual choice and group needs, between the need for individual freedom and for belonging and togetherness—conflicts that derail less capable families. The optimal families studied showed capability in many areas, organized around the following eight variables.

## A Systems Orientation

This concept includes at least four basic assumptions:

1. An individual needs a group, a human system, for identity and satisfaction.
2. Causes and effects are interchangeable.
3. Any human behavior is the result of many variables rather than one "cause"; therefore, simplistic solutions are questioned.
4. Human beings are limited and finite. No one is absolutely helpless or absolutely powerful in a relationship.

Optimal family members know that people do not prosper in an interpersonal vacuum; human needs are satisfied in relationships. As children develop and mature, they leave their families, not for isolated independence but for other human systems. Whether they enter college or marriage, the military or the swinging singles, the need for community continues, and interpersonal skills are required to adapt to these various networks.

The second hallmark of a systems view, the recognition that causes and effects are interchangeable, is equally significant. Optimal family members know, for example, that hostility in one person promotes deception in the other and that deception promotes hostility. Efforts at tyrannical control increase the possibility of angry defiance, just as uncooperative defiance invites tyrannical control. Stimuli are responses, responses are stimuli, in a process with shape and form but with no clearly defined villains or victims.

The third concept, that human behavior results from many variables, is evident in optimal families and painfully absent in dysfunctional families. For instance, when a child of 3 spills milk at the table, possible explanations include the following: (1) It happens accidentally, and no motive should be attached to the behavior. (2) It has interpersonal meaning; for example, the child has a score to settle with the mother. (3) The child has to express hostile, destructive drives, unrelated to the mother. (4) The child is tired or anxious and therefore apt to make mistakes. (5) The problem is mechanical; the glass is too large for the child's small hands. A characteristic of dysfunctional families is that they believe one or another of these explanations almost fanatically. In contrast, optimal families use all these possibilities and more; they are not locked into an idea of single causation, and their responses vary with the situation in a pragmatic fashion.

Finally, a systems orientation includes an awareness that humans are finite, that they have limited power, and that self-esteem comes from achieving relative competence rather than from attempting some sort of omnipotence. Optimal family members know that success in human endeavors depends on variables beyond anyone's control; yet, if they possess goals and purpose, they can make a difference in their own lives and in others' lives.

People are terribly vulnerable if they try to control others absolutely. Negotiation is essential for success in human enterprise, and individual choice must be taken into account.

## Clear Boundaries

A useful parallel to the external boundary of an optimal family system is that of a living cell, possessing enough strength and integrity to allow a highly involved interaction within its borders, yet permeable to the outside world, allowing a satisfying interchange. Optimal family members are actively involved in the world beyond the family, relate to it with optimism and hope, and from their encounters outside bring varied interests and excitement back into the family. Openness to other viewpoints, lifestyles, and perceptions contribute to the congruent mythology seen in the optimal families studied. Their perception of their own family strengths and weaknesses coincides with observations of outside raters. In addition, these optimal families have very clear boundaries between members. It is easy to distinguish a mother's feelings from a father's and one child's view of a specific situation from another child's view. Negotiation consists of accepting differences and working toward shared goals. In such a differentiated family unit, individual choice is expected, family members speak up, and even the youngest children are respected as significant sovereign individuals with valuable contributions.

These are clear generational boundaries. Though overt power is shared freely, there is no question as to who is parent and who is child. No parents feel obligated to disclaim their adult power, and no children feel called upon to assume a premature responsibility. Parents forego any possibility of exploiting their children by defining them as pseudoadults.

Respect for individual boundaries invites intimacy. Members of optimal families have the opportunity to share their innermost selves, experiencing each other as different but empathic. In deciding on plans and goals, compromise is usually unnecessary, as the family members consider individual and family goals generally compatible. Negotiation is qualitatively different from compromise, since compromise suggests an oppositional set with the expectation of settling for "half a loaf." Optimal family members expect that the whole system must function for the individuals to prosper. They consider the negotiating process an aspect of being an individual within the family rather than an incessant compromising of personal goals. This affiliative orientation is quite significant in defining an optimal family.

## Contextual Clarity

In any social context—family, friendship, patient–therapist—there is a useful rule of thumb in defining the degree of craziness or sanity: How clear is the context? When an optimal family interacts, it is generally clear to whom comments are addressed and what the relationship is between the speaker and the audience. There is a shared theme, and members can continue discussions over a period of time with effective results. Social roles, though flexible, are clear.

In disturbed families a major source of context confusion is unresolved Oedipal issues. One can be a parent, a spouse, a lover, or a child, but not to the same person. The central issue in adequate developmental resolution of these basic relationships is *renunciation*. A 4-year-old child says, "I am going to grow up and marry Daddy (or Mommy)." (Parents smile, unperturbed.) As the child grows older, he or she becomes capable of dealing with triangles and limitations. In optimal families, children have assistance in accepting these limitations from parents who present clear role definitions and a solid parental coalition.

### Relatively Equal Power and the Process of Intimacy

A human being, when frightened, seeks some kind of power. Two choices are available:

1. The power of a loving relationship with others—the experiencing of closeness without coercion.
2. The power of control—control over one's inner self and/or control over others.

In an optimal family, there is a clear hierarchy of power, with leadership in the hands of the parents who form an egalitarian coalition. Children are less overtly powerful than their parents, but their contributions influence decisions, and their power becomes more nearly equal as the children grow toward adulthood. Frustrating, self-defeating power struggles seldom occur, and family tasks are undertaken with good-humored effectiveness. These fortunate individuals have learned to deal with fear by relating rather than by controlling.

Because the parents have relatively equal overt power, they must have complementary roles in order to avoid constant competitive conflict. There are either overt or tacit agreements as to areas of responsibility and authority. In recent times, an occasional definition of female equality prescribes highly symmetrical roles for marital partners; for example, both should work, and they should share the same housework and child care tasks. None of the healthy families studied had this kind of symmetry. Quite the contrary, it is in poorly differentiated families that symmetrical relationships, along with continuing unresolved conflicts, are found. Long- and short-term complementarity and role differentiation are apparently necessary for pleasant interaction with shared dignity. To illustrate this point, an analogy may help—say, in basketball. On unskilled teams, everybody tries to get the ball and shoot baskets, while on very skilled teams, players cooperate and have complementary roles. While some authors (Watzlawick, Beavin, & Jackson, 1967) have used "complementarity" to include an overt power differential, the term as used here does not imply such overt power differences. Overt power is one dimension of family interaction, and role complementarity or symmetry is another relationship dimension.

Optimal family members recognize and utilize both relationship and coercive controls. Authoritarian control is occasionally used to enforce family rules. It is neither compulsively denied nor virtuously touted. The family under pressure can thus revert to a more control-oriented style, but can enjoy relating intimately when relatively stress-free by throwing aside the overt power differences and sharing as fellow humans.

There is little sexual stereotyping in these optimal families. Instead of gender dictating character, the Timberlawn study found an interesting relationship between the children's birth order and personality. Oldest children were generally more controlled in emotional expression, better disciplined, and more achievement-oriented. Second children showed more affective openness, spontaneity, and less concern with achievement or with personal discipline. The younger children were often slightly retarded in social development.

One of the striking features of the optimal group in the study was the high degree of emotional energy, drive and performance level found in almost everyone because the members did not fear moving toward others or moving into the world. They found rewards in pursuing active solutions to everyday problems. It seems probable that individuals develop passive and inhibited characteristics not so much from biological variations but from family systems that cripple initiative.

### The Encouragement of Autonomy

Westley and Epstein have stated that "autonomy seems to be essential to the development of a satisfactory ego identity, for one must be permitted to consider oneself as a separate person and to experience oneself as such, to find an identity. Without such autonomy, it seems likely that the child will be unable to solve the basic problems of separation from his family of origin and will remain overdependent" (1969, p.23).

Optimal family members take responsibility for their thoughts, feelings and behavior. They are open to communication from others and respect the unique and different subjective views of reality found in any group of people. These family members express feelings and thoughts clearly. They show a striking absence of blame and personal attack, and there is no scapegoating within the family. Because the family system accepts uncertainty, ambivalence, and disagreement, members risk little in being known and open. These families recognize people as mistake makers. The parents can issue pronouncements that later prove to be erroneous with little loss of face. Children can fail without being attacked or defined as inadequate. Because of this tolerance of uncertainty, ambivalence and imperfection, family members can be honest; this creates a climate in which mutual trust flourishes. If people are not punished for telling the truth as they experience it, then lying is unnecessary.

### Joy and Comfort in Relating

Transactions among optimal family members are notable for their warm, optimistic tone of feeling and also for their intensity. Empathy for each other's feelings, interest in what each other has to say, and expectation of being understood encourage them to respond to each other with concern and action. Their orientation is affiliative, with each person expecting satisfaction and reward from relationships, and this reinforces the involvement with and investment in each other. Assessment of this affiliative attitude in a family is based on a complex synthesis of behavior, voice tone, verbal context and communicative patterns.

As a corollary to an affiliative expectation, optimal family members see human nature as essentially benign. Human needs for sexual expression, intimacy, and assertiveness are recognized with a minimum of apprehension. People are understood to be struggling to do as well as possible under their particular circumstance, rather than to be fundamentally hostile or destructive. There is, as might be expected, variability in the extent to which people outside the family are seen as benign, but all optimal families include at least their own members in this assumption.

### Skilled Negotiation

In shared tasks, optimal families excel in their capacity to accept directions, organize themselves, develop input from each other, negotiate differences, and reach closure coherently and effectively. Parents act as coordinators, bringing out others' ideas and voicing their own. They usually alternate this role several times in a short planning session. All the variables important in family systems come into play, including clarity of context, relatively equal power, affiliative expectations, and encouragement of choice. In the studies, family performance in specified small-scale tasks was correlated with overall competence in parenting (Beavers, Lewis, Gossett, & Phillips, 1975).

### Significant Transcendent Values

Capable families accept change. Children grow up, themselves becoming parents. Parents grow old and die. To accept the inevitable risks and losses of loving and being close, families and individuals appear to require a system of values and beliefs which transcend (go beyond) the limits of their experience and knowledge. With such transcendent beliefs and values, families and their members can view their particular reality, which may be painful, uncertain, and frightening, from a perspective that makes some sense of events and allows for hope. Without such beliefs and perspectives, families and individuals are vulnerable to hopelessness and despair.

Every culture must provide its members with mythic truths that make sense of the larger world, the processes of human living, and the passage of time. Western society, though now highly secular, nevertheless offers its members belief in their country, in science, or in other values ranging from capitalism, Communism, or technology, to psychology, Zen Buddhism, and many others.

The ability to accept change and loss is closely tied to the acceptance of the idea of one's own death. Ernest Becker has pointed out that "The human animal is characterized by two great fears that other animals are protected from: the fear of life and the fear of death" (1973, p.53). Only by using the human capacity for symbolism, defining ourselves as part of a meaningful whole, can these threats be faced openly and courageously. Just as no individual person can survive and prosper without relating to a larger system—usually a family—no family can survive and prosper without a yet larger system. A transcendent value system, whether conventional or unique, allows persons and families to center themselves in the universe, to define themselves and their activities as meaningful and significant.

Implicit in the behavior and relationships of all families are certain attitudes about the nature of man and the nature of truth. For optimal families, these attitudes encompass a positive view of humanity as essentially good, or at least as neutral, and of human behavior as a response to experiences and an effort to deal with problems. The behavior and relationships of these family members also imply an understanding of truth as relative rather than as absolute; or, expressed another way, of reality as subjective and different for each person. With these two underlying assumptions about people and reality, healthy families are able to relate with trust, without erecting ponderous interpersonal defenses.

It is important to put the foregoing description of optimal families in perspective. Yes, these skills are present; these attitudes are found; but the overall description suggests a near perfection that is wondrously absent! Healthy families, like healthy plants, have defects and weaknesses resulting from the very processes that produce this health. Along with the capabilities, there are also relative fears of the unusual, or a need to control through affluence, or concerted efforts to blot out the seamy or disturbing. Such defects are a part of health and part of the charm of any competent family. These real defects represent vulnerability; probably no family can be confident that its skills can encompass all possible environmental stresses.

## ADEQUATE FAMILIES

At the next level of competence, adequate families are in some respect similar to optimal families. Their boundaries are clear; they are seldom invasive; and individuals in the families assume responsibility for their own feelings, thoughts, and acts. Unresolvable conflict is minimal.

In other respects, adequate families resemble moderately dysfunctional families. The parental coalition tends to be less sturdy, and overt power is more likely to be unequal than in the optimal family. Members are less receptive to and less empathic with each other. In performing tasks and negotiating differences, they are less successful, and their interaction is observed to be less spontaneous with more tension and discouragement. There is considerable evidence of a family referee who judges all things; hence members have less awareness of and less respect for their own and others' subjective views of reality, and, correspondingly, have reduced potential for personal growth and development. Members evidence definite fear of normal human drives, and there are some fairly painful efforts to control themselves and others. Members are more likely to have an oppositional rather than an affiliative expectation, and they are more likely to distance themselves as part of the process of individuation, though they can break through at times with genuine warmth and intimacy.

These adequate families raise competent children, but they do so with more strain and apparently at the expense of some family members. Often the mother expresses considerable self-doubt, relies on tranquilizers, or is somewhat depressed. Nevertheless, the family members value the responsibility and process of rearing children and work hard at it, and their investment and tenacity compensate for somewhat modest skills.

After this description of healthy families, with its differentiation between optimal and adequate family groups, we are ready to describe less fortunate families that are apt to have members defined as emotionally ill, and families that are organized and function in quite different ways from those of the healthy families.

## FAMILY CLASSIFICATION

In conceptualizing different possible family groupings, both healthy and dysfunctional, I have used two dimensions: a continuum of competence and one of family style. Figure 2-1 presents the 13 subscales that are used to evaluate family competence. The stylistic dimension utilized is similar to that advanced by Stierlin and his coworkers (Stierlin, 1972; Stierlin, Levi, & Savard, 1973), that of "centripetal" and "centrifugal" family styles. The family classifications system derived from these two dimensions has proven clinically useful and valuable in family research.

Family Name ................................................      Rater .....................................................

Segment ......................................................      Date .................................................

*Instructions:*   The following scales were designed to assess the family functioning on continua representing interactional aspects of being a family. Therefore, it is important that you consider the entire range of each scale when you make your ratings. Please try to *respond on the basis of the videotape data alone,* scoring according to what you see and hear, rather than what you imagine might occur elsewhere.

I.   *Structure of the Family*

   A.  Overt Power:   Based on the entire tape, check the term that best describes your general impression of the overt power relationships of this family.

| 1 | 1.5 | 2 | 2.5 | 3 | 3.5 | 4 | 4.5 | 5 |
|---|---|---|---|---|---|---|---|---|
| Chaos | | Marked dominance | | Moderate dominance | | Led | | Egalitarian |
| Leaderless; no has enough power to structure the inter-action. | | Control is close to absolute. No nego-tiation; dominance and submission are the rule. | | Control is close to absolute, Some nego-tiation, but dominance and submission are the rule. | | Tendency toward dom-inance and submission, but most of the inter-action is through respectful negotiation. | | Leadership is shared between parents, changing with the nature of the interaction. |

   B.  Parental Coalitions:   Check the terms that best describe the relationship structure in this family.

| 1 | 1.5 | 2 | 2.5 | 3 | 3.5 | 4 | 4.5 | 5 |
|---|---|---|---|---|---|---|---|---|
| Parent-child coalition | | | | Weak parental coalition | | | | Strong parental coalition |

   C.  Closeness

| 1 | 1.5 | 2 | 2.5 | 3 | 3.5 | 4 | 4.5 | 5 |
|---|---|---|---|---|---|---|---|---|
| Amorphous, vague and indis-tinct boundaries among members | | | | Isolation, distancing | | | | Closeness, with distinct boundaries among members |

II.  *Mythology:*   Every family has a mythology; that is, a concept of how it functions as a group. Rate the degree to which this family's mythology seems congruent with reality.

| 1 | 1.5 | 2 | 2.5 | 3 | 3.5 | 4 | 4.5 | 5 |
|---|---|---|---|---|---|---|---|---|
| Very congruent | | Mostly congruent | | | | Somewhat incongruent | | Very incongruent |

FIGURE 2-1. THE BEAVERS–TIMBERLAWN FAMILY EVALUATION SCALE. SUB-SCALES USED TO DETERMINE COMPETENCE LEVELS.

III. *Goal-Directed Negotiation:* Rate this family's overall efficiency in negotiating problem solutions.

| 1 | 1.5 | 2 | 2.5 | 3 | 3.5 | 4 | 4.5 | 5 |
|---|-----|---|-----|---|-----|---|-----|---|
| Extremely efficient | | Good | | | | Poor | | Extremely inefficient |

IV. *Autonomy*

  A. Clarity of Expression:  Rate this family as to the clarity of disclosure of feelings and thoughts. This is not a rating of the intensity or variety of feelings, but rather of clarity of individual thoughts and feelings.

| 1 | 1.5 | 2 | 2.5 | 3 | 3.5 | 4 | 4.5 | 5 |
|---|-----|---|-----|---|-----|---|-----|---|
| Very clear | | | | Somewhat vague and hidden | | | | Hardly anyone is ever clear |

  B. Responsibility:  Rate the degree to which the family members take responsibility for their own past, present, and future actions.

| 1 | 1.5 | 2 | 2.5 | 3 | 3.5 | 4 | 4.5 | 5 |
|---|-----|---|-----|---|-----|---|-----|---|
| Members regularly are able to voice responsibility for individual actions | | | | Members sometimes voice responsibility for individual actions, but tactics also include sometimes blaming others, speaking in 3rd person or plural | | | | Members rarely, if ever, voice responsibility for individual actions |

  C. Invasiveness:  Rate the degree to which the members speak for one another, or make "mind reading" statements.

| 1 | 1.5 | 2 | 2.5 | 3 | 3.5 | 4 | 4.5 | 5 |
|---|-----|---|-----|---|-----|---|-----|---|
| Many invasions | | | | Occasional invasions | | | | No evidence of invasions |

  D. Permeability:  Rate the degree to which members are open, receptive and permeable to the statements of other family members.

| 1 | 1.5 | 2 | 2.5 | 3 | 3.5 | 4 | 4.5 | 5 |
|---|-----|---|-----|---|-----|---|-----|---|
| Very open | | Moderately open | | | | Members frequently unreceptive | | Members unreceptive |

*(continued)*

FIGURE 2-1. (*continued*)

V. *Family Affect*

A. Range of Feelings: Rate the degree to which this family system is characterized by a wide range expression of feelings.

| 1 | 1.5 | 2 | 2.5 | 3 | 3.5 | 4 | 4.5 | 5 |
|---|---|---|---|---|---|---|---|---|
| Direct expression of a wide range of feelings | | Direct expression of many feelings despite some difficulty | | Obvious restriction in the expressions of some feelings | | Although some feelings are expressed, there is masking of most feelings | | Little or no expression of feelings |

B. Mood and Tone: Rate the feeling tone of this family's interaction.

| 1 | 1.5 | 2 | 2.5 | 3 | 3.5 | 4 | 4.5 | 5 |
|---|---|---|---|---|---|---|---|---|
| Usually warm, affectionate, humorous and optimistic | | Polite, without impressive warmth or affection; or frequently hostile with times of pleasure | | Overtly hostile | | Depressed | | Cynical, hopeless and pessimistic |

C. Unresolvable Conflict: Rate the degree of seemingly unresolvable conflict.

| 1 | 1.5 | 2 | 2.5 | 3 | 3.5 | 4 | 4.5 | 5 |
|---|---|---|---|---|---|---|---|---|
| Severe conflict, with severe impairment of group functioning | | Definite conflict, with moderate impairment of group functioning | | Definite conflict, with slight impairment of group functioning | | Some evidence of unresolvable conflict, without impairment of group functioning | | Little, or no unresolvable conflict |

D. Empathy: Rate the degree of sensitivity to, and understanding of, each other's feelings within this family.

| 1 | 1.5 | 2 | 2.5 | 3 | 3.5 | 4 | 4.5 | 5 |
|---|---|---|---|---|---|---|---|---|
| Consistent empathic responsiveness | | For the most part, an empathic responsiveness with one another, despite obvious resistance | | Attempted empathic involvement, but failed to maintain it | | Absence of any empathic responsiveness | | Grossly inappropriate responses to feelings |

VI. *Global Health-Pathology Scale: Circle the number* of the point on the following scale that best describes this family's health or pathology.

| 10 | 9 | 8 | 7 | 6 | 5 | 4 | 3 | 2 | 1 |
|---|---|---|---|---|---|---|---|---|---|
| Most Pathological | | | | | | | | | Healthiest |

Centripetal family members look for gratification predominantly from within the family and are less trustful of the world beyond the family boundaries. Centrifugal family members, on the contrary, expect gratification from beyond the family and trust activities and relationships outside the family unit more than those within it. Ambivalent feelings in family members are handled quite differently: centripetal families try to repress, suppress, or deny negative feelings and to play up the positive, caring ones (hence the "glue" for the centripetal style), while centrifugal family members are wary of affectionate statements and more comfortable with negative or angry feelings (hence the force for outward or centrifugal movement). Centripetal families tend to bind children and make leave-taking difficult; centrifugal families tend to expel children before optimal individuation is complete.

The most clear-cut, readily evident styles will be found in the most severely disturbed families, since they are the least flexible and the most resistant to adaptive change. Families that are midrange in functioning competence show these stylistic differences clearly but less dramatically, and they possess more mixed patterns than are seen in the severely disturbed group, since midrange families are more differentiated and relatively more adaptive. Stylistic differences are mostly irrelevant for healthy families, who possess enough flexibility to vary styles.

Figure 2-2 describes a systems model of family structure, flexibility, and competence on one dimension and of family styles on the other. The horizontal continuum represents family competence, and the vertical continuum represents the degree of centripetal or centrifugal behavior, assessed by the family's tendency to pull members in or to push them outward for major satisfaction.

The V-shaped notch on the left of Figure 2-2 represents the finding that severely disturbed families show centripetal or centrifugal styles most strongly, since their rigidity and limited coping skills preclude variation in their styles. On the high end of the competence scale, the stylistic variable disappears, since healthy families adapt their styles as family and individual members' needs change. The continuum of family functioning shows progression from extreme rigidity (chaotic, noninteractive), through marked dominance–submission patterns, to greater and greater capacity for equal-powered transactions. It parallels clinical data from both family systems and individual development, and it is offered as a tool for family assessment. It is a cross-sectional model representing a moment in time; families are placed in the various categories depending on interactive, process data, rather than on historical or individual information. The subscales of Figure 2-1 illustrate the process orientation of data collection. Although many variables, such as current stress, social class, and conditions in the larger community, may impinge on family functioning at a given time, a family assessment can point toward intervention methods.

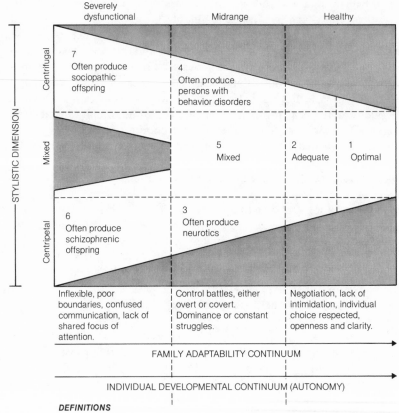

FIGURE 2-2.   A SYSTEMS MODEL COMBINING CONTINUA OF FAMILY COMPE-
TENCE AND STYLE, LEADING TO SEVEN FAMILY TYPES.

This classification system defines seven family types based on competence and style. "Optimal" and "adequate" families have already been described. "Midrange centripetal," "midrange centrifugal," and "midrange mixed" are discussed in the next section of this chapter. Finally, there are "severely disturbed centripetal" and "severely disturbed centrifugal" families, described in the last section of the chapter.

Though such a classification offers no more about a family than an individual diagnosis (e.g., acute psychosis or depression) says about a person, it is a useful means of organizing information about the family and assisting the evaluation of intervention, treatment strategies and outcome.

## MIDRANGE FAMILIES

Returning to the central concept of family competence as a continuum from "severely dysfunctional" to "optimal," a very large group of families are found in the middle of this continuum. These families evidence considerable pain and difficulty in functioning. Healthy families seek intimacy; these families seek control. Parents are engaged in a never-ending effort to control (and inhibit) themselves, their spouses, and their children.

Since they exclude from their definition of what is good or acceptable much of what is essentially human, they usually drive much of their expression of self underground, either into fantasy or illicit behavior. A rigid and often harsh invisible referee rules family interactions. If other members' wishes and behavior coincide with this referee's rules, he or she can speak and behave directly—even smugly! Frequently, these direct declarations are negative: "I'm not angry at you." "I'm not going to act up again." If the other members' feelings and behavior are not in accord with the referee's rules, they see themselves, and others see them, as bad, and they try to control themselves or others in order to bring the forbidden feelings and behavior in line. Excluded feelings are hidden or are expressed with much shame or guilt.

The family referee may be either personified (as a dominating father or mother, or a powerful grandparent understood to be the spokesman for the referee), or abstract. In many families, it is a "they" ("good" people); in others, it is a formal religious code perfectionistically adhered to; or it may be science or reason. In any case, the resulting family interaction is pervaded with intimidation, "shoulds" and "oughts."

The parental coalition in these families is never both equal and unconflicted. Either one parent dominates and the other defers, or there is endless battling. The parent–child interaction is characterized by power struggles, either overt or hidden.

Family members typically resist taking personal responsibility for feelings, thoughts and actions, instead taking shelter behind the referee ("I'm punishing you for your own good"), or obscuring the issue with blame and attack ("You got me so upset, I forgot").

### Painful Encounters

A variety of unpleasant feelings are typical of midrange families. When individuals are overcontrolled, there are two possible responses: submission or rebellion. Power struggles are expressed within the family either in open competition with angry overtones, or in hidden conflict with a depressed atmosphere and little spontaneity. Moves toward intimacy are spoiled by overt intimidation or efforts to induce guilt.

### Unresolved Developmental Issues

The boundary problems most noticeable in midrange families are those of subtle Oedipal coalitions between parents and children (father–daughter, mother–son). These are enjoyable to the family members involved, but are covert and interfere with acknowledged transactions. They are an ongoing factor in difficulties experienced by children growing up and forming new families, adding to their anxiety and conflict about separating from the family of origin and to their attempts to recreate this family in their adult relationships. Individuals in these families do not develop the essential ability to renounce total possession of a loved person or the skills to trade gains in other relationships for reductions in primary attachments (i.e., if I don't try to have Mother all to myself, I can have Dad *and* Mother).

In the family and in society, children develop their definitions of self—who they are, what they can do and strive for, what they are not and cannot be. Supression of those qualities that do not fit his family or society creates longings and rebellious feelings. Midrange families, with their referee system and belief in absolutes, narrow the range of available behaviors and responses. An easily recognized example is the stereotyped role model of the "correct" male or female. Men are expected to be powerful, oblivious to feelings and relationships, action-oriented, aggressive, and monetarily successful. Women are to be weak, intuitive about feelings and relationships, and emotive and dependent. There are, in addition, many personality stereotypes implanted in individuals growing up. "Tom is our hard-working, conscientious son." "Mollie is our scatterbrain." "Bill is timid and won't compete." "Betty is stubborn and wants her own way." These limited and limiting roles become fixed and self-perpetuating.

The midrange family members' narrow definition of what is good or acceptable does not include ambivalence, perhaps the most ubiquitous of all human characteristics. They perceive evidence of strong ambivalence toward family members as part of the willful and evil self, calling for greater efforts at personal and interpersonal control. One side of mixed feelings must be hidden, yet fears of its presence in themselves and others are constantly troublesome.

### Underlying Attitudes and Assumptions

The belief, explicit or implied, that people are essentially willful sinners is central to the interaction of midrange families. If people are by nature lazy, greedy, lustful, and destructive, it follows that they must battle with their own wishes and control others. There is usually a hope that life could be more satisfying, but little ability to make changes toward that end.

### Products of These Families

Children in these families are likely to grow up sane but limited in their ordinary life tasks. As adults, their limitations can be categorized under the general headings of neuroses and behavior disorders. The neurotics are in emotional pain from depression or excessive anxiety, but they do not have trouble conforming to social rules. People with behavior disorders, on the other hand, are in pain from their continuing difficulty in following accepted rules of society. Some members of midrange families are also susceptible to reactive schizophrenic illness (typically an acute psychosis with recovery).

Midrange family members, then, develop a self-definition that is clear and coherent but quite vulnerable to stress because of its narrowness and limits. Their interpersonal skills are fewer than those of the healthy family, and they are far more likely to be guilt-laden.

## MIDRANGE CENTRIPETAL FAMILIES

In these families (see Classification 3, Figure 2-2), rigid structure is maintained. Coercive control methods are used and are generally successful. The parental coalition is characteristically reasonably competent, because one parent (usually the husband) has greater overt power and the other submits. Young children are coerced into following the rules. The credo of this family might be stated as follows: "To be good, you must do, think, and feel according to the family rules. Behave properly, and hide your feelings."

Ambivalence is usually handled by denying or repressing the ugly or improper half of mixed feelings. In these centripetal families, the referee approves of positive feelings and attempts to eradicate negative ones. There is a pervasive belief that people "really" have only one feeling, as, "He really loves me though he never says anything." There is little spontaneity and great concern for rules and authority. Sex stereotyping is greater in this group than in all other family classifications; women are expected to be nurturing and unambitious, while men are expected to be powerful and acquisitive.

The classic neurotic (appreciated by psychotherapists for coming into treatment, paying his bills, and not "acting out") is the expected product of the midrange centripetal family. He or she may become compulsive or hysteric, chiefly differing in the expectation each has had of becoming socially powerful (effective, significant). If a family expects the child to be powerful, this encourages the person to behave as a compulsive; if he or she is expected to be weak or vulnerable, then the neurotic illness will be hysteric, and these expectations are strongly related to the sex of the child. Family members have trouble with autonomy and with choice, a predictable result of the family assumption that all encounters must be a struggle for control, with winners and losers. Each family member mistrusts close encounters because of this assumption. If a midrange centripetal family scapegoats one child, a severe behavior disorder can develop. For this one child, the family roles are reversed, and he or she takes on all the denied negative feelings and characteristics.

At the point of contact with psychotherapists, the family members are fearful of exposure, and usually one member reluctantly accepts the role of the identified patient requiring treatment. When these families are doing well, they are likely to be quite visible in the community. When they are doing poorly, they try to hide their difficulty.

## MIDRANGE CENTRIFUGAL FAMILIES

These families (see Classification 4, Figure 2-2), in contrast to the midrange centripetal group, lack an effective parental coalition. Both parents feel inadequate to follow the rules, and they habitually and ineffectually battle for control of the children, blaming each other for their failures. Unstable illicit alliances between one or the other parent and children are common. Children learn to play one parent against another, typically developing a rather cynical attitude, which is transferred to their expectations of authorities in the outside world. The parents believe in the cultural sexual stereotypes of a strong male and nurturing female, but fail to live up to them. Fathers are more inadequate and mothers more aggressive than they believe acceptable. As a result, they have overt conflict and ineffectual guilt, and they frequently engage in blaming and attacking. Expressions of warmth and caring provoke anxiety. Easily unleashed negative feelings provide the energy for centrifugal movement; mothers and fathers spend little time in the home, and children move out into the neighborhoods and streets much earlier than the norm.

The children behave poorly in social and work situations. The norms of other groups are as difficult for them to accept, as are the conflicting and ineffective family rules. They learn from their parents to be disappointed in each other and in themselves. This kind of family and individual appears to be increasing. As the mores of our culture become more uncertain and contradictory, and as very young children are less likely to be supervised by one consistent adult, behavior disorders increase and classical neuroses decrease. More therapeutic ingenuity and energy are required in developing a treatment alliance with clients who are suspicious of authority, fearful of close relationships, and skeptical of the value of words.

The centrifugal family occasionally will produce a neurotic, who rejects the turmoil and dramatic emotionality of other family members, perceives himself as the "odd duck" therein, and controls his own feelings, thoughts and behavior to a high degree. He looks to outside authority to reward him, and may be a high achiever at the expense of gratifying relationships.

Centrifugal families seen by professionals may be expected to have many open and repeated crises, calling attention in the wider world to internal family problems. Children run away to express the feeling that parents don't care. Spouses separate, threaten suicide, and have dramatic brawls. When these families are in trouble, their initial reaction is often to get an authority to agree that one member is responsible. They distrust words, are action-oriented, and not only watch the therapist's behavior closely, but act out their responses—for example, by missing appointments. Their fear of the therapist/referee is expressed either in defiance or in superficial compliance. The therapist's authority is used as a club to blame (not to change) other family members.

## MIDRANGE MIXED FAMILIES

Another category of midrange families (see Classification 5, Figure 2-2) has alternating and competing centripetal and centrifugal behaviors, representing characteristics of both styles. In this mixed style, the parental coalition typically varies in one interview from dominance–submission to petty bickering; the children alternate between accepting and resisting parental control.

## SEVERELY DYSFUNCTIONAL FAMILIES

We now move to the low end of the functional continuum of families, those who are most inflexible, undifferentiated, and ineffective in meeting stress and developmental demands. These families have a variety of difficulties in relation to systems variables. They have poorly defined power structure; unclear, ineffective, and unsatisfying communication; extreme problems in interpersonal boundaries; few negotiation skills; and a pervasively depressed or cynical feeling tone.

The family power structure is difficult to define, and communication is chronically ineffective. Family members characteristically have no shared focus of attention (Singer, Wynne, & Toohey, 1978). The parental coalition is in shambles. Family members deny the passage of time and its implications as to growth and development, aging and death. Behavior and feelings are quite often unresponsive to the changing abilities of family members, and the family members have great difficulty in looking forward to the future and making effective plans. Ambivalence is characteristically expressed in a sequential fashion. That is, family members tend to express first one side and then another of the strong mixed feelings that they feel toward one another. There is little "glue" in these ambivalent communications, and the listener is left to interpret and to make some sense out of quite opposite communications (Beavers, Blumberg, Timken, & Weiner, 1965).

The lack of individuality or differentiation of self in these families leads to profound difficulties in members' ability to decide on and move toward goals, as well as in the family's capacity to resolve conflicts and deal with pressing problems. The system wallows like a rudderless ship. The mood and tone of feeling is the most painful found in any families. Expressions of warmth and affirmation are rare. Severely disturbed families feel chronically disappointed, frustrated, angry, resentful, and guilty. In these families and individuals, a basic developmental task, that of evolving trust, remains unfinished.

The child growing up in such a family develops only a rudimentary sense of self, and choice is characteristically ignored. When individual choice is ignored, hopelessly irresolvable conflict is inevitable, and a loss of individual identity frequently occurs.

## SEVERELY DYSFUNCTIONAL CENTRIPETAL FAMILIES

This group of severely disturbed families has a tough (see Classification 6, Figure 2-2), nearly impermeable outer boundary or perimeter. The family is usually seen as strange or odd by neighbors, and family loyalty requires remaining in the family and either physically or emotionally never leaving home. Family members are expected to think and feel alike, with no comprehension of uniquely subjective human responses to the world. There are severe boundary problems. Children receive few clear messages and many confusing ones. Parents speak for children ("You don't really mean that; you actually love your sister, you don't hate her"). Members of these families are unable to experience or express a sense of individual identity.

Because of the lack of a shared focus of attention and the pervasive communicational obscurity, dealing with loss by sharing is quite impossible. Clinicians have long observed the connection between unfinished grief, or inability to deal with loss, and the schizophrenic process (Paul & Grosser,

1965; Searles, 1961). Families need to face and adapt to the inevitable losses brought by time and change. Marital relationships and the ability of family members to reach outside the family for satisfaction and meaning are important factors in healing the pain of human loss.

The children in these families are characteristically quite inhibited and overcontrolled; for them, one solution to the conflict between developmental pressures toward separation and family rules of remaining loyal and static is a schizophrenic level of functioning.

## SEVERELY DYSFUNCTIONAL CENTRIFUGAL FAMILIES

This group of families (see Classification 7, Figure 2-2) is characterized by an extremely diffuse boundary with the outside world. Family organization is unstable. Parents move in and out, children run away, and the very definition of who constitutes the family is often ambiguous. Family interaction is marked by competition, teasing manipulation, and open conflict that is never resolved. Interpersonal skills are so limited that, though parents and children may leave home, they are usually unsuccessful and return to the family as needful and hostile as before. Discipline is attempted through intimidation, which usually fails because of the shifting, ineffective power structure and the lack of positive relationships. Family members are unreceptive to each other's efforts to communicate, and there is a marked lack of empathy. The quarrelsome, angry family interaction and the hostile, antisocial behavior of individual members can be seen as a defense against the pain and sadness of emotional deprivation. These family members find hostility easy to express, but tenderness, loneliness, and emotional pain are difficult or impossible to admit openly.

Centrifugal severely disturbed families are likely to produce sociopathic offspring (antisocial personalities). Children in these families can find no way to be loved by obeying the rules, since the rules shift and no behavior patterns are rewarded consistently by closeness or caring. They learn to present an "I don't care" facade and to share the family viewpoint that all those within its boundaries are bad, even evil. The resulting unacceptable behavior of these children provokes social rejection and punishment, which further encourages self-loathing. Self-defeating behavior expresses rage to an uncaring world.

## SUMMARY

This chapter summarizes material derived from both clinical observations and extensive family research concerning the nature of family processes in emotional health and illness. The characteristics found in optimal families are presented as the highest level of a continuum of competence. It is valuable for clinicians to know these characteristics; intervening in troubled families is facilitated by knowing what system changes are needed, in addition to knowing what is wrong with the system. Healthy families have a capacity for and seek intimacy. Less fortunate families in the midrange of functioning competence seek control, and family members endlessly attempt to obtain a power edge and to intimidate others successfully. Severely dysfunctional families flounder in unsuccessful efforts at achieving coherence and reaching out to others. The data provide a framework for family classification that can be useful in deciding on intervention techniques and in developing outcome studies.

## REFERENCES

Beavers, W. R. *Psychotherapy and growth.* New York: Brunner/Mazel, 1977.

Beavers, W. R., Blumberg, S., Timken, K. R., & Weiner, M. D. Communication patterns of mothers of schizophrenics. *Family Process,* 1965, *4,* 95–104.

Beavers, W. R., Lewis, J. M., Gossett, J. T., & Phillips, V. A. Family systems and ego functioning: Midrange families. *Scientific Proceedings,* 128th Meeting, American Psychiatric Association, Anaheim, Calif., May 1975 (Summary #265).

Becker, E., *The denial of death.* New York: Free Press, 1973.

Lewis, J. M., Beavers, W. R., Gossett, J. T., & Phillips, V. A. *No single thread: Psychological health in family systems.* New York: Brunner/Mazel, 1976.

Offer, D., & Sabshin, M. *Normality.* New York: Basic Books, 1976.

Paul, N., & Grosser, G. H. Operational mourning and its role in conjoint family therapy. *Community Mental Health Journal,* 1965, *1,* 339–345.

Searles, H. F. Schizophrenia and the inevitability of death. *Psychiatric Quarterly,* 1961, *35,* 631–664.

Singer, M. T., Wynne, L. C., & Toohey, M. L. Communication disorders and the families of schizophrenics. In L. C. Wynne, R. L. Cromwell, & S. Matthysse (Eds.), *The nature of schizophrenia: New approaches to research and treatment.* New York: Wiley, 1978.

Stierlin, H. *Separating parents and adolescents.* New York: Quadrangle, 1972.

Stierlin, H., Levi, L. D., & Savard, R. J. Centrifugal versus centripetal separation in adolescence: Two patterns and some of their implications. In S. Feinstein & P. Giovacchini (Eds.), *Annals of the American Society for Adolescent Psychiatry* (Vol. 2). New York: Basic Books, 1973.

Watzlawick, P., Beavin, J., & Jackson, D. D. *Pragmatics of human communication.* New York: Norton, 1967.

Westley, W. A., & Epstein, N. B. *The silent majority.* San Francisco: Jossey-Bass, 1969.

# 3

# RESEARCH ON "NONLABELED" FAMILIES: A LONGITUDINAL STUDY

## JULES RISKIN

## INTRODUCTION

The purpose of this chapter is to report on a pilot project for a prospective longitudinal research study on "healthy" or "nonlabeled" families.[1] The data analysis phase of the work is still continuing, and this chapter is therefore a "progress report" (see Riskin, 1976, and Riskin & McCorkle, 1979). We interviewed two families over a period of 4½ years. After presenting background material, I describe the methods used, the data collected, an analysis of the data, preliminary findings, and some implications for future research. Our primary focus has been on family interaction and on the relationship between that interaction and the mental health of the family members. This paper emphasizes methodological issues and empirical findings rather than the development of a conceptual framework. It should be stressed at the onset that the findings are only suggestive and that more investigation on a larger sample is essential.

## BACKGROUND

Objective, longitudinal data about effective or "healthy" whole-family interaction and its relationship to the children's development, as well as methods for collecting these data, are extremely limited. Existing knowledge from the

---

[1] It is difficult to discuss the complex concept of "mental health" without value judgments or extremely difficult theoretical issues being raised. This study uses an operational criterion: "families whose members do not bear formal psychiatric labels at the start of the project," and whose members meet some other specific exclusion and inclusion criteria to be described below, are abbreviated as "nonlabeled" families. When the words "healthy" or "normal" appear, they mean "nonlabeled."

Jules Riskin. Mental Research Institute, Palo Alto, California.

clinical research tradition in the family field has been primarily based on a pathology model. This reflects the traditional clinical approach: identifying those factors that produce disease and developing therapeutic procedures. To the extent that there is a body of knowledge about "nonlabeled" families, it has been obtained almost entirely through cross-sectional studies. Hypotheses have typically been tested by cross-sectional correlations or through analysis of data obtained retrospectively, and these kinds of data are often unreliable.

The early history of clinically based family interaction research is embedded in the origins of the family therapy movement. Troubled families who sought therapy were available for ongoing study, and the treatment situation provided a strong motive for them to stay in contact with the clinical researchers. Research inevitably was intertwined with a concern for "what went wrong" and "how to bring about improvement." The dominant research questions were directed towards identifying different patterns of dysfunctional family interaction, especially as they might relate to schizophrenia. Seminal hypotheses relating individual pathology to pathological family interaction were generated in the ongoing therapeutic setting (Ackerman, 1962; Bateson, Jackson, Haley, & Weakland, 1956; Lidz, Fleck, & Cornelison, 1965; Wynne, Ryckoff, Day, & Hirsch, 1958).

Following the early clinical–impressionistic studies, quantitative approaches came into vogue. These studies have usually been short-term (a few minutes to a few hours of observation) and have stressed methodology and measurement. Objective instruments have been developed, but most are so complex that their applicability is limited. Many researchers developed their own scoring systems; not surprisingly, however, significant overlap exists among variables in the different systems. Researchers frequently used "microanalytic" techniques; that is, they examined small segments of behavior in great detail. They typically dealt with some variation of the pathology/nonpathology dichotomy—for example, "schizophrenogenic" versus "neurotic" versus "normal" families. The major substantive concern, however, was with troubled families; "normal" families were used primarily as controls. In these works, operational procedures, coding categories, and scoring criteria were strongly emphasized (e.g., Ferreira & Winter, 1965, 1968; Goldstein, Judd, Rodnick, Alkire, & Gould, 1968; Haley, 1964; Lennard & Bernstein, 1969; McPherson, 1968; Mishler & Waxler, 1968; Reiss, 1971; Riskin & Faunce, 1968, 1970a, 1970b; Faunce & Riskin, 1970; Riskin & Faunce, 1972; Wynne & Singer, 1963a, 1963b; Singer & Wynne, 1966). Several family sociologists also focused on quantitative methodology (e.g., Bales, 1950; Strodtbeck, 1951; Straus & Tallman, 1970).

A few groups of nonclinical families have been studied. In general, these studies have combined qualitative–impressionistic evaluations with quantitative data. Although they include data obtained over several interviews and spread over a period of a few months, they are essentially cross-sectional (e.g., Hess & Handel, 1959; Westley & Epstein, 1969). Also, reports of "live-in" observers (Hansen, 1981, with "normal" families; Henry, 1971, with schizophrenic families) cover a fairly short time span. Kantor and Lehr (1975) published their findings based on living in with several families, but it is not clear how long and under what conditions the observers were actually in the homes. Wynne and Whitaker (1974) interviewed one "normal" family once a year for 4 years; their material is quite impressionistic and has not been formally written up. Lewis, Beavers, Gossett, and Phillips (1976) have studied a group of "healthy" families whom they apparently intended to follow longitudinally; they have not, however, actually done so.

Some longitudinal studies of families are under way. Again, they focus on pathology—that is, on families having children at high risk for mental illness (e. g., Jones, Rodnick, Goldstein, McPherson, & West, 1977). The Child Development Group at the National Institute of Mental Health (NIMH) conducted a longitudinal study restricted to the mother–child dyad, and subsequently Ryder (Ryder & Goodrich, 1966; Ryder, 1974) from that group studied couples, but not families, longitudinally. There has been some longitudinal research on "healthy" individuals (Grinker, 1962; Offer & Offer, 1968); however, the family interaction component has been secondary or inferential. While the long-term Berkeley Growth Study recently has given attention to the family interactional aspects of the subjects' lives, this appears to be essentially retrospective analysis.

Conceptually, advances have been made. A plethora of high-level abstractions and conceptual schemes, relating, for instance, to power, cohesiveness, affiliation, systems theory, adaptability, and self-esteem, have been developed (e.g., Beavers in Lewis *et al.*, 1976; Olson, Sprenkle, & Russell, 1979). But the field is noticeably weak in concepts and hypotheses that can be operationalized and subjected to empirical tests.

A particularly important area that has been seriously neglected in much of the family research literature is the matter of the effects, for good or bad, on "healthy" families that result from the very processes of the researchers' studying them (Rosenthal, 1963). This aspect of studying "nonlabeled" families, with its ethical implications, must in itself be most carefully evaluated.

To summarize, there are several major areas of deficiency in knowledge about "healthy" families. These include direct, empirical observation of whole families interacting over time; valid, reliable, and useful instruments for objectively assessing family interaction; operational hypotheses relating the family interaction to the functioning of its members; methods for involving and studying families over time; and the ethics involved in research of this nature. The present research addresses these areas.

## GOALS

Work was started on this project in mid-1974. The goal was to conduct a pilot longitudinal study (originally set at 2 years) of psychiatrically "nonlabeled" families. The guiding substantive question was this: What family interaction patterns are related to raising psychologically "healthy" children? The guiding methodological question was this: What data should be collected and how should it be managed? In the pilot phase, two families were studied. The objectives of this preliminary work were as follows:

1. To conduct a pilot project to develop a methodology for a prospective long-term study of "nonlabeled" family interaction.

2. To investigate whether certain formal, stylistic patterns of family interaction (i.e., communication patterns) remain stable over time, and to determine how they might vary with differing content.

3. To explore the range and heterogeneity of interactional patterns of "nonlabeled" families.

4. To investigate how "nonlabeled" families identify and cope with expected and unexpected stresses.

5. To begin identifying "positive" coping characteristics of families especially those that might relate to the psychological health of the children.

6. To generate—but not to test—operational hypotheses relating the family interaction to the behavior of its members.

7. To adapt my own Family Interaction Scales for "macroscopic" use.

8. To develop additional appropriate methods for processing the data.

9. To assess the impact of this kind of study on the subject members; to identify the ethical issues involved in longitudinal studies.


## PROCEDURES

In order to provide a framework, I shall start with an outline of the methodological and conceptual positions which have guided this research. First, we use an interactional approach, which involves the following assumptions: (1) Causality is not linear but involves feedback loops. (2) Recurrent or redundant patterns of interaction, or family styles, especially those which persist across different areas of content, are particularly significant. (3) The family group is different from the sum of the behaviors of its individual members. Second, we are concerned with individual development as it relates to family interaction. We are particularly interested in the development of self-esteem, individuality, and autonomy. We do not find our interest in the family as a unit and our interest in the individual person to be mutually exclusive points of view. Third, the observation time needed to identify and follow family communication patterns may vary from a few seconds to a year or longer, depending on the issues involved. Fourth, the direct observation and recording of fairly "natural" family interaction as it can be seen to evolve over time has been our primary unit of study.

## Selection Criteria

Families were to be biologically intact, white, middle-class with at least two children (none younger than 6 nor older than 17), at least third-generation American, and living in a professional-class, suburban community. We wanted families in which the youngest child was old enough to participate in verbal interactions and the oldest child was becoming increasingly independent, even preparing to leave home. While the psychiatric criteria used are crude and rely primarily on exclusion factors, they are typical of those used in this field today (Lewis *et al.*, 1976; Ryder, 1974; Wynne & Whitaker, 1974). They included the following:

1. No family members have been in psychotherapy for at least 3 years prior to participating in the project. (Seeking therapy *after* this project began would be irrelevant in terms of this criterion.)

2. No family members have had serious police contact during the past 3 years.

3. All family members are effectively functioning in ways expected of people of their age and sex in their community.

4. All family members are in good physical health, and none has had any of the classically defined psychosomatic symptoms.

5. In the independent judgments of two experienced clinical interviewers based on a "recruitment/screening" interview at home, no symptoms of unlabeled but significant pathology are present in family members.

## Recruitment and Final Screening

First, the Principal Investigator (PI) met with several local clergymen to explain the study and seek their endorsements. All of them believed that the study would be important. We asked one of the clergymen to screen his congregation informally for eligible families. We then asked him to inform several families that he thought would meet our criteria about the project.

After initial telephone calls, the PI and a colleague did "recruitment/ screening" interviews with several families (all members present) at their homes. They were told that the researchers wanted to study the ordinary, day-to-day interaction of families who are otherwise not investigated by psychiatrists and psychologists. The demographic and psychiatric criteria were reviewed with the families. The researchers deemphasized such terms as "healthy" and "normal," in order to minimize creating any expectations that might influence the families' behavior. The researchers informed the families that the study might touch upon topics of a sensitive nature, which they could choose not to discuss. Families were told that they would function as "pilot" families; this would include their helping to identify appropriate topics for investigation. The length of the project, observation and audio-taping of interviews, confidentiality, frequency of contacts, the possibility that the project might have an effect on the family, and a consent form were all discussed. The researchers emphasized that very little was known about *ongoing* processes of family functioning, and that the families could make a significant contribution to the advancement of scientific knowledge in this area. The researchers stated further that they were not offering therapy, but that if a participating family ever requested it, they would be referred elsewhere for treatment, which need not be incompatible with continuing on the project. They were told that they would be free to withdraw from the project at any time. Families were informed that they would be given copies of published material if they so wished. They were asked to wait a week before reaching a decision, so that they could discuss the project by themselves. Also, the researchers wanted time to discuss privately whether the families fit the criteria.

Five families were telephoned; four agreed to home visits, which were then held. One family was not accepted because both interviewers were concerned about unspoken tensions. (Several days after the home visit, the mother called to ask for a referral to a marriage counselor.) Another family declined to participate, stating that the father would be traveling too much. Two families met the criteria and agreed to participate. A contract was made to meet monthly for 2 years; this period was later extended. Reasons the families initially gave for participation included "to help in a research project," "to be of community service," and "to learn more about communication." Compositions of the participating families were as follows:

*Family 1.* As of 1974, members were the father, age 44, business executive; the mother, age 43, homemaker; a daughter, age 17, student; a son, age 14, student; a daughter, age 13, student.

*Family 2.* As of 1974, members were the father, age 45, accountant; the mother, age 45, homemaker; a daughter, age 16, student; a son, age 12, student, a daughter, age 11, student.

It was quite fortuitous that the members of the two families were so closely matched in ages and sexes.

### Data Collection

A major guideline was to avoid collecting so much data that they could not be effectively and efficiently analyzed.

### Interview Frequency and Format

The interviews started in the fall of 1974. They were set at monthly intervals in order to develop rapport and to observe how the families coped with a variety of expected and unexpected stresses. After 2 years, both families agreed to a 6 month follow-up interview and subsequently agreed to three more. The follow-up interviews extended over the next 2½ years. The interviews were terminated in the summer of 1979. One family moved to another city, and the other family decided to discontinue the project.

Whole-family interaction was the principal unit of observation, although various subgroups met for certain discussions. In addition, each family member was interviewed individually three times. With the exception of two home dinner meetings, all interviews were held at the Mental Research Institute (MRI) and at night, for the families' convenience. Interviews, lasting about an hour, were audiotaped and were observed from behind a one-way mirror. The PI conducted most of them. We were quite concerned from the start about being overwhelmed by too much data; for this reason (as well as for financial ones), videotapes were not made. During the first 2 years of the study, the interviewer stayed behind the one-way mirror except when he introduced a new topic to the families.

Since the researchers' expectations might influence the families, the focus was on "communication" and "coping" rather than on "sickness" or "health." There was no effort to suppress discussion of problem areas, but the interviewer avoided making "therapeutic" interventions.

Interview questions were designed to generate family interaction across a variety of topics, to facilitate comparing and contrasting the two families, and to permit the emergence and development of issues unique to each family. Both families were asked their opinions about appropriate topics for discussion and were asked the same general questions in approximately the same time sequence.

Examples of topics for the whole family were as follows (in sequence):

1. Plan something together as a family (first interview).

2. Respond to TAT and Blackie cards (first interview and repeated after 1 year).

3. Give an opinion about tonight's questions and the questions coming up next month (at end of each interview).

4. Describe the past month (at start of each interview).

5. Tell how "who has what responsibilities around the house" gets decided (second interview).

6. Plan a trip to Mars (third interview).

7. (For parents without the children present) discuss your perceptions of each child today and your predictions about each child 10 years from now (fifth interview and repeated in 1 year).

8. Build something together with Lego building blocks.

9. Discuss the following hypothetical situation (first the parents without the children, then the children without the parents, then all together):

> Mr. and Mrs. Carter's 16-year-old son sometimes leaves home for a few hours without telling his parents where he is going. His parents feel they have a right to know how he spends his time, and he believes he is entitled

to some privacy in this matter. Discuss how you would handle this situation, and the reasons why.

10. Discuss a problem similar to the preceding one (first the father and children, then mother and children, then all together).

11. Discuss several semantic differential adjectives as they apply to each person: for example, assertive–unassertive, trusting–distrusting.

12. Discuss the terminal illness of grandparents (which occurred in both families).

13. Discuss the impact of the children's leaving home.

As the interviews proceeded, there was increasing focus on the actual experiences unique to each family. The interview format encouraged the families to introduce their own topics. Some of these topics took only a few minutes, and some recurred for 2 years or longer. We were able to observe directly how these issues were dealt with over time. Examples are as follows:

1. One couple had strong differences over whether they should remodel their house or buy a new one; this was a major issue for over 4 years.

2. A family dealt with the poor school performance of one child in a subject in which he had no interest.

3. The parents were concerned about one child's being shy. They encouraged her to take a summer job in a distant town where her cousin lived; she worked with a group of young men and women as a fellow house painter.

4. A child had a serious orthopedic problem. She wore a brace for several years. With her family's support, she became a poised, self-confident, attractive young woman.

5. A family had to decide whether the father would take a more challenging job for 3 years in a distant community; they used part of the interview time to discuss the pros and cons of the move, and its implications for the family.

6. A father was experiencing serious pressures at his job and was working quite long hours.

7. A son took a summer job away from home, with which he was quite dissatisfied. He consulted his parents, and then made his own decision about continuing with it.

8. A mother had major surgery, with a very slow convalescence and distressing side effects; the family was quite unhappy with the lack of adequate explanation from her doctor about the postoperative symptoms.

9. (At a home interview) the children argued for a few seconds over who would clear the dishes from the table.

### Individual Interviews

Each family member was interviewed individually three times: during the first, the second, and the third years. These interviews were conducted by the PI and audiotaped, but not observed. All family members, especially the parents, tended to be more candid in these interviews than in the family interviews.

### Home Interviews

In addition to the initial screening interviews, both families were visited by the PI and a colleague at their homes twice: after the first and the second years. The purpose was to assess whether the family interaction patterns on their own territory, and without specific topics being assigned, would be different from their interaction at MRI. Each home meeting lasted several hours and was centered around the evening meal. The families' interactional styles at the dinner table were quite similar to their styles in the MRI interview rooms.

### Observers

Every family interview held at the MRI during the first 2 years was observed by two to six people, including the interviewer. 37 observers, all white, middle-class professionals—25 clinicians with a wide range of orientations and 12 nonclinicians—participated.

### Measurement: Family Interaction Scales

Immediately following the interviews and before any discussion, the observers rated the family on the current, global form of the Family Interaction Scales (FIS) (Riskin, 1974). The original FIS was "microanalytic," that is, designed to assess interaction through a speech-by-speech analysis (Riskin & Faunce, 1968). This system was reliable and valid, but was extremely complex and cumbersome. Therefore the scoring procedures were modified to rate globally, or "macroanalytically," 17 dimensions of family interaction. The entire family interview was rated on each of the following:

1. Clarity (vs. unclarity).
2. Topic continuity (vs. topic change).
3. Appropriate topic change (vs. inappropriate topic change).
4. Commitment (vs. lack of it).
5. Request for commitment (vs. lack of it).
6. Information exchange (vs. lack of it).
7. Agreement (vs. lack of it).
8. Disagreement (vs. lack of it).
9. Support (vs. lack of it).
10. Attack (vs. lack of it).
11. Intensity (high vs. low).

12. Humor (much vs. little).

13. Interruptions (many vs. few).

14. Laughter (much vs. little).

15. Who speaks (all participating vs. not all participating).

16. Intrusiveness (much vs. little).

17. Mind reading (much vs. little).

Raters were given the following instructions:

1. Use as a baseline *all* families in the white middle class whom you know—for example, treatment families, friends, own family.

2. All ratings should be made about the family group as a *whole unit*.

3. You should evaluate the *whole* interview. Make an overall judgment about the interview.

4. All ratings should be made from the observer's point of view.

5. All ratings should be based on *observations*; minimize inferences.

6. There are 17 variables. Each one should be rated *independently* of all the other ones. For example, there can be high "laughter" but low "humor." And there can be high "agreement," but low "clarity" plus high "attack."

7. In scoring, the rater should consider both the verbal aspects and the tone of voice. Exception: For "agreement" or "disagreement," use the verbal statement only. For example, a sarcastic "agreement" *is* agreement.

8. The scoring is set up in terms of a 5-point scale. "5" = "very much" or "high." "1" = "very little," "a lack of," or in some cases (e.g., clarity) "an opposite."

9. The rater should not be too heavily swayed by one person's being deviant. Make a marginal note for that person. For example, if 4 of 5 family members are actively participating and one is rather quiet, give a score of 4 (medium-high for "who speaks"), and note that Johnny is very quiet.

Each rater was also supplied with a list of the 17 variables, with brief definitions and examples, and a scoring sheet.

Most of the raters were unfamiliar both with the earlier microanalytic scoring system and with the current macroanalytic form. A few minutes were spent in discussing and clarifying the definitions, and then the scoring was done; the entire procedure took about 10 minutes.

### Postinterview Discussions

After the observers and the interviewer scored the interview, they held a discussion to elicit each person's impressions and clinical judgments. General framing and facilitating questions included the following: What "rules" would seem to govern the family interaction? What interactional patterns are observed? Do any patterns seem particularly "healthy"? How might the present interaction affect the family members in the future? What might the children be learning from the actual interaction during the hour? Observers' comments were used in the writing of the initial clinical summaries of the family interviews and as a source for generating hypotheses.

All postinterview discussions were audiotaped, providing a record of the observers' impressions, the concepts they used to describe the family, and the hypotheses or predictions generated by their direct observation of family interaction. The contents of these taped discussions are currently being intensively reviewed.

### Summary of Data Base

Using the general research format presented above, the following data have been obtained on the two pilot families: approximately 50 hours of recorded family interviews; 30 hours of individual interviews; 35 hours of clinical discussions; and quantitative ratings for each interview. The data base is summarized in the following list:

*Family 1*

1. 19 family interviews (tape recordings of 17 sessions; 2 home sessions not recorded).

2. 19 clinical discussions by observers (tape recordings of 14).

3. 15 taped individual interviews (3 per person).

4. 4 taped follow-up interviews (6, 12, 18 and 24 months).

5. FIS ratings; mean ratings on 17 dimensions (for 2 years).

*Family 2*

1. 18 family interviews (tape recordings of 16 sessions; 2 home sessions not recorded).

2. 18 clinical discussions by observers (tape recordings of 14).

3. 15 taped individual interviews (3 per person).

4. 4 taped follow-up interviews (6, 12, 18, and 24 months).

5. FIS ratings; mean ratings on 17 dimensions (for 2 years).

### Data Analysis (1974–1979)

In order to analyze the data most efficiently, we strove to organize the data base in a way that would facilitate the interplay between empirical and conceptual levels.

### Data Analysis: Quantitative Aspects

Observers rated the whole-family interaction on each of the 17 FIS variables for the first 18 interviews. Mean ratings were derived for each family on each interview by combining the scores given by the several raters (two to six raters per interview). This procedure yielded a set of 18 mean ratings for each dimension.

Preliminary assessment of the FIS suggests that it is a useful scoring system. The FIS accurately reflected both salient similarities and differences between the families that the observers identified through clinical discussions. Some dimensions showed more stability than others, and some appeared to reflect changes in the family system over the 2-year span. Statistical findings on these dimensions will be discussed below.

The table of mean ratings (see section A of Table 3-1) indicates that several FIS dimensions discriminated between our pilot families. The following scales strongly discriminated between families: "commitment" ($p <$ .002), "information exchange" ($p < .05$), "disagreement" ($p < .01$), "attack" ($p < .002$), "intensity" ($p < .002$), "humor" ($p < .002$), "interruptions" ($p < .002$), and "laughter" ($p < .002$). The FIS dimensions "topic continuity," "support," and "intrusiveness" showed differences between families at the $p < .10$ level; and there were suggested differences between families on "appropriate topic change" and "who speaks" ($p < .20$). $t$-tests were not

TABLE 3-1.  MEAN RATINGS AND RELIABILITY FOR FAMILY INTERACTION SCALES

| | (A) Overall mean ratings for each FIS dimension[a] | | | (B) Reliability of global FIS[b] | | |
|---|---|---|---|---|---|---|
| | Overall mean | | | | | |
| FIS dimension | Family 1 | Family 2 | $p$ | $W$ | $\chi^2$ | $p$ |
| Clarity | 4.31 | 4.19 | NS | .4655 | 33.52 | $<.10$ |
| Topic continuity | 4.06 | 4.31 | $<.10$ | .4005 | 30.04 | $(.10<p<.20)$ |
| Appropriate topic change | 4.32 | 4.51 | $(.10<p<.20)$ | .5151 | 37.09 | $<.05$ |
| Commitment | 4.05 | 3.33 | $<.002$ | .6670 | 48.023 | $.001<p<.01$ |
| Request for commitment | 3.01 | 3.14 | NS | .3996 | 27.57 | NS |
| Information exchange | 3.82 | 3.34 | $<.05$ | .4675 | 32.26 | $<.10$ |
| Agreement | 3.44 | 3.47 | NS | .4426 | 31.87 | $(.10<p<.20)$ |
| Disagreement | 2.79 | 1.89 | $<.01$ | .5386 | 38.78 | $<.05$ |
| Support | 3.95 | 3.61 | $<.10$ | .5829 | 41.97 | $.01<p<.02$ |
| Attack | 1.73 | 1.23 | $<.002$ | .4693 | 33.79 | $<.10$ |
| Intensity | 3.86 | 2.59 | $<.002$ | .7647 | 55.06 | $<.001$ |
| Humor | 3.67 | 2.44 | $<.002$ | .6362 | 45.80 | $.001<p<.01$ |
| Interruptions | 3.10 | 1.91 | $<.002$ | .6619 | 47.66 | $.001<p<.01$ |
| Laughter | 3.30 | 2.51 | $<.002$ | .5897 | 42.456 | $<.01$ |
| Who speaks | 3.53 | 3.23 | $(<.20)$ | .3415 | 23.57 | NS |
| Intrusiveness | 1.66 | 1.34 | $<.10$ | .5622 | 38.79 | $.02<p<.05$ |
| Mind reading | 1.49 | 1.58 | NS | .3349 | 24.115 | NS |

[a]Part A shows the pilot families' mean ratings for each FIS variable (columns 1 and 2). $t$-tests were used to look for differences between the two families' mean scores, and the resulting probabilities are reported in column 3.

[b]Part B shows the reliability for the global FIS ratings, using Kendall's coefficient of concordance ($W$). Chi-square values computed from $W$ were used to estimate the probability that the observed ranking of the family interviews was random (i.e., that the rankings were unrelated). The $W$, chi-square, and probability values for each FIS variable are reported.

significant for "clarity," "request for commitment," "agreement," or "mind reading."

The reliability of global rating procedures was assessed by Kendall's coefficient of concordance ($W$). The probabilities associated with the obtained chi-square values are reported for each scale in section B of Table 3-1. The probabilities that the obtained ratings resulted from chance ordering were less than .01 for "commitment," "intensity," "humor," "laughter," and "interruptions"; the probabilities were less than .05 for "appropriate topic change," "disagreement," "support," and "intrusiveness"; and they were less than .10 for "clarity," "information exchange," and "attack." The following scales did not show sufficient agreement among raters to be considered reliable: "topic continuity," "request for commitment," "agreement," "who speaks," and "mind reading."

Additional data on one variable and one ratio between two variables are presented below.

*Commitment Scale.* The "commitment" scale measures the degree to which the family members take clear, definite stands—that is, commit themselves to ideas, issues, suggestions, and so on. Using the global ratings based on the entire interview, Family 1's mean ratings ranged from 3.0 to 4.5, with an overall mean of 4.1, and Family 2's mean ratings ranged from 2.2 to 4.0, with an overall mean of 3.3. Although both families show considerable variation on this dimension, there was a significant difference between them ($t = 4.65$, $p < .002$). Figure 3-1 shows a graph of the mean ratings over the first 18 interviews. The mean interrater agreement on the "commitment" scale for

FIGURE 3-1. "COMMITMENT" SCALE RATINGS.

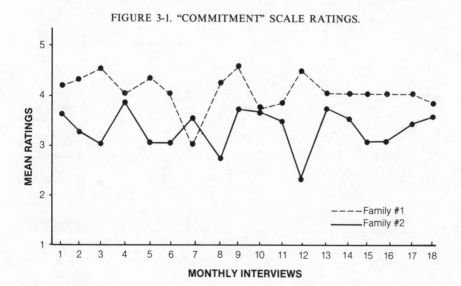

both families is 83.96%. Reliability, using Kendall's coefficient of concordance, is high ($W = .6670$, $\chi^2 = 48.023$, $.001 < p < .01$). Plots of running medians (Tukey, 1977) show Family 1 rated consistently higher than Family 2.

*The Ratio of "Agreement" to "Disagreement."* The "agreement" and "disagreement" scales measure whether family members explicitly agree or disagree with one another. Ratios between variables will often highlight differences that are present. Figure 3-2 shows a graph of the mean ratings for the ratio of "agreement" to "disagreement" over the first 18 interviews. Family 1's mean ratings ranged from .71 to 2.80, with an overall mean ratio of 1.36 ($SD = .50$). Family 2's mean ratio ranged from 1.32 to 3.00, with an overall mean ratio of 1.91 ($SD = .48$). The difference on this ratio between the two families is significant ($t = 3.52$, $p < .002$).

To summarize the quantitative findings, the families are perceived as quite different in some of the formal, stylistic aspects of their interaction, and as alike in other aspects. Family 1 expresses more "commitment," more "information exchange," more "disagreement," more "support," more "attack," more "intensity," more "humor," more "interruptions," more "laughter," and more "intrusiveness" than does Family 2. Family 2 expresses more "topic continuity" and more "appropriate" (vs. "inappropriate") "topic change" than does Family 1. Both families are medium-high on "clarity" (but not extremely so), are medium on "request for commitment" and "agreement," and very low on "mind reading." The objective measures correspond quite closely to the observers' clinical descriptions of the families; they are

FIGURE 3-2. RATIO OF "AGREEMENT" TO "DISAGREEMENT" RATINGS.

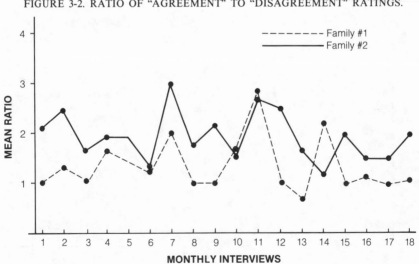

also quite similar to impressions of others who have listened to the tapes but have not observed or rated the families by the FIS variables. Thus we believe that there is preliminary evidence for content validity of the FIS.

### Data Analysis: Clinical-Qualitative Aspects

Synopses of all family interviews and observers' discussions have been written. From these two sets of data, "clinical" summaries have been constructed. These include statements about the whole family, the marital dyad, the children, and each individual member. By examining the summaries sequentially, one can obtain, for example, a longitudinal picture of the marriages over the 4½ year period. In addition, during 1978–1979, two research groups who did not observe the interviews have separately reviewed the tapes. In general, the comments of these groups are consistent with those of the original observers. These clinical summaries have served as an important source for generating hypotheses about the family interaction.

In order to facilitate the articulation of a theoretical framework for the data, we have created a file of "concept cards." These cards contain concepts used by observers and listeners when they discuss the interviews, as well as concepts that appear in the literature on "normal" families. They are arranged by topic, are crossreferenced, and refer to specific footages of or topics on the interview tapes. This procedure allows one to move back and forth between the empirical data (the tapes and transcripts) and the more abstract ideas that are used to "explain" the data. Some examples of these concept cards are given here:

1. Family 1, Interview 17, footage 153–203. *Emotional climate, shifts in—* from arguing to friendly. Ability to shift from arguing to being friends and cooperating occurs quickly. No lingering grudges.

2. Family 2, Interview 17, footage 1009. *Sarcasm—how used.* Mother is sarcastic, but everyone—including her—acknowledges and openly identifies sarcasm, and clearly picks up the underlying intent. It is safe to "metacommunicate" about sarcasm.

3. Family 2, Follow-up interview 4. (See family discussion about children's jobs.) *Rebellion.* Son seems to have a strong sense of autonomy without significant rebellion. Is rebellion present, but so subtle we're missing it? Is he expressing assertiveness by wanting to continue with a job, even though parents think it's better to quit?

4. Family 1, Follow-up Interview 4. (See family discussion about father's job transfer.) *Emotional climate: Commitment without attack.* In discussing father's job transfer to another city, mother candidly expresses her fears without criticizing or blaming father.

5. Family 1, Interview 4, footage 356. *Parents and children.* Parents accept (within limits) a child's being critical of a parent, without countercriticism.

6. Family 1, Interview 11, footage 728. *Conflict*: effectively dealing with disagreements. When the family is faced with a problem about which they have clearly differing opinions, they look at the problem to see if they are all interpreting it the same way. This tends to depersonalize it: "Let's get clarification of *what* we're disagreeing about before we continue to disagree."

Clinical "portraits" of the two families have been written by researchers who independently only listened to segments of the tapes but did not observe the families. These portraits serve as an additional validity check on the FIS scores and provide another source for generating hypotheses. Here are some examples:

> *One family (by Writer A):* This family is polite, subdued, somewhat fundamentalist in its values and ethics. They are orderly and nonintrusive and in general are warm and supportive. There is a decided absence of disagreement or disparagement. The spouses do not describe themselves as having a gratifying marriage, and yet they agree that commitment and optimism about the future has kept them together. They both feel that their mutual agreement on raising their children has been important in providing common ground.

> *Same family (by Writer B):* This family is a close, caring group who are well-educated, successful, with sensible, conventional values. Each member is autonomous. Father is acknowledged head of the family, the spokesman. Son is being trained to emulate him. Mother is very strong in the home. Children are intelligent, well-behaved, and well-mannered. All are careful to preserve the family homeostasis, and there is a guarded atmosphere. While the *marriage* is lacking in intensity and good communication, the *family* has good communication and commitment.

### Summaries of Dimensions Used to Characterize Families

Observers of the interviews and auditors of the tapes tend to describe the two families in terms of similar major dimensions. The families are seen as alike in some dimensions and different in others. For example, both families are viewed as having a high degree of mutual respect ("support" is greater than "attack"), much acknowledgment of others (there is good "topic continuity" and explicit "agreement" and "disagreement"), a virtual absence of "mind reading" and "intrusiveness," an absence of sustained "attacks" or scapegoating, and high commitment to traditional values, including "family and marriage." They are confident that they can handle their own problems—which they easily acknowledged as existing—without relying primarily on external resources. The fathers are the family spokesmen in public, and all four parents tend to be supportive at home.

The separation of generations is clear, and the parents are in charge. The parents expect their children to obey, while simultaneously encouraging the children to strive towards independence; they are not troubled by any apparent contradiction in these expectations. The children's moves towards independence are well within the parents' range of tolerance, and autonomy is encouraged. Differentness—within limits—is accepted and valued. Power struggles do not seem to dominate family interaction. All four parents show much caring (high on "support" statements) for the children, though there are clear differences in this respect, especially between the fathers and sons, in the two families. Family 1 is seen as more "spontaneous" than Family 2 (more "commitment," "disagreement," "interruptions," "humor," and "laughter"). The marital relationship in one family is more satisfying than in the other, but both sets of adults appear to be good parents.

Statements such as those made in the preceding two paragraphs might be clinically interesting, but, as expressed, the implicit hypotheses are difficult to subject to empirical test. Therefore, they must be reformulated as more general and explicit hypotheses, which can be operationalized and then empirically tested on a larger sample.

### Hypotheses

In order to investigate whether descriptions such as the foregoing apply more generally, we have begun to formulate hypotheses. This project was designed to generate hypotheses, not to test them. We therefore do not have adequate direct evidence either to support or to contradict most of them. Some were suggested by the FIS scores, others by clinical observation and discussion. Whenever possible we have attempted to cite specific empirical references for the hypotheses, in order to facilitate making them operational. They range from the correlational to the etiological, and from the rather concrete to the fairly abstract. They refer to white, middle-class, American families. Some examples follow:

*Quantitative hypotheses, in terms of FIS scores, which focus on family "emotional climate" and communication patterns:*

1. "Nonlabeled" families speak quite, but not extremely, clearly. ("Clarity" is more than 3.5 and less than 4.5.)

2. "Nonlabeled" families do not maintain a rigidly rationalistic stance in their discussions, nor are they chaotic. ("Appropriate topic change" is greater than 3 and less than 4.5. "Inappropriate topic change" is less than 3.5 and greater than 1.5.)

3. "Nonlabeled" families tend to agree more than to disagree. (Scores for the ratio of "agreement" to "disagreement" are greater than 1.)

4. "Nonlabeled" families are able to assert themselves. ("Commitment" is greater than 3.)

5. "Nonlabeled" families have a friendly environment; there is mutual goodwill. (The ratio of "support" to "attack" is greater than 1.)

6. "Nonlabeled" families can disagree in a friendly way. ("Disagreement" is greater than 3; "support" is greater than 3; "attack" is less than 3.)

7. "Nonlabeled" families manifest variations in expressed affect. ("Intensity" fluctuates during interviews and from one interview to the next.)

8. "Nonlabeled" families tend to have a sense of humor. (Score is more than 2.5 on "humor.")

9. "Nonlabeled" families are relatively nonintrusive. ("Intrusiveness" is less than 2.)

10. "Nonlabeled" families rarely exhibit "mind reading," and when it does occur the interactions are quickly labeled as such: "I realize I spoke for you." ("Mind reading" is less than 2.)

*Qualitative hypotheses focusing on coping styles:*

1. "Nonlabeled" families avoid prolonged "scapegoating" of any one member.

2. Arguments are quickly followed by friendly interactions (grudges are not held).

3. Individual differences are respected and encouraged.

4. In working on a task, family members cooperate and collaborate rather than bicker.

5. A misbehaving child is not allowed to disrupt the family's work on a task.

6. Members' comments are acknowledged by other family members.

7. "Nonlabeled" families do not use attributions with negative connotations; a quiet child is seen as "shy" rather than "immature."

*Qualitative hypotheses focusing on parent–child relationships:*

1. Parents share similar perceptions and expectations of their children.

2. Children need not rebel aggressively in order to assert their independence.

3. Parents encourage children to make their own decisions, even when they may privately judge the decisions to be mistaken ones.

4. Successful parenting can occur in the absence of a "happy" marriage.

5. Generational differences are clear; parents are in charge.

6. Parents set limits clearly and firmly, as appropriate.

7. If parents have differences about dealing with a child, they discuss their differences and do not draw the child in as an intermediary.

8. Children are allowed—within rather clear limits—to defy their parents.

9. Parents support their children's successes, without overdoing it; the support is appropriate to the given situation and context.

10. Parents express ambivalence quite explicitly about a child's increasing independence: "I'm glad son is going off to college and I wish he weren't going."

### "Facts" Contradicted by Data

We have collected data that are inconsistent with some hypotheses that many clinicians treat as fact. Two of them are as follows:

1. It is a widely held notion that a necessary condition for parents to function effectively is that they have a "happy," mutually satisfying marriage. In one family, it is clear, both from their behavior in the family meetings and from direct statements in the individual interviews, that the parents have *not* had a consistently happy marriage. Yet they do function effectively as parents—they agree on how to raise the children; they provide a warm, caring atmosphere with appropriate limits; and so on.

2. Another widely held belief is that, at least in the white middle class, children need to "rebel" or to have overt clashes with their parents in order to establish autonomy and independence. In Family 2, the children are quite well-mannered, accept and follow their parents' value systems, and do not defy the parents (e.g., come home late or neglect their homework). And yet each one does convey strongly his or her own sense of individuality. Assertiveness is present, but rather subtle (e.g., a quiet but firm "no" when asked to play the piano for the interviewers during a home visit).

It is imperative, in light of those observations, that *all* beliefs about family interaction—including marital and parent–children relationships—be subjected to empirical scrutiny.

### Significant Incidents

During the 4½ years of interviewing, several fairly brief interactions occurred that the observers believed were significant because they were particularly clear examples of underlying rules and dynamics. Some appear to be strong indicators of "health," and others primarily reveal the quality of the family interaction. Some examples follow.

When a family arrived for an interview one evening, it was obvious that the son was quite annoyed. While they were discussing a family incident, he remained silent and began thumbing through a magazine. His mother whispered, "Put the magazine down," and he didn't. She whispered the same words two more times, with increasing intensity, over the next few minutes. The other members disregarded him and continued to discuss the topic. The mother finally whispered, "I will not tolerate that—put it down!" and he laid the magazine down. We were told later that his sisters had felt mortified by his behavior and that during the ride home they had "given him hell" for being so rude. The observers were impressed that the family discussion was not disrupted by the mother–son interaction.

As a family entered the interview room, the children were angrily bickering with one another, apparently continuing an argument that had started earlier. The parents sat quietly, appearing quite at ease. After a few minutes, they all began discussing a family matter, and everyone spoke pleasantly. The children's argument seemed to have run its natural course; the parents were not anxious, and the family was able to switch easily to a friendly mode.

After the whole family had actively and with enjoyment discussed "planning something together," the interviewer escorted the children to the waiting room, and for a few minutes the parents were alone without an assigned topic. Observers noted that they did not speak to each other and appeared rather ill at ease. When the interviewer then returned and asked the parents to plan something for themselves, they were much less spontaneous than when they were discussing the same topic with the children.

A family came for an interview shortly after their first child had moved away to college. The two younger children started arguing over who was going to move into the vacant, and largest, bedroom. The parents listened a few minutes with amusement, then suggested a solution. The children discussed it and then arrived at their own solution.

The mother in one family had major surgery and subsequently developed mild hyperventilation. She complained that these symptoms interfered with her housework. She and the father discussed the possible basis and concluded it was due to a biochemical imbalance related to the surgery. They expressed resentment that her doctor had not taken more time to explain the reasons for the hyperventilation to them. After a few months, the symptoms disappeared.

The PI told both families that he was planning an extended and somewhat exotic trip in a distant country. Before the trip, all members of both families asked many questions about it, and upon his return, both families were very interested in hearing about the subjective aspects of his experience. The project and the interviewer had become an important part of their lives.

### Effect of Project on Families

Several changes occurred in the two families over the 4½ years, and at least some of these changes may have in part been related to their participation in the project. This aspect of the study will be discussed in more detail below.

### Data Retrieval System

We have recently developed a formalized system for organizing and retrieving the material on the taped interviews. This procedure is in an early stage but is already making possible a more effective "mining" of the primary data than before.

## DISCUSSION OF FINDINGS

Extreme caution is clearly required in making even preliminary generalizations from experiences with only two families. However, given that many observers made many observations on these families and that some findings are compatible with findings from other studies, some tentative generalizations may be stated.

## Availability and Interest of Families

Families are generally willing to participate in research, but it is essential that the project and sponsoring agency be endorsed by a person whom the family respects (such as a minister, a physician, or a school principal). Once families have agreed to participate, they follow through; in our project no interviews were missed. Much has been expected, and the families have given generously of themselves

It is extremely important that an explicit contract be made, that it be adhered to, and that the family's wishes be thoroughly respected. If the researchers plan for any change in the initial contract, the changes should be candidly discussed and the contract should be renegotiated. The two pilot families' motives for participating have not been explored in depth, but it was emphasized that they would not receive explicit advice or therapy. Both families have stated that they enjoyed participating.

## Interview Frequency and Format

Regular, ongoing meetings are esssential to establish rapport. One parent recently stated, "You would have offended and scared us if you had asked about the physical problems of [our child] in the first meeting." The monthly meetings have enabled direct observation, rather than retrospective reconstruction, of how the families dealt with emerging problems and stress situations. To recapitulate, the question of whether to remodel their house or buy a new one has preoccupied one family; they first disagreed, then negotiated their differences. The other family experienced the terminal illness of a grandparent. Both families had eldest children who would soon leave home for college, and each family discussed for several months the many aspects of the child's leaving. One family has dealt with a child's serious physical problem without allowing it to damage her self-esteem. The other family successfully guided a shy child in developing confidence away from home. How the families cope with these common, ordinary situations without their becoming overwhelming "problems" becomes clear when researchers directly observe them identifying and grappling with an issue as it evolves.

Having a group of families discuss similar topics in approximately the same order and during parallel interviews facilitates comparing and contrasting their interactional styles. Asking different subgroups as well as the whole family—for example, father and children, and then mother and children—to discuss the same topic permits assessing the differential effects of various members' presence.

In hindsight, the PI might have been more aggressive in introducing certain potentially emotionally charged subjects. However, a different interviewer did take a considerably more aggressive stance with one family in the fifth interview. They maintained the same style we had already seen, but they backed away from the interviewer's assertive moves and revealed virtually nothing substantive. At the next interview, which was conducted by the PI, the family stated they did "not feel at ease" with the more aggressive interviewer. Also, other colleagues conducted the first interviews at MRI, and the families' styles were essentially the same as with the PI. If researchers want families to continue with the project, we must be guided by their own tolerance for novel and possibly stressful topics.

## Family Interaction Scales: Reliability and Validity

Even with limited training in the use of the FIS system by the observer–raters, meaningful levels of reliability and significant differences between the two families were obtained on several scales. These results are encouraging in terms of the validity and usefulness of the instrument.

## Generalizability of Methodology

The methods we have developed for recruiting, engaging, and following families appear to be useful and applicable to studying a larger group longitudinally. Regular monthly meetings encourage families to become increasingly candid about themselves without feeling so stressed that they might not return, and the meetings also permit the prospective investigation of family interactional processes. Cross-sectional studies, by their nature, not only rely upon retrospective reports for longitudinal data, but also need not necessarily be hampered by concern about whether a family might return the following month, after a series of intensive interviews and testing. Our strong impression is that once families have made a commitment they will stay with a project, barring unforeseen external events. Attrition could be a serious problem with a larger group, and appropriate measures would have to be taken to deal with this factor.

The FIS has shown promise, and further work with it, including formal training of new raters, is indicated. The findings in the current study suggest that with appropriate rater training the FIS would be a useful contribution as a method for studying family interaction quantitatively and objectively.

## Generalizability of Substantive Findings

The findings on these two families are quite consistent with findings from other studies of "healthy" families. The characteristics of the project families resemble those of Group E ("normal") families in my earlier methodology study (Riskin & Faunce, 1970b); and Family 1 appears similar in many respects to those whom Lewis *et al.* call "optimal families," while Family 2 seems like their "adequates" (Lewis *et al.*, 1976). Additionally, the two families impressed the observers as being similar in many ways to families of the same socioeconomic status (SES) whom the observers have treated or known socially. Therefore, it seems reasonable to suggest that their styles of interaction might be characteristic of other families coming from the white professional middle class. It should also be noted that the two families are quite closely matched demographically, and those interactional patterns in which they are different cannot be attributed to family differences in developmental stages.

Since the families' styles may well be representative of their SES group, it would seem appropriate to test the hypotheses that we have generated on a larger sample. Little is known, however, about how nontraditional (e.g., single-parent) and minority families function and cope successfully. It remains to be empirically determined how these hypotheses and related procedures would need to be modified in order to study families of other SES and ethnic groups.

From studying these two families, we have doubts about the applicability of a unitary dimension of "family health" (Lewis *et al.*, 1976). The two families have strengths in similar and in different areas. To conclude that one is "more" healthy than the other does not seem too useful. Perhaps the purpose for which "health" is being assessed needs to be more clearly specified.

### Observer Bias

It was often quite difficult, especially for the professionally trained observers, to shift from a pathology orientation to a nonpathology perspective. For example, several times the postinterview discussions became snarled on the question of whether the parents in one family were *so* polite that there *must* be serious neurotic hostility underneath the surface. This bias suggests the importance of having nonprofessionals participate as observers.

The background of the observers also may have contributed a bias. For example, several visiting European observers had notions of "appropriate" behavior for children that differed from those of the American observers. This suggests that it would be important, if ethnic minority families are studied, that there also be observers of similar ethnic background.

## STUDY EFFECTS: ETHICAL ASPECTS OF LONGITUDINAL STUDY

The study effects of this kind of project are particularly important (Rosenthal, 1963). Families are not requesting treatment, yet it is probably inevitable that they *will* be affected when there is long-term participation in a research project that directly and explicitly focuses on their interaction. The reader will recall that the reasons the two families gave for participating included their interest in making a contribution to science and in contributing to community betterment; they also stated that they would like to learn more about communication. We did not probe their stated reasons. This kind of study, by its nature, is intrusive to some degree, and the families are affected; but there is no way to study families longitudinally without having some influence. A related factor is that they might attempt to meet implied expectations about being "healthy," and thereby minimize—or exaggerate—whatever problems they do have.

Investigators have a responsibility to minimize any impact and to be especially alert to the possibilities of a negative effect. The researchers stated at the initial "screening" interview at the families' homes that the study might have some effect on them, and they explicitly added that therapy would not be offered. Whatever their covert motives were, the families did *not* explicitly seek therapy.

Several factors indicate that the families have in fact been influenced. The two research teams who reviewed the tapes have independently concluded that Family 2 was less subdued after 2 years of interviews than they were at the start. One possible contributing factor is the effect, month after month, of the researchers asking the families to discuss situations that are potentially emotionally charged and that they would not typically discuss (Riskin & McCorkle, 1979). Family members spontaneously mentioned many times, "You give us some situation to discuss, and we get in the car and on the way home continue the discussions." They added that they normally did not talk about many of their own family matters that now were being discussed. A father said: "I learn a lot about my son at the MRI discussions that I don't otherwise know." A mother was asked what the effects were of her oldest child going off to college. She replied: "You've been asking us about children leaving for so many months now that we really were well prepared for it!" (This mother suggested, at the final interview, that we should send a tape recorder with families on their trip home from MRI.)

When directly asked whether and how they have been affected, members commented that they discuss some family-related topics more than they used to, and that they view this change as positive. (They may also have been trying to reassure the PI as they responded to his concerns about the effect of the project.) Also, both families have said that they would endorse the project to any new study families.

At times it has been difficult for the researchers to avoid playing the role of therapists and making comments when, for example, one mother experienced an anxiety episode, or when observing a father being close to his daughters but rather impersonal with his son.

In hindsight, the PI may have focused too much with the families on the possible effects of the project on them. At times, as indicated above, the tapes sound as if the families are reassuring him that they were not being harmed. The PI also raised the question of whether the families would want to read any published material—a commitment that they could do so had been made at the initial screening interview. Both families vacillated back and forth on this point, perhaps having picked up some of the interviewer's own ambivalence.

Some guidelines have been established for minimizing observer impact: (1) The screening criteria should be followed most scrupulously. (2) Researchers should be quite aware at the outset that there will be *some* impact on families from participating in an ongoing study. (3) Observers should be present at all interviews to monitor the interviewer if he or she is switching to a therapist mode. (4) The interviewer should be neutral and be out of the interview room whenever possible. (5) The interviewer must respect the family's wishes not to discuss a topic. (6) The interviewer should monitor his own anxieties about the impact of the project.

## FUTURE PLANS

As stated in the beginning, this chapter is a "progress report." Much productive analysis continues on the present data. This includes compiling a glossary of concepts, cross-referenced and with specific examples from the taped interviews; grouping the hypotheses into major dimensions and themes; indexing and cross-referencing the taped interviews, which will make the empirical data more accessible for following major themes and for comparing and contrasting the two families; constructing a composite demonstration tape, which will contain examples of "critical incidents" (Flanagan, 1954); and refining the FIS in order to improve its reliability and validity.

For the future, longer-term longitudinal studies should be considered. Considerable difference of opinion exists as to whether longitudinal family studies are in fact necessary or desirable (Hill, 1964). I believe that they should be carried out, both to collect baseline data that presently are not available, and to test hypotheses. They should also include the study of alternative families, such as single-parent families, blended families, and ethnic minority families.

What are the applications of this kind of research? We believe that people in the helping professions who work with families—therapists, clergymen, educators, counselors—are too often working from a perspective of assisting families to change *from some negative* condition. The helpers lack a solid framework which would serve as a guide to aid troubled families in moving *toward specific positive* goals. Additionally, much more emphasis should be devoted to prevention—for example, conducting "well family" clinics; longitudinal research on "nonlabeled" families provides data for constructing a body of knowledge on which to base effective prophylaxis. The family as we know it may be becoming an "endangered species." The field of "healthy" family research is in a position, through properly conducted studies to elucidate the *strengths* in families as well as the pathology, and thus to contribute towards counteracting that process.

## ACKNOWLEDGMENTS

This work was supported in part by the Luke B. Hancock Foundation, the Distribution Fund, the Louise M. Davies Foundation, and other private contributions.

## REFERENCES

Ackerman, N. Adolescent problems: A symptom of family disorder. *Family Process*, 1962, *1*, 202–213.

Bales, R. F. *Interaction process analysis: A method for the study of small groups.* Cambridge, Mass.: Addison-Wesley, 1950.

Bateson, G. Jackson, D. D., Haley, J., & Weakland, J. H. Toward a theory of schizophrenia. *Behavioral Science*, 1956, *1*, 251–264.

Faunce, E. E., & Riskin, J. Family interaction scales: II. Data analysis and findings. *Archives of General Psychiatry*, 1970, *22*, 513–526.

Ferreira, A. J., & Winter, W. D. Decision-making in normal and abnormal two-child families. *Family Process*, 1968, *7*, 17–36.

Ferreira, A. J., & Winter, W. D. Family interaction and decision-making. *Archives of General Psychiatry*, 1965, *13*, 214–223.

Flanagan, J. C. The critical incident. *Psychological Bulletin*, 1954, *51*, 327–358.

Goldstein, M. J., Judd, L. L., Rodnick, E. H., Alkire, A. A., & Gould, E. A method for studying social influence and coping patterns within families of disturbed adolescents. *Journal of Nervous and Mental Disorder*, 1968, *147*, 233–251.

Grinker, R. R., Sr., with Grinker, R. R., Jr., & Timberlake, J. Mentally healthy young males (homoclites): A study. *Archives of General Psychiatry*, 1962, *6*, 405–453.

Haley, J. Research on family patterns: An instrument measurement. *Family Process*, 1964, *3*, 41–65.

Hansen, C. Living-in with "normal" families. *Family Process*, 1981, *20*, 53–76.

Henry, J. *Pathways to madness.* New York: Random House, 1971.

Hess, R. D., & Handel, G. *Family worlds.* Chicago: University of Chicago Press, 1959.

Hill, R. Methodological issues in family development research. *Family Process*, 1964, *3*, 186–206.

Jones, J., Rodnick, E., Goldstein, M., McPherson, S., & West, K. Parental transactional style deviance as a possible indicator of risk for schizophrenia. *Archives of General Psychiatry*, 1977, *34*, 71–74.

Kantor, D., & Lehr, W. *Inside the family.* San Francisco: Jossey-Bass, 1975.

Lennard, H. L., & Bernstein, A. *Patterns in human interaction.* San Francisco: Jossey-Bass, 1969.

Lewis, J. W., Beavers, W., Gossett, J. T., & Phillips, V. A. *No single thread.* New York: Brunner/Mazel, 1976.

Lidz, T., Fleck, S., & Cornelison, A. R. Family studies and a theory of schizophrenia. In T. Lidz, S. Fleck, & A. R. Cornelison (Eds.), *Schizophrenia and the family.* New York: International Universities Press, 1965.

McPherson, A. *A manual for multiple coding of family interaction.* Unpublished manuscript, 1968.

Mishler, E. G., & Waxler, N. E. *Interaction in families: An experimental study of family processes and schizophrenia.* New York: Wiley, 1968.

Offer, D., & Offer, J. Profiles of normal adolescent girls. *Archives of General Psychiatry*, 1968, *19*, 513–522.

Olson, D., Sprenkle, D., & Russell, C. Circumplex model of marital and family systems, I. *Family Process*, 1979, *18*, 3–28.

Reiss, D. Intimacy and problem solving: An automated procedure for testing a theory of consensual experience in families. *Archives of General Psychiatry*, 1971, *25*, 442–455.

Riskin, J. *Global family interaction scales scoring manual.* Unpublished research instrument, 1974. (Available from the author.)

Riskin, J. "Nonlabeled" family interaction: Preliminary report on a prospective study. *Family Process*, 1976, *15*, 433–439.

Riskin, J., & Faunce, E. E. *Family interaction scales scoring manual.* Published privately, 1968.

Riskin, J., & Faunce, E. E. Family interaction scales: I. Theoretical framework and method. *Archives of General Psychiatry*, 1970, *22*, 504–512. (a)

Riskin, J., & Faunce, E. E. Family interaction scales: III. Discussion of methodology and substantive findings. *Archives of General Psychiatry*, 1970. *22*, 527–537. (b)

Riskin, J., & Faunce, E. E. An evaluative review of family interaction research. *Family Process*, 1972, *11*, 365–455.

Riskin, J., & McCorkle, M. "Nontherapy" family research and change in families: A brief clinical research communication. *Family Process*, 1979, *18*, 161–162.

Rosenthal, R. On the social psychology of the psychological experiment: The experimenter's hypothesis as unintended determinant of the experimental results. *American Scientist*, 1963, *51*, 268–283.

Ryder, R. G. *Describing variation among marriages.* Unpublished manuscript, 1974.

Ryder, R. G., & Goodrich, D. W. Married couples' responses to disagreement. *Family Process*, 1966, *5*, 30–42.

Singer, M., & Wynne, L. C. Principles of scoring communication defects and deviances in parents of schizophrenics: Rorschach and TAT scoring manuals. *Psychiatry*, 1966, *29*, 260–288.

Straus, M. A., & Tallman, I. *SIMFAM: A technique for observational measurement and experimental study of families.* Unpublished manuscript, 1970.

Strodtbeck, F. L. Husband–wife interaction over revealed differences. *American Sociological Review*, 1951, *16*, 468–473.

Tukey, J. W. *Exploratory data analysis.* Menlo Park, Calif.: Addison-Wesley, 1977.

Westley, W. A., & Epstein, N. B. *The silent majority.* San Francisco: Jossey-Bass, 1969.

Wynne, L. C., Ryckoff, I., Day, J., & Hirsch, S. Pseudo-mutuality in the family relations of schizophrenics. *Psychiatry*, 1958, *21*, 205–220.

Wynne, L. C., & Singer, M. T. Thought disorder and family relations of schizophrenics: I. A research strategy. *Archives of General Psychiatry*, 1963, *9*, 191–198. (a)

Wynne, L. C., & Singer, M. T. Thought disorder and family relations of schizophrenics: II. Classification of forms of thinking. *Archives of General Psychiatry*, 1963, *9*, 199–206. (b)

Wynne, L. C., & Whitaker, C. *The normal family.* Unpublished manuscript, 1974.

# 4

# FAMILY STYLES OF CONSTRUING THE SOCIAL ENVIRONMENT: A PERSPECTIVE ON VARIATION AMONG NONCLINICAL FAMILIES

## MARY ELLEN OLIVERI
## DAVID REISS

For the past several years, we have been engaged in a series of studies aimed at identifying and elucidating variation among families who, at the time of study at least, are under no particular acute stress and manifest no serious psychopathology. We have studied these "nonclinical" families with an eye toward understanding crucial mechanisms underlying families' interchanges with their social environments. Having adapted and extended concepts derived from previous research on clinical samples, we have begun to explore how families without particular clinical problems vary in the ways they interpret and interact with their social worlds. This chapter presents an overview of our current research on nonclinical families, with a focus on how insights developed through research on specific clinical concerns can inform research of a more nonclinical nature, and also on how the latter can, in turn, offer insight to practitioners concerned with issues of family diagnosis and evaluation.

This chapter is organized into four major sections. In the first section we describe how our current research on nonclinical samples is derived from insights gained from previous research on clinical samples, and we note some important links between the two realms of study. The second section describes our central method of study—a laboratory problem-solving procedure—and the primary dimensions along which variation among families is

Mary Ellen Oliveri and David Reiss. Center for Family Research and Department of Psychiatry and Behavioral Sciences, George Washington University School of Medicine, Washington, D.C.

examined. The third describes those aspects of variation in families' social perceptions and interactions that are predictable from their problem-solving behavior. Finally, in the fourth section, we consider the areas of potential applicability of this work to ongoing clinical concerns.

## BACKGROUND: APPLYING CONCEPTS DERIVED FROM WORK ON SPECIFIC CLINICAL CONCERNS TO THE STUDY OF NONCLINICAL FAMILIES

During the late 1960s and early 1970s, David Reiss was engaged in a series of studies (Reiss, 1967a, 1967b, 1968, 1969, 1971b, 1971c) that, at the outset, were aimed at discovering a particular style of information processing in families of schizophrenic patients that might help to explain a comparable information-processing deficit in the identified patient. Using a variety of laboratory problem-solving tasks and two different "control" groups (families with delinquent patients and families whose children had no particular psychiatric abnormality), he found a number of differences between families of schizophrenics and the other two groups, and differences between the two control groups as well.

A number of observations during the testing of these families, however, contributed to an interpretation of the findings in a way that could not have been predicted before the studies began: the focus in interpretation shifted from differences in families' skills in solving problems—specifically, their modes of information processing—to differences among families in the ways they perceived the laboratory setting in which they were being tested. The patterns of behavior observed suggested that families with schizophrenic adolescents perceived the laboratory as dangerous and threatening to the viability of intensely felt intermember ties; that families with delinquent adolescents viewed the laboratory as an arena for each individual to demonstrate independence from the others and thus to maintain intermember distance; and that families with "normal" adolescents saw the laboratory and its procedures as a challenging game—an opportunity for the family to explore and master a new situation collectively.

The differences among the three groups of families in their problem-solving behaviors were readily explainable in these terms, and these interpretations were buttressed by observations of other clinical investigators. Several investigators (e.g., Kaufman, Durkin, Frank, Heims, Jones, Ryter, Stone, & Zilbach, 1963; Minuchin, Auerswald, King, & Rabinowitz, 1964) had spoken of a pervasive sense of isolation and subjectively experienced distance among members in families with delinquent adolescents, and others (Stabenau, Tupin, Werner, & Pollin, 1965) had provided data suggesting conflict between members. Fleck, Lidz, and Cornelison (1965) and Wynne, Ryckoff, Day, and Hirsch (1958) had pointed to the existence, in families of schizophrenics, of estrangement from the social environment, and Scott and Askworth (1967) and Hoover (1965) had spoken of the extraordinary mutual involvement—in fact, "embroilment"—among members of these families.

Along with the emergence of these kinds of explanations for families' behavior in the laboratory came an increasing appreciation of the salience of the laboratory testing situation itself for promoting meaningful variation in families' behavior. Several related aspects of the laboratory testing experience—the unfamiliarity of the setting, the personnel, and the procedures, as well as the somewhat mysterious, partially hidden, nature of the research aims—seemed to combine to allow families considerable leeway to develop their own views of the setting's properties and demands, and to behave *vis à vis* the setting accordingly. Given that none of the families had actually had previous experience with this particular setting, it was additionally plausible that their orientations to the laboratory derived from their typical modes of perceiving and interacting with their everyday social milieus. The novelty and ambiguity of the laboratory appeared to encourage families to project onto it their feelings and views regarding the not fully understood aspects of the wider social environment.

These early observations and interpretations of families' behavior in the laboratory gave rise to the development of a theoretical model of shared construing in families that focused specifically on the issue of how families perceive the fundamental character of the social environment and their place within it. Originally, the model consisted of a small set of general propositions concerning processes by which families, as unitary groups, explore and interpret their immediate social worlds (Reiss, 1971a). A set of related propositions concerned how and why certain shared interpretations—shared constructs—arise; what serves to maintain or to modify them; and how they differ from family to family.

The development of the model was supported and shaped by Kelly's personal construct theory (1955), Heider's naive psychology (1958), concepts about the subjective world of families from Hess and Handel (1959), and ideas on social process by Berger and Luckman (1966). The central notion is that just as individuals develop their own personal modes of construing people and events in their environments, so family units, through a process of integrating and reconciling the construing styles of all members, develop a *shared* mode of perceiving and interpreting their social world. A family's set of shared assumptions about the fundamental nature of the social world— more recently termed its *paradigm* (Reiss, 1981)—has been seen to shape the family's typical mode or style of interacting with the environment, thus influencing to a considerable degree the outcome of the family's everyday interchanges with its social environment.

Several empirical studies using laboratory problem-solving behavior as an indicator of variation in selected aspects of families' paradigms have been inspired by this model. The model's promise of applicability to a broader range of families than that examined in the early studies, however, made the issue of clinically pertinent psychopathology matter less as time went by. A subsequent series of studies (Costell, Reiss, Berkman, & Jones, 1981; Reiss, Costell, Berkman, & Jones, 1980; Reiss, Costell, Jones, & Berkman, 1980) was conducted with families of psychiatrically hospitalized adolescents but without specifying subgroups by means of the adolescents' specific diagnosis. Most recently, as will be seen in the body of this chapter, our work has aimed to track important kinds of variation among nonclinical families— those not manifesting any particular psychiatric symptomatology in any member. The early work, however, continues to inform the current work, both through its parallels with the current work and through its contrasts.

An important parallel comes from having observed both clinical and nonclinical samples of families in similar contexts; the early work differentiating among families of adolescents with different forms of psychiatric disturbance has had significant interpretive utility in the current work with nonclinical samples. That is, the kinds of variation previously observed among families with different clinical problems now serve as *prototypes* for interpreting variation among nonclinical families. Consider the following example.

As noted above, in the early studies families of delinquent adolescents showed one pattern of behavior in the laboratory, and families of schizophrenics showed another. For the moment, let us call the pattern of behavior shown by families of delinquents Type D and that shown by families of schizophrenics Type S. Our latest work makes it clear that not all families displaying Type D behavior in the laboratory have delinquent children. However, the earlier characterization of the orientation to the environment expressed in the behavior of families of delinquents (buttressed by the insights of other investigators) may be applied as well to other families showing Type D behavior; thus, Type D behavior in general can be considered indicative of an experienced sense of isolation among members and a disjointed approach to the environment. Such an interpretation of the meaning of the behavior of all Type D families is further specified by knowing that Type D behavior, while not associated with delinquency in every case, still bears no systematic association with other forms of psychopathology—for example, schizophrenia. The Type S behavior pattern suggests a qualitatively different kind of orientation to the environment that is consistent with other information on the characteristics of schizophrenic families (but that, we argue, need not be associated with the presence of schizophrenia in every instance).

A final comment regarding relationships between the early and current work has to do with some salient contrasts. An obvious advantage of the early work was that different patterns of problem-solving behavior (and the corresponding orientations to the environment that they were seen to express) were tied to relatively concrete "markers" (i.e., psychiatric disturbances in children). Whether the specific forms of children's psychopathology were the outcome or the cause of the family patterns observed could not be determined; but it was clear, nonetheless, that families who differed from one another in problem-solving behavior were also different from one another in at least one other, unequivocally important, way. As will be seen, we have less dramatic and obviously salient independent or dependent variables in our current work with nonclinical families. Precisely because these families are not, as far as we can tell, widely different in psychological health, we must depend on more subtle manifestations of the variations in family patterns that we observe.

On the other hand, a problematic aspect of the early work (and of other studies using clinical samples) does not beset our current work. That is, it was unclear in the early studies if and how other experiences connected with children's conditions systematically influenced the patterns of family behavior observed in the laboratory; the assessments might have been colored to an unknown degree by stress engendered by the illness or by the influence of other professionals with whom the families came into contact concerning the illness. In contrast, our present focus on nonclinical families has the advantage of allowing us to study family–environment interactions without systematic contamination by any particular stress.[1] Also, by not concentrating specifically on issues of health versus pathology, we have the opportunity to investigate a range of ways in which variation among families in their orientations to the environment are manifested in the course of their everyday lives.

## METHODS: SAMPLES, LABORATORY ASSESSMENT, AND DIMENSIONS OF FAMILY PARADIGM

In this section, we describe the central features of our method of studying variation among nonclinical families: the nature of the samples studied, the laboratory problem-solving procedure that is our primary assessment instrument, and the dimensions of variation in families' paradigms—their shared assumptions about the nature of the social world—that are estimable from objectively recorded problem-solving behaviors.

---

[1]As we discuss below, we do not mean to imply that our samples of nonclinical families are without stress. Our method of recruitment, however, is not aimed at eliciting the cooperation of families with any particular forms of stress, and, as far as we have been able to tell, variation in the nature and extent of those family stresses that exist has not been systematically associated with the central variables we study. A study of ours that is currently under way examines the relationships between characteristics of family paradigm and families' modes of dealing with stressful events with which they are faced in everyday life. According to theory, the results of that study should demonstrate that variation in families' paradigms is related less to the *incidence* of stress than to the family's style of *coping* with it.

## Samples

The operational definition of nonclinical families in our current studies derives primarily from the mode and source of recruitment; these families are not recruited through clinical sources, nor are any specific clinical issues emphasized in the advertising for volunteers. Our samples consist of middle- to upper-middle-class families whose cooperation is elicited as a result of recruitment efforts within suburban Washington, D.C., area PTAs; recruitment efforts do not indicate that any particular family problems or clinical conditions are the foci of study or requirements for participation. Requirements for participation pertain only to such issues as the intactness of the family, age of parents, absence of major physical conditions that could hamper or be aggravated by the mechanics of data collection, and fluency in the English language. Subject families are paid a modest fee for their participation; although clinical referrals are provided if requested by families, provision of any kind of clinical services is not part of the researcher-subject family contract. The problems and stresses that exist in these families should approximate the range typical of middle- to upper-middle-class families of high school students in a large metropolitan area. Approximately 33% of the families report prior or concurrent participation in individual, marital, or family counseling or therapy.

In practice, only the father, mother, and one high-school-age child usually participate in our studies, regardless of the size of the family. This use of family triads rather than entire nuclear families is primarily for the purpose of controlling for the number of family members participating and the age of the child participating. Because we do not study complete families, we have been concerned about the possibility that systematic error might intrude into our assessments because of the particular composition of the triad studied. We have, therefore, examined various indices of family composition (size of family; sex and birth order of child tested), but have, as we note below, found no consistent or strong relationships between such indices and the dimensions of family paradigm estimated from problem-solving behavior.

## Laboratory Assessment

Our laboratory problem-solving procedure—the card sort procedure—is a standard situation in which the family triads participating are asked to work toward solution of a series of logical puzzles, both individually and with the possibility of consulting one another. The most recent version of the procedure is described in detail in a forthcoming paper. It is sufficient to note here that although families are given detailed concrete instructions for completion of several phases of the task, the procedure is designed to allow families considerable latitude in behaviors relevant to the problem-solving dimensions of interest. Families may choose to work closely together, exchanging information and deciding on very similar solutions to the puzzles, or they may choose to work independently, barely talking to one another. They may choose highly complex and organized or extremely simple, superficial solutions. They may reach decisions quickly, indeed before all relevant information is available, or they may labor over the task indefinitely, considering every scrap of information presented and every comment coming from one another, and only coming to a final solution after lengthy deliberation.

Families do, in fact, vary widely in these sorts of ways, and it is important to note that we have found as much variability within nonclinical samples as had previously been observed both within clinical samples and between clinical and nonclinical samples. Variations in these types of behaviors form the basis for our evaluation of families' positions along three dimensions of problem-solving performance; these are interpreted as estimates of three dimensions along which characteristics of family paradigm vary.

The first dimension is "configuration"; this refers to variation in families' levels of belief that the social world is inherently ordered, understandable, and masterable by them. Families high on this dimension experience a sense of optimism that they can meet and deal effectively with challenges posed by the social environment, that fundamental rules governing the social world can be discovered and understood by them. Families with low "configuration" are pessimistic that, by their own efforts, they can have an impact on the world; for these families, environmental principles seem hidden, not discernible by them. Variation in this sense of potential mastery and trust that problems in the environment are soluble is measured in the problem-solving setting by the degree of complexity and organization of family members' solutions to the externally given puzzles. That this is not a simple reflection of problem-solving *skills*, but rather a reflection of a sense that such problems *can be solved*, is supported by the consistent lack of association (over several samples) of this dimension with the verbal or abstract intelligence of family members.

The second dimension is "coordination." This refers to variation in families' levels of belief that the environment has a uniform impact on all family members, and it is manifested in families' propensities to take a unitary and collaborative approach to the social environment. Families high on this dimension adopt a unitary stance toward the environment, resulting from a fundamental sense that consensus on the meaning of environmental events is possible. In families low on this dimension, members interpret and deal with environmental events as separate individuals, since the environment is seen as functioning differently for each member; input from other family members is seen as of little use, perhaps even detrimental, to one's own environmental interactions. "Coordination" is measured in the problem-solving setting by the degree of close temporal pacing among family members as they progress through the task, and by the similarity of members' solutions to the puzzles.

The third dimension is "closure." This refers to variation in families' perceptions of events in the social world as continually familiar (readily interpretable on the basis of past experience) versus uniquely fresh and new (warranting consideration of new modes of interpretation). In families with "delayed closure," each new piece of information coming from the environment is interpreted afresh as each new situation is encountered; previous approaches to similar situations are suspended until all current input is available for consideration. Families with "early closure" seem dominated by their past; consideration of new and immediate experience is foregone so that decisions can be reached as quickly as possible before information that might indicate a change from previous approaches can accumulate. In the problem-solving setting, variation in families' tendencies to delay "closure" is measured by the degree of their adaptation to information input in the form of changes in solutions as information accumulates throughout the task, and by the amount of time taken overall in dealing with the externally given tasks.

In practice, we employ several discrete indices, all based on nonverbal family behaviors, to measure each dimension. Within the nonclinical samples we have studied, the resulting three dimensions have been shown to be independent of measures of social class (occupation, income, education), family composition, intelligence, and reported participation in individual, family, or marital therapy. The three dimensions also have been shown repeatedly to be independent of one another. That is, a family's level of "coordination," for example, cannot be used to predict its levels of "configuration" and "closure." Since every family is assessed along each of three independent dimensions, all dimensions can be considered simultaneously to describe distinctive family "types"; in this chapter, however, we consider each dimension separately in describing how families who differ from one another in problem-solving behavior have also been shown to differ systematically from one another in other patterns of social interpretation and interaction.

## LABORATORY CORRELATES: EVIDENCE THAT PROBLEM-SOLVING BEHAVIOR TAPS VARIATION IN CHARACTERISTICS OF FAMILY PARADIGM

The validity of measures of family problem-solving behavior as markers of variation in families' fundamental assumptions about and orientations toward the social environment has been supported by results of several studies demonstrating that problem-solving behavior is predictive of families' actual patterns of social interpretation and interaction. A series of recent studies utilizing clinical samples (Costell *et al.*, 1981; Reiss, Costell, Berkman, & Jones, 1980; Reiss, Costell, Jones, & Berkman, 1980) demonstrated relationships between families' problem-solving behavior and their modes of adaptation to a family-oriented treatment program for psychiatrically hospitalized adolescents. Evidence obtained from two recent studies of nonclinical families is presented here. In the first study we examined relationships between problem-solving behavior and families' perceptions of family and family-environment relationships, using a semiprojective felt-figure technique. In the second, we examined variation in families' orientations to the social environment by studying the structure of families' experienced ties to networks of extended family. (More detailed information on the results of the first study will be described in a subsequent paper; see Oliveri & Reiss, 1981, for a fuller explication of the results of the second study.) It should be noted that data analyses for both studies are not complete at this writing. Thus, the findings we present here are illustrative rather than definitive, and our interpretations, while consonant with theory, may be modified and elaborated as more information becomes available.

### Perceptions of Family and Family-Environment Relationships

Data from 69 family triads recruited through one high school PTA in suburban Washington were used to investigate the usefulness of laboratory problem-solving behavior in delineating theoretically pertinent patterns of variation in families' perceptions of social relationships. These families completed both the card sort procedure described above and a procedure aimed at tapping perceptions of both family and family-environment relationships through nonverbal means; this is called the figure placement procedure.

The figure placement procedure is an adaptation of Kuethe's felt-figure technique (1962); it was designed to assess certain general properties of families' perceptions of the social and inanimate environment. It is a semiprojective technique that requires family members to make spatial arrangements, on a felt board, of small figures representing family members, strangers, and inanimate objects. The central assumption in the use of the procedure, following Kuethe, is that actual distances between certain kinds of figures as arranged by the family represent experienced distances—for example, feelings of closeness versus alienation. The procedure has three sequential phases. In the first, only figures representing members of the same family are arranged; in the second, figures identified as "people the family does not know" are added to the arrangement; in the third, geometric shapes—seen as representing inanimate, impersonal aspects of the social environment—are added. Family members work individually and without seeing each other's arrangements, although they may discuss (by means of earphone-microphone arrangments) the figure arrangements if they wish.

Overhead still cameras photograph each member's figure arrangements at the end of each phase.

During observations of how families performed during the procedure, four kinds of ways in which families differed in their arrangements struck us as particularly noteworthy. The first concerned how families dealt with the figures representing members of the same family. Most families immediately identified these as members of their own family, but, beyond that, families varied widely in the ways they chose to arrange these figures. Some families took care to arrange them in ways they seemed to feel represented their family's own distinctive characteristics, while others simply arranged the figures according to conventional age and/or sex stereotypes (e.g., adults together and separate from children, or father with son and mother with daughter, or a combination of both). This latter type of arrangement seemed to us, in observing it, a superficial response—perhaps a facade that allowed the family to avoid grappling with more subtle and complex issues and feelings characterizing relationships within the family. (This interpretation was supported by subsequent findings of significant negative correlations between stereotypic arrangements and the amount of time families invested in each phase of the task.)

A second aspect of the arrangements was the way the figures representing strangers were placed *vis à vis* the family figures. Some families kept these two kinds of figures at great distance, and others brought the strangers quite close to the family—almost embracing them within the family group. A third way in which arrangements varied concerned placement of geometric shapes *vis à vis* family and stranger figures. Again, some families kept the geometric shapes at some distance from the family or stranger figures, making no effort to integrate them into a unified array. At the other extreme were those families who included the shapes within the arrangements of family and stranger figures, making them into buildings, trees, or sometimes more abstract "markers" of the other figures' positions—that is, demarcations of these figures' places on an otherwise blank field.

Finally, we were struck by variations in how families progressed through the three phases of the task. Some families changed previous arrangements when new figures were introduced; in other families, an arrangement in an early phase was kept intact or merely added to when new figures came on the scene. In this connection, we were particularly interested in the ways the relationships among the family figures changed when the strangers were introduced.

After these initial observations, we developed a series of indices that could be objectively derived in order to quantify the kinds of variation we had observed. These indices were computed by means of mathematical manipulations of actual pairwise distances between various types of figures on the board. Indices were computed separately for each family member participating, and family total indices were also computed. Preliminary analyses indicated that the amount of similarity or dissimilarity among the three family members was not systematically related to the three problem-solving dimensions; thus, further analyses concentrated primarily on family total indices.

Factor analysis revealed that three orthogonal dimensions could describe much of the variation in family behaviors in response to the task. "Conventional family structure" marked variation in the extent to which family figures were arranged according to stereotypic age and sex relationships; "family accommodation to strangers" assessed the degree of inclusion of strangers among family figures and the amount of change in previous arrangements of family figures when strangers were introduced; and "inclusion of inanimate objects" assessed the closeness with which geometric shapes were placed *vis à vis* family and stranger figures.

In order to examine patterns of association between problem-solving behavior and these styles of figure arrangements, factor scores from each of these three figure placement dimensions were used as dependent variables in three-way ("configuration," "coordination," and "closure") analyses of variance. (Scores on each problem-solving dimension were divided at the median to describe low and high levels.) Table 4-1 presents a summary of the findings for each of the three problem-solving dimensions. (These result from statistically significant main effects; the complexities involved in the

TABLE 4-1. SUMMARY OF ANALYSES OF ASSOCIATION BETWEEN FAMILY PROBLEM SOLVING AND FIGURE PLACEMENT BEHAVIOR[a]

| Dimensions of problem-solving performance | Figure placement dimensions | | |
|---|---|---|---|
| | Conventional family structure | Accommodation to strangers | Inclusion of inanimate objects |
| Configuration | $F(1,61) = 15.96$*** $\bar{x}_H = -.39$ $\bar{x}_L = .40$ | $F(1,61) = 3.82$* $\bar{x}_H = .19$ $\bar{x}_L = -.19$ | $F < 1$ |
| Coordination | $F(1,61) = 5.65$** $\bar{x} = -.27$ $\bar{x} = .27$ | $F < 1$ | $F < 1$ |
| Closure | $F(1,61) = 2.93$ | $F(1,61) = 1.66$ | $F(1,61) = 5.67$** $\bar{x}_D = .25$ $\bar{x}_E = -.26$ |

[a]Explanation of symbols: $\bar{x}$ = group mean for variable yielding significant main effect; for configuration and coordination, subscripts $H$ and $L$ refer to high and low; for closure, subscripts $D$ and $E$ refer to delayed and early.
*$p < .055$
**$p < .02$
***$p < .001$

interaction effects that were obtained necessitate their report elsewhere.) We describe these for each figure placement dimension in turn.

"Conventional family structure" was found to be inversely associated with both configuration and coordination. Families high on "configuration" and those high on "coordination" tended to arrange the family figures with the least regard for stereotype. Since the "conventional family structure" variable showed strong associations with each of these two orthogonal problem-solving dimensions, it is clear that this variable has more than one meaning, that is, that it measures more than one particular aspect of family perception. We can identify two plausible components of the measure that are helpful in interpreting both the "coordination" and "configuration" effects. As we noted previously, one contributor to the tendency to portray one's family in a nonstereotypic way is a strong investment in the unique qualities of one's own family, an investment that one would expect in families with high coordination. Another is a preference for novelty, subtlety, and complexity rather than for conventional or superficial structure. We have discussed this elsewhere (Oliveri & Reiss, 1981; Reiss, Costell, Berkman, & Jones, 1980) as a characteristic of families high on "configuration" that promotes their sense of potential mastery over complex and challenging events and issues arising in the social environment. Also, an analogous finding emerged in a study of family perceptions of an inpatient treatment program; "configuration" was positively associated with the level of subtlety, organization, and structure of families' perceptions of other families and staff (Costell *et al.*, 1981; Reiss, Costell, Berkman, & Jones, 1980).

Another finding consistent with the conceptualization of "configuration" as a manifestation of a sense of mastery over the social environment is the marginally significant association of "configuration" with "family accommodation to strangers." Families high on "configuration" adjusted their previous arrangements of family figures and brought the strangers close to the family, suggesting a comfort with the environment characteristic of an optimistic, masterful orientation. Families low on "configuration", on the other hand, displayed a more rigid and distant stance toward the strangers, suggesting fearfulness and pessimism that the environment can be effectively dealt with by the family.

"Inclusion of inanimate objects" is the most ambiguous of the three figure placement tasks, since it is not at all clear to families what the geometric shapes are actually supposed to mean. The ways in which families accommodated to this ambiguity, however, supported our prior notion that these abstract figures represent, quite generally speaking, inanimate, impersonal aspects of the environment (e.g., institutions, governments, cities) with which families have quite variable degrees of comfort. The association seen in Table 4-1 of this variable with "closure" enhances the plausibility of that interpretation. Families most open to new and immediate experience ("delayed closure") demonstrated the most openness to the inclusion of "inanimate" with "animate" figures, suggesting a flexibility in approach to the environment and a sense of permeability of family and other social boundaries consistent with our conceptualization of the manifestations of "delayed closure."

### Families' Ties to Their Kin

Data from 82 family triads recruited through seven suburban Washington PTAs were used to study variation in families' interactive relationships with the social environment. Families who had completed the card sort procedure also completed a lengthy and detailed social network inventory that requested information pertaining to structural, functional, and contextual aspects of families' ties to kin, friends, and other acquaintances. We present here only a portion of the data collected; these are findings pertaining to the structure of families' ties to their kin, and they are described more fully in Oliveri and Reiss (1981).

The inventory is self-administered; each family member completes it independently of the others. First, respondents define the composition of their networks by listing all individuals outside their nuclear families that they deem important or significant in some way. Two major categories of individuals are requested: a maximum of 12 relatives living outside a nuclear family's household, and a maximum of 18 friends or other significant individuals (neighbors, coworkers, etc.). After answering a series of questions on functional and contextual aspects of each relationship, respondents indicate who among the listed individuals know one another. A "linkage" is indicated if two listed individuals know one another. The information on linkages, as well as on the number of individuals listed, forms the base for examining structural aspects of networks. Three structural descriptors of kinship networks are considered here. "Size" is computed simply by counting the number of extended family individuals listed as important or significant to respondents. "Degree" which is a measure of the closeknit, interconnected, character of networks—the extent to which the individuals important to respondents also know one another—is computed by dividing two times the number of linkages by the total number of individuals listed. "Shared connection," which is a measure of the extent to which family members are jointly invested in the same network groupings, is computed by counting the number of specific linkages reported in common by family members and dividing by the total number of linkages reported.

"Size" and "degree" were computed on various levels (family, parental, and individual), although "shared connection" is by definition a group- or dyad-level score, and thus was computed only on family and parental levels. We concentrate on results pertaining to family-level indices here. To compute

TABLE 4-2. SUMMARY OF ANALYSES OF ASSOCIATION BETWEEN FAMILY PROBLEM SOLVING AND KINSHIP NETWORK STRUCTURE[a]

| Dimensions of problem-solving performance | Network structure dimensions | | |
|---|---|---|---|
| | Size | Degree | Shared connection |
| Configuration | $F < 1$ | $F < 1$ | $F\,(1,74) = 6.26*$ $\bar{x}_H = .05$ $\bar{x}_L = .09$ |
| Coordination | $F < 1$ | $F\,(1,74) = 8.22**$ $\bar{x}_H = 7.7$ $\bar{x}_L = 6.4$ | $F\,(1,74) = 5.91*$ $\bar{x}_H = .09$ $\bar{x}_L = .05$ |
| Closure | $F\,(1,74) = 7.71*$ $\bar{x}_D = 17.5$ $\bar{x}_E = 15.2$ | $F < 1$ | $F\,(1,74) = 2.19$ |

[a]Explanation of symbols: $\bar{x}$ = group mean for variable yielding significant main effect; for configuration and coordination, subscripts $H$ and $L$ refer to high and low; for closure, subscripts $D$ and $E$ refer to delayed and early.
*$p < .02$
**$p < .005$

a family-level index, we first constructed combined lists of individuals and linkages by consolidating the lists of all three family members. Redundancy within a combined list was eliminated by deleting any duplicate names or linkages. Then the formulas described above were applied.

Table 4-2 presents a summary of the results of three-factor ("configuration," "coordination," and "closure") analyses of variance using the three family-level indices of kinship network structure as dependent variables. Again, only main effects are presented. We describe the findings pertaining to each network index in turn.

The dimension of "size" for the significant kin network showed a strong association with "closure."[2] "Delayed closure" families, those most open to environmental experience, were invested in the largest number of relationships outside the nuclear family; we suggest that this is a reflection of their commitment to insuring maximal influx of new ideas and information into the family.

[2]Note that this does not necessarily mean that delayed closure families simply have more relatives than early closure families, although this may be true. The inventory specifically asks for the listing of the relatives important to the respondent, and we cannot assume that the number of "important" relatives necessarily covaries positively with the actual number of relatives available.

"Degree"—the measure of the close-knit character of the significant kin network—was positively associated with "coordination." Bott (1957) has suggested that the level of interconnectedness in a network increases the likelihood of a sharing of values and norms within it. Thus, this finding suggests that the level of "coordination" in a nuclear family runs parallel to the level of "coordination" of prevailing attitudes and values among significant members of the extended family. Another aspect of close-knit networks is that their members are more embedded within a system of relationships than they tend to be if the network is more loose-knit. In this regard, the association of coordination with degree is consistent with earlier findings (Costell et al., 1981; Reiss, Costell, Jones, & Berkman, 1980) that families high on coordination manifested the most "fit" and engagement with an inpatient treatment program, most likely as a reflection of similar feelings of themselves as family units.

"Shared connection," the measure of family members' joint investment in the same groupings within extended family, was, as is shown in Table 4-2, positively associated with "coordination" and negatively associated with "configuration." Again, as in findings on figure placement, one variable has shown associations with two orthogonal problem-solving dimensions, indicating possibilities of more than one interpretation. Another factor to consider in interpretation is that additional analyses (see Oliveri & Reiss, 1981) indicate that, for both "configuration" and "coordination," significant variation in the family-level "shared connection" measure was specifically due to differences between adolescents and parents (rather than to interparental differences or to differences among all three members).

Adolescent–parent differences in kinship ties may reflect two related but conceptually distinct family processes. They may signify simple lack of closeness between adolescents and parents, or they may reflect adolescents' developing autonomy in social relationships. Additional data of ours suggest that the former circumstance might underlie the "coordination" effect on "shared connection" and that the latter might underlie the "configuration" effect. These data show adolescents in families high on "configuration" to be invested in larger and more connected peer groups than those in families low on "configuration" appear to be; this suggests that the low shared connection in families high on "configuration" reflects age-appropriate autonomy of adolescents from parents in social interactions, which is a plausible offshoot of the sense of potential mastery hypothesized to characterize these families. An absence of an analogous association of adolescents' peer group involvements with "coordination," however, suggests that the association of low "shared connection" with low "coordination" reflects a simple lack of close engagement with parents around issues of kin ties, which is consistent with the conceptualization of these families' disjointed approach to the social environment.

## Summary

The patterns of association between families' problem-solving behavior, figure placement behavior, and kinship ties that we have presented result from our first efforts at studying the kinds of variation among nonclinical families that had been previously observed among clinical families. As additional information accumulates, our interpretations of particular findings may be modified, but they are, for the most part, consistent both with previous work and with theory. The present findings, summarized in Table 4-3, provide continuing support for the notion that patterns of problem-solving behavior in the laboratory signal variation in families' perceptions of and orientations to the broader social environment. In the final section of this chapter, we discuss the implications of awareness of these kinds of variation for issues relevant to clinical practice.

## A RETURN TO SOME CLINICAL CONCERNS

In concluding this chapter, we briefly consider some aspects of our current research on nonclinical samples that have potential clinical applicability: we discuss parallels between our method of family assessment and more traditional assessment instruments; we consider some issues relating to definitions

TABLE 4-3.  SUMMARY OF PATTERNS OF ASSOCIATION OF FAMILY PROBLEM-SOLVING BEHAVIOR WITH (*a*) PERCEPTIONS OF SOCIAL RELATIONSHIPS, AND WITH (*b*) ORIENTATIONS TOWARD KIN

| High levels of: | (*a*)<br>. . . were associated with<br>high levels of: | (*b*)<br>. . . and with high levels of: |
|---|---|---|
| Configuration<br>  Belief in a masterable environment | Nonstereotypic view of family<br>Openness to individuals outside the family | Child–parent independence in kin ties |
| Coordination<br>  Sense that the environment functions similarly for all members | Nonstereotypic view of family | Child–parent congruence in kin ties<br>Investment in close-knit networks of kin |
| Closure (delayed)<br>  View of the environment as source of new and changing experience | Openness to inanimate aspects of the environment | Investment in large networks of kin |

of family health versus pathology that our research has raised; and we touch on some ways in which this perspective on family variation has implications for the help-giving process.

## Family Evaluation in the Laboratory

Although the card sort procedure in itself may seem to have little to do with families' everyday lives, it has been shown to be able to predict interesting variation in families' styles of perceiving and interacting outside the laboratory, just as some more standard clinical assessment instruments (e.g., Rorschach, TAT) have been able to detect important kinds of variation in individuals' psychological states. Given the obvious surface contrasts between the card sort procedure and, for example, the Rorschach, it may be useful to point out some parallels in order to clarify some areas of potential linkage between this research and issues of evaluation confronting individuals in clinical practice.

A central feature of the Rorschach is ambiguity. While certain instructions to subjects are clear and to the point, the stimuli to which the subjects must respond—the inkblots—are decidedly ambiguous, and for good reason. The point of the Rorschach procedure is, after all, to learn how the subjects respond to the ambiguous stimuli—how they construe their meaning. Following years of experience with the procedure, much is known about the kinds of psychological problems or syndromes most likely to be associated with various patterns of response to the inkblots, although these responses may not in themselves seem so startling or significant to an observer unfamiliar with the test's aims and background.

In our laboratory, many aspects of our procedures are clear and concrete. The puzzle stimuli are not inkblots, but series of letters or numbers, and the instructions for completing necessary phases of the task are clear. Nonetheless, a central feature of the procedure as an evaluation instrument is ambiguity. The family's task in the laboratory has much in common with the task of an individual taking the Rorschach; family members must decide how to respond as a group to the setting, and there is little in the concrete instructions or task stimuli to guide them in that regard. Their mode of response to the setting, then, must be governed by the view of reality they project onto it.[3] Our experience with the procedure and its correlates gives us confidence that the three dimensions of problem-solving behavior do

---

[3]Viewing the card sort procedure as a form of projective test should clarify our position that it is, despite some of its surface features, not a group intelligence test. A family group projects its feelings as well as its thoughts onto the problem-solving procedures. The substantial contribution of a family's feelings about itself and the testing situation to its performance probably account for the lack of correlation of that performance with such variables as intelligence and education.

signal variation in three aspects of such family projections: whether the setting is masterable or uncontrollable ("configuration"), whether the task is a family or an individual one ("coordination"), and whether the setting provides new information useful to the family or irrelevant to them ("closure"). Like the Rorschach, an added advantage of the procedure is that the underlying dimensions it is designed to tap, as well as the relationships of these dimensions to actual behaviors, are not obvious to the subject family itself. The quality of ambiguity inherent in the procedure, in addition to allowing families to project their own views onto it, also makes it more difficult for them to know what it is about them that is being evaluated and thus reduces the likelihood of success of attempts to "fake good" (or "bad").

Thus, as an evaluation instrument, the card sort procedure has many features in common with more traditional assessment instruments, and, as we have noted at several points, it has already proven useful in making clinically pertinent predictions regarding the process of engagement in treatment. Like other instruments, however, it cannot detect *all* clinically pertinent kinds of variation—an issue we consider below.

### Definitions of Health versus Pathology

Our experience with assessing both clinical and nonclinical samples of families in the same kinds of settings has proven profitable in several ways, but it has also caused us to become exceedingly circumspect about what actually defines family health or pathology. In the problem-solving situation, we have found the same variability among extremely troubled families as we have among families, who, as far as we can tell, are managing to function pretty well in life. We cannot infer from this that the dimensions we study are of little significance, since, as we have shown, they have predicted other aspects of families' functioning in several contexts. Rather, this evidence causes us to hold in abeyance any judgments of what exactly is unhealthy or maladaptive that might follow from our method of family evaluation, and to suggest that caution is warranted in the interpretation and application of other models of family assessment as well.

The fact that some severely troubled families in our prior clinical samples would, on the basis of our assessment techniques, be described as identical to some families in our current nonclinical samples suggests that the same might occur using other evaluation models based on dimensions comparable to ours (e.g., Olson, Sprenkle, & Russell, 1979; Wertheim, 1973). Our experience suggests that, to the extent that such models define certain "maladaptive" extremes with accompanying implications for preferred directions of family change, they may be vulnerable to serious error unless the extent of variability among different kinds of samples is systematically assessed. If an appreciable amount of variability exists, decisions as to whether any specific directions of family change are warranted must be determined by means of multiple criteria—certainly more than these sorts of evaluations alone.

This recommendation is not meant to imply that our and other methods of family evaluation have no clinical relevance (our own previous research indicates important areas of clinical concern for which they do have relevance); rather, it simply suggests that considerably more research is needed before we will have confident knowledge of exactly what family characteristics or patterns necessarily signal pathological extremes and what patterns simply fall within a "normal" range of reasonably adaptive functioning.

### Families and the Help-Giving Process

Having pointed out what we feel our method of family evaluation *cannot* do (i.e., diagnose family health or pathology), we offer some final words about what it apparently *can* do: it can identify variation in the ways families construe and respond to their social environments. Since social environments include hospitals, treatment programs, and therapists, the central clinical relevance of this work lies in any insights it might offer to practitioners, treatment planners, and clinical researchers about how widely families differ in their interpretations of and responses to social input, including attempts to help them.

For example, we have noted at several points the demonstrated value of knowledge of families' orientations to the environment for tracking variation in families' modes of response to treatment; future clinical research might test the utility of designing different forms of treatment to correspond to different kinds of family orientations. For practitioners, our research reinforces the view that families are hardly passive entities in relation to the social environment; they form their own constructions of the meaning of health and illness, the efficacy of treatment, and the motives of therapists, and these constructions must have a decided influence on the process and outcome of clinical interventions. We have pointed to three kinds of variation among families that may enhance or impede practitioners' efforts to help them: their openness to influence from outside the family, their reliance on individual or group efforts, and their level of conviction that problems confronting them can, in fact, be solved.

## ACKNOWLEDGMENT

The research described in this chapter was supported by DHEW grant MH 26711.

# REFERENCES

Berger, P. L., & Luckman, T. *The social construction of reality.* New York: Doubleday, 1966.

Bott, E. *Family and social network.* New York: Free Press, 1957.

Costell, R., Reiss, D., Berkman, H., & Jones, C. The family meets the hospital: Predicting the family's perception of the treatment program from its problem-solving style. *Archives of General Psychiatry,* 1981, *38,* 569–577.

Fleck, S., Lidz, T., & Cornelison, A. The understanding of symptomatology through the study of family interaction. In T. Lidz, S. Fleck, & A. Cornelison, *Schizophrenia and the family.* New York: International Universities Press, 1965.

Heider, F. *The psychology of interpersonal relations.* New York: Wiley, 1958.

Hess, R., & Handel, G. *Family worlds: A psychosocial approach to family life.* Chicago: University of Chicago Press, 1959.

Hoover, C. The embroiled family: A blueprint for schizophrenia. *Family Process,* 1965, *4,* 291–310.

Kaufman, I., Durkin, H., Frank, T., Heims, L., Jones, D., Ryter, Z., Stone, E., & Zilbach, J. Delineation of two diagnostic groups among juvenile delinquents: The schizophrenic and the impulse-ridden character disorder. *Journal of the American Academy of Child Psychiatry,* 1963, *2,* 292–318.

Kelly, G. *The psychology of personal constructs.* New York: Norton, 1955.

Kuethe, J. Social schemas. *Journal of Abnormal and Social Psychology,* 1962, *64,* 31–38.

Minuchin, S., Auerswald, E., King, C., & Rabinowitz, C. The study of treatment of families that produce multiple acting-out boys. *American Journal of Orthopsychiatry,* 1964, *34,* 125–133.

Oliveri, M. E., & Reiss, D. The structure of families' ties to their kin: The shaping role of social constructions. *Journal of Marriage and the Family,* 1981, *43* (2), 391–407.

Olson, D., Sprenkle, D., & Russell, C. Circumplex model of marital and family systems: I. Cohesion and adaptability dimensions, family types, and clinical applications. *Family Process,* 1979, *18,* 3–28.

Reiss, D. Individual thinking and family interaction: I. Introduction to an experimental study of problem solving in families of normals, character disorders, and schizophrenics. *Archives of General Psychiatry,* 1967, *16,* 80–93. (a)

Reiss, D. Individual thinking and family interaction: II. A study of pattern recognition and hypothesis testing in families of normals, character disorders and schizophrenics. *Journal of Psychiatric Research,* 1967, *5,* 193–211. (b)

Reiss, D. Individual thinking and family interaction: III. An experimental study of categorization performance in families of normals, those with character disorders and schizophrenics. *Journal of Nervous and Mental Disease,* 1968, *146,* 384–403.

Reiss, D. Individual thinking and family interaction: IV. A study of information exchange in families of normals, those with character disorders, and schizophrenics. *Journal of Nervous and Mental Disease,* 1969, *149,* 473–490.

Reiss, D. Varieties of consensual experience: I. A theory for relating family interaction to individual thinking. *Family Process,* 1971, *10,* 1–28. (a)

Reiss, D. Varieties of consensual experience: II. Dimensions of a family's experience of its environment. *Family Process,* 1971, *10,* 28–35. (b)

Reiss, D. Varieties of consensual experience: III. Contrasts between families of normals, delinquents, and schizophrenics. *Journal of Nervous and Mental Disease,* 1971, *152,* 73–95. (c)

Reiss, D. *The family's construction of reality.* Cambridge: Harvard University Press, 1981.

Reiss, D., Costell, R., Berkman, H., & Jones, C. How one family perceives another: The relationship between social constructions and problem-solving competence. *Family Process,* 1980, *19,* 239–256.

Reiss, D., Costell, R., Jones, C., & Berkman, H. The family meets the hospital: A laboratory forecast of the encounter. *Archives of General Psychiatry,* 1980, *37,* 141–154.

Scott, R., & Askworth, P. "Closure" at the first schizophrenic breakdown: A family study. *British Journal of Medical Psychology,* 1967, *40,* 109–145.

Stabenau, J., Tupin, J., Werner, M., & Pollin, W. A comparative study of families of schizophrenics, delinquents, and normals. *Psychiatry,* 1965, *28,* 45–59.

Wertheim, E. Family unit therapy and the science and typology of family systems. *Family Process,* 1973, *12,* 361–376.

Wynne, L., Ryckoff, I., Day, J., & Hirsch, S. Pseudo-mutuality in the family relations of schizophrenics. *Psychiatry,* 1958, *21,* 205–222.

# 5

# MCMASTER MODEL
# OF FAMILY FUNCTIONING:
# A VIEW OF THE NORMAL FAMILY

## NATHAN B. EPSTEIN
## DUANE S. BISHOP
## LAWRENCE M. BALDWIN

## INTRODUCTION

The concepts contained in the McMaster Model of Family Functioning (MMFF) have evolved from studies of normal as well as clinical populations; as a result, they define family health as well as pathology.

In what follows, we discuss our view of normal family function, the MMFF, and findings from our research that relate to normal families. In presenting the MMFF, we highlight the significant historical issues in its development, define the model and its concepts, describe one family as an example, and discuss variations that could occur within a normal range.

### Health and Normality

The MMFF does not cover all aspects of family functioning. It focuses on the dimensions of functioning that are seen as having the most impact on the emotional and physical health or problems of family members. We have defined each dimension as ranging from "most ineffective" to "most effective." We hypothesize that "most ineffective" functioning in any of these dimensions can contribute to a clinical presentation, whereas "most effective" functioning in all dimensions supports optimal physical and emotional health.

In this chapter, we take the position that it is useful to equate the notion of "health" with "normality." This position requires some justification.

Nathan B. Epstein, Duane S. Bishop, and Lawrence M. Baldwin. Butler Hospital and Section of Psychiatry and Human Behavior, Brown University, Providence, Rhode Island.

Normality is an ill-defined concept. It often seems to mean "not display-ing any particular problems." For instance, when we conducted a computer search of papers on the normal family, "normal" was not a category; we had to specify "not reconstituted," "not psychiatric," "not alcoholic," etc. When defined in this exclusionary way, "normal" is not a very useful concept. A normal family is described as not having a number of features, but there is no positive statement about what a normal family is.

Another common approach has been to equate "normal" with the statistical average. Using this approach, measurements are taken on some sample, and the average score is taken to be the normal score for the population. If the sample is representative of the total population, then something is known of the distribution of the characteristic being measured in the whole population. But, for example, if the characteristic is the frequency with which husbands and wives discuss financial problems, and the average is once a week, it does not tell us much of use about families. For one thing, the current life situation of the family may influence the amount of discussion that is required. For another thing, if it could be assumed that other families were in similar life situations, could we think that families discussing finances once a week are functioning better than those discussing finances more or less often?

We argue that a clinically useful concept is "health." A healthy family is neither necessarily average nor merely lacking in negative characteristics. Rather, it has described positive features. The MMFF contains a description of such a set of features.

## MCMASTER MODEL OF FAMILY FUNCTIONING

### Overview

The MMFF has evolved over a period of more than 25 years. The initial study in the evolution of the model was conducted in the late 1950s at McGill University and was reported in *The Silent Majority* (Westley & Epstein, 1969). (This research is discussed in more detail in a later section of this chapter.) The next stage in the development, described in the *Family Catego-ries Schema* (Epstein, Sigal, & Rakoff, 1962), occurred in the early 1960s, also at McGill. In the late 1960s and through the 1970s, work on the model took place at McMaster University. The model in its current form was described by Epstein, Bishop, and Levin (1978). Currently, work on the model is taking place at both McMaster and Brown Universities.

Useful ideas from the family therapy literature, as well as from clinical, teaching and research experience, have been incorporated into the model. The model has been continually refined and reformulated. Aspects of family functioning were conceptualized and then tested in clinical work, research,

MCMASTER MODEL OF FAMILY FUNCTIONING

and teaching. Problems arising in applying the model became the basis for reformulations. The result is a pragmatic model containing ideas that have worked. Those not meeting the test in treatment, teaching, or research have been discarded or modified.

The model has been used extensively in a variety of psychiatric and family practice clinics (Comley, 1973; Epstein & Westley, 1959; Guttman, Spector, Sigal, Rakoff, & Epstein, 1971; Guttman, Spector, Sigal, Epstein, & Rakoff, 1972; Postner, Guttman, Sigal, Epstein, & Rakoff, 1971; Rakoff, Sigal, Spector, & Guttman, 1967; Sigal, Rakoff, & Epstein, 1967; Westley & Epstein, 1960) and by therapists who treated families as a part of a large family therapy outcome study (Guttman *et al.,* 1971; Santa-Barbara, Woodward, Levin, Streiner, Goodman, & Epstein, 1975; Woodward, Santa-Barbara, Levin, Goodman, Streiner & Epstein, 1975; Woodward, Santa-Barbara, Levin, Epstein, & Streiner, 1977; Woodward, Santa-Barbara, Levin Goodman, Streiner, Muzzin, & Epstein, 1974). The framework has also been used in a number of family therapy training programs and found to be readily teachable (Bishop & Epstein, 1979).

The model is based on a systems approach.

> In this approach the family is seen as an open system consisting of systems within systems (individual, marital dyad) and relating to other systems (extended family, schools, industry, religions). The unique aspect of the dynamic family group cannot be simply reduced to the characteristics of the individual or interactions between pairs of members. Rather, there are explicit and implicit rules, plus action by members, which govern and monitor each other's behavior. (Epstein & Bishop, 1973, p. 176)

The crucial assumptions of systems theory that underlie our model can be summarized as follows:

1. The parts of the family are interrelated.
2. One part of the family cannot be understood in isolation from the rest of the system.
3. Family functioning cannot be fully understood by simply understanding each of the parts.
4. A family's structure and organization are important factors determining the behavior of family members.
5. Transactional patterns of the family system shape the behavior of family members.

In addition to the systems approach, another feature we should note is that of values. We describe how a healthy, or, in our view, a normal family should look on each of the dimensions. Often such a description involves a value judgment. For instance, we would say that family members ought to be able to show sadness at the appropriate times and to the degree called for by the situation. The judgment of appropriateness with respect to sadness is not clear-cut and varies among cultures. We take the position that knowledge of the culture to which a family belongs is necessary for understanding a family and that judgments of health or normality are relative to the culture of the family. We comment more on values later.

We assume that a primary function of today's family unit is to provide a setting for the development and maintenance of family members on the social, psychological, and biological levels (Epstein, Levin, & Bishop, 1976, p. 1411). In the course of fulfilling this function, families will have to deal with a variety of issues and problems or tasks, which we group into three areas. These are the Basic Task Area, the Developmental Task Area, and the Hazardous Task Area.

The Basic Task Area is the most fundamental of the three; it involves instrumental issues. For example, families must deal with the problems of providing food, money, transportation, and shelter.

The Developmental Task Area encompasses those family issues that arise as a result of development over time. These developments are often conceptualized as a sequence of stages. On the individual level, these include crises of infancy, childhood, adolescence, and middle and old age. On the family level, these might be the beginning of the marriage, the first pregnancy, or the last child's leaving home. Developmental concepts and family functioning have been referred to by a research of authors (Berman & Lief, 1975; Brody, 1974; Carter & McGoldrick, 1980; Group for the Advancement of Psychiatry, 1970; Hadley, Jacob, Milliones, Caplan, & Spitz, 1974; Scherz, 1971; Solomon, 1973).

The Hazardous Task Area involves the handling of crises that arise as a result of illness, accident, loss of income, job change, and so on. There is also substantial literature dealing with these topics (Comley, 1973; Hill, 1965; Langsley & Kaplan, 1968; Minuchin & Barcai, 1969; Parad & Caplan, 1965; Rappaport, 1965).

We have found that families who are unable to deal effectively with these three task areas are most likely to develop clinically significant problems and/or chronic maladaptive problems.

### Dimensions of Family Functioning

To understand the structure, organization, and transactional patterns of the family, we focus on the following six dimensions: "problem solving," "communication," "roles," "affective responsiveness," "affective involvement," and "behavior control." These are outlined briefly in Table 5-1.

> The McMaster model does not focus on any one dimension as the foundation for conceptualizing family behavior. We argue that many dimensions need to be assessed for a fuller understanding of such a complex entity as the family. Although we attempt to clearly define and delineate the dimensions,

we recognize the potential overlap and/or possible interaction that may occur between them. Further clarification will undoubtedly result from our continuing research. (Epstein & Bishop, 1981a, p. 448)

We discuss the dimensions separately and present brief definitions of each. We then describe how one very effectively functioning family appeared on that dimension. (This particular family, whom we call the Simpsons, consisted of father, mother, and two sons, aged 3 and 4. The description we present is excerpted from material obtained during an in-depth interview.) Finally, we consider the range of functioning that we consider healthy or normal. The case material and the description of the range of effective functioning provide other ways to understand the workings of the model.

A more detailed discussion of the model is presented elsewhere (Epstein & Bishop, 1981a; Epstein, Bishop, & Levin, 1978). The 1978 presentation discusses the relationship of family functioning to preventive medicine, which might also be of interest to some readers.

### Problem Solving

*Definition.* The term "family problem solving" refers to a family's ability to resolve problems to a level that maintains effective family functioning. Prior to Epstein's earlier research studies (Westley & Epstein, 1969), it had been postulated that ineffective families would have more problems than would more effectively functioning families. Surprisingly, studies showed that this was not the case; in fact, all families encountered more or less the same range of difficulties. However, differences did occur. Effective families solved their problems, while ineffectively functioning families did not deal with at least some of their problems.

Family problems can be divided into two types: "instrumental" and "affective." Instrumental problems relate to issues that are mechanical in nature, such as provision of money, food, clothing, housing, transportation, and so on. Affective problems relate to issues of emotion or feeling, such as anger or depression. Families whose functioning is disrupted by instrumental problems rarely, if ever, deal effectively with affective problems. However, families whose functioning is disrupted by affective problems may deal adequately with instrumental problems.

Effective problem solving can be described as a sequence of seven steps:

1. Identifying the problem.
2. Communicating with appropriate people about the problem.
3. Developing a set of possible alternative solutions.
4. Deciding on one of the alternatives.
5. Carrying out the action required by the alternative.

TABLE 5-1.   SUMMARY OF DIMENSION CONCEPTS IN THE MCMASTER MODEL OF FAMILY FUNCTIONING

*Problem solving*
Two types of problems:
  Instrumental and affective
Seven stages to the process:
  1. Identification of the problem
  2. Communication of the problem to the appropriate person(s)
  3. Development of action alternatives
  4. Decision on one alternative
  5. Action
  6. Monitoring the action
  7. Evaluation of success
Postulated:
  Most effective when all seven stages are carried out.
  Least effective when families cannot identify problem (stop before step 1).

*Communication*
Instrumental and affective areas
Two independent dimensions:
  1. Clear and direct
  2. Clear and indirect
  3. Masked and direct
  4. Masked and indirect
Postulated:
  Most effective: Clear and direct.
  Least effective: Masked and indirect.

*Roles*
Two family function types:
  Necessary and other
Two areas of family functions:
  Instrumental and affective
Necessary family function groupings:
  A. Instrumental
    1. Provision of resources
  B. Affective
    1. Nurturance and support
    2. Adult sexual gratification
  C. Mixed
    1. Life skills development
    2. Systems maintenance and management
Other family functions:
  Adaptive and maladaptive

TABLE 5-1.  (*continued*)

Role functioning is assessed by considering how the family allocates responsibilities and handles accountability for them.
Postulated:
   Most effective when all necessary family functions have clear allocation to reasonable individual(s) and accountability is built in.
   Least effective when necessary family functions are not addressed and/or allocation and accountability are not maintained.

*Affective responsiveness*
Two groupings:
   Welfare emotions and emergency emotions
Postulated:
   Most effective when a full range of responses is appropriate in amount and quality to stimulus.
   Least effective when range is very narrow (one or two affects only) and/or amount and quality is distorted, given the context.

*Affective involvement*
A range of involvement with six styles identified:
   1. Absence of involvement
   2. Involvement devoid of feelings
   3. Narcissistic involvement
   4. Empathic involvement
   5. Overinvolvement
   6. Symbiotic involvement
Postulated:
   Most effective: Empathic involvement
   Least effective: Symbiotic involvement and absence of involvement

*Behavior Control*
Applies to three situations:
   1. Dangerous situations
   2. Meeting and expressing psychobiological needs and drives (eating, drinking, sleeping, eliminating, sex, and aggression)
   3. Interpersonal socializing behavior inside and outside the family
Standard and latitude of acceptable behavior determined by four styles:
   1. Rigid
   2. Flexible
   3. Laissez-faire
   4. Chaotic
To maintain the style, various techniques are used and implemented under "role" functions (systems maintenance and management)
Postulated:
   Most effective: Flexible behavior control
   Least effective: Chaotic behavior control

6. Monitoring to ensure that the action is carried out.

7. Evaluating the effectiveness of the problem-solving process.

Effective families solve most problems efficiently and easily. Therefore, at times, it can be difficult to elicit information about the problem-solving steps that they have gone through. In families that have difficulty solving problems, it is easier to analyze their stepwise attempts at solving problems.

Families range along a dimension of problem-solving ability. Most effective families will have few, if any, unresolved problems. Problems that exist are relatively new, and they are dealt with effectively. When a new problem situation occurs, the family approaches the problem systematically. As family functioning becomes less effective, family problem-solving behavior becomes less systematic, and fewer problem-solving steps are accomplished.

### Clinical Description

The Simpsons cannot identify any major unresolved problems. A visit by the maternal grandmother led to some difficulties with the children. They describe one son as cuddly, while the other is more active and independent. The independent grandson, who did not receive as much attention from his grandmother, became jealous and acted up a bit when she visited. When his grandmother scolded him, his behavior then became mildly problematic. Mrs. Simpson first identified this problem and then discussed it with her husband. At the earliest reasonable opportunity, they discussed it with the grandmother. This was done in such a way that she was able to support them in maintaining discipline; at the same time, they helped her relate more appropriately with each boy. The couple was flexible and made reasonable allowances for the grandmother, as she came from a great distance and was only with them for a brief time; they respected her individuality.

They described another problem with the older son. He would not follow the rules they had laid down regarding where he could and couldn't play. Initially, they tried a number of disciplinary measures. Then the mother realized that this was not working, and they reverted to a previously effective pattern of using rewards. Returning to a previously adaptive approach quickly led to positive results.

This family can discuss all problems in an open and clear way and can also identify both the instrumental and the affective components of each. They communicate about problems at the earliest possible time, process alternatives quickly, make a decision, and begin to act. They make sure their actions are carried out, and they can describe reviewing previously effective and ineffective methods.

*Variation within Normal.* Not all normal families demonstrate problem solving as effective as that just described. The Simpsons represent the positive extreme of healthy functioning. We conceptualize that a normal family can have some minor unresolved problems. However, such problems will not be of a degree or duration that creates major disruption in the family. A normal family can also be a little slower than the Simpsons to identify problems, to communicate with each other about them, and to act. Despite this reduction in efficiency, however, they will still manage to resolve the majority of problems. They will resolve all instrumental problems; affective problems may present a little more difficulty. We also expect that only the most effective families will actually evaluate the problem-solving process.

## Communication

*Definition.* We define "communication" as the exchange of information within a family. "Communication" is also subdivided into instrumental and affective areas, with the same ramifications for each as are discussed for the dimension of "problem solving."

In addition, two other aspects of communication are also assessed. Is the communication clear or masked, and is it direct or indirect? The clear versus masked continuum focuses on whether the content of the message is clearly stated or is camouflaged, muddied, or vague. The direct versus indirect continuum focuses on whether messages go to their appropriate targets or tend to be deflected to other people. These two aspects are independent, and we can therefore identify four styles of communication as follows: clear and direct; clear and indirect; masked and direct; masked and indirect.

While we focus primarily on verbal communication, we pay attention to nonverbal behavior when it is in direct contradiction to verbal information exchange. Contradictory nonverbal behavior contributes to masking and may reflect indirectness of communication as well.

At the healthy end of the dimension, the family communicates in a clear and direct manner in both the instrumental and the affective areas. As we move towards the less effective end of the dimension, communication becomes less clear and less direct.

### Clinical Description
The Simpson family is clear and direct in all their patterns of communication. There was no sense of hesitation or holding back, no talking around the issue; in addition, they always direct their comments to the person for whom they are intended. Their talking is efficient and effective. This is equally true of the children, who were open and straightforward with the parents and the interviewer.

*Variations within Normal.* Toward the lower end of the normal functioning range, communication about conflictual issues may not be clear and direct. There can be some brief occasions of hesitation or beating around the bush (masking); having trouble clearly hearing each other (masking and/or indirectness); or not clearly stating a personal point of view (indirectness).

## Roles

*Definition.* "Family roles" are defined as the repetitive patterns of behavior by which family members fulfill family functions. There are some functions that all families have to deal with repeatedly in order to maintain an effective and healthy system. We identify five such necessary family functions, and they are the basis for necessary family roles. Each of these areas subsumes a number of tasks and functions.

1. Provision of resources. This area includes those tasks and functions associated with providing money, food, clothing, and shelter.
2. Nurturance and support. This involves the provision of comfort, warmth, reassurance, and support for family members.
3. Adult sexual gratification. Both husbands and wives must personally find satisfaction within the sexual relationship and also feel that they can satisfy their partners sexually. Affective issues are therefore prominent. A reasonable level of sexual activity is generally required. It has been our experience that in some instances, however, both partners may express satisfaction with little or no activity.
4. Personal development. This includes those tasks and functions necessary to support family members in developing skills for personal achievement. Included are tasks relating to the physical, emotional, educational, and social development of the children, and those relating to the career, avocational and social development of the adults.
5. Maintenance and management of the family system. This area includes a variety of functions.

   a. Decision-making functions include leadership, major decision making, and the question of final decisions when there is no agreement. In general, these functions should reside at the parental level and within the nuclear family.

   b. Boundary and membership functions include functions and tasks concerned with extended families, friends, neighbors, the taking in of boarders, family size, and dealings with external institutions and agencies.

   c. Behavior control functions include disciplining of children and the maintenance of standards and rules for the adult family members.

   d. Household finance functions include the tasks of dealing with monthly bills, banking, income tax, and household money handling.

   e. Health-related functions include making appointments, identifying appropriate health problems, and maintaining compliance with health prescriptions.

We consider two additional aspects of role functioning: "role allocation" and "role accountability."

1. Role allocation is concerned with the family's pattern in assigning roles and it includes a number of issues. Does the person assigned a task or function have the power and skill necessary to carry it out? Is the assignment done clearly and explicitly? Can reassignment take place easily? Are tasks distributed and allocated to the satisfaction of family members?

2. Role accountability looks at the procedures in the family for making sure that functions are fulfilled. This includes the presence of a sense of responsibility in family members and the existence of monitoring and corrective mechanisms.

At the healthy end of this dimension, all necessary family functions are fulfilled. Allocation is reasonable and does not overburden one or more members. Accountability is clear.

*Clinical Description*
The Simpsons are very clear regarding who carries out each of a variety of family tasks. They discuss the jobs each has, are comfortable with them, and do not feel overburdened. They share tasks in many areas but are also clear about their separate areas of responsibility. For example, the wife does the flower garden, while the husband does the vegetable garden, lawns, and shrubbery.

The task of getting up with the children on weekend mornings is split, one taking Saturday, the other Sunday. Their mutual involvement in dealing with the children was repeatedly demonstrated during the course of the interview, and the children showed no preference for one parent or the other.

The couple are satisfied with their financial resources but would not mind a larger income. They are quite clear about their roles in handling budgeting and financial organization. They set priorities and handle their finances so that they can maximize their resources. The children clearly go to both parents for nurturance and support as appropriate, and the parents obtain their main support from each other.

Both partners are satisfied with their sexual functioning. They can discuss this in an open and straightforward manner and can indicate their enjoyment in being personally satisfied as well as in satisfying each other. In the course of their marriage, the wife has increasingly become more active in initiating sexual activity. They can handle issues such as one partner's saying "no" to sex with tact and sensitivity and without either of them having a sense of being rebuffed.

The wife is actively involved in decisions regarding the husband's career and his pursuit of avocational interests. He is aware of her need to be active outside the home, and he organizes his schedule to support this. She is a Girl Guide commissioner and had an active job early in the marriage. They fully discussed her leaving the job to have children and their long-range plans. The wife enjoys her active role with the children, which led after discussions to their involvement in a parent–therapist program [which we discuss later]. They are always able to agree on major decisions.

In all of the above role functioning, this family is amazingly clear in their ability to discuss the allocation of roles; in doing so, they play to individual strengths and interests. They keep track of whether the jobs allocated to each are carried out. When one does not carry out a task, the other will either fill in or point out the problem.

*Variations within Normal.* Functioning somewhat less effective than the Simpsons' would still fall appropriately within the normal range. In our society, normally functioning families will generally not have difficulties with provision of resources except when circumstances are out of their control (e.g., times of economic depression, labor action, etc.). Nurturance and support will be provided, although it may not always be immediately available. The couple may have minor dissatisfaction with the sexual relationship. Similarly, slight deficiencies in personal development and systems management and maintenance may also occur.

In general, these deviations from effective role functioning should not lead to conflict. In some normal families, roles can be effectively handled even though most functions are carried out by one individual. In the most effective families, there is role sharing. This allows the family to deal with changes from the usual pattern (e.g., those that might be caused by illness). Within the normal range of families, individuals carry out role functions willingly and possess the required skills and abilities. Individuals are not overburdened. Normally functioning families do not always maintain complete accountability, and there can be occasions when some tasks are not carried out or there is a delay. But, again, this should not lead to conflict.

### Affective Responsiveness

*Definition.* In this dimension, we examine the family's potential range of affective responses, both qualitatively and quantitatively. We define "affective responsiveness" as the ability to respond to a given stimulus with the appropriate quality and quantity of feelings.

We are concerned with two aspects of the quality of affective responses. First, do family members demonstrate an ability to respond with the full spectrum of feelings experienced in human emotional life? Second, is the emotion experienced at times consistent with the stimulus and/or situational context?

The quantitative aspect focuses on the degree of affective response and can be described along a continuum from absence of response through reasonable or expected responsiveness to overresponsiveness. While this dimension considers the overall pattern of the family's responses to affective stimuli, it focuses more than any other dimension on the behaviors of individual members.

It is important to remember that this dimension does not assess the ways in which family members will convey their feelings. How affect is conveyed is an aspect of affective communication.

We distinguish between two categories of affect: "welfare emotions" and "emergency emotions." Welfare emotions consist of affection, warmth, tenderness, support, love, consolation, happiness, and joy. Emergency emotions consist of responses such as anger, fear, sadness, disappointment, and depression.

At the healthy end of the dimension, we conceive of a family that possesses the capability of expressing a full range of emotions. In most situations, they experience the appropriate emotion, and when an emotion is experienced, it is of reasonable intensity and of reasonable duration. Obviously, cultural variability must be considered in evaluating the affective responsiveness of families.

*Clinical Description*
All members of the Simpson family display a wide range of affect that is appropriate and in keeping with the situation. They have suffered no major losses in their extended family but can describe periods of sadness and loss in other circumstances. They respond with appropriate anger and disappointment to situations. They have a good sense of humor and are able to be affectionate and caring. They describe how earlier the husband was more responsive across the range of emotions than the wife but also how he has helped her to become more responsive. They communicate all feelings in a clear and direct manner.

*Variations within Normal.* Even at a fairly healthy level on this dimension, families may contain a member who is not capable of experiencing a particular affect. There may also be instances where members occasionally respond with inappropriate affect and/or experience occasional episodes of underresponding or overresponding. However, the inappropriateness is not disruptive.

### Affective Involvement

*Definition.* "Affective involvement" is the extent to which the family shows interest in and values the particular activities and interests of individual family members. The focus is on the amount of interest the family demonstrates, as well as the manner in which the family members show interest in and invest themselves in one another. There is a range of styles from a total lack of involvement at one end of the continuum to extreme involvement at the other. We identify six types of involvement as follows:

1. Lack of involvement. No interest or investment in one another.

2. Involvement devoid of feelings. Some interest and/or investment in one another. This interest is primarily intellectual in nature.

3. Narcissistic involvement. Interest in others only to the degree that their behavior reflects on the self.

4. Empathic involvement. Interest and/or investment in one another for the sake of the others.

5. Overinvolvement. Excessive interest and/or investment in one another.

6. Symbiotic involvement. An extreme and pathological interest and/or investment in others. Symbiotic involvement is seen only in very disturbed relationships. In such families, there is marked difficulty in differentiating one person from another.

We consider empathic involvement optimal for health. As families move in either direction away from empathic involvement, family functioning becomes less effective in this area.

*Clinical Description*
In the Simpson family, all members show an active interest in each other. The children respond appropriately for their age. The parents take an active interest in what is important to each other, even though their interests vary in several areas. They can respond to what is going on with each other without overidentifying or personalizing.

*Variations within Normal.* The Simpsons function very effectively on this dimension. However, some variation can occur within the healthy range. There may be some instances of narcissistic interest of some members in others. There may also be occasional episodes of overinvolvement. However, these patterns are focused on a single individual and are not consistent.

### Behavior Control

*Definition.* This dimension is defined as the pattern a family adopts for handling behavior in three areas: physically dangerous situations; situations that involve the meeting and expressing of psychobiological needs and drives; and situations involving interpersonal socializing behavior both between family members and with people outside the family.

We are interested in the standards or rules the family sets in these areas and in the latitude they allow around the standard. We describe four styles of behavior control based on variations of the standard and latitude:

1. Rigid behavior control. Standards are narrow and specific for the culture, and there is minimal negotiation or variation across situations.

2. Flexible behavior control. Standards are reasonable, and there is opportunity for negotiation and change, depending on the context.

3. Laissez-faire behavior control. At the extreme, no standards are held, and total latitude is allowed, regardless of the context.

4. Chaotic behavior control. There is unpredictable and random shifting between other styles, so that family members do not know what standards apply at any one time or how much negotiation is possible.

We view flexible behavior control as the most effective style and chaotic behavior control as the least effective.

*Clinical Description*
Mr. and Mrs. Simpson are very clear about rules of behavior. They take a basic stance of allowing considerable exploration and activity by the children, and they tolerate a higher level of activity and noise than many couples would. However, they are very clear about what behavior is unacceptable, and they intervene consistently when such behavior occurs.

They support each other in this regard. They handle the children in a mutually supportive and consistent fashion. They make allowances when the situation calls for it (for example, a visit by grandmother), but they still maintain consistent patterns within that framework. They demonstrate superior techniques for handling the children's behavior. For example, during the interview when one child went to leave the room, he was politely told to stay and close the door. When he persisted, he was told again, in a clear and slightly more forceful way. He responded and was immediately told, "Thank you, that's very good." On another occasion, when one boy was making quite a bit of noise, the father said, "Please yell more quietly." The child immediately spoke in a quieter voice.

This family was considering becoming foster parents for a disturbed child. They could indicate with considerable insight the problems they felt they would face in this role. They knew that taking a disturbed child into the family setting would require a shift in their standards of behavior and control. While they had standards for their own children, they realized that tighter standards might initially be required when the disturbed child came to stay with them.

*Variation within Normal.* Within the range of normal functioning, there can be a number of variations on the above example of very effective functioning. The family may be clear about the rules of behavior in general, while being indecisive, unclear, or lacking in agreement in one or two relatively minor areas (e.g., the parents may disagree about minor aspects of table manners, but the family members are aware of the general range). Such inconsistency should not, however, be a source of major conflict. Normally functioning families also may not use the most effective of techniques and therefore may require more time to establish control.

It should be noted that this dimension also applies to the parents in the family. In normally functioning families, parents are able to describe what they expect from their partners and what their partners expect of them. When one partner does not meet the other's expectations, they address the problem.

## RESEARCH ON NORMAL FAMILIES

### Silent Majority Study

*The Silent Majority* (Westley & Epstein, 1969) reports on a large study of college students and their families carried out from 1955 to 1964 at McGill University in Montreal. The aim of the study was to determine how the emotional health of individuals relates to the overall structure and function of their families.

The study was carried out in two phases. The first was a pilot phase in which nine families were intensively studied. The second and final phase was based upon the findings and methods developed during this pilot study. During this second major phase, 97 families were chosen for the study. Only 59 of these 97 families agreed to be studied; however, partial data were available from the 38 refusing families. The second phase of the study concentrated on the families of the 10 healthiest and the 10 most disturbed subjects. There were one to three psychiatric interviews, leading to a psychiatric evaluation, a sociological interview (a 70-page questionnaire covering all aspects of personal and family life), TAT protocols, and a psychological evaluation. In addition, for each of the index subjects, a battery of 38 pencil-and-paper tests drawn from the Minnesota Multiphasic Personality Inventory (MMPI), the Vassar Personality Scale, the California Psychological Inventory, and the Guilford–Zimmerman Inventory was administered. The members of the families in the middle group were seen only by the psychologist who gave each of them the TAT and Rorschach tests and by the sociological research assistant who administered the sociological questionnaire. Further details are given in the book.

On reviewing this study, one becomes aware of how rapidly our society has undergone changes in values and mores in the two decades since the completion of this study. These changes have not only affected family life, but have altered the methods of examining and evaluating families in many important areas. The largest value shifts are those arising from the changes that have occurred with regard to women's place in society, especially their role in today's family. These changes have obviously affected both spouse and parent–child relationships. The fact that the majority of women now work outside the home, and the common occurrence of single-parent families, have enormous impact on the family organization.

Work, power, status, roles, and psychodynamics were the aspects of families examined in detail in *The Silent Majority*. We do not have comparable data currently available, but an educated guess would be that the attitudinal and behavioral changes in society since then would significantly change the findings today. Consequently, there is no need to go into detail in these areas; we merely refer the curious to the original findings.

We do feel that two of the basic findings in the original study are still applicable. This notion is based on clinical impressions only, as we have no experimental or empirical information. We hope to rectify this with studies over the coming years. First, the organizational, structural, and transactional pattern variables are more powerful in determining the behavior of family members than are the intrapsychic variables. This statement merely refers to the relative power of the variables and does not mean that intrapsychic factors are unrelated to behavior.

Second, the most important finding of the *Silent Majority* study was that the children's emotional health is closely related to the emotional relationships between their parents. When these relationships are warm and supportive, so that the husband and wife felt loved, admired, and encouraged to act in ways that they themselves admired, the children were happy and healthy. Couples who were emotionally close, met each other's needs, and encouraged positive self-images in each other were good parents. This positive relationship between husband and wife did not depend on their being emotionally healthy themselves as individuals, though obviously this was a great help. In some cases, one or both of the parents were emotionally disturbed, but they still managed to develop a good marital relationship. When this happened, the children were emotionally healthy. It seemed that the good marital relationship had insulated the children and prevented contagion from the individual parental deficiencies.

We continue to be impressed by the importance of such a loving and mutually supportive relationship between the parents. The presence of such strong support, genuine concern, and loving care, and the absence of chronic, persistent, naggingly destructive hostility in the relationships of the parental couple, apparently serves as a foundation that can bear the weight of much strain inside and outside the family group in a manner that protects the ongoing interrelationships and development of the family members. We would go so far as to predict that in the absence of such a relationship between parents, no family system could be expected to function at a really satisfactory level.

## Parent-Therapist Study

Colleagues in our research group have carried out a project that tested the idea that if poor family functioning could negatively influence the behavior of children, then placing disturbed children in very effectively functioning families could have a remedial influence (Levin, Rubenstein, & Streiner, 1976; Rubenstein, Armentrout, Levin, & Herald, 1978). The study, "The Parent-Therapist Program: An Innovative Approach to Treating Emotionally Disturbed Children," compared the relative effectiveness of placing emotionally disturbed children in superior-functioning families (i.e., with parent-therapists) and placing them in residential child treatment centers.

Several issues and findings are relevant to the issue of normal family functioning. First, the families involved were interviewed and assessed using the MMFF. Superior-functioning families were quite identifiable. This supported our view that the model can be applied to and discriminate between families of widely varying levels of functioning.

Second, the families were as effective as the institutions in treating the children. This supports the assumption that the behavior of individuals is strongly influenced by the structure and organization of the family of which they are a part.

Third, the original study design called for children to be placed in institutions, in families that were part of a collaborative network of parent–therapist families, and with individual parent–therapist families. The latter group was unable to deal with the assigned children. Apparently, even these very effective families had limits to the amount of stress they could handle. Less effective but still healthy families are probably even less able to handle such stresses. Presumably, they too can cope more effectively if they are part of a social network for support.

Finally, it is interesting to note that none of the children treated was incorporated to the level of complete family membership. This supports the notion that aberrant behavior in an individual is not tolerated by a healthy family and that healthy, well-functioning families clearly deal with boundary and membership issues.

### London Study

In 1979, one of our group, Byles, collected data using an early version of our Family Assessment Device for the problem-solving dimension. The instrument was completed by 30 couples who had at least one child. The children were seen at a family medicine clinic for nonpsychiatric problems in London, Ontario, Canada. This population differs from the parent–therapist families. While they did not seek help with psychiatric problems, there is no evidence that they were functioning very well according to our model. They probably can be considered "normal" in the statistical sense discussed at the beginning of this chapter.

Demographically, these are two-parent families with one to four children (mean 2.4). The fathers ranged in age from 28 to 51 (mean 35.8). The mothers ranged in age from 26 to 41 (mean 33.6). The oldest child in these families was aged 2 to 19 (mean 8.83). The youngest child was aged 1 to 13 (mean 4.8). The families were all relatively young, with few if any of the children having yet moved out of the house. The families had moderate yearly incomes, ranging from $10,000 to over $30,000, with most in the $20,000 to $30,000 range. Most of the parents were born in Ontario, some in other parts of Canada, and a few outside Canada.

The problem-solving scale that these families filled out was in draft form and had not been used previously. Thus, its psychometric properties were unknown. Persons filling out the test simply indicated whether each of about 80 statements was true or false for their families. Scales were constructed on which scores ranged from .0 to 1.0. These can be interpreted as the proportion of items answered in an unhealthy direction. The husbands' and wives' responses were very similar in form, so they were combined to provide a family score.

We constructed two scales. The first contained 20 items that assessed the problem-solving process described in the MMFF. The second was made up of 22 items that assessed the frequency and extensiveness of the problems that the families had. For each scale, scores can range from .0 to 1.0, with a score of 0 indicating good functioning or healthy responses to all items, and a score of 1 indicating poor functioning or unhealthy responses to all items.

There was considerable variation on scores among the families sampled. The problem solving process scale score had a mean of .26 and ranged from .05 to .61. The problem extensiveness scale score ranged from .045 to .432, with a mean of .164. Because this was an untried instrument, there are no baseline data with which to compare these findings. However, clearly, some of these nonclinical families have ineffective problem-solving techniques and a fairly high incidence of problems. The families that had the most problems with the process of problem solving had the most areas of difficulty ($r = +.80$). These data are consonant with the findings in *The Silent Majority*.

We also investigated the relationship between the demographic information and the problem-solving scores. Interestingly, the only demographic variable that had much effect was the age of the oldest child. Families in which the oldest child was an adolescent had more difficulty with problem solving on both scales. (Given the restricted range of families tested, these were the only families with adolescent children.) Thus, we have verified a piece of cultural and clinical lore—that adolescents are problematic for the family. If this finding holds up, it provides an interesting example of how an individual developmental change (i.e., entering adolescence) can affect the normal family system.

## COMPARISON OF THE MCMASTER MODEL
## WITH OTHER FAMILY RESEARCH

In this section we compare the MMFF to five other approaches and their views of normal family functioning. The five were selected because they all have been used in research and have developed methods of assessing family functioning that provide for empirical testing of the models. In making comparisons, we will sketch out the differences among the views of the normal family that the models provide.

## Beavers–Timberlawn Approach

In the book *No Single Thread* (1976), Lewis, Beavers, Gossett, and Phillips provide two not totally congruent models of the normal, healthy family. Beavers gives one description in his theoretical chapter, but the set of scales developed for rating taped therapy sessions provides a slightly different one. For example, three scales (negotiation, conflict, and closeness) do not correspond to Beavers' theory, and there is no scale assessing the family's handling of separation and loss.

In general, the view of the healthy family is not very different from the one we present. There are some differences, however:

1. Because the MMFF focuses on current functioning, separation and loss are not treated as separate issues; they would get picked up under "problem solving," "communication," "affective involvement," and in some aspects of "roles."

2. The MMFF puts less emphasis on the formal structure of the family system and more on the ability of the system's components (dimensions) to do the job. Some difficulties in one area can be offset by strengths in others. For example, one Beavers–Timberlawn scale is called "overt power." The healthy end of this scale is egalitarian; leadership is shared between the parents. The MMFF asserts that there should be clear leadership patterns within the family and that these patterns should be perceived as fair and reasonable by family members. The MMFF does not assume that a specific structure is best for healthy functioning, as does the Beavers–Timberlawn approach.

3. The MMFF is incorporated into a system of therapy described in detail elsewhere (Epstein & Bishop, 1981a, 1981b). One of the distinctive characteristics of this therapy system is that it stresses an active collaboration between the family and the therapist throughout therapy. The family's perceptions are accepted as accurate (providing there is not disagreement among family members or contradictions between perceptions and behavior in therapy sessions). This stance of accepting data from families that cannot be directly verified by the therapist has several benefits. One result of this is that the MMFF considers aspects of family functioning that are not easily observable in the therapeutic setting. General areas that thus appear in MMFF and not in Beavers–Timberlawn are instrumental issues—for example, much of the "roles" and "behavior control" dimensions cover aspects of family functioning that are not especially evident in the behavior of families in laboratory or therapeutic settings.

## Reiss's Model

Reiss has developed a model over a period of 10 years that approaches family functioning by looking at how families go about solving problems (Reiss, 1971, 1980). Families are observed doing analogue tasks in a laboratory setting, and their interactions are meticulously recorded. Reiss's model involves two dimensions: "coordination" of family problem-solving efforts, and "configuration" (or the degree to which the family problem-solving process fosters the individual family members' understanding of that process). A healthy family, according to this model, is one high in "coordination" and "configuration." Such a family is labeled "environment-sensitive." The other three combinations of high and low "coordination" and "configuration" are given three other labels, and the four together constitute a typology of families.

1. In terms of content, the MMFF would label high "coordination" as clear and direct "communication," and it would assess well-handled systems maintenance, management, and allocation under "roles." High "configuration" would be reflected in empathic involvement and fostering of personal development in "roles." There are clearly many areas of functioning in the MMFF that are not a part of Reiss's model. Where the two models overlap, they agree as to what they consider healthy.

2. Reiss, like the Beavers–Timberlawn group, focuses on observational data, and it is not clear whether he feels that family perceptions of their own functioning are relevant. He argues that families' behavior in a laboratory while being videotaped generalizes to real-life behavior. (He provides some tangential evidence for this in his 1980 paper.) But like Beavers–Timberlawn, this approach excludes from consideration any aspect of family functioning that cannot be readily observed in a laboratory.

3. Another way in which Reiss's model differs from the MMFF is his use of a four-case typology. We would argue that this typologizing is premature. While typologizing is one way to establish groups that can be compared in statistical tests, such a classification seems to be begging the question, given the current state of knowledge. A more fruitful strategy at this time is to try to identify important dimensions of variation and to see how families distribute themselves along these dimensions. If, with empirical study, they fall into clusters, then the set clusters may become a useful typology.

4. The clinical utility of this model seems questionable. The collecting of data to assess family functioning is too time-consuming to be used by a front-line clinician. At this point in time, a four-category typology is too gross a measure to have sufficient accuracy or predictive value in terms of guiding clinical work. Finally, it leaves out many aspects of family functioning that are, in our experience, very relevant to understanding families and clinical work.

### Olson's Circumplex Model

Olson and his associates developed a typology system (16 types instead of four), based on two underlying dimensions of family functioning (Olson,

1977). One of these incorporates "cohesion," which refers to emotional bonding of family members, and the autonomy of individuals within the system. The dimension ranges from "enmeshment" (extreme bonding–no autonomy) to "disengagement" (extreme autonomy–no bonding). Families falling in the middle of the dimension are healthy. A healthy family on this dimension should have internal and external boundaries, but these should not be too rigid. Its members should spend time together and alone, and should have public and private space, individual and family friends, individual and family activities, and moderate independence and interdependence. Decisions should be made by individuals and by the family as a whole.

The second dimension is "adaptability," which refers to the modifiability of the family system in response to environmental changes. This dimension ranges from "extreme rigidity" to "extreme pliability" (or essentially no structure). Again, a middle range on the dimension is considered to be healthy. A healthy family should display egalitarian leadership and have democratic discipline. Family members should be successful in negotiating, should share roles, and should have negative and positive feedback. Individuals should be assertive but not passive or aggressive.

The typology is formed by defining four levels on each dimension, crossing the two dimensions and labeling the 16 cases thus produced.

1. FACES (Family Adaptability and Cohesion Evaluation Scales), a family self-report measure, has been developed to assess family functioning according to this model. By implication, Olson's group is willing to accept family perceptions as useful in family assessment. Unfortunately, they seem somewhat restricted with respect to the variety of aspects of functioning they attempt to measure.

2. Again, typologizing seems premature and not fruitful (see our third comment on Reiss). Having 16 categories rather than one provides for more variation; however, there may be so many types that the system is hard to use.

3. The "adaptability" dimension assumes that certain structures (i.e., egalitarian–democratic) are better than others. MMFF would not necessarily do this (see our second comment on Beavers–Timberlawn).

4. The "cohesion" dimension is a combination of two unipolar dimensions. Extreme positions on either have been observed to be associated with pathology. This is a case in which health is being defined as an absence of pathology.

5. The MMFF taps areas included in the circumplex model and some others as well. The MMFF places more emphasis on problem solving and on the instrumental aspects of family life.

### Moos's Family Environment Scale

Moos and his group developed a scale to assess family environments but were not especially involved in clinical work (Moos, 1974; Moos & Moos,

1976). As a result, they look at different aspects of families than do the other groups whose work is clinically oriented. The Moos group describes the family settings in which individuals function. Their approach is a more traditional psychometric one. They generated a large pool of items in a fairly systematic way (but not with any particular theoretical position on the nature of families). They administered this item set to a large number of individuals and used factor analysis to identify ten sets of items, which became the subscales of the instrument. Any areas of family functioning not represented in the original item pool could not be included in the scale.

The ten subscales fall into three clusters. One cluster, labeled "personal growth," is especially interesting because it assesses areas which most clinically oriented models ignore—for example, achievement orientation, intellectual cultural orientation, active recreational orientation, and moral religious orientation. These are all areas that the MMFF would view as more or less independent of the dimension of emotional health.

A second cluster is labeled "system maintenance" and contains subscales assessing the importance of orderliness of the family and degree of hierarchy in the family structure. This is similar to Olson's "adaptability" dimension and some of the Beavers-Timberlawn scales, such as "negotiation." The MMFF attends less to these formal structural qualities and more to how well the structure works.

The third cluster is labeled "relationships" and contains items related to the affective aspects of family functions. This dimension is similar to the affective dimensions in all the other models, yet different in reflecting the environmental orientation. Instead of describing the family as expressing emotion, they describe it as a setting in which individuals are free to express emotion.

1. The environmental approach does not look at some aspects of family functioning that the MMFF attends to—for example, most instrumental areas. Other areas, such as personal growth, are emphasized much more than in the MMFF.

2. This measure does not have a clinical model associated with it. Rather, this is a research-oriented device, and so its clinical utility is unclear.

3. This scale is an example of the statistical approach to defining normality discussed at the beginning of the chapter. Families falling at the extremes of the subscales are presumably not normal. As argued previously, we do not see this as a clinically useful way to view families. Just because a family is unusual in some way does not mean they are functioning poorly; they may be functioning very well.

### Van der Veen's Family Concept Test

Over the last 20 years, Van der Veen and his associates have developed an 80-item scale for rating families (Van der Veen, 1960, 1966; Van der Veen, Howard, & Austria, 1970; Van der Veen, Huebner, Jorgens, & Neja, 1964).

The original item set appears to have been arrived at in a standard psycho-metric fashion, and reliability and validity are established. There are no subscales that can be scored separately, so the measure can really be used to provide only a general rating of the family. A factor analysis of the items that distinguishes between a set of family integration items and a set of adaptive coping items is reported. Individual family members rate their real and ideal families; in addition, the ratings of professional clinicians' concepts of an ideal family are available. From these ratings, several global scores can be generated. A "family adjustment" score is a comparison of a person's rating of his or her real family and the clinician's ideal family ratings. A "family satisfaction" score compares a person's real and ideal ratings. A "family congruence" score compares the husband's and wife's ratings of their real family, while a "family compatibility" score compares the husband's and wife's ideal family ratings.

1. The instrument is not associated with a model of family functioning and does not appear to have been used to guide clinical intervention. The measures comparing family members' perceptions of their real and ideal families can provide useful information, but it is not clear how differences affect family functioning.

2. The clinicians' ratings of the ideal family provides an ingenious way to compare a family to clinicians' views regarding a healthy, normal family. However, the "family adjustment" score only tells us how much an actual family is observed to differ from the ideal. We cannot tell in what direction it differed. There is insufficient detail in the scoring method provided.

3. The clinicians' ratings constitute the description of the normal family. However, the description provided is not coherent. It only indicates that clinicians feel that a healthy family would agree with certain items and disagree with others. Therefore, we must extensively and intuitively con-struct a picture of how such a family would function.

## SUMMARY

In this chapter, we argue that it is useful to equate normality with health. Given this definition of normality, the MMFF provides a clear description of a normal family. For each of the six dimensions of the model, we describe normality in a general theoretical fashion and describe the characteristics of a very effectively functioning family on the dimension. Having presented the model, we describe several studies that provide some support for the asser-tions of the model. Finally, we compare the MMFF with five other research-oriented models of family functioning.

In general, the different models tend to identify similar aspects of family functioning as healthy. They differ in how complex a description they provide. The MMFF is the most complex; it makes more assertions than most of the other models. We also argue that the MMFF is more useful to a practicing clinician than are many of the other models. This is due, in part, to the richness of the description the model provides. It is also due to the fact that the model was developed through a process of clinical and empirical testing. As we see it, all the models contribute to the understanding of the normal family and suggest future lines of research. Perhaps, if we focus on empirical testing of the models, it will be possible to avoid some of the ideological conflicts that seem so common in the field.

## ACKNOWLEDGMENTS

The development of these concepts, the research, and the training programs were supported by a number of grants from the Firestone Foundation. The special skills and contributions of Dr. Ian Goodyer, Dr. Richard Sippe, Louis Vlok, Beth Vetter, Carolyn Barlow, Lorraine Branch, Lori Krop, and Pam Degnan in the preparation of this chapter are also gratefully acknowledged.

## REFERENCES

Berman, E. M., & Lief, H. I. Marital therapy from a psychiatric perspective: An overview. *American Journal of Psychiatry*, 1975, *132*, 583–592.

Bishop, D. S., & Epstein, N. B. *Research on teaching methods*. Paper presented at the International Forum for Trainers and Family Therapists, Tavistock Clinic, London, England, July 1979.

Brody, E. M. Aging and family personality: A developmental view. *Family Process*, 1974, *13*, 23–37.

Carter, E., & McGoldrick, M. (Eds.). *The family life cycle: A framework for family therapy.* New York: Gardner Press, 1980.

Comley, A. Family therapy and the family physician. *Canadian Family Physician*, 1973, 78–81.

Epstein, N. B. Concepts of normality or evaluation of emotional health. *Behavioral Science*, 1958, *3*, 335–343.

Epstein, N. B., & Bishop, D. S. State of the art—1973. *Canadian Psychiatric Association Journal*, 1973, *18*, 175–183.

Epstein, N. B., & Bishop, D. S. Problem centered systems therapy of the family. In A. S. Gurman & D. P. Kniskern (Eds.), *Handbook of family therapy.* New York: Brunner/Mazel, 1981. (a)

Epstein, N. B., & Bishop, D. S. Problem centered systems therapy of the family. *Journal of Marital and Family Therapy,* 1981, *7*, 23–31. (b)

Epstein, N. B., Bishop, D. S., & Levin, S. The McMaster model of family functioning. *Journal of Marriage and Family Counseling*, 1978, *4*, 19–31.

Epstein, N. B., Levin, S., & Bishop, D. S. The family as a social unit. *Canadian Family Physician*, 1976, *22*, 1411–1413.

Epstein, N. B., Sigal, J. J., & Rakoff, V. *Family categories schema.* Unpublished manuscript, Family Research Group of the Department of Psychiatry, Jewish General Hospital, Montreal, in collaboration with the McGill Human Development Study, 1962.

Epstein, N. B., & Westley, W. A. Patterns of intra-familial communication. *Psychiatric Research Reports II*, American Psychiatric Association, December 1959, 1–9.

Group for the Advancement of Psychiatry. The field of family therapy. *Report 78*, 1970, 7.

Guttman, H. A., Spector, R. M., Sigal, J. J., Epstein, N. B., & Rakoff, V. Coding of affective expressions in conjoint family therapy. *American Journal of Psychotherapy,* 1972, *26,* 185–194.

Guttman, H. A., Spector, R. M., Sigal, J. J., Rakoff, V., & Epstein, N. B. Reliability of coding affective communication in family therapy sessions: Problems of measurement and interpretation. *Journal of Consulting and Clinical Psychology,* 1971, *37,* 397–402.

Hadley, T. R., Jacob, T., Milliones, J., Caplan, J., & Spitz, D. The relationship between family developmental crisis and the appearance of symptoms in a family member. *Family Process,* 1974, *13,* 207–214.

Hill, R. Generic features of families under stress. In H. N. Parad (Ed.), *Crisis intervention: Selected readings.* New York: Family Services Association of America, 1965.

Langsley, D. G., & Kaplan, D. M. *The treatment of families in crisis.* New York: Grune & Stratton, 1968.

Levin, S., Rubenstein, J., & Streiner, D. L. The parent–therapist program: An innovative approach to treating emotionally disturbed children. *Hospital and Community Psychiatry.* 1976, *27,* 407–410.

Lewis, J. M., Beavers, W. R., Gossett, J. T., & Phillips, V. A. *No single thread: Psychological health in family systems.* New York: Brunner/Mazel, 1976.

Minuchin, S., & Barcai, A. Therapeutically induced family crisis. In J. H. Masserman (Ed.), *Childhood and adolescence* (Vol. 14 of *Science and psychoanalysis*). New York: Grune & Stratton, 1969.

Moos, R. H. *Family environment scale: Preliminary manual.* Palo Alto: Consulting Psychologists Press, 1974.

Moos, R. H., & Moos, B. S. A typology of family social environments. *Family Process,* 1976, *15,* 357–371.

Olson, D. H. *Circumplex model of marital and family systems.* Unpublished manuscript, University of Minnesota, 1977.

Olson, D. H., Bell, R., & Portner, J. *Family adaptability and cohesion evaluation scales.* Unpublished manuscript, University of Minnesota, 1978.

Olson, D. H., Sprenkle, D. H., & Russell, C. S. Circumplex model of marital and family systems: I. Cohesion and adaptability dimensions, family types, and clinical applications *Family Process,* 1979, *18,* 3–28.

Parad, H. J., & Caplan, G. A framework for studying families in crisis. In H. J. Parad (Ed.), *Crisis intervention: Selected readings.* New York: Family Services Association of America, 1965.

Postner, R. S., Guttman, H. A., Sigal, J. J., Epstein, N. B., & Rakoff, V. Process and outcome in conjoint family therapy. *Family Process,* 1971, *10,* 451–473.

Rakoff, V., Sigal, J. J., Spector, R., & Guttman, H. A. *Communication in families.* Unpublished paper based on investigation aided by grants from Foundations Fund for Research in Psychiatry, Laidlaw Foundation, 1967.

Rappaport, L. The state of crisis: Some theoretical considerations. In H. J. Parad (Ed.), *Crisis intervention: Selected readings.* New York: Family Services Association of America, 1965.

Reiss, D. Varieties of consensual experience: I. A theory for relating family interaction to individual thinking. *Family Process,* 1971, *10,* 1–28.

Reiss, D., Costell, R., Jones, C., & Berkman, H. The family meets the hospital. *Archives of General Psychiatry,* 1980, *37,* 141–154.

Rubenstein, J., Armentrout, J., Levin, S., & Herald, D. The parent–therapist program: Alternative care for emotionally disturbed children. *American Journal of Orthopsychiatry,* 1978, *48,* 654–662.

Russell, C. S. Circumplex model of marital and family systems: III. Empirical evaluation with families. *Family Process,* 1979, *18,* 29–45.

Santa-Barbara, J., Woodward, C. A., Levin, S., Streiner, D., Goodman, J., & Epstein, N. B. *The relationship between therapists' characteristics and outcome variables in family therapy.* Paper presented at the Canadian Psychiatric Association, Baniff, Alberta, September 1975.

Scherz, F. H. Maturational crises and parent–child interaction. *Social Casework*, 1971, *52*, 362–369.

Sigal, J. J., Rakoff, V., & Epstein, N. B. Indicators of therapeutic outcome in conjoint family therapy. *Family Process*, 1967, *6*, 215–226.

Solomon, M. A. A developmental, conceptual premise for family therapy. *Family Process*, 1973, *12*, 179–188.

Sprenkle, D. H., & Olson, D. H. Circumplex model of marital systems: An empirical study of clinic and non-clinic couples. *Marriage and Family Counseling*, April 1978, 59–74.

Van der Veen, F. *The family concept Q sort.* Unpublished mimeo, Dane County Mental Health Center, Madison, Wisconsin, 1960.

Van der Veen, F. *The family concept Q sort: A brief review of findings and studies in progress.* Unpublished mimeo, University of Kansas, 1966.

Van der Veen, F., Howard, K. I., & Austria, A. M. Stability and equivalence of scores based on three different response formats. *Proceedings of the 78th Annual Convention of the American Psychological Association*, 1970, *5*, 99–100. (Summary)

Van der Veen, F., Huebner, B., Jorgens, B., & Neja, P., Jr. Relationships between the parent's concept of the family and family adjustment. *American Journal of Orthopsychiatry*, 1964, *34*, 45–55.

Westley, W. A., & Epstein, N. B. Report on the psychosocial organization of the family and mental health. In D. Willner (Ed.), *Decisions, values and groups* (Vol. 1). New York: Pergamon Press, 1960.

Westley, W. A., & Epstein, N. B. *The silent majority.* San Francisco: Jossey-Bass, 1969.

Woodward, C. A., Santa-Barbara, J., Levin, S., Epstein, N. B., & Streiner, D. *The McMaster family therapy outcome study: III. Client and treatment characteristics significantly contributing to clinical outcomes.* Paper presented at the 54th Annual Meeting of the American Orthopsychiatric Association, New York, April 1977.

Woodward, C. A., Santa-Barbara, J., Levin, S., Goodman, J., Streiner, D., & Epstein, N. B. *Client and therapist characteristics related to family therapy outcome: Closure and follow-up evaluation.* Paper presented at the Society for Psychotherapy Research, Boston, 1975.

Woodward, C. A., Santa-Barbara, J., Levin, S., Goodman, J., Streiner, D., Muzzin, L., & Epstein, N. B. *Outcome research in family therapy. On the growing edginess of family therapists.* Paper presented at the Nathan W. Ackerman Memorial Conference, Margarita Island, Venezuela, February 1974.

# 6

# HEALTHY FAMILY COMMUNICATION PATTERNS: OBSERVATIONS IN FAMILIES "AT RISK" FOR PSYCHOPATHOLOGY

LYMAN C. WYNNE
JAMES E. JONES
MANHAL AL-KHAYYAL

Past psychiatric research on family communication and interaction patterns has tried to identify disturbances of those patterns that appeared relevant to schizophrenia and other forms of psychopathology. Up until recent years, there has been a notable lack of attention to the presence of healthy communication patterns and other aspects of healthy family functioning that may coexist with disturbed family relationships and, indeed, that may reduce the risk of severe psychopathology and promote healthy or even superior functioning in the offspring. Garmezy's (1974) and Anthony's (1974) work on relatively "invulnerable children" has brought this issue to our attention. Even when a parent has been schizophrenic, only 8%–10% of the children became schizophrenic later in life. Despite their presumed genetic predisposition and adverse life circumstances, a substantial proportion, perhaps a majority, of offspring at "high risk" for later psychiatric illness remain relatively "invulnerable," or, more accurately, stress-resistant, to the development of psychopathology (Garmezy, Masten, Nordstrom, & Ferrarese, 1979). Not only do they remain free of serious symptoms, but an unexpectedly large proportion of them also have been found to be quite gifted and to show unusual talent, skill, and creative potential (Anthony, 1974; Heston & Denney, 1968; Karlsson, 1973; Kauffman, Grunebaum, Cohler, & Gamer, 1979).

Lyman C. Wynne, James E. Jones, and Manhal Al-Khayyal. Department of Psychiatry, University of Rochester, Rochester, New York.

In the past several years, Garmezy, among others, has devoted a considerable amount of attention to understanding the nature of competence in normal and high-risk children. He believes that the study of competence and incompetence might provide the key to understanding why some children who have a heightened genetic predisposition for the development of psychopathology become vulnerable to the development of later behavior disorder, while other children remain "invulnerable" (Garmezy, 1974).

It is our thesis that understanding the nature of existing competencies in high-risk children is but one element in the mosaic of the "invulnerable child." A broader understanding of "invulnerability" will require a search for "antecedents to health" in normal as well as in disturbed families. The present literature on family interaction is replete with studies concerned with searching for "antecedents to psychopathology." This literature has been valuable in expanding our understanding of the nature of deviance and in pointing to productive areas for exploration in a search for antecedents to health. The family environment, especially the modes of communicating and relating, has repeatedly emerged as critical in the development of psychopathology.

What, then, might be some of the elements of family interaction and communication that provide the high-risk child with resources and coping strategies that promote resilience and healthy functioning? In recent years, several investigators have begun to explore patterns of healthy family functioning in normal and disturbed families. Several family interaction variables have been identified tentatively as being associated with greater competence on the part of the high-risk child's functioning: for example, maternal warmth (Kauffman *et al.*, 1979), a warm, active, and balanced family interaction (Cole, Al-Khayyal, Baldwin, Baldwin, & Fisher, 1980a), and healthy and benign parental attributions toward the child (Yu, 1979) have each been associated with greater competence in the high-risk child. However, the studies have not yet focused systematically on healthy parental communciation and its relationship to the adjustment of the high-risk child. It is the purpose of the present investigation to move ahead in this important but unexplored area of healthy family communication, using a sample in which "health" may stand out vividly because of the "high risk" for disturbance associated with past hospitalization of a parent for schizophrenia or another psychiatric disorder.

It is our belief that "healthy communication" on the part of parents is a domain of family functioning that is important in promoting healthy adjustment in offspring, particularly through providing children with a model for developing the cognitive capacities of attending, focusing, remaining task-oriented, and communicating ideas and feelings clearly and directly. These cognitive capacities of attending and transactional focusing have consistently been found to be impaired in parents of schizophrenics (Singer, 1967; Singer & Wynne, 1965b; Wynne, Singer, Bartko, & Toohey, 1977). It is therefore to be expected that the presence of these capacities in the family environment of high-risk children would provide them with the cognitive resources needed to make a healthy adjustment in the academic and social spheres of their lives. These familial cognitive resources would be particularly important for children who already show attention deficits and are in need of attention-focusing skills. In this report, we shall identify some of the kinds of healthy parental communciations that contrast with deviant communication and that may counteract the potentially disturbing impact of deviant parental communications on the offspring; further, we shall examine the relationships between these measures of healthy parental communication and the cognitive and socioemotional functioning of the offspring.

Because of the traditional focus on pathology in much of the literature on family interaction and communciation, normal families typically have been characterized merely as showing an *absence* of pathological communication. It is our belief that "normal, healthy, productive communication" has distinctive qualities and can be meaningfully contrasted with measures of communication deviance. The present measures of "healthy communication" (HC) were specifically designed to contrast with the Singer–Wynne measures of "communication deviance" (CD). Since the present HC measures were originally intended to represent the opposite end from CD, along a continuum of "communication," we felt that HC could be profitably considered in conjunction with CD when examining the relation between family communcation styles and offspring functioning. (We now believe that the relationship between HC and CD is too complex to be conceptualized as a single continuum.)

## THE DOMAINS OF FAMILY VARIABLES

In order to place our recent studies of healthy family communication in historical and conceptual context, we wish to sketch out briefly a formulation of four domains of family variables of which "communication," quite arbitrarily but conveniently, constitutes the first.

### Communicational/Cognitive/Attentional Domain

For many years, the work of Wynne and Singer on communication in the families of schizophrenics has strongly emphasized attentional problems of schizophrenics as a starting point. For example, Singer and Wynne hypothesized that "communication in the families of schizophrenics is especially disturbed at the attentional level, whereas in the families of borderline and neurotic individuals, communication disorders are more prominent later on after an attentional focus has been shared (1965a, p. 191)." In this respect, our emphasis on the concept of attention converges with much other recent research on schizophrenia (Goldstein, 1981; Wynne, Cromwell, & Matthysse, 1978).

Although we have viewed communicational problems as *initially* attentional, we go on to consider the attentional level as a component of broader communicational and transactional formulations. These broader issues become crucial when one considers how two or more persons try to *share* the same focus of attention and to derive shared meaning during this effort. The manifestations of cognitive and attentional problems at the individual level have reverberations in the communicational framework of the family systems.

## The Concept of Communication Deviance (CD)

This term is a construct that we have used to designate collectively those various features that have the impact of making it difficult for the listener to visualize, and therefore to share with the speaker, what the speaker means or is focusing upon. Some forms of CD are similar to what has been called "thought disorder" in the schizophrenia literature (cf. Johnston & Holzman, 1979). But other more common types of CD are clearly not examples of thought disorder, or at least are not the markedly incoherent forms that are used to make a diagnosis of schizophrenia (Singer & Wynne, 1966; Singer, Wynne, & Toohey, 1978).

The CD concept can be studied wherever communication can be precisely recorded, but, for comparative research purposes, standardized administration and experience with normative samples are obviously helpful. Although we now have applied the concept using several procedures, our first systematic studies used the Rorschach procedure as a means of sampling communication. For example, in the Rorschach transaction, hopping around among responses and partial disqualifications without carrying the listener along can divert and puzzle the listener (tester) about which ideas the speaker has selected, or about whether the speaker's commitment to the idea is firm enough for the listener to bother to attend. Such selection and labeling problems can be illustrated in a Rorschach response such as: "Two people upon—you can call it a patio, call it a cliff, or it might be a garden." Another example of CD is: "Here is a bat, but when I look here, his head has moved down here, but I've never seen a bat. First of all, I said [actually, no prior comments have been made] this looks like a bat's ear." Note that with traditional scoring in which the Rorschach is used to reveal intrapsychic projections, the content ("bat") would be unremarkable. Nevertheless, a complete tape-recorded transcript of the same passage conveys a perplexing, even bewildering impact that impairs the listener's ability to share an attentional focus and meaning.

After reviewing Rorschach protocols from many parents of young adult schizophrenics, we identified 41 categories of deviances (Singer & Wynne, 1966) that could be scored in several samples, with interrater reliabilities and intrarater reliabilities from .80 to .96 (intraclass correlation coefficients) (Wynne *et al.*, 1977). In a sample of 114 families at the National Institute of Mental Health (NIMH), with offspring that included a "normal" (nonclinical) group and groups encompassing a range of diagnoses—diverse hospitalized neuroses, borderline syndromes, and both remitting and nonremitting schizophrenia—32 of the 41 categories each separately differentiated ($p < .01$) the parents of the schizophrenics from the other three groups (Singer *et al.*, 1978).

We also found that clinical ratings of severity of parental psychopathology and frequency of parental CD are statistically separable measures, each significantly related to severity of the psychiatric disorder in the late adolescent and young adult offspring (Wynne *et al.*, 1977). Finally, pilot data and several lines of correlative evidence suggested that attentional and cognitive aspects of communication styles (as contrasted with content and perhaps with affect) are relatively stable over time.

Applying these findings to our Rochester sample, in which parents, not offspring, had been psychiatrically hospitalized, we hypothesized that parental CD might be a risk variable (Wynne, 1978b)—that is, a precursor of later serious psychiatric disorders in preadolescent, *non*clinical children, as well as a concurrent predictor of what, in retrospective studies of schizophrenia, is called poor premorbid adjustment. It should be noted that the Goldstein-Rodnick-Jones-McPherson-West (1978) studies of parental CD as a risk variable (in the TAT) have been confirmatory of this hypothesis, although the UCLA offspring at risk were already disturbed enough to come for outpatient clinical services when first studied at about age 15.

Another development in this work has extended the applicability of the individual Rorschach CD manual to two consensus Rorschach procedures. Doane (1977), building upon an earlier manual by Singer and Faunce, has scored CD in the Spouse and Family Consensus Rorschach procedure devised by Loveland, Wynne, and Singer (1963). In the Spouse Rorschach, the parents as a couple are first instructed by a staff member about the consensus task, which is videotaped with the staff member out of the room. The task given to the parents is to discuss with each other what each of them believes the inkblot looks like or resembles, and to reach as many agreements as they can. In the Family Rorschach that follows, the parents take over the instructions. First, they instruct the children in the consensus task, and then the whole family shifts to the second task of sharing and agreeing on their perceptions. From verbatim transcriptions of their verbal interaction in the Family Rorschach, a range of family variables has been scored, including "agreement" and "disagreement"; "negative relationship" and "positive relationship"; "clarity"; "task focus"; "acknowledgment" and "nonacknowledgment"; and "parental CD" (defined as frequency of CD divided by word count).

Working with these variables from the Family Rorschachs of the first 65 children (aged 7 and 10) in the Rochester risk research program, Fisher and Jones (1980) have recently used multiple regression analyses to predict to teacher and peer ratings of the children, obtained concurrently in time but completely independently from the family data. Three conceptually overlapping family variables ("parental communication deviance," "nonacknowledgment of comments," and "clear communication") consistently and linearly related to problem-solving competence of the children at school. In the social-emotional area, only parental CD displayed a linear relationship to the children's functioning at school.

### The Concept of Healthy Communication (HC)

In this paper, our special interest is another construct in the communicational domain, namely, healthy parental communication, which was not included in the analyses by Fisher and Jones, but which we now have compared with parental communication deviance as a concurrent predictor of child competence or incompetence.

But what do we mean by "healthy communication"? In a broad preliminary formulation, Singer and Wynne noted:

> In our conceptualization of "normal" development, which goes astray with schizophrenics, we reason that there needs to be a reasonably appropriate "fit" between the innate characteristics of each child at successive stages of maturation and the characteristics of the environment. The latter include the patterns with which the parents focus attention, share meaning, and communicate with one another and with their children. . . . Personality development is affected from birth onward not only by the person's own capacities to engage and become oriented to significant caretakers from whom he can then learn, but by the caretakers' ability to engage his attention and to orient him to those aspects of speech, reasoning behavior, and other events that will be important in his expectable life experiences. Thus, it is at the stage of engagement, orientation, and what, broadly speaking, can be called shared attentional processes that the first difficulties can arise which may lead into schizophrenic forms of ego impairment. In an effort to formulate these processes into a unified concept, we speak of impairment of "shared focal attention." (1966, pp. 261–266)

Thus, CD and HC are different aspects of the same cognitive/attentional domain. Recently, Al-Khayyal (1980) has developed a scoring manual for the Family Rorschach that serves as the healthy communication counterpart to the CD Consensus Rorschach scoring manual. Without attempting to assess all conceivable aspects of HC, Al-Khayyal delineated five groups of scoring categories and established satisfactory interrater reliability:

1. *Instructions* for the consensus task given by the parents as a pair to the children; the clarity, accuracy and completeness of their presentation, followed by a scoring of their clarity in making a transition to the family discussion of the inkblot.

2. *Parental structuring/orienting statements and questions*, directing family members to the task, contributing to a shared focus, and seeking clarification of confusing or ambiguous comments.

3. *Presentation of percepts*, the "visualizability" (Singer, 1967), specificity, and commitment with which the parents introduce and embellish percepts, including their ability to bring in multiple and diverse percepts and, sometimes, task-appropriate fantasy and whimsy.

4. *Parental consensus statements*, assessing progress toward reaching agreement.

5. *Closure on the task*, evaluating whether a mutually agreeable, full consensus about all the percepts has been reached before they decide to terminate the discussion.

### Affective/Relational Domain

The second domain is what we now call the "affective and relational domain." In earlier publications, we have conceptualized "communication" more broadly to encompass affective components and the level of the relationship context, as well as the levels of message and task (Wynne, 1970). It should be noted that the CD scoring, with both the Rorschach and the TAT, includes factors that are highly affectively loaded and are not purely "cognitive" by any means. For example, categories of nihilistic, derogatory, disparaging, and critical remarks are both cognitively disrupting and clearly important affective manifestations (Wynne, 1978a). Although a generalized formulation of "communication" that includes affect remains theoretically sound, several pragmatically useful though arbitrary distinctions between "affect" and "cognition" have emerged that are linked to specific family research procedures.

Among the measures explicitly constructed to tap affectivity in family relationships, "expressed emotion" (EE) has attracted the most attention in recent years (Brown, Birley, & Wing, 1972; Vaughn & Leff, 1976). Critical comments, hostility, and emotional overinvolvement are prominent features judged from content and tone of voice of key relatives in speaking about psychiatric patients during semistructured interviews conducted at the time of psychiatric admissions. Although EE ratings in the British studies have been impressive predictors of later relapse of schizophrenic (and depressive) episodes 9 months after discharge from the hospital, caution is needed in generalizing to families in which the issues are pathogenesis, prevention, and risk of illness, *prior* to actual diagnosis and hospitalization of the offspring. Thus far, EE has not been explicitly assessed except through the use of a special interview (in its present form called the Camberwell Family Interview [CFI]). Whether EE, assessed during patients' hospitalization, has links to family relationships prior to illness and in later follow-up remains to be determined.

Although the EE measure, using the CFI, has not been incorporated into risk research samples, a different approach to affect has very recently been introduced by Doane and her UCLA colleagues (Doane, West, Goldstein, Rodnick, & Jones, in press). Her concept of "affective style" includes aspects of EE but, instead of the CFI as the data source, uses a family discussion procedure, with *direct* interaction of family members. A combination of CD, measured from individual TAT protocols (Jones, 1977) and the affective style measure, afforded the most precise prediction of psychiatric outcome 5 years later in the UCLA risk research sample. An important problem that is being examined at both UCLA and Rochester is the study of the *components* or factors in family relationships that are predictive of *particular* features of schizophrenia—for example, florid episodic turmoil versus the deficit problems of chronic schizophrenics with amorphous attentional drift and social withdrawal. This dimensionalized approach was used in earlier work by Wynne and Singer (Singer & Wynne, 1965b; Wynne & Singer, 1963) in which specific aspects of patient thought disorder were linked to family communication patterns. This strategy, in contrast to more global clinical measures and *total* CD scores, has been reintroduced in current longitudinal studies. We need to examine more regularly, in the *same* samples of families, both attentional/cognitive variables *and* affective/relational features, ultimately building up a picture of factors that reduce or accentuate vulnerability developmentally.

Another new approach that offers promise of integrating affective, relational, and cognitive features has been developed by Yu (1979), in which affective attributions by parents about child figures and parent–child relationships in the TAT are systematically associated with independent child competence measures in the Rochester school setting.

### Structural/Contextual Domain

The third domain that concerns us is what we call "family structure and context." This includes both internal family structure and the contextual matrix of the extended family and social network. The internal organization of the family is a concept that has been studied clinically and sociologically in a number of ways. One of the more interesting research notions, recently developed by Cole in our Rochester program, is the balance of activity among the family members during their direct interaction with one another. Balance has been studied in such procedures as the Family Rorschach (Cole, Al-Khayyal, Baldwin, Baldwin, & Fisher, 1980a) and the Family Free Play procedure (Baldwin, Baldwin, & Cole, 1980), and can, in principle, be applied to family discussion tasks such as the Revealed Differences and the Plan-Something-Together. In such procedures, it is appropriate that each family member take part in the transaction. If participation is unbalanced too much in the direction of one person, or toward the parents in comparison to the children, this is an ominous predictor about the competence of the child, and thus is an important family risk factor. This measure can be looked at in terms of family dyads as well as across generational boundaries, taking the parents as a couple versus all of the children.

Balance measures must be examined in relation to norms for both task and family composition. Unstructured, free-play situations call for different leadership roles and different percentages of activity between parents and children than do structured, problem-solving tasks, such as the Family Rorschach. Also, when children are younger and more numerous, vigorous parental leadership is more appropriate than it is when the children are older (Cole *et al.,* 1980a, 1980b).

Another aspect of the structural domain is the extrafamilial, the social support network for the family. The social networks of schizophrenics have received much attention recently (e.g., Beels, 1978). The network concept is linked to the issue of the extent to which the family maintains its isolation or not. A number of years ago the metaphor of a family "rubber fence" was coined to describe a particular kind of all-encompassing and isolating family boundary (Wynne, Ryckoff, Day, & Hirsch, 1958). Families of schizophrenics seem to be cut off from a meaningful support network and to have difficulty making use of supports, even in times of crisis and turmoil. They have problems in negotiating with others and in evolving relationships outside the family, especially in working out transitions of exit from and entry into the family. In therapy this problem comes up both about the crisis of hospitalization and the issue of returning home, as noted in the EE literature (Leff, 1976). An alternative approach is to develop family surrogates as in the Soteria model (Mosher & Menn, 1978).

## Domain of Family Subculture, Values, and Myths

The fourth domain, "family subculture," cannot be discussed here at length. This area has been neglected in both outcome research and in risk research. We need to look further at the hypotheses—for example, those of Murphy (1972)—that certain ideas and beliefs concerning "responsibility" for an illness not only affect the relationships within the family and the attitudes toward helping with the problems caused by the illness (matters affecting outcome), but also may be predisposing to the illness. These idiosyncratic family subcultural issues certainly also need to be considered as partly derivative from broader ethnic and religious value patterns, as well as from the kind of world view that is associated with, for example, the lower-social-class orientation on which Kohn (1972) has commented.

## MULTIMETHOD FAMILY APPROACHES TO RISK

In our risk research program at Rochester, we have tapped the first three of these family domains systematically with a multimethod approach. When one conceptualizes the domains of family functioning, as we have above, then the limitations of any one measure become obvious. No single research procedure can be expected to tap equally well all of these domains, or even all of the salient components within a domain. Because of such considerations, the Rochester program has incorporated an extensive and systematic multimethod approach to family risk variables. Flexible adaptability to changing situations or problems is a crucial aspect of well-functioning families and individuals; hence, a diversity of assessment procedures, with comparisons across procedures, is invaluable (Cole, Perkins, Al-Khayyal, Baldwin, Baldwin, & Kokes, 1980).

At the initial research evaluation, we began with index sons in three age groups (4, 7, and 10). The data reported here will be restricted to the relatively homogeneous 10-year-old sample. We are greatly interested in examining later developmental changes, especially the question of the most strategic age for preventive intervention in relation to the age when significant risk variables are manifest. The three-year follow-up data will be completed shortly, and then longitudinal analyses can proceed. While we are still looking at the initial data of parents and children obtained at the same time, the data about the children are most satisfactory for research purposes if obtained independently from the family. Thus, the dependent variables that we are using here are school measures developed by Fisher (1980). He has obtained a great variety of measures of school functioning, particularly of academic, cognitive competence, and social–emotional competence, based on both teacher and peer ratings; each index child is blindly compared with age mates in the same classroom.

In addition to a number of psychophysiologic measures, we have used two primary sets of parental risk variables: parental *psychopathology* and current parental and family *relationship* features (Wynne, 1978b). At least one of the parents in each of these families has been hospitalized with a mental disorder, including typical DSM-III schizophrenia, schizoaffective disorder, bipolar (manic–depressive) psychosis, unipolar psychotic depression, neurotic depression, and personality disorders—all severe enough to require hospitalization.

The Rochester risk variables associated with parental psychopathology are being studied in detail and have been recently reported using preliminary assessments by Fisher (Fisher, Harder, & Kokes, 1980), Kokes (Kokes, Harder, Fisher, & Strauss, 1980), and Harder (Harder, Kokes, Fisher, & Strauss, 1980). Briefly, the findings suggest that traditional typologic diagnoses appear less predictive of child functioning than do dimensional aspects of parental psychopathology, such as chronicity and severity. Episodic affective symptom pictures, including "schizoaffective" and bipolar psychotic syndromes are associated with surprisingly favorable child functioning. Tentatively, the results indicate that the use of narrowly defined disorders or disease entities as predictor variables may not be the most fruitful risk research strategy, compared to enduring dimensions of parental functioning, such as chronicity and affective lability, that are likely to be of clear importance in family interaction and family relationships.

Fortunately, in the Rochester program we do not need merely to infer how parental psychopathology may be associated with family interaction variables, because these classes of variables have been independently assessed. In Table 6-1, we have listed the family risk variables for which methods of family data collection and scoring of direct measures are available.

In this report, we have selected 20 representative variables from this array—7 in the domain of "communication," including HC; 8 in the "affective/relational" domain, and 5 in the domain of "family structure." In Table 6-2, these variables are listed along with the tasks used to elicit them. Within each of the three domains, we carried out multiple regression analyses initially on only half ($n = 27$) of the sample of families with 10-year-old sons; the second half of the sample can be used for statistical replications.

First, these analyses were conducted across tasks *within* each domain. A number of interesting findings emerged:

1. *Communicational domain.* Both the healthy and the deviant ends of the mothers' communicational functioning were significant, with mothers' healthy communication in the Family Rorschach procedure being the most consistent predictor in the whole array of the children's school measures. Although the fathers' communication is predictive short of statistical significance, it is especially noteworthy that the mothers' communication was much more significant in the *Family* Rorschach, with the fathers present, than in the mothers' individual Rorschach with testers. Also, the HC scores for the portion of the Family Rorschach in which the parents function as a couple (while giving instructions, making the transition to the family discussion, and reaching closure) are significantly predictive of favorable child functioning.

2. *Affective/relational domain.* The "affective/relational" findings were also interesting but rather more complicated. In the unstructured Family Free Play task, *both* hostile and nonsupportive affect ($\beta = .55$) *and* warmth and supportive affect ($\beta = .46$) predicted highly significantly to the social-emotional competence of the children in school. One interpretation could be that freedom of mothers' emotional expression, positively *or* negatively, is a favorable feature of their relationship with their sons. Dynamically, of course, this makes good sense. On the other hand, one must pause to consider how this finding relates to the EE literature in which criticism predicts to relapse. But the hostility in the Free Play task was nearly always less caustic than were the critical comments scored in the CFI. The context in

TABLE 6-1.   MULTIPLE-METHOD VARIABLES FOR THREE DOMAINS OF PARENT FUNCTIONING

| Methods | Domains of parent functiong | | |
| --- | --- | --- | --- |
| | Communicational/ cognitive/attentional | Structural/ contextual | Affective/relational |
| *Individual parent* | | | |
| Rorschach | *Parental communication deviance* (CD)[a] [Healthy communication] (HC) | × | DeVos–Singer Affective Scales |
| TAT | Parental CD | Kinship content | Affective attributions (Yu) |
| Camberwell Family Interviews (Vaughn & Leff, 1976) | [CD] | × | Expressed emotion (EE) |
| Five Minute Speech Sample (Wynne–Gift modification of Gottschalk procedure) | [CD] | × | EE Hostility Scales (Gottschalk, Winget, & Gleser, 1969) |
| *Family pairs and groups* | | | |
| Spouse Consensus Rorschach | Parental CD | × | × |
| Family Consensus Rorschach | *Parental CD HC* Acknowledgment Focus measures | *Mother/child balance Father/child balance Couple/children balance* | *Mother, father positive and negative relationship statements* Acknowledgment |
| Family Free Play | × | Mother/child balance Father/child balance | *Mother, father warmth Mother, father hostility* |
| Family Discussion Procedures (including Revealed Differences) | Acknowledgment Focus measures Set-correction (Lieber) | Centrality of parent (Lewis) [Balance/activity] | Affective style (Doane) Nonlinguistic expression (Lewis) |

[a]The variables that are italicized were included in the multiple regression analyses reported in this chapter. Other variables for which scoring methods are presently available are not italicized, while those variables in brackets involve scoring procedures that are still being developed.

which parental affect is expressed surely is highly relevant, as is the developmental status of the offspring's vulnerability to stimuli.

   Affect in the more structured consensus Rorschach task was measured in terms of positive and negative relationship messages (these scoring codes were introduced into the program by Faunce). In contrast to the Free Play setting, a greater frequency of negative relationship messages by mothers

TABLE 6-2.  TWENTY FAMILY VARIABLES ANALYZED ACROSS TASKS WITHIN
THREE DOMAINS

---

I. Cognitive/attentional domain
   A. Individual Rorschach Task
      1. *Mother's communication deviance* (CD) (number of CD/word count)[a]
      2. Father's CD
   B. Consensus Family Rorschach Task
      1. *Mother's CD*
      2. Father's CD
      3. *Mother's healthy communication* (HC) (3 components)
      4. Father's HC (3 components)
      5. *Parental shared HC* (2 components)

II. Affective/relational domain
   A. Family Free Play Task
      1. *Mother's warmth toward index son* (frequency)
      2. Father's warmth
      3. *Mother's hostility and nonsupport toward son*
      4. Father's hostility
   B. Consensus Family Rorschach Task
      1. Mother's positive relationship messages toward other family members
      2. *Father's positive relationship*
      3. *Mother's negative relationship*
      4. Father's negative relationship

III. Structural/contextual domain
   A. Family Free Play Task
      1. Activity/balance in mother–son dyad
      2. Activity/balance in father–son dyad
   B. Consensus Family Rorschach Task
      1. Activity/balance between mother and rest of family
      2. Activity/balance between father and rest of family
      3. *Activity/balance between parental couple and child group*

---

[a]Family variables that are italicized were statistically significant predictors of one or more integrated measures of school functioning of the 10-year-old sons (first split-half, $n = 27$).

predicted to greater *in*competence of the children, *but* only when fathers' *positive* relationship messages also entered the equation. Thus, a contradictory constellation of supportive and nonsupportive expressions from the two parents may impair a child's functioning in a cognitive, problem-solving task, whereas contrasting parental affect in the Free Play setting seems not to be associated with child disturbance, but interestingly appears to have a favorable impact. At this stage of data analyses, these findings should not be regarded as definitive. Nevertheless, such details about family risk variables certainly seem to reflect the complexity that is so well known in family life.

3. *Family structure domain.* Cole's structured measure of the balance of activity by the family members also reveals significant predictors. Here the most powerful variable is the balance between father and son—that is, when neither is shut out by the other in the Free Play interaction. In the Family Rorschach, the balance between the parental generation as a couple and the children as a subgroup is also a significant predictor of child competence.

Having identified ten key family variables *within* each domain (italicized in Table 6-2), we then carried them into multiple regression analyses *across* the three domains and eventually replicated the most significant variables both on the second split-half of the sample and on the total sample. In Table 6-3 are the results of the latter multiple regression analyses. Both the structured Family Rorschach and the unstructured Family Free Play procedures, and representative measures in each of three conceptual domains of family functioning, remain highly significant ($p < .01$) concurrent predictors of academic and social–emotional school competence of 10-year-old sons.

## COMMENTS ON THE DATA ANALYSES

1. Wynne (1969, 1978b) has contended that parental mental disorder is inadequate as a solitary variable in the study of children at risk for later psychopathology. Rather, direct assessment of both parental psychopathology and family relationship patterns should be incorporated into the

TABLE 6-3.  MULTIPLE REGRESSION, PARENTAL VARIABLES PREDICTING TO CHILD SCHOOL COMPETENCE (ACROSS TWO METHODS AND THREE DOMAINS)

| Domain | Method | Predictor variables | $F$ | $\beta$ | Adj. $R^2$ |
|---|---|---|---|---|---|
| | | Dependent variable: Academic competence (teacher–peer ratings) | | | |
| Structural | Free Play | Father–son balance/ activity | 19.59 ⎫ | .46 ⎫ | |
| Structural | Family Rorschach | Parent–children balance/activity | 9.56 ⎬ 14.49 | .35 ⎬ | .43 |
| Communicational | Family Rorschach | Mother's healthy communication | 5.49 ⎭ | .27 ⎭ | |
| | | Dependent variable: Social/emotional competence (teacher–peer ratings) | | | |
| Communicational | Family Rorschach | Mother's healthy communication | 18.77 ⎫ | +.51 ⎫ | |
| Affective | Family Rorschach | Mother's negative relationship statements | ⎬ 10.84 4.12 ⎭ | −.24 ⎭ | .27 |

design of risk research. Additionally, of course, the way in which the children's "innate" biological and psychological assets and vulnerabilities "fit" and unfold in the context of family patterns should be considered, together with child measures obtained outside the family context. This point of view is transactional (Wynne, 1968). We are not talking about unidirectional etiologic factors, but *reciprocal* effects within family systems. Origins can only arbitrarily be located within one person as an interchange unfolds. Hence, we have urged study not only of the end point of symptom manifestation, but also of the sequences in the unfolding transactions within family relationships and within the entire family system repeatedly over time in longitudinal studies (Wynne *et al.*, 1977).

2. In the area of family relationships, a Rochester team headed by Romano and Geertsma (1978) obtains retrospective family data reported by the parents. Current family patterns, at initial research evaluation and at three-year follow-up, are examined both indirectly through study of parental communication styles with a tester and directly through a series of procedures in which the interaction of family members is observed and tape-recorded (see Wynne, Toohey, & Doane, 1979, for a review of these methods).

3. Whereas past clinical and research work with families has tended to emphasize pathogenic and deviant features, the present report introduces and identifies positive, healthy family communication as a significant component of family functioning. Even in a sample in which a parent in each family has had a serious mental disorder requiring past psychiatric hospitalization, the children show a wide range of healthy and deviant levels of functioning, separately assessed in the school setting (Fisher, 1980). Our data suggest that when the parents as individuals, both the patient–parent and the spouse, and the couple working together as a pair, communicate in a clearly focused, well-structured, flexible, and task-appropriate manner, their 10-year-old sons are typically regarded as competent academically and socially by their teachers and peers. In families in which there has been reciprocity and balance in the amount of activity between father and son, and between the parental couple and the children as a subsystem, the sons also function more competently in the school setting. And, if one regards task-relevant emotional expressiveness by parents as contributory to healthy child development, our findings appear to support this hypothesis.

4. Methodologically, we have found that multiple situations or tasks in which families are studied are necessary to tap the diverse family domains. The multimethod approach appears helpful in assessing healthy as well as deviant forms of family functioning.

5. Although these findings seem encouraging, a number of cautions about their interpretation are in order. We have not yet included in the analyses all of the family measures that are available in our program; the overall results may throw a different light on our conclusions. We have not yet studied comprehensively how parental diagnoses and the various dimen-

sions of parental psychopathology fit together in multivariate matrices with the family interaction variables. Because of statistical pitfalls in doing multivariate analyses in a piecemeal fashion, we are planning to carry out such analyses in the near future when the data are coded satisfactorily for all of the specific measures. In the child assessment area, additional measures bringing psychological test and clinical data together with the school ratings will deepen our picture of the children. Finally, the findings reported here, one should remember, are concurrent, not longitudinal; the family measures in the research setting predict to the ratings of the children obtained independently in school but at the same point in time. Longitudinal, prospective results from this program will be reported at a later date and are needed for developmental formulations.

6. The concept of communication deviance is not restricted to specific procedures. It differs, in this respect, from EE, which has not yet been applied to methods other than the CFI. (Research to expand the applicability of the EE concept is in progress at the Universities of Rochester and Pittsburgh.) We introduce here the concept of HC, with a manual that thus far has been explicitly applied to only one procedure, the Consensus Family Rorschach. Nevertheless, as demonstrated with CD and anticipated with EE, we expect that the principles underlying this manual will be applicable, with appropriate modification of details, to other methods of sampling family communication. Schuldberg, working with Singer, is currently developing a manual for scoring HC in individual Rorschach protocols. Additionally, many of the family relationship codes that we have been scoring in the Rochester risk research already have both "healthy" and "disturbed" components. For example, this is readily apparent in the codes for "acknowledgment": "complete acknowledgment," "partial acknowledgment," "recognition," and "nonacknowledgment" scores. Also available are the codes for "clarity" and the codes for "past" and "present task focus," which are obviously part of the communicational domain. Some of these codes already have a substantial past history, but further data analyses are needed to map out how these variables overlap and supplement one another. The computer files in the Rochester risk program are suitable for such comprehensive analyses at both initial evaluation and three-year follow-up, and these will be carried out during the coming year.

7. This is not a chapter on family therapy. Nevertheless, we are active clinicians and therapists as well as researchers, and we have found these research results provocative and helpful in our thinking about treatment and prevention. Mapping out the domains of both assets and liabilities is, we believe, fully as crucial for successful therapy as for satisfactory research. Family therapists and educators need to recognize more clearly and to nurture more knowledgeably those aspects of family communication and relatedness that generate rally and resilience, despite, or conceivably because of, the distress and disorder of an individual family member.

## APPENDIX: A MANUAL FOR SCORING
## HEALTHY FAMILY COMMUNICATION

The following categories provide an outline of the manual used by Al-Khayyal (1980) in scoring HC in the Consensus Family Rorschachs, as reported above. Although interrater reliability has been satisfactory in the work carried out thus far, we recommend direct contact and training with one of us by other investigators who may wish to use this method. Such direct training will insure consistency of method and will forestall methodologic questions when new samples are examined.

I. *Presentation of Instructions*
  A. Quality of instructions: Rating scale
    1. The primary presenter
      4: Clear, explicit, adequate     also: $\begin{cases} 4+, 4- \\ 3+, 3- \\ 2+, 2- \\ 1+, 1- \end{cases}$
      3: O.K.
      2: Less than adequate
      1: Inadequate
    2. The secondary presenter
      3: Enhances
      2: Neutral
      1: Impairs
    3. Joint product
      4: Clear, explicit, adequate     also: $\begin{cases} 4+, 1- \\ 3+, 3- \\ 2+, 2- \\ 1+, 1- \end{cases}$
      3: O.K.
      2: Less than adequate
      1: Inadequate
  B. Checking: Tabulation
  C. Transition: Rating scale
    3: Clear
    2: Muddled
    1: Unclear

II. *Structuring Statements/Questions Related to Percept/Group Process*
  A. Group structuring/task refocusing statements: Tabulation
    1. Parent structures how the group should proceed in completing the task (usually done at the beginning of the task); language used must be clear and explicit.
    2. Parent structures the group during the task to prevent or limit chaos or confusion.
      a. Parent asks group to slow down.
      b. Parent asks group to slow down and deal with one person at a time.
      c. Parent asks group to slow down and deal with one percept at a time.

    d. Parent restructures statements around proceeding.
3. Parent (re)focuses group or family member on the task.
4. Parent repeats parts of task instructions during the task; parental statements need to be clear and accurate.

B. Percept-related structuring statements/questions: Tabulation
1. Parent asks family members:
    a. for their percepts in the beginning of the task.
    b. for their percepts during the task.
    c. for additional percepts.
    d. for one's percepts of a given location.
    e. for a percept in response to another's request to be heard.
    f. for a previously stated percept.
    g. for additional percepts (by supplying encouragement or orientation).
2. Parent requests clarification on a stated percept and asks members to point it out, explain it, describe it:
    a. Requesting *general* clarification; half score for indirect requests for clarification.
    b. Requesting more *specific* clarification on the stated percept.
    c. Requesting clarification on the *dimensions* of the percept.
    d. Asking member to point out the *location* of the percept, to point out or *describe* the *parts*.
3. Parent makes statements/questions about percepts that help to clarify the stated percept and make it more visualizable. Parental statements must be clear and understandable; this includes parental statements that refer to one's own and another's percept:
    a. Statements that *orient* family members to the percept and help them see it.
    b. Statements that *specify* a stated percept, that point out the parts, the location, or describe the features.
    c. Statements that *restate* or point out a percept in response to a request by another or an indication by another that he or she does not follow or agree.
    d. Statements/questions that *restate* or explain another's percept to make sure that he or she is following it correctly, or to point out that one follows.
    e. Statements/questions that appropriately *clarify*, reflect, reword, or restate another's percept or explanation.
    f. Statements that appropriately *correct* another person's misperception or misunderstanding.

III. *Acknowledgment: Rating Scale* (Mishler & Waxler, 1968)
    1: Complete acknowledgment
    2: Partial acknowledgment

> 3: Recognition
> 4: Nonacknowledgment

IV. *Percept Statements*

A. Score each presentation of a new and different percept: Rating Scale

4+, 4, 4−: Percept is stated clearly and directly and includes some specification of the different parts.

3+, 3, 3−: Percept is stated clearly and directly, but does not include specification of the parts.

2+, 2, 2−: A score of "2" is given in any of the following situations:

   a. Statement of percept is given in question form.
   b. A less clear/direct statement of the percept than "3"; statement of percept may lack confidence or assertion, and/or includes disqualifying remarks.
   c. Parent specifies the parts of the percept but is unable to commit himself or herself to what it looks like.
   d. Parent indicates two percepts that could potentially fit with that location, but cannot commit himself or herself to either.
   e. Parent states the percept for the first time as if it has been stated before and/or presumes that others are familiar with it.

1+, 1, 1−: A score of "1" is given in any of the following situations:

   a. Parent gives vague statement of the percept with if's, but's, maybe's, or contradictions, leaving the rater unclear as to what the parent is describing, or with the feeling that the parent is uncommitted to the precept.
   b. Parent presents incompatible percepts for a given location.
   c. Parent derogates his or her own percept during the presentation.

B. Score as elaborations each time a stated percept is expanded or elaborated upon; there are two types:

   1. A stated percept is described more fully and includes additional parts of the blot.
   2. A stated percept is enlarged into a more general category that allows members to achieve consensus more easily.

C. Score variations on a stated theme: Score here instances where a parent states a percept that has not been stated before, but falls into the same category or class as a previously stated percept.

V. *Consensus: Tabulation*

1. Questions that assess agreement or elicit confirmation from other family members about a stated percept, with the aim of reaching consensus.

   a. Assessing agreement—checking to see whether others agree on a stated percept.

   b. Eliciting confirmation—checking with members to see if they follow or see the percept as described.
2. Statements or questions that summarize or categorize percepts in order to get consensus.
3. General summarizing or concluding statements or questions that initiate the process of closure or of reviewing the agreed-upon percepts.
4. Statements that list or point out agreed-upon percepts, or list members who agree on a given percept.
5. Statements regarding group consensus about whether agreement has or has not been reached about a given percept or by different family members.

VI. *Closure: Rating Scale*
   4+, 4, 4−: Complete and adequate
   3+, 3, 3−: Partial closure
   2+, 2, 2−: Incomplete closure
      1+,1: Clear ending with no closure or closure with no clear ending
        1−: No closure
         9: Interrupted by the examiner

*Additional Scoring Category*

VII. *Reinforcement: Tabulation*
   1. a. Positive reinforcement for another's percept/positive validation.
      b. Positive reinforcement for one's cognitive style.
      c. Statements allowing for independent thought.
   2. a. Negative reinforcement for another's percept; denying/not allowing for independent thought.
      b. Derogating or criticizing another's percept.
      c. Derogating, criticizing another's cognitive style.

## ACKNOWLEDGMENTS

Portions of the research reported in this paper were supported by NIMH grant MH22836, Lyman C. Wynne, Principal Investigator. The authors are indebted for essential contributions in this work to Margaret T. Singer and Barry Ritzler (particularly in scoring of communication deviance in individual parental Rorschachs), Elaine Faunce and Jeri Doane (scoring in the Family Rorschach), Lawrence Fisher (school ratings of offspring), Robert E. Cole (assessment of family structural balance), and Nancy Hartwick and Howard Iker (statistical assistance and consultation).

Portions of this paper are also published in "Familial Risk Factors in Psychopathology" by L.C. Wynne, J.E. Jones, M. Al-Khayyal, R.E. Cole, and L. Fisher. In M. Goldstein (Ed.), *Preventive Intervention in Schizophrenia.* Washington, D.C.: U.S. Government Printing Office, 1981, in press.

# REFERENCES

Al-Khayyal, M. *Healthy parental communication as a predictor of child competence in families with a schizophrenic and psychiatrically disturbed nonschizophrenic parent.* Unpublished doctoral dissertation, University of Rochester, 1980.

Anthony, E. J. The syndrome of the psychologically invulnerable child. In E. J. Anthony & C. Koupernick (Eds.), *The child in his family: Children at psychiatric risk* (Vol. III). New York: Wiley, 1974.

Baldwin, A. L., Baldwin, C. P., & Cole, R. E. *Family free play interaction: Setting and methods.* Manuscript submitted for publication, 1980.

Beels, C. C. Social networks, the family, and the psychiatric patient: Introduction to the issue. *Schizophrenia Bulletin,* 1978, *4,* 512–521.

Brown, G. W., Birley, J. L. T., & Wing, J. K. Influence of family life on the course of schizophrenic disorders: A replication. *British Journal of Psychiatry,* 1972, *121,* 241–258.

Cole, R. E., Al-Khayyal, M., Baldwin, A. L., Baldwin, C. P., & Fisher, L. *A cross-setting assessment of family interaction and the prediction of school competence in children at risk.* Paper presented at the Schizophrenia High Risk Consortium Conference, San Juan, Puerto Rico, 1980. (a)

Cole, R. E., Al-Khayyal, M., Baldwin, A. L., Baldwin, C. P., & Fisher, L. *Controlling for the effect of family configuration on family behavior in the Consensus Rorschach.* Paper presented at the Schizophrenia High Risk Consortium Conference, San Juan, Puerto Rico, 1980. (b)

Cole, R. E., Perkins, P., Al-Khayyal, M., Baldwin, A. L., Baldwin, C. P., & Kokes, R. F. *Family flexibility: The ability to adapt to varying task demands.* Paper presented at the Schizophrenia High Risk Consortium Conference, San Juan, Puerto Rico, 1980.

Doane, J. A. *Parental communication deviance as a predictor of child competence in families with a schizophrenic and nonschizophrenic parent.* Unpublished doctoral dissertation, University of Rochester, 1977.

Doane, J. A., West, K. L., Goldstein, M. J., Rodnick, E. H., & Jones, J. E. Parental communication deviance and affective style. Predictors of subsequent schizophrenia spectrum disorders in vulnerable adolescents. *Archives of General Psychiatry,* 1981, *38,* 679–685.

Fisher, L. Child competence and psychiatric risk: I. Model and method. *Journal of Nervous and Mental Disease,* 1980, *168,* 323–331.

Fisher, L., Harder, D. W., & Kokes, R. F. Child competence and psychiatric risk: III. Comparisons based on diagnosis of hospitalized parent. *Journal of Nervous and Mental Disease,* 1980, *168,* 338–342.

Fisher, L., & Jones, J. E. Child compentence and psychiatric risk: II. Areas of relationship between child and family functioning. *Journal of Nervous and Mental Disease,* 1980, *168,* 332–337.

Garmezy, N. Children at risk: The search for the antecedents of schizophrenia Part I. Conceptual models and research methods. *Schizophrenia Bulletin,* Spring 1974, 14–90.

Garmezy, N., Masten, A., Nordstrom, L., & Ferrarese, M. The nature of competence in normal and deviant children. In M. W. Kent & J. E. Rolf (Eds.), *The primary prevention of psychopathology: Promotive social competence and coping in children* (Vol. 3). Hanover, NH.: University Press of New England, 1979.

Goldstein, M. J., Rodnick, E. H., Jones, J. E., McPherson, S. R., & West, K. L. Familial precursors of schizophrenia spectrum disorders. In L. C. Wynne, R. L. Cromwell, & S. Matthysse (Eds.), *The nature of schizophrenia: New approaches to research and treatment.* New York: Wiley, 1978.

Goldstein, M. J. (Ed.). *Preventive intervention in schizophrenia.* NIMH Primary Prevention Series. Washington, D.C.: U.S. Government Printing Office, 1981, in press.

Gottschalk, L. A., Winget, C. N., & Gleser, G. C. *Manual of instructions for using the Gottschalk-Gleser Content Analysis Scales: Anxiety, Hostility, and Social Alienation-Personal Disorganization. Berkeley: University of California Press, 1969.

Harder, D. W., Kokes, R. F., Fisher, L., & Strauss, J. S. Child competence and psychiatric risk: IV. Relationships of parent diagnostic classifications and parent psychopathology severity to child functioning. Journal of Nervous and Mental Disease, 1980, 168, 343-347.

Heston, L., & Denney, D. Interactions between early life experience and biological factors in schizophrenia. In D. Rosenthal & S. Kety (Eds.), The transmission of schizophrenia. Oxford: Pergamon Press, 1968.

Johnston, M. H., & Holzman, P. S. Assessing schizophrenic thinking. San Francisco: Jossey-Bass, 1979.

Jones, J. E. Patterns of transactional style deviance in the TAT's of parents of schizophrenics. Family Process, 1977, 16, 327-337.

Karlsson, J. L. An Icelandic family study of schizophrenia. British Journal of Psychiatry, 1973, 123, 549-554.

Kauffman, C., Grunebaum, H., Cohler, B., & Gamer, E. Superkids: Competent children of psychotic mothers. American Journal of Psychiatry, 1979, 36, 1398-1402.

Kohn, M. L. Class, family and schizophrenia: A reformulation. Social Forces, 1972, 50, 295-313.

Kokes, R. F., Harder, D. W., Fisher, L., & Strauss, J. S. Child competence and psychiatric risk: V. Sex of patient parent and dimensions of psychopathology. Journal of Nervous and Mental Disease, 1980, 168, 348-352.

Leff, J. P. Schizophrenia and sensitivity to the family environment. Schizophrenia Bulletin, 1976, 2, 566-574.

Lewis, J. M. Family interaction behaviors associated with a communication disorder index of risk for schizophrenia. Doctoral dissertation, University of California, Los Angeles, 1979.

Loveland, N. T., Wynne, L. C., & Singer, M. T. The Family Rorschach: A method for studying family interaction. Family Process, 1963, 2, 187-215.

Mishler, E. G., & Waxler, N. E. Interaction in families. New York: Wiley, 1968.

Mosher, L. R., & Menn, A. Z. The surrogate "family," an alternative to hospitalization. In J. C. Shershow (Ed.), Schizophrenia: Science and practice. Cambridge: Harvard University Press, 1978.

Murphy, H. B. M. The evocative role of complex social tasks. In A. R. Kaplan (Ed.), Genetic factors in "schizophrenia." Springfield, Ill.: Charles C Thomas, 1972.

Romano, J., & Geertsma, R. H. Parent assessment and research on the vulnerability of children and families to mental disorder. American Journal of Psychiatry, 1978, 135, 812-815.

Singer, M. T. Family transactions and schizophrenia: I. Recent research findings. In J. Romano (Ed.), The origins of schizophrenia. Amsterdam: Excerpta Medica Foundation, 1967.

Singer, M. T., & Wynne, L. C. Thought disorder and family relations of schizophrenics: III. Methodology using projective techniques. Archives of General Psychiatry, 1965, 12, 187-300. (a)

Singer, M. T., & Wynne, L. C. Thought disorder and family relations of schizophrenics: IV. Results and implications. Archives of General Psychiatry, 1965, 12, 201-212. (b)

Singer, M. T., & Wynne, L. C. Principles for scoring communication defects and deviances in parents of schizophrenics: Rorschach and TAT scoring manuals. Psychiatry, 1966, 29, 260-288.

Singer, M. T., Wynne, L. C., & Toohey, M. L. Communication disorders and the families of schizophrenics. In L. C. Wynne, R. L. Cromwell, & S. Matthysse (Eds.), The nature of schizophrenia: New approaches to research and treatment. New York: Wiley, 1978.

Vaughn, C. E., & Leff, J. P. The influences of family and social factors on the course of psychiatric illness: A comparison of schizophrenic and depressed neurotic patients. British Journal of Psychiatry, 1976, 129, 125-137.

Wynne, L. C. Methodological and conceptual issues in the study of schizophrenics and their families. Journal of Psychiatric Research, 1968, 6, 185-199.

Wynne, L. C. Family research in the pathogenesis of schizophrenia: Intermediate variables in the studies of families at high risk. In P. Doucet & C. Laurin (Eds.), *Problems of psychosis*. Amsterdam: Excerpta Medica Foundation, 1969.

Wynne, L. C. Communication disorders and the quest for relatedness in families of schizoprenics. *American Journal of psychoanalysis*, 1970, *30*, 100–114.

Wynne, L. C. Knotted relationships and communication deviance. In M. Berger (Ed.), *Beyond the double bind*. New York: Brunner/Mazel, 1978. (a)

Wynne, L. C. Family interaction: An alternative starting point for evaluating risk of psychosis. In E. G. Anthony, C. Koupernick, & C. Chiland (Eds.), *The child and his family: Vulnerable children* (Vol. IV). New York: Wiley Interscience, 1978. (b)

Wynne, L. C., Cromwell, R. L., & Matthysse, S. (Eds.). *The nature of schizophrenia: New approaches to research and treatment*. New York: Wiley, 1978.

Wynne, L. C., Ryckoff, I. M., Day, J., & Hirsch, S. I. Pseudo-mutuality in the family relations of schizophrenics. *Psychiatry*, 1958, *21*, 205–220.

Wynne, L. C., & Singer, M. T. Thought disorder and family relations of schizophrenics: II. A classification of forms of thinking. *Archives of General Psychiatry*, 1963, *9*, 199–206.

Wynne, L. C., Singer, M. T., Bartko, J. J., & Toohey, M. L. Schizophrenics and their families: Recent research on parental communication. In J.M. Tanner (Ed.), *Developments in psychiatric research*. London: Hodden & Stoughton, 1977.

Wynne, L. C., Toohey, M. L., & Doane, J. A. Family studies. In L. Bellak (Ed.), *Disorders of the schizophrenic syndrome*. New York: Basic Books, 1979.

Yu, P. *Parental attributions as predictors of child competence in families with a parent with a history of psychiatric disturbance*. Unpublished doctoral dissertation, University of Rochester, 1979.

# I I I

## NORMAL FAMILIES
## IN TEMPORAL CONTEXT

# 7

# THE FAMILY LIFE CYCLE

## MONICA MCGOLDRICK
## ELIZABETH A. CARTER

Time present and time past
Are both perhaps present in time future,
And time future contained in time past.—T. S. ELIOT

The family life cycle perspective views symptoms and dysfunction in relation to normal functioning over time. It frames problems within the course the family has moved along in its past, the tasks it is presently trying to master, and the future toward which it is moving. It is surprising how little explicit attention therapists have paid to this framework of the developmental processes of the family. Perhaps the dramatically changing patterns of the family life cycle in our time are what are drawing our attention more toward this perspective. In any case, it is becoming increasingly difficult to determine what family life cycle patterns are "normal," and this in itself is often a cause of great stress for family members, who have few models for the passages they are going through.

It is our view that the family is more than the sum of its parts and that the family life cycle is the major context for the development of family members. The family, in our view, is the basic unit of emotional development, the phases and course of which can be identified and predicted. We think that this perspective is crucial to understanding the emotional problems that people develop as they move together through this basic process.

In this chapter we look at the family life cycle in relation to three aspects: (1) the predictable stages of the "normal" family life cycle in middle-class America in the late 20th century, and typical clinical fallout when

Monica McGoldrick. Family Training, College of Medicine and Dentistry of New Jersey–Rutgers Medical School, Community Mental Health Center, Piscataway, New Jersey, and Faculty, Family Institute of Westchester.

Elizabeth A. Carter. Faculty, Family Institute of Westchester.

families have trouble negotiating these transitions; (2) the changing patterns of the family life cycle in our time and the shifts in what is considered "normal"; and (3) a clinical perspective that uses the family life cycle as a framework and that views therapy as helping families who have become derailed in the family life cycle to get back on their developmental track.

## THE FAMILY AS A SYSTEM MOVING THROUGH TIME

Haley and Solomon were the first to point us in the direction of a family life cycle framework for viewing clinical problems. Haley's book, *Uncommon Therapy*, a presentation of the brilliant techniques of Milton Erickson, is organized conceptually around the stages of the family life cycle. Haley viewed family stress as highest at the transition points from one stage to another of the family developmental process, and symptoms as most likely to appear when there is an interruption or dislocation in the unfolding family life cycle. Symptoms signal that the family is stuck and having difficulty moving through the transition to its next phase. Therapeutic efforts need to be directed toward remobilizing the family life cycle so that normal developmental progress can continue (Haley, 1973).

Solomon (1973) outlined the tasks at each stage for a five-stage family life cycle and suggested that this could be used as a diagnostic base from which a treatment plan for therapy could be developed. Others have divided the family life cycle into a different number of stages. The most widely accepted is the breakdown of the sociologist Duvall (1977), who has been working for many years to define normal family development. An important addition to the life cycle perspective was offered by Hill (1970), who emphasized the three-generational aspects of the life cycle, describing parents of married children as forming a "lineage bridge" between the older and the younger generations of the family. His view is that at each stage of the family life cycle there is a distinctive role complex for family members with one another. Obviously, the many ways in which family members of one generation rely on those of another in a mutual interdependence are part of the richness of the family context as generations move through the life cycle.

Our view of "family" is that it comprises the entire family emotional system of at least three generations. This, we are convinced, is the operative emotional field at any given moment. We do not consider the influence of the family to be restricted to the members of a particular household or to a given nuclear family branch of the system. Thus, although we recognize the dominant American pattern of separately domiciled nuclear families, they are, in our view, emotional subsystems, reacting to past, present, and anticipated future relationships within the larger three-generational family system.

Although family process is by no means linear, it exists in the linear dimension of time. From this we can never escape. It has rarely been taken adequately into account that the family life cycle is a complex process involving at least three and now more often four generations moving along together in time. The tremendous impact of one generation on those following is hard to overestimate. For one thing, the three or four different generations must accommodate to life cycle transitions simultaneously. While one generation is moving toward older age, the next is contending with the empty nest, the third with young adulthood and the forming of couples, and the fourth with the process of becoming the newest members of the system. Naturally, there is an intermingling of the generations, and events at one level have a powerful effect on relationships at each other level. The impact of events in the grandparental generation is routinely overlooked by therapists focused on experiences of the nuclear family. And yet there is clear indication that illness or death in the grandparental generation can have profound effects on the parents' relationships with their children many years later (Orfanidis, 1977; Walsh, 1978). Painful experiences such as illness and death are particularly difficult for families to integrate; they are thus most likely to have a long range impact on relationships in the next generations, as has been shown in the impressive work of Paul (Paul & Grosser, 1965; Paul & Paul, 1974; see also Chapter 9, this volume).

As we have outlined elsewhere (Carter & McGoldrick, 1980), our view of the normal family includes a vertical and a horizontal axis. The vertical flow in the system includes patterns of relating and functioning that are transmitted down the generations in a family, primarily through the mechanism of emotional triangling (Bowen, 1978). It includes all the family attitudes, taboos, expectations, labels, and loaded issues with which people grow up. One could say that these aspects of people's lives are like the hand they are dealt: these are the given. What people choose to do with them is the issue.

The horizontal flow in the system includes the anxiety produced by the stresses on the family as it moves forward through time, coping with the changes and transitions of the family life cycle. It includes both the predictable developmental stresses, and those unpredictable events, "the slings and arrows of outrageous fortune" that may disrupt the life cycle process (untimely death, birth of a defective child, chronic illness, war, etc.). Given enough stress on the horizontal axis, any family will appear extremely dysfunctional. Even a small horizontal stress on a family in which the vertical axis is full of intense stress will create great disruption in the system.

While we generally share Haley's concept that symptoms reflect family life cycle derailment and that therapy should aim at change that reestablishes the forward developmental momentum of the system, Haley's formulation does not address the enormous impact of the vertical stresses passing down the generations of the family. In our view, the degree of anxiety engendered by the stress on the vertical and horizontal axes at the points where they converge is the key determinant of how well the family will manage its transitions through life. It becomes imperative, therefore, for the family therapist to assess not only the dimensions of the current life cycle stress, but also their connections to family themes, triangles, and labels coming down in the family over historical time (Carter, 1978). Although all normative change is to some degree stressful, we have observed as clinicians that when the horizontal (developmental) stress intersects with a vertical (transgenerational) stress, there is a quantum leap in anxiety in the system. If, to give a global example, one's parents were basically pleased to be parents and handled the job without too much anxiety, the birth of the first child will produce just the normal stress of a system expanding its boundaries from two to three members. If, on the other hand, parenting was a *cause célèbre* of some kind in the family of origin of one or both spouses, and has not been dealt with, the birth of a baby may produce heightened anxiety for the couple in making the transition to parenthood. The greater the anxiety generated in the family at any transition point, the more difficult or dysfunctional the transition will be.

In addition to the stress "inherited" from past generations and the stress experienced while moving through the family life cycle, there is, of course, the stress of living in this place at this time. One cannot ignore the social, economic, and political context and its impact on families moving through the life cycle at this point in history. Cultural issues naturally play a major role in this. Not only do cultural groups vary greatly in their breakdown of life cycle stages and definitions of the tasks at each stage (Falicov & Karrer, 1980), but it is clear that even several generations after immigration the family life cycle patterns of various groups differ markedly (Gelfand & Kutzik, 1979; Lieberman, 1974). One must also recognize the strain that the vastly accelerated rate of change puts on families today, whether the changes themselves are for better or worse.

Even the stages of the life cycle are rather arbitrary breakdowns. The notion of childhood has been described as the invention of 18th-century Western society, adolescence as the invention of the 19th century (Aries, 1962), related to cultural, economic, and political contexts of those eras. The notion of young adulthood as an independent phase could easily be argued to be the invention of the 20th century, and, for women, of the late 20th century, if it is accepted even now. The phases of the empty nest and older age are also developments primarily of this century, brought about by the smaller number of children and the longer life span of families in our era. Developmental psychology has tended to take an ahistorical approach. In virtually all other contemporary cultures and during virtually all other historical eras the breakdown of life cycle stages has been different from our current definitions (Kenniston, 1971).

The development of a life cycle perspective for the individual has been greatly facilitated by the creative work of Erikson (1950), Levinson (1978), and others in defining the transitions of adult life. Recent studies of the couple over the life cycle have helped us gain a time perspective on the two-person system (Campbell, 1975; Gould, 1972; Harry, 1976; Schram, 1979). The three-person or family model has been elaborated most carefully by Duvall, who focuses on child rearing as the organizing element of family life. We would like to go beyond this model to consider the motion of the entire three- or four-generational system as it moves through time. Relationships with parents, siblings, and other family members go through stages as one moves along the life cycle, just as parent-child and spouse relationships do. It is extremely difficult, however, to think of the family as a whole because of the complexity involved. As a system moving through time, the family has basically different properties from all other systems. Unlike all other organizations, families incorporate new members only by birth, adoption, or marriage, and members can leave only by death, if then (Terkelsen, 1980). No other system is subject to these constraints. A business organization can fire members it views as dysfunctional, or, conversely, members can resign if the structure and values of the organization are not to their liking. The pressures of membership with no exit available can, in the extreme, lead the family down the road to psychosis, if no way can be found to function within the system (Cecchin, 1979). In nonfamily systems the roles and functions of the system are carried out in a more or less stable way, by replacement of those who leave for any reason, or else the system self-destructs. While families also have roles and functions, the main value in families is in the relationships, which are irreplaceable. If a parent leaves or dies, another person can be brought in to fill a parenting function, but this person can never replace the parent in his or her most important aspects.

One of the most complex aspects of the status of family members is the confusion that occurs over whether one can choose membership and responsibility in a family or not. People often act as though they can choose in this matter, when in fact there is very little choice. Children, for example, have no choice about being born into a system; nor do parents have a choice, once children are born, as to the existence of the responsibilities of parenthood, even if they neglect these responsibilities. In fact, no family relationships except marriage are entered into by choice. Even in the case of marriage, the freedom to marry whomever one wishes is a rather recent option, and the decision to marry is probably much less freely made than people usually recognize at the time (McGoldrick, 1980). While one person can choose not to continue a marriage relationship, the fact of having been married continues to be acknowledged with the designation "ex-spouse." People cannot alter whom they are related to in the complex web of family ties over all the generations. Obviously, family members frequently act as if this were not so—they cut each other off because of conflicts or because they claim to have "nothing in common"—but when family members act as though family relationships were optional, they do so to the detriment of their own sense of identity and the richness of their emotional and social context.

We want to emphasize two cautions about a life cycle perspective that we have noted before (Carter & McGoldrick, 1980). A rigid application of psychology to the "normal" life cycle can have a detrimental effect if it promotes anxious self-scrutiny that raises fears that deviating from the norms is pathological. The opposite pitfall, overemphasizing the uniqueness of the "brave new world" faced by each new generation can create a sense of historical discontinuity by devaluing the role of parenthood and rendering meaningless the relationship between generations. Our aim is to provide a view of the life cycle in terms of the intergenerational connectedness in the family. We believe this to be one of our greatest human resources. We do not mean to oversimplify or to encourage stereotyping by promoting classifications of "normality" that constrict our view of human life. On the contrary, our hope is that by superimposing the family life cycle framework on the natural phenomenon of lives through time, we can add to the depth with which clinicians view family problems and strengths.

There is ample evidence by now that family stresses, which are likely to occur around life cycle transition points, frequently create disruptions of the life cycle and produce symptoms and dysfunction. The death of any family member, for example, leads to disruption in the family equilibrium. According to Herz (1980), the degree of disruption in the family system is affected by a number of factors, the most significant of which are the timing of the death in the life cycle of the family, the nature of the death, the openness of the system, and the family position of the dying or dead family member.

Hadley and his colleagues found that symptom onset correlated significantly with family developmental crises of addition and loss of family members (Hadley, Jacob, Milliones, Caplan, & Spitz, 1974). Walsh and Orfanidis both found that a significant life cycle event (death of a grandparent), when closely related in time to another life cycle event (birth of a child), correlated with patterns of symptom development at a much later time in the family life cycle (the transition from adolescence to young adulthood in the offspring) (Orfanidis, 1977; Walsh, 1978). There is growing evidence that life cycle events have a continuing impact on family development over a long period of time. It is probably clinicians' own limited perspective that inhibits our noticing these patterns. Research is rarely carried out over periods of more than a few years, and thus longitudinal connections can easily get lost. One research group, headed by Thomas, studied the family patterns of medical students at Johns Hopkins and then followed them over many years. They found numerous life cycle connections between early loss or life cycle disruption and later symptom development (Thomas & Duszynski, 1974). Such research supports the clinical method of Bowen, who tracks family systems through their life cycle patterns over several generations, focusing especially on nodal events and transition points in family development in seeking to understand family dysfunction at the present moment (Bowen, 1978).

Clinical families characteristically lack time perspective when they become stuck. They tend generally to magnify the present moment, overwhelmed and immobilized by their immediate feelings; or they become fixed on a moment in the past that they cannot recapture or cannot escape. Others focus on a moment in the future that they dread or long for. They lose the awareness that life means continual motion and transformation of familial relationships and contexts. As the sense of motion becomes lost or distorted, therapy involves restoring a sense of life as process and movement from and toward.

## THE CHANGING FAMILY LIFE CYCLE

Within the past generation, the changes in family life cycle patterns have escalated dramatically, due especially to the lower birth rate, the longer life expectancy, and the increasing divorce and remarriage rate. While it used to be that childrearing occupied adults for their entire active life span, it now occupies less than half the time span of adult life prior to old age. The meaning of the family is changing drastically, since it is no longer organized primarily around this activity.

The changing role of women in families is central in these shifting family life cycle patterns. Women have always been central to the functioning of the family. Their identities were determined primarily by their family functions as mother and wife. Their life cycle phases were linked almost exclusively to their stages in child-rearing activities. For men, on the other hand, chronological age has been seen as a key variable in life cycle determinations. But this description no longer fits. Today's women are moving through the life cycle more rapidly than their grandmothers; while they may put off developing personal goals beyond the realm of the family, they can no longer ignore such goals. Even women who choose a primary role of mother and home-maker must now face an "empty nest" phase that equals in length the years devoted primarily to child care. Perhaps the modern feminist movement was inevitable, as women have come to need a personal identity. Having always had primary responsibility for home, family and child care, women necessarily began to struggle under their burdens as they came to have more options for their own lives. Given their pivotal role in the family and their difficulty in establishing concurrent functions outside the family, it is perhaps not surprising that women have been the most prone to symptom development at life cycle transitions. For men, the goals of career and family are parallel. For women, these goals come into conflict and present a severe dilemma. While women are more positive than men about the prospect of marriage, they are less content than men generally with the reality of it (Bernard, 1972). Women, not men, are likely to become depressed at the time of childbirth; this appears to have a great deal to do with the dilemma that this shift creates in their lives. Women, more than men, seek help as their children reach adolescence and leave home and as their spouses retire or die. Women, not men, have had primary responsibility for older relatives. Surely this has much to do with the different ways in which women are socialized to seek help, but it also reflects the special life cycle stresses on women.

Actually, at an ever-accelerating pace over the decades of this century, women have radically changed—and are still changing—the face of the traditional family life cycle that had existed for centuries (Gluck, Dannefer, & Milea, 1980). In fact, the present generation of young women is the first in history to insist on their right to the first phase of the family life cycle—the phase in which the young unattached adult leaves the parents' home, establishes personal life goals, and starts a career in work. Historically, women were denied this most crucial step in adult development and were handed, instead, from their fathers to their husbands. In the next phase, that of the newly married couple, women are establishing two-career marriages, having children later, having fewer children, or choosing not to have children at all. In the "pressure cooker" phase of the family life cycle—that of families with young children—the majority of divorces take place, many of them initiated by women; in the next phase, that of families with adolescents, couples have the fastest growth in divorce rates at present. It is during this phase that the "midlife crisis" sends unprecedented numbers of women back to school and work. Finally, when the children are gone, a married couple—if they are still married—can expect an average of 20 years alone together, the newest and longest phase of the family life cycle. In former times one spouse, usually the husband, died within two years of the marriage of the youngest child. Old age, the final phase of the family life cycle, has almost become a phase for women only, both because they outlive men and because they live longer than they used to. At ages 75 to 79, only 24% of women have husbands, while 61% of men have wives. At ages 80 to 84, 14% of women have husbands, and 49% of men have wives. At age 85, 6% of women have husbands, while 34% of men have wives.

The recent changes in these patterns make our task of defining the normal family life cycle even more difficult. Given that 7% of women never marry, 4% never have children, and 38% end their marriages in divorce, many families do not go through the "normal" phases at the "normal" times. If one adds to this the number of families who experience the death of a member before old age and those who have a chronically ill or handicapped family member, which alters their life cycle pattern (Herz, 1980), the number of "normal" families is even smaller. Another major factor affecting all families at one time or another is immigration. The break in cultural and family continuity created by immigration affects family life cycle patterns for several generations. Given the enormous number of Americans who have immigrated within the past two generations, the percentage of "normal" families is diminished still further. Thus our paradigm for middle-class American families is more or less mythological, though statistically accurate, relating in part to existing patterns and in part to the ideal standards against which most families compare themselves.

## THE STAGES OF THE FAMILY LIFE CYCLE

We now provide a very brief outline of the statistically predictable developmental stages of American middle-class families in the last quarter of the 20th century. Our classification of family life cycle stages highlights our view that the central underlying process to be negotiated is the expansion, contraction, and realignment of the relationship system to support the entry, exit, and development of family members in a functional way. We offer suggestions about the process of change required of families at each transition, as well as hypotheses about the clinical fallout at each phase.

### The Unattached Young Adult

In outlining the stages of the family life cycle, we have departed from the traditional sociological depiction of the family life cycle as commencing at courtship or marriage and ending with the death of one spouse. Rather, considering the family to be the operative emotional unit from the cradle to the grave, we see a new family life cycle beginning at the stage of the "unattached young adult," whose completion of the primary task of coming to terms with his or her family of origin will most profoundly influence whom, when and how he or she marries and carries out all succeeding stages of the family life cycle. Adequate completion of this task requires that the young adult separate from the family of origin without cutting off or fleeing reactively to a substitute emotional refuge. Seen in this way, the "unattached young adult" phase is a cornerstone. It is a time to formulate personal life goals and to become a "self" before joining with another to form a new family subsystem. The more adequately young adults can differentiate themselves from the emotional program of the family of origin at this phase, the fewer vertical stressors will follow them through their new family's life cycle. This is the chance for them to sort out emotionally what they will take along from the family of origin and what they will change for themselves. Of great significance is the fact that until the present generation this crucial phase was never considered necessary for women, who were traditionally handed directly from their fathers to their husbands. Obviously, this tradition has had profound impact on the functioning of women in families, as the current attempt to change the tradition is now having.

We have found it useful to conceptualize life cycle transitions as requiring second-order change, or change of the system itself. Problems within each phase can often be resolved by first-order change, or a rearranging of the system, involving an incremental change. We have outlined the shifts in status required for successful accomplishment of life cycle transitions in column 2 of Table 7-1, which outlines the stages and tasks of the life cycle. In our view, it is important for a therapist not to get bogged down with a family

TABLE 7-1.   THE STAGES OF THE FAMILY LIFE CYCLE

| Family life cycle stage | Emotional process of transition: Key principles | Second-order changes in family status required to proceed developmentally |
|---|---|---|
| 1. Between families: The unattached young adult | Accepting parent–offspring separation | a. Differentiation of self in relation to family of origin<br>b. Development of intimate peer relationships<br>c. Establishment of self in work |
| 2. The joining of families through marriage: The newly married couple | Commitment to new system | a. Formation of marital system<br>b. Realignment of relationships with extended families and friends to include spouse |
| 3. The family with young children | Accepting new generation of members into the system | a. Adjusting marital system to make space for child(ren)<br>b. Taking on parenting roles<br>c. Realignment of relationships with extended family to include parenting and grandparenting roles |
| 4. The family with adolescents | Increasing flexibility of family boundaries to include children's independence | a. Shifting of parent–child relationships to permit adolescents to move in and out of system<br>b. Refocus on midlife marital and career issues<br>c. Beginning shift toward concerns for older generation |
| 5. Launching children and moving on | Accepting a multitude of exits from and entries into the family system | a. Renegotiation of marital system as a dyad<br>b. Development of adult to adult relationships between grown children and their parents<br>c. Realignment of relationships to include in-laws and grandchildren<br>d. Dealing with disabilities and death of parents (grandparents) |
| 6. The family in later life | Accepting the shifting of generational roles | a. Maintaining own and/or couple functioning and interests in face of physiological decline; exploration of new familial and social role options<br>b. Support for a more central role for middle generation<br>c. Making room in the system for the wisdom and experience of the elderly; supporting the older generation without overfunctioning for them<br>d. Dealing with loss of spouse, siblings, and other peers, and preparation for own death. Life review and integration. |

in first-order details when they have not made the required second-order shifts in relationship status to accomplish the tasks of the phase.

In the "unattached young adult" phase, problems usually center on either young adults' or their parents' not recognizing the need for a shift to a less interdependent form of relating, based on their now all being adults complementing each other. Problems in shifting status may take the form of parents' encouraging the dependence of their young adult children, or of young adults' either remaining dependent or breaking away in a pseudo-independent cutoff of their parents and families. It is our view, following Bowen (1978), that cutoffs never resolve emotional relationships and that young adults who cut off their parents do so reactively and are in fact still emotionally bound to rather than independent of the family "program." The shift toward adult-to-adult status requires a mutually respectful and personal form of relating, in which young adults can appreciate parents as they are, needing neither to make them into what they are not, nor to blame them for what they could not be. Neither do young adults need to comply with parental expectations and wishes at their own expense. As outlined by Meyer (1980), therapy at this phase most often involves coaching young adults to reengage with their parents in a new way that accomplishes the shifting of roles and status in the system. When the parents are the ones seeking help, therapy usually involves helping them to recognize the new status of their adult children and to let them go. An example may clarify the way in which family members can get stuck in a "more of the same" struggle, where the harder they try, the worse it gets. Therapy focuses on helping them make the necessary second-order change, as in this case example:

David G., a 24-year-old computer programmer, applied for therapy with vague complaints of depression and the inability to form close relationships. The picture that emerged was of an isolated young man who had trouble keeping himself motivated at work. He also had trouble feeling connected with friends, especially women. When asked about his parents, he said they were not worth discussing. He described them as critical, cynical, having a poor marriage and little to give. Further questioning revealed that he knew very little about his parents as people. They were Jewish immigrants whose families had struggled through the Depression. As we explored the family relationships, it became clear that David saw his parents as wounded people, felt guilty and resentful that they had not given more to him, and sensed their emptiness as he, the younger of two sons, left home. He did not want to reach back for fear that they would pull him into their depression and bitterness and he would never be able to leave. Yet, by cutting off, he had no sense of who he was or how to make other connections. He was not free to move on as an adult. He was reluctant at first to make moves with his family of origin and insisted, "I am an adult and can handle my own problems." Questions about his parents' lives gradually helped him to alter his view of them and to redefine his relationship with them as a relationship of adults. Other relatives were called on for information about the family background, and the details they gave David about his parents' lives helped him in making this shift to a different view of his parents and the nature of their hold on him. As he gave up rigidly resisting his parents, he began to get to know them and became freer to make contacts with peers as well. He also found himself having more energy for his work.

It seems clear in this case that the more David tried to cut himself off from his parents and disassociate himself from traits he identified with in them, the less able he became to get on with his own life and to develop a truly personal identity. By reconnecting with them in a new way and shifting his status in relation to them, he became able to move on developmentally.

### The Joining of Families through Marriage: The Newly Married Couple

Becoming a couple is one of the most complex and difficult transitions of the family life cycle. However, along with the transition to parenthood, which it has long symbolized, it is seen as the easiest and the most joyous. The positive and romanticized view of this transition may add to its difficulty, since everyone wants to see only the happiness of the shift. The problems entailed may thus be pushed underground, only to intensify and surface later on.

Weddings, more than any other rite of passage, are viewed as the solution to a problem, such as loneliness or extended family difficulties. The event is seen as terminating a process instead of beginning one. The myth "And they lived happily ever after" (with no further effort) causes couples and families considerable difficulty. Weddings, far from resolving a "status problem" of young unmarried adults, come in the middle of a complex process of changing family status.

Marriage requires that a couple renegotiate a myriad of personal issues that they have previously defined for themselves or that were defined by their parents, from when to eat, sleep, have sex, or fight, to how to celebrate holidays or where and how to live, work, and spend vacations. The couple must renegotiate their relationships with their parents, siblings, friends, and other relatives in view of the new marriage, and this will to some degree affect all personal relationships. It places no small stress on the family to open itself to an outsider who is now an official member of its inner circle. Frequently no new member has been added for many years. In addition, marriage involves a shifting of family boundaries for the members on both sides to some degree or other. Not only is the new spouse now a factor for each family, but priorities of both systems must now be negotiated in a complex set of arrangements of each system. As mentioned earlier, relationships with the third generation are of utmost importance in understanding the family life cycle, not only because of their historical importance to the system, but because of their direct, ongoing impact on the life of the next generations' family experiences.

In the animal kingdom, mating involves only the two partners. For mankind, it is the joining of two enormously complex systems. In fact, Haley has commented that the fact of having in-laws is the major distinguishing characteristic between man and all other forms of life. In any case, it is surely a complex transition and one that our rituals hardly prepare us for. And, although couples are marrying later and delaying having children more than ever before, the average age of marriage for women in 1975 was 21.3 and for men 23.8; the birth of the first child came, on the average, 1½ years later. This means that there is still a relatively short time in which the couple and both families must adjust to this phase of their life cycle, with its accompanying stresses, before moving on. It may also be worth noting that there seems to be an optimum timing for this phase, with those who fall outside it often having more difficulty. Women who marry before the age of 20 (38% of women) are twice as likely to divorce as those who marry in their 20s. Those who marry after 30 (6%) are half again as likely to divorce as those who marry in their 20s (Glick & Norton, 1977). Thus it appears that in our culture there is a time for coupling; while it may be better to marry later than sooner, those who fall too far out of the normative range on either end are more likely to have trouble making the transition. A number of other factors appear to make the adjustment to this life cycle transition more difficult:

1. The couple meets or marries shortly after a significant loss.

2. One or both partners wish to distance from family of origin.

3. The family backgrounds of each spouse are significantly different (religion, education, social class, ethnicity, age, etc.).

4. The couple have incompatible sibling constellations (Toman, 1976).

5. The couple reside either extremely close to or at a great distance from either family of origin.

6. The couple are dependent on either extended family financially, physically, or emotionally.

7. The couple marries before age 20 or after age 30.

8. The couple marries after an acquaintanceship of less than 6 months or after more than 3 years of engagement.

9. The wedding occurs without family or friends present.

10. The wife becomes pregnant before or within the first year of marriage (Christensen, 1963; Bacon, 1974).

11. Either spouse has a poor relationship with his or her siblings or parents.

12. Either spouse considers his or her childhood or adolescence as an unhappy time.

13. Marital patterns in either extended family were unstable.

Most of these factors have already been given support by sociological data on divorce (Becker, 1977; Bumpass & Sweet, 1972; Burchinal, 1965; Goodrich, Ryder, & Raush, 1968; Mott & Moore, 1979; Ryder, 1970). A number of other factors also add to the difficulty of adjusting to marriage in our time. Changing family patterns as a result of the changing role of women, the frequent marriage of partners from widely different cultural backgrounds, and the increasing physical distances between family members are placing a much greater burden on couples to define their relationship for themselves than was true in traditional and precedent-bound family structures. While any two family systems are always different and have conflicting patterns and expectations, in our present culture couples are less bound by family traditions and freer than ever before to develop male–female relationships unlike those they experienced in their families of origin. This is particularly so because of the changing role of women in families. It appears that the rise in women's status is positively correlated with marital instability (Pearson & Hendrix, 1979) and with the marital dissatisfaction of their husbands (Burke & Weir, 1976). When women used to fall automatically into the adaptive role in marriage, the likelihood of divorce was much lower. In fact, it appears very difficult for two spouses to be equally successful and achieving. There is evidence that either spouse's accomplishments may correlate negatively with the same degree of achievement in the other (Ferber & Huber, 1979). Thus, achieving a successful transition to couplehood in our time, when we are moving toward the equality of the sexes (educationally and occupationally), may be extraordinarily difficult.

Surprisingly few couples ever seek premarital counseling, in spite of the obvious difficulties in negotiating this life cycle transition. If couples do seek therapy at this phase, it is more often for difficulty in tolerating closeness, sexual problems, problems in negotiating their differences (particularly male–female issues), or difficulty in settling the question of whether to have children (more common for couples where the wife is over 30). Although we hypothesize that failure to renegotiate family status is the main reason for marital failure, it appears that couples are very unlikely to present with extended family problems as the stated issue. Problems reflecting the inability to shift family status are usually indicated by a lack of boundaries around the new subsystem. In-laws may be too intrusive and the new couple afraid to set limits, or the couple may have difficulty forming adequate connections with the extended systems, cutting themselves off in a tight twosome. At times the inability to formalize the couple relationship indicates that the partners are still too enmeshed in their own families to define a new system and accept the implications of this realignment.

It is useful in such situations to help the system to move to a new definition of itself (second-order change) rather than to get lost in the details of incremental shifts they may be struggling over (sex, money, time, etc.).

Carol and Steve were both assistant professors at a local university when they applied for help with relationship conflicts. They had been living together for 3 years, to the disapproval of both extended families. Carol said that she wanted to get married, but Steve was ambivalent. Three times they had become engaged and then called it off at Steve's insistence. He feared that Carol's tendency to be demanding might in the long run mean she would not make a good wife. On further investigation, it seemed that Steve's upper-middle-class, white Anglo-Saxon Protestant family disapproved of Carol's lower-middle-class, Jewish background. In return, Carol disapproved of what she perceived as Steve's snobbish concern with manners, and at times she acted intentionally unconventional with him or his family as part of a reactive pattern that was her tendency in her own family. Her parents also disapproved of Steve's "uptightness" and his "not being Jewish." In part, Steve's ambivalence about marriage served Carol's purposes, since she herself was quite unsure about the commitment of a marriage. Both partners struggled with each other over details of their habits, but the underlying difficulty related to the failure of both of them to be able to view themselves in a new way in relation to their families of origin.

The therapist listened carefully to their discussion of the numerous nuances of their conflicts. When more direct ways of breaking their fruitless arguments about who was "right" failed, the therapist finally told them that there was only one way they could be sure to resolve their problems, and that this was for each of them to make a much more concerted attempt to win parental approval for the other in whatever way possible. When this was accomplished, they would be ready for marriage. This intervention helped push the couple to a different view of themselves. Shortly after this time they did get married and soon after left therapy. They were able to stay in emotional contact with their parents in spite of the parents' continuing disapproval of them as a couple, which did not soften until their first child was born two years later.

The shift in their view of themselves had allowed Carol and Steve to move ahead in the difficult couple negotiations of this phase, in which they were initially blocked because they had not taken the necessary steps in shifting their relationships with their families of origin.

## The Family with Young Children

The shift to this stage of the family life cycle requires that adults now move up a generation and become caretakers to the younger generation. Typical problems that occur when parents cannot make this shift are struggles with each other about taking responsibility, or refusal or inability to behave as parents to their children. Often parents find themselves unable to set limits and exert the required authority, or they lack the patience to allow their children to express themselves as they develop. Typically, parents with children who present clinically at this phase are somehow not accepting the generation boundary between themselves and their children. They may complain that their 4-year-old is "impossible to control." Given their relative size, the difficulty here relates to the parents' difficulty exerting authority.

From this perspective, whether parents placate and spoil their children, or whether they are endlessly critical, they are reflecting a failure to appreciate the new change in family status required in this stage of the family life cycle.

It should be added that many factors in our social system make this stage especially difficult. Social supports that formerly reinforced generational boundaries are now often lacking, and parents frequently find that the community or family resources that in the past reinforced and supported parental roles are unavailable. This makes it extraordinarily difficult to maintain appropriate boundaries and authority.

In any case, therapy is typically addressed at helping parents gain a view of themselves as part of a new generational level with specific responsibilities and tasks in relation to the next level of the family. Parents may be encouraged to recognize their power in relation to children who have been acting as "little tyrants." If parents are engaging with their children as equals—for example, when parents let children's criticisms "get" to them— they need help in realizing that children's criticisms are not of the same quality as those of peers and that it is usually counterproductive to take such comments personally. The same thing can be said about children's "bad behavior." Parents often present with complaints that their children are "mean" to them. These feelings immobilize them just at the time when children need parental limits, authority, and security that there is an order to the family structure that will be controlled by the parents.

The Brown family presented for therapy because their 5-year-old daughter, Angela, was impossible to manage, in contrast tho their 4-year-old son, Jerome, who was described as "cherubic." Angela had apparently "always been willful and contrary," and in fact, Mrs. Brown said she had never even looked like a baby. The litany of her misbehaviors was endless. The therapeutic problem was how to help the parents recognize that they were of a different generation and were, by their intimidation, granting Angela a power in the family that was making their situation impossible to resolve. Inquiring into the history, the therapist learned that Mrs. Brown's own mother had been hospitalized many times during Mrs. Brown's childhood for mental illness and that Mrs. Brown had functioned as a parental child to her younger siblings for most of her childhood. Establishing appropriate parent–child boundaries was a task she had never fully learned. Therapeutic strategies were geared to forming a "collusion," with the parents as adults having to "handle" difficult children, and especially to outwit clever youngsters for their own benefit. Moves were geared toward shifting the parents' view of themselves in relation to their daughter, and to their son as well, since their "cherubic" view also involved an inadequate sense of parental boundaries.

As the Brown family was proceeding before therapy, the harder they tried to win a "power struggle" with their daughter, the more ineffective they became. They needed to shift to a different view of themselves, in which the idea of an equal "power struggle" between parents and young children is meaningless;

the parent–child relationship is one between unequals, in which the younger generation needs the protection and guidance of the older. When families cannot make this shift, they may struggle endlessly. The harder they try, the more stuck they become.

## The Family with Adolescents

While many have broken down the stages of families with young children into different phases, in our view the shifts are incremental until adolescence, which ushers in a new era because it marks a new definition of the children within the family and of the parents' roles in relation to their children. Families with adolescents must establish qualitatively different boundaries than families with younger children. The boundaries must now be permeable. Parents can no longer maintain complete authority. Adolescents can and do open the family to a whole array of new values as they bring friends and new ideas into the family arena. Families that become derailed at this stage are frequently stuck in an earlier view of their children. They may try to control every aspect of their lives at a time when, developmentally, this is impossible to do successfully. Either the adolescent withdraws from the appropriate involvements for this developmental stage, or the parents become increasingly frustrated with what they perceive as their own impotence. For this phase the old Alcoholics Anonymous adage is particularly apt for parents: "May I have the ability to accept the things I cannot change, the strength to change the things I can, and the wisdom to know the difference." Flexible boundaries that allow adolescents to move in and be dependent at times when they cannot handle things alone, and to move out and experiment with increasing degrees of independence when they are ready, put special strains on all family members in their new status with one another. This is also a time when adolescents begin to establish their own independent relationships with the extended family, and it requires special adjustments between parents and grandparents to allow and foster these new patterns.

Parents of adolescents often get stuck in attempting to get their children to do what the parents want at a time when this can no longer be done successfully, or they let the children do whatever they want and fail to exert the needed authority. Children may become overly independent and adult-like, or they remain immature and fail to develop sufficient independent functioning to move on developmentally.

Therapy in such situations needs to help families make the appropriate transformation of their view of themselves to allow for the increasing independence of the new generation, while maintaining appropriate boundaries and structure to foster continued family development.

The Martin family presented for therapy for John, the younger of their two sons who at age 15 was "skipping school, smoking pot, and hanging around with the wrong type of friends for someone as smart as he." The parents were obsessed with whether he was smoking pot and which friends he was hanging around with. When asked about John's functioning at home, the therapist was told that he did nothing and his room was a mess. They were, however, not that concerned about his responsibilities for chores, since both parents had had to work hard during their own adolescent years and felt they had missed a great deal of youthful fun and freedom because of this. They wanted it to be better for John. However, in their attitude toward John, Mr. and Mrs. Martin were still locked into a view of him related to the previous developmental stage—when parents may take considerable responsibility for children and do much for them, and when there are not too many areas of functioning that are really beyond parental control. Now the parents were not demanding the responsibilities appropriate for a child moving toward adulthood in terms of taking on a share of responsibilities for family functions, but were trying to gain full control over John's outside functioning, which was impossible. The more energy the parents focused on the things they could not control, the worse their relationship became and the more frustrated they were. The parents were helped to see that they were treating their fast-maturing son as a spoiled brat who was accountable for nothing at home and would get picked up after, served, and waited on, with no effort on his part. On the other hand, he was being treated as though he had no ability to choose friends or make proper judgments about his own behavior outside the home, when he needed to take responsibility there himself. The major hindrance to their shifting to a more mature view, as they had in fact done quite well with their older son, lay in their reluctance to start letting go of parenthood and examining the state of their marriage and their personal lives in light of the stages of life looming ahead.

Once the parents could come to view themselves as ready to move to a new level, they shifted their handling of John and became able to apply appropriate limits at home, where they had control over what was given to him, and to let him take the consequences outside the home.

Again, focus on the details of the parents' complaints would have missed the important fact that they had failed to make the transition emotionally to this life cycle phase.

### Launching Children and Moving On

This phase of the family life cycle is the newest and the longest, and for these reasons, it is in many ways the most problematic of all phases. Until about a generation ago, most families were occupied with raising their children for their entire active adult lives until old age. Now, because of the low birth rate and the long life span of most adults, parents launch their children almost 20 years before retirement and must then find other life activities. The difficulties of this transition can lead families to hold on to their children or can lead to parental feelings of emptiness and depression, particularly for women who have focused their main energies on their children and who now feel useless and unprepared to face a new career in the job world. The most significant aspect of this phase is that it is marked by the greatest number of exits and entries of family members. It begins with the launching of grown children and proceeds with the entry of their spouses and children. Meanwhile, it is a time when older parents are often becoming ill or dying; this, in conjunction with the difficulties of finding meaningful life activities during this phase itself, may make it a particularly difficult period. Parents must not only deal with the change in their own status as they make room for the next generation and move up to grandparental positions, but they must deal also with a different type of relationship with their own parents, who may become dependent, giving them considerable caretaking responsibilities. This can also be a liberating time, in that finances may be easier than during the primary years of family responsibilities and there is the potential for moving into new and unexplored areas—travel, hobbies, new careers. For some families this stage is seen as a time of fruition and completion and as a second opportunity to consolidate or expand by exploring new avenues and new roles. For others it leads to disruption, a sense of emptiness and overwhelming loss, depression, and general disintegration. The phase necessitates a restructuring of the marital relationship now that parenting responsibilities are no longer required. As Solomon (1973) has noted, if the solidification of the marriage has not taken place and reinvestment is not possible, the family often mobilizes itself to hold onto the last child. Where this does not happen the couple may move toward divorce.

The family that fails to appreciate the need for a shift in relationship status at this stage may keep trying to fill their time with the old tasks, or the spouses may begin to blame each other for the emptiness they feel. If they can recognize the new efforts required in this period, they are much more likely to be able to mobilize the energy to deal with them than if they go along on the assumptions of the previous phase.

Nat and Marcia were in their late 40s when they applied for therapy for marital problems. Their two sons were in their last years of college and were about to move to the dormitories on campus at the local college. Nat was an accountant who had never been as successful as he had wished and who frequently changed jobs. This had been a source of continued irritation and frustration to Marcia, who had been a teacher since her sons were small. Now, for the first time, because she felt less need to hold the family together, she began to voice and act on her frustration with the marriage. She was angry at Nat for all the years he had not shared the family responsibilities or given her the appreciation she wanted. She began to unleash feelings she had bottled up for years because, as she said, she had "nothing to lose any more." The more she expressed her feelings, the more frustrated she felt, because her husband did not change. Therapy was aimed at normalizing the difficulty the couple was facing and at helping them realize how hard it is to be confronted suddenly with issues that have not been resolved for many years. Marcia was helped to see that her frustration was not because her husband was a bad person or because she had been so unassertive she had tolerated misery when she should have protested. Both spouses were helped to see that they now had new choices because their life was at a new stage, and that working out a comfortable marriage would require much energy even if they had not let it slide for a long time. This helped to take some of the pressure off the couple; they began to see that they now had a whole process ahead of them of renegotiating their marriage and their future lives, together or separately, and that these were large tasks for any family.

The relief of recognizing the extent to which they were at a new stage of their lives and of becoming conscious of the tasks it required was an enormous relief to this couple. For Marcia in particular, it enabled her to do some long-range thinking about how she wanted to spend the next portion of her life, and to begin planning constructively. Until she realized this, she was continuously recycling old arguments with her husband about things he had not done for her in the past or about ways she wished he would relate to their sons, though their job was now substantially done in this area.

### The Family in Later Life

As Walsh (1980) has pointed out, few of the visions we are offered in our culture for old age provide us with positive perspectives for healthy later-life adjustment within a family or social context. Pessimistic views of later life prevail. The current myths are that most elderly people have no families; that those who do have families have little relationship with them and are usually set aside in institutions; or that all family interactions with older family members are minimal. On the contrary, the vast majority of adults over 65 do not live alone but with other family members. Over 80% live within an hour of at least one child (Walsh, 1980).

Another myth about the elderly is that they are sick, senile, and feeble and can be best handled in nursing homes or hospitals. Only 4% of the elderly live in institutions (Streib, 1972), and the average age at admission is 80. There are indications that if others did not foster their dependence or ignore them as functional family members, even this degree of dependence would be less.

Among the tasks of families in later life are adjustments to retirement, which may not only create the obvious vacuum for the retiring person but may put a special strain on a marriage that until then has been balanced in different spheres. Financial insecurity or dependence are also special difficulties, especially for family members who value managing for themselves. And while loss of friends and relatives is a particular difficulty at this phase, the loss of a spouse is the most difficult adjustment, with its problems of reorganizing one's entire life alone after many years as a couple and of having fewer relationships to help replace the loss. Grandparenthood can, however, offer a new lease on life, and opportunities for special close relationships without the responsibilities of parenthood.

Difficulty in making the status changes required for this phase of life are reflected in older family members' refusal to relinquish some of their power, as when a grandfather refuses to turn over the company or make plans for his succession. The inability to shift status is reflected also when older adults give up and become totally dependent on the next generation, or when the next generation does not accept their lessening powers or treats them as totally incompetent or irrelevant.

Even when members of the older generation are quite enfeebled, there is not really a reversal of roles between one generation and the next, because parents always have a great many years of extra experience and remain models to the next generations for the phases of life ahead. Nevertheless, because valuing older age is totally unsupported in our culture, family members of the next generation often do not know how to make the appropriate shift in relational status with their parents.

Clinically, it is rarely the older family members themselves who seek help, although they do suffer from many clinical problems, primary among which is depression. More often it is members of the next generation who seek help, and even they often do not present with their problem defined as relating to a parent. It is often only through careful history taking that one learns that an aging grandparent is just about to move in or to be taken to a nursing home, and that the relationship issues around this shift have been left totally submerged in the family. Helping family members recognize the status changes and the need for resolving their relationships in a new balance can help families move on developmentally.

Joan and Peter Green, a couple in their mid-50s, presented for marital therapy for what appeared to be very long-standing marital problems. Their youngest child had been out of the home for several years. Obtaining an extended family history was difficult, as both spouses saw this information as irrelevant to their problem and were impatient with the discussion. Peter's parents were apparently in good health and lived a considerable distance away. Joan's parents were divorced, and her father was remarried in California. Her mother, with whom she had a very stormy relationship, had been ill with cancer on and off for the past 2 years. She did not want to talk about it, however, saying that her mother would probably die soon anyway. Details were requested about the mother's condition and support system. It turned out that Joan's only brother had totally cut the mother off years before, that the mother's live-in companion had recently become ill and hospitalized herself, and thus that the mother had no place to go. Joan felt obligated to take her in, but said that, given the marital problems, it didn't make sense. Peter said he had agreed to let the mother come as long as Joan did not fight with her constantly. It became evident that Joan's fighting with Peter was a way of distracting herself from her unhappiness about her mother and about her relationship with her. Once this became clear, the therapist suggested that an even more pressing issue than the marital problems, which appeared to flare up whenever there was stress, was the unresolved relationship with her mother that Joan was ignoring. The recommendation was made that she take time to renegotiate her relationship with her mother, who might now be more ready than in the past to sort out a relationship that would fit them for the present. Reluctantly Joan brought her mother into a therapy session, not warning the therapist beforehand that her mother spoke no English, since she had immigrated to this country from Hungary at age 50. To everyone's surprise, Joan conducted the session herself, raising many long-buried issues in her relationship with her mother, making use of the mother's limited time to fill in family history, and showing a respect for the mother's background she had never even known she felt. The mother responded warmly and with much reflection on her past life, her regrets, and the things she felt proud of, particularly her daughter's education, for which she had sacrificed a great deal. She talked frankly about her own death and her regrets that she had not been able to talk with her son.

While this shift did not solve the daughter's problems, it freed her considerably to carry on her own responsibilities, with a certain strength from the generational continuity and bond added. Without recognizing the need to face the status shift required, and the opportunity it offered for her to renegotiate a relationship with a mother with whom much had been lacking in earlier years, frustration and tension might only have been added to the system as she struggled even more intensely to make the marriage "come out right."

## MAJOR VARIATIONS IN THE FAMILY LIFE CYCLE

### Divorce and Remarriage

While the statistical majority of the American middle and upper classes still go through the traditional family life cycle stages as outlined above, the largest variation from that norm consists of families in which divorce has occurred. With the divorce rate currently at 38% and the rate of redivorce at 44% (Glick & Norton, 1976), divorce in the American family is close to the point at which it will occur in the majority of families and will thus be thought of more and more as a normative event.

In our experience as clinicians and teachers, we have found it useful to conceptualize divorce as an interruption or dislocation of the traditional family life cycle, which produces the kind of profound disequilibrium that is associated throughout the entire family life cycle with shifts, gains, and losses in family membership. As in other life cycle phases, there are crucial shifts in relationship status and important emotional tasks that must be completed by the members of divorcing families in order for them to proceed developmentally. As in other phases, emotional issues not resolved at this phase will be carried along as hindrances in future relationships.

Therefore, in this view, we conceptualize the need for families in which divorce occurs to go through one or two additional phases of the family life cycle in order to restabilize and go forward developmentally again at a more complex level. Of women who divorce, 25% do not remarry. These families go through one additional phase and can restabilize permanently as divorced families. The other 75% of women who divorce remarry, and these families can be said to require negotiation of two additional phases of the family life cycle before permanent restabilization.

Our concept of divorce and postdivorce family emotional process can be visualized as a roller-coaster graph, with peaks of emotional tension at all of the transition points.

In divorcing families, emotional tension peaks predictably at these points:

1. at the time of the *decision* to separate or divorce;

2. when this decision is announced to family and friends;

3. when money and custody–visitation arrangements are discussed;

4. when the physical separation takes place;

5. when the actual legal divorce takes place;

6. when separated spouses or ex-spouses have contact about money or children and at life cycle transition points of all family members;

7. as each spouse is making the initial adjustments to rebuilding a new life.

These emotional pressure peaks occur in all divorcing families—not necessarily in the above order—and many of them occur over and over again, for months or years. A more detailed depiction of the process appears in Table 7-2.

The emotions released during the process of divorce relate primarily to the work of *emotional* divorce—that is, the retrieval of self from the marriage. Each partner must retrieve the hopes, dreams, plans, and expectations that were invested in *this* spouse and in *this* marriage. This requires mourning what is lost and dealing with hurt, anger, blame, guilt, shame, and loss in oneself, in the spouse, in the children, and in the extended family.

In our clinical work with divorcing families, we subscribe to the basic systems view that cutoffs are emotionally harmful, and we work to help divorcing spouses continue to relate as cooperative parents and to permit maximum feasible contact between children and natural parents and grand-parents. Our experience supports that of others (Hetherington, Cox, & Cox, 1977), who have found that it takes a minimum of 2 years and a great deal of effort after divorce for a family to readjust to its new structure and proceed to the next developmental stage. Families in which the emotional

TABLE 7-2. DISLOCATIONS OF THE FAMILY LIFE CYCLE REQUIRING ADDITIONAL STEPS TO RESTABILIZE AND PROCEED DEVELOPMENTALLY

| Phase | Emotional process of transition: Prerequisite attitude | Developmental issues |
|---|---|---|
| | Divorce | |
| 1. The decision to divorce | Acceptance of inability to resolve marital tensions sufficiently to continue relationship | Acceptance of one's own part in the failure of the marriage |
| 2. Planning the breakup of the system | Supporting viable arrangements for all parts of the system | a. Working cooperatively on problems of custody, visitation, finances <br> b. Dealing with extended family about the divorce |
| 3. Separation | A. Willingness to continue cooperative coparental relationship <br> B. Work on resolution of attachment to spouse | a. Mourning loss of intact family <br> b. Restructuring marital and parent-child relationships; adaptation to living apart <br> c. Realignment of relationships with extended family; staying connected with spouse's extended family |
| 4. The divorce | More work on emotional divorce: Overcoming hurt, anger, guilt, etc. | a. Mourning loss of intact family: giving up fantasies of reunion <br> b. Retrieval of hopes, dreams, expectations from the marriage <br> c. Staying connected with extended families |
| | Postdivorce family | |
| A. Single-parent family | Willingness to maintain parental contact with ex-spouse and support contact of children with ex-spouse and his or her family | a. Making flexible visitation arrangements with ex-spouse and his or her family <br> b. Rebuilding own social network |
| B. Single-parent (noncustodial) | Willingness to maintain parental contact with ex-spouse and support custodial parent's relationship with children | a. Finding ways to continue effective parenting relationship with children <br> b. Rebuilding own social network |

issues of divorce are not adequately resolved can remain stuck emotionally for years if not for generations.

At the transition into remarriage, the predictable peaks of emotional tension occur at the time of serious commitment to the new relationship; at the time the plan to remarry is announced to families and friends; at the time of the actual remarriage and formation of the stepfamily; and as the logistics of stepfamily life are put into practice.

The family emotional process at the transition to remarriage consists of struggling with *fears* about investment in a new marriage and a new family:

one's own fears, the new spouse's fears, and the children's fears (of either or both spouses); dealing with hostile or upset reactions of the children, the extended families, and the ex-spouse; struggling with the ambiguity of the new model of family structure roles and relationships; rearousal of intense parental guilt and concerns about the welfare of children; and rearousal of the old attachment to ex-spouse (negative or positive). Table 7-3 depicts the process in somewhat greater detail.

Our society offers stepfamilies a choice of three conceptual models, none of which work: the intact family next door; *The Brady Bunch* of TV fame; and the wicked stepparents of the fairy tales. Our first clinical step, then, is to validate for stepfamilies the lack of social support and lack of clarity in the relationship models they are offered. Clinicians can try to offer them the challenge of helping to invent a new form of family structure, with the following guidelines making good systems sense: giving up the old model of family and accepting the complexity of a new form; maintaining permeable boundaries to permit shifting of household memberships; and working for open lines of communication between all sets of parents and between all natural parents and grandparents and their children or grandchildren. (McGoldrick & Carter, 1980).

In our experience, the residue of an angry and vengeful divorce can block stepfamily integration for years or forever. The rearousal of the old emotional attachment to an ex-spouse, which characteristically surfaces at the time of remarriage and at subsequent life cycle transitions of children, is usually not understood as a predictable process and therefore leads to denial, misinterpretation, cutoff, and assorted difficulties. As in the case of adjustment to a new family structure after divorce, stepfamily integration seems also to require a minimum of 2 years before a workable new structure permits family members to move on emotionally.

### The Family Life Cycle of the Poor

The adaptation of multiproblem poor families over decades and centuries to a stark political, social, and economic context has produced a family life cycle pattern that varies significantly from the middle-class paradigm so often and so erroneously used to conceptualize their situation. Colon (1980) offers a thought-provoking breakdown of the family life cycle of the poor into three phases: the "unattached young adult" (who may actually be 11 or 12 years old), on his or her own virtually unaccountable to adults; families with children—a phase that occupies most of the life span and commonly includes three- and four-generation households; and the phase of the nonevolved grandmother, still involved in a central role in old age—still actively in charge of the generations below.

Since this area is a very specialized one, no attempt will be made here to do more than mention that middle-class family assumptions are obviously

TABLE 7-3. REMARRIED FAMILY FORMATION: A DEVELOPMENTAL OUTLINE

| Steps | Prerequisite attitude | Developmental issues |
|---|---|---|
| 1. Entering the new relationship | Recovery from loss of first marriage (adequate "emotional divorce") | Recommitment to marriage and to forming a family with readiness to deal with the complexity and ambiguity |
| 2. Conceptualizing and planning new marriage and family | Accepting one's own fears and those of new spouse and children about remarriage and forming a stepfamily<br>Accepting need for time and patience for adjustment to complexity and ambiguity of the following:<br>1. Multiple new roles<br>2. Boundaries: space, time, membership, and authority<br>3. Affective issues: guilt, loyalty conflicts, desire for mutuality, unresolvable past hurts | a. Work on openness in the new relationships to avoid pseudomutuality<br>b. Plan for maintenance of cooperative coparental relationships with ex-spouses<br>c. Plan to help children deal with fears, loyalty conflicts, and membership in two systems<br>d. Realignment of relationships with extended family to include new spouse and children<br>e. Plan maintenance of connections for children with extended family of ex-spouse(s) |
| 3. Remarriage and reconstitution of family | Final resolution of attachment to previous spouse and ideal of "intact" family; acceptance of a different model of family with permeable boundaries | a. Restructuring family boundaries to allow for inclusion of new spouse–stepparent<br>b. Realignment of relationships throughout subsystems to permit interweaving of several systems<br>c. Making room for relationships of all children with biological (noncustodial) parents, grandparents, and other extended family<br>d. Sharing memories and histories to enhance stepfamily integration |

*Note.* Variation on a developmental schema presented by Ransom, Schlesinger, and Derdeyn (1979).

inappropriate in approaching poor families clinically. In addition to the study referred to above, readers are referred to Aponte (1976, 1974) and Minuchin and Montalvo (1967) for clinical approaches to the poor family.

### Cultural Variations

Most descriptions of the typical family life cycle (including ours) fail to convey the considerable effects of ethnicity and religion on all aspects of how, when, and in what way a family makes its transitions from phase to phase. Although we may ignore these variables for the theoretical clarity of focus on our commonalities, a clinician working with real families in the real world cannot afford to ignore this. According to Falicov and Karrer, "To the clinician, awareness of cultural variations in the family life cycle has important application in several areas relevant and even crucial to the treatment process, such as recognizing family crisis points, differentiating functional from dysfunctional behavior, and selecting treatment goals and interventions which are culturally appropriate" (1980, p. 384).

## CONCLUSION

In concluding this chapter, we direct the reader's thoughts toward the powerful (and preventive) implications of family life cycle celebration: those rituals, religious or secular, that have been designed by families in every culture to ease the passage of its members from one status to the next. As Friedman (1980) points out, all family relationships in the system seem to unlock during the time just before and after such events, and it is often possible to shift things with less effort during these intensive periods than could ordinarily be expended in years of struggle.

## REFERENCES

Aponte, H. Psychotherapy for the poor: An eco-structural approach to treatment. *Delaware Medical Journal,* 1974, *46,* 15–23.

Aponte, H. Underorganization in the poor family. In P. J. Guerin (Ed.), *Family therapy.* New York: Gardner Press, 1976.

Aries, P. *Centuries of childhood: A social history of family life.* New York: Vintage, 1962.

Bacon, L. Early motherhood, accelerated role transition and social pathologies. *Social Forces,* 1974, *52,* 333–341.

Beal, E. Separation, divorce and single parent families. In E. A. Carter & M. McGoldrick (Eds.), *The family life cycle: A framework for family therapy.* New York: Gardner Press, 1980.

Becker, G. Economics of marital instability. *Journal of Political Economy,* 1977, *85,* 1141–1187.

Bernard, J. *The future of marriage.* New York: Bantam, 1972.

Bowen, M. *Family therapy in clinical practice.* New York: Aronson, 1978.

Bumpass, L., & Sweet, J. Differentials in marital instability, 1970. *American Sociological Review*, 1972, *37*, 754–766.

Burchinal, L. G. Trends and prospects for young marriages in the United States. *Journal of Marriage and the Family*, 1965, *27*, 243–254.

Burke, R. J., & Weir, T. The relationships of wives' employment status to husband, wife and pair satisfaction. *Journal of Marrige and the Family*, 1976, *2*, 279–287.

Campbell, A. The American way of mating: Marriage si, children only maybe. *Psychology Today*, May 1975, pp. 37–43.

Carter, E. A. Transgenerational scripts and nuclear family stress: Theory and clinical implications. In R. R. Sager (Ed.), *Georgetown Family Symposium* (Vol. 3, 1975–1976). Washington, D.C.: Georgetown University, 1978.

Carter, E. A., & McGoldrick, M. (Eds.). *The family life cycle: A framework for family therapy.* New York: Gardner Press, 1980.

Cecchin, G. Personal communication, 1979.

Christensen, H. T. The timing of first pregnancy as a factor in divorce: A cross-cultural analysis. *Eugenics Quarterly*, 1963, *10*, 119–130.

Colon, F. The family life cycle of the multiproblem poor family. In E. A. Carter & M. McGoldrick (Eds.), *The family life cycle: A framework for family therapy.* New York: Gardner Press, 1980.

Duvall, E. M. *Marriage and family development* (5th ed.). Philadelphia: Lippincott, 1977.

Erikson, E. *Childhood and society.* New York: Norton, 1950.

Falicov, C., & Karrer, B. Cultural variations in the family life cycle: The Mexican-American family. In E. A. Carter & M. McGoldrick (Eds.), *The family life cycle: A framework for family therapy.* New York: Gardner Press, 1980.

Ferber, M., & Huber, J. Husbands, wives and careers. *Journal of Marriage and the Family*, 1979, *41*, 315–325.

Friedman, E. Systems and ceremonies: A family view of rites of passage. In E. A. Carter & M. McGoldrick (Eds.), *The family life cycle: A framework for family therapy.* New York: Gardner Press, 1980.

Gelfand, D. E., & Kutzik, A. J. (Eds.). *Ethnicity and aging.* New York: Springer, 1979.

Glick, P., & Norton, A. J. Number, timing and duration of marriages and divorces in the U.S.: June 1975. In *Current Population Reports.* Washington, D.C.: U.S. Government Printing Office, October 1976.

Glick, P., & Norton, A. J. Marrying, divorcing and living together in the U.S. today. In *Population Bulletin*, *32*, No. 5. Washington, D.C.: Population Reference Bureau, 1977.

Gluck, N. R., Dannefer, E., & Milea, K. Women in families. In E. A. Carter & M. McGoldrick (Eds.), *The family life cycle: A framework for family therapy.* New York: Gardner Press, 1980.

Goodrich, D. W., Ryder, R. G., & Raush, H. L. Patterns of newlywed marriage. *Journal of Marriage and the Family*, 1968, *30*, 383–390.

Gould, R. The phases of adult life: A study in developmental psychology. *American Journal of Psychiatry*, 1972, *129*, 33–43.

Hadley, T., Jacob, T., Milliones, J., Caplan, J., & Spitz, D. The relationship between family developmental crises and the appearance of symptoms in a family member. *Family Process*, 1974, *13*, 207–214.

Haley, J. *Uncommon therapy: The psychiatric techniques of Milton H. Erickson.* New York: Norton, 1973.

Harry, J. Evolving sources of happiness for men over the life cycle: A structural analysis. *Journal of Marriage and the Family*, 1976, *2*, 289–296.

Herz, F. The impact of serious illness and death on the family life cycle. In E. A. Carter & M. McGoldrick (Eds.), *The family life cycle: A framework for family therapy.* New York: Gardner Press, 1980.

Hetherington, E. M., Cox, M., & Cox, R. The aftermath of divorce. In J. J. Stevens, Jr., & M. Matthews (Eds.), *Mother-child, father-child relations.* Washington, D.C.: National Association for the Education of Young Children, 1977.

Hill, R. *Family development in three generations.* Cambridge, Mass.: Schenkman, 1970.

Kenniston, K. Psychological development and historical change. *Journal of Interdisciplinary History*, 1971, *2*, 329–345.

Levinson, D. *The seasons of a man's life.* New York: Knopf, 1978.

Lieberman, M. *Adaptational patterns in middle-aged and elderly: The role of ethnicity.* Paper presented at the Gerontological Society Conference, Portland, Ore., October 1974.

McCullough, P. Launching children and moving on. In E. A. Carter & M. McGoldrick (Eds.), *The family life cycle: A framework for family therapy.* New York: Gardner Press, 1980.

McGoldrick, M. The joining of families through marriage: The new couple. In E. A. Carter & M. McGoldrick (Eds.), *The family life cycle: A framework for family therapy.* New York: Gardner Press, 1980.

McGoldrick, M., & Carter, E. A. Forming a remarried family. In E. A. Carter & M. McGoldrick (Eds.), *The family life cycle: A framework for family therapy.* New York: Gardner Press, 1980.

Meyer, P. Between families: The unattached young adult. In E. A. Carter & M. McGoldrick (Eds.), *The family life cycle: A framework for family therapy.* New York: Gardner Press, 1980.

Minuchin, S., & Montalvo, B. Techniques for working with disorganized low socio-economic families. *American Journal of Orthopsychiatry*, 1967, *37*, 248–258.

Mott, F. J., & Moore, S. F. The causes of marital disruption among young American women: An interdisciplinary perspective. *Journal of Marriage and the Family*, 1979, *41*, 355–366.

Orfanidis, M.M. *Some data on death and cancer in schizophrenic families.* Paper presented at Pre-Symposium Meeting of the Georgetown Symposium, Washington, D.C., 1977.

Paul, N., & Grosser, G. Operational mourning and its role in conjoint family therapy. *Community Mental Health Journal*, 1965, *1*, 339–345.

Paul, N., & Paul, B. B. *A marital puzzle.* New York: Norton, 1974.

Pearson, W., & Hendrix, L. Divorce and the status of women. *Journal of Marriage and the Family*, 1979, *41*, 375–386.

Ransom, W., Schlesinger, S., & Derdeyn, A. P. A stepfamily in formation. *American Journal of Orthopsychiatry*, 1979, *49*, 36–43.

Ryder, R. Dimensions of early marriage. *Family Process*, 1970, *9*, 51–68.

Schram, R. W. Marital satisfaction over the family life cycle: A critique and proposal. *Journal of Marriage and the Family*, 1979, *41*, 7–12.

Solomon, M. A developmental conceptual premise for family therapy. *Family Process*, 1973, *12*, 179–188.

Streib, G. Older families and their troubles: Familial and social responses. *The Family Coordinator*, 1972, *21*, 5–19.

Terkelsen, K. G. Toward a theory of the family life cycle. In E. A. Carter & M. McGoldrick (Eds.), *The family life cycle: A framework for family therapy.* New York: Gardner Press, 1980.

Thomas, C. G., & Duszynski, D. R. Closeness to parents and the family constellation in a prospective study of five disease states: Suicide, mental illness, malignant tumor, hypertension, and coronary heart disease. *The Johns Hopkins Medical Journal*, 1974, *134*, 251–270.

Toman, W. *Family constellation* (3rd ed.). New York: Springer, 1976.

Walsh, F. Concurrent grandparent death and the birth of a schizophrenic offspring: An intriguing finding. *Family Process*, 1978, *17*, 457–463.

Walsh, F. The family in later life. In E. A. Carter & M. McGoldrick (Eds.), *The family life cycle: A framework for family therapy.* New York: Gardner Press, 1980.

# 8

# PSYCHOLOGICAL AUTONOMY AND INTERDEPENDENCE WITHIN THE FAMILY

BERTRAM J. COHLER
SCOTT GEYER

Popular discussions of family life in contemporary society have provided a rather bleak characterization of a social institution more fragile and disorganized than it has been in past times. These discussions point to high rates of divorce, increasing rates of voluntary childlessness among otherwise fecund couples, and isolation of the aged from meaningful family ties, in support of a pessimistic view of the future of the family. This portrayal of the family in American society is not very consonant with findings from studies of family relations, which show that high rates of contact and exchange of resources and services across generations are characteristic of family life in our urban society; that high rates of divorce, never modal for first marriages, are on the wane; and that only a small number of fecund couples do elect to remain childless.

The discrepancy between myth and reality in present-day family life reflects a more significant paradox within American society regarding appropriate forms of relationships, particularly among adults, across the generations within the family. While autonomy and independence are valued as the ideal mode of relationship among adults, interdependence and maintenance of "invisible loyalties" (Boszormenyi-Nagy & Spark, 1973) are more characteristic of actual relationships among these family members. In addition to the feelings of obligation attendant to family loyalties, family members also struggle with an inevitable internal conflict between the wish to be

Bertram J. Cohler and Scott Geyer. The Committee on Human Development, The Department of Behavioral Sciences, The University of Chicago, Chicago, Illinois.

cared for and the fear of being overly dependent and thus losing a sense of autonomy. This ambivalent stance towards one's need for others is a lifelong problem and is especially sharply defined in family relations. This continuing relationship among three or even four generations within the family has important implications for socialization and psychological development across generations. The very interdependence that has been reported in a number of studies may, itself, be a source of conflict for family members to an even greater extent than the anomie believed to be characteristic of contemporary urban life.

The present chapter provides a framework for understanding the interplay between psychological and social factors determining socialization within the family, leading to particular solutions for the essential problem of separation and closeness within the family (Cohler & Grunebaum, 1980; Hess & Handel, 1959). It is useful at the outset to distinguish between the development and maintenance of intrapsychic and interpersonal autonomy. While both types of autonomy are involved in the process of separation and individuation, they represent different aspects of development. At the level of analysis of individual family members, this issue is understood as the development of intrapsychic autonomy resulting from the resolution of the issue of separation and individuation in the terms discussed by Mahler and her colleagues (Mahler, Pine, & Bergman, 1975; Panel, 1973a, 1973b, 1973c). With the attainment of object constancy during early childhood, enduring mental representations of sources of comfort and assistance are available; these are sustaining in the physical absence of caretakers and, later, of others with whom intimate relationships are formed. As a result, increased intrapsychic autonomy is achieved from the external environment, which permits a more flexible adaptation (Hartmann, 1939/1958; Jacobson, 1964). However, even when considering optimal development, there may be still an internal tension between the wish to merge with the idealized mother and the fear of engulfment and of the loss of identity (Panel, 1973a).

At the level of analysis of the family as a psychosocial unit, resolution of tensions associated with the problem of remaining interdependent continues as a salient issue from initial stages of family formation during courtship and marriage, through phases of parenting during the preschool and school years, through the "postparental" phase of the family after children are grown and beginning families of their own, and finally to that period of the family life cycle in which adult children assume responsibility for the care of their own aged parents (Grunes, 1980). Earlier socialization of family members, leading to particular solutions regarding the issue of separation–individuation, is related both to prevailing value preferences regarding the desirability of particular modes of interrelationship and to unique historical cohort factors (Elder, 1979) in determining the manner in which the issue of separation and closeness is resolved across the family life cycle.

## SOCIAL CONTEXT OF PSYCHOLOGICAL DEVELOPMENT
## WITHIN THE FAMILY

### The Modified Extended Family

From the perspective of sociological studies of the family across social strata and within diverse subcultures, it is clear that the modal family arrangement in American society is that of a modified extended family in which, while not necessarily sharing a common household, family members live close to each other and exchange not only tangible resources, but also help and assistance (Adams, 1970; Litwak, 1960a, 1960b, 1965). It is part of the American romance with our rural past to believe that urbanization resulted in the destruction of a tightly knit extended family. Available evidence suggests that this form of family organization never really existed in American society (Demos, 1979), and it is possible that this form of family organization never even existed in European society (Laslett, 1977). Critics of urbanization such as Park, Burgess, and McKenzie (1925/1967) and Wirth (1938) had maintained that the diversity of city life tends to dissolve primary group bonds, such as those of the family.

While fostering the individuality which makes possible greater freedom to innovate, both Wirth and Park, Burgess, and McKenzie believed that such creativity was only possible when persons were freed from the constraints imposed by such traditional roles as those among members of the family. Other social theorists (Parsons, 1949) have suggested that the emphasis upon geographic and social mobility in American society is incompatible with the preservation of extended family ties. However, as Haller (1961) notes, the very heterogeneity and diversity of the city makes possible a variety of occupational choices not available in the small town.

Results reported in the studies of Litwak (1960a, 1960b), as well as those reported by Reiss (1962), Leichter and Mitchell (1967), Adams (1968), and Shanas (1961, 1973, 1979), all show that urban life actually helps to draw the family together. Greater population density makes it possible for several generations of the same modified extended family to live in geographic proximity. Mass transit and the automobile make it possible for family members to visit together frequently, and the telephone permits easy communication at any hour of day or night. Indeed, it is interesting to note that in Shanas's (1968) report of contact between members of urban families, fully 62% of older persons in her survey reported living within walking distance of at least one daughter or son.

### Patterns of Intergenerational Contact

Research regarding relations between the generations in American society leads to two particularly important conclusions: (1) There is a greater degree of shared agreement in attitudes and values among working-class than among middle-class families (Fried, 1973; Rosenberg, 1970; Rosenberg & Anspach, 1973; Rubin, 1976; Sussman, 1960), and (2) The single most important source of intrafamily agreement is the mother–daughter tie, which is particularly strong within working-class families (Aldous, 1967; Glick, 1957; Komarovsky, 1962; Townsend, 1957).

Findings supporting these conclusions come from studies of kinship and social organization within working and middle class communities in England and the United States. Young and Wilmott (1957), describing family life in a London housing project, report that 55% of the women interviewed had talked with their own mothers in the past day, as contrasted with 31% of the men who had talked with their fathers in this period of time. In a subsequent report of family life in a London suburb (Wilmott & Young, 1960), it was reported that women in this suburb maintained more frequent contact than did their husbands with parents on either side of the family, but parents are somewhat less frequently seen than among urban families, largely because the generations live farther apart and transportation is more difficult to arrange.

Comparison of these English results with those reported for a California suburb suggests that the extent of intergenerational continuity may be even greater within the American community. The community surveyed by Young and Geertz (1961) was largely middle-class and generally comparable in social background characteristics with the London suburb. Women in both suburban communities visited with their own mothers less than was true for the London housing project, but California women saw their mothers with somewhat greater frequency than did women in the London suburb. In each community, more than 40% of the women interviewed had some daily contact with their own parents, primarily their mothers, either by phone or in person. In each community, less than a quarter of the respondents had contact with their own parents less often than once a month.

The California findings are particularly interesting, since the stereotyped picture of California is of an area with a high degree of geographic mobility, where young adults have infrequent contact with their own parents. Indeed, results of several studies regarding mobility and kinship in American society show that geographic and occupational mobility has a less disruptive influence on relations with own parental family than had previously been believed (Adams, 1968; Haller, 1961; Litwak, 1960a, 1960b; Reiss, 1962). Other findings are similar to those reported for the California community. On the basis of a probability sample of U.S. households, Shanas (1961, 1968) reports that nearly 90% of the older persons in the United States with children had seen at least one of the children within the week preceding the survey. Frequency of contact was somewhat greater between working-class parents and their young adult offspring than it was between middle-class parents and their offspring. However, across all social strata, parents were more likely to have visited with adult daughters than with sons.

Similar results, based on intensive interviews with a group of working-class wives in a northeastern United States community, have been reported by Komarovsky (1962), who notes in addition that frequency of contact is greatest between these working-class women and their own mothers during the first seven years of marriage, declining somewhat in the succeeding years. Since women often regard their own mothers as the first and most important source of child-rearing information, it is probable that presence of young children in these families provides a focal point of communication during the first years after the daughters' marriage and further strengthens the role convergence that is fostered by the daughters' marriage and assumption of the maternal role.

A third study, which bears out the findings of both the California and the northeastern findings as well as the national sample findings, has been reported by Adams (1968), and is based on a group of young adults and their parents in the South. Once more, in the category of face-to-face contact, women reported more frequent contact with their own parental families than with their husbands' families. This contact with own parental families was greater among working-class than among middle-class families; geographic mobility had little effect on frequency of contact. Indeed, Adams reports that, at least for the husbands' parental families, there was a curvilinear relationship, with visits more likely when husbands' own families lived in the same community or at a distance of more than 100 miles than when the husbands' families lived at some intermediate distance.

Consistent with the findings of Litwak (1960a) regarding families in upstate New York, and of Bott (1971) regarding families in England, Adams's study shows that occupational mobility has had little effect on the extent of intergenerational continuity. The only group of persons reporting decreased contact with their own parents were downwardly mobile women. Overall, more than 50% of both husbands and wives had contact with their respective families at least weekly, with a larger number of husbands having their own family living in geographic proximity than has typically been reported.

It is interesting to note that in evaluations of the degree of affection that women feel towards their own mothers, a greater proportion of middle-class than of working-class women reported close affectional bonds, a finding that is consistent with results reported by Firth, Hubert, and Forge (1970) among urban English families. In contrast with most other studies, Adams also reports little difference in the degree of intergenerational value consensus among the families of his study, considering either social status or social mobility. It is also interesting to note that neither expressed feelings of closeness nor value consensus are associated with extent of contact; Adams finds little relationship between feelings towards parents and amount of actual contact with them.

Although adult offspring and their own parents in modified extended families typically live apart, it is not uncommon for the generations to share common residences, particularly during the period just after marriage when young couples have not achieved economic self-sufficiency, or at a later point in the family life cycle when parents of the adult offspring are no longer able to live alone (Smith, 1965; Streib & Thompson, 1955). Nor is it uncommon for parents, adult offspring, and unmarried children of the adult offspring to live together in three-generation residences or households, even when economic self-sufficiency is not an issue (Koller, 1954).

Typically, such living arrangements are "asymmetrical"; the average three-generation family includes parents of the wife rather than those of the husband. Indeed, Sweetser (1966) reports that 60% of young couples living with either set of parents choose to live with the wives' parents. Leichter and Mitchell (1967) report that 93% of the women in their study of extended Jewish families in New York had lived with their own mothers at some time since marriage, and that 54% of these women still lived no farther away from their own mothers than the same building. This finding is consistent with results reported by Smith, Britton, and Britton (1958) that 75% of the young couples in two Pennsylvania communities studied by them had shared a common residence with their own parents for some period of time since marriage.

The literature reviewed by Sweetser (1966) shows that in contemporary American and Western European society, when parents and their adult offspring share common residences or establish common households, these are almost always with the wives' parents. This pattern is also consistent with observations by Fischer and Fischer (1963), based on an ethnographic study of a New England community, that the normative pattern was for adult children to live as near as possible to wives' parents. Even in a case where, as a result of the husband's work, the young couple was forced to move to another community, it was considered desirable to move back to the community of the wife's parents as soon as such a move could be arranged.

## PSYCHOSOCIAL ORIGINS OF KINSHIP ASYMMETRY IN AMERICAN SOCIETY

Within contemporary American society, the generations are much less isolated than has often been claimed for the nuclear family as a structural unit (Ogburn, 1953; Parsons, 1949); individual families of the parental and grandparental generations are linked through the continuing relationships between adult daughters and their own mothers. While such relationships are most striking among working-class families, it is clear that, across social strata, women maintain greater contact than men do with their own parental families. This conclusion obtains even when considering factors such as occupational and geographic mobility and region of the country (Aldous & Hill, 1965; Bernardo, 1967; Farber, 1971; Fried & Stern, 1948; Hagstrom &

Hadden, 1965; Komarovsky, 1962; Leichter & Mitchell, 1967; Reiss, 1962; Robins & Tomanec, 1962; Rubin, 1976); such asymmetry, emphasizing the importance of relations with wives' parental families in spite of the supposed bilaterality of kinship, naturally affects not only patterns of visiting, but the decision regarding which family the young couple will share a household with when the two generations do live together. In the English studies of Wilmott and Young, as well as in studies of American families, a majority of cases in which parents and children share a common residence are those in which mothers come to live with their daughters or in which daughters and their husbands and children come to live with the wives' mothers (Sweetser, 1964, 1966).

Two reasons have generally been advanced in explaining the greater tendency for a family to share a household with the wife's parents than with the husband's parents. In the first place, there is likely to be greater conflict between a woman and her in-laws than between a woman and her own parents. Having lived together for so many years, mothers and daughters typically are more likely to agree on desirable ways of keeping house and raising children—issues that would have to be negotiated from scratch if the residence or household were to be shared with husbands' parents. In the second place, as Komarovsky (1950, 1956), Young and Geertz (1961), and Robins and Tomanec (1962) have shown, the culture itself intensifies the continuing dependence of women on their own families during adulthood, with daughters expected to be more available than sons for family errands, for fulfilling kinship obligations, and for serving as "kin-keepers." Women are socialized from earliest childhood into the roles of caretakers and kin-keepers.

Komarovsky (1950, 1956) suggests that while parents encourage independence from the family among boys, they encourage dependence upon the family among girls. Boys are provided with greater incentive for activities that are independent of the family, and they are permitted greater privacy in personal affairs. Girls are encouraged to run errands and to help other family members, and they are more likely than boys are to be pressured into attending family rituals. Komarovsky suggests that this childhood socialization is functional in training boys and girls in their respective sex roles. This greater sheltering of girls within the home, while it provides socialization into the "domestic" role, may subsequently impair young women's ability to develop more independent lives outside their families, and later to adapt successfully to their roles as wives and mothers.

Both the asymmetry of the American kinship system and socialization into a dependent–expressive role within families make it more difficult for women than for men to relinquish their ties to their own parental families. In addition, continuing attachment to their own parents means that additional conflict is engendered between wives and their husbands' parental families, for couples characteristically choose to spend holidays with the wives' paren-

tal families. Wives typically place kinship obligations toward their own family
above those toward their husbands' families. Wallin (1954) and Gray and
Smith (1960) both report that, among young couples living some distance
away from their own parents, wives were more homesick for their own parents
than husbands were for their parents. Stryker (1955), Kerr (1958), Rainwater,
Coleman, and Handel (1959), Komarovsky (1962), and Rubin (1976) all
report that the typical wife is more attached to her own parental family than to
that of her husband.

The pattern of women's continued dependence on their own parental
families for advice and assistance during the time they are caring for young
children is particularly striking among working-class families (Glick, 1957;
Komarovsky, 1962). Fried (1973), in discussing this greater dependence of
working-class women on their own parental families, suggests that working-
class persons generally value comfort and pleasure in interpersonal relationships to a greater extent than middle-class persons do: enjoyment of interpersonal closeness is more important to them than is technical mastery, an
observation that is consistent with findings reported by Rainwater and
colleagues (Rainwater et al., 1959; Rainwater & Handel, 1964) in their study
of working-class wives, as well as by Aldous (1967) on the basis of results of
a survey study of three-generation families.

Support for this position, which suggests that working-class families are
more conformist and dependent, is also found in a number of interesting
studies of working-class "culture" (Dyer, 1956; Miller & Riessman, 1961;
Paterson, 1964). An explanation for this more conformist, dependent orientation toward the world found among working-class persons has been provided by Kohn (1969), who notes that the critical factor is not social status as
such, but rather the degree of responsibility and judgment required by the
jobs held by most working-class persons. While middle-class occupations
typically demand reliance upon internal standards of excellence and call for
professional competence in making decisions on the basis of judgment rather
than on that of specific directives, working-class occupations typically demand harmony among fellow workers, conformity to externally determined
standards for performance of the job, dependence upon the leadership of
others, and the capacity to follow orders in an exact manner. The same skills
required on the job are carried into the home and govern both interpersonal
relations within the family and parental socialization practices.

## AFFECTIONAL DEPENDENCE AND THE
## DEVELOPMENTAL TASK OF SEPARATION-INDIVIDUATION:
## THE MOTHER-GRANDMOTHER RELATIONSHIP AS AN EXAMPLE

Particularly within working-class families, as previously stated, mothers of
young children are likely to maintain close ties with their own mothers. As

Bott (1971) has noted, social relations within working-class families are typically arranged in such a way that husbands and wives lead quite separate lives. While the husbands' free hours are often spent away from home, typically with friends from work, the wives' social contacts are oriented primarily towards members of their own extended families. As the wives' situation comes increasingly to resemble that of their own mothers, there is increased convergence of attitudes and values and greater role colleagueship (Hagestad, 1974), leading to increased positive feelings between the two generations.

At the same time that such role convergence is perceived by both mothers and daughters (Fischer, 1979), issues of autonomy and control continue to be important as a factor determining the relationship between these two generations of adult women in the family (Abrahams & Varon, 1953; Ackerman & Franklin, 1965; Cohler, 1975; Rheingold, 1964; Vollmer, 1937). Sussman (1953), Boyd (1969), Neisser (1973), and Hammer (1975) all note that the best relationship between the two generations, viewed from the adult daughters' perspective, is that in which the grandparental generation is willing to provide help and assistance when requested, while recognizing the need of the young adult generation for autonomy and independence. Issues of autonomy are also important from the grandmothers' perspective. Having "launched" their children into marriage, careers, and parenthood, these middle-aged women look forward to decreased responsibility for child care (Deutscher, 1964; Hill & Rodgers, 1964; Lowenthal & Chiriboga, 1972; Neugarten, 1970; Robertson, 1977; Rosow, 1967; Spence & Lonner, 1971; Wood & Robertson, 1970, 1976).

Particularly within working-class families, where daughters have been socialized since childhood into the roles of caretakers and kin-keepers, their middle-aged mothers' newly expressed desire for increased freedom from such "person-oriented" activities is often a source of great disappointment. While daughters ordinarily do not expect their mothers to be their children's primary caretakers, the anxiety that many new mothers report upon the assumption of this previously unrehearsed role compels them to call upon their own mothers for help and advice, particularly during the first weeks after returning home from the hospital.[1] At a time in their own lives when the new mothers feel most in need of assistance, their own mothers have become increasingly concerned with their own privacy and with the need for increased time for personal pursuits (Cohler & Grunebaum, 1981; Cohler &

[1]This emphasis upon self-reliance among mothers of young children has sometimes been mistaken to mean that the mother is isolated from extended family ties in ways that are not true among families in traditional societies. It is not so much true that a mother is isolated from her extended family as it is expected that she will not depend upon her own mother's help and assistance for extended periods of time. Even where, as is quite usual, mother and grandmother live in geographic proximity, it is still the case that the mother is expected to provide the care for her own children.

Lieberman, 1980). Should a daughter object to her mother's demand that she be more independent, or should she ignore the mother's stated wish not to assume greater responsibility for the grandchild's care, serious conflict may arise between the generations. In such a situation, the middle-aged mother may withdraw from her previously close relationship with her daughter; or, as a result of her own ambivalent feelings, she may first attempt to provide the nurturant care that her daughter seeks and then, feeling pressured and resentful, suddenly become angry and explosive in her criticism of her daughter. The daughter, in her turn, may become frustrated, disappointed, confused, and angry over her mother's unpredictable responses to her request for help and assistance.

## The Development of Affectional Dependence

The conflicting expectations of middle-aged mothers and their adult daughters shows the importance, in studying intergenerational relations, of considering not only the amount of intergenerational contact, but also the psychological significance of this contact for each generation. In this particular situation, it is necessary to consider the ambivalent and highly charged feelings of both middle-aged mothers and their young adult daughters about their complex continuing relationship.

Conflict over the issues of dependency and mutual obligations between adults and their own parents is one of the most important of the interpersonal conflicts that adults in our society confront (Freud, 1905/1953). It is generally expected that adults in this society will strive to become autonomous and self-reliant, remaining independent of their own parents and expressing little continuing need for their own parents' assistance and affection (Kluckhohn & Strodtbeck, 1961; Papajohn & Spiegel, 1975; Spiegel, 1971). This Western pattern is in striking contrast with traditional Japanese society, where, as a number of observers have reported, it is expected that adults will permit themselves to become dependent upon others and permit others to become dependent upon them (Caudill & Doi, 1963; Doi, 1962, 1963, 1973; Vogel & Vogel, 1961). In the Japanese family, closeness between family members is emphasized to such an extent that members of several generations may sleep together in one common room, even when alternative arrangements are possible (Caudill & Plath, 1969). The expression of this wish to remain dependent upon another causes such discomfort among American families that, as Boszormenyi-Nagy and Spark (1973) observe, helping family members to remain interdependent and to acknowledge this interdependence is perhaps *the* central issue in family treatment.

Such striking cultural differences in the manner in which family members deal with this issue of interdependence raises the question of the origins of this conflict regarding dependency in our society. The single most important determinant of this conflict is the manipulation of children's wish to remain dependent and to obtain affection as a way of producing socially desirable behavior in them. Writing from the perspective of social learning theory, Jones and Gerard (1967) distinguish between "effect dependency"— represented by children's ties to their caretakers, which function to motivate performance in accordance with a specified standard by using the children's need for love or care as a resource that can be withheld until the desirable behavior is elicited—and "information dependency," or children's reliance upon others for information about the real world around them.

Using a psychoanalytic perspective, Parens and Saul (1971) draw a similar distinction between "libidinal dependence," or "affectional dependence," and "ego-developmental dependence," or "informational dependence." While informational or ego-developmental dependence contributes to the child's developing mastery over reality, libidinal or affective dependence represents the child's need for emotional support, protection, and care. As is true of Jones and Gerard's formulation, this distinction between the two kinds of dependency recognizes that each form influences the other. However, libidinal or affectional dependency serves primarily the function of "emotional refueling" as described by Pine and Furer (1963) and Mahler, Pine, and Bergman (1975), enhancing feelings of safety, security, and support.

Although this process has been described most clearly within the more narrowly defined context of the mother–infant relationship, ties based on affectional dependence, with the goal of obtaining emotional security, continue throughout the life cycle (Freud, 1965; Bowlby, 1970/1979). For example, in considering the problems involved in intergenerational relations among adults, Goldfarb (1965) distinguishes between what he terms "type-1" socialization, which "produced" rationally nondependent adults able to distinguish between the need for information contributing to further ego development and to the emotional refueling characteristic of affectional dependence, and "type-2" socialization, which produces adults who are dependent and who maintain ambivalent, symbiotic relationships with others, even if masked by a showy pseudoindependence.

According to Goldfarb, the dependent person, the product of type-2 socialization, spends much time and effort searching for emotional refueling as a response to feelings of helplessness. The need for affectional dependence becomes a central motive, leading to the use of informational dependence as a way of initiating and perpetuating dependency relationships that were appropriate during childhood but that, at least in our culture, are considered inappropriate among adults. The expected relationship between a young adult couple and their parents is that in which the young couple maintains some friendly contact, with occasional visits and more frequent phone calls and letters, and in which financial assistance is provided at times of family emergency. In additon, a young adult woman with one or more children may rely upon her mother for limited advice regarding housekeeping and child care (informational or ego-developmental dependence) but is not expected to depend on her for emotional refueling (effect or affectional dependence). Yet findings reviewed in this chapter, based on empirical study of groups of mothers and adult daughters from different social strata and different regions of the country, do not correspond with this norm. In fact, most studies point to the interdependent tie that is maintained between young adults and their own parents.

Goldfarb also notes that intergenerational ties based on shared dependency are much more common than those based on "rational, affectionate fulfillment of generational roles." In contrast to the ideal intergenerational relationship emphasizing self-reliance, intergenerational relations among adults and their own parents in our society are most often characterized by the demand, particularly on the part of the younger generation, for the perpetuation of interdependence through the continuing use of affectional dependence, which serves important needs and yet which evokes great discomfort for members of each generation (Boszormenyi-Nagy & Spark, 1973). The developmental line of separation–individuation may be used not only in describing the developing relationship between a mother and her young child, but in describing the relationship between parents and offspring across the entire life cycle (Mahler, 1972a; Panel, 1973a, 1973b, 1973c).

## SEPARATION-INDIVIDUATION AND THE DEVELOPMENT OF PSYCHOSOCIAL DIFFERENTIATION: IMPLICATIONS FOR INTERGENERATIONAL RELATIONS

At birth, an infant's tie to the mother is governed almost entirely by biological factors in both mother and infant (Bowlby, 1969, 1973, 1980). Through socialization, this bond of attachment shifts from a purely biological attachment to emotional dependence upon the mother. The mother–infant tie represents a child's first and most enduring human relationship (Ainsworth, 1964, 1969, 1973; Ainsworth, Blehar, Waters, & Wall, 1978). Children who cannot develop this attachment never achieve the capacity for closeness and remain unable to allow others to become involved in their care, a deficit which leads to the profound intellectual and emotional retardation known as autism (Bettelheim, 1967).

### The Paradigm of Separation-Individuation

Among adults in our culture, while there may continue to be conflict in the development of the capacity for closeness or intimacy, it is more likely that the initial attachment has been formed. Adults often find it difficult to resolve issues associated with the continuing need for affectional dependence, or to attain a "mature dependence" in which one's own needs are clearly differentiated from those of others, based on a mutuality among persons appreciated for their own unique qualities (Fairbairn, 1941/1952, 1951/1952). Attaining "mature dependence" in interpersonal relationships is always a matter of degree. From the psychoanalytic perspective, the ability to view others objectively is directly influenced by the degree of individually expressed needs. If others are *necessary* in order to regulate self-esteem or to provide a sense of purpose, then the degree of need is very high and likely to cause distortion in perceptions of others (Pollock, 1964). Angel (1972), using the term "mature object constancy," describes a state in which "the object is loved, valued, and cared for even under prolonged frustration, i.e., need fulfillment has more or less ceased" (p. 543). Such maturity is thought to be achieved late in life or even not at all. Adult relations can be characterized as more or less reliant upon this need for immediate mutual gratification.

It is clear from the findings reported here that interdependence rather than total independence characterizes these family relationships, and that adults must be able to feel comfortable depending upon others for support and assistance. Some balance must be struck between the attainment of appropriate autonomy and the continuing need that all adults have for help from others, including such important family members as adults' own parents or, as a result of aging, adult offspring. Fleming (cited in Panel, 1973c) has commented on the need for role flexibility in the process of separation–individuation across the life cycle. She asserts that this process is not complete unless both adult offspring and their aging parents can permit a reversal of the direction of the early symbiotic relationship. Boszormenyi-Nagy and Spark (1973) point out that such alterations do not mean simply becoming a parent to one's own parents. Rather, having become mature adults, these offspring have the capacity to fulfill their filial obligations in a new way.

Kohut (1977) and Kohut and Wolf (1978) suggest that adults across the life cycle continue to make use of the attributes of others, perceived as psychological functions of the self, or "self-objects," which have the power to be sustaining during times of crisis and conflict. Modes of tension regulation, based on care initially provided by the mother during the first years of life but perceived by the young child as a part of self, remain as a source of self-soothing throughout life. If initial modes of tension regulation have not successfully provided such soothing, regardless of whether the failure was due to problems in mothering or in the child's experience of mothering, a deficit may develop in this capacity for regulating tension; it appears in adulthood as the lack of the ability to provide self-soothing and to use comforting provided by others successfully in the service of tension regulation. Such adults show problems in successfully maintaining intrapsychic autonomy, together with conflict in resolving issues of dependence and independence or separation and individuation.

The most clearly articulated discussion of the developmental line of dependence to independence (Freud, 1965) has been provided by Mahler and her colleagues (Mahler, 1972a, 1972b; Mahler, Pine, & Bergman, 1975). Her work, based on careful longitudinal study of groups of both psychotic and well children and their mothers over about the first 3½ years of life, suggests that development from infantile dependence to mature dependence or psychological individuation is always problematic and, as Mahler (1972a) has noted, has implications for intrapsychic development across the life cycle (Panel, 1973a, 1973b, 1973c).[2] For example, Blos (1967, 1972) suggests that adolescence represents a second phase of individuation. Not since early childhood has the person been so vulnerable to disorganization or so vulnerable in terms of conflicts in self–other differentiation. This process takes place on both intrapsychic and interpersonal levels. The former involves a gradual modification of childhood images of parents as omnipotent beings, together with growing stability in self and object representations. "These structural changes establish constancy of self-esteem and of mood as increasingly independent from external sources, or at best, dependent on the external sources of one's own choosing" (Blos, 1972, p. 163). Adolescents gain intrapsychic autonomy both by freeing themselves from internal dominance by representations of their parents and by learning that they can choose rather than feel compelled to rely on others.

From the interpersonal perspective, the issue of attaining appropriate autonomy from one's parents and establishing comfortable interdependence remains a central issue across adolescence and adulthood (Bowen, 1978). Much of the adolescent's vacillation and apparently contradictory actions—one day helplessness and dependence, but independence and even defiance the next—can be understood in terms of this struggle for individuation from the family. The fluidity of ego processes in adolescence—the frequent regression to forms of behavior more characteristic of childhood, and the paradoxical wish to be both a child and an adult at the same time—intensifies the conflict that the adolescent feels in the search for differentiation from the family.

### Separation–Individuation in Adulthood

Among adolescent girls, difficulties in achieving individuation are particularly pronounced. Having been socialized into a dependent role as mother's helper, a daughter is now expected to go out into the world, find herself a

---

[2]Although we have stressed the extent to which there is continuity across the life cycle in dealing with the issue of separation–individuation, we must also recognize that this approach emphasizes continuities in socialization, rather than possible discontinuities. Further, we must not assume that the meaning of separation and the desire for reunification with the lost person are necessarily the same for the 2-year-old searching for the mother whom he or she lost sight of while absorbed in play, and the middle-aged mother whose own mother has recently died. Changes in the context in which this issue appears are such that there may be little direct continuity in reactions to the issue of separation from childhood through adulthood and middle and old age.

spouse, and establish her own family. Mothers watch this struggle for greater differentiation among their adolescent and young adult daughters with particularly mixed feelings, especially when they are not satisfied with their own lives. Much of the concern that mothers express about the apparent preoccupation of their adolescent daughters with sexuality represents a projection of maternal wishes and fears (Cohler, 1977). In addition, within many families, just as the daughter is beginning to date, the mother may be encountering menopause, which many women experience as indicating diminishing sexual attractiveness and capacity for sexual enjoyment. As Anthony (1970) observes, this unfortunate timing of the mother's menopause only increases her envy of her daughter's increasing psychological differentiation and, as a result of the mother's use of projection, may lead the mother to overcontrol her daughter's activities outside the home.[3]

While attainment of young adult status may mark the resolution of the adolescent crisis of individuation, more often this conflict between separation and interdependence continues into adulthood. All too often, both parents and offspring see few alternatives other than rigid independence or continued dependence. At least within middle-class families, there are institutional supports that facilitate a gradual individuation process. Typically, entrance into college follows upon graduation from high school, and this represents a break with adolescence. Although parents may maintain their young adult offspring's rooms for occasional visits home, there is a gradual decrease in such visits during the college years as the young people make new friends and develop more autonomous lives. Murphey, Silber, Coelho, Hamburg, and Greenberg (1963) have reported that the parents of college students most capable of such autonomous relationships were themselves better able to differentiate between their own needs and those of their children, and had succeeded to a greater extent than parents of nonautonomous young adults in fostering individuation appropriate to the young adults' own needs. Sullivan and Sullivan (1980), comparing groups of male college students residing at home and at college, report that those living away perceive communication with their parents to be better as a result of living independently, and they feel increased affection for their parents. For boys living away at college, parents—in particular, mothers—also report increased

[3]When conflict regarding separation and individuation has been prevalent throughout the daughter's childhood socialization, the conflict between mother and daughter regarding this second individuation of adolescence may be so pervasive that they become involved in a *folie à deux* (Anthony, 1971), sharing common psychiatric symptoms and describing common delusions and hallucinations. Similar dynamics have been shown to exist in the development of anorexia nervosa, in which, as a result of basic confusion regarding bodily signals due to the daughter's difficulty in her perception of herself as separate from her mother, the adolescent girl loses her appetite and becomes emaciated (Ehrensing & Weitzman, 1970; Bruch, 1973; Palazzoli, 1971; Cohler, 1977; Thompson, 1980).

feelings of affection. As was true in the earlier study of Murphey and his colleagues, the capacity to resolve the adolescent separation–individuation conflict leads to more satisfying and mature relationships among young adults and their parents, with each generation showing increased satisfaction with the relationship as a result of this appropriate resolution.

Within working-class families, there is often no such institutional support as college in fostering individuation, making it somewhat more difficult to realize a more comfortable and appropriate mode of interdependence. Particularly in the case of young adult daughters, it is common for the daughter to live at home while working and preparing for marriage. Studies of family relations among working-class young adults and their parents show that fully 40% of young adults and their spouses share their parents' home for some period of time following marriage (Cohler & Grunebaum, 1981). Ultimately, most couples do establish a separate household; even if this new household is just down the street, there may at least be some recognition given to the belief that the young adult couple should have a separate life. The extent to which this separation can be negotiated in a manner that is satisfying for both the parental and young adult generation depends upon the life experiences both of their parents and of the young people themselves, including the capacity of members of each generation to achieve individuation, which includes awareness of the importance of "interdependent" ties in adulthood.

In a series of studies, Stierlin (1973, 1974) and Stierlin and his colleagues (Stierlin, Levi, & Savard, 1971, 1973; Stierlin & Ravenscroft, 1972) have described the process by which young adults and their own middle-aged parents negotiate this issue of individuation. Stierlin views the developmental task of separation and individuation during late adolescence and early adulthood as that of establishing mature relations between the generations; successful resolution of this task is contrasted with uncompleted or immature outcomes. An immature resolution leads either to "centripetal separation," in which the young person views the world as dangerous and less capable than the parental family of satisfying basic needs, or to a "centrifugal separation," in which the young person is pushed out of the family by virtue of the lack of commitment among family members to the stability of the family unit itself.

According to Stierlin and Ravenscroft (1972), the centripetal pattern of separation has the effect of binding the young person to the family. The young person, in turn, becomes overly dependent on the parents who, while continuing to infantilize their young adult child, also feel resentful about the limitations that the continuing relationship places on their own autonomy. Feelings of ambivalence and guilt characterize both generations in this separation pattern. The centrifugal separation pattern involves either delegation (sending the young person out into the world while fostering a feeling of obligation to the family) or expulsion (sending the young person out into the world at a fixed time, largely in order to relieve intrafamilial conflicts regarding available emotional and/or financial resources).

Delegation as a separation pattern may lead to particularly intense conflict between young adults and their parents. Young persons serving as delegates of their parental families feel a conflict between commitment to their own parents and to their in-laws. To the extent to which parents send young persons out as delegates of their own needs, hoping to achieve "vicarious gratification" through the offspring, the young adults fail to achieve autonomy and remain family captives (Giovacchini, 1970; Shapiro, 1972). The young persons' attempts to become autonomous are compromised, because the meaning of actions is misappropriated by the family and emphasizes the sameness of parents and children rather than their individuality.

Continued conflict between young adults and their own parents regarding the issue of separation–individuation is generally a result of the ambivalent feelings of members of each generation about this issue. Nowhere is this perspective better demonstrated than in Sampson, Messinger, and Towne's analysis (1964) of extended interview data from a group of women hospitalized for mental illness during the first few years after becoming mothers. These authors differentiate women whose hospitalization appeared most closely associated with the fear of becoming like their own mothers ("crisis of identification") from women whose hospitalization appeared most closely associated with disruptions in their efforts to maintain their mothers' continuing help and support ("crisis of separation"). Unable to sustain affection over time, and feeling depleted as a result of the demands imposed upon them from having to care for babies, these women needed to return home at frequent intervals to obtain "emotional refueling" (Pine & Furer, 1963). Centripetal binding to their mothers was reflected in the ambivalent relationship between the generations. Hospitalization for psychiatric illness was most often a direct consequence of the loss of the mother through the death or of a family move in which the two generations were forced to live apart from each other without the daily contact so important for each. Abrahams and Varon (1953) and Lyketsos (1959) have also reported that issues of closeness and separation between mentally ill women and their own mothers played an important role in the exacerbation of the illnesses and in the most immediate hospitalizations.

While this crisis of separation has been described in greatest detail among families in which the young adult offspring has been hospitalized for psychiatric illness, this crisis of separation may also be observed among women in the community who have not developed serious psychiatric impairment. Continuing ambivalence between adult offspring and their parents, together with problems in being able to obtain satisfaction from adult family relationships, continues as a major problem in contemporary American society. Adults within each generation are often unable to acknowledge their desire for comfort in an interdependent relationship with other family members. This wish for interdependence is often viewed as inconsistent with the values placed upon individual achievement in contemporary society. Particularly among working-class urban families, in which intergenerational ties have traditionally been of importance in such diverse aspects of family life as job opportunities and emotional support, stereotyped reliance upon such autonomous modes of interpersonal relationships may actually increase problems in resolving this issue of interdependence, intensifying the crisis of separation for each generation.[4]

Problems in obtaining satisfying interdependence among members of families may be further exacerbated as a result of the prevalent belief among many mental health professionals that personal individuation in adulthood must necessarily mean renouncing the comfortable interdependence and use of others as a means of support and soothing that appears to be so essential for continued personal adustment across adulthood. Boszormenyi-Nagy and Spark (1973) point out that often the amount of guilt experienced by young people after a highly ambivalent move away from the family erodes the benefits of a physical separation. Since guilt undermines the feeling of autonomy, increasing the need to make reparation, an abrupt departure may do more harm than good; actual living arrangements play little specific role in the ability of a family to relate as an interdependent unit.

## IMPLICATIONS FOR INTERVENTION

The paradox between culturally determined values stressing individual achievement and the reality of the continued interdependence of the modified extended family in contemporary urban society causes conflict within the family as a whole; this conflict is intensified among those families in which there is some crisis, such as the hospitalization of a family member as a result of a psychiatric disturbance. For example, hospitalization of mothers of young children may pose problems both for the patients themselves and for their multigenerational family units (Grunebaum, Weiss, Cohler, Hartman, & Gallant, 1975). A mentally ill mother may feel intense guilt about what she

---

[4]An interesting contrast with this dilemma characteristic of American families regarding family interdependence and adult psychological development has been provided by Rudolph and Rudolph (1976/1978). In their discussion of the diary of a Rajput nobleman (circa 1900) living in a complex patrilineal family system, the Rudolphs show that psychological autonomy in adulthood was actually enhanced by the extended family system of Indian society. The corporate family identity supported Amar Singh's efforts in realizing his own achievement goals as an adult within his society. This interpretation of Indian society is supported by Kakar's discussion (1978) of interdependence within the Indian family in the context of a culture that, as expressed through the Hindu world view, stresses relations and connections both in time and in space. Interdependence among adults in the Hindu family is the realization of this world view in interpersonal relations.

believes to be her abdication of the roles of housewife, wife, and mother. She is frightened both of her wish for her mother to assume the duties of housework and child care and of the destructive merger that might result from this increased dependence upon her mother. As a result of her use of projective identification (Jaffe, 1968; Ogden, 1979; Meissner, 1980), the mentally ill mother often develops delusions of persecution so well described by Burnham (1969) as the "need–fear dilemma."

Feelings of guilt, resentment, anger, and fear further adversely affect the relationship between the mother hospitalized for psychiatric illness and both her husband and her own parents. For the husband–father, the very fact of his wife's hospitalization means increased conflict between his responsibilities at work, caring for the children, and visiting his wife in the hospital (Schuerman, 1972). Further, as a result of the asymmetry within the family, he must now perform the "kin-keeping" duties formerly assumed by his wife. Often, in order to manage his many responsibilities, the husband–father calls upon his own parents or his wife's parents for help. If it is his wife's parents who provide the majority of the assistance, there may be a particularly serious problem, since the tension which usually exists within our society between in-laws is compounded by the complex feelings of his wife's parents about their daughter's illness and hospitalization.

Particularly for the wife's own mother, her daughter's hospitalization leads to feelings of guilt arising from her belief that her own parenting must have been in some respect inadequate, contributing to the development of her daughter's disturbance. Such feelings of guilt may be compounded by the daughter's socialization into the patient role during hospitalization, including views inculcated by mental health professionals that events earlier in her life actually did contribute to her later illness. Problems in the relationship between the mentally ill daughter and her own mother may be further compounded by the daughter's intense feelings of guilt about the burden her illness has placed upon her mother; this guilt itself may be defended by additional projective identification, leading to additionally hostile interchanges between the daughter and her parents.

For the grandmother, feelings of guilt are often mixed with feelings of anger and resentment as she attempts to maintain two households and to care for her grandchildren during her daughter's hospitalization. This responsibility upsets the grandmother's own domestic responsibilities and her own outside obligations and interests. Indeed, her daughter's hospitalization may even affect the grandmother's relationship with her own elderly parents, who, in turn, may be critical of the grandmother for raising a daughter who has required psychiatric hospitalization. The daughter's hospitalization further intensifies the grandmother's own ambivalence towards baby-sitting and other household chores which, as Cohler and Grunebaum (1981) and Cohler and Lieberman (1980) have shown, is characteristic of middle-aged and older mothers in their relationship with their young adult offspring. If,

as is so often the case, there have been multiple hospitalizations, the grandmother and other relatives become increasingly resentful, while the recurrently disturbed daughter becomes also increasingly despairing of any change
in her adaptation.

The daughter's hospitalization in such a family represents the outcome
of a complex process both within and across generations, in which there is a
systematic interplay between aspects both of the patient's relationship with
her own parents and of her relationship with her husband and children
(Meissner, 1978). Hospitalization may symbolize complex and enduring
aspects of the relationship between the daughter and her parents; these may
include an expression of the grandmother's own needs, as well as the young
mother's attempt to involve both her husband and her own parents more
directly in her life. Haley (1967) has described this multigeneration pattern as
a "perverse triangle" (p. 16), in which various coalitions between two members of the triangle are established against the third. Haley notes that a large
number of such triangles are possible within the family. While a coalition
may be "adaptive" in terms of the needs of each participant, such as the
interdependent relationship between mother and daughter or between husband and wife, exclusion of the third member of the triangle may have
disruptive effects within the larger family unit (Bowen, 1978).

Particularly within those multigeneration families in which there is a
continuing tie between the wife–mother and her own mother, this tie has the
often unintended consequence of excluding the husband–father. Consistent
with Bott's formulation (1971) of the impact of intense intergenerational
family ties on the marital relationship, fathers in such families may understand their own roles in particularly instrumental terms. When the wife–
mother is hospitalized, the husband–father feels even more excluded from
his relationship with his wife. His relative lack of involvement with his wife's
mother and his wife's extended family makes it additionally difficult for him
to ask for help with housework and child care, while his understanding of his
role as father in particularly instrumental terms makes it difficult to provide
the kind of help that is possible among those families in which the husband
and wife have more involvement in the marital family, including less explicit
division of labor within the family.

As coping resources are "used up" with the family, the husband gradually
renounces efforts at preserving the family as a marital and child-rearing unit
(Dunigan, 1969), while the grandmother and other family members become
increasingly reluctant to assume a burden that grows in magnitude over
time. Wishes and fears become intensified and are expressed increasingly
through projective identifications with the mentally ill young adult offspring,
in which anger erupts in an ever less controlled manner. Finally, the family
unit implodes upon itself; children are placed in foster care, while the husband–father becomes so depressed that separation and divorce become the
only viable alternatives (Grunebaum, Gamer, & Cohler, in press).

Intervention within these families in which the wife–mother is recurrently hospitalized for a psychiatric disturbance is always difficult. Both the nature of the patient's own difficulties and the contribution of both intergenerational and family dynamics must be simultaneously considered (Musick, Cohler, & Stott, 1981). When the family conflict has reached the point at which the husband–father begins to withdraw, intervention within the family unit becomes particularly complex. Grunebaum *et al.* (in press) report that the father's continued involvement in child care is essential for the children's own subsequent adjustment. Provision of homemaker services, family treatment designed to foster increased understanding of conflicts within the multigenerational and marital families on the part of all family members, and particular support for the husband–father in his attempt to care for the children during hospitalization are important aspects of the treatment process. If long-standing coalitions within the larger family unit can be highlighted, and if, in addition, the husband–father can be helped to gain increased understanding of his own role within the family, together with his contribution to the present crisis, there is some hope that an alternative to divorce and dissolution of the family unit can be achieved.

The recurrent hospitalizations that are so characteristic within these families in which the young adult mother has become mentally ill are often responses to the conflict that erupts within the family during the course of the mother's illness from hospitalization to discharge. While men discharged from psychiatric hospitals have at least the option of leaving home and going to work, the discharged mentally ill mother remains enmeshed in an increasingly painful set of domestic relationships. The contact that has already been shown to characterize relationships between the two generations of young adult women and their own middle-aged and older mothers means that the women in the two generations will remain involved with each other on a daily basis. Studies by Brown (1959) and his colleagues (Brown, Carstairs, & Topping, 1958; Brown, Monck, Carstairs, & Wing, 1962; Brown & Rutter, 1966; Brown, Birley, & Wing, 1972) have shown that recently discharged psychiatric patients living with their own families are more likely to be rehospitalized than are patients living independently, even former patients living in isolated lodgings such as rooming houses. The single most critical factor linking hospitalization with continued residence in the parental family is not merely the nature of the expectations of other families regarding instrumental performance, as was earlier suggested by Freeman and Simmons (1963), but the intensity of the feelings expressed within the family, or the level of "emotional expressiveness." It is the continued intense expression of ambivalent feelings that so adversely affects such a patient's adjustment during the first critical year after discharge from the hospital.

Brown's findings have been based on groups of chronic schizophrenic men and need to be replicated among women, but the conclusions drawn from his studies suggest that women are even more "at risk" for rehospitalization than the men. Indeed, there is no group of women so much "at risk" in terms of the dimension of emotional expressiveness as the mother of young children who is at home with her children and her mother on a daily basis and who, as a result of the continuing relationship between the generations, has particularly intense and continuing opportunity for precisely those sorts of interactions that Brown and his colleagues have shown to be most insidious in terms of later outcome among schizophrenic patients.

In sum, the extensive interaction between young mothers and their own mothers that is characteristic of contemporary society becomes particularly problematic among these poorly adjusting former mental patients. Relations between these mothers and their mentally ill daughters are typically intensely ambivalent; repeated contact without substantial improvement may create an environment for the newly discharged patient that hastens rehospitalization. Intervention efforts must be directed towards increased understanding among both mothers of young children and their own mothers of this problem, and must provide both support for the formerly hospitalized mother during the first important year of readjustment after hospitalization, and support for the mother and grandmother as they continue to negotiate their important but often difficult relationship (Musick *et al.*, 1981).

## CONCLUSION

In contrast to the prevailing stereotype of distant intergenerational relations in contemporary American society, there is considerable contact between young adults and their own parental families. While, from an analytic-structural perspective, the nuclear family is isolated from the larger kinship group, from the perspective of actual relationships among family members, exchange of resources and provision of continuing assistance across generations is far more common than has often been realized.

It is not at all clear that successful adaptation to urban life demands the creation of a highly mobile and self-contained nuclear family unit. On the contrary, the very diversity of the city makes possible the availability of a large number of jobs and prevents the necessity of moving far away from the parental family to another location in order to find work. In addition, there is considerable evidence that the modified extended family continues as an important resource in finding employment for its members. In spite of the norm in bureaucratic–technological society that individuals' achievements count for more than their family connections, family life promotes particular avenues of achievement, which are then useful in providing employment.

While there is considerable evidence to support the extensive contact between the generations in American families, it is not clear that such contact necessarily leads to more harmonious or mutually satisfying relations within the family. In the first place, there is much evidence that the American family is asymmetrical and that the norm is for a daughter and her husband and children to live in geographical proximity to her own family. In addition, because the wife—mother does much of the family planning for holidays and vacations, it is likely that husband, wife, and children will visit with the wife's extended family rather than with that of her husband. However, this asymmetry can sometimes cause marital conflict, with the husband feeling split between his allegiance to his in-laws and his own parents.

Even when the asymmetry of the family does not lead to conflict between husband and wife, the extensive contact between a woman and her own mother that characterizes relations within the generations may lead to tension within the family. Contrary to the popular stereotype, grandmothers seldom feel abandoned by their children and grandchildren. Having raised their own children, grandmothers look forward to the greater autonomy that is permitted by the postparental years and do not welcome demands that they provide baby-sitting or that they be available to have their grandchildren live with them for extended periods of time while the parents take a vacation.

Mothers are often quite disappointed that their own mothers do not provide greater help with housework and child care, and they are surprised and confused when their requests for assistance are rebuffed. Dependency is not a psychological issue that is comfortably resolved in American society, in contrast with societies like Japan, which encourage the continued dependence of adult children on their own parents; an American daughter's expression of dependency needs often evokes psychological discomfort for both mother and grandmother. At the same time, young married women, faced with problems in learning to meet the challenges associated with the assumption of the parental role, typically turn to their own mothers for help.

Contemporary society first advocates young children's development of dependency upon their parents and then encourages the manipulation of this dependency relationship as the basic instrument of preadult socialization. It is expected that young adults will be able to forego such dependency relations, relying instead upon reciprocity and mutual obligation as the basis for interpersonal relations. However, theories of socialization and a variety of clinical and empirical studies show that, once learned, this dependence upon others endures across the life cycle as the paradigm for subsequent interpersonal relations and can provide the basis for enjoying satisfying relationships in adulthood. Relationships based on dependency are particularly characteristic of working-class women, who are socialized from childhood into the domestic role. It is the little girl who is discouraged from showing independence from the family or from assuming the role of the competent worker.

Having first fostered the dependence of the little girl upon her mother and established that the rightful place of the girl is in the kitchen, learning her mother's techniques of cooking and housekeeping, society then demands that this dependence of the young girl upon her mother be surrendered and replaced by self-reliance during the first years after marriage, when, with little prior preparation, the young woman is expected to run her own household, perform the role of wife, and care for her own dependent children. Particularly within working-class families, the conflict between cultural valuing of autonomous achievement and the reality of socialization, which stresses continuing dependence of young adults and their parents, has important consequences for the continuing adult relationship between the generations. Further, as a result of the very powerful effects of socialization into the dependent role during early childhood, together with the unique conflicts faced by young married women and their middle-aged mothers, this conflict is transmitted to the young mothers' own daughters with particularly great force echoing across the generations. While Chodorow (1978) has suggested that this socialization pattern could be altered if fathers were to take a primary role in raising their young children, Gutmann (1975) has noted that the fact of becoming a parent has a particular imperative that leads to definitions of the parental roles along more sex-stereotyped lines than at any other point in the life cycle.

At least to some extent, problems in achieving a sense of comfort or ease, both in providing and in accepting care from other family members, is an issue that is central for both men and women within the contemporary family. Issues in recognizing enduring ties among family members, as well as conflicts in achieving flexible but appropriate differentiation, are also important for both men and women (Bowen, 1978). In the present discussion, this issue of interdependence has been considered particularly in terms of women because of the centrality of this issue for women within each generation in the family. As a result of continuing socialization across the life course, women remain more interdependent with their relatives than men do. Beginning with childhood socialization into interdependence and kin-keeping, and continuing through expanding reciprocal relationships with relatives in adulthood, present social ties with relatives enhance early learned psychological interdependence. This involvement with relatives also fosters kinship asymmetry, as a result of which ties to wives' families are likely to take precedence over those to husbands' families. As Fischer and Fischer (1963) have noted, when there is an option, the norm among American families is to move as close as possible to the wives' families.

Much less is known about relations of men within the family than about those of women. Findings reviewed in this chapter suggest that the husband–father is rather less involved with relatives than is characteristic for the wife–mother. As a result of lifelong socialization into interdependence among women and into self-reliance and independence among men (Chodorow, 1978; Komarovsky, 1950), together with the impact of parenthood in creating stereotyped definitions of sex roles (Gutmann, 1975), men become involved principally in the world outside the family, while women become involved principally in the tasks of child care and kin-keeping. Even in the large number of families in which husband and wife both work, this division of labor within the family is maintained. Such role differentiation and accompanying asymmetry appears particularly characteristic of working-class families.

Even within middle-class families, men appear to be much less involved than women are in relations with the larger family unit. Study of exchange of particular forms of influence, such as those concerning life styles, values, child rearing, or choice of friends among both men and women, within three-generation middle-class families has shown that men (particularly within the middle-aged and young adult generations) participate markedly less than women do in such efforts at influencing other family members and are less often the targets of such efforts at influence.[5]

While middle-aged men reported some definite attempts at influencing other family members, this influence was not perceived by others, at least as reported in interviews designed to obtain such reciprocal patterns of influence. Reports by grandparents, spouses, and young adult offspring all showed that these men in the middle generation were rather isolated from exchanges with other family members, except when there were issues between the family and the outside world in which instrumental activity could assist in resolution of outstanding problems. These findings suggest that much more needs to be learned about the quality of interdependence that exists between middle-aged men and their relatives. While it is possible that a greater degree of reciprocal exchange takes place within working-class families, the combined effects of socialization across childhood and adulthood, developmental tasks, expected and eruptive life events, and cohort and generation within the family all contribute to the problems that men characteristically show, particularly in the middle years, in attaining comfortable interdependence within the multigeneration family unit.

Much of the tension that exists between culturally shared assumptions about the importance of independence and autonomy in contemporary society and the reality of interdependence within the family of adulthood is reflected in contemporary theories of personality and socialization. Clearly, some adults feel pressed to maintain throughout life the symbiotic ties to others that have been described by Mahler and her colleagues between young children and their mothers. Such adults show incomplete intrapsychic autonomy and cannot function in the physical absence of supporting family members, maintaining a lifelong need for "emotional refueling." However, much of what has been viewed as an incomplete resolution of the issue of

[5]Findings reported from study of Patterns of Influence among Urban Families, Bertram J. Cohler, Gunhild Hagestad, and Bernice L. Neugarten, coinvestigators, supported in part by NIA grant AG00123.

separation–individuation, particularly among women, may be better understood as the preservation of psychological interdependence among persons who care very much for each other, and who maintain satisfying mutual ties of caring and sharing across adulthood. Only recently, as a result of such studies of families as those of Hess and Handel (1959), Cohler and Grunebaum (1981), and others, together with the emergence of new formulations of the social psychological basis of family ties (Boszormenyi-Nagy & Spark, 1973), there has been increased appreciation of the importance of continuing ties across generations for the continued psychological adjustment of family members. Such interdependent ties are particularly important among working-class families, in which these ties represent important continuing exchange of resources.

It is important to revise prevailing views of the importance of psychological ties among adults in discussions of intergenerational relations, and to emphasize the interdependence within the family, rather than to view such ties as representing childish dependence or symbiosis maintained in adulthood. While much of the ideology in the mental health literature has focused on the importance of fostering autonomy between adults and their parents, this ideology is in conflict with the important sources of caring and support which are critical for continued adjustment across the life course. Increased attention must be devoted to coalitions of help and care across generations and to the means used for repairing relationships between adults and their parents that have been severed as a result of family conflict.

The reality of family life in contemporary urban society is not that the family has ceased to be a viable institution for socialization and for the maintenance of social life; it is rather, that the family is still an important locus for the exchange of resources and services, as well as of continuing complex feelings engendered by investment in relationships between the generations across the course of life. Problems of adjustment in adulthood are often more a consequence of conflicts stemming from continuing relationships among family members, than a result of feelings of anomie engendered by lack of meaningful ties with others. Particularly among working-class mothers of young children, in whom feelings of futility and despair are particularly prevalent (Cohler & Grunebaum, 1981), the relationship between mothers and their own middle-aged mother can be a source both of support and of increased inner turmoil as the mothers attempt to resolve intense conflicts regarding individuation within the context of interdependence in daily life.

Information dependence and affective dependence compound both the wish for closeness and the fear of loss of autonomy which might result. Attempts at intervention with family members showing psychological disturbance that emphasize only the need for family members to remain autonomous and independent do not account sufficiently for the impact of the interdependence that characterizes relations between members of the three or four generations within the family. Members of each generation have to become aware not only of conflict regarding the attainment of autonomy, but of the desire for comfortable interdependence that will permit continued personal satisfaction and enhanced adult development within the modified extended multigeneration family.

## REFERENCES

Abrahams, J., & Varon, E. *Maternal dependency and schizophrenia: Mothers and daughters in a therapeutic group.* New York: International Universities Press, 1953.

Ackerman, N., & Franklin, P. Family dynamics and the reversibility of delusional formation: A case study in family therapy. In I. Boszormenyi-Nagy & J. Framo (Eds.), *Intensive family therapy: Theoretical and practical aspects.* New York: Harper-Hoeber, 1965.

Adams, B. Isolation, function and beyond: American kinship in the 1960's. *Journal of Marriage and the Family,* 1970, *32,* 575–597.

Ainsworth, M. Patterns of attachment behavior shown by the infant in interaction with his mother. *Merrill-Palmer Quarterly,* 1964, *10,* 51–58.

Ainsworth, M. Object relations, dependency, and attachment: A theoretical review of the mother–infant relationship. *Child Development,* 1969, *40,* 969–1025.

Ainsworth, M. The development of infant–mother attachment. In B. Caldwell & H. Ricciuti (Eds.), *Review of child development research.* Chicago: University of Chicago Press, 1973.

Ainsworth, M., Blehar, M., Waters, E., & Wall, S. *Patterns of attachment: A psychological study of stranger situations.* Hillsdale, N.J.: Erlbaum/Halstead/Wiley, 1978.

Aldous, J. Intergenerational visiting patterns: Variation in boundary maintenance as an explanation. *Family Process,* 1967, *6,* 235–251.

Aldous, J., & Hill, R. Social cohesion, lineage type, and intergenerational transmission. *Social Forces,* 1965, *43,* 471–482.

Angel, K. The role of internal objects and external objects in object relationships, separation anxiety, object constancy and symbiosis. *International Journal of Psychoanalysis,* 1972, *53,* 541–546.

Anthony, E. J. The reactions of parents to adolescents and to their behavior. In E. Anthony & T. Benedek (Eds.), *Parenthood: Its psychology and psychopathology.* Boston: Little, Brown, 1970.

Anthony, E. J. Folie à deux: A developmental failure in the process of separation–individuation. In J. McDevitt & C. Settlage (Eds.), *Separation–individuation: Essays in honor of Margaret Mahler.* New York: International Universities Press, 1971.

Bernardo, F. Kinship interaction and communication among space-age migrants. *Journal of Marriage and the Family,* 1967, *29,* 541–554.

Bettelheim, B. *The empty fortress.* New York: Free Press, 1967.

Blos, P. The second individuation process of adolescence. *Psychoanalytic Study of the Child,* 1967, *22,* 162–186.

Blos, P. The epigenesis of the adult neurosis. *Psychoanalytic Study of the Child,* 1972, *27,* 106–135.

Boszormenyi-Nagy, I., & Spark, G. *Invisible loyalties: Reciprocity in intergenerational family therapy.* New York: Harper & Row, 1973.

Bott, E. *Family and social network* (2nd ed.). London: Tavistock, 1971.

Bowen, M., *Family therapy in clinical practice.* New York: Aronson, 1978.

Bowlby, J. *Attachment and loss* (Vol 1: *Attachment*). New York: Basic Books, 1969.

Bowlby, J. *Attachment and loss* (Vol. 2: *Separation, anxiety, and anger*). New York: Basic Books, 1973.

Bowlby, J. *Attachment and loss* (Vol. 3: *Loss, sadness and depression*). New York: Basic Books, 1980.

Bowlby, J. Self-reliance and some conditions that promote it. In *The making and breaking of affectional bonds.* London: Tavistock, 1979. (Originally published, 1970.)

Boyd, R. The valued grandparent: A changing social role. In W. Donahue (Ed.), *Living in the multigeneration family.* Ann Arbor, Mich.: Institute of Gerontology, 1969.

Brown, G. Experiences of discharged chronic schizophrenic patients in various types of living group. *Milbank Memorial Fund Quarterly,* 1959, *37,* 105-131.

Brown, G., Birley, J., & Wing, J. Influence of family life in the course of the schizophrenic disorders: A replication. *British Journal of Psychiatry,* 1972, *121,* 241-258.

Brown, G., Bone, M., Dalison, B., and Wing, J. *Schizophrenia and social care.* London: Oxford University Press, 1966.

Brown, G., Carstairs, G., & Topping, G. Post-hospital adjustment of chronic mental patients. *Lancet,* 1958, *2,* 685-689.

Brown, G., Monck, E., Carstairs, G., & Wing, J. Influence of family life in the course of schizophrenic illness. *British Journal of Preventative and Social Medicine,* 1962, *16,* 55-68.

Brown, G., Parkes, C., & Wing, J. Admissions and readmissions to three London mental hospitals. *Journal of Mental Science,* 1961, *107,* 1070-1077.

Brown, G., & Rutter, M. The measurement of family activities and relationships: A methodological study. *Human Relations,* 1966, *19,* 241-263.

Bruch, H. *Eating disorders: Obesity, anorexia nervosa and the person within.* New York: Basic Books, 1973.

Burnham, D., Gladstone, A., & Gibson, R. *Schizophrenia and the need-fear dilemma.* New York: International Universities Press, 1969.

Caudill, W., & Doi, L. T. Interrelations of psychiatry, culture, and emotions in Japan. In I. Galdston (Ed.), *Man's image in medicine and anthropology.* New York: International Universities Press, 1963.

Caudill, W., & Plath, W. Who sleeps by whom? Parent-child involvement in urban Japanese families. *Psychiatry,* 1969, *32,* 12-43.

Caudill, W., & Weinstein, H. Maternal care and infant behavior in Japanese and American urban middle class families. In R. Hill & R. Konig (Eds.), *Families in East and West: Socialization process and kinship ties.* The Hague: Mouton, 1970.

Chodorow, N. *The reproduction of mothering: Psychoanalysis and the sociology of gender.* Berkeley: University of California Press, 1978.

Cohler, B. Character, mental illness and mothering. In H. Grunebaum, J. Weiss, B. Cohler, C. Hartman, & D. Gallant (Eds.), *Mentally ill mothers and their children.* Chicago: University of Chicago Press, 1975.

Cohler, B. The significance of the therapist's feelings in the residential treatment of anorexia nervosa. In S. Feinstein & P. Giovacchini (Eds.), *Adolescent psychiatry* (Vol. 5). New York: Basic Books, 1977.

Cohler, B., & Grunebaum, H. *Mothers, grandmothers, and daughters: Personality and child-care in three generation families.* New York: Wiley, 1981.

Cohler, B., & Leiberman, M. Social relations and mental health among three European ethnic groups. *Research on Aging: A Quarterly of Social Gerontology,* 1980, *2,* 445-469.

Demos, J. Images of the American family: Then and now. In V. Tufte & B. Meyerhoff (Eds.), *Changing images of the family.* New Haven: Yale University Press, 1979.

Deutscher, I. The quality of post-parental life: Definitions of the situation. *Journal of Marriage and the Family,* 1964, *26,* 52-59.

Doi, L. T. Amae: A key concept for understanding Japanese personality structure. In R. Smith & R. Beardsley (Eds.), *Japanese culture: Its development and characteristics* (Viking Fund Publications in Anthropology). New York: Werner-Gren Foundation, 1962.

Doi, L. T. Some thoughts on helplessness and the desire to be loved. *Psychiatry,* 1963, *26,* 266-272.

Doi, L. T. *The anatomy of dependence*. Tokyo: Kodansha International, 1973.

Dunigan, J. *Mental hospital career and family expectations*. Unpublished doctoral dissertation, Case Western Reserve University, 1969.

Dyer, W. The interlocking of work and family social systems among lower occupational families. *Social Forces*, 1956, *34*, 230–233.

Ehrensing, R., & Weitzman, E. The mother–daughter relationship in anorexia nervosa. *Psychosomatic Medicine*, 1970, *32*, 201–208.

Elder, G. Family history and the life course. In T. Hareven (Ed.), *Transitions: The family and the life course in historical perspective*. New York: Academic Press, 1979.

Fairbairn, W. R. D. A revised psychopathology of the psychoses and psychoneuroses. In *Psychoanalytic studies of the personality*. London: Tavistock, 1952. (Originally published, 1941.)

Fairbairn, W. R. D. A synopsis of the author's views regarding the structure of personality. In *Psychoanalytic studies of the personality*. London: Tavistock, 1952. (Originally published, 1951.)

Farber, B. *Kinship and class: A Midwestern study*. New York: Basic Books, 1971.

Firth, R., Hubert, J., & Forge, A. *Families and their relatives: Kinship in a middle class sector of London*. New York: Humanities Press, 1970.

Fischer, J., & Fischer, A. The New Englanders of Orchard Town. In B. Whiting (Ed.), *Six cultures: Studies of childrearing*. New York: Wiley, 1963.

Fischer, L. *When daughters become mothers*. Unpublished doctoral dissertation, University of Massachusetts at Amherst, 1979.

Freeman, H., & Simmons, O. *The mental patient comes home*. New York: Wiley, 1963.

Fried, E., & Stern, K. The situation of the aged within the family. *American Journal of Orthopsychiatry*, 1948, *18*, 31–54.

Fried, M. *The world of the urban working class*. Cambridge: Harvard University Press, 1973.

Freud, A. *Normality and psychopathology in childhood*. New York: International Universities Press, 1965.

Freud, S. *Three essays on the theory of sexuality*. In *Standard edition* (Vol. 7). London: Hogarth Press, 1953. (Originally published, 1905.)

Giovacchini, P. Effects of adaptive and disruptive aspects of early object relationships upon later parental functioning. In E. Anthony & T. Benedek (Eds.), *Parenthood: Its psychology and psychopathology*. Boston: Little, Brown, 1970.

Glick, P. *American families*. New York: Wiley, 1957.

Glick, P. Updating the life cycle of the family. *Journal of Marriage and the Family*, 1977, *39*, 5–14.

Goldfarb, A. Psychodynamics and the three-generation family. In E. Shanas & G. Streib (Eds.), *Social structure and the family: Generational relations*. Englewood Cliffs, N.J.: Prentice-Hall, 1965.

Gray, R., & Smith, T. Effect of employment on sex differences in attitudes toward the parental family. *Journal of Marriage and the Family*, 1960, *22*, 36–38.

Grunebaum, H., Weiss, J., Cohler, B., Hartman, C., & Gallant, D. (Eds.). *Mentally ill mothers and their children*. Chicago: University of Chicago Press, 1975.

Grunebaum, H., Gamer, E., & Cohler, B. The spouse in depressed families. In H. Morrison (Ed.), *Children of depressed parents*. New York: Grune & Stratton, in press.

Grunes, J. *On becoming a child to one's own children*. Paper presented at Conference on Parenting as an Adult Experience, Psychosomatic and Psychiatric Institute for Research and Training, Chicago, 1980.

Gutmann, D. Parenthood: A comparison key to the life-cycle. In N. Datan & L. Ginsberg (Eds.), *Life-span developmental psychology: Normative crises*. New York: Academic Press, 1975.

Hagestad, G. *Middle aged women and their children: Exploring changes in a role relationship*. Unpublished doctoral dissertation, University of Minnesota, 1974.

Hagstrom, W., & Hadden, J. Sentiment and kinship terminology in American society. *Journal of Marriage and the Family*, 1965, *27*, 324–332.

Haley, J., Toward a theory of pathological systems, In G. H. Zuk & I. Boszormenyi-Nagy (Eds.), *Family therapy and disturbed families.* Palo Alto: Science & Behavior Books, 1967.

Haller, A. O. The urban family. *American Journal of Sociology,* 1961, *66,* 621–622.

Hammer, S. *Daughters and mothers.* New York: Quadrangle, 1975.

Handel, G. The analysis of correlative meaning. In G. Handel (Ed.), *The psychosocial interior of the family.* Chicago: Aldine 1967.

Handel, G. (Ed.). *The Psychosocial interior of the family.* Chicago: Aldine, 1967.

Hartmann, H. [*Ego psychology and the problem of adaptation*] (D. Rapaport, trans.). New York: International Universities Press, 1958. (Originally published, 1939.)

Hess, R., & Handel, G. *Family worlds.* Chicago: University of Chicago Press, 1959.

Hill, R., & Rodgers, R. The developmental approach. In H. Christensen (Ed.), *Handbook of marriage and the family.* Chicago: Rand McNally, 1964.

Jacobson, E. *The self and the object world.* New York: International Universities Press, 1964.

Jaffe, D. The mechanism of projection: Its dual role in object relations. *International Journal of Psychoanalysis,* 1968, *49,* 662–677.

Jones, E., & Gerard, H. *Foundations of social psychology.* New York: Wiley, 1967.

Kakar, S. *The inner world: A psychoanalytic study of childhood and society in India.* New York: Oxford University Press, 1978.

Kerr, M. *The people of Ship Street.* London: Routledge & Kegan Paul, 1958.

Kluckhohn, F., & Strodtbeck, F. *Variations in value orientations.* New York: Harper & Row, 1961.

Knudtson, F. Life-span attachment: Complexities, questions, and considerations. *Human Development,* 1976, *19,* 182–196.

Kohut, H. *The restoration of the self.* New York: International Universities Press, 1977.

Kohut, H., & Wolf, E. The disorders of the self and their treatment: An outline. *International Journal of Psychoanalysis,* 1978, *59,* 413–425.

Koller, M., *Families: A multigenerational approach.* New York: McGraw-Hill, 1974.

Komarovsky, M. Functional analysis of sex roles. *American Sociological Review,* 1950, *15,* 508–516.

Komarovsky, M. Continuities in family research: A case study. *American Journal of Sociology,* 1956, *62,* 466–469.

Komarovsky, M. *Blue-collar marriage.* New York: Random House, 1962.

Laslett, P. Characteristics of the Western family considered over time. *Journal of Family History,* 1977, *2,* 89–115.

Leichter, H., & Mitchell, W. *Kinship and casework.* New York: Russell Sage Foundation, 1967.

Lerner, R., & Ryff, C. Implementation of the life-span view of human development: The sample case of attachment. In P. Baltes (Ed.), *Life-span development and behavior.* New York: Academic Press, 1978.

Litwak, E. Occupational mobility and extended family cohesion. *American Sociological Review,* 1960, *25,* 9–21.(a)

Litwak, E. Geographical mobility and extended family cohesion. *American Sociological Review,* 1960, *26,* 258–271.(b)

Litwak, E. Extended kin relations in an industrial democratic society. In E. Shanas & G. Streib (Eds.), *Social structure and the family: Generational relations.* Englewood Cliffs, N.J.: Prentice-Hall, 1965.

Lowenthal, M. & Chiriboga, D. Transition to the empty nest: Crisis, challenge, or relief? *Archives of General Psychiatry,* 1972, *26,* 8–14.

Lyketsos, G. C. On the formation of mother–daughter symbiotic relationship patterns in schizophrenia. *Pyschiatry,* 1959, *22,* 161–166.

Mahler, M. Thoughts about development and individuation. *Psychoanalytic Study of the Child,* 1963, *18,* 307–323.

Mahler, M. On the significance of the normal separation–individuation phase: With reference to research in symbiotic child psychosis. In M. Schur (Ed.), *Drives, affects, behavior: Essays in memory of Marie Bonaparte.* New York: International Universities Press, 1965.

Mahler, M. *On human symbiosis and the vicissitudes of individuation* (Vol. 1: *Infantile psychosis*). New York: International Universities Press, 1968.

Mahler, M. On the first three phases of the separation–individuation process. *International Journal of Psychoanalysis*, 1972, *53*, 333–338.(a)

Mahler, M. Rapprochement subphase of the separation–individuation process. *Psychoanalytic Quarterly*, 1972, *41*, 487–506.(b)

Mahler, M., & Furer, M. Certain aspects of the separation–individuation phase. *Psychoanalytic Quarterly*, 1963, *32*, 1–14.

Mahler, M., & La Perriere, K. Mother–child interaction during separation–individuation. *Psychoanalytic Quarterly*, 1965, *34*, 483–498.

Mahler, M., Pine, F., & Bergman, A. *The psychological birth of the human infant*. New York: Basic Books, 1975.

Meissner, W. Conceptualization of marriage and family dynamics from a psychoanalytic perspective. In T. Paolino, Jr., & B. McCrady (Eds.), *Marriage and marital therapy: Psychoanalytic, behavioral and systems theory perspectives*. New York: Brunner/Mazel, 1978.

Meissner, W. W. A note on projective identification. *Journal of the American Psychoanalytic Association*, 1980, *28*, 43–68.

Miller, S., & Riessman, F. The working-class subculture: A new view. *Social Problems*, 1961, *9*, 86–97.

Murphey, E., Silber, E., Coelho, G., Hamburg, D., & Greenberg, I. Development of autonomy and parent–child interaction in late adolescence. *American Journal of Orthopsychiatry*, 1963, *33*, 643–652.

Musick, J., Cohler, B., & Stott, F. The treatment of psychotic parents and their children. In M. Lansky (Ed.), *Major psychopathology and the family*. New York: Grune & Stratton, 1981.

Neisser, E. *Mothers and daughters: A lifelong relationship* (Rev. ed.). New York: Harper & Row, 1973.

Neugarten, B. Dynamics of transition of middle age to old age: Adaptation and the life-cycle. *Journal of Geriatric Psychiatry*, 1970, *4*, 71–87.

Ogburn, W. F. The changing function of the family. In R. Winch & R. McGinnis (Eds.), *Selected readings in marriage and the family*. New York: Holt, Rinehart & Winston, 1953.

Ogden, T. On projective identification. *International Journal of Psychoanalysis*, 1979, *60*, 357–373.

Palazzoli, M. Anorexia nervosa. In S. Arieti (Ed.), *World biennial of psychiatry* (Vol. 1). New York: Basic Books, 1971.

Panel. The experience of separation–individuation in infancy and its reverberations through the course of life: I. Infancy and childhood. *Journal of the American Psychoanalytic Association*, 1973, *21*, 135–154.(a)

Panel. The experience of separation–individuation in infancy and its reverberations through the course of life: II. Adolescence and maturity. *Journal of the American Psychoanalytic Association*, 1973, *21*, 155–167.(b)

Panel. The experience of separation–individuation in infancy and its reverberations through the course of life: III. Maturity, senescence, and sociological implications. *Journal of the American Psychoanalytic Association*, 1973, *21*, 633–645.(c)

Papajohn, J., & Spiegel, J. *Transactions: The interplay between individual, family and society*. New York: Science House, 1975.

Parens, H., & Saul, L. *Dependence in man: A psychoanalytic study*. New York: International Universities Press, 1971.

Park, R., Burgess, E., & McKenzie, R. *The city*. Chicago: University of Chicago Press, 1967. (Originally published, 1925.)

Parsons, T. The social structure of the family. In R. Anshen (Ed.), *The family: Its function and destiny*. New York: Harper & Row, 1949.

Paterson, J. Marketing and the working class family. In A. Shostak & W. Gomberg (Eds.), *Blue collar world: Studies of the American worker.* Englewood Cliffs, N.J.: Prentice-Hall, 1964.

Pine, F., & Furer, M. Studies of the separation–individuation phase: A methodological overview. *Psychoanalytic Study of the Child,* 1963, *18,* 325–342.

Pollock, G. On symbiosis and symbiotic neurosis. *International Journal of Psychoanalysis,* 1964, *45,* 23–28.

Rainwater, L., Coleman, R., & Handel, G. *Workingman's wife.* New York: Oceana, 1959.

Rainwater, L., & Handel, G. Changing family roles in the working class. In A. Shostak & W. Gomberg (Eds.), *Blue collar world: Studies of the American worker.* Englewood Cliffs, N.J.: Prentice-Hall, 1964.

Reiss, P. The extended kinship system: Correlates of an attitude on frequency of interaction. *Journal of Marriage and the Family,* 1962, *24,* 333–339.

Rheingold, J. *The fear of being a woman: A theory of maternal destructiveness.* New York: Grune & Stratton, 1964.

Robertson, J. Grandmotherhood: A study of role conceptions. *Journal of Marriage and the Family,* 1977, *39,* 165–174.

Robins, L., & Tomanec, M. Closeness to blood relatives outside the immediate family. *Marriage and Family Living,* 1962, *24,* 340–346.

Rosenberg, G. *The worker grows old: Poverty and isolation in the city.* San Francisco: Jossey-Bass, 1970.

Rosenberg, G., & Anspach, D. *Working class kinship.* Lexington, Mass.: D. C. Heath–Lexington Books, 1973.

Rosow, I. *Social integration of the aged.* New York: Free Press/Macmillan, 1967.

Rudolph, S., & Rudolph, L. Rajput adulthood: Reflections on the Amar Singh diary. In E. Erikson (Ed.), *Adulthood.* New York: Norton, 1978. (Originally published, 1976.)

Rubin, L. *Worlds of pain: Life in the working class family.* New York: Basic Books, 1976.

Sampson, H., Messinger, S., & Towne, R. *Schizophrenic women: Studies in marital crisis.* New York: Atherton Press & Prentice-Hall, 1964.

Schuerman, J. Marital interaction and post-hospital adjustment. *Social Casework,* 1972, 163–172.

Shanas, E. Living arrangements of older people in the United States. *The Gerontologist,* 1961, *1,* 27–29.

Shanas, E. Family–kin networks and aging in cross-cultural perspective. *Journal of Marriage and the Family,* 1973, *35,* 505–511.

Shanas, E. Social myth as hypothesis: The case of the family relations of old people. *The Gerontologist,* 1979, *19,* 3–9.

Shapiro, D. A. Symbiosis in adulthood. *American Journal of Psychiatry,* 1972, *129,* 65–68.

Smith, H. Family interaction patterns of the aged: A review. In A. Rose & W. Peterson (Eds.), *Older people and their social world: The subculture of aging.* Philadelphia: F. A. Davis, 1965.

Smith, W., Britton, J., & Britton, J. *Relationships within three-generation families.* University Park, Pa.: Pennsylvania State University College of Home Economics, 1958.

Spence, D., & Lonner, T. The "empty nest": A transition within motherhood. *The Family Coordinator,* 1971, *20,* 369–375.

Spiegel, J. *Transactions: The interplay between individual, family and society* (J. Papajohn, Ed.). New York: Science House, 1971.

Stierlin, H. Interpersonal aspects of internalizations. *International Journal of Psychoanalysis,* 1973, *54,* 203–213.

Stierlin, H. *Separating parents and adolescents.* New York: Quadrangle, 1974.

Stierlin, H., Levi, L. D., & Savard, R. Parental perceptions of separating children. *Family Process,* 1971, *10,* 411–427.

Stierlin, H., Levi, L. D., & Savard, R. Centrifugal versus centripetal separation in adolescence:

Two patterns and some of their implications. In S. Feinstein & P. Giovacchini (Eds.), *Adolescent psychiatry* (Vol. 2: *Developmental and clinical studies*). New York: Basic Books, 1973.

Stierlin, H., & Ravenscroft, K. Varieties of adolescent "separation conflicts." *British Journal of Medical Psychology*, 1972, *45*, 299–313.

Streib, G., & Thompson, W. The older person in a family context. In C. Tibbitts (Ed.), *Handbook of social gerontology*. Chicago: University of Chicago Press, 1960.

Stryker, S. The adjustment of married offspring to their parents. *American Sociological Review*, 1955, *20*, 149–154.

Sullivan, K., & Sullivan, A. Adolescent–parent separation. *Developmental Psychology*, 1980, *16*, 93–99.

Sussman, M. The help pattern in the middle class family. *American Sociological Review*, 1953, *18*, 22–28.

Sussman, M. Intergenerational family relationships and social role changes in middle age. *Journal of Gerontology*, 1960, *15*, 71–75.

Sweetser, D. Asymmetry in intergenerational family relationships. *Social Forces*, 1963, *41*, 346–352.

Sweetser, D. Mother–daughter ties between generations in industrial societies. *Family Process*, 1964, *3*, 332–343.

Sweetser, D. The effect of industrialization on intergenerational solidarity. *Rural Sociology*, 1966, *31*, 156–170.

Thompson, M. *Eating disorders and anorexia nervosa*. Unpublished doctoral dissertation, University of Chicago, 1980.

Townsend, P. *The family life of old people*. London: Routledge & Kegan Paul, 1957.

Vogel, E., & Vogel, S. Family security, personal immaturity, and emotional health in a Japanese sample. *Marriage and Family Living*, 1961, *23*, 161–166.

Vollmer, H. The grandmother: A problem in childrearing. *American Journal of Orthopsychiatry*, 1937, *7*, 378–382.

Wallin, P. Sex differences in attitudes to "in-laws." *American Journal of Sociology*, 1954, *50*, 466–469.

Wilmott, P., & Young, M. *Family and class in a London suburb*. London: Routledge & Kegan Paul, 1960.

Wirth, L. Urbanism as a way of live. *American Journal of Sociology*, 1938, *40*, 1–24.

Wood, V., & Robertson, J. *Grandparenthood: A significant role to older individuals: Fact or fancy?* Paper presented at the meeting of the Gerontological Society, Houston, 1970.

Wood, V., & Robertson, J. The significance of grandparenthood. In J. Gubrium (Ed.), *Time, roles, and self in old age*. New York: Human Sciences Press, 1976.

Young, M., & Geertz, H. Old age in London and San Francisco: Some families compared. *British Journal of Sociology*, 1961, *12*, 124–141.

Young, M., & Wilmott, P. *Family and kinship in East London*. London: Routledge & Kegan Paul, 1957.

# 9

# DEATH AND CHANGES
# IN SEXUAL BEHAVIOR

## NORMAN L. PAUL
## BETTY B. PAUL

In the midst of life we are in death. . . .—*The Book of Common Prayer*

Of all the different topics considered representative of normal family processes, the one experienced as the least normal and most abnormal is the
mourning process. The problem here is that it is generally regarded as
normal in the literature, only to be resisted consciously and unconsciously
with great force when it actually occurs in oneself. The main paradox is that
while there exists a constant shadow of death in everybody's life, everybody
is entertaining notions of his or her own immortality.

An inherent paradox of American life is that a person's role in a family
is dual. It is to reproduce and to participate in family life, and at the same
time to achieve some semblance of self-fulfillment. In addition, parents
naturally become unconscious conduits between the generations. The pro-
creative act, while representing the height of pleasure, paradoxically also
represents the symbolical expression of the parent's preparation for and
participation in being succeeded by the next generation. Therefore, it is not
unusual for an intense degree of emotional projection onto the children to
occur, so that the children very often are in the position of being expected to
carry out the unfulfilled dreams of parents or grandparents.

In this chapter, we describe and suggest a relationship between aborted
grief and abrupt changes in sexual behavior. Three cases will be used to

Norman L. Paul. Department of Neurology, Boston University School of Medicine, Boston,
Massachusetts; Department of Psychiatry, Harvard Medical School, Boston, Massachusetts;
and New England Center for the Study of the Family, Newton, Massachusetts.

Betty B. Paul. Social Work Staff, Arlington, Massachusetts, Public Schools; Wheelock College
Center for Parenting Studies, Boston, Massachusetts; New England Center for the Study of the
Family, Newton, Massachusetts; and private practice of family therapy.

demonstrate this relationship, which we have frequently observed in over 20 years of family systems practice. A family systems practice consists, for us, of planned interventions in a family of procreation, after a transgenerational analysis of at least three generations of the dynamic system in each spouse's extended family. We look at the chain reaction of affects from such occurrences as deaths, life-threatening events, births, and divorces; these have a significant impact on the couple and its children, as naturally occurring entities based on the human projection systems. People are generally unaware of these connections.

## HISTORY TAKING

Prior to a first meeting with any clients, we will send out instructions to guide them in making a genogram (see Appendix A). The instruction sheet also suggests that they read our book *A Marital Puzzle* (1975) prior to that first visit. Of particular importance in the data to be included in the genogram are dates of birth, dates of death, and causes of death for family members, including siblings, their spouses, and their children, for the past three generations. Usually, clients will indicate some degree of mystification about doing the genogram (Figure 9–1).

Each of the three cases we will describe offers an example of a different type of sudden change in sexual relationship and function. Rather than treating the symptoms directly, the therapist and the clients collaborate in searching the genogram for the existence of deaths in either the immediate or extended families, as well as for the history of life-threatening illnesses. This focus is based on the recognition that the projective tendencies in families unconsciously conspire to recreate earlier family scenes. Because of unconscious images in family members' minds operating as unrecognized forces, they tend to recreate early scenes from either our own history or those of our parents or grandparents.

The transgenerational focus developed in these cases is similar to that described in detail in *A Marital Puzzle*. It includes the use of audiotapes to permit clients to review the interview experience, as well as the use of videotape playback for self-confrontation assessment. The reader is referred to *A Marital Puzzle* for a more comprehensive review of these elements.

These cases are taken from the private practice of Norman L. Paul. All identifying data have been altered to insure anonymity. The material was organized and edited by Betty B. Paul. Interpretation and analysis was contributed by both authors. Presenting these cases poses a difficult problem, insofar as we are attempting to translate a variety of complicated experiences into linguistic instruments (i.e., words); this creates considerable difficulty in conveying the essence of what actually transpired. However, given these constraints, these situations provided for us interesting and unusual ways of viewing some connections between lovemaking and the grieving process.

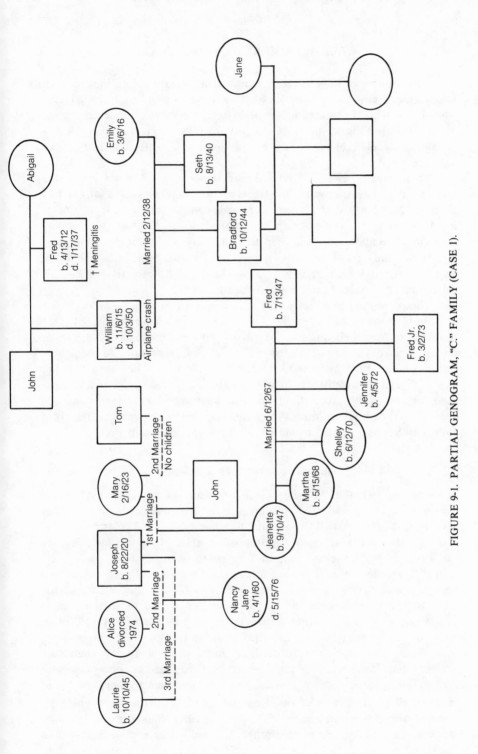

FIGURE 9-1. PARTIAL GENOGRAM, "C." FAMILY (CASE 1).

231

## CASE 1: FRED AND JEANETTE C.

This case illustrates how an early death of a parent created in a man an unrecognized emotional complex that became unconsciously reactivated when his own child of the same sex and sibling position approached the age of the man when the original loss was sustained. It also gives an example of a change in sexual involvement in a woman immediately after the death of her half-sister.

At the time of referral, Fred and Jeanette were both 29 years old, attractive, and articulate; they were the parents of three daughters and a son and had been married for 9 years. They were both college graduates from upper-middle-class, white Anglo-Saxon Protestant families. Fred was a practicing orthodontist and Jeanette a housewife with a variety of community interests. The names and ages of their children were as follows: Martha, 8; Shelley, 6; Jennifer, 4½; and Fred, Jr., 3½. The youngest child, Fred, Jr., had had his third birthday 7 months previous to the office visit.

The presenting problem was that Jeanette was having an affair with a neighbor. Jeanette and Fred had, at Jeanette's insistence, separated for 1 month. Jeanette "fell out of love with Fred" and claimed that he never communicated with her or related to the children. Her affair had been going on since a few months after Fred, Jr.'s first birthday. She stated that her husband needed immediate help and that she felt certain she knew where her own life was going. Tom, the man with whom she was now in love, was married and had five children. According to Jeanette, he was increasingly in love with her and wanted to marry her after obtaining a divorce.

### Interview 1—10/6/76: Jeanette

Jeanette was seen alone. During this first session, she indicated that she was the product of her parents' first marriage and that both her father and her mother had been married three times. She had a brother 2 years her junior. She said that her marriage had gotten worse about 4 months ago; that she and Fred had had no sexual relations for about a year; and that she was determined to get out of this "wretched marriage." She had told Fred 2 years ago that she was dating Tom, and had informed him at that time that the only way she would continue to live with him would be to maintain a secret relationship with Tom. A year later, Fred had "accidentally" found her diary containing detailed descriptions as to how much she loved Tom. After that, the marriage continued at more of a standoff. Jeanette described that, while she had achieved orgasm on several occasions with Fred prior to their getting married, she had not done so since they were married. She further revealed that from the age of 9 until the onset of menses, she had engaged in sexual activities, including fellatio and occasional vaginal penetration, with her second stepfather. She had felt obliged to comply with her stepfather's wishes lest he desert her mother. She had also been resentful of her mother's rejecting behavior toward her and had been very concerned about giving up her attachment to this special stepfather.

At the time of her first therapy visit she was also particularly distressed at the breakup of her father's third marriage. When the therapist suggested to her that she might be following in her mother's footsteps, she became angry and stated that she didn't want to return for therapy.

### Interview 2—10/8/76: Fred

Fred's father had died in an airplane crash when returning home for a visit from active duty in the Air Force early in the Korean conflict. Fred was 3 years old at the time and the youngest of three sons. As a child, Fred had been told that he had not seen his father for about 6 months before his death because he had been in active duty. Fred recalled suffering from moderate bouts of depression in the fall of each of his last 3 years at Dartmouth, which had also been his father's college. He described his mother as a domineering person, who, with financial support from her family, managed to maintain a household adequately for her three sons. Fred had never visited his father's grave. When confronted by his own picture on a closed-circuit TV monitor, he was struck by his aloofness and a look that he described as one of "hardened stone." He was surprised at his lack of aliveness.

### Interview 3—10/11/76: Couple

In Fred and Jeanette's first session together, the Lewis stressor tape (see Appendix C) was used. A stressor tape is a 10- to 15-minute audio- or videotape segment designed to immerse listeners or viewers in the emotions of the experience of grief. Clients can then tune in or empathize with such an experience if they have had similar experiences in their own past.

Because Fred's father had died when Fred was 3, and Jeanette had sustained the loss of a home with two parents due to divorce when she was 4 years old, the hypothesis was that the Lewis tape might catalyze into awareness hidden experiences of grief. In reaction to hearing this tape, they each were saddened, but neither of them had a tearful reaction. However, Fred was reminded of the intensity of his loneliness because of growing up without a father, and he mentioned that one of Jeanette's attractions had been that her father was very responsive toward him.

### Interview 4—10/16/76: Jeanette

Jeanette stated that she was more than ever intent on marrying Tom, who was now pursuing a divorce after consulting an attorney. However, her daughters were acting up and had difficulties sleeping at night. They were harassing her during the night, pleading with her to have their father return. Jeanette had been taking sleeping pills for her insomnia. She was at this point also particularly distressed at the recent suicide of a younger half-sister. She also reviewed her distress about the time when her relationship with her stepfather came to an end as a result of her mother's third divorce. She was very vague about and unable to remember whether her mother had found out about her sexual experiences with this stepfather.

### Interview 5—10/18/76: Fred

Fred and Jeanette had talked about a lot of difficult subjects a few nights earlier and he was incensed that that "SOB Tom would be raising my children." His perception of Jeanette after they had married was that she was completely numbed to any kind of sexual activity with him—something she had continued to deny.

### Interview 6—10/25/76: Fred

Fred had just leased an apartment in response to Jeanette's insistence that she "had had it." He had had severe nightmares the previous weeks, wherein he was chased by a vague, unidentified mist, which, on touching him, kept him from breathing and terrified him. (In a later session, he associated this mist with his father's presence.)

Jeanette had refused to come in, insisting that since "it was all over" there was no point in returning. Fred stated that she continued to be distressed at the idea that she might be following in her mother's footsteps.

### Interview 7—11/8/76: Fred

Fred arrived smiling and feeling a sense of relief at the lessening tension between Jeanette and himself. He seemed more resigned to a divorce and recently had talked to his oldest daughter, Martha, about this event. Martha had been visibly shaken, indicating that she wanted to live with her father since she found her mother disagreeable. Jeanette had mentioned to Fred that Martha had started to masturbate in the classroom, which had become embarrassing to Jeanette after she had been made aware of it. When describing his own masturbatory fantasies over the years, he mentioned that they included images of Jeanette and Tom having intercourse, which suggested that he possibly had had a role in promoting the affair.

### Interview 8—11/20/76: Fred

Fred described a conversation with his mother-in-law, wherein he stated that he was in a quandary about the whole point of marriage. He had also learned from his sister-in-law that Jeanette had had an intense affair with one of his colleagues only a month after they were married. Yet he described an increased sense of well-being and ascribed it to his transient involvement with a new woman.

### Interview 9—12/4/76: Fred

On reflection, it seemed to Fred that their problems increased after Jeanette's half-sister, Nancy, committed suicide. Nancy, the daughter of her father's second wife, had been viewed by Jeanette as especially bright, sensitive and beautiful. Nancy had been hospitalized in Chicago because of a suicidal depression after her father's separation from his second wife; she had viewed herself as the cement between her parents. She had been the source of Jeanette's considerable envy, who felt that Nancy had all the attributes of confidence, charm, and polish that she herself felt she lacked. Coincident with Nancy's walking into the ocean and drowning in May of 1976 in Florida, Jeanette became distressed and sexually involved with Tom.

### Interview 10—12/14/76: Fred

The goal of this session was to neutralize the bitterness Fred had toward Jeanette. He was particularly distressed at his son's refusal to see him for the previous 3 weeks. This had caused him to become depressed and to feel that there was little point in living. At times, he wished he were dead, and he began thinking about suicide; however, he did not think of any concrete way of doing this. At the same time he was still searching for a replacement for Jeanette.

### Interview 11—12/22/76: Fred

Fred reported on what he had recently discovered about his father. He had learned that his father had been "forced" to attend Dartmouth by his maternal grandmother. Also, his father's brother, Fred's uncle, was to have married Fred's mother, but had died of meningitis 2 months before the wedding. Fred's father later married her. In the early years of the father's marriage, and before he went into the Air Force as a pilot, he had been periodically depressed, unable to make a living after having failed in a variety of business enterprises. Fred had also learned that his paternal grandfather had been totally dominated by his wife and, as a result, had refused to speak to her for weeks on end. Fred had been expected to go into his mother's family's textile business, but managed to avoid that by becoming an orthodontist.

Fred had told Jeanette that he was not going to agree to an immediate divorce and that he wanted to have some time to figure out just what had transpired in his life. He said that Jeanette seemed relieved by that suggestion.

Fred continued to speak about his lingering sense of embarrassment and oscillating inadequacy at having no father, vividly remembering his tearfulness when filling out school forms that required information as to fathers, or when only his mother arrived at school functions for parents. He was very critical of himself, wishing he could make this whole scene evaporate. He reviewed his prior reactions to the Lewis tape, focusing on his chronic search for a father and his feelings that in some ways, Jeanette had functioned as a father substitute in the marriage.

The next meeting was planned to include his mother and his two older brothers. The rationale for this projected family-of-origin meeting was to assess the family's perceptions of how the death of Fred's father had affected them collectively and individually, and to find out to what extent that event had contributed to Fred's current marital difficulties.

### Interview 12—1/11/77: Fred's Family

Fred arrived with his mother and his two older brothers, John and Frank. The mother described Fred's frantic search for his father after the airplane crash on December 6, 1950. Fred had been the only one not attending the military funeral. He was later found constructing a telescope from Tinkertoys in order to search for his father in heaven. As she described this in much detail, Fred broke into convulsive sobbing. The mother, contrary to what seemed to have been her customary behavior, moved over and sat beside him and comforted him. It seemed that Fred had for the first time experienced for himself his own grief at the death of his father. The two older brothers were also tearfully reflecting on their father's death.

The therapist recommended that the family further complete this belated process of grief by going to the father's grave site, which they did 2 weeks later. When doing this, they shared their respective experiences of him. Many tears were shed. After this visit to the cemetery, Fred felt the beginning of his reintegration into his family of origin, from whose members he had felt disconnected over time.

### Interview 13—1/27/77: Fred

Fred came alone and described that he seemed to have "descended into hell" as he had become acutely aware of his longing for a father whom he felt he had never known. He had, for the first time, accepted a dinner invitation from his older brother and his wife. He felt that he had returned to his original family after a long absence. He also reported that, over Christmas 1976, his daughter Martha had told him that she was fearful that he would desert her.

The intervention with Fred and his family of origin, as noted above, was an intervention designed to thwart his persistent attempt to retrieve Jeanette. The neutralization was intended to occur by directing his attention and energy to completing the task of a belated grief reaction in the context of his family of origin. Often, such mourning brings about an increased sense of space, as occurred here, permitting the spouse (in this instance, Jeanette) to reflect on the widson of whatever position she might take regarding her marriage—for example, the question of whether or not to attempt new negotiations. The intervention was based upon the systemic principle that a more neutral reaction on Fred's part could lead indirectly to Jeanette's being less reactive to his wish for a reconciliation.

### Telephone Call—1/27/77, 11P.M.: Fred

The therapist received an "emergency" phone call at home from Fred, who was flustered because he had just received a phone call from Jeanette. She wanted to have lunch with him at his convenience to review the possibilities of a reconciliation. He wanted the therapist's advice about this. Fred was told that considering a reconciliation was appropriate, provided that he kept in mind that he had had much to do with Jeanette's involvement with Tom. If he felt that he had to blame her for this affair, a genuine reconciliation would be impossible. The therapist stressed that it was vitally important for him to see the responsibility for the affair as one to be shared by both partners.

### Interview 14—1/29/77: Fred

Fred had had lunch with Jeanette the previous day. Jeanette wanted to see if they could make it together, indicating that she would like to have him back. She had told Tom that she did not want to see him any more. As a result of this, Tom had decided to return to his own analyst, whom he had last seen 5 years ago.

Jeanette's behavior was almost predictable, once she had the space to consider the consequences of her behavior in regard to remaining married or getting divorced. She was able to review her mother's three marriages and those of her father and to note that their successive marriages did not resolve their own respective problems. They were only distracted from their problems by the new spouse-to-be. It obviously took courage to see the same process occurring in herself. This insight would not have occurred without Fred's willingness to review his own personal and family history.

### Interview 15—2/28/77: Fred

Fred was back home and overcome with joy at his reunion with Jeanette and the children. The children were thrilled to have him back, though bewildered that everything had worked out. Jeanette was discovering that Fred was not bitter at her involvement with Tom. The therapist instructed them to listen to the first tapes made of them together. Fred related that Jeanette felt he was more responsive and capable of being loving to her than she had previously believed.

### Interviews 16 and 17—3/18/77 and 4/4/77: Fred and Jeanette

Fred and Jeanette were seen together, and the case was closed. During the last meeting, a few things were sorted out; for example, Jeanette described their son's third birthday party, when Fred had been in a total trance while being completely unaware of that fact. It was on that day that Jeanette concluded that Fred would never be responsive to her.

They both mentioned that their sexual experience with each other had improved and that Jeanette was capable of experiencing orgasm with him again. Their review of the first sessions on tape had been startling for them, as they had had no recognition of the multiple elements that had been contributing at that time to the destruction of their marriage.

Follow-up after 2 and 3 years indicated that Fred and Jeanette are happily married and that the family is mutually supportive. Jeanette has become professionally involved as a community leader.

## DISCUSSION OF CASE 1

The C. family's situation, like most similar crises, is very complicated and requires a systemic overview to determine the nature and quality of the experiences required to neutralize what appears to be an impasse. Fred's failure to mourn the death of his father adequately was a key element in his subtle but forceful rejection of his son and wife. It would appear that from the moment that his son was born, Fred had experienced an unconscious dread that when his son reached the age that he himself had been at the time of his father's death, in some magical way he himself would die. The inference was that, for him, life beyond this unconscious death date would put him in the position of being envious of his son's having a father and of his wife's having a husband, unlike himself and his mother. As he himself put it, it was reminiscent of his early years in school, when he was continually reminded of his paternal void and experienced various degrees of envy and jealousy of his male schoolmates. When Fred, Jr. turned 3 years old, Fred unconsciously relived the trauma of the death and then the absence of his own father. Out of unconscious loyalty to his own father, Fred behaved as though he were dead in relation to his wife and son. The connection between aborted grief and sexual rejection of a spouse is dramatically highlighted here.

It is interesting to observe that children will very often say they feel that they were the cause of a marital crisis or divorce, and that then the parents often get involved in attempts of disabusing them of their self-implication. When viewed from a transgenerational perspective, such children may be more insightful than they are usually given credit for, because on some unconscious level they may be keenly aware that the birth of children re-stimulates an awareness of the relationship between their parents and themselves; this was the case when Fred, Jr.'s existence catapulted his father into the role of father to a son. It would follow that, had Fred, Jr. not been born or had Fred had another daughter instead, there would have been less likelihood of marital tumult at that particular time.

The C. family is similar to the Lewis case in *A Marital Puzzle*, in which part of Mr. Lewis's hostility toward his wife, which in that instance had precipitated his having an affair, was his envy of his son's being conceived and born in wedlock while he himself was not.

Obviously, much of such interpretive reflection represents, at best, a meager attempt at assessing such a situation. The interesting aspect of these marital scenes is that when a mourning experience is induced in the family, the trajectory toward dissolution is very often neutralized, and satisfactory (if not always exciting) sexual behavior is resumed.

## CASE 2: DAVID AND NATALIE J.

David and Natalie J. were seen together in various combinations a total of 39 times between January 17, 1978, and September 16, 1979. A complicating feature of this course of therapy was the intense anxiety and acting out of their three adolescent daughters, aged 14, 19, and 21. This acting-out behavior, coupled with hostility toward both parents but particularly toward Natalie, seemed by all accounts not to have been present prior to their grandfather's fatal illness. The focus herein will be restricted to the relationship between the adults, the death of David's father, and the impact this had on David's sexual functioning.

David, 46, and Natalie, 45, both Jewish, had been married for 23 years. David was the younger of two boys. Natalie was the youngest of four children and the only daughter of living parents. While they had had their differences over the years, they both stated that there had been an overall sense of comfort and well-being in their marriage until the beginning of David's father's fatal illness in December of 1976. He died on March 12, 1977. David had worked as a partner in his father's stock brokerage firm ever since he left college.

The presenting problem was that David had become sexually involved with his father's secretary, Barbara, beginning on New Year's Eve 1976. When Natalie found out that David had gotten Barbara pregnant, she threw David out of the house with great alacrity, and David moved in with his mother. While living with his mother, David learned from her that after he was born, his father had disappeared into Peru. There he remained for three years, apparently living with another woman who had a son by him.

During subsequent office visits, it became quite apparent that David had been experiencing tremendous sexual anxiety and a sense of terror when in bed with Natalie. Natalie described how very much attached David had been to his father, and how shocked he was after hearing about his father's escapades in South America. David also felt unhappy that he had not been able to provide his father with a grandson. Whatever unhappiness there had been in the marriage had intensified after David's father's death. At times, David appeared suicidal, since he no longer seemed to know what to do with his life.

When David was seen alone, he described the following: When in bed with Natalie, he was unable to have an erection and he felt that he was dying. He was terrified that something was happening to him that he was unable to understand. Suddenly, at times, he would have the feeling of his body shrinking in size down to a few inches. If he opened his eyes, he was able to freeze this sensation and return slowly to his normal size. These sensations had started in the beginning of 1977, after the onset of his father's illness, and had intensified after his father's death.

In tracing the beginning of the dissolution of this marriage, it became very clear that the key date was December 26, 1976. David described how his father had arrived home from the office of his physician, who had informed him that tests had indicated that he had cancer of the liver, secondary to a primary cancer in the stomach. Four days after hearing this information, David first got sexually involved with Barbara. The development of David's phobia about Natalie was also coincidental with this.

Subsequently, Barbara went to the West Coast and had a baby boy. David, not wanting to desert the baby, followed her and resettled on the West Coast. Natalie moved back to her original home in Wisconsin, taking their three daughters with her.

Before David left treatment, he found out that Barbara had had an affair with his father a few years before his death. David spent 5 months near the cemetery where his father was buried, planning and constructing an obelisk in his father's memory. He wanted it positioned on a high piece of land, in such a way as to achieve the maximum degree of visibility from all points of the cemetery and beyond.

## DISCUSSION OF CASE 2

The case of Natalie and David graphically illustrates the emergence into consciousness of the principle of loyalty to the dead or to the one about to die. David's unconscious loyalty to his father was such that it transcended the relationship he had had with his wife and children. His behavior of impregnating a single woman, who subsequently bore him a child, was identical to what had transpired when his father had disappeared into Peru.

Ironically, he had chosen as the woman to have his child the same woman with whom his father had had an affair.

Over the years, we have often observed that, if a wife learns that her husband has recently impregnated another woman, and if that pregnancy is allowed to go to term, it becomes impossible for the marriage to continue. However, in five of the seven instances we have encountered in which a married woman has become pregnant by another man, the husband has chosen to stay with his wife and to accept the child as his own.

The case of David and Natalie beautifully demonstrates what we have playfully labeled "the Whammo syndrome." The rapid shift in both relationships and sexual behavior consequent to an unexpected death of a parent in an enmeshed family are features of this entity. "Whammo" signifies the unexpected flash in which the family picture changes dramatically.

## CASE 3: SALLY O.

Sally O., 24, was a college graduate, a practicing RN, and single. Her family of origin consisted of two living parents, a brother 2 years younger, and a sister 5 years her junior.

Sally had been engaged three times over the previous 2½ years. Within a week after each engagement, she would begin to find herself increasingly anxious and tense while making love with her fiancé. Suddenly she would become inorgasmic, even though she felt that she was not basically fearful of having an orgasm, because she could have one easily through masturbation.

### Interview 1—9/26/74: Sally

Sally described her first heterosexual encounter during her sophomore year in college as a tense and anxious experience. She also recalled that, as a youngster, she talked about sex with her father, whom she found very seductive. Between the ages of 8 and 12, she and her father would have periodic episodes of mutual masturbation. She mentioned that the manner of dress in her original home was "like a bunch of nudists," except for her mother.

A week before her first visit, there had been a fire in her apartment; her dog, to whom she was very attached, had been hit by a car; and her third engagement had broken up. She was desperate and seemed quite frantic during that first visit. Her reaction to seeing herself on videotape playback was that she liked herself much more than she thought she would. She had had a fair amount of experience with LSD, which had brought about intense hallucination at the time of ingestion and occasional flashbacks since then. She had been a regular user of marijuana.

### Interview 2—10/14/74: Sally

During her second visit, upon hearing a stressor tape, she recalled vividly the beginning of her intense loneliness at the age of 8, when she had broken her right leg and a very close friend had moved far away. She spoke of her very estranged relationship with her mother, adding that the mother heard on the stressor tape had features very similar to those of her own mother.

At the end of this second session, the therapist suggested that she plan to come in for an office visit with her parents in a month's time. During that projected visit, the plan was to have her review and share her memories of her masturbating experience with both her father and her mother. The therapist indicated to her that he thought this was a reasonably common problem and that her reaction to intercourse with her fiancés suggested that her genitals were rejecting them, symbolically indicating a preference for her father. Between the first two visits, Sally and her close friend Jane listened to the tape of the first session. Jane had told her that she had had a similar problem with her father between the ages of 15 and 18, during which time she had had repeated intercourse with him.

### Interview 3—11/18/74: Sally and Parents

The therapist used a videotape segment of Sally's review of her experience between 8 and 12 years of age, in which she described the mutual masturbation with her father and her father's excitement with her body next to his. It was played in the following sequence: first, it was played for Sally and her father alone, principally to get corroboration of Sally's story from him. Her father did corroborate the events as described, and the therapist suggested that he discuss all this with his wife during the upcoming lunch break.

When Sally and her parents returned, the therapist observed great tension in the father, who, with Sally, okayed the use of the videotape they had made earlier that morning for the mother to view alone that afternoon. The therapist had tremendous anxiety as to what might happen, fearing some kind of explosion. After seeing the videotape, the mother responded by saying that she was sorry that both of them had had to suffer with this secret over the years.

This led to an emerging resolution of the problem among the three of them. It became very clear that the mother and father had had a reasonably good sexual relationship until the mother's mother died on Sally's eighth birthday, after which Sally's mother's sexual desire abated drastically.

### Later Interviews

The therapist subsequently used heterosexual and homosexual films with Sally to desensitize her feelings of disgust about sexual fantasies regarding her father and mother. Her parents came in during the early part of the following year for a few sessions as a couple to review and enhance their relationship.

A month after the first office encounter with her parents, Sally met a new man, a journalist. They were seen together for eight sessions. Sally was orgasmic through vaginal intercourse in a very satisfying sexual relationship with him. They eventually got married, had two children, and are living on the West Coast.

## DISCUSSION OF CASE 3

Sally's mother was a woman who, in identifying with her dead mother, shut herself off sexually from her husband, who, in turn, used his older daughter initially as a wife surrogate. The search for the role of death and aborted grief and its impact on sexual behavior ended in this case when it was determined that the first incestuous contact between the father and the daughter occurred around the first anniversary of the death of the maternal grandmother, which happened to be Sally's ninth birthday.

The particular problem in this case was to neutralize the obvious parental sexual dissatisfaction, while at the same time exploring the possibility of assisting the parents in evolving a more satisfying relationship. The first chore was to establish whether the purported incest was a fantasy, however vivid, or whether it had indeed occurred. This required the presence of the father without the mother. When there was agreement that the events had indeed occurred as stated by Sally, it was essential to have the mother involved. Here television was used creatively to show the mother, with permission of the father and the daughter, the discussion that had taken place between them, which validated that the incestuous contact had indeed taken place. The mother's reaction to this was interesting in that she regretted that they both had had to suffer for so long with the secret of what had transpired.

In this case, the father was a timid, somewhat stiff and reticent person, who was quite distressed at Sally's breaching this secret. Yet he was able to assume and accept responsibility for what had happened. The issue was to see what constructive resolution could be afforded that would include a redefinition of the family relationship.

It is interesting to note that there is a movement afoot suggesting that father–daughter or mother–son incest is not really that damaging to the developing child (deMott, 1980). It may not be that damaging to the child during the child's development in adolescence. However, as seen in this case, it becomes a great stumbling block for any child in his or her attempt to achieve a satisfactory heterosexual relationship as an adult.

## CONCLUSION

In the family, the biological thrust to regenerate the species is reflected in the transgenerational sequencing of death, sex or lovemaking, and birth. There is a disproportionate interest in sex in our culture, with an "allergy" or aversion to the experience of death and grief. Aries (1975), in a very penetrating and compelling overview of the problem of death and mourning, suggests that the escalating terror about death is such that it has become the contemporary taboo *par excellence*.

Among the multiple considerations of factors that influence the nature of sexual behaviors, there has been a sparsity of references to the role of death and grief. The three cases described herein clearly demonstrate that, however intense the aversion to death and grief in an individual or family, the grief force will be expressed nonetheless. We have focused on the specific intrusion of unrecognized grief trauma into the area of sexual behavior. Part of the problem we have in the appreciation of the role of aborted grief in any area of human functioning has to do with the fact that grief is a very intense experience that defies linguistic expression. The particular problem has to do with the fact that language is not a reality, while at the same time our verbal world conditions us to conceive of reality as derived from a linguistic mode.

A factor that generally militates against the recognition of the relationship between aborted grief and changes in behavior, sexual and otherwise, is the general cultural aversion to death and grief. If this aversion leads to an inability to diagnose a family systemic problem correctly as grief-related, and if secondary derivations (e.g., sexual dysfunctions) are imputed as the condition requiring treatment, then the consequences of such a lack of appropriate diagnosis will occur.

Each case presented a "normal" family reaction to grief when viewed from the family's own perspective. The reaction is generally regarded as undesirable, but not pathological. The therapeutic task here is to bring the aborted grief out into the open so that the family can regard it as normal.

> We shall not cease from exploration
> And the end of all our exploring
> Will be to arrive where we started
> And know the place for the first time.—T. S. ELIOT

## DEFINITIONS

"Mourning" (Bowlby, 1961) denotes the psychological processes that are set in train by the loss of a loved object and that commonly lead to the relinquishing of the object. This process can begin before the actual loss of the loved person, starting with the first fantasy of that loss. It is important that these predeath fantasies be encouraged in children so that, in the event of death, they can be prepared to experience themselves as not causing the other's death.

"Grief," by contrast, denotes the sequence of subjective states that follow loss and accompany mourning (Bowlby, 1961). Although a common outcome of mourning is relinquishment of the object, this is not always so. By defining the term "mourning" to cover a fairly wide array of psychological processes, even including those that lead to a retention of the object, the different courses that mourning may take—healthy or pathological—are, we believe, more easily understood.

"Mourning," because it includes both the subjective and behavioral consequences of the trauma of death, appears to be the preferred term to convey both the paradoxical nature of behaviors observed and the process initiated. We conceive of "mourning" to be both conscious and unconscious.


## APPENDIX A: HOW TO DO YOUR FAMILY TREE— INSTRUCTIONS FOR CLIENTS

(*Note*: These instructions are for *both* spouses.)

Before our first session together, we expect that you will have completed a family tree. This family tree is essential in our being able to assist you in the resolution of your marital/family problem. We used to send forms to be completed by the prospective clients, but we have become very interested in how they will organize the relevant data, as it gives us a sense as to how they orient themselves to their original family. It is critical that all the information be completed to the extent that it is available or can be obtained.

Starting with yourself as a point of reference, give your date of birth and of marriage, as well as the birth date of each of your children, including any stillbirths or miscarriages. Then list brothers and sisters, again including stillbirths and miscarriages, giving date of birth (and death). We are interested in knowing to whom your brothers and sisters are married, and how often they have been married. We need their dates of marriage and the dates of birth (and death) of their spouses and their children, as well as of your spouse's siblings and their children.

Birthdates are very important; many people will put down "1962" as an example of a date of birth, which from our perspective suggests that the whole year was spent being born. Actually, people are born on a given date or point in time.

Then move back a generation and provide the same information about your parents, their siblings, spouses, and children. Finally, it is important to have whatever relevant information you are able to obtain about your respective grandparents.

For each member of your family tree, you should include information about chronic physical disease (such as stroke, cancer, etc.), as well as chronic emotional disorders and other chronic disorders that you feel are important. Here, dates of onset of illness, hospitalizations, and so on should be supplied wherever possible.

Although some of the information requested may be difficult to obtain, the more you can find, the more helpful we can be in our joint enterprise to try and figure out what unrecognized factors are feeding into the problem that you are currently having.

Before our first session, we also require that you and your spouse read *A Marital Puzzle,* by Norman L. Paul and Betty B. Paul, published by W. W. Norton, New York, 1975. This book will help you to begin to experience how we will work together, and it also contains an example of a family tree as described above.

## APPENDIX B: THE LEWIS TAPE

This example of a stressor tape is an excerpt from the fourth session with the Lewis couple. At that time, the Lewises were both 39 years old; they had been married for 20 years and had six children. At the beginning of this meeting, Mr. Lewis had announced that he had consulted an attorney the previous evening to initiate a separation from his wife. He was planning to marry a woman by the name of Charlotte, 21 years old, who was living in another city. He informed us that this was going to be our last meeting.

The level of acrimony between the spouses was reminiscent of the dialogue in *Who's Afraid of Virginia Woolf?*. On an examination of their premarital history, a crucial factor seemed to have been that Mr. Lewis was born out of wedlock, but had successfully persuaded his father to marry his mother when he was about 12 years old. Another important factor was that both Mrs. Lewis's parents committed suicide—her mother when she was 16 and her father when she was 32.

At the point at which this excerpt begins, Mr. Lewis was discussing his feelings that he and his father had both been trapped into marriage. During the excerpt, he exposed previously unrecognized, intense feelings of grief, of which his wife had also been unaware until that moment.

Some 4 months after this interview, Mr. Lewis abandoned his plans to marry Charlotte and returned home to his wife and children.

### Excerpted Transcript of Lewis Couple's Interview—Fourth Meeting

DR. PAUL: How often did you ask your father to marry your mother?

MR. LEWIS: Oh, quite often.

DR. PAUL: Beginning at what age?

MR. LEWIS: Oh, probably when I was about 9.

DR. PAUL: And how would he greet you?

MR. LEWIS: He would be very indulgent. He would be, we, we, my father and I, when we got along very well, we can have very friendly pleasant relationships, I mean, at times.

DR. PAUL: Again, I draw the parallel between you and your wife; you get along, you have pleasant relationships. Go ahead.

MR. LEWIS: But, I mean, for example, I'd say, I've usually, in fact I think this has been one of the reasons I was successful in my own work is that I've always had to persuade, I mean, I was a kid, my parents were older. They were, they were foreigners in this country. They couldn't speak English. I was sort of the educator, the critic, and the persuader.

DR. PAUL: You were assuming leadership in some ways in the home?

MR. LEWIS: Oh . . .

MRS. LEWIS: Oh, yes.

MR. LEWIS: I led that family from the time I was probably 5 years old, and, uh, in many, many ways, in many ways. I really marshalled the family's direction in many ways. And they appreciated it. They were very proud of me for this. I mean they . . . But I would say to my father sometimes when we were alone, I would say, "Pop, you know it would be very nice if you married Mom. After all, she is a woman, and she, she'd feel better if she were married." Incidentally, my mother would sometimes mention this to me.

DR. PAUL: That she'd like to be married.

MR. LEWIS: Yes. I mean she would mention it. See, I don't know how I ever got the impresssion that I was illegitimate because no one ever said it to me. It's a funny thing. Now, speaking of hearing things. No one ever told me that.

DR. PAUL: Did you ever see any documents?

MR. LEWIS: No. There's a funny thing. It's a funny thing. I just knew. I don't know.

DR. PAUL: Do you believe in the supernatural?

MR. LEWIS: No. But something must have told me.

DR. PAUL: The vapor in the air, sort of . . .

MR. LEWIS: No, no, but I think maybe my mother must have said, I remember, I know what, I was with my mother and aunt and one of the things I think has influenced me a lot, my Aunt Mary was a most wonderful person. Oh, she was . . .

DR. PAUL: Her sister?

MR. LEWIS: Yeah, my mother's sister.

DR. PAUL: Older?

MR. LEWIS: Younger, and we were, we would go on vacation, not vacation but we'd go to visit my Aunt Mary in North Carolina, and I would be in bed with the two women as a boy.

MRS. LEWIS: Yes, you told me that you used to overhear the women talking.

MR. LEWIS: And they were talking. They wouldn't see each other for a year and they talked for all night.

DR. PAUL: You'd sleep what, on the end or between . . .

MR. LEWIS: I'd sleep on the end, and they'd be in the other . . .

DR. PAUL: What age?

MR. LEWIS: Oh, I must have been 8, 7. And they would talk all night about men, and all night they'd be, the sisters, having a real personal and intimate relationship and . . .

DR. PAUL: What?

MR. LEWIS: A personal and intimate relationship, discussing men and discussing life with men and the problems of men and every so often, I'd just get, just wake up and hear . . . men are so and so, men are so and so.

DR. PAUL: Did that make you feel sort of positive about growing up to be a man?

MR. LEWIS: Make me feel positive? Well, I don't know about that.

DR. PAUL: What do you think?

MR. LEWIS: I don't know. My mother would always criticize my father. You know, she'd, she'd always be very critical at some times. Then she'd be nice at other times. My Aunt Mary was wonderful, though. There was a remarkable woman. She was a remarkable person.

DR. PAUL: When did she die?

MR. LEWIS: She was 35.

DR. PAUL: And you were how old?

MR. LEWIS: I was about, oh, 10 or 11. She was a remarkable, nice person.

DR. PAUL: And how did you feel when she died?

MR. LEWIS: Oh, I felt sadder about my aunt's death than anybody.

DR. PAUL: How's that?

MR. LEWIS: Miserable, miserable.

DR. PAUL: How miserable?

MR. LEWIS: Terrible.

DR. PAUL: What do you remember, huh?

MR. LEWIS (*weeping*): I feel terrible.

DR. PAUL: Do you feel that you still miss her?

MR. LEWIS: Oh, yes, I do. She was so nice (*weeping*). She was so nice.

MRS. LEWIS: She had, she did all the things, you know, for him, you know, when he was a little boy that little kids need that he didn't get at home. You know, she had animals around the house and things, you know, his parents never understood things like that.

MR. LEWIS: She's really the woman I've been looking for, really. She was so nice. She was a beautiful woman. She was so kind.

DR. PAUL: She was single?

MR. LEWIS: No, she was married. She had a family. She had her children, and, uh, but she was always understanding.

DR. PAUL: Do you ever see her family?

MR. LEWIS: No. Never had any really close relationship with her family.

DR. PAUL: Since she died.

MR. LEWIS: Since she died. She was a remarkable, kind person.

DR. PAUL: Do you know where she's buried?

MR. LEWIS: Yeah, Charlotte, North Carolina. I've never been to her grave.

DR. PAUL: Never?

MR. LEWIS: No. You see, I don't know why I've never been to her grave, but I haven't been to anybody's grave. She's the only person I ever, the only close person that's ever died in our family, you know.

DR. PAUL: Do you feel that, uh, she's the only one that you really loved that way? (*Mr. Lewis weeping, then silence.*)

MR. LEWIS: I've always loved her. She was very kind to me.

DR. PAUL: She loved you?

MR. LEWIS: Yes, she did (*sobbing*). I don't know what I'm crying about.

DR. PAUL: You don't know what you're crying about.

MR. LEWIS: I don't know.

DR. PAUL: You don't? You still miss her.

MR. LEWIS: She was so nice. It wasn't anything she did, especially, it was just . . . she was always so nice (*sobbing*). She always, she was always so sweet and so kind, and there was never a mean or a bad word (*sobbing loudly*) coming from her lips. She always liked me. There was never anything phony, she was always accepting me as I am. Being with her was like peace, just peace, just absolute peace.

DR. PAUL: So, in many ways you have been looking for her over the years.

MR. LEWIS: Yeah, I think I've found her. I think I have.

## REFERENCES

Aries, P. The reversal of death: Changes in attitudes toward death in Western societies. In D. E. Stannard (Ed.), *Death in America*. Philadelphia: University of Pennsylvania Press, 1975.

Bowlby, J. Process of mourning. *International Journal of Psycho-Analysis*, 1961, *42*, 317–340.

deMott, B. The pro-incest lobby. *Psychology Today*, March 1980, pp. 11–16.

Paul, N. L., & Paul, B. B. *A marital puzzle*. New York: Norton, 1975.

## RECOMMENDED READING

Becker, E. *The denial of death.* New York: Free Press, 1973.

Bowlby, J. *Attachment and loss* (Vol. 3: *Loss*). New York: Basic Books, 1980.

Borszormenyi-Nagy, I. Loyalty implications of the transference model in psychotherapy. *Archives of General Psychiatry,* 1972, *27,* 374–380.

Borszormenyi-Nagy, I., & Spark, G. M. *Invisible loyalties: Reciprocity in intergenerational family therapy.* New York: Harper & Row, 1973.

Engel, G. E. Is grief a disease? *Psychosomatic Medicine,* 1961, *23,* 18–22.

Masters, W. H., & Johnson, V. E. *Human sexual inadequacy.* Boston: Little, Brown, 1970.

Paul, N. L. Cross-confrontation. In P. J. Guerin, Jr. (Ed.), *Family therapy: Theory and practice.* New York: Gardner Press, 1976.

Selvini Palazzoli, M., Boscolo, L., Cecchin, G., & Prata, G. *Paradox and counterparadox.* New York: Aronson, 1978.

Stierlin, H. *Conflict and reconciliation.* New York: Science House, 1969.

Stierlin, H. *Separating parents and adolescents.* New York: Quadrangle, 1974.

Williamson, D. S. New life at the graveyard: A method of therapy for individuation from a dead former parent. *Journal of Marriage and Family Counseling,* 1978, *4,* 93–101.

# 10

# FAMILY MICROEVENTS: COMMUNICATION PATTERNS FOR PROBLEM SOLVING

JILL METCOFF
CARL A. WHITAKER

> The meaning or function of an event is not contained in itself but in its relation to the context. —GREGORY BATESON

Theoretical definition of a microevent: A repetitive loop of family interactions leading over and over to the same behavioral outcome for family members, thereby functioning to define, sustain, or provide a springboard for modification of interpersonal relationships.

## INTRODUCTION: THE FAMILY AS A CONTEXT FOR MICROEVENTS

The normal human family can be described as a negentropic biological system that is continuously open to growth and change (self-actualizing). Growth and change for individuals and for the family as a whole can be stimulated from within or without. In our view, the healthy family carries a sense of esteem for itself that is openly coordinated with children, grandparents, and the wider world of neighborhood and community. This family is focused in the present, holds its past in minor perspective, and envisions the future with comfort and without pain.

The group is qualitatively alive with an atmosphere of play and with a freedom for aggression. This group acknowledges separating and uniting currents within the subgroups; currents such as an adolescent's need to leave

Jill Metcoff. Consultant in Videotape Observation and Intervention in Family Interaction, Chicago, Illinois.

Carl A Whitaker. Department of Psychiatry, University of Wisconsin Medical School, Madison, Wisconsin.

home or a father's need for emotional support during a job crisis. The rules for group function are flexible, and the customs include secrecy rights, easy rotation in and out of triangles, and teaming without rigid fixation in the teams. The communication patterns are replete with affective recall and free associative material. The variety of available communication styles enables the family to be comfortable with the irrational as well as the logical and to protect these flexible mind sets with an overall sense of the absurd.

The group has freedom to admit nonmembers to intimate status as the situation warrants. Such expansions of the group indicate a strong sense of community with its neighbors.

The subgroups of the family structure the generation gap for comfort in the established role states but allow for flexible interchange so that children may play at parenting and parents may regress for fun and growth. The nuclear pair has developed a free sharing of roles without a duty-bound structure. Their relationship is stable enough to serve as the foundation for a sensitivity to nonverbal cues from within and without the entire system.

The suprasystem of the extended family includes the two sets of grandparents, who are intimates of their children and close friends with their children's other parents and grandparents. The children venerate these grandparents and enjoy parenting them and being parented by them.

The role of nourishing mother does not shadow that parent's person-hood, just as the father's role maintains the marriage and family as his central focus. These two persons are primarily individuals; secondarily, partners; and, thirdly, parents.

In our model, the individuals in this normal family enjoy a casual freedom in joining and separating from the group and its subgroups. Each dares to be tender enough to be available to the affect of any significant other, yet tough enough to tolerate interpersonal pain without residual bitterness. The courage to lose oneself in the group is balanced by the capacity to defend oneself if needed. Freedom to aggress is matched with a freedom to love without major reservation, in spite of the vulnerability entailed. Finally, the individuals stand free of the disorder of deliberate awareness and hold access to the kind of "sacred disorder" that, for example, Jackson Pollock attained.

*All* families, regardless of normality, develop characteristic redundant patterns of communication. For many years, the observation of such patterns stimulated clinicians and researchers to theorize about the meaning of such patterns in families. A confusion quickly developed: descriptions of these patterns (such as a "double bind" or a "generational boundary") were combined with hypotheses about their function, often in the same sentence. The newfound "vocabulary" of family theory, which included redundant transactional patterns (behaviors), was mixed together with a "grammar," the hypothesized regulation of family relationships through transactional patterns (rules). The result was a lack of straightforward behavioral descriptions of different kinds of redundant patterns that might be found in a variety of families.

Haley (1976) and Hoffman (1976) identified this quandary, and each has undertaken to rectify the situation, Hoffman in her description of the repetitive "homeostatic cycle," and Haley in his description of redundant family "sequences." Their separate analyses, derived from studies of similar repetitive family communication patterns, led them to two conclusions:

1. These sequences are regulatory or homeostatic—"a homeostatic mechanism which redirects tension away from some other area of the family" (Hoffman, 1976, p. 504).

2. "When [each type of repetitive] sequence changes, the individuals in the group undergo change" (Haley, 1976, p. 105).

In this chapter we focus on repetitive family patterns, but we theorize that they are not as much homeostatic mechanisms as they are continuously self-modifying, evolving structures for family communication around perceived problem areas. In this view, *such redundant patterns can be identified as the creative edge, the source of change in all families.* Such a view supports Haley's and Hoffman's second point: "When that sequence changes, the individuals in the group undergo change."

For convenience, the observable, redundant pattern we are describing is called a "microevent." All families are seen to have at least one such redundant pattern as part of their organizational structure. The most chaotic family could be seen to have repetitive loops of chaos; the most rigid schizophrenic family could be seen to be embedded in unending repetition of their ritual communication. Many families, particularly normal ones, have many different microevents. *All microevents involve a repetitive loop of observable interpersonal behaviors—both verbal and nonverbal—with a redundant outcome that affects most family members.* The term "microevent" suggests (1) that it is not necessarily a linear sequence of behaviors, but more of an event, a circular grouping of behaviors performed by several participants; (2) that this group of behaviors is embedded in a broader context (the microevent behaviors are not themselves of topical interest to the family); and (3) that each microevent has historical roots in some hypothetical "macroevent"—the microevent is the visible legacy of the macroevent.

In this chapter, we describe these patterns as created, modified, passed on and remodified through the generations as a structure to negotiate and resolve the day-to-day problems that arise as family members interact and grow older together. Each microevent can be simply described as a way, developed through the generations, in which people operate in families. Then we provide a detailed behavioral description of a microevent as seen in a clinical interview in order to clarify the type of redundant sequence we are describing. Finally, we examine the effects of therapeutic intervention in these sequences to illustrate the microevent as a family structure for growth and change.

## THE NORMAL EVOLUTION OF A MICROEVENT

The study of a family's repetitive interactional patterns offers a methodology for the study of the* family. We speculate that each distinctive redundant pattern, a microevent, develops as a creative family strategy that enables all family members to deal with internal stressful/developmental events that occur at crucial family transition points, or with external events that impinge on the family's functionings. As a strategy it is not an end in itself (content-oriented), but a means (process) to an end: the microevent interaction acts as a procedure for problem solving by sustaining a manner of relating to one another (a sort of parliamentary rule) that works well for all concerned.

*Example: The T. Family (Mom; Dad; Sue, aged 12; Bill, aged 15)*

When Sue was just entering her teens, she frequently "'almost' got into serious trouble." Her friends encouraged her to cut classes and go to the movies; her brother Bill requested her to meet a friend and "pick up something owed him" after school, and so led his sister to make drug connections for him. Sue's parents were anxious about the ease with which her peers could push her around. Yet, during family discussions, Sue's parents used her susceptibility to pressure (and her desire to be helpful) to ensure her compliance with *their* values. Over time, family discussions that focused on obtaining Sue's compliance were characterized by the following pattern of interaction:

1. Mom (or Bill) would find out about one of Sue's escapades.
2. Mom would bring Sue's "problem" to her father's attention.
3. Dad would get angry at Sue and demand "the whole story."
4. Mom would appear as if she might take Sue's side, thus encouraging Sue to "tell all" to her father.
5. Sue would tell the whole story, and Dad would become more upset.
6. Mom (or Bill, if present) would then agree with Dad's negative interpretation of the episode.
7. Sue would begin to cry.
8. Dad would cap the discussion with a last word, usually a permanent prohibition on an activity and an additional temporary punishment, such as "no television all week."

This pattern of interaction was functional for the whole family. Sue was protected from her own naïveté; the parents ensured her compliance with their family values; and Bill avoided having parental anxiety and punishment focused on him at a time when he was actually far closer to serious trouble. This interactional pattern suited both a value system and individual needs, while helping all family members to negotiate stresses particular to a moment in the family life cycle (adolescence). This useful interactional pattern became the distinctive family microevent for those times when Sue appeared to be getting into trouble. As a strategy for handling issues, *this microevent permitted family members to define interpersonal relationships and maintain acceptable family positions, while simultaneously providing a structure for dealing with each new stressful event.*

Hypothetically, the T. family microevent evolved from a major event, a "macroevent." For example, the T. family had a family secret: Sue's grandmother's adolescent pregnancy. That pregnancy, counter to values held by the family, was handled by Grandma's father's forcing her to give up the baby for adoption. Great-Grandma openly agreed with her husband, but secretly wished the baby could be kept. *The macroevent is hidden by the singleness of its occurrence and by time; the microevent is its visible legacy.* In the T. family, the strategy by which Grandma's family responded to her pregnancy was so effective (despite unresolved ambivalencies) that it became part and parcel of the family's operating procedures when Grandma came even close to trouble. Although perhaps Grandma never told Sue's mother of the pregnancy, Grandma and Grandpa kept Sue's mother out of trouble by using Great-Grandma and Great-Grandpa's tactics. In turn, Sue's mother internalized this pattern of problem solving—along with the original ambivalencies—and brought a modified version of the original pattern into play in her new family.

Because the microevent is so much a part of the family's fabric, the presumption is that no director stands outside the family to lead the family through a script; the family system instigates the microevent, precipitating it from within. *Causation of the microevent is circular in that any one of the family may precipitate it; there are no distinct beginnings.*

Although the microevent is expected to lead to an outcome that is useful to the family system, over time it could become a formula independent of family needs. For example, as Sue grew up, it was important for her own development to get into and out of predicaments on her own.

Returning to our example, let us presume that some years passed. Sue wanted more independence, but whenever a crisis flared she was unable to deviate from her part in the microevent pattern. That is, a potential issue with Sue would be focused on by Mom, often through brother Bill's tattling. In Sue's mother's eyes, the issue might take on crisis proportions, leading her to "deputize" herself to elicit a history of the issue in front of Dad. This history would so anger Dad as to provoke a Dad–Sue confrontation in which Dad always had the final word, Sue complied, and Mom and Bill remained on the emotional outskirts of both the confrontation and the final solution.

When Sue began to date Tom openly at the age of 18, she considered it "a good thing for her." Her family even liked Tom. But when Sue and Tom decided a few months later to marry, the family opposed this decision. The old microevent was triggered, but for Sue it was no longer functional: it had developed a life of its own by becoming a rigid, dysfunctional communicational structure.

In a normal family, we speculate that the microevent would be modified to remain functional in the face of family change and growth. In Sue's normal family, the microevent might undergo fission of a sort in response to Sue's desire to marry Tom: the old microevent (Type X) might continue in force for a limited number of problems relating to Sue, or might be used for another sibling altogether (Bill), while a new microevent (Type Y) might be developed in which Sue, not her father, has the final word. A benefit of a "new" microevent (Type Y) might include the freeing of Sue's mother to confront Sue directly, perhaps as Sue's great-grandmother would have liked to handle directly the issue of her daughter's adolescent pregnancy. *In normal families, the microevent as a familiar procedural strategy continues— through modification—to facilitate the handling of problems instead of becoming the problem itself.*

A microevent is useful to families becaue it streamlines the process of problem solving. It develops as a procedure to handle the family's problems of growth and stress. A sizable part of this streamlining is the trying on of individual roles and of behaviors characteristic of these roles. Once roles are agreed upon, problem solving occurs. As an analogue, imagine how a company makes product decisions through channels created by the following roles: corporation president, production engineer, assembly line foreman, director of marketing. In a family, the microevent exemplifies a similar allotment of roles; these roles, however, deal not with company production but with system functioning, generational boundaries, sibling position, marital or parental stance, and so forth.

Sue's family is not limited to one microevent. A thoroughly different repetitive interactional pattern might occur in response to a psychological crisis created by the death of a relative. Hypothetically, the greater the variety of microevents in a family, the greater the variety of roles available to family members, both within and across generational boundaries (Haley, 1976). Roles are acquired through growth, experience, and practice. A parent has had life experience as a parent, a marital partner, a son or daughter, a sibling, a neighbor, and a friend. Yet in dysfunctional families, a mother or father may still be locked into an old role, such as that of sibling or child in the family of origin. When this occurs, the parenting role is not readily available to him or her in the current family. That failure to acquire a variety of roles and to maintain a flexibility between them is directly observable in the repetitive frequency of a single type of microevent.

From our observations, a very dysfunctional family is limited to one or two main, rigid microevents. Theoretically, a microevent of many years' standing has failed to evolve as participants grew and changed. The old microevent still in operation is observed as mechanical interaction, since the issue around which family members might be interacting has become less important than the interaction itself.

Sometimes a dysfunctional family appears continuously chaotic or rigid. In either instance, they might be described as being dominated by one microevent. That microevent plays itself out, behavior by behavior, over and over. The redundancy suggests that the family system is closed; its boundaries are impermeable and its process is maintained by patterned ritual. The microevent has become in essence a "false process." Situational problems and information communicated are not "real," because the word-for-word content communicated from one family member to the next is overshadowed by the redundant process of the microevent. The interchangeability of content within a repetitive interactional pattern suggests that the microevent is in itself the major family problem.

Thus the microevent is a way of studying the process of family interaction. One can also assume (or presume) that the microevent process is itself identical to or modified from a larger process, the macroevent. Normal family *change,* as presented in this chapter, involves a change in the outcome of the family's microevent(s). Such change is precipitated from within, as in the T. family, or stimulated from without by some external trauma or by counseling.

## DETAILED BEHAVIORAL DESCRIPTION
## OF THE MICROEVENT IN CLINICAL INTERVIEWS

The microevent that we see in a clinical interview is a short, 5- to 10-minute repetitive drama that involves a tightly knit group of characters, usually most or all nuclear family members. Each character's behaviors appear to fit smoothly with a larger, well-rehearsed program, so that each action appears as a cue to another character. The actions of all the characters lead to a final conclusion or outcome that affects the entire group.

*Example (from Weclew, 1974)*

*First Occurrence of Sequence*

MOTHER TO FATHER (*in loud voice, wagging finger*): You're home with us so little. I'm beginning to think you don't care about us. Why don't you act like a father should?

FATHER (*leans forward in chair*): Don't you know why?

SON, AGED 5 (*stands up, walks over to mother*): Can I go to the bathroom? (*Mother answers, gives directions to bathroom. Father slumps in seat.*)

*Outcome:* Son interrupts mother and father, and thus conflict between them is avoided.

*Second Occurrence of Sequence (Variation of Above)*

MOTHER TO FATHER (*in loud voice*): You never help me with the housework. I have to do everything.

FATHER (*in sarcastic voice*): Poor you! (*He leans forward in chair.*) I do my best.

MOTHER (*getting louder*): Are you kidding? You . . .

(*Son slaps sister.*)

MOTHER TO SON: Leave her alone.

(*Father slumps in seat.*)

*Outcome*: Son interrupts their argument by slapping sister, so disagreement is discontinued, and conflict is avoided once again.

Under the observation conditions of our study, microevents appeared at least twice during an hour-long family therapy interview.[1] Variation within each character's behaviors are thought of as "cues" and not as "script"; all cues lead to the same final outcome. Thus, for a wife who might be seen as a shrew, her actions during different occurrences of a microevent might vary from screaming to hitting to slamming doors, but they will always be shrewlike, tend to occur at a particular moment during the drama, and contribute inexorably to a final outcome. The final outcome is the same in each occurrence of the microevent.

Up to now, it is clear that the microevent is describable as a nonlinear set of observations. The observations, verbal or nonverbal, are recognizable as interpersonal *cues*. This notion gains support from the familiar concepts that "all behavior is communication" and that "one cannot not communicate" (Watzlawick, Beavin, & Jackson, 1967). The repetitious nature of the microevent and the identical consequences to the family from each microevent suggest that an individual's behaviors (i.e., communications) are meaningless unless they are considered as cues, each of which triggers the next individual to act. The consequences (outcome) to the family group of the *entire* sequence of such behaviors is observably meaningful indeed:

Every time the husband $\begin{cases} \text{scratched his ear} \\ \text{rubbed his nose} \\ \text{tapped his left foot} \end{cases}$ during an argument with his

---

[1]Potentially, and conceptually, other microevents (in any family) may occur less frequently than twice per hour. Some life traumas or developmental stages occur so infrequently—for example, the transition from parenthood to grandparenthood—that the microevents that may have developed around those macroevents are not readily accessible to the observer. Similarly, some microevents might exceed an hour, a month, or years in length. However, we cannot know these, because they are not readily studied. Nonetheless, this variability in the time dimension should be kept in mind by the reader.

wife, one of the children would

$$\left.\begin{array}{l} \text{ask to go to the bathroom} \\ \text{slap a sibling} \\ \text{begin to cry} \end{array}\right\}\text{, so that the}$$

husband–wife dispute was never resolved.


*Example: The S. Family*

| Description of the S. Family Microevent | Key Behavioral Cues |
|---|---|
| A family of three—mother, father, and 24-year-old son—sat down for a consultation interview with the family therapist. The son slumped in his seat and cradled his head in his hands while explaining that his problem—finding his "identity" and "having a meaningful relationship"—was uniquely his. He strongly felt that his parents need not be involved in the interview. The mother, seated beside her son, agreed with him. In fact, when the son failed to find words to articulate his position, his mother helped him out with examples of previous failures to solve his problem, such as moving in with his girlfriend and then immediately breaking off the relationship. The father, seated on the other side of the mother but further away from the other three, remained aloof and "tuned out" except when he was questioned directly by the therapist. In those instances, the father would react to all questions as an intellectual dealing with hypothetical situations. | (1) Son's slumped, infantile posture; head cradled in hands. Frequent rubbing of forehead. (2) Mother and son's physical proximity; father's relative distance. (3) Son (or mother) verbally expresses son's problems, particularly developing his own "identity" and having a "meaningful relationship." |
| When the therapist questioned the reality of the son's problems or asked if the father's examination of the situation suggested that the son could relate to others, the mother would intervene "on behalf" of her son. She explained that the father hadn't understood what the son had said. She would supply examples of her son's inadequacies to the therapist. After she had spoken a few sentences, the son would agree with her and resume his slumped, infantile posture. The family became silent for almost a minute | (4) Son sits upright, looks therapist (or father) in eye. (5) Mother restates son's position. (6) Son resumes slumped posture, cradles head in hands. |

| Description of the S. Family Microevent | Key Behavioral Cues |
|---|---|
| then, until the son returned to his claim, "I have always been a problem to myself and my family," or until the therapist asked a question. | (7) Family silence. |

*Repeated Outcome of This Microevent.* Mother thwarted any attempt by son to abandon his "childlike" position in the family. Her success in prohibiting her son's change was strongly assisted by her husband's silence and her son's enthusiastic collusion in his role.

*Occurrence of This Microevent.* This microevent occurred five times during the interview. Spacing between occurrences decreased until, after 30 minutes, each microevent immediately followed the previous one.

| Continuation of Session | Key Behavioral Cues |
|---|---|
| After some conversation about the son's problems, the therapist suggested that all the problems might not be the son's alone. The son reacted strongly. He sat up straight and looked the therapist in the eye; he also disagreed strongly with the therapist, insisting with numerous examples that he had always been a problem to himself and to his family. Then he would run his fingers through his hair, wrap his hands on his face, and resume the slumping, infantile posture. Yet the therapist persisted. Most times, the reaction to these "crazy" suggestions was the same. At other times, the son—although still straightening up and looking the therapist in the eye— stayed quiet and appeared attentive to the therapist's ideas. At this juncture, the mother restated the son's failure to make and sustain relationships. | (Therapeutic intervention)<br><br>(4) (repetition)<br>Son sits upright, looks therapist in eye.<br><br><br>(5A) (variations of 5)<br>Son verbally restates his problems. He speaks to therapist as if therapist ought to understand.<br><br>(5B)<br>Mother restates son's position. |
| Another distinctive variation in this pattern was apparent. The mother did *not* challenge the therapist's viewpoint *although* the son appeared attentive to the therapist when (1) the son glanced at the mother *before* answering the therapist *and* (2) he retained the infantile, slumped posture. | (5C)<br>Son maintains his verbal position by *not* sitting upright and glancing at his mother prior to speaking. |

*Effect of Therapeutic Intervention.* The strength of this family pattern was demonstrated when the father substituted for the mother at the end of the interview. This event was triggered when the therapist built an alliance with the mother during the penultimate microevent occurrence: rather than continuing to insist that the son's problem was the family's, the therapist began to sympathize with the mother for the father's aloofness and failure to assist with their son. She began to cry and borrowed the therapist's handkerchief. The therapist had speeded up the microevent until it finally exploded here. The son, acting distraught, began to retell his problems in a loud voice. The therapist said, "Shut up. I'm having a conversation with your mother," while moving his chair closer to the mother's. At this point, the father voluntarily entered the conversation to tell the therapist that the son *always* had been *the* problem, and the microevent resumed.

The observer of this repetitive pattern is struck by three characteristics of the microevent:

1. The microevent is identifiable through a series of behaviors.
2. The nature of these behaviors is equifinal.
3. The microevent is reactive to positive and negative feedback.

The microevent's chain of behaviors (both verbal and nonverbal) appear as cues: "Such interactional sequences trigger and regulate the steps in a communicational program; they do not cause them" (Scheflen, 1965). Different family members may "fill in" for others in the performance of these cues, just as a dramatic understudy substitutes for a sick actor. This type of substitution indicates the operation of equifinality—a characteristic of all systems: "The principle of equifinality means that the same result may spring from different origins, because it is the nature of the organization which is determinate" (Watzlawick, *et al.,* 1967). In the example of the S. family above, cue 5 indicates equifinality: If the son doesn't justify his viewpoint in the face of a challenge to this viewpoint, then the mother does. If the mother is vacillating during his challenge, the father steps in and takes her place. As Scheflen (1965) succinctly states:

> The point is that when a step is [precipitated] in a program, if one person fails to peform it another person will, and if one's performance does not come off, someone else may repeat it until the step is completed and the group can go on in its task. (p. 51)

Thus, however idiosyncratic some behaviors might appear during the unfolding of a microevent, the presence of equifinality suggests that we are observing in the microevent a family communications system.

Like any system, the microevent is guided by and responsive to negative and positive feedback. Feedback is input into a system that affects and is affected by other parts of the system. Negative feedback is input that promotes stability in the system, as in the following example of an employee-employer relationship: An employee, Bill, always performs his duties well. His employer, Jim, invariably pats him on the back at the end of the day, saying, "That was a great job, Bill," and both employer and employee go home feeling pleased. Despite the positive nature of the employer's comment and the positive spirit in which each departs, Bill and his employer are part of a negative feedback loop: their system remains the same and stable. Positive feedback, on the other hand, promotes dissonance in the system; positive feedback is a change mechanism. For example: Sam, an employee, always performs his duties poorly. He expects his employer to say to him, "Sam, you've got to do this over. If you don't improve, I'm sorry, but we'll have to let you go." Sam's negative expectations are usually met, and he frequently must redo an activity. In exasperation one day, his employer says (with only a hint of sarcasm), "That was a great job, Sam! One of these days you'll have to show me just how you do that." This feedback so surprises Sam that he responds, "I can actually do it better and I will—it will just take 15 minutes." And he does so. In this instance, the behavior of one individual in the system has changed, triggering change in another and probably escalating further change in the first individual (because feedback, whether positive or negative, operates in loops).

The microevent of the S. family indicates successive operations of negative *and* positive feedback loops. The negative loops were these: Usually, the boy remained in a slumped posture, asserting that he was the one with problems. His position was agreed to by the parents and appeared comfortable to them. The mother remained physically close to and concerned about her son, while the father remained apart from the two of them; physical and emotional distance between the parents was evident. This interactional pattern was stable. The positive loops were these: If the family was challenged enough times in their belief that the son had all the problems, deviation from the original loop was visible. The mother would become convinced that the act of speaking for her son is too much of a "burden" for her; the father would force himself to replace her in the equation. The very act of replacement brought the father into a closer, more active relationship with the family, while allowing the mother to begin a move away from her son and/or to confront the distance in the marital relationship.

When positive feedback was injected repeatedly by the therapist into the microevent, this family seemed to teeter-totter. Negative feedback could have restabilized the microevent, but in a new configuration: the father would have become close to the son, and the mother might have gone back to school or gotten a job to increase her distance from both men. On the other hand the dissonance already present within the microevent might have amplified: The mother, resentful of her "burden," might have confronted the father with his distance from her. Attempts by the son to reaffirm his closeness with either parent would have been rebuffed while his parents were altering the nature of their relationship.

These ideas are speculative; what is clear and observable is that *external inputs of feedback were handled within the context of the family's microevent.* If the family were a house, then the microevent would be the front hall through which all strangers must pass. In real life, such external inputs or "strangers" include the passage of time, developmental processes, and life event stresses. A family's microevent vibrates like an invisible, permeable membrane between the family and its world. Thus, in its reactivity to negative and positive feedback, *the microevent embodies themes of stability and change within the family system.*

## THERAPEUTIC IMPLICATIONS OF THE MICROEVENT

### Overview

One particular microevent usually dominates family interaction during a clinical interview. It is composed of a distinctive, observable set of behaviors that includes seating position, posture, language use, speaking and gesture orders, and exits and entrances. The observation that one microevent predominates in an interview is perhaps attributable to the idea that the microevent is a well-developed family pattern for problem solving (or negotiating) that is activated by the presence of a therapist, new surroundings, and a presenting problem. Theoretically, it should repeat frequently during a family interview: the family unit puts on its most comfortable and characteristic problem-solving pattern as an individual would put on his or her most comfortable shoes for a walk.

The microevent is a ritualistic structure that the family lives in and through. A mass of microevents is possible in *every* family, ranging from the infrequently activated rituals for special "hello" (birth) and "good-bye" (death) occasions to the events in between: for example, going off to school, bringing home a girlfriend, or settling on who is going to carry out the garbage. Some families have not developed this range or have become stuck in one or two of these rituals, leaving them with a depleted communicational structure through which they must manage the variety of life's events. The variety of microevents available to families can be compared to the number of songs a family incorporates: The healthy family uses Mendelssohn for weddings, *Dies Irae* for death, and "Happy Birthday to You" for birthdays; the communicationally depleted family uses one song for all occasions.

The more rigid the family, the more limited the variety of microevents. The more flexible, adaptable, and well-integrated the family system, the more variety in type, length, duration, and intensity of microevents. A rigid family "stuck" in the communicational glue created by a few but highly redundant microevents "feels" monotonous, repetitious to the observer; they live in their process, not with life's content. The healthy family is alive with a mass of microevents, many of which are hidden to the observer because they rarely appear, others of which are undergoing constant modification to keep the family structure concurrent with internal and external events.

Although a therapist cannot prevent a microevent from happening, he or she can disrupt an occurring microevent to prevent its outcome. Any change in the outcome of the microevent is therapeutic because it introduces flexibility into family interaction. The disruption of one microevent precipitates another one, which may not be a repetition of the first one.

The therapist needs to let a microevent unfold to the degree that he or she can jump in and join in. By this intrusive action, the therapist acts as the hero who jumps on the fast-going stagecoach, scares the driver into dropping the reins, and causes the horses to deviate to a new trail—thereby missing arrival at the usual time and place. By intruding in the microevent, the therapist pushes someone else out of an interactional niche or behavior, thereby modifying the course and the outcome of the entire process.

The therapist's role in the microevent is to disrupt it while it is happening in such a way that its outcome cannot be accomplished. Although not necessarily verbalizing it, the therapist makes the implicit interactional game explicit so that the possibility of reactivating the identical microevent is decreased.

*Example*

In Minuchin's paper, "The Family Lunch Session" (1976), he describes a methodology used in treatment of anorexia nervosa that consists of the therapist having lunch with the family. In one such case, videotaped by Dr. Minuchin, the microevent was a very conspicuous part of the episode. Mother, father, therapist, and patient ordered a lunch. The secretary brought the lunch, and the daughter hesitated to eat. The father remonstrated with her. Minuchin then said, "Why can't you make your daughter eat?", and the father became more and more irate. The daughter got up out of her chair at the table and was gradually backed into the corner by the father, who was becoming more and more infuriated. At the point of almost physical contact, the father and daughter stopped their face-to-face confrontation and backed away. The daughter went back and sat down at the table, and the father sat down in obvious defeat. Almost within a matter of minutes, the mother reenacted the same scene: she began to harangue the daughter, got the daughter up from the chair, and backed her over into the corner. In the middle of this stressed confrontation, when it looked as though mother and daughter would strike each other, the mother also backed down and moved back to the table. The daughter also went back and sat down to her food. At this point, Dr. Minuchin quietly asked the girl if she had changed her mind about what she wanted to eat. The girl said "Yes, I'd like some ice cream." Dr. Minuchin ordered the ice cream; when it was brought, the daughter ate it and then went back to eat the hamburger she had previously ordered.

In essence, the family's therapeutic effort to help the daughter change her disruptive behavior was a failure because it failed to reach resolution. The microevent was creative but dysfunctional. In a manner of speaking, there was foreplay but no orgasm. Dr. Minuchin, on the other hand, utilized simple caring and compromised his own control system; he offered the daughter part of the control and won the cooperation of the patient. He modeled for the family the creative (nonhomeostatic) way out of the narrow path provided by the family's routinized microevent. Thus he helped them to shift from an old to a new outcome and thereby to create a new microevent.

### A Description of the Process of Disrupting Microevents

In live and videotaped observation of therapists, we saw consistently the following three "ingredients" in the successful disruption of microevents. Each of these strategic points is described in the next few pages.

1. The therapist needs to acknowledge the power of the family system as represented by the microevent. Simultaneously, he needs to make the attempt to promote change in the family, a subgroup, or an individual by disrupting the microevent.

2. When the usual outcome of the microevent is prevented, family change occurs. Change is short-lived unless the therapist reassures the family unit while also supporting the individual's efforts to disrupt the cycle, so that the individual's change is accommodated in the larger system.

3. In both of the above instances, the therapist needs to act and to discredit his very action so that the system or individual perceives change as precipitated by the family unit and therefore useful to them.

#### Proposition 1: Acknowledging the Family While Undermining It

Family members communicate to others from at least two standpoints during an interview: they display idiosyncratic thinking and influences from nonfamily spheres, such as work, friends, and school; and they are also advocates of the family system, as indicated by participation in the microevent.

When the thrust of a family member's dialogue with the therapist is framed by his or her participation in the microevent (instead of being idiosyncratic), the therapist internally keeps in mind that the current conversation is not as much one with an individual as it is a conversation with a family system. The therapist can then adopt a special therapeutic role characterized by a "skewed statement set." (Metaphorically, a "skewed statement set" can be imagined as the pitching of curve balls, one after the other, to family members as they come up to bat.) These statements deliver a "punch" to the system and then a "shock absorber" that supports the system on another dimension. A further confusion occurs when the therapist "acknowledges" the delivery of both "punch" and "shock absorber," a tactic that leaves the family open to choose which message they wish to answer. The three messages, "punch," "shock absorber," and "acknowledgment," may operate in three basic combinations (in either direction): (1) Verbal-verbal-verbal; (2) Verbal–nonverbal–verbal; (3) Nonverbal–verbal–non-verbal.

Here are two examples of the process. In the first example, a description of the process is found in the left column, and the specific example—from an Ackerman videotape—is found in the right column. The second example continues the description of Whitaker's intervention with the S. family—the mother, the father, and the 24-year-old son with "identity problems."

*Systemic Approach: Example 1*

| Process | Illustration |
|---|---|
| 1. The therapist interrupts a microevent with a comment that redefines family roles. | 1. (Therapist to 6-year-old Johnny): "In all families like yours where the son is accused of lying, the son thinks his parents are lying. How do your parents lie to you?" |
| 2. This redefinition challenges a family rule as presented in the microevent (Sluzki, 1978). | 2. Rule: Johnny is the only liar in the family. |
| 3. This challenging redefinition contains a contradictory (paradoxical), ambiguous, or skewed aspect that enables a family member to respond to the therapist without overtly admitting or rejecting the redefinition. | 3. The therapist sat beside the parents while he spoke to Johnny and he gave the mother an encouraging smile. |
| 4. The skewed aspect does not negate the challenge if the communication set is linked by "acknowledgment." | 4. "Acknowledgment": The combination of 1 and 3. The system and Johnny were given support. |

In the preceding example, the therapist first generalized about all families with liars. The generalization that challenges the rule was immediately combined with another statement, that Johnny-plus-someone is lying. By challenging rules, the therapist then redefined family roles in interpersonal terms. A role such as "family liar" is no longer perceived by the therapist (or family) as a static niche, but rather as a dynamic factor of relationships (if one lies, everyone has to lie). Finally, the therapist extruded himself from his own statement *before* the family extruded him by sitting beside the parents and smiling at the mother. Such self-disqualification is "acknowledgment": it implies recognition of the power of the system as represented by the micro-event.

*Systemic Approach: Example 2*

In the example of the mother, father, and 24-year-old son, Whitaker used his own brand of strategic communication. The boy's presenting problem was that he "can't build a meaningful relationship." The microevent, previously described, suggested that any change in the boy's usual form of infantile relationship would cause the mother to intervene. Whitaker's strategy was directed along the following lines:

BOY (B) TO WHITAKER (W): I'm miserable without anyone. Can I expect no happiness in life?

W TO B: Probably not. Why don't you ask your mother?

B: My mother?

W TO B: Sure, there's nothing worse than an unemployed mother.

Here, Whitaker challenged the idea that the boy can't build relationships by suggesting to him that all along he had maintained a positive (and un-recognized) relationship with his mother—he kept her employed worrying about him. By directly addressing his comments to the boy, Whitaker indirectly communicated a new viewpoint to the mother. She was offered the opportunity to think over this new idea without being put in a position where she was forced to respond. In fact, she was encouraged *not* to respond: Whitaker's "acknowledgment" of the power of the family unit, through his description of the mother's activity in the microevent (being·employed), made the micro-event undesirable to both the mother and the son because a completed microevent would now indicate a "meaningful relationship" between mother and son. The mother was put in a very uncomfortable position: if she rejected or accepted Whitaker's viewpoint, she would be *continuing* the old outcome of the microevent, that of interrupting her son when he begins to relate to someone else; the best position for her was to remain quiet. Whitaker's verbal strategy rendered the mother powerless. Thus Whitaker singled out the son and asked him to change (as the family ineffectually requests), while simul-taneously acknowledging the family system. Family change was promoted by encouraging mother or son to forestall the outcome of the microevent, which is redefined—in their eyes—as undesirable.

This strategic verbal communication has a nonverbal component as well. While the verbal "punch" to the family rule is being delivered ("Your son *can* build a relationship—with you"), Whitaker provides a nonverbal "shock ab-sorber": he leans toward the mother and assumes an identical position with her as if to suggest an alliance between them (Scheflen, 1964).

Whitaker escalated each of these dialogues with the son to the extent that the buildup of verbal exchanges resembled a boxing round. Each round began with the boy assuming his habitual infantile posture and whining voice. It ended when the boy was sitting upright; the mother would lean farther and farther away from him until she was finally determined to challenge Whitaker.

Each round lasted for less time than the previous one. In each round, the therapist verbally joined with one family member, while nonverbally he paralleled whichever one, mother or son, was getting "punched." Finally, the mother, of her own accord, overtly redefined the rule about the son by saying she didn't want him living at home any more. Thus the microevent was fundamentally changed.

The therapists' use of themselves in both examples was what is termed "systemic": each *reflected back* the family system to the family when a family member was acting and speaking as part of a microevent. We may interpret this systemic role as a metacommunication in which the therapist offered a symmetrical relationship to the family. He was in effect saying, "You and I are equally powerful because we understand each other—but it's your ball game." A runaway competitive relationship occurred in each case. The runaway situation resulted from the positive feedback going into the system; this disrupted each microevent and redefined its outcome.

### Proposition 2: Helping the Family System to Accommodate Changes in a Subgroup or Individual

Now we turn to the second proposition: If change occurs in a subsystem or an individual member of the system, the therapist needs to inject some positive feedback into the dominant pattern to alter its powerful control so that the individual's change is accommodated in the larger system.

First, we describe some dynamics of this second situation. Observation of the S. family showed that as the microevent was challenged, its reappearance occurred more frequently, and each occurrence was shorter than the previous one. It appears that this disruption of the microevent by Whitaker interrupted the pattern so as to change the outcome only briefly. Mother and son were not able to sustain their attempts to separate and change until after many "rounds" were played out. In theoretical terms, we presume that the system's parts are interdependent and that shifts in one area will reverberate throughout the system. The reverberation indicates that the system is—or may become—open, and that it will flexibly tolerate change. Nonetheless, the system-rigid (or closed system) behaviors of other members, or even of the member who changes for a moment, may regain their salience at any moment, since a family system tends to function along patterned lines. When the system-rigid (closed) behaviors reoccur, they may increase in frequency, rigidity, or flexibility. Such behavioral shifts toward a more closed or more open system will be echoed by shifts in the original parameters (verbal, nonverbal, and durational) of a specific microevent.

The therapist, according to his or her judgment, style, and expertise, can and does manipulate such shifts in the direction of a flexible, open system by utilizing a structure similar to the "skewed statement set" of Proposition 1.

For convenience, this second intervention and the therapist's role are called "individualistic." Here are the process and some examples.

### Individualistic Approach: Example 1

| Process | Illustration |
|---|---|
| 1. A family member shifts from the closed- to the open-system mode. | 1. W TO B: So what's with you?<br>B: Sometimes I think I'm very arrogant . . .<br>W: I don't. I think you're lonely, paralyzed, not arrogant. I like you.<br>B (*surprised look*): You know, I'm frightened of you. |
| 2. The therapist joins the individual or subgroup. | 2. W TO B: I understand. |
| 3. The therapist's acceptance of the individual challenges a system rule. | 3. Rule: Boy can't engage in expressive relationship. |
| 4. To mitigate the challenges to the system, the therapist can then acknowledge another family member or subsystem by | 4. |
|    a. soliciting a comment from another family member. |    a. W addressed the father: "So what's with you, Dad? How do you feel about me?" |
|    b. posturing himself symmetrically with another family member without loosening the verbal tie to the individual. | |
|    c. doing the reverse of (b). |    c. W sat close to son in identical posture. |
|    d. shifting his voice tone, posture, and/or verbal content so as to rapidly leave his individualistic input to stand alone. | |

After Whitaker strengthened his relationship to the boy, he gave full attention to the parents. Then the boy tried to shift back to the old pattern. He constantly interrupted to talk about his "relationship problem." Meanwhile, Whitaker worked to strengthen a bond to the mother—thus momentarily loosening her bond to the boy. To keep the boy in the new pattern (a different microevent), Whitaker smiled at him, patted him on the knee, sat close to him, and said "Shut up!"

### Individualistic Approach: Example 2

The microevent: A mother talked to the therapist while her 10-year-old son first echoed her comments and then interrupted them. Finally she stopped speaking to the therapist and addressed her son.

| Process | Illustration |
|---|---|
| 1. A family member makes a shift from the closed- to the open-system mode. | 1. The mother talked to the therapist, ignoring son's increasingly strong attempts to interrupt. |
| 2. The therapist joins the indivdual by accepting that individual's role redefinition. | 2. The therapist responded to mother in kind: he talked to the mother while ignoring the interrupting son. |
| 3. The therapist's acceptance of the individual challenges a system rule. | 3. Rule: The son can interrupt the mother. |
| 4. To mitigate the challenges to the system, the therapist can then acknowledge another family member or subsystem by<br><br>    a. soliciting a comment from another family member.<br>    b. posturing himself symmetrically with another family member without loosening the verbal tie to the first individual.<br>    c. doing the reverse of (b).<br>    d. shifting his voice tone, posture, and/or verbal content so as to rapidly leave his individualistic input to stand alone. | 4. The mother heard the therapist out, then spoke to her son. While she spoke to the son, the therapist began to clean his fingernails absent-mindedly. |

In this approach, the therapist waited until a family member took the initiative in changing the microevent pattern. Since the mother's relationship with the therapist broke a family rule, the therapist then chose to "leave" the family to create its own new outcome and new microevent by extruding himself from the situation (cleaning his nails). On the content level, the mother was complaining about the son's unhelpfulness in household chores. On the new relationship level, she was defining a complementary relationship with the son and a symmetrical one with the therapist. The therapist accepted the symmetry by participating in exactly the same pattern and then kept the situation from becoming either "runaway" or extrusive by withdrawing to clean his nails.

### Proposition 3: A Discussion of the Therapist as Catalyst

In our view, the therapist regards the normal or pathological family as both seedbed and nurturer of its own change. The therapist is no more—and no less—than the catalyst who intervenes at the proper moment (the unfolding of the microevent) to assist the individual, subgroup, or family towards change. *"Change" is defined as a lasting disruption of the outcome of the microevent.* Thus the therapist's interventions are tied to the occurrence of the microevent.

These interventions are geared to the relative degree of openness or closure in the family's system as indicated by the frequency, intensity, and rigidity of the microevent(s). When the system is relatively open, individuals comfortably risk change. The therapist, when dealing with openness, operates from an "individualistic" standpoint: he or she supports the individual's efforts to change while simultaneously working to permit accommodation of individual change in the larger system (see Proposition 2). When the system is relatively closed, the therapist proceeds "systemically"; that is, while acknowledging the power of the family's system, the therapist also undermines it by sabotaging the attempts of one or more family members to continue his, her, or their participation in the microevent.

The therapist does not openly challenge the system or its rules as these are reflected in the microevent. He or she may "wrap" the intervention around seemingly "innocent" information collection, such as history taking or "let's define this problem" (see the example of 6-year-old Johnny as "family liar"). The therapist may also enact this strategy while planning a family task or creating a paradoxical situation. The "systemic" or "individualistic" processes of communicating with a family can be used, regardless of a therapeutic "school" that might guide the overall structure of a therapist's strategy.

Our observations suggest that failure to be "systemic" or "individualistic" when appropriate indicates to the family that the therapist sanctions covert rules or roles that are dysfunctional for the family or identified patient. The sanction enables the family to accommodate the therapist in its system without motivating the family to change. Another possibility is that the therapist, when failing to be "systemic" or "individualistic," acts as an individual outside of the system and remains out of synchrony with the system. Such action is alien to the microevent pattern and causes such an increase in the intensity and/or frequency of the microevent pattern that the therapist is extruded from ever "joining" with the family. The result of both sanctioning and being out of synchrony is that there is no change in the outcome of the microevent.

In keeping with the notion that families precipitate their own changes through modification of microevents, the therapist can readily free himself from either the glory or the responsibility of change. Once the catalytic interventions are performed, the therapist acknowledges a family's strength by momentarily disengaging himself or herself from their interactions with one another. The therapist is like a workman building a house alone in a comic film: he nails on a window and the roof begins to fall out. Eventually he gets the window and the roof in place. If the therapist is successful, the building remains standing, welcoming tenants, while the therapist twirls his cane and goes off into the sunset.

## CONCLUSION

Normal families have the capacity to change over time.

*Example*

Bowen, who was interviewing a couple, was convinced that the wife pre-cipitated the husband's alcoholic bouts. He said to the wife, "Have you ever considered doing it on purpose, for fun?" On the way home from the inter-view, the wife said to her husband, "Your mother is a bitch." The husband started drinking as soon as he got home. He was "drunk as a skunk" 12 hours later, and his wife said, "That was just great. It worked just like Murray said." But they were never able to do it again.

When the implicit interactional game was made explicit, this microevent could never be reconstructed, reactivated. Any time that a therapist invades the unconscious successfully, he or she destroys the microevent, even the internal microevent of the individual's communication with himself or herself.

*Example*

A patient attempted suicide, and the family was brought together for a family therapy interview. The therapist's gathering together of the family suggests that he believed that someone in that family felt murderous towards that person; suicide is a two-person event. The therapist stated this to the family. Then the patient was pushed into a fantasy: "What would have happened if you'd been successful this time and you were now dead? What kind of funeral would you have; what kind of flowers would come; who would attend; what will they do with your high school memorabilia?" This was an immunizing process; it disturbed the intrapsychic microevent, "They'll be sorry when I'm dead and gone." This intervention defused the charge to suicide.

Once having gone through a disruption of the microevent, individuals find it easier to go through it next time. No therapist is ever so powerful as to be able to break up a pattern evolved over a period of time in a matter of minutes. The family must sustain a number of disruptions to alter its microevent. If the entire family (or even an extended family) participates in the disruption of the microevent, their input, however minimal, to the next microevent will be altered—possibly enough so as to change the whole episode.

Thus family change, as presented in this chapter, means a change in the outcome of that family's microevent(s). The visibly redundant nonlinear behaviors, verbal and nonverbal, that make up the micro-event pattern provide the family with a strategy, a process for dealing with life's events. Its repetitive operation on a day-to-day basis gives the family a framework for dealing with one another, possibly because it is a codification of rules by which each can live with the others. As years pass, one particular microevent may have outlived its usefulness. It becomes a "false process," a hollow ritual that bogs down the family so that they cannot cope creatively with life's normal developmental crises. When this occurs, a therapist can use the microevent as a key to family change. The therapist can model a new microevent in which he or she triangulates an individual (e.g., the family hero, the mother or father, or the family scapegoat) and the family, thereby changing the dynamic relationship between the whole family and one or more of its members. For example, a male therapist may attempt to seduce the mother to make the father jealous so that she will spend less time being a drudge for her family and so that father will want to take her away from the children. This change will become apparent in a new ritual of interaction, a new microevent.

This chapter has attempted to present redundant family interactional patterns that have a consistent outcome for each family member as microevents. A microevent exists in three dimensions: it is a set of verbal and nonverbal behaviors; it is a family communicational format (a process); it is a reflection of a family in time. In normal families, these behavioral patterns, although repetitious, are not rigid and homeostatic in nature; they are continuously self-modifying, evolving structures for family communication around family issues. Without continuous evolution, a single type of microevent becomes not a structural channel for communication, but rather a dam in the stream of communication. If the family is to maintain the openness characteristic of normality, then this dam must be exploded; the microevent must change.

Microevents come into being over time. Each microevnt is, in our view, a reflection of some macroevent in family history. Examples of macroevents might include an external stress that impinged on the family system (such as an abrupt wartime dislocation) or an internal crisis around a transition point in the family life cycle (such as the birth of a stillborn first child/first grandchild). Whether the original macroevent is known or unknown, the microevent is its visible legacy. As such, the microevent reflects the communicational strategy to handle the stress that the family developed at that key time.

As normal families grow in time, their microevents change. Some old ones give way to new ones; others simply disappear while new ones develop in response to new situations. Thus, change in the outcome of microevents reflects evolutionary growth and change in families.

## ACKNOWLEDGMENTS

The repeated viewing in 1972 of videotaped family therapy interviews at Chicago's Institute for Juvenile Research/Family Systems Program gave rise to this study of microevents. Videotapes from virtually all the major family therapists, as well as from lcoal and student family therapists, were included. The range of therapists' styles, combined with their universal attempts to interrupt redundant interactional patterns, stimulated Metcoff to involve Whitaker in the group immediately. Celia J. Falicov contributed invaluable ideas and feedback from 1972 to the present. Carol Weclew and Randall O'Brien spent a year working on an instrument to identify microevents for therapeutic and teaching purposes. From this instrument, it may be possible to assess different degrees of dysfunctionality in families. Both have continued to devote time and ideas to this study. Finally, a debt of thanks is due to Nathan Lyons, photographer and teacher, whose teaching about serial imagery trained Metcoff to view interpersonal behaviors serially.

# REFERENCES

Bateson, G. *Steps to an ecology of mind.* New York: Ballantine, 1972.
Haley, J. *Problem-solving therapy: New strategies for effective family therapy.* San Francisco: Jossey-Bass, 1976.
Hoffman, L. Breaking the homeostatic cycle. In P. Guerin (Ed.), *Family therapy in theory and practice.* New York: Gardner Press, 1976.
Minuchin, S. The family lunch session. *Harper's,* 1976.
Scheflen, A. The significance of posture in communication systems. *Psychiatry,* 1964, *27;* 316–331.
Scheflen, A. The bowl gesture in the Whitaker–Malone program. In O. S. English (Ed.), *Strategy and structure in psychotherapy.* Philadelphia: Eastern Pennsylvania Psychiatric Institute, 1965.
Sluzki, C. E. Marital therapy from a systems theory perspective. In T. Paolino & B. McCrady (Eds.), *Marriage and marital therapy.* New York: Brunner/Mazel, 1978.
Watzlawick, P., Beavin, J., & Jackson, D. *Pragmatics of human communication: A study of interactional patterns, pathologies and paradoxes.* New York: Norton, 1967.
Weclew, C. *Research instrument for the micro-event.* Unpublished manuscript, Chicago, 1974.

# I V

## NORMAL FAMILY STRUCTURAL VARIATIONS

# 11

# INTERPERSONAL ARRANGEMENTS IN DISRUPTED FAMILIES

## BRAULIO MONTALVO

Dislocation is the experience of having lost one's place in relation to other people. It is the result of fractured relationships, of major shifts in the ties among people one depends or relies upon. To deal effectively with the experience of dislocation in children, it is necessary to understand the triangular arrangements in which children exist. This chapter examines such arrangements, drawing first a brief example from the situation of children who lose their home to go into a foster home, and then introducing more detailed examples from the situation of children of divorced parents. The discussion reflects a structural orientation—a traditional concern with the fate of disrupted coalitions and hierarchical boundaries that alter the caretaking processes between generations. (For an orientation to concepts used in the discussion see Minuchin's *Families and Family Therapy*, 1974, and Haley's *Problem-Solving Therapy*, 1976.) Its emphasis is on the means that participants employ to ease the sense of dislocation and prevent dysfunctional adjustments.

## FOSTER PLACEMENT AND DISLOCATION

One of the most common sources of dislocation experiences in children is the political and economic upheaval that in different countries produces children removed from parents. Some are fortunate and later receive care from sensitive observers. A foster mother who works with Vietnamese boat children, for example, noticed that they have a rare fascination for garbage cans.

Braulio Montalvo. Philadelphia Child Guidance Clinic, Philadelphia, Pennsylvania; Bryn Mawr College, Graduate School of Social Research and Social Work, Bryn Mawr, Pennsylvania; and Aspira Research Project, Philadelphia, Pennsylvania.

She found out that they meant food and survival during the periods of stress and scarcity through which the children lived in their culture before they came to her. She came to understand why the children find Big Bird of *Sesame Street* not as interesting as the familiar monster who lives in the garbage can. So she decided to make garbage cans available to the children as objects of free exploration, and discovered that this helped them to ease their restlessness.

Since familiarity with the children's language would certainly seem to help bridge the gap between her and the children, a psychologist asked her whether she had mastered some Vietnamese words and, if so, whether she used them with the children. Her answer was a quick and surprised "No." "I learned differently; you must not talk to them in their language right away. They take it as an unwarranted intrusion in their lives, as if you wanted to steal the place of their real parents." Boundary keeping around language became for these children a way of preserving their ties to that original source of security which they suddenly lost. This foster mother worked intuitively from the notion that she was, in effect, only one side of these children's triangular arrangements. On the other side were their lost parents. At the apex of the triangles were the children, holding on for dear life to whatever they could of their original families. To respect that hold, the foster mother was also inventive in supplying the children with small ways to show gratefulness, ways to repay her favors. She would, for instance, allow extra use of the vacuum cleaner whether the house needed cleaning or not. She learned that by repaying her care as "favors," the children felt less threatened. In this way, they could keep her as a stranger, a temporary caretaker who did not endanger their ties with their real families.

This was the first home to which the children would come right off the boat before being assigned for permanent placement. By skillfully managing the triangular arrangement between her, the children, and the next foster homes, this foster mother also learned to provide some possibility of repair for the children's first traumatic loss. For instance, she would get a call from a permanent foster mother: "He would like to go and visit with you and the other kids, maybe stay overnight. Is that possible?" Though caring for 12 youngsters at one time, she would answer, "That is always possible with me. This home is always open. They can come back and forth as they wish, but it must be that you want it and that you allow it." She was not only helping the new mothers like this one to become secure and really in charge, but also communicating to the youngsters that their home could not be lost again. She offered a kind of basic headquarters from which they could come and go, this time more under their own control. The losing and recovering of her home proved to be a corrective experience which eased the children's sense of dislocation.

What confuses the professional who tries to assist with the process of transition for such youngsters is that the practical way to help is not

immediately accessible to common sense. The professional may think com-
monsensically that to close a clear language gap between a foster mother and
a youngster could be helpful, but from a vantage point of triangular dynamics, it turns out not to be so. Similarly, a professional may think common-
sensically that in working with a foster family of a neglected youngster, it
would help to support the family's efforts to make the youngster feel loved
and feel special. Many youngsters are placed in foster families who receive
them with honest affection, provide them with rooms of their own, and so
on, only to see too late that they seek refuge by a psychotic reaction. One
such youngster revealed to a worker the acute triangular dislocation he
experienced. He was overcome with a feeling of strangeness and guilt, but
had to conceal that from his nice foster parents because he did not want
them to think him ungrateful. He felt undeserving of their favors and hoped
that he would not be continually singled out for good things while his
siblings, his friends, and his parents were left behind still in need. The sense
of dislocation and anxiety had become unbearable as he saw himself unable
to justify his good fortune and unable to reciprocate the love of his new
parents. Only by erupting in "sick" behavior and forcing his removal from
the foster home had he interrupted an impossible situation. Now, he was
betraying no one and in debt to no one. His psychosis had solved a situation
in which neither foster parents nor agency professionals saw their roles as
worsening the triangular arrangement.

## DIVORCED FAMILIES AND DISLOCATION

The most common source of dislocation experiences in children is divorce. It
could be argued that to look at divorce as a natural triangular arrangement
producing the experience of dislocation in children is to understate the
significance of a major pathological event. From this viewpoint, the rate of
divorce is primarily an indicator of the erosion of the family as an institution
in a dangerously unstable society. The viewpoint taken here is different. It
follows Murdock's cross-cultural observations of 30 years ago (1950), in
which he saw that in practically all societies, excepting perhaps the Incas,
some provision for ending marriage through divorce had or has developed.
From this standpoint, divorce is a most natural though not necessarily
unstressful process, to which we have as a country no special claim. Only 16
societies have a lower divorce rate than the United States; 24 have higher
rates. In 19 of these societies, the rate of permanent separation exceeded that
of the United States. "The comparative evidence makes it clear that we still
remain well within the limits which human experience has shown that
societies can tolerate with safety" (Murdock, 1950).

What can be tolerated with safety at a societal level is different, however,
from what can be tolerated with safety at the more immediate level of the

children in the divorcing family. The issue as to whether the triangular arrangement becomes dysfunctional or not often hinges on whether children can actively modulate the change process so as to keep their sense of dislocation within tolerable limits. To illustrate this point, four arrangements that appear with variations among divorcing families will be discussed.[1]

### Arrangement 1: System with Only One Compass

Consider the triangular arrangement of a girl whose mother was just beginning to be visited by her new boyfriend. This girl took her mother aside and said to her, "Let's not get personal, now." She just had witnessed the mother giving a backrub to the boyfriend. This would have been an inconsequential event were it not for the fact that the mother used to sit in exactly the same place on the sofa when giving a backrub to the girl's father. To the girl, the mother's gesture had become acutely uncomfortable; it implied a betrayal of her father. Through her comment, the girl was cuing her mother to be more sensitive when displaying affection to this still distant and new person in her life. This is a perfectly common interaction that becomes pathological only when adults depend mainly on this indirect communication from children as a way of finding out where they themselves stand in new relationships. It is then the adult's own discomfort and uncertainty that prompts children to utter such statements.

What a therapist usually has to clarify in such situations is whether the adults can modulate their own behavior without the children producing such statements or equivalent behavior. The aim is to determine the extent to which the children are caught in a system where the lack of synchronicity between them and their parents is dangerous. An example is the parent who wants a child to move as fast as he or she is moving. When the child resists by saying, "You expect us to love Larry just like you do," the parent is unable to modify the intensity or the pace of his or her relationship in such a way as to ease the sense of dislocation in the child. In such cases, parents proceed on the premise that families operate through uniform movement, as if all parts had to move at the same time and in the same direction. With this idea, all sense of individuality among members of families is violated. Children in such families are in trouble because they question the premise whenever they convey that they are not as tied to their parents as the parents assume.

Dysfunctional triangular patterns of this sort can be easily mistaken for just another instance of intrusive children inappropriately moving into the parents' domain, from which they must be moved out through parental

---

[1]Based on income and residence, the families range from working-class to middle-class. We do not consider here the situations among certain low-income families where the impact of multiple external disruptions (job loss, frequent residence change, fragmented and shifting family/household membership, etc.) mixes with that of coalitions and hierarchies shaken or broken by divorce.

efforts at behavior modification. The issue clarifies as the parents begin to look distressed and disoriented when the behavior modification means are applied. The children turn out to be essential tools in the parents' testing of reality, and any attempt to remove the children from that function will expose an inability to regulate the pace at which new relationships are pursued. This diminishes the chances for a sound postdivorce adjustment.

### Arrangement 2: The Crippled Executive

During and after divorce, there usually follows a period of oscillation between overstrictness and overindulgent behavior on the part of custodial parents. The parents may have indulged the children in an attempt to support them during the period of loss. One common way of indulging the children is to relax the rules that usually prevail and to allow the children some temporary regression, hoping that after a while the children will recover their sense of safety. This may entail such a simple move as allowing the children to come to sleep in the beds of the grownups. A problem arises only when the parents slip into a position of helplessness and cannot get the children to move out of their beds, to follow routines, to do homework, or to follow curfew expectations.

The temporary regression threatens then to become permanent and has many useful functions. This is the situation of the mother who became helpless toward her daughter, who, she said, "screams a lot when I make demands, to the point that she embarrasses me and scandalizes the neighbors, who come rushing in." This mother was caught in a pattern that was dysfunctional in terms of child rearing and discipline, but quite effective in compelling the ex-spouse to reenter the family to respond to the child's deviance or the mother's own helplessness. If a mother like this also happens to be afraid to venture forth socially, as she sees other single parents doing, the arrangement conveniently distracts her from having to become immediately self-sufficient. Unable to take charge of her daughter right away, she cannot possibly enter the world of competitive new relationships. To determine then what is a natural or unnatural process, what is a functional or dysfunctional pattern, is relative to the multiple purposes that the participants pursue in the different interpersonal contexts that matter to them.

The triangular arrangement of the custodial parent going weak in order to get the noncustodial parent to come in becomes most dysfunctional when it blocks the new existence of the noncustodial parent. This parent can be facing so many calls requiring advice or ideas that efforts to make a new life away from the old family are subverted. We have then a full-fledged failure of the process of transition and family splitting. The natural work of social restoration in which both the custodial and noncustodial parent have to engage is sabotaged. They cannot make and solve their own child-rearing mistakes; they cannot make new commitments, explore new friends, find new jobs, or learn to hold jobs in a new way. They cannot learn to feel at home as single parents or to meet effectively the demands of their new situations.

One way in which therapists confuse themselves with this arrangement is by insisting on working with both fathers and mothers at once. This looks appropriate from a family therapy standpoint. Since both fathers and mothers play a vital role in the life of the children, the work must be with fathers and mothers together, having them close ranks and reach agreements without utilizing the children. The problem with this approach is that it too often misses the main consideration, which is that one adult in a family must now recover leverage where two adults had it. A more economic focus is on strengthening the custodial parent as executive, as enforcer of child care rules, while proceeding to intensify negotiations between the parents. The most outstanding problem is the custodial parent's problem solving with the children, and the securing of leverage and authority over them now, without the other parent's remote control and directives. Recovery of leverage over the children by dealing constantly with the noncustodial parent in sessions must be avoided because it tends to make the custodial parent feel that his or her authority was not earned independently.

The children's contribution to this process is in maintaining the merry-go-round of the adults' getting together through constant rescue calls. Notable exceptions are, of course, available. Many preadolescent youngsters express openly that they want the "hassle to be over" and display enormous self-restraint, becoming "good" in order to help helpless parents to look competent and thus stopping conflict between mothers and fathers, although often paying a great price internally. This becomes an especially stressful problem for determined parents, who, finding no way to provoke such children, must develop new reasons for pulling ex-spouses back. Among these reasons show up personal symptoms.

The therapist during this period must be careful not to fall into inadvertent coalition with helpful relatives, who intensify the parent's sense of dislocation by treating every relationship as an opportunity for possible remarriage. The parent's freedom is enhanced by supporting, instead, the natural wish for guarded experimentation. By shifting the emphasis to whether an experimental relationship proves enjoyable rather than useful, the therapist will hasten recovery of competence and well-being. The goal is to prevent the parent from being pushed into a dysfunctional extreme by helpful relatives who urge him or her into new relationships, compounding the problem of adjustment.

Another consideration in helping the custodial parent to disconnect from the ex-spouse is to help him or her manage relatives who treat all instances of child care as part of an unfair load—a load that they claim should have been shared with the noncustodial parent. According to them, the noncustodial parent must be getting away with a lot, simply because he or she has fewer caretaking duties. This notion is often a trap, leading the custodial parent away from taking charge and away from the fact that he or she must be able to cope with these problems alone in any case.

To prevent further troubles during this period, it is also important to build on the understanding that both custodial parent and children are undergoing a severe dislocation. Since both are removed from their usual relationship context, therapy must deal with two contexts almost simultaneously, one for the children and one for the parents. The goal is to attend to the defenses of the children and to the replacement of defenses for the adults while the adult moves the children into new behavior. For instance, a mother tried to help a daughter to deal with the loss of the father by bringing her into her bed. She found out soon enough that she couldn't get her out. To ease the mother into a position of being able to let go of the girl, it was important to consider the needs that were met by having the girl in bed with her. The mother was concealing from herself that she really wanted the girl's company, despite her open wish for a change in the daughter, whom she wanted out of bed and independent. The therapist dealing with the situation organized a ritual in which the mother was helped to keep her loneliness concealed. The important issue became for the mother to move the girl out of bed gradually, slowing down the change, while also engaging in small moves that would mitigate her own loneliness. The mother was to go to sleep with the girl, but when the girl was asleep, she was to get up and do something strictly for herself. She could read a book, call a friend, or think of the theater activities that she liked so much.

A similar two-context-oriented approach became available in dealing with the problem of the screaming girl mentioned earlier. The mother eventually controlled the screaming in a way that at the same time allowed her to deal with her neighbors. She had the girl make a sign for the door—"A Screamer Lives Here. Don't Worry. Everything under Control."—and, through use of the sign and through physical restraint of the girl, this mother effectively lessened this girl's hold on her. She achieved competent leverage over the girl in many sectors of her life. She became also more assertive with her own mother, withstanding the mother's intrusions, and resisting the help of her ex-husband whenever it was unnecessary. She moved ahead to cultivate her own interests. Like many other parents in this situation, she prevented the development of that dysfunctional extreme in which a single parent stagnates in orbit around a helpful grandmother and other helpers. She utilized therapy as a training ground in which to assert herself and differentiate herself from other people. By differing with the therapist, she learned to cope better with her own mother and especially with her husband.

This woman, however, managed an incomplete change in dealing with the problem of the girl sleeping in her bed, leaving for herself one domain where she maintained control. This manner of changing seems to be common in parents who feel that with change in all sectors, control would be lost. Another brief example underscores this point. A couple came in, struggling over joint custody of a 3-year-old and an 11-month-old baby. The father wanted 5 days with him and 5 days with the mother. The mother, of course, began to resist. After much work, the father made a momentous change. He allowed that the baby, after all, needed his mother much more. But he was insistent to the end that, despite the acute symptoms of separation anxiety shown in school and at home by the 3-year-old, he still wanted joint custody for this child.

In many other triangular arrangements, particularly those where the loss of the spouse is soon to be followed by a potential loss of the children, the need to harness change and prevent another loss increases. By maintaining one symptomatic area unchanged, many parents keep control not only over children, but over therapists, who as agents of change can be experienced as too powerful, potentially capable of producing another loss. In some cases, by keeping one area half-changed, parents ensure against losing their therapists. In others, they merely ensure that, upon ending the process of therapy, they are in charge.

### Arrangement 3: The Uneven Race

This arrangement includes situations in which parents are attempting hard to maintain a correct front of proper caretaking behavior while maintaining a relationship in which they check each other's behavior for potential ammunition. The children do not necessarily show immediate symptoms; however they appear tense, concerned with being "good" and appearing happy and polite to the grownups, as if to say, "If I remain good at all moments, I will maintain their togetherness and intactness."[2] Generally, in such situations, one of the adults has left. If it is the mother, she feels that in all her actions she must be totally proper in order to counter her husband's poor opinion of her. To restore the image of herself as a responsible, care-taking person, she keeps all visits; she is careful to phone the child every day; she is very careful about avoiding mistakes. She tries very hard to provide no ammunition to her husband, and feels she must do all this to secure some custody rights. In effect, she is in an uneven race in which she starts from behind, just because she is a female in this culture and *she* left her husband with the children. The husband presents himself as mainly concerned with

[2]The "good" facade is rarely seen in adolescents. When it shows, it reflects a very disturbed youngster in an exceptionally disturbed family situation. More commonly, adolescents are differentiated enough to develop a "busy and slippery" demeanor to avoid having to take sides. The "good" facade conceals, of course, the children's fear that they are causing the split and their hope that maybe they can still stop it.

his wife's return and willing at any time to negotiate sensible custodial arrangements.

A therapist can get confused with this pattern because if the party who leaves a spouse is the wife, she looks appropriately assertive, careful, and defended in the beginning, impressing the therapist with her good awareness that the adversary, the husband, could utilize any mistake in order to penalize her. The surprise comes later, as the therapist attempts to get them to negotiate in the sessions. It becomes clear that the arrangement is rather skewed, not as symmetrical as it looked in the beginning. The husband is not so reasonable or so ready to negotiate, and the wife is not as well defended or as ready to deal from a position of strength as she appeared to be. Toward the end of a session, it can be noticed that they are engaged in courting behavior. This becomes confusing, because no one wants to step in to the possibility of an honest reconciliation, so the therapist will hesitate and not move ahead to help the partners resume problem solving. The next stage presents the therapist with the fact that more than courting has developed. For instance, the mother, when taking her daughter home, may have had sex with the ex-husband. Afterwards, she may claim she did it just to protect her visitation rights. He may feel he did it to get her to return to him. She may feel that she cannot "redeem" herself with him or with society fast enough. She is running a risk of reaching a custody battle and not looking good enough. In the end, "he is going to prevail anyway." He, in turn, may feel deflated, beginning to wonder whether she really "did love me or used me" and whether or not it is worthwhile to try to have her return. Maybe she did it just to get custody and visitation arrangements "the way she wants them, not because she loved me." In these situations, sexual reencounters turn out to be delaying and detouring tactics that prolong the suffering of all participants, but especially the children (Isaacs, 1981).

In dealing with the "uneven race" arrangement, it behooves therapist and supervisor to detect the first signs of courting and to rush forward, explaining that to use love and sex in order to secure visitation rights and custody arrangements is rather common and that they should anticipate whether it would help solve things or delay them. This becomes a way of making them responsible before they get into "accidental" events of sexual blackmail. In this situation, it is also of crucial importance to give special support to the wife who feels like a "sinner" for leaving. By reviewing the original justifications for leaving, it is often possible to reawaken the sense of indignation that is necessary for pursuing a sound adjustment. This usually means helping a wife not to settle for less than she is entitled to. It means countering the feeling of being dominated by the other partner. This may entail slow and elaborate discussions outlining the many ways in which, for instance, the husband's family co-opted her right to be mother of her child or children; the innumerable ways in which she was made to feel different and incompetent; the particular instances in which her husband's family treated her as an outsider; the detailed manner in which her goodness as a mother was not allowed to show because of the activities of her husband's mother; and so on. By dwelling on these justifications, rightful anger and assertiveness usually returns, stopping the process of self-devaluation and the fears that she cannot ever catch up to her husband. There is also a lessening of those depressive states that promote the search for some other "strong" protector. What needs to be avoided is the extreme dysfunction of the wife who becomes so sad and helpless that she compounds her troubles by choosing another "bad" partner.

### Arrangement 4: The Abdication Contest

The most trying and disturbing of all arrangements is the "abdication contest." In situations of this type, the custodial parent is paralyzed by helplessness and sadness as a result of separation or divorce. The typical instance is that of a mother who can't get over the feeling of being abandoned by her husband; she cries constantly and cannot control her youngsters. One example of this was a mother with four adolescent daughters whom she could not handle in many ways. The basic routines—meals, homework, rules for dates, curfew limitations, and proper care of the house—were all erratically supervised. As the mother became obsessed with her terrible situation, rule breaking became frequent among the girls. One girl was having her second abortion; another was overworried, guilty, and focused on consoling her mother. The other two were involved in occasional petty delinquent activities and were always surly, resisting any demands from the mother. The father in this case stepped in sporadically to offer support to the girls. But his efforts at enforcing rules were feeble, and he never really inquired as to the whereabouts of the girls or questioned in depth any of their disturbing activities.

The therapist dealing with this arrangement based his strategy on the obvious acting out of the youngsters and on one of the purposes of mother's depression—calling for help from the husband. To go along with this purpose, the therapist tried to work at establishing the father as a help to control the children. These attempts quickly failed. As is typical in the "abdication contest," the father held a firm stance over the youngsters, but only briefly. He could not measure up to handling their delinquent activities. The net result was that the vacuum of executive leadership left by the mother was also left by him. In a dynamic "abdication contest" such as this one, neither adult wants to take over the responsibility of boundary setting for the youngsters. Yet, each expects the other to step in to control and change the situation somehow, and this usually goes on until anarchic developments are inevitable. The youngsters escalate their delinquent activities until the therapist must compel the father to contain them or until some other external interference becomes necessary, such as the appearance of the police, the courts, or school authorities.

The "abdication contest" comes out of the very natural and temporary phase of sadness and confusion that besets almost any divorcing family. Inner turmoil and grief can so disengage adults from the needs of their youngsters as to produce some temporary loosening of rules. Ordinarily, parents come back and recover their executive stance, restoring the rules with their youngsters. They usually do so before the situation becomes extremely dysfunctional and the youngsters become involved in serious criminal activity. If the arrangement has become destructive and chronic, it is necessary to explore the multiple sources maintaining the situation. The therapist must step in and discover whether the arrangement is kept in place essentially by means of a still-existing marital contract, by means of a parent's relationship with a new partner (a new girlfriend or boyfriend), or by virtue of a parent's relationship with the youngsters.

One procedure to clarify such situations is to approach it in terms of how the noncustodial parent can help the youngsters to settle down without doing it so well that the custodial parent is embarrassed. If the noncustodial parent finds a way to take charge in a manner that does not embarrass the custodial parent, then the reason for the avoidance of the executive function can be assumed to have been basically related to marital conflicts. By not rescuing the custodial parent, the noncustodial parent tries to protect the other from coming in contact with his or her own sense of failure. If the custodian becomes busy with trying to become firm with the youngsters, his or her inadequacy and helplessness may be exposed even more. On the other hand, if successful, such activity would signal the termination of his or her relationship to the noncustodial parent, which would complete the split of the family in transition. By hesitating to take over the youngsters, the noncustodial parent leaves open the possibility that after some struggle and defeat, the custodial parent may finally emerge as an effective executive. If the noncustodian does not respond to the request that he or she take over the situation in ways that would not embarrass the custodian, a different basis for the problem is usually disclosed. The noncustodian, it is found out, is already more thoroughly anchored than may have been apparent, in a relationship with a new partner. The ties to the previous marriage are by now weaker than the ties to the new relationship. To really motivate him or her to take over parental duties with the youngsters, he or she must then be helped to see that the possibility for happiness in the new relationship will be spoiled or sabotaged unless the youngsters' needs are taken care of now. "Would your girlfriend like to visit courts and hospitals as soon as you two get started in this new life?" is often an effective question.

The most difficult "abdication" pattern usually entails both an intense old contract of the noncustodian with the youngsters, as well as an investment in protecting the relationship to the new partner. In this kind of arrangement, the noncustodian is reluctant to be firm with the youngsters because of not wanting to be "the bad parent," the one who gets rejected by the children. He or she always wants to be the "good" parent who keeps the children's support. Long ago in this failing marriage, the present noncustodian may have made a coalition with the youngsters to cope with the other parent. The unspoken contract might be phrases as follows: "I will not be a boundary enforcer, so that you can be my support in dealing with the other parent. By being my ally against the other parent, you give me what is sorely missing between him or her and me." With this contract in the background, the "abdication contest" has been growing for a long time by the time the marriage fully splits, and then becomes an almost unstoppable runaway.

An "abdication contest" can be managed by working carefully around one of the frequent crises that will be presented by one or more youngsters. This means working on setting the parents to achieve a minimal closing of ranks and a minimal enforcement and maintenance of standards. When this is done correctly, the parent-youngster contract from long ago immediately surfaces. For instance, a daughter may use her father's apartment to sleep over with her friends, and leave the place in total chaos—the toilet clogged, Valium pills stolen, everything else disordered. Prompted by the therapist, the father may try for new heights of firmness and indignation. He may demand to know the whereabouts of the drugs and who took them, and he may push hard on the daughter until she is repentant, gives some excuses for her behavior, and promises that she will search for the pills. A session or two after this, the therapist is puzzled: some kind of short circuiting seems to have happened, since the tempers have cooled quite fast. By probing, the therapist finds that father's investigation of the Valium pills has become a whitewash. The father has stopped pushing. When the therapist presses the request that he continue in his executive stance, since he or she does not know yet what happened, the youngsters operate predictably—they gang up on the parent. For example, they may attack him because at one time he left to go see his girlfriend when he was supposed to have stayed throughout the night with them in the apartment. At this point, the father will retreat completely under the threat that the extent of his neglect and delinquencies will be exposed even more. The contract that is now revealed seems to be this: "You have promised not to expose us so that we would not expose you."

At this crossroads, the therapist usually must go on to prevent the father from abdicating, in spite of the fact that the father feels really caught and feels that he has no right to enforce any rules since he doesn't want rules enforced on him. The "abdication contest" will finally be resolved when the father manages, through a coalition with the therapist or his girlfriend, to let go a bit on his coalition with the youngsters against their mother. He then goes back to demand accountable conduct from the youngsters, though he may be delinquent himself. Soon after that, a new stage emerges, in which the father cannot sustain himself in the new position without feeling like an unfair executive and somehow tries to generate another reciprocal contract among equals. The new contract may be this: "I will stop being delinquent so that I can feel justified in asking you not to be delinquent."

To appreciate the tenacity of youngsters like these in rebelling against the noncustodial parent's efforts to assert control, we must understand that, by acting out, the youngsters are not simply moving the parents to get together in a typical triangular dynamic. They are also attempting desperately to protect their own power and freedom, the life of privilege into which they fell by adult default. By exposing their parent's delinquencies whenever a parent tries to control them, they also postpone that time when the adult may prevail. If they accommodate to parental demands, they fear that they will be vulnerable once more. To trust the adult is to risk being let down again.

What is unique in the "abdication contest" is that youngsters escalate the acting out so that the adults expect each other to step in but do not step in enough. What is maintained is a curiously ineffectual triangle, which is more alive by what it promotes itself not to do than for what it manages to do. The tension it generates does not lead to the fulfillment of functions that can stop the delinquent activity. The delinquent activity only leads the adults to the point of attempting to get together to take over the executive functions and then abandoning each other. In this repeating cycle, retreat occurs just at the right moment.

A very special problem worth mentioning in working with the "abdication contest" is that of how to deal with depressed partners. Most therapists find themselves thinking of ways to shorten or to lessen the depression so that these parents can, as significant executives, become related to the urgent needs of the youngsters. One way that has been found effective is based on discovering the commanding obsessions of the depressed parents and working on those intensely. An example is offered in the work of Abelson, who searches until he finds these commanding obsessions. In a particular case, a mother was obsessed about her husband's new partner, whom she had seen and thought a masculine-looking woman. She was wondering constantly whether her husband was, after all, a homosexual. To this concern, the answer from the therapist was this: "That's fine: continue to think about that as long and as hard as you can. It will help you to integrate this experience and to process it, so that you will be able to go on with the business of getting yourself together." By phrasing this same message in many other ways, clearly sponsoring the mother in her search for clarification as to whether this man was or was not a homosexual, the therapist worked on the depression as a major obstacle to the mother's becoming responsible with the youngsters. Since the woman was protecting herself from narcissistic injury through this obsession, the therapist helped her to conceal from herself the possibility that she was not loved. But while keeping the obsession going, the therapist was at the same time introducing the idea that it had to be checked, that it had to finish so that she could continue to do whatever she needed to do with her life. For many parents, this means working actively to relieve the loss and depression of the youngsters, and not only their own.

### Simultaneous Management of Coalition and Depression

Before a split, divorcing parents may have existed in a poorly practiced dual-command system or in no flexible system at all. The mother may have carried responsibility, but only with the father's implicit backing, seldom exercising independent control without his sanction. No model for transferring control, for trustfully switching responsibilities between executives, may have been worked out. (In a recent sample of 20 families, only one was found to have been successful at switching efforts in preparation for the changeover.) Taking over skills may appear to be only erratically developed, and confident child-rearing responsibility may not have been practiced by each separate parent before it was shared. Yet, as the parents split, the one who remains with the children usually mobilizes enough of a protective and organizing response toward them and toward himself or herself to prevent extreme dysfunctional adjustments. This is nowhere better seen than in the handling of the dislocations that arise when one parent moves out and siblings realign their relationships. These realignments may involve severely stressful double blows for a particular child. A little boy, for example, may get depressed because his father left and more depressed because his father was his ally; now alone, without him, the child faces a mother and an older sister who don't like him. For the mother, the test is extraordinary. She must disengage from her coalition with the older daughter to help the youngster at risk. She must stand by and help him negotiate with his older sister until he feels that she won't pick on him with license. Most remarkable in this event is the capacity on the part of the adult to leave the side of the older daughter to allocate support compensatorily on the side of the youngster most in need. This move substitutes, at the level of hierarchy, for the ally who left; in one stroke, it reorders siblings' boundaries and helps the child under stress cope with loss and depression.

This ability to take and leave sides with children in a fair way remains one of the most obvious instrumental factors preventing dysfunctional extremes among divorcing families. The conditions associated with this ability should be the subject of prospective studies. Also warranting study is the ability to take and leave sides with relatives. The elaborate social processes shaping, amplifying, and unbalancing the conflicting forces in the family until it splits are best revealed in the making and unmaking of coalitions

around relatives. It is there that we see the resulting interpersonal arrangement on its way to becoming functional or dysfunctional, to closing or
opening possibilities for new beginnings.

### Hazardous Exiting

Most of the dysfunctional extreme states associated with these arrangements
represent incomplete splits and hazardous exiting from a marriage, as Table
11-1 makes clear.

In the "system with only one compass," parents may be trying to
manage transitions without relying on relatives or friends, but may be
closing the exits by overrelying on the children and fostering possibilities of
phobic developments. This will keep these parents tied to an enmeshed and
burdened single-parent status and unable to move on to being an adequate
single parent or a candidate for an unproblematic remarriage.

"Crippled executives" may successfully negotiate roads to nowhere
instead of roads out of the marriage by relying on the remote control of the
noncustodial parents, closing not only their own exits, but those of the
noncustodians as well.

Parents in "uneven races" are almost culturally preorganized into trying
to manage transitions through rivalrous tug-of-war over the children, and
the parents who feel "behind" see no exit except through making coalitions
with outside figures who will pull them out. This way of exiting entails
jealousy and betrayal possibilities that can run out of control. It is hazardous
at the beginning because it creates psychosomatic problems among children,
and later because it moves the participants toward explosive resolutions as
the only way of finalizing the split.

Adults in "abdication contests" display well how lack of success in
reengaging responsibly as executive parents compels them to stay in contact
as bitter ex-spouses. Since they divorce not only as spouses, but as parents,
this arrangement is the most hazardous in that it disables the basic traditional
function of families—the socialization of youngsters.

For each of these arrangements it may eventually be possible, through
clinical and prospective studies, to gather and establish confirmed rules for
mobilizing therapeutic progress. These would be demands that generally
tend to facilitate transitions leading away from dysfunctional extremes.

In the "system with only one compass" it is often useful to rule out,
temporarily, the use of children as sources of orientation. This exacerbates
the mechanisms for retrieving the children and permits analysis and development of alternative ways of organizing around relationships.

In "the crippled executive" arrangement, it is almost mandatory that
one instance emerge in which the call or contact with a noncustodial parent
occurs *after*, not before, a custodial parent has managed to control a child's

## TABLE 11-1. FOUR INTERPERSONAL ARRANGEMENTS AMONG DIVORCING FAMILIES

| Triangular arrangement | Problem of child (example) | What is concealed | What is confusing | Usual divorce locus | Dysfunctional extreme |
|---|---|---|---|---|---|
| *System with only one compass*<br>Mother uses child as compass to find out where she is in uncharted new relationships. Child's comments and behavior are used to slow down or accelerate the relationship's progress. Child modulates the sense of dislocation which is experienced during the transition to becoming a new threesome. Child is not free not to comment by word or deed; mother mostly conscious only of childs "intrusiveness" not the "help" child is offering. | Child hyperalert, feels mother is going too fast in bringing new person into her life, demanding a betrayal or abandonment of father. Child handles dislocation experiences for self and mother, for example, mother's back-rub to new boyfriend gets "you are getting too personal now," you are in Daddy's turf. Can I slow you down? Child feels occasional fear when seeing mother cannot make up her mind about new relationships. | Mother ostensibly sees child as "intrusive" but conceals that she welcomes the intrusion, because without it she feels rudderless and needs it as a cue. Child conceals that it is not just his or her anxiety over betraying Dad that bothers her. It is mother's looking helpless without child orientation. Mother's front "it is not me who is unsure of the new linkage. It's my daughter." In some cases mother unconsciously demands: "Go as fast as I go," denying child's independence. | Looks like a problem of an intrusive child that will yield to behavior modifications. Mother appears to control her relationship pace. It's just my child is "in my business." Blocking the child as critic, pacemaker, or commentator, reveals that mom becomes less organized without child's input. | Divorced as spouses, but not as parents; caretaking problematic but not endangered. | Mother lost, disoriented, dependent without child's comments and choice. Child enmeshes further and becomes phobic to protect mother. Erratic choice of new partners; possibilities of another divorce. |

| *The crippled executive* | | | | | |
|---|---|---|---|---|---|
| Wife becomes helpless as mother to ensure husband's participation; child contributes unmanageability, straining mother's executive capacities. Husband contributes a remote control executive stance which fails to definitely resolve the cycle of defeat, insuring that he'll be called in again. | Child screams and cannot be stopped; wants to sleep in mother's bed all the time; resists attempts to get her out. Child overestimates power over mother, which is based on coalition with grandmother and father. | Mother ostensibly wants child to stop screaming, and to go to sleep in own bed. Mother conceals that she really wants child's company to mitigate loneliness, to replace husband's presence, and to delay or avoid facing her own social restoration tasks. | Change will be offered in many areas but withheld in others. Mother stops the child's screaming, develops her own interests, asserts herself with grandmother's relatives, resists husband's help, but allows child to stay in bed. Mother retains one area unchanged in order to prove independent control. | Divorced as spouses, but not as parents; caretaking problematic but not endangered. | Mother cannot recover effectiveness in child rearing unless husband participates and disrupts his life: regresses child, restricts her own interpersonal field; stagnates. Mother jumps into another marriage pushed by relatives who support her helplessness; remains tied to grandmother, and/or other helpful relatives. |
| *The uneven race* | | | | | |
| Mother behaves perfectly in keeping with caretaking and visitation routines, she fulfills all duties carefully. Picks up child and returns punctually, calls child regularly and predictably. The child detects something wrong, tense, but cannot pinpoint it. Father is polite and | Child uncertain, overalert, happy facade. By being good the children feel they'll keep intact, together, what remains of the couple. Child's happiness front eventually breaks into delayed psychosomatic expressions of chronic stress, for example, | Wife who left presents herself as strong, as not willing to give in, or to forfeit her rights. Wife conceals that "only if I give in to what he wants /ill I be allowed visitation as I want it." She fears she cannot catch up with his advantaged supervisory position. | Initially they look like a balanced seesaw, a fair contest of evenly matched antagonists. The asymmetry in the skewed arrangement, and the accompanying feeling of dislocation experienced by both, but particularly the wife, is not projected | Divorced as spouses, but not as parents; caretaking problematic but not endangered. | Sexual blackmail. Child develops chronic severe psychosomatic illness. Wife feels she cannot escape husband, unless she links to a strong protector that will pluck her from the husband's domination. Double dealing, dangerous jealousy triangle, |

*(continued)*

293

TABLE 11-1. (*continued*)

| Triangular arrangement | Problem of child (example) | What is concealed | What is confusing | Usual divorce locus | Dysfunctional extreme |
|---|---|---|---|---|---|
| cooperative as he "watches" mother for failures in visitation and caretaking routines. A subtle tug-of-war. | losing hair, skin rashes; problems in school follow. | Conceals fear that she may not buy enough time to "redeem" herself fast enough. At first husband looks reasonable, benevolent, ready to negotiate. Conceals fears that he cannot deal with her as equal and must dominate her into returning, or be rejected. | clearly. Wife and husband look fairly balanced, defended. Sexual reencounters are difficult to judge. Are they using each other to get what they want? Can they honestly reconcile? Therapist hesitates and the conflict and tension is prolonged. | | violence possible unless she is helped to move from one relationship to another, going first through a nonrelationship stage. High risk for parental kidnapping. |
| *The abdication contest* Husband about to respond to his ex-wife's call and act as father but does | Youngsters constantly elicit and yet sabotage feeble executive moves. | Father: "I must pretend that I am out to stop them and socialize | Looks as if husband is going to take over, but doesn't quite do it. In- | Divorced as spouses and as parents; caretaking is endangered. | Anarchy, delinquency, psychosis. High risk for joining religious cults. |

not carry through. She acts as if she will pick up as mother, but really drops it, for him to pick up. A repeating cycle in which the youngsters continue acting out and parents continue ineffectual until the outside steps in. Courts, police, hospitals, and so forth.

Multiple and escalating acting out, anarchy, stealing, confrontation, and intimidating of parents. Parental child emerges to console mother in her sadness. Youngsters conceal a fear that if they act responsibly they will be let down once more. Youngsters conceal that they are out to protect their own freedom at parental expense.

them, I really want my kids approval and consolation. I want them to take my side." Mother conceals from herself and others that "he may be leaving me because he does not love me." She protects self-esteem. "He is leaving me because of something wrong in him," for example, he is homosexual.

vestigative and supervisory moments that look encouraging turn out to be "whitewash." Mother's depression is not capable of keeping and holding husband in. Difficulty in determining which are the most influential relationships—coalition with youngsters, with new partner, with ex-wife, in motivating new parental efforts to modify acting out.

behavior adequately. This unleashes new interactional possibilities toward a cleaner disengagement of the ex-spouses.

In "the uneven race," at some point in time it becomes essential to encourage the parent to go through a reflective period without a partner. The establishment of clear closure in one relationship before shifting fully to another becomes a necessary step toward preventing an explosive split and smoothening out the transition.

In "the abdication contest," at least one instance of rule breaking from youngsters must be met by a firm closing of ranks of the executives, with the binding rule for the adults being that whichever parent dumps blame on the other must take all responsibility for the next round of acting out.

## ACKNOWLEDGMENTS

For the material on Vietnamese children I am indebted to a foster mother called Vicky, and to Jay Lappin of the Service for Indo-Chinese Families of the Philadelphia Child Guidance Clinic. The material on divorced families comes from the Pew Memorial Trust-supported work of Marla Isaacs, Director of the Families of Divorce Project at the Philadelphia Child Guidance Clinic, and from the project's clinicians, particularly Jenny Simmons and David Abelson, to whom I am grateful for sharing their experiences.

## REFERENCES

Haley, J. *Problem-solving therapy.* San Francisco: Jossey-Bass, 1976.
Isaacs, M. Treatment for families of divorce: A systems model of prevention. In I. R. Stuart & L. E. Abt (Eds.), *Children of separation and divorce: Management and treatment.* New York: Van Nostrand Reinhold, 1981.
Minuchin, S. *Families and family therapy.* Cambridge: Harvard University Press, 1974.
Murdock, G. P. Family stability in non-European cultures. *The Annals,* 1950, *272,* 197-199.

# 12

# THE POSTDIVORCE FAMILY SYSTEM

## JEAN GOLDSMITH

## INTRODUCTION

A decade ago, the inclusion of a chapter on postdivorce families in a book on normal family processes would have seemed a contradiction in terms. Even now, there are many who view the postdivorce family as a pathological variation on the (healthy) theme of the married, two-parent family, the latter being held as the exclusively appropriate environment in which to rear a child. The price that has been paid for this view is the failure to identify those processes and patterns that are normative for postdivorce families and that result in successful adaptations for family members. For clinicians, the absence of this information has resulted in lack of clarity and greater difficulty in helping postdivorce families move toward growth and development.

In this chapter, the postdivorce family[1] is seen essentially as a normal family form; that is, divorce is not viewed, *ipso facto*, as generating an aberrant unit. Data that converge from several areas of investigation support this viewpoint.

From a purely statistical perspective, the postdivorce family is currently the largest minority form, and its frequency is increasing (Glick, 1979). Each year since 1972, more than one million children under 18 years of age have experienced parental divorce (Carter & Glick, 1976), and it has been estimated that 32% to 46% of children who have grown up in the United States during the 1970s will experience the separation or divorce of their parents (Bane, 1979). For certain subgroups of the population, the number of children

---

[1]In this chapter, the focus is on families with children in which legal divorce has taken place. The concepts and clinical implications are also generally applicable to permanently separated families and to separated families moving toward divorce.

Jean Goldsmith. Center for Family Studies/The Family Institute of Chicago, Institute of Psychiatry, Northwestern Memorial Hospital and Northwestern University Medical School, Chicago, Illinois.

living in postdivorce family situations is even greater; for example, even though less than one-sixth of all children under 18 are black, they represent one-third of those living with a separated or divorced parent (Glick, 1979).

Within the mental health field, it has been established that divorce does not automatically result in an unhealthy family environment. Reviewing the literature, Bloom, White, and Asher (1979) conclude that while separation and divorce are major life stressors associated with physical and emotional disorder, these events must be viewed in the larger context: "most persons who go through a marital disruption do not appear to be at excess risk of developing illness or disability" (p. 200). Certainly there is transitory disruption and difficulty for both adults and children involved in divorce (Hetherington, Cox, & Cox, 1976; Wallerstein & Kelly, 1979). However, under certain conditions,[2] there are many individuals for whom the postdivorce family environment provides opportunities for growth (Abarbanel, 1979; Longfellow, 1979; Roman & Haddad, 1978); and just as certain aspects of married family[3] life (e.g., conflict-ridden relationships) are pathogenic, so in the postdivorce family it is the quality of the emerging environment, rather than the divorce itself, that determines the mental health of family members (Longfellow, 1979).

As a sociological unit, it is apparent that the postdivorce family continues to take on the same functions, roles and responsibilities as the married family (Fleck, 1966): it continues to process growth for its members; it copes with family problems and crises; and it plans and carries out routine events and social occasions. While the divorce experience does generally require that families alter the ways they handle these basic functions, it does not necessarily result in a disintegration of family functioning.

Based on the view that the postdivorce family is essentially a normal unit, this chapter identifies those processes and patterns that are normative or common to postdivorce families, and also those that result in successful adaptations for family members. The implications of this information for clinicians helping postdivorce families move toward growth and development are articulated. Specifically, a paradigm for understanding the postdivorce family, based on general systems theory, is presented. The postdivorce family is examined first as an overall system and then in terms of its relevant subgroups, including the coparental, the custodial parent–child, the noncustodial parent–child, and the individual subsystems. The results of a recent research study I have conducted on postdivorce families are described.

---

[2]Some key factors influencing adjustment to divorce appear to include the predivorce family situation, sex and age of adults and children, postdivorce quality of family relationships, custody arrangements, and prior mental health of adults (Abarbanel, 1979; Longfellow, 1979; Roman & Haddad, 1978).

[3]The term "married family" is used in this chapter to describe a family situation involving children living with their mother and father, in which the mother and father are married to one another and it is the first marriage for both adults.

Throughout, the clinical implications of the conceptual material are explicated. Since space limitations prohibit discussion of specific techniques in the present chapter, the clinical focus is on assessment and treatment goals and strategies.

## THE POSTDIVORCE FAMILY AS A REORGANIZED FAMILY SYSTEM

### General Systems Theory Paradigm

A major problem confronting clinicians who work with postdivorce families is the absence of a conceptual framework to guide their work. Without such a paradigm, clinical practice is frequently value-laden if not stereotypical, because it has been based on implicit assumptions that are not always congruent with available data. For example, the noncustodial parent (usually the father) has often been viewed as a relatively unimportant member of the postdivorce family, and yet there is considerable evidence that points to the opposite conclusion (Keshet & Rosenthal, 1978). Similarly, women have been perceived and treated as "victims" of the divorce process, while the data show that women initiate divorce more often than men (Goldsmith, 1980).

To remedy this conceptual deficiency, I suggest the application of general systems theory to postdivorce families. Information under this theoretical framework has been steadily accumulating (Hall & Fagen, 1978; Bertalanffy, 1978), and its utility for understanding and treating married families has been demonstrated (Watzlawick, Beavin, & Jackson, 1967; Weiting, 1976). The paradigm coheres with available clinical and research data and is consonant with the view that the postdivorce family is a normal family form.

Within the general systems theory paradigm, the married family is viewed as a "system" of which family members are the components and their attributes or characteristics are the properties. The members and their relationships bind the system together. Every part of the system is, by definition, related to its member parts, so that a change in one will cause a change in all members and in the total system. It is in this sense that family members are interdependent.

Family systems have the property of self-regulation; that is, any input to the family (e.g., change in one member) is acted upon and modified by the system itself through the mechanism of feedback. Family stability or equilibrium is generally maintained through negative feedback mechanisms, while change (learning, growth, or crisis) is maintained and increased by positive feedback.

The family system is also nonsummative: while the characteristics of individual family members partially determine the characteristics of the family system, the total system generates a unitary complexity and an emergent quality or "style" that cannot be accounted for by the sum of its individual members and their attributes. Within the family system, there are subsystems. These are smaller groups (e.g., the parents) defined by boundaries establishing who will participate and how (Minuchin, 1974). These subsystems possess all of the basic systems properties of the overall family system.

## The Postdivorce Family System

### Continuity and Change

Divorce is a crisis in the life cycle of a family which results in change to the original system. When parents[4] end their spousal relationship but continue, to some extent,[5] to participate in child rearing, the postdivorce family system still involves the same members, although their attributes and the relationships between them will have changed. The family system is not dissolved, but altered.

Despite the structural changes, the tasks facing the postdivorce family remain the same as those of the married one (Brandwein, Brown, & Fox, 1974). Changes that occur in the system generally focus around a redivision of labor (who will do what tasks) and new methods of organization (how tasks will be accomplished). The children, for example, may now become more responsible for the chores. Many roles do not necessarily change: fathers may continue to assume major financial responsibility, and mothers may maintain the role of chief caretaker for the children.

### Disequilibrium

Following separation, the family system goes into a state of marked disequilibrium that may last for varying lengths of time and may vary in intensity, depending upon the specific family and the circumstances of the separation. Over time, a new but temporary equilibrium is attained, one commensurate with the development of adjusted roles and relationships among the family members. This state, too, is usually short-lived, and the system swings through additional cycles, although the instability tends to be progressively less intense. Most families in which divorce does not occur go through similar periods of disequilibrium at critical transitions in their life cycles, as in an adolescent's leaving home; however, the divorce crisis is of such

---

[4]The postdivorce family situation in which children are involved is the focus of this chapter. The family situation in which there are no children presents a different picture and challenge to clinicians.

[5]The situation in which the noncustodial parent does not continue to be involved in child rearing to any extent is discussed in the section on the custodial parent–child subsystem.

magnitude that it usually takes the postdivorce family at least several years to develop a fairly stable new family system (Hetherington *et al.,* 1976).

Restoring equilibrium to the system may result in long-term consequences for the family; these may be either positive or negative, depending upon how the crisis itself is resolved. On the negative side, equilibrium is regained in some families by members' taking on maladaptive roles: for example, a child may take the absent father's place and thereby stabilize the system. Subsequently, however, it may be difficult for the child to separate from the family. Or, on the positive side, the crisis may stimulate personal growth and development in ways that were not available to family members in the married system: for example, a woman who felt unable to cope with financial and occupational responsibilities when married may now get a job, develop financial competence, and feel much better in general, about herself as an achiever.

### Continued Interdependence

Every member of the postdivorce family system is related to his or her fellow members in such a way that a change in one will cause a change in all of them and in the total system. Thus, family members, including divorced parents who share child rearing, continue to be interdependent and to have impact on one another. The following example illustrates how change in the behavior of one member results in reverberating consequences for the entire family, including the initiator of the change.

A divorced father forgets to pick up his son at the appointed time, and, as a result, the mother is forced to cancel her plans. The mother is angry and tells the child that she is having to sacrifice her plans because of the father's irresponsibility. The child is torn between loyalty to each parent but sides with the mother, his primary caretaker. The next time the father comes to pick up his son, he refuses to go, saying that his father isn't a good person. The father feels hurt and blames the mother. He sends his next child support payments two weeks late. . . .

Interdependence among postdivorce family members is not necessarily based on extensive and direct interaction. Family members, particularly the divorced parents, are often interdependent although they have little or no direct interaction. Children may function as "split field relayers" (Hogg, 1972), carrying messages between the parents. The effect of this pattern is to maintain interconnectedness between the adults but at the cost of stress to the children (Hogg, 1972), as in this example:

Having just returned from a weekend spent with her father, a little girl begins to eat candy before dinner. Her mother tells her that she knows this is not allowed, but the child says, "Daddy lets me have candy before dinner." The mother becomes angry or guilty and tells the child that her father would do better to provide more financial support and act more responsibly in general. When the child next spends time with her father, she tells him that mother said that he should give them more money. The father then responds that he would give more if the mother stopped squandering it, and so on. . . .

Based on the premise of continued interdependence, it becomes apparent that while spouses may end their marital relationship, they continue to have impact on each other as parents. In the past, this impact was minimized or ignored, perhaps because it seemed to be inconsistent with the fact that former spouses had terminated their relationship as marital partners. This apparent inconsistency may be clarified or resolved from a systems theory perspective. As illustrated in Figure 12-1, the divorced couple may alter the structure of their relationship in the direction of greater separation in regard to their spousal functions, but at the same time or subsequently, may develop or maintain a highly interdependent relationship in regard to their child-rearing functions. Through a process of "progressive segregation" (Hall & Fagen, 1978), they move from interdependence to greater independence in their husband–wife relationship, while through a process of "progressive systematization" (Hall & Fagen, 1978), they maintain (and sometimes increase) their interdependence as parents.

### *Functionality of Symptomatic Behavior*

The concept of interdependence among postdivorce family members, including the divorced parents, allows a clearer understanding of symptomatic behavior in the postdivorce family to develop. As in any family system, symptomatic behavior may function to maintain the family equilibrium (Jackson, 1957). Within the postdivorce family, this has sometimes been

FIGURE 12-1. THE POSTDIVORCE FAMILY AS A REORGANIZED FAMILY SYSTEM. THIS FIGURE ILLUSTRATES THE SITUATION IN WHICH BOTH DIVORCED PARENTS STAY INVOLVED IN CHILD REARING TO SOME EXTENT. ↔ INDICATES CONTINUED INTERDEPENDENCE VIA PROGRESSIVE SYSTEMATIZATION; # INDICATES TERMINATION OF RELATIONSHIP OR INDEPENDENCE VIA PROGRESSIVE SEGREGATION.

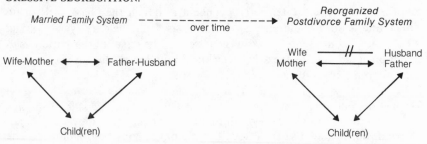

difficult to perceive or understand without considering all of the family members, particularly the divorced spouses. A clinical case example illustrates this point.

In a postdivorce family, it emerges that the father did not want the divorce and is still attached to his former wife; he is lonely and wants to get back together. The mother will hear none of this—she says she wants to start a new life, but she is afraid to start moving out on her own. When the mother sets limits on her adolescent son, he runs away to his father, who seizes the opportunity to communicate with the mother, emphasizing her inability to control their son alone. The mother feels insecure about her parenting and latches on to the father for support. As the mother moves toward a life of her own, the child acts out in school.

Here, the child's symptomatic behavior functions to maintain a postdivorce family system equilibrium in which the mother and the father continue to be actively intertwined. Only when one considers the father as a family member and the relationship between the parents as a critical aspect of the family does the systemic function of the child's symptomatic behavior become apparent.

### *"Parental Child" and "Spousal Child" Roles*

In addition to the development of symptomatic behavior, a child may take over roles vacated by a departing spouse, thus maintaining postdivorce family equilibrium. There is a blurring or breaching of generational boundaries (Walsh, 1979), in which the child is expected and, indeed, agrees to behave in ways more typically associated with the parental generation. This situation can have negative or positive repercussions for the child and the family.

Most commonly, a child will take over a parental role (Hajal & Rosenberg, 1978), acting as a parent toward siblings or toward a parent. This is particularly evident in postdivorce families in which the noncustodial parent has entirely abdicated a parental role, or in which the custodial parent, feeling overwhelmed or insecure, gives up or diminishes his or her own parental involvement. It is less likely to occur if the parents maintain a shared cooperative coparenting relationship.

The "parental child" role is not exclusively negative and, in fact, may facilitate a child's growth and development: for example, the child may develop a sense of responsibility, learn child-rearing skills, or develop a positive sense of self as an important family member. However, when the "parental child" role is rigid and extreme, and the child must play the parental role to the exclusion of more age-appropriate roles, problems arise. Such a child may have difficulty separating from the family, have problems getting personal needs fulfilled, and may feel deprived of nurturance as well as resentful of increased responsibilities.

A child may also take over a spousal role within the family. This may involve acting as a confidante, accompanying the parent on weekend excursions, partaking of "intimate" dinners at home, and so on. Or the divorced spouse may have functioned as the "bad one" or the "irresponsible–inconsiderate one" in the marital relationship. With the spouse now absent, the child becomes the focus of the remaining parent's critical attention, often receiving the label "just like your father (mother)." While the "spousal child" role may at times provide gratification, it often involves unproductive behavior for the child and hinders the development of more appropriate peer relationships for both the child and the parent.

### Custody

At first reading, it would appear that custody is the quality that truly differentiates divorced from married families. Certainly this is true if custody is viewed from a purely legal point of view, because there is no legal equivalent of custody in married family situations. From a systems perspective, however, it becomes clear that the elements of custody are also evident in married families.

Custody basically determines questions of control, rights, and responsibilities in relation to the children (Abarbanel, 1979; Benedek & Benedek, 1979), issues shared by both married and postdivorce families. In any family, there will be a "decider subsystem" (Hall & Fagen, 1978)—that part of the system that maintains control and order. The decider subsystem obtains information on all parts of the system, compares this information with the family's goals, and, where necessary, sends back commands correcting the dispositions. For decisions to be of maximum benefit to the whole family, the decider subsystem must be provided with the fullest information about the whole system and about details of any conflicts between other subsystems before any choice is made (Skynner, 1976).

In married families, this function is endogenous—that is, it is determined within the system. In postdivorce families, the decider subsystem is exogenously (i.e., legally) determined. The legal arrangement, however, must be differentiated from the actual control structure that develops. For example, within the traditional mother-custody situation, the degree of shared parenting can vary from no sharing of control and decision making to almost equal sharing between the parents.

In postdivorce families, mothers still receive legal custody in 90% of all cases. Although more fathers overall are receiving sole custody, the ratio of mothers to fathers receiving custody has remained stable for several decades (U.S. Bureau of the Census, 1975). Recently, joint custody as a legal alternative and shared parenting as a structural alternative for postdivorce families have received wide attention (Abarbanel, 1979; Benedek & Benedek, 1979; Roman & Haddad, 1978). This shift in focus is consistent with a growing body of research and clinical data indicating that continued free access to both parents after a divorce is of optimal benefit for family members (Wallerstein & Kelly, 1979). It is also consistent with systems principles in that joint custody—shared parenting—increases the likelihood of providing the decider subsystem with the fullest information about the whole system, thus optimizing decision making.

However, even advocates of joint custody or shared parenting caution that it is extremely difficult to maintain successfully and that it requires a high level of cooperation and mutual support (Abarbanel, 1979). Should joint custody or shared parenting be undertaken by an actively conflictual and hostile couple, the effect might well be to impede decision making. Such an arrangment would be more detrimental to family members than would one requiring less interaction between parents. The question of which custody arrangements work better with which kinds of postdivorce families is an intriguing one, requiring continued research and clinical investigation.

### Remarriage

The postdivorce family has been defined as a reorganized family system involving the original married family members. It is often true that at some point in the postdivorce process, new family members will be added through remarriage (or living together), and new family systems will develop. (For a discussion of these types of families, see Chapter 13, in this volume.) The addition of new family members, however, does not change the basic conceptualization of mother, father, and children as a continuing system. Rather, as illustrated in Figure 12-2, the original mother–father–child postdivorce family, as well as the newer stepparent family (composed of mother or father, new spouse/stepparent, and children), can now be considered to be subsystems of a larger, general remarried family system. Individual family members (e.g., mother and children) are members of both subsystems. The remarriage of one or both parents, therefore, does not result in the dissolution of the mother–father–child system. In fact, this subsystem has been found to be critical to an understanding of the new stepfamily system, because many problems in remarried families stem from continuing difficulties in the relationships among the original family members (Visher & Visher, 1978).

## GOALS AND STRUCTURE OF CLINICAL INTERVENTION

### Goals

In general, the goal of clinical intervention with postdivorce families is to help resolve the divorce crisis in ways that reconstitute normal family functioning and that permit new opportunities for growth and development

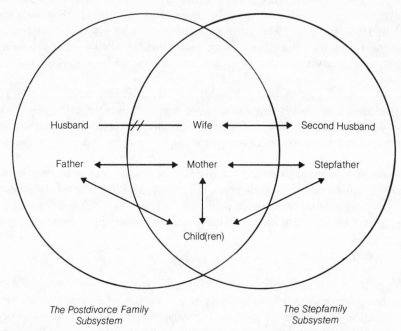

The Postdivorce Family
Subsystem

The Stepfamily
Subsystem

FIGURE 12-2. THE REMARRIED FAMILY SYSTEM. THIS FIGURE ILLUSTRATES A
FAMILY IN WHICH ONLY THE MOTHER HAS REMARRIED. ↔ INDICATES INTER-
DEPENDENCE; ╫ INDICATES TERMINATION OF RELATIONSHIP.

for family members. As noted earlier, the divorce crisis stimulates systemic
disequilibrium, and it is useful to view such disruption not only as a period
of increased stress, but also as a moment of opportunity. When a system is in
flux, it is open to change: the increased permeability of boundaries, temporary suspension of rules, momentary confusion of roles, and loss of controls—all of these factors permit fresh input to be heard. Under these
circumstances, the clinician can help to develop new roles and relationships
that, in turn, will move the family system to a healthier and perhaps more
satisfying equilibrium. In fact, as most clinicians know, it may be considerably more difficult to accomplish this when the family is in a stable but
unsatisfactory state.

## Structure

When a child of divorced parents develops symptoms that lead the family to
seek help, the question arises as to which members should be involved in
treatment. Should the therapist see the custodial parent and child, all per-

sons living in the same household, or all of the original members of the married family? The way in which this decision gets made will be explicitly or implicitly determined by the way in which the therapist defines the postdivorce family. It is a critical determination, for the structure of the therapy will shape the ensuing therapeutic process (Goldsmith, 1981).

From a systems theory perspective, it is apparent that when the non-custodial parent continues to be involved in child rearing, it is important to include all of the original family members as part of a treatment plan. This position is consistent with an understanding of these family members as comprising an ongoing postdivorce family system, for all of the original family members will be expected to affect and be affected by the presenting problem.

One way to illustrate the importance of including all family members is to describe some common repercussions of not following this strategy. Consider this continuation of the clinical example of the boy who acts out in school:

On the school's recommendation, the mother calls a therapist who, because the parents are divorced and the mother has custody of the child, decides to see only the mother and the child. In excluding the father from the sessions, the therapist does not learn that the father never wanted the divorce and is still very attached to his former wife. What emerges in therapy is only that the mother sets limits on the child but then backs down because, she says, she is insecure about her ability to rear her children alone. Therapeutic efforts are consequently directed toward helping the mother to control the child, whose behavior indeed temporarily improves. Several weeks later, however, the mother calls the therapist to indicate that, following a visit with the father, the child's behavior has taken a downturn. In fact, the child has again run away to the father's house and will not be attending the next scheduled therapy session.

Based on an understanding of the continuing interdependence between postdivorce family members, it is apparent that a reduction in this child's symptomatic behavior has resulted in disequilibrium for this postdivorce family system. No longer able to maintain his rescuer role, the father sabotages the gains made in therapy, reestablishing the family stability.

Clearly, the inclusion of all postdivorce family members in this case would have provided a more complete picture of the family system, and by offering more points of intervention, it might have increased the likelihood of therapeutic success. Had the father been included in the treatment plan, it would have been possible to work on developing a new family stability that would not require the child's continued symptomatic behavior. This might have involved exploring other ways for the parents to stay connected (e.g., routine meetings to talk about the children's accomplishments). It might also have involved "working through" the strong emotional entanglement between the former spouses (for example, by working with the father on acceptance of the divorce, and with the mother on her fear of new relationships) to reduce the need for continued maladaptive involvement.

The recommendation that all of the original family members be included in assessment and treatment planning does not mean that all members should be seen together *all of the time*. At the outset, it is essential to develop an understanding of the overall postdivorce family system by including all original family members in assessment and treatment planning. It is preferable, but not essential, that this involve at least one session with all family members present. Once the overall system has been evaluated, much of the subsequent therapeutic work may be undertaken with smaller units—with mother and children, with father and children, and/or with father and mother. It is important to develop a structure for each session that reflects the particular problem being addressed while supporting clear boundaries between subgroups. For example, when working on behavior control with an acting-out child, it is best for both parents to be with the children in the session. When, however, the therapeutic issue involves the mother developing new dating relationships, it is clearly inappropriate to include the former spouse in the same session.

Involving all of the family members (particularly the former spouses) in therapy requires ingenuity, flexibility, and perseverance, since family members are often quite resistant to such an endeavor. Any strategy effective in bringing in resistant family members in other family situations may be applied equally effectively to the postdivorce family. Unique to the divorce situation is the importance of communication to the former spouses that their relationships *as coparents* is critical to the therapeutic effort; that the sessions will be problem-focused; and that conjoint therapy will be time-limited rather than open-ended. Above all, it must be made clear that the purpose of therapy is not to reunite them.

When either parent still refuses to be seen with the other, or when there is a great deal of hostility between the former spouses, it may be necessary to meet with each separately. Only when the resistance or hostility has diminished will it be constructive to see them together.

In addition to the resistance of family members, the therapist's own reluctance often inhibits the inclusion of both former spouses in treatment. Therapists sometimes feel uncomfortable meeting together with two people who have divorced, because they assume that divorced spouses do not have direct contact with one another. In fact, recent data show that the majority of former spouses who participate in child rearing continue to have direct, although episodic, contact with one another following divorce (Goldsmith, 1980). It is highly unlikely that the initial assessment session with both parents will be the first time that they have been together since their divorce.

Another possible objection to including both former spouses is that the therapeutic process will maintain or encourage reunion fantasies that hinder family members in working through and accepting the reality of the divorce. Certainly it is true that one or both former spouses, as well as the children, may have ambivalent feelings about the divorce that will be stimulated by meeting together. (This will be particularly true if therapy is successful and the former spouses are able to work together cooperatively.) Rather than inhibiting the process, however, including all of the members may in fact facilitate it. Seeing their parents together in therapy sessions and not re-uniting helps children to confront their fantasies and to see that they will not materialize. So too, for the adults, meeting together makes it equally difficult for them to maintain an idealized picture of a former spouse or a marriage. Instead, it provides an opportunity for the surfacing of reunion fantasies that may have been interfering with individual and family growth and develop-ment, and for work on the fantasies within the therapeutic context.

At times, the divorce crisis results in a family being left with a sole parent (the other having entirely given up child-rearing responsibilities). In such instances, it will usually not be feasible to include both parents in assessment and treatment planning. Before excluding the noncustodial par-ent from clinical attention, however, it is important to determine whether he or she has actually cut off all ties with the family. Therapists may be too quick to accept the story that one parent has no ongoing connection, when probing may uncover information which shows continued involvement. Even when the former spouse is not physically present in the family in any way, it is important to assess his or her role in the ongoing system. A father who has left town permanently and does not see his children may still be "alive" for them, so that when family problems emerge, the adolescent children introduce his opinion (and perhaps undermine the mother's). Thus, the father's role as "good parent" in such a family system is maintained, even though he is not physically present. It may be helpful to use an empty chair in the therapy room to represent the absent parent as a means of assessing his or her role in the family.

When one or both divorced parents have remarried, the question of which family members to include in treatment becomes a more complicated issue, and the resistance to including both divorced parents is often height-ened. In making this decision, it is important to recognize that the original mother–father–child system remains a viable and often critical subsystem of the overall remarried family. This subsystem has an impact on the stepfamily subsystem, and vice versa. In order to obtain the most complete picture of the family system as it affects the presenting problem, it is still necessary to include all of the original family members, as well as the new family mem-bers, in assessment and treatment planning (Suarez, Weston, & Hartstein, 1978). When and in what combinations members should be included will depend on the specific situation; one remarried mother may feel comfortable meeting together with her former spouse and her new spouse, while another may first need to meet with her former spouse alone.

Thus far, this discussion has focused on the nuclear family. A brief note should be made regarding the importance of the extended family—in particular, the grandparents—in the life of the postdivorce family system. Extended family members can play a critical role in facilitating or impeding growth in the family. Relatives may stand in for an absent parent in a way that enhances the development of the children (Lovelene & Lohman, 1978); on the other hand, they may fuel anger at the absent parent, sabotaging the family members' movement toward adaptive emotional separation. At the very least, an assessment of the role of the extended family must be a part of an evaluation of the postdivorce family system. When relatives play an active role in the life of the family, particularly if they influence the presenting problem, it will be important to include them in the therapeutic process.

Clinicians working with the postdivorce family have often viewed it as so different from its counterpart, the married family, that knowledge and skills long developed in working with the latter tend not to be used. Viewing the postdivorce family as a reorganized family system suggests that many of the same basic issues and clinical skills needed for working with all families will be appropriate and applicable. In a word, "divorce therapy" is not some unique brand; rather, it is the application of the family systems principles, together with congruent strategies and techniques, to the issues involved in the postdivorce family situation.

These issues, as stated earlier, involve the entire family system and as such require an evaluation of the interrelationships among all family members in order to obtain an accurate and complete analysis. However, much of the clinical work on these issues will take place within subsystems. For this reason, the principal subsystems are here identified, and the issues and clinical implications as they apply to each are presented. Common patterns as well as successful adaptations to problems for each subsystem will be presented.

## WORKING WITH POSTDIVORCE FAMILY SUBSYSTEMS

Subsystems are of particular importance in understanding and treating postdivorce families. The earlier emphasis on the continuing interdependence among mother, father, and children is not meant to negate the importance of establishing clear and separate identities for subgroups operating within this overall system.

The clinical strategy stated in this chapter—that is, obtaining an assessment of the overall family and following this by work with subgroups—is consistent with establishing or validating a distinct identity for each sub-system. It allows the therapist to identify and then to work with those subgroups of the family system that seem most stressful for individual members (Kaplan, 1977) and most relevant to the presenting problem. At the same time, it maintains an awareness of the repercussions that change in any particular subsystem would have on overall family functioning.

Each parent and his or her child(ren) comprise a separate and critical subsystem of the postdivorce family. Where there are two households, there is a physical as well as a psychological boundary differentiating each parent–child(ren) subsystem. The custodial parent–child and the noncustodial par-ent–child subsystems will often differ markedly from each other in their rules and roles. In one household, a child may be expected to be polite and respectful under all circumstances; in the other, the child may feel free to express feelings toward the parent directly. In one setting, a child may be the "little spouse" and in the other the "little brat."

At first reading, this kind of family situation would appear to be both confusing and harmful to the children involved. However, there is clinical evidence that if the two households maintain clear and consistent character-istics, the children will learn to switch from one situation to the other without major psychological disruption, even if those characteristics are markedly dissimilar (Galper, 1978). Clarity, rather than symmetry, appears to be the necessary ingredient in facilitating a child's adjustment (Minuchin, 1974).

In addition to the parent–child subsystems, the coparental subsystem (mother and father) emerges from the previous analysis as a significant part of the postdivorce family. Particular emphasis is given here to this sub-system, because it appears to be of particular importance to the health of the postdivorce family, and yet has received little attention in prior literature and clinical work.

### The Coparental Subsystem

Consistent with systems theory, recent research and clinical data show that a mutually supportive and cooperative relationship between divorced parents has a positive impact on postdivorce family functioning (Longfellow, 1979). Such a relationship has been found to be a salient factor in predicting a custodial mother's effectiveness in child rearing and has been related to a child's positive adjustment to divorce (Hetherington et al., 1976). Moreover, a supportive and cooperative divorced coparenting relationship has been found to be an essential ingredient in the successful implementation of joint custody or shared parenting arrangements, which tend to maximize a child's continued access to both parents (Abarbanel, 1979). With cooperation on the part of both parents in the maintenance of their parenting roles, there is also less need for children to take on age-inappropriate parental role functions, and there is less likelihood that the divorced couple will need to return to court to settle any disagreements that may emerge (Goldsmith, 1980).

Despite the importance of this subsystem, there is little current or systematic information concerning the nature of the relationships between former spouses who both continue to act as parents. In the absence of such information, divorced parents face the formidable task of terminating their marital relationship while reorganizing their relationship toward one another as parents, all without knowing how or whether this is accomplished by others in similar circumstances. Former spouses frequently express interest in how other divorced parents work out their relationships, and they express concern about their own lack of knowledge of how to do so successfully. Moreover, an increasing number of professionals who are attempting to help parents develop successful postdivorce relationships do so with little information about what constitutes normative as well as successful adaptations for this population (Bohannan, 1971; Goetting, 1978).

To begin filling the information deficit surrounding the coparental subsystem, I have been conducting a research study investigating the nature of relationships between divorced parents. (For more detailed information about the research study, see Goldsmith, 1980.) The study provides norms regarding divorced couples' relationships and identifies those intrapersonal and interpersonal factors that account for successful adaptation. The research has involved 129 divorced adults (representing 85 divorced couples) with children under 18 years of age. They were interviewed 1 year after their legal divorce (couples had been separated for from 2 months to 2 years prior to legal divorce), and again at 3 years after divorce. Their names were obtained from a random selection of the Cook County, Illinois, divorce court records. Whenever possible, both male and female members of the divorced couple were interviewed individually. The sample was selected to represent the most common divorced family form (Hetherington et al., 1976): the subjects were all Caucasian, and the mother was the custodial parent in each case. Because the focus was on coparental relationships, only those couples in which the father had seen the child at least once in the 2 months preceding the interview (90% of the couples contacted) were included in the study. For those who were interviewed, the amount of father–child involvement ranged from once every 2 months to every day.

The interview[6] was an in-depth, semistructured procedure designed to evaluate multiple dimensions of the former spousal relationship. Self-report scales were developed from the interviews to assess each aspect of the relationship. These scales were found to have good internal consistency and

---

[6]The interview and research design for 1 year after divorce was developed in collaboration with Constance R. Ahrons.

yielded adequate consensus between reports by the members of each divorced couple.

The Quality of Divorced Coparental Relationship Scale was developed as a self-report measure of successful adaptation for this subsystem. It is composed of items measuring cooperation, mutual support, and satisfaction between divorced parents. In addition to measures of reliability and validity used to evaluate other self-report scales, a behavior test was specifically constructed to determine whether the self-report of quality was associated with the way in which the couple actually interacted in a structured situation. The results lend support to the use of the self-report measure of quality of the divorced coparental relationship; there was a strong association ($r = +.787$) between what the couple said about their relationship and the amount of support and attack (measured by the Family Interaction Scales—Global Form; Riskin, 1980) they actually manifested in their interaction.

The results and clinical implications that follow are based only on the completed analysis of the data for 1 year after divorce (analysis of the data for 3 years after divorce is underway). As mentioned above, the data and the clinical implications that emerge therefrom are based on a sample of Caucasian, mother-custody families in which the father maintained at least minimal contact with the children. While the conclusions may apply to other populations or types of families (e.g., other racial/ethnic groups or joint custody families), it is also possible that others present a different picture. Unfortunately, these data await collection, and research in this area is essential. However, until this material is available, clinicians must individually evaluate the extent to which the conclusions of the present study generalize or can be applied to different types of client families at different points in the postdivorce reorganization process.

The results of the research study indicated that the majority of the divorced parents surveyed experienced some degree of conflict or stress in their coparental relationships. Common problems included the following: disagreements and arguments about raising children; dissatisfaction with the other parent's "using" a child (e.g., as a go-between or as a way of getting back at the other parent); the other parent's way of relating to a child in general; the former spouse's personality (e.g., "too immature") or living arrangements (e.g., living with a friend of the opposite sex); and competition with the other parent. Problems raised exclusively by mothers included fathers' spoiling the children and lack of support and caring from fathers. Problems reported exclusively by men involved lack of input into and control over the child-rearing process because of restrictions imposed by former wives. It is interesting, in light of the common myth that women suffer more from the divorce process, that noncustodial fathers in general were more dissatisfied with the coparental relationship than were custodial mothers.

On the positive side, there were a number of couples (13%) in which both parents consistently agreed that they had achieved an ideal or at least a highly successful (cooperative, supportive, and satisfying) divorced coparental relationship. In addition, many couples who reported stress or conflict as one characteristic of their relationship also described their relationships as involving cooperation and mutual support. Thus, while the maintenance of a cooperative and supportive divorced coparental relationship may be difficult to accomplish, some couples were able to do so consistently, while others were able to maintain elements of such a relationship at some times in their coparental relating.

The data on problems in coparental relationships should not be altogether surprising, in view of the fact that, in each case, two people who were previously unable to work out a spousal relationship (and whose marriage probably terminated under a high degree of distress) are now required to work out a relationship for which norms and rules have never been mapped. The evidence does suggest, however, that it is possible for divorced couples to accomplish, or at least to move closer to, the goal of cooperative divorced coparenting. Most divorced parents will need direction in this undertaking, but there are few current clinical resources available to help them.

The importance of successful divorced coparenting relationships underscores the need to develop intervention programs for divorced couples. This should be a major goal of clinicians working with postdivorce families. At the present time, clinical access to divorced couples is generally obtained through the presenting problem of one of the family members. In keeping with the strategy of including all original family members in such therapy, the clinician will then have access to both divorced parents and the possibility of engaging the divorced couple in an effort to improve their coparental relationship emerges. As information about the importance of the divorced coparental relationship becomes more widely disseminated, clinicians may increasingly find that divorced couples present themselves directly for help with these relationships.

Clinical intervention directed toward facilitating divorced coparental relationships must involve a number of overlapping strategies suitable for particular divorced couples. Direct behavioral intervention strategies will sometimes facilitate change. To illustrate, mediation techniques (Coogler, 1979) have been found to be effective in resolving conflict for some divorced couples. In addition, clinicians will need to take an active role in educating their clients about the coparental relationship options available to them. For example, couples who might be able to work out such an arrangement need to be informed about the possibility of joint custody as a parenting option.

For many couples, direct behavioral intervention and education regarding coparenting options will not be enough. It will be necessary to work on those interpersonal and intrapsychic factors that inhibit the development of successful divorced coparental relationships. To date, it has not been clear which factors determine the development of these relationships. My own research project investigates some of those factors that appear to be most relevant, including the amount and content of coparental communication; the nonparental relationship between former spouses; feelings of one former spouse toward the other; psychiatric symptoms; and the willingness of noncustodial parents to participate. In order to provide information relevant to clinical work with divorced parents, a description both of the norms for these areas and of their association with successful divorced coparental relationships is presented below.

### Coparental Communication

The study indicated that when both former spouses continued to be involved with their children after divorce, they generally also continued a direct relationship with each other as divorced parents. Only 16% of divorced spouses who shared child rearing (to any extent) did not communicate directly with each other as parents.

The contact maintained by most divorced parents tended to be regular and periodic (e.g., once a week), but it was more likely to increase in regard to a special occasion or a problem with the child(ren). Divorced couples exhibited wide differences in the degree to which the parents stayed involved with each other concerning the children (from every day to not at all). There was also considerable variation in the extent to which divorced parents maintained communication, depending on the child-rearing area involved. While school or medical problems stimulated the highest frequency of communication, other child-rearing areas, such as day-to-day decisions regarding the children, were much less likely to be shared.

In addition to communicating about child-rearing issues, the majority of divorced parents also reported that they occasionally spent time with each other and with the children as a "family." These tended to be special occasions, such as birthdays, outings, school and church functions, or visits to grandparents.

Of particular importance to any understanding of the development of successful divorced coparental relationships was the finding that those divorced couples who maintained a high degree of coparental involvement were more likely to experience their relationships as cooperative, mutually supportive, and satisfactory. It appears that successful divorced coparental relationships implied not only parent–child interaction, but also parent-to-parent relating. Divorced parents generally felt more satisfied and supported when there was a sharing of interest and responsibility toward the children.

These findings on coparental communication have immediate clinical relevance, because they suggest that continued contact between divorced parents concerning child rearing should not be perfunctorily interpreted by clinicians as a reflection of an inability to separate, and therefore as something to be discouraged. On the contrary, since active coparental communication is associated with successful coparental relationships, clinicians should generally facilitate this kind of interaction. This will involve not only encouraging the active involvement of the noncustodial parent, but also helping the custodial parent to allow the former spouse to contribute to child rearing.

Of course, if the nature of continued contact between divorced parents is inappropriate (e.g., reinforcing essentially hostile communication), coparental relationships will not be enhanced by this strategy. In such instances, these feelings must be explored before active sharing between the parents will be useful. It must be stressed, however, that clinicians should not automatically assume that because a couple is divorced, their interaction will be hostile. Many divorced parents who maintained active communication with each other found that it enhanced their experience of support and cooperation, instead of increasing conflict and hostility.

Coparental communication is one area in which divorced parents reported a great deal of confusion because of the lack of information concerning existing norms and options. Role models are not generally available, and parents are unable to judge their efforts against the experience of others in comparable situations. They often need to be informed that continued contact concerning child rearing is not only normal but may also be beneficial to their family situation. Moreover, divorced parents who spend time together with each other and their children on a special occasion, but who hide this information from disapproving family and friends, need to know that such behavior is common among divorced families and is not necessarily pathological.

The findings on coparental involvement also have implications for the vocabulary used by clinicians and the general public to describe postdivorce family relationships. The term "coparents" might be used to supplement the term "ex-spouses" in describing divorced couples who maintain active coparental relationships. The latter term is not only mildly pejorative (carrying with it the stigma of failure) but is also not an accurate picture of the current relationship. One divorced father described a situation in which he was called upon to introduce his former wife to a group of his friends. In thinking about introducing her as his ex-wife, he felt that this was somehow derogatory and that it denied the reality of the past 10 years in which they had actively and cooperatively shared parenting. He coined a term on the spot and introduced her as his "coparent," which more accurately characterized their relationship. The use of this term, "coparents," may well be a means of identifying and validating this important and ongoing subsystem in the postdivorce family.

### Nonparental Involvement

Former spouses may also continue to relate to each other quite apart from child-rearing concerns. These relations vary from friendly, "kin-type" contacts (e.g., talking about extended family members or discussing mutual friends) to more romantic or sexual involvement (e.g., dating). The results of the study indicate that the majority of divorced couples had maintained "kin-type" contacts on a periodic basis, while very few divorced parents had maintained romantic or sexual involvement with each other. For those in the study, any physical expression of affection was generally restricted to kissing and hugging; none reported continuing sexual intercourse. Of particular interest was the finding that couples who maintained friendly "kin-type" contact were also more likely to develop mutually supportive and cooperative coparental relationships.

Nonparental contact between former spouses has stimulated contradictory interpretations by clinicians. Some view this contact as a healthy outcome of the divorce process (Kressel & Deutsch, 1977), but most view it as a pathological inability to separate (Kressel & Deutsch, 1977) and as a contaminant of the coparental relationship (Wiseman & Lindner, 1977). The results of the present study point to the importance of revising traditional clinical views about former-spousal interaction. It is suggested that continued nonparental contact be looked at closely for each divorced couple *before* it can be evaluated. Key criteria in clinically evaluating continued nonparental contact are whether the boundaries for such interaction are clear and agreed upon (Minuchin, 1974), and whether each former spouse actively continues to develop new relationships.

Many former spouses in the present study were able to relate in friendly ways without becoming involved with one another sexually or romantically, and while continuing to develop new relationships. There were some couples, however, for whom the boundaries were unclear and there was continued enmeshment and distress. One woman, for example, related that whenever her former husband came to pick up the children, the two of them spent time together, ostensibly to talk about child-rearing issues. This progressed to sharing information about friends and relatives. In the course of their conversations, her former husband would begin to wander around the house, "checking into things." Inevitably, he would end up in the bedroom opening drawers, including those containing her lingerie; he would also query her about her recent sexual experiences. Although the situation distressed her, she did not know what to do about it. For this couple, the parameters of their relationship as coparents were not clear-cut, and the continued nonparental interaction contaminated their coparenting and inhibited their ability to separate and develop new relationships.

The nonparental contact maintained by a majority of former spouses suggests that divorced parents may be thought of as members of a new kinship network resulting from the divorce. Since, under certain circumstances, maintenance of this network may facilitate coparental relationships, clinicians should focus in such cases on clarifying boundaries around friendly contacts between former spouses, rather than on immediately discouraging such interaction.

### Feelings toward the Former Spouse

There is considerable agreement that termination of a marriage stimulates a process of emotional separation that involves a corresponding set of feelings toward the former spouse (Weiss, 1975). These feelings, including hostility, caring and guilt, not only affect the individual's own adjustment to divorce (Kitson & Sussman, 1976), but also influence interaction with the former spouse (Weiss, 1975).

In the present study, moderately negative feelings of blame or anger toward the former spouse were experienced by a majority of subjects. The majority also believed that their former spouses were angry and blamed them. Extremely negative feelings (e.g., wanting revenge or wanting the former spouse to be punished) were much less commonly experienced.

The study also showed that negative feelings critically affected the quality of divorced coparental relationships. The single best predictor of problems in these relationships was the belief that the former spouse had angry and hostile feelings about oneself. In addition, if *either* former spouse experienced his or her own negative feelings, the couple was more likely to have problems with their coparental relationships. If *both* former spouses were angry with the other, this led to even greater difficulties.

The findings on the prevalence and importance of negative feelings are consistent with the clinical picture developed from working with divorced couples; they support the need for direct clinical intervention aimed at modifying these feelings with *both* former spouses. Often it will not be enough to work with one former spouse, because if the other is still hostile, or if the client perceives that the former spouse has angry feelings, there will still be problems in the coparental relationship.

Any clinical strategy that is effective in modifying negative feelings between married partners may be equally applicable to divorced spouses. When hostile feelings are maintained in the face of clinical intervention, it may be best to work toward a divorced coparenting situation that minimizes direct hostile interaction or the use of the children as instruments for expressing hostility. This usually requires a clearly defined policy about when the children will be seen and should involve the minimal possible negotiation between the parents necessary to deal with child-rearing issues.

The feelings expressed toward one another by former spouses were not exclusively negative. Indeed, in the present study, positive feelings (such as caring and compassion) were the most frequently reported; one-third of the former spouses even expressed loving feelings. It should be noted that one former spouse's having positive feelings toward the other did not mean that negative feelings were not also present. In fact, as other studies have shown (Weiss, 1975), many individuals experienced ambivalent feelings (i.e., both positive and negative concurrently).

In our study, positive feelings about former spouses were associated with more successful coparental relationships: those former spouses who felt caring, compassion, and even loving feelings toward each other—particularly when those feelings were mutual—were also more cooperative and supportive in their coparental interaction. While these results indicated that positive feelings between former spouses facilitated coparenting, it should be noted that clinicians have had difficulty in accepting such positive feelings, especially those in which love is expressed (Brown, 1979); these feelings have been labeled "inappropriate" or "pathological," because they have been attributed to the inability of the former spouses to achieve an emotional separation.

It is critical, however, to distinguish between positive feelings and continued attachment (Kitson & Sussman, 1976). In our study, most former spouses who experienced positive feelings toward the other did *not* experience themselves as unable to separate. Based on these findings, clinicians should not prejudge and label positive feelings as "inappropriate"; rather, they should help former spouses (who themselves are often confused about having positive feelings toward someone they have recently divorced) to understand that such feelings are commonplace and may actually facilitate their postdivorce family life. When positive feelings are, however, associated with continued attachment, the clinical focus should be on helping the separation process, not on eliminating positive feelings.

Spouses who divorce must face the death of their marriage. As with other "deaths," they must go through an emotional process (involving, for example, denial, anger and depression) that ultimately leads to acceptance of their changed situation (Kubler-Ross, 1969). When former spouses do not work through the emotional separation, negative psychiatric and medical repercussions usually ensue (Kitson & Sussman, 1976). Moreover, on the basis of the findings of our study, continued attachment (of noncustodial father to his former wife, but not vice versa) also had negative repercussions on the coparental relationship. For divorced spouses who have been unable to separate emotionally, intervention should be aimed at working through grief over the separation and loss, and then at facilitating the development of new directions in their lives (Bridges, 1977).

### Psychiatric Symptoms

Difficulties involved in working out successful divorced coparental relationships may be related to psychiatric symptoms experienced by the divorced parents. In the present study, psychiatric symptoms (measured by the Hopkins Symptom Checklist; see Derogatis, Lipman, Rickels, Uhlenhuth, & Covi, 1974) in the noncustodial fathers were associated with greater problems in coparental relationships; the association was not found for custodial mothers. The overall results for this factor indicated that while psychiatric symptoms have some effect on the coparental relationship, it was not nearly so powerful a predictor as were the above-mentioned variables. Clinical efforts aimed at reducing psychiatric symptoms in divorced parents will be useful but probably not sufficient to facilitate successful divorced coparenting. Moreover, as with the findings on continued attachment to the former spouse, it is the father's psychological state that appears to have impact on the coparental relationship. Perhaps his position as the noncustodial parent is more difficult and requires a greater degree of emotional separation and stability.

### Fathers' Involvement

The present study indicated that divorced couples in which the noncustodial fathers were more actively involved in spending time with their children and in child-rearing tasks experienced more successful coparental relationships. Clinical work with divorced fathers and their children (discussed in the section on the noncustodial parent–child subsystem) will be important to the development of successful divorced coparental relationships, and vice versa.

Participation of fathers in the research project emerged as an important variable. There were a number of couples (33 of 85) in which the fathers either could not be contacted or refused to participate. Their former wives were interviewed and reported significantly greater difficulties in their coparental relationships than did those women whose former husbands participated. If we assume that fathers who did not participate in the research are also those who would not participate in treatment, the discouraging conclusion may be that those divorced couples who require the most help may present the greatest difficulty in getting the fathers involved. Since the father is a critical element in the functioning of a divorced couple, this indicates a need for developing more effective ways of reaching noncustodial fathers and for refining our clinical skills for engaging resistant family members in general. It may also be that providing greater social recognition for the importance of the noncustodial father's role on a societal level will contribute toward his increased willingness to participate in intervention programs in the future.

### Summary

The overall picture that emerges from this study is that divorced parents who develop cooperative, mutually supportive coparental relationships are more likely to maintain greater involvement with each other regarding coparental issues; to maintain friendly, "kin-type" contact; and to experience positive feelings toward each other. These parents are less likely to experience hostility. The noncustodial fathers in these cooperative coparenting couples are more likely to stay actively involved with their children and to achieve emotional separation from their former wives; they are also less likely to experience psychiatric symptoms.

In general, these findings call into question current thinking about coparental relationships. They indicate a need for making clinical judgments on the basis of a careful evaluation of the divorced couple, rather than on the basis of prevailing myths or the therapist's own discomfort; for exercising extreme care before interpreting divorced couple's interaction as "pathological"; for including noncustodial fathers in clinical programs aimed at helping postdivorce families; and for developing research programs to examine postdivorce coparental relationships (particularly with different client groups), in order that clinical intervention can become increasingly data-based.

### The Custodial Parent–Child Subsystem

This is the subsystem of the postdivorce family that is typically referred to as "single-parent" and, as such, is viewed as the normative postdivorce family. As the research and clinical data already presented indicate, this description is not accurate; nor is it congruent with a systems perspective, because it includes many postdivorce families in which both parents continue to be involved in child rearing. For these families, the term "custodial parent–child subsystem," or "one-parent *household*" (rather than "family"), is more appropriate. In a family in which the divorce crisis *does* result in a sole parent (the other having given up child-rearing responsibilities), it would be appropriate to label the unit as a single-parent family. The development of the single-parent family system is illustrated in Figure 12-3.

It follows that clinicans need to evaluate the postdivorce family in order to determine whether it is a single-parent family system or whether it is a family that includes, among other subsystems, a one-parent household. When it is the former, it is appropriate to focus primarily on this family unit. When the one-parent household is part of a larger postdivorce family system, it should be one of several subsystems included in the treatment plan. Under either circumstance, working with the custodial parent–child subsystem will be an especially critical aspect of any intervention effort, because family contacts most often take place among members of this family unit.

The custodial parent–child subsystem (under the name "single-parent family") has received the greatest attention in the literature on divorce and families, and only the key findings need be highlighted here. Historically,

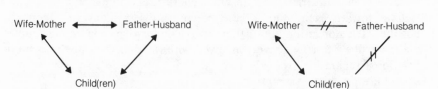

FIGURE 12-3. THE SINGLE-PARENT FAMILY. THIS FIGURE ILLUSTRATES THE
MOST COMMON SINGLE-PARENT FAMILY FORM, IN WHICH THE MOTHER
BECOMES THE SOLE PARENT. ⇠⇢ INDICATES CONTINUED INTERDEPENDENCE;
⫫ INDICATES TERMINATION OF RELATIONSHIP OR INDEPENDENCE.

this material has been based on mothers as the custodial parents (Biller,
1974; Brandwein *et al.*, 1974). Recently, studies have focused exclusively on
fathers (Bartz & Witcher, 1978) or else have included both mothers and
fathers in their investigations (Barry, 1979). The issues for a custodial parent
of either sex are generally identical, and there are no data to indicate that
fathers do any worse or better than mothers do under these circumstances
(Bartz & Witcher, 1978). Investigators studying fathers as custodial parents
argue for the viability of this postdivorce family situation and for the
importance of clinical acceptance and support of this option for families
considering it (Bartz & Witcher, 1978).

Researchers and clinicians working with custodial parent–child subsystems assert the need for a change in our basic viewpoint (Mendes, 1976).
One-parent households have been viewed from a two-parent perspective,
with the expectation that many family needs of the former must perforce go
unmet. By extension, this "deficit model" carries with it the clinical assumption that one-parent households are detrimental to their members. It follows
that this perception maladaptively reinforces the family members' opinions
that they are living in less highly esteemed, if not deficient, family situations.

In opposing this model, researchers have pointed to the mounting
evidence suggesting that one-parent households are a heterogeneous group
with the potential for successful family formation (Mendes, 1976). Proponents of this view emphasize the need to investigate and understand
different types of one-parent household lifestyles as the basis for differential
clinical intervention. They also stress the importance of determining those
factors that make for "success" for each family; not only are one-parent
households heterogeneous in style, they also exhibit wide variation in what
they themselves consider successful family situations (Barry, 1979).

Barry (1979) suggests that one-parent households are more or less
successful to the degree that they adequately complete a series of tasks
necessary for positive adjustment to one-parent household life. She groups
these as "Tasks for The Adjustment Period" (an example of which would be

recognition that important changes affecting all family members have taken place) and "Tasks of The New Family Period" (a typical task here would be coping with the financial and practical needs of the new family structure). She also suggests a task-oriented, clinical approach to working with one-parent households that initially assesses which tasks have not been adequately completed and then helps families to complete them. For example, one household may be unable to work through grief issues, while another cannot manage financial matters. The clinical focus in these two instances would, of course, be different.

All custodial parent–child subsystems experience a number of tasks that are commonly difficult to resolve and so are of particular clinical relevance. At the outset, the custodial parent and child(ren) will need to grieve the loss of the previous family situation. Failure to do so is manifested in such outcomes for parent and child(ren) as chronic depression, feelings of responsibility and guilt over the loss, angry feelings about what is missing, and a failure to develop the necessary skills to cope with the new situation. Here, clinicians must facilitate a process that moves the family toward acceptance of the loss and the new family situation. In this regard, it is important to be aware that adults and children will usually grieve in different ways; for example, children will tend to idealize missing parents (Hajal & Rosenberg, 1978), while adults may depreciate former spouses. When the grieving process is being inhibited by reunion fantasies of either a parent or a child, these fantasies will need to be surfaced so that the mourning may progress.

Another task common to one-parent households is that of learning to cope with being understaffed (Bloch, 1979). Where previously there were two parents in the household contributing to maintenance of family functions, now there is only one. (Of course, it is also the case that in some married families only one parent carries the weight of family responsibilities.) Failure to cope with this situation successfully may take many forms. As indicated earlier, a child may take over parenting responsibilities. Or one parent may try to fulfill the role of both parents, denying the reality of the situation and depleting his or her own resources. At the other extreme, a parent may simply give up trying to fulfill what are still crucial family functions (such as dealing with medical problems).

The problem of being understaffed often sets into motion a maladaptive family pattern common to one-parent households. Parent and child(ren) become immobilized in a "guilt–anger bind": in response to demands, the parent feels angry about fulfilling them but guilty about not fulfilling them; at the same time, a child may feel guilty about asking and angry about not getting. The unfortunate result is that what time there is available to spend together as a family is tension-filled and unrewarding.

Helping such a parent to develop an active support network is one clinical strategy designed to meet the problem of understaffing (Barry, 1979); this network may include neighbors and relatives, and, whenever appropriate, the former spouse. Bringing the "anger–guilt bind" out into the open in therapy and acknowledging the validity of both a parent's limits and a child's needs will help to negotiate a more adaptive arrangement. A specific therapeutic objective of this strategy would most likely be getting the parent to be more precise about his or her availability, and thereby more responsive to the child's needs during those periods. For the child, the reciprocal goal would be clarification of what could be expected from the parent and when it could be expected, so that the child could develop alternatives for getting needs met when the parent is not available (e.g., spending time with friends after school before the parent arrives home from work). Still other strategies for dealing with understaffed families involve the development of better parenting skills, as well as better utilization of those skills already present. As previously indicated, such strategies may make a virtue out of necessity, since the skills that are developed may enhance the parent's sense of personal esteem and lead to more successful life styles in general.

Another issue common to one-parent households is the parent's need for peer intimacy. Divorced parents may deny this need or incorporate a quick series of "intimate others" into the family unit. Clinical intervention should be directed toward acknowledging needs and should stress the importance of fulfilling them with peer contacts, rather than through use of the child(ren) in maladaptive roles. The issue of when and how to incorporate new members into the family unit is complicated and will be different for each family situation. Obviously, however, it is important and useful for parent and child(ren) to talk openly about this with one another and with the new members. But, although children need the opportunity to share their feelings and express their opinions, ultimately it is the parents in these situations who must make the decisions about what is best for all.

A pattern frequently seen with one-parent households is a return to the parent's family of origin (Kaplan, 1977). This may be adaptive to the extent that within this setting the parent can share child-rearing responsibilities with the grandparents and be more free to develop vocationally and socially. Often, however, a parent's return to the family of origin signals an abdication of the parental role and a blurring of generational boundaries, so that the grandparents are now responsible for both their own (adult) child and grandchild(ren). Parent and child(ren) may now act like siblings, competing for attention from grandparents. This can develop into a stable pattern, in which the grandparents are gratified by the caretaker role and the parent is comfortable in a childlike posture. Clinical intervention under these circumstances will need to include all three generations, since grandparents will resist efforts at change if the *status quo* is meeting their needs. The parent should be encouraged to reestablish a parental role, and boundaries between all three generations must be redefined. More appropriate participation by the grandparents in the family life will need to be developed in a way that provides support but does not require the parent's relinquishing the parental role.

Finally, the clinician should be aware that a common pitfall in working with a custodial parent–child subsystem is that both parent and child(ren) are often in search of a replacement for the "lost" parent (Hajal & Rosenberg, 1978). It is easy for the therapist to be seduced into this role, if only because it provides such ready validation. But the role should be avoided, not only because it inhibits an appropriate solution to the family's problem, but also because it is particularly draining of the therapist's own resources in the long run. To avoid this pitfall, strategies such as helping family members to accept their loss, mobilizing alternative resources, and maximizing the "lost" parent's involvement with the family as a coparent will often be useful.

### The Noncustodial Parent-Child Subsystem

Until recently, this subsystem has been neglected in both the divorce literature and in clinical practice. Consistent with a systems paradigm, however, the research that is available has demonstrated the unquestionable importance of this family unit for postdivorce functioning. To date, research and clinical data on noncustodial parents have been based, almost exclusively, on fathers; loss of access to father has been associated with greater problems in children's adjustment to divorce (Greif, 1979; Jacobson, 1978; Wallerstein & Kelly, 1979), while loss of access to children has been associated with more dissatisfaction and problems for fathers (Dreyfus, 1979; Greif, 1979; Keshet & Rosenthal, 1978; Wallerstein & Kelly, 1979). On the other hand, an active, continuing involvement between fathers and children has been linked to successful adaptation for other subsystems, such as the coparental subsystem (Goldsmith, 1980) and the one-parent household (Hetherington et al., 1976).

Research indicates that noncustodial fathers generally do stay involved with their children after divorce (Goldsmith, 1980; Lovelene & Lohmann, 1978); however, as a group, they tend to decrease their involvement over time (Hetherington et al., 1976). Notwithstanding its importance, it appears that the father–child relationship is constrained by a number of problems that make it difficult to sustain. Perhaps the most important of these is the development of a satisfying family life when the time spent together by fathers and children is often limited. Many noncustodial fathers feel that they are merely visitors in their children's lives (Goldsmith, 1980), and that as such they are somehow obliged to entertain continuously, a situation that eventually becomes unsatisfying and exhausting for all involved.

Clinicians should work directly with father–child subsystems, one goal being to transform the time fathers spend with their children from "visiting" to "family living." In order to accomplish this, it is important for fathers and children to establish a household that includes a well-defined physical space for the children, as well as a routine that allows them to feel and behave like a family (e.g., cooking meals at home, doing homework together, etc.). Moreover, the time spent by fathers and children together should be routinized on a long-term basis, rather than negotiated by the coparents each week or month. It should be stressed, too, that the more time fathers and children are able to spend together, the more likely they are to be satisfied with the relationship (Keshet & Rosenthal, 1978).

Fathers and children who had formerly not spent much time together may now feel uncomfortable or awkward in each other's company. Fathers may feel insecure about their parenting skills or, if they feel guilty over a divorce, may trap themselves into a "candy man" role that inhibits the development of this family unit. Children may want to please their fathers but not know how to do so, or they may want to spend time alone (e.g., in reading) but may not want to hurt their fathers' feelings. When this is the case, clinical work should focus on surfacing and resolving these underlying feelings. Fathers and children often benefit from direct help in learning how to relate in each other's presence.

Lack of cooperation or active sabotage by the custodial parent may also be a factor inhibiting the development of a father–child subsystem: for example, the child(ren) may be led to expect that if they are good to the father, they will lose their relationship with their mother. In such instances, facilitating the development of the father–child relationship will depend heavily on the success of clinical work with the mother and with the father–mother subsystem.

Another problem evidenced in the father–child subsystem is the apparent lack of societal sanction and support in maintaining this relationship. For example, in one postdivorce family in which the father was very actively involved with his children, a confirmation ceremony program listed only the mother under "Parents of the Confirmees" (although information about both parents had been provided); it was as though the father were no longer a parent. Widespread dissemination of information about the viability and importance of the father–child relationship after divorce would help provide needed societal support and recognition. From a clinical perspective, the strategy of having separate sessions with fathers and children together also accomplishes the purpose of reinforcing the identity of these units as critical parts of overall family systems.

Finally, clinical strategies involved in the development of successful noncustodial parent–child subsystems, in most respects, flow from the same list of issues already described for other subsystems. These include the development of clear boundaries, support networks, acceptance of the loss of the previous relationship, and so on. To the extent that fathers and children hold on to the wish to regain the past, it is as difficult for them to develop healthy and satisfying relationships in the present as it is for custodial parents and children. When fathers and children are able to develop active postdivorce relationships, they may find that their relationships are in fact more rewarding and satisfying than they were when they all lived together as a married family unit (Hetherington *et al.*, 1976).

## The Individual Subsystems

Each individual family member may be understood as a separate subsystem, although the relevant individual characteristics affecting the properties of postdivorce family systems are only just beginning to be understood. There is some indication that the age, sex, and personality of a child (Longfellow, 1979), as well as the level of maturity of an adult (Hetherington *et al.*, 1976) will affect the reorganization process. The stage of each individual's adjustment to the divorce process (Brown, 1976) is also likely to affect postdivorce family formation.

Viewing the postdivorce family from a systems perspective does not negate the importance of working with individual family members. It is critical, however, for the clinician to evaluate what the impact of the change on the overall system will be. Without such an understanding, the effect of working with one member may be to stimulate negative feedback from other family members that ultimately undermines the treatment.

Individual work can be done within the structure of individual or family sessions. It is generally better to work with young children together with their families rather than in individual sessions. The focus is on helping parents to help children. In this way, a child avoids being isolated from the family as a "problem" requiring special attention (this often feeds into the child's initial fantasy of being responsible for the divorce). Children must often be helped to find alternatives to their maladaptive behavior that will still provide gratification for them. For example, a child who has obtained gifts from her parents by "playing them off" against each other may learn that she can get similar rewards by earning them with productive behavior at home.

In other instances, it may be useful and necessary to meet with each parent alone in order to work on issues of personal growth and new relationships, as well as reinforce generational boundaries. For example, a father who has isolated himself since his divorce may benefit from individual sessions dealing with his relationships with women, his self-esteem, or his social skills. Or a mother whose feelings of sexual inadequacy are inhibiting her developing peer relationships may benefit from individual sessions focused on her sexuality. As an alternative to individual therapy, divorce adjustment groups for adults and adolescents have proved particularly useful in working with these issues (Shelton & Nix, 1979).

## CONCLUSIONS

The main thesis of this chapter is that the postdivorce family is essentially a normal family form and may be understood through the application of general systems theory. Specifically, those processes and patterns that are normative for postdivorce families and that result in successful adaptations for family members have been identified. In this way, clinicians are provided with a conceptual framework within which they may facilitate postdivorce families' movement toward healthy growth and development.

To the maximum extent possible, the conclusions presented in this chapter are based on or supported by research data. However, research on postdivorce families is in its infancy, and available data are generally restricted to the mother–child dyad. Future research should be directed toward developing our understanding of the overall family and the relevant subsystems.

With the increasing number of families experiencing divorce, it is equally important that effective intervention strategies and programs aimed at this population be developed and that this work not be restricted to mother–child dyads. The development and refinement of clinical practice with postdivorce families is, however, not sufficient. The myths about divorce are pervasive and continue to overpower the reality. Change will require a fundamental reorientation—by clinicians, by the divorcing population, and by social institutions. This reorientation may be accomplished through generating new knowledge about postdivorce families and incorporating this knowledge not only into clinical intervention, but also into educational programs for the divorcing population and into a widespread program of disseminating information about postdivorce families for the general population.

## REFERENCES

Abarbanel, A. Shared parenting after separation and divorce: A study of joint custody. *American Journal of Orthopsychiatry*, 1979, *49*, 320–329.

Bane, M. Marital disruption and the lives of children. In G. Levinger & O. Moles (Eds.), *Divorce and separation*. New York: Basic Books, 1979.

Bartz, K. S., & Witcher, W. C. When father gets custody. *Children Today*, September–October, 1978, pp. 1–6.

Barry, A. A research projection on successful single-parent families. *American Journal of Family Therapy*, 1979, *7*, 65–73.

Benedek, E. P., & Benedek, J. D. Joint custody: Solution or illusion? *American Journal of Psychiatry*, 1979, *136*, 1540–1544.

Bertalanffy, L. General systems theory. In B. D. Ruben & J. Y. Kim (Eds.), *General systems theory and human communication*. Rochelle Park, N.J.: Hayden, 1978.

Biller, H. B. *Paternal deprivation*. Lexington, Mass.: Lexington Books, 1974.

Bloch, D. Interview reported in *Marriage and Divorce Today*, 1979, *5*, 1-2.

Bloom, B., White, S., & Asher, S. Marital disruption as a stressful life event. In G. Levinger & O. Moles (Eds.), *Divorce and separation.* New York: Basic Books, 1979.

Bohannan, P. (Ed.). *Divorce and after.* New York: Anchor Books, 1971.

Brandwein, R., Brown, C., & Fox, E. Women and children last: The social situation of divorced mothers and their families. *Journal of Marriage and the Family*, 1974, *36*, 498-514.

Bridges, M. Grief training. *Conciliation Courts Review*, 1977, *15*, 34-36.

Brown, E. A model of the divorce process. *Conciliation Courts Review*, 1976, *14*, 1-11.

Brown, H. Interview reported in *Marriage and Divorce Today*, 1979, *5*, 1-2.

Carter, H., & Glick, P. *Marriage and divorce: A social and economic study.* Cambridge: Harvard University Press, 1976.

Coogler, O. Divorce mediation for "low income" families: A proposed model. *Conciliation Courts Review*, 1979, *17*, 21-26.

Derogatis, L., Lipman, R., Rickels, K., Uhlenhuth, E., & Covi, L. The Hopkins symptom checklist (HSCL): A self-report symptom inventory. *Behavioral Science*, 1974, *19*, 1-15.

Dreyfus, E. Counseling the divorced father. *Journal of Marital and Family Therapy*, 1979, *5*, 79-85.

Fleck, S. An approach to family pathology. *Comprehensive Psychiatry*, 1966, *7*, 307-319.

Galper, M. *Co-parenting: Sharing your child equally.* Philadelphia: Running Press, 1978.

Glick, P. Future American families. *The Washington Coalition of Family Organization Memo*, 1979, *2*, 2.

Goetting, A. *The normative integration of the former spouse relationship.* Paper presented at the meeting of the American Sociological Association, San Francisco, 1978.

Goldsmith, J. The relationship between former spouses: Descriptive findings. *Journal of Divorce*, 1980, *4*, 1-20.

Goldsmith, J. The divorced family: Whom to include in therapy. In A. Gurman (Ed.), *Practical problems in family therapy.* New York: Brunner/Mazel, 1981.

Greif, J. B. Fathers, children, and joint custody. *American Journal of Orthopsychiatry*, 1979, *49*, 311-319.

Hajal, F., & Rosenberg, E. Working with the one-parent family in family therapy. *Journal of Divorce*, 1978, *1*, 259-269.

Hall, A., & Fagen, R. Definition of system. In B. D. Ruben & J. Y. Kim (Eds.), *General systems theory and human communication.* Rochelle Park, N.J.: Hayden, 1978.

Hetherington, E. M., Cox, M., & Cox, R. Divorced fathers. *The Family Coordinator*, 1976, *25*, 417-428.

Hogg, W. F. The split field relayer system as a factor in the etiology of anxiety. *Psychiatry*, 1972, *35*, 126-138.

Jackson, D. The question of family homeostasis. *Psychiatric Quarterly Supplement*, 1957, *31*, 79-90.

Jacobson, D. The impact of marital separation/divorce on children: I. Parent-child separation and child adjustment. *Journal of Divorce*, 1978, *1*, 341-360.

Kaplan, S. Structural family therapy for children of divorce: Case reports. *Family Process*, 1977, *16*, 75-83.

Keshet, H. F., & Rosenthal, K. M. Fathering after marital separation. *Social Work*, 1978, *23*, 11-18.

Kitson, G., & Sussman, M. *The processes of marital separation and divorce: Male and female similarities and differences.* Paper presented at the meeting of the American Sociological Association, New York City, August 1976.

Kressel, K., & Deutsch, M. Divorce therapy: An in-depth survey of therapists' views. *Family Process*, 1977, *16*, 413-443.

Kubler-Ross, E. *On death and dying.* New York: Macmillan, 1969.

Longfellow, C. Divorce in context: Its impact on children. In G. Levinger & O. Moles (Eds.), *Divorce and separation.* New York: Basic Books, 1979.

Lovelene, E., & Lohmann, N. Absent fathers and black male children. *Social Work*, 1978, *23*, 413–415.

Mendes, H. A. Single fathers. *The Family Coordinator*, 1976, *25*, 439–449.

Minuchin, S. *Families and family therapy*. Cambridge: Harvard University Press, 1974.

Riskin, J. *Family interaction scales—global form*. Unpublished manuscript, 1980.

Roman, M., & Haddad, W. *The disposable parent*. New York: Holt, Rinehart & Winston, 1978.

Shelton. S., & Nix, C. Development of a divorce adjustment group program in a social service agency. *Social Casework: Journal of Contemporary Social Work*, 1979, *24*, 309–312.

Skynner, A. *Systems of family and marital psychotherapy*. New York: Brunner/Mazel, 1976.

Suarez, J., Weston, N., & Hartstein, N. Mental health interventions in divorce proceedings. *American Journal of Orthopsychiatry*, 1978, *48*, 273–283.

United States Bureau of the Census. *Household and Family Characteristics Series P-20*. Washington, D.C.: U.S. Government Printing Office, 1975.

Visher, E., & Visher, J. Major areas of difficulty for stepparent couples. *International Journal of Family Counseling*, 1978, *6*, 70–80.

Wallerstein, J., & Kelly, J. Children and divorce: A review. *Social Work*, 1979, *24*, 468–477.

Walsh, F. Breaching of family generation boundaries by schizophrenics, disturbed, and normals. *International Journal of Family Therapy*, 1979, *1*, 254–275.

Watzlawick, P., Beavin, J., & Jackson, D. *Pragmatics of human communication*. New York: Norton, 1967.

Weiss, R. S. *Marital separation*. New York: Basic Books, 1975.

Weiting, S. G. Structuralism, systems theory, and ethnomethodology in the sociology of the family. *Journal of Comparative Family Studies*, 1976, *7*, 375–395.

Wiseman, R., & Lindner, D. *For the sake of the children*. Paper presented at the meeting of the American Orthopsychiatric Association, New York, April 1977.

# 13

# STEPFAMILIES AND STEPPARENTING

JOHN S. VISHER
EMILY B. VISHER

## INTRODUCTION

In the United States, the divorce rate has increased 79% between 1970 and 1977, and it is projected that one-third of married persons who were aged 25 to 35 in 1979 will eventually be divorced. A total of 80% of these adults will remarry, with 60% of the remarriages involving at least one child from a previous marriage (Baker, Druckman, & Flagle, 1980). At the present time, it is estimated that over 35 million adults are stepparents and that one child in six is a stepchild. In many sections of the country, the figures are higher, so that one child in four is a stepchild.

As many as 40% of second marriages end in divorce within 5 years, with the presence of children from a previous marriage being a predisposing factor in favor of the divorce—the opposite of which is true in original marriages (Becker, Landes, & Michael, 1977). This figure supports research studies indicating that remarriage families have more stress and are less cohesive than nuclear families (Bitterman, 1968; Bowerman & Irish, 1962; Fast & Cain, 1966).

Cherlin (1978) summarizes the situation this way:

> Persons who are remarried after a divorce and have children from previous marriages face problems unlike those encountered in first marriages. The institution of the family provides no standard solutions to many of these problems, with the result that the unity of families of remarriages after divorce often becomes precarious. The incomplete institutionalization of

John S. Visher. Clinical Faculty, Department of Psychiatry, Stanford University, Stanford, California, and Adult Services, San Mateo County Mental Health Services, Daly City, California.

Emily B. Visher. Stepfamily Association of America, Inc., and private practice, Palo Alto, California.

remarriage shows us, by way of contrast, that family unity in first marriages is still supported by effective institutional controls, despite claims that the institutional nature of family life has eroded in the twentieth century. (p. 634)

## PATTERNS OF STEPFAMILIES

All stepfamilies have a complicated family structure, due to the number of people involved either directly or more peripherally with these families. There are also numerous family patterns represented among stepfamilies, each with its own common characteristics. To name only a few, there are women with no children of their own married to divorced men with custody of their children, or to divorced men without custody; there are divorced women with children remarried to men with no children of their own; there are marriages in which each adult is divorced and has children, some or all of whom may be living together for most of the time, or for only short periods of time; there are widows with children married to widowers with children, widows married to men with no children, or widowers married to women with no previous experience of being parents; finally, there are stepfamilies of all these types that also include children from the present marriage.

While there are cultural and structural characteristics present in all types of stepfamilies, certain stepfamily patterns do have common characteristics. For example, Duberman's study (1973) indicates that women with no children of their own, as a group, have a particularly difficult time. They do not know what to expect from their stepchildren, since they have no experience in child rearing. They may look forward to suddenly "having a family," only to find walls of hostility separating them from children who fear a takeover by these new persons, or from children who may wonder what will happen to their relationship with their biological mothers. Even children whose mothers have died may resist the attentions of stepmothers because they feel that to accept them would be a betrayal of their love for their biological mothers. "A stepfather who has had no children of his own appears to have an easier time because of minimal guilt about his previous relationship and no feelings that he has abandoned his children. On the other hand, a man with no experience as a parent has a certain handicap as he confronts the 'new experience of being a stepparent'" (Visher & Visher, 1979, p. 88).

When both adults bring children into the present marriage, there can be a quantum leap as far as complexity is concerned: more children, more grandparents, more opportunity for jealousies and varying alliances. One positive aspect, however, is that each adult is aware of differences in feelings that can exist, particularly at first, between parent and child and between stepparent and stepchild. Because of this awareness, there is often a bond of empathy and understanding between the couple that does not exist when one is a stepparent but not a parent and the other is a parent but not also a stepparent.


## CULTURAL MILIEU OF STEPFAMILIES: THREE COMMON MYTHS

At the present time, stepfamilies may be considered culturally deprived. They are the result of "broken homes" and "failed marriages." The word "stepchild" connotes neglect and second-class status. Three common myths cast their shadows across the landscape: the myth of the "reconstitution of the nuclear family," the myth of instant love (Schulman, 1972) or instant adjustment (Jacobsen, 1979), and the myth of the wicked stepmother.

For many years, it has been recognized that raising children can be fraught with difficulties, and there has been a myriad of governmental and community-based support systems for biological families—to say nothing of the books on child rearing that line the shelves of bookstores and libraries. With the escalating divorce rate, society has become aware of the problems of separation and single parenting, and "Parents without Partners," singles groups of many kinds, and mental health programs for children and adults have been developed. An unfortunate myth, however, surrounds stepfamilies: namely, that the remarriage is the "reconstitution of the nuclear family."

Their failure to find a familiar family structure and community acceptance and support is a disappointing experience for many children, parents, stepparents, and grandparents involved in remarriage families. Stepparenting is different from original parenting; being a remarried parent is different from being a parent in a biological family; and growing up in a stepfamily may be more complicated than growing up in a nuclear family.

The biological family is still considered the "ideal" family pattern, and other family types trail far behind in terms of acceptability. Because stepfamilies are compared unfavorably to biological families, adults in stepfamilies try to return to the acceptable image, to the tightly knit nuclear family of their dreams. Remarried parents usually agree that their new families are very different from their first-marriage families; yet they set out to remake these new family units into biological families like their first families.

Many adults remarry expecting the impossible of themselves and of the rest of the family. Stepmothers may try too hard to be superMoms so they won't be mistaken for Cinderella's stepmother. Stepfathers may rush in full of guilt at having separated from their own children and try to take command immediately. Stepchildren may balk and drag their heels in resentment at being asked to participate in this new venture that has been no choice of theirs.

It is indeed true in a stepfamily that there is once again an adult couple in the household, but there is another biological parent elsewhere either in reality or in memory; parent-child relationships precede the newer—and perhaps more fragile—couple relationship; and everyone in the household, children as well as adults, comes with memories and expectations from previous family histories. There is no time for couple adjustment without the existence of children, and often there is constant upheaval and change as transition crowds upon transition, with children going to or coming from a household with different roles and different rules. The homeostatic balance of the household is often in constant flux; for individuals who are particularly uncomfortable with ambiguity and transitions, the lessened control and stability produces severe tension and feelings of helplessness.

The work of Wallerstein and Kelly (1980) indicates that, with very few exceptions, it is important for children after a divorce to maintain contact with both biological parents. Thus, for a stepfamily to ignore these needs and to attempt to recreate the tightly knit cohesiveness of an "ideal" biological family is diametrically opposed to what seems needed to produce stepfamily growth and integration. Since trying to fit a stepfamily into a biological family mold is doomed to failure, it is important for the helping professions, for the community at large, and for stepfamilies themselves to relinquish their expectations of the past and to recognize the value of stepfamily uniqueness and potential for richness and growth.

Instant love or adjustment is a myth because relationships take time to grow. They cannot be forced. In all families, parent-child relationships run from hot to cold, and to expect caring from individuals who suddenly find themselves living together after remarriage usually leads to disappointment, insecurity, and anger.

The members of any merging group require time to adjust to one another and to work out new roles and rules. New ways of doing things can be worked out much faster than can feelings between people. The first critical step toward developing satisfying stepfamily relationships is for stepparents not to try to replace the missing biological parents. If the adults can relax and let the children set the pace of the relationships, many times friendships, caring, and love do develop.

One stepmother said, "When I remarried I was totally naive. Although 40 years old, I expected everything to work out smoothly from the first. We would all get along fine. How could I be so ignorant?" She was no more naive than most who believe this destructive myth and think that by simply joining two families they will automatically love the children of the adult they love so dearly—and that the children will show them love and affection in return.

Younger children respond more freely to developing relationships with stepparents. Teenagers, struggling with their sense of who they are and what they want, have a more difficult time; they are already growing away from

4

whatever family in which they live. As one teenager in a stepfamily said, "Two parents are more than enough. I don't need another telling me what to do." Teenagers in stepfamilies often separate earlier from their parents and stepparents than they might have in their biological families. But, as in any family, if the door remains open, they often return as young adults to form mature and independent relationships with their parents and stepparents.

Often remarried parents and stepparents cling to the myth of "instant love" because of their strong desire to erase past hurts for themselves and their children. They frequently feel guilty about their children's reactions to the divorce or death of parents, and they wish to make up for the children's pain. Some stepparents and remarried parents push for a loving stepparent–stepchild relationship; but, try as they will, stepparents cannot suddenly feel love for half-grown children who do everything absolutely "wrong"—for example, who leave bikes in the driveway or track mud onto the carpet.

The pressure to *feel* a certain way, and then not to feel that way, creates anger and guilt for stepparents and stepchildren. It takes time to get to know new people, to form any kind of relationship. Attempts to force friendship and caring create a pressure that usually leads to just the opposite. When everyone tries too hard, "pussyfoots" around the issues, and finds it impossible to relax, then anger rather than love reigns. When this myth is understood and accepted, then stepfamily members can relax their expectations about their feelings. Their relationships often blossom into caring and loving relationships that last a lifetime.

Every culture has its stories about wicked stepmothers, but unlike the goblins and giants of the fairy tales, there are in fact flesh-and-blood stepmothers in our society.

> Children learn at a very early age just what a stepmother is like. As an attorney said recently, "If you were to ask my seven-year-old daughter about stepmothers, she'd say they were very bad people because she knows Cinderella's stepmother." And little girls grow up to be women, and mothers, and stepmothers. And if they do become stepmothers, *deep* inside themselves they carry the stereotypes of the culture. They vow to themselves that they will not become wicked stepmothers and as a result they try to be super-perfect stepparents. And, unfortunately, these efforts very frequently lead to frustration—and to a perpetuation rather than an evaporation of the myth. (Visher & Visher, 1979, p. 56)

Simon (1964) comments:

> It is more than coincidence that almost all stepmothers seem to share the legendary traits; they come to resemble the stepmother stereotype because they become stepmothers. Behavioral science now allows us to understand that the situation has little to do with the character of the woman, or, for that matter, of the child. It is the relationship between them that sparks the fire. . . . There is a kernel of truth in the stepmother fiction, but it is the result of interaction, a generic, not a personal truth. (p. 139)

Recently, college students were asked to rate the behavior of a woman toward a child misbehaving in public. Each student received identical stories, with the exception that in 50% of the stories, the woman was identified as the "mother" of the little girl, and in the other half the woman was identified as the "stepmother" of the little girl. The rating scales were identical. In keeping with the cultural stereotype, there was a definite tendency for the students to rate the behavior of the "stepmother" toward the child more harshly than they rated the behavior of the "mother" toward the child.

Parenting is a role taken seriously in our society, and partially because of the negative myths surrounding the stepmother role, difficulties with this role are the rule rather than the exception. Of course there are stories about cruel stepfathers, but they appear in literature written for an older age group, and as a result apparently do not hold the same psychological weight carried by the earlier fairy stories.

## STRUCTURAL CHARACTERISTICS OF STEPFAMILIES

Stepfamilies differ structurally from biological families in several ways:

1. All stepfamily members have experienced important losses.
2. All members come with past family histories.
3. Parent–child bonds predate the new couple relationship.
4. There is a biological parent elsewhere, either living or deceased.
5. Children often are members of two households.
6. No legal relationship exists between stepparent and stepchild.

### All Have Experienced Important Losses

Remarriage with children is a stage in a process that begins with death or divorce, continues through a time of single parenting, and goes on into the remarriage. A spouse has died, or there has been a tearing apart of a once-existing love relationship. Children and parents have been separated totally or to a lesser or greater extent, depending on the custody and visitation arrangements. Sometimes brothers and sisters have been separated. A severing of relationships with grandparents, or alienation from friends and from a familiar community, may have occurred. And for many adults, many cherished dreams of marriage may have been lost in the chaos of instant children and former spouses. Thus, remarriages, unlike first marriages, are born of many losses.

Parents may have been able to communicate to their children their own feelings of distress and pain at the breakup of a former marriage. This helps the children express their own feelings of hurt and anger at the losses they have been experiencing. Individuals differ in the time it takes them to mourn the losses, and frequently adults form new meaningful relationships while children are still adjusting to a new home, a new school, new friends, and separation from a parent. Children often need continuous reassurance that their behavior was not responsible for a parent's death or for a divorce. They also need to know that divorce is an adult decision and that it does not mean that they will necessarily lose one or both parents, even though their parents are no longer married to each other.

The children's view of remarriage is usually very different from the adults' view. Children often hope and dream that their biological parents will get back together again, and these hopes are dashed by remarriage. Many children worry whether they will continue to see their other parents. For example, 7-year-old Kim began to whine and demand ice cream cones and trips to the zoo when she was with her father, who was soon to be remarried. During the week, when she was with her mother, she became cranky and disobedient. One day Kim blurted out, "Will I ever see my Daddy again?" Her fears of further loss were clear. Parental reassurance and continued contact with her father reduced Kim's anxiety, and even though she had some difficulty sharing her father with his new wife, Kim's behavior gradually changed as she realized that she would be able to be with her father as before.

The new couple may be happy and excited and may be making plans to give the children a "full family life" again. In contrast, the children experience loss; they now need to share their remarried parent with another person, and often with other children as well. An only child may be dropped into the middle of three stepsiblings, or the favored youngest may become displaced by a cute 3-year-old, posing a difficult adjustment. If parents and stepparents can be sensitive and accepting of the fears of their children at this important time, these new marriages can get off to a much easier start.

Children wonder how they are going to fit into the new household. During the period of single parenting, children have assumed new roles, and although they may have complained bitterly about cleaning the bathroom, doing the cooking, or walking the dog, they may feel displaced and devalued when a stepparent or stepsiblings take over these tasks. In one single-parent family, 16-year-old Laura had been doing all the cooking for her father— until her new stepmother rearranged the kitchen and made it her own; in another single-parent household, 12-year-old Bruce had taken pride in being allowed to mow the front lawn, but after his father remarried, the mowing was turned over to Bruce's 15-year-old stepbrother. Such role changes need to be made slowly or not at all, if feasible.

After a death or divorce, parents often turn to their children for emotional support. If they have been close, when the parent remarries, it takes more time and thought to make a space for the new person or persons in the stepfamily group.

Ellen married Bill, who had two children from a previous marriage. Depressed after his divorce, Bill had spent his weekends and all his vacations relating constantly with his two children. The three of them enjoyed sports of all kinds, and they camped together over long weekends. Bill dated only when his children were not with him. When Bill and Ellen were married, the children and Bill continued their usual activities together and were reluctant to have Ellen join them. Ellen had not been interested in sports previously, but she was willing to go camping, since she wished to become a part of the group. The children, however, wanted to continue as before, and Bill felt guilty when he suggested some other recreation or when he included Ellen in the familiar activity. There was no room for Ellen in the closed family group.

In contrast, when Agnes and Eric were married, Agnes had little difficulty being absorbed into the family. After his divorce, Eric had dealt with his loneliness by participating in a wide variety of activities. When his two children were with him, they often took friends along when they went camping, and sometimes friends of the children came to stay on weekends when Eric had other plans. After his remarriage, Eric and Agnes continued to include the children's friends from time to time, and since the group had always been variable and flexible, Agnes soon found a place for herself in the new family unit.

### Adults and Children All Come with Past Family Histories

There are no identical family histories. In a first marriage, the couple comes together with expectations and experiences from the families in which they grew up. Together, the couple works out a unique family pattern, a combination of parenting styles, and a set of traditions. Adding children to the unit is a gradual process.

In remarriages, all individuals come together suddenly. They bring with them previous experiences and deeply felt beliefs about "rights" and "wrongs" and the way things "ought" to be done. In stepfamilies where everyone arrives complete with diverse family histories, new traditions need to be negotiated and implemented. Ways of doing things that were previously taken for granted suddenly are questioned. How is the French toast to be made? Is the Christmas tree to be large or small? White or green? Decorated with tinsel, or not? There are differences. Old traditions were not "wrong" or "right"—just different and unique to the former family units. The important question at hand is to work out traditions acceptable to the present stepfamily unit.

Everyone in the new family needs to be heard. The older the children, the longer the family history and the surer they are of how things are done. Satisfactory solutions usually can be found if fights over what is "right" and what is "wrong" are stopped immediately, and if the concept of "differences" is understood and supported. Compromises can be made. A small, live Christmas tree can stand by the front door trimmed with lights and tinsel, while a larger white tree decorates the living room. Variation in making and serving French toast can become acceptable. To expect similarity is betting on million-to-one odds. As one stepchild said to her stepmother, "I can't be like you because I didn't come from you." The two do not share the same genes, and they have not shared a common family history. If there is respect for the uniqueness of each individual, from these differences a new and rich family heritage can be developed.

### Parent-Child Bonds Predate the New Couple Relationship

In first marriages, partners have the opportunity to adjust to each other and to form a solid couple bond before adding children to the family unit. In addition, with the birth of a baby in a biological family, each adult is a parent to the child and can influence and experience the unfolding of this tiny person.

In a remarriage, there is no honeymoon. The older parent–child relationships may be very strong, while the new couple relationship is a fragile union that needs nourishing—shared, loving time together. The presence of children, uncertain of their own future in the new family, can add turmoil that erodes rather than enhances the new couple relationship. Children may cling to their parents for security, bang on the bedroom door whenever the adults disappear for a few minutes, and erupt with jealousy. Rather than the gradual progression of first marriage families, merging a stepfamily may yield instant pandemonium.

Marriage is based on adult love, not on adult–child love. The new adult–child relationships mature slowly and depend on many factors: the age of the children, the stepfamily structure, and the individual needs of the family members. The adults need to give themselves and the members of their family the time and space they need to relate to one another. They can do interesting and fun things as a couple, as a family, or in twos and threes. New bonds can be encouraged when stepparents and stepchildren relate to each other; former bonds can be maintained when biological parents and children spend some time alone together. At other times, the stepfamily may wish to do things together as a total unit.

Some remarried parents feel that they are betraying their prior relationships with their children when they form a new primary bond with their new spouses. Such a primary commitment, however, is of vital importance for the children as well as for the adults. If the couple relationship is tentative or fragmented, the children become insecure and may fear family disintegration. The life of the family depends on the ability of the adults to form a strong couple bond.

As the children grow and form their own family units, it is easier to do so if they leave a couple who have maintained a caring relationship. The model provided by the couple also influences the children in their own future adult couple relationships.

### A Biological Parent Exists Elsewhere

In stepfamilies, one of the children's parents is somewhere else. Even if the parent has died, the influence of that parent remains. Memories linger and dictate present behavior. It seems disloyal to form new relationships in the shadow of old friends and neighbors. One widower commented that it took him 2 years after his remarriage to act spontaneously rather than as he believed his former wife would have wished and as his neighbors would approve. It is particularly difficult for new spouses to break into preexisting units if they move into the homes of the former couples. It is as though such houses are haunted by the ghosts of the previous relationships. A new home can do much to provide a nurturing environment for any stepfamily. It can be especially important when there has been a death and the ties of the past remain unchanged.

As Kalish and Visher (in press) remind us, the impact of divorce and remarriage falls also upon the grandparents whose children are divorced and remarried, often taking with them much-loved grandchildren and tearing apart close bonds that have been forged during the years of growth and single parenting. Grandparents may worry about what role they will have, and even whether they will have any contact with their grandchildren. If there are stepgrandchildren in the new family, how do they treat them at Christmas, or in decisions about inheritance? Gift giving may become a time of trial and tribulation, and visits are often tense. Stepgrandparents have no legal rights, and their emotional rights are dependent on establishing a workable relationship with a new family group that has somehow been grafted onto the family tree, bearing strange and unfamiliar fruit.

Changes are difficult for all human beings, particularly changes over which people have little or no control. Grandparents come from another generation, and they may have difficulty accepting the new directions their children and grandchildren are taking. However, they can play an important role in the success or failure of the remarriage of their children—they can build bridges, or they can build walls. It is to be hoped that an understanding of their parents' feelings will enable the new couples to bring them into the picture and guide them to play positive roles that will assist the process of stepfamily integration. Hopefully, this older generation will respond positively and enjoy a richness of experience as they relate to stepgrandchildren as well as to grandchildren.

When both biological parents are alive, it is difficult for parents to share children. It is also difficult for children to share parents. The insecurities and pain involved in sharing children are difficult to imagine. For ex-spouses who are angry and bitter, the sharing of children can stir deep and powerful emotions. There is a sense of helplessness and lack of control, especially on the part of noncustodial parents. For example, a father makes reservations for a ski weekend, and at the last minute the children telephone to say they cannot come because their mother is taking them to Disneyland. Or the children are to be with their father for the weekend, and the phone rings and he says he cannot take them; as a result, the mother's weekend plans suddenly crumble.

One of the greatest gifts that divorced parents can give their children is to leave them out of adult battles. Unfortunately, all too often, children get caught in the crossfire as ex-spouses try to hurt each other, try to protect themselves, or find it necessary to fight to maintain a relationship with their children.

One way to help children feel loved and accepted and to help them adjust to divorce and remarriage is to respect their need to maintain contact with both biological parents. Even minimal contact helps children maintain a sense of worth. Of course, there are a few situations where the emotional climate between the ex-spouses is so negative that contact with both parents erodes children's self-esteem. However, it has been found that even when there is some friction between the two parents, it is still beneficial for the children to have access to both (Wallerstein & Kelly, 1980).

Adults who are divorced because they have not been able to maintain their couple relationship can still be loving parents to their children. By respecting parenting skills and maintaining civil contact with regard to the children, ex-spouses can minimize the pain of sharing children.

An unmarried ex-spouse frequently has great difficulty in accepting a remarriage, particularly when the divorce was wanted by the person getting remarried. For one thing, the dream of possible reconciliation seems permanently dashed when word filters back that a new relationship is being legalized. Fears of the unknown and feelings of being out of control are likely to be very strong, as well as angry feelings of rivalry and intensified feelings of rejection. Unmarried ex-spouses often ask questions like these:

> Will the children's new stepparent be a better parent? Will they like him (or her) better than they do me? Their lifestyle is so different from mine. What effect will it have on the children when they visit at the other house and find that there is pot-smoking at parties, and that table manners are not considered a very high priority? Perhaps the new stepparent will not take as good care of the children as I do when they get sick, or protect them from danger.

Support, reassurance of the children's continued need for both parents, and help in adjusting to changes can be very beneficial for ex-spouses at this time, as these can help restore a sense of self worth.

Recently a woman wrote "Dear Abby" this letter:

> We were both kids when we married . . . but we drifted apart . . . I've been alone for four years. He is now married to a younger, stylish woman who is very pretty and active socially. I frequently see her picture (usually with him) in the society section of the newspaper. Abby, every time I see a picture of that woman with my ex-husband, I get so upset I have to go to bed for a week! What should I do? (Signed) Jealous.

When such angry feelings remain strong, they are often expressed in ways that are harmful to the children, who try to maintain a relationship with both parents. Children who are go-betweens are often caught in the middle and are sometimes used as pawns to express vengeful feelings towards an ex-spouse. It is frequently a challenge to therapists and counselors to try to get the children out of the middle, so that they can move back and forth between their two families and benefit from the experiences and love that is available in both places. Sometimes, a family meeting involving all the adults and strictly focused on what is best for the children can help to clear the air.

### Children Are Often Members of Two Households

Linked to the fact that biological parents no longer live together is the fact that children in many stepfamilies are members of two households. If the adults in both households can work together with regard to the children, then the children go back and forth relatively easily. But competitiveness and insecurity are difficult to avoid, and children may well find themselves swinging between two warring camps. It may be a hot war, a cold war, or only a minor skirmish, but in each case the children are torn by their loyalty to each of their two parents. They are half of each of the two adults, and anger by these adults toward one another is felt by the children as dissatisfaction with part of themselves. Older children often withdraw from both families, and younger children often choose sides. It is best if ex-spouses do not argue in front of the children. When conversation is kept to issues involving the children, this is easier to accomplish.

A recent doctoral dissertation assessing the stress perceived by teenage stepchildren underscores the need for easing the two-household situation: "Experiencing one natural parent talking negatively about the other natural parent, not being able to visit a parent who does not live with you, hearing your parent and stepparent argue, and 'feeling caught in the middle' between your two natural parents, were listed as the four most stressful aspects of their lives" (Lutz, 1980).

Adults can help children deal with "culture shock" as they go from one household to another—from American cooking to French cooking, from modern apartment to colonial home, from no TV to unlimited TV. Every household is different, and children must adjust as they go back and forth. If the adults do not attempt to label one household as "wrong" and the other one as "right," then the children feel less pulled, and they can enjoy the variety of experiences offered to them. This diversity is a plus for children, for it provides more options for them. "I learned sewing and basket weaving in one home, and an appreciation of music in the other," said one grown stepchild. Adults as well as children can have a kaleidoscope of experiences resulting from increased diversity in stepfamilies.

No longer does a single set of parents or a single home provide a total family setting. In stepfamilies, the responsibility for guiding a child to maturity may be shared by more than two parental adults. Such sharing reduces the load for any one adult and offers a wide variety of experiences for the children. Parents are at a place in history where they are being asked to make another leap in thought and feelings: to accept the fact that being raised in two households can be a positive "given" rather than a negative influence on children.

As change crowds upon change, many remarried adults want thinking, feeling, and behavior to shift at the same pace. Human emotions do not change this quickly, however, and at many levels, stepfamilies are too impatient. They are reluctant to accept the fact that change is unsettling and that the healing of memories takes time. They need time to adjust, time to work things out, time to feel and deal differently. Even when stress and cutoff relationships remain, present-day stepfamilies can be good places for adults to find emotional satisfaction and for children to grow into effective and productive adults. The children have a number of adults to relate to and to use as models for their own lives. They have sampled diverse family styles and have a variety of patterns to choose from and make their own.

## DEVELOPMENTAL TASKS OF STEPFAMILIES

All families have the same basic goals: to introduce independent children into society, and to provide personality growth and stability for the adults in the family (Lewis, Beavers, Gossett, & Phillips, 1976). The developmental stages and tasks that stepfamilies face in achieving their goals differ in some important ways from those of biological families because of the cultural and structural variables previously discussed. There are four tasks immediately faced by stepfamilies before they can begin the individuation process that takes place in all types of families:

1. Mourning of losses.
2. Negotiation and development of new traditions.
3. Formation of new alliances and preservation of old alliances that are still important.
4. Stepfamily integration.

## Mourning of Losses

All choices, changes, and transitions involve loss. There are losses in first marriages with moves, new jobs, and new homes. A stepfamily, however, can be said to be a family born of loss, because important interpersonal losses have preceded the formation of the family. Even when a divorce has been desired by adults, there is the loss of an expectation or hope of what a marriage might have been; for those who have never been married before, the presence of former spouses and instant children means the loss of many barely conscious fantasies of what a marriage might have been.

Children have experienced either the loss of a parent by death, or a partial or total disruption in the relationship with at least one biological parent. An additional loss is felt if grandparents have become less accessible. All too often, remarried parents, particularly those without custody of their children, have not dealt sufficiently with these previous losses. Children, still hurt and angry, find that in remarriages they must share parents with other adults and perhaps with other children as well. These losses, together with loss of familiar communities, schools, homes, jobs, and friends, stir many sad and angry feelings—and individuals in stepfamilies often need help and support in recognizing and dealing with their anger, depression, and sadness.

## Negotiation and Development of New Traditions

Stepfamilies come together with few if any shared memories. With understanding and creativity, stepfamilies can immediately begin to join together around shared activities, special rituals developed for this particular household and arrived at by input from all members. The participation of older children is especially important, since they have had a number of years of a different "sentimental order" (Stern, 1978) in which family activities and roles have followed certain paths. Now, perhaps, a family can shift household duties and define new shared pleasurable activities.

## Formation of New Alliances and Preservation of Old Alliances

At the same time that new ways of doing things are being negotiated, it is important for the individuals concerned to move gradually into new relationships and also to maintain important relationships from the past. Continuity of contact with relatives and friends is helpful. The couple needs to maintain "alone" time, instead of slowly sinking into the quicksand of children and family demands and decisions. The children need to relate to stepparents without the biological parent present; however, since the couple relationship is still not solid, these parent–child or stepparent–stepchild times need to be casual and initially of short duration—a walk to the store, watching a favorite TV program, or building a model together.

Adolescents, already growing away from their families, may not wish to be included in "stepfamily" activities, but they may be willing to relate on a one-to-one basis with the adults in the family around time-limited activities. At this age, the peer group is their important concern, and remarried parents and stepparents often tend to forget this developmental growth pattern. When reminded of their own teenage years, the adults often are able to relax, and their perhaps unreasonable expectations of the adolescents no longer produce unnecessary tension in the new household.

The boundaries in stepfamilies are "permeable" (Messinger, 1976), because children often spend time in two households. "When the former spouse maintains a role with the children, all members of the reconstituted family are required to sort through feelings of loyalty, anger, jealousy, abandonment, and guilt . . ." (Ransom, Schlesinger, & Derdeyn, 1979, p. 38). As stated earlier, "sharing" children and "sharing" parents is an emotionally difficult task, and the success with which the adults involved are able to come to terms with this process seems closely related to the success of the integration of the new stepfamily unit.

### Stepfamily Integration

Knowing what to anticipate can make stepfamily integration much easier. Stern (1978) studied stepfamily integration by looking at the time it takes for stepfathers to gain a "comanagement" role with their wives in the area of discipline. Parents have two primary emotional tasks in raising their children: nurturance and limit setting. In biological families there is a natural and necessary sequence—nurturance, and then, as children grow, an increasing degree of limit setting to accompany the nurturance. The area of limit setting or discipline is a difficult one for stepfamilies, because stepparents enter the household and wish to have input into decisions about limit setting without first going through the period of nurturance. The way has not been paved for the children to care about or want to please the adults. Stern found that in the stepfather families it took 1½ to 2 years for the stepfathers to form a friendly relationship with their stepchildren and to achieve an equal disciplinary role with their wives. Recognizing that they are "on schedule" in this difficult area of discipline has enabled many stepparents to "back off" without feeling that doing so is somehow "wrong" or that they have failed. Allowing 2 or more years for the household to shift and define its rules and roles facilitates integration by reducing the "pressure cooker" atmosphere and forestalling the inevitable blowup if changes are forced too rapidly.

The couple usually needs to clarify expectations and arrive at a few important family rules in private before attempting to involve the children. Trying to change everything at once and create a "new" family leads to nothing but frustration. As the couple relationship becomes less tenuous, the children are less likely to amplify differences between the adults, and the need for private adult discussions in regard to family functioning may become less necessary.

## DYNAMIC ISSUES IN STEPFAMILY SYSTEMS

As a family system, stepfamilies are more complex in their structure, with a greater number of built-in subsystems and greater ambiguity than is found in nuclear families. Boundaries are less clear, and homeostatic stability is lacking because of the constant fluctuations within the household. "We have an accordion family," said one parent/stepparent. "One day there are the two of us, the next there are nine." There are continual transitions, greater stress, and less cohesiveness (Fast & Cain, 1966). The household must deal with the following major dynamic issues:

1. Outsiders versus insiders.
2. Boundary disputes.
3. Power issues.
4. Conflicting loyalties.
5. Rigid, unproductive triangles.
6. Unity versus fragmentation of the new couple relationship.

### Outsiders versus Insiders

While individuals in nuclear families may experience being "left out" in stepfamilies with the many types of "mergers" that take place, there is a constant problem of helping outsiders to become insiders if there is to be household unity. Very often the outsider is a stepfather joining an ongoing group of a mother and her children; or it may be a woman marrying a man with custody of his children; or children coming to stay in the household every other weekend, or for the summer; or a teenager changing residence from the mother and stepfather's household to the father and stepmother's household. Being a newcomer in any type of group can cause discomfort, both for the person or persons trying to be "one of the gang," and for the original group, who may feel intruded upon and protective of its original position. In the less "neutral" emotional climate of the stepfamily group, the feelings of exclusion, intrusion, rejection, and resultant anger and depression can be extremely strong. Working out ways of dealing with the shifts and transitions takes time and understanding, patience, and tolerance for ambiguity.

## Boundary Disputes

Because children are often members of two separate households, the stepfamily boundaries may get blurred, as the adults in the two households need to cooperate in arrangements involving the children. It is, however, necessary in most instances for each household to recognize that there are boundaries to that particular unit. The individuals in that household do have control over how they decide to deal with the individuals and events that take place within that sphere. In fact, if some separation is not made, there is little chance for a stepfamily to develop any sense of cohesiveness and unity.

Within the household there are also many "turf" problems to be worked out as well: who sleeps where; what personal privacy is possible; what space can be reserved for whom? As an example of what can happen, consider the stepfamily in which the husband's three children joined the household every 3 to 4 days for a few days' time. The house was small, and the mother's three children who lived in the household had to shift where they slept, where they put their clothes, and where they could go to read or to be alone in order to make the available space accommodate the extra family members. Bedrooms became dormitories, and the continual chaos created tension and instability for everyone. This family needed to work out ways in which to eliminate the major changes so that "property rights" became clear and consistent and that there was a stable place for each person.

## Power Issues

Power issues in stepfamilies can be exaggerated for many reasons. Women who have been on their own for the first time in their lives because of a divorce or the death of a husband, and who take pride in having "proved" their capabilities, frequently have no desire to return to a relationship in which there is not an egalitarian couple relationship. They have discovered that they can indeed take care of themselves, and of their children too if they have children. For many, there is a fear of sharing this new-found control or power for fear of falling back into previously unsatisfying patterns.

Money is often equated with power, and men who are divorced and remarried often feel that they have been robbed of their power and control and have become "walking wallets." Secrecy in regard to financial matters may be practiced by both adults, and this often exacerbates power issues that affect many relationship areas.

In stepfamilies, children can often gain power in the age-old game of "divide and conquer." Because their two biological parents now live in two separate households, and, in addition, may maintain minimal and hostile contact with each other, there is a built-in system that makes it extremely easy for children to gain tremendous power. "If you don't treat me right, I'll go live with my Dad." "You are really mean! My mother lets me watch TV until midnight." And while the children want and need to feel a sense of mastery and power, they also need and want to know that there are adults who are stronger than they are and on whom they can depend.

### Conflicting Loyalties

Loyalty conflicts for children and for remarried parents can hardly be avoided. In a biological family, children may feel more comfortable with one parent than with the other, but they are not placed in the position of choosing whom to ask to a special event, or with whom they are to spend the weekend. They are part of each parent and feel torn apart when their parents are no longer together, with divided loyalties perhaps increasing when another adult enters the picture because of a parental remarriage. Naturally, the more amicable the relationships between all the parental adults, the fewer loyalty conflicts the children will have. When the parent has died and the remaining biological parent remarries, this marriage is often seen by the children as a betrayal of the former spouse. It may appear to the children that this new relationship negates the former couple relationship. Therefore, the stepparent stirs many strong emotions, particularly in older children who have lived with their other biological parent longer, and it is difficult for the children to accept this new person.

As for remarried parents, since the parent–child relationships have preceded the new couple relationship, the adults often feel caught between their children and their new partners. It may, indeed, seem to remarried parents that it is a betrayal of the older parent–child bonds to form new primary adult relationships. However, a satisfactory couple bond is usually necessary for a remarriage to continue. Therefore, if a new primary couple bond is not established, it is likely that the children of this stepfamily will experience still more loss and disruption in their lives as their second family unit breaks apart.

### Rigid, Unproductive Triangles

There are triangles in all families. However, the subgroupings present in stepfamilies can produce particularly rigid, unproductive triangles. Unproductive triangles involve three individuals in a struggle so that clear dyadic relationships are not possible. Important triangles in stepfamilies include the following:

1. Remarried parent in the middle, not allowing a direct relationship between a stepparent and a stepchild.

2. Remarried parent and stepparent standing united against an ex-spouse.

3. Remarried child in the middle, not allowing direct relationship between his or her parents and their new daughter or son-in-law.

4. Child caught in the middle between hostile ex-spouses.

Because of the complexity of the subgroups in a stepfamily, and because of the heightened emotions involved and the long duration of some of the relationships, it can become difficult to break down these groupings so that simple and direct dyadic relationships are possible.

### Unity versus Fragmentation of the New Couple Relationship

There are many internal and external pulls on the new couple relationship. A number have already been mentioned, such as the feelings of betrayal at forming a primary couple relationship, and the pull of grandparents who are having difficulties adjusting to new branches being grafted onto their family tree. There is also the divisiveness of children who still hope that disruption can lead to the reuniting of their biological parents; the insecurity of being a "second" and perhaps not the "real" mate; and, initially, the absence of a shared family history or way of doing things.

The interface between the stepfamily and the community can also produce tensions that strain the couple. Schools, churches, the legal system, and social institutions of all types continue to consider the biological parents together and to leave out stepparents, even though these persons may in fact have been primary parental figures in children's lives for many months or even years. Often, stepparents do not receive graduation tickets, are not included in PTA activities, are not asked to help with the Little League, or are not included in legal discussions when a stepchild may in fact be joining the household in which they live. Human flexibility exceeds institutional flexibility, and the social system is only now becoming responsive to the need for many changes in these areas.

## IMPORTANT FACTORS FOR SUCCESSFUL STEPFAMILY FUNCTIONING

Research is indicating that many factors can and do influence the development of cohesiveness and a sense of integration in a stepfamily, as Sirulnick (1980) points out. Although the original purpose of her study was to explore the marital relationship and, in particular, the coparental alliance as a component in stepfamily integration, it became apparent that each aspect which was reviewed to better understand the couple partnership was powerful and important in its own right. It was demonstrated that even when the couple bond is secure and there are clear parental role definitions, such elements as the previous marital history, the custody and visitation agreements, the current relationship with a former spouse, the early stepfamily formation, the ages of the stepchildren, the reactions of family and friends, and the denial of stepfamily identity can affect the solidarity and strength of the current blended family. Obviously, more research is needed to tease out these factors and to understand the complexity more fully, in order to be of more assistance to stepfamilies during the integration process.

From information available at the present time, there appear to be four major ingredients necessary for the successful functioning of a stepfamily:

1. Knowledge and recognition of what to expect in this type of family.
2. Good couple unity.
3. Space for children to continue to relate to both biological parents.
4. Civil relationships between all the parental adults.

Parents are concerned about the impact of divorce and remarriage on the lives of their children.

> The research studies of Bohannan and Erickson (1978), Duberman (1973), and Wilson, Zurcher, McAdams, and Curtis (1975) are helpful to these couples, since the studies indicate that children are able to cope with stepfamily situations and grow into adults with similar positive character-istics as children from biological families. Vaillant's (1977) study of normal adult males again gives an optimistic picture of human flexibility and adaptability. (Visher & Visher, 1979, p. 212)

Dealing creatively and successfully with the complexity of a stepfamily springs from the sense of self-esteem and mastery experienced by the people involved. Knowledge is an important key to the existence of such feelings. Therefore, as more is learned about what to expect in these types of families, members of stepfamilies will be better prepared and less anxious about what lies ahead. As realistic expectations replace unrealistic ones, the stresses can become less severe, and the functioning of these families can improve accordingly.

Lewis and his colleagues (1976) have found that in optimally func-tioning biological families, a major characteristic is the solidity of the bond between the spouses. With the added complicating dimensions in stepfam-ilies, it is even more difficult to attain such a couple bond; once again, however, the importance of a good couple relationship appears to be of paramount importance in the successful functioning of a stepfamily.

More difficult to attain, yet important to the relationships between parents and children and between stepparents and stepchildren, is the ability of the adults involved to allow children to feel free to relate to both bio-logical parents and to stepparents. One stepmother expressed it very clearly:

It's in my best interest to make it easy for my stepchildren to see their mother and show their love for her. This makes them feel comfortable with us and we all gain. At times, I catch myself not wanting to share them with another woman, but I find I'm able to tell myself that we each have very different things to contribute to the children—and they respond so positively to all of us and then I know it's what I want to do!

With the increase in understanding and support for new family patterns, it is to be hoped that adults will find it easier to share children; then, in turn, they will receive the gains inherent in the sharing.

## THERAPEUTIC IMPLICATIONS

Many stepfamilies need education and support to assist them in their journey together. Educational groups and mutual help groups are forming around the country in answer to this need. In addition, several organizations have been formed to meet the need for an ongoing educational and/or support network for stepfamilies. (Examples of such organizations include the following: Remarrieds, Inc., Box 742, Santa Ana, Calif. 92701; and Stepfamily Association of America, Inc., 900 Welch Road, Suite 400, Palo Alto, Calif. 94304.)

An increasing number of individuals in stepfamilies are also seeking professional help. While the basic therapeutic skills used with stepfamilies are the same as with other families, there are a few specific guidelines that make a great deal of difference when working with individuals in stepfamilies, either singly, in different subgroup combinations, or as a family unit:

1. It is difficult but extremely important to overcome the emotional concept of the "ideal" American family, so that there is not an attempt to fit a stepfamily into a nuclear family mold.

2. It is helpful to have a different assessment scale operating. Due to the cultural and structural characteristics producing added external stress, individuals in stepfamilies may seem to be falling apart right there in the office. However, unlike similar behavioral signs in individuals living in nuclear families, these signs in stepfamily members may simply indicate a need for support and validation of their experience rather than medication and in-depth therapy to start them on the road to increased self-esteem and the ability to make productive choices. As they begin to experience a sense of mastery, the chaos can be controlled. Any deeper couple or individual issues will then emerge if they are in need of attention.

3. While it may not be necessary later on, educational material and

direct information about stepfamily expectations is often helpful in the beginning stages of therapy.

4. It may be important at times to include ex-spouses, grandparents, or other significant adults in the therapeutic process in some way. Even if more than one therapist is working with different individuals or subgroups, when they all meet together, the focus of the meeting needs to be clearly stated ahead of time: the focus should be on issues involving the children, and not on an attempt to resolve spousal relationship problems. Such meetings occur most frequently in regard to custody and visitation questions.

5. Countertransference, both positive and negative, can be particularly difficult to deal with in stepfamily situations, where the feelings are so strong and the situations may be so familiar (or, conversely, so unfamiliar) to the experience of the therapist. For this reason, consultation or the use of cotherapists can be extremely valuable.

## SUMMARY

Stepfamilies are families emerging out of loss as well as out of hope. Stepparenting is different from parenting; being a remarried parent is different from being a parent in a first-marriage family; and growing up in a stepfamily can be more complicated than growing up in a biological family. To work effectively with these individuals and families, therapists need to be aware of stepfamily structure and of common feelings and situations, so that they are able to provide the needed emotional validation, education, support, and appropriate therapeutic interventions.

## REFERENCES

Baker, O. V., Druckman, J. M., & Flagle, J. E. *Helping youth and families of separation, divorce and remarriage.* Palo Alto: American Institutes for Research, 1980.

Becker, S., Landes, E. M., & Michael, R. T. An economic analysis of marital instability. *Journal of Political Economy,* 1977, *85,* 1141–1187.

Bitterman, C. M. The multi-marriage family. *Social Casework,* 1968, *49,* 218–221.

Bohannan, P. J., & Erickson, R. J. Stepping in. *Psychology Today,* January 1978, pp. 53–59.

Bowerman, C. E., & Irish, D. P. Some relationships of stepchildren to their parents. *Marriage and Family Living,* 1962, *24,* 113–131.

Cherlin, A. Remarriage as an incomplete institution. *American Journal of Sociology,* 1978, *84,* 634–650.

Duberman, L. Step-kin relationships. *Journal of Marriage and the Family,* 1973, *35,* 283–292.

Fast, I., & Cain, A. C. The stepparent role: Potential for disturbances in family functioning. *American Journal of Orthopsychiatry,* 1966, *36,* 485–491.

Jacobsen, D. S. Stepfamilies: Myths and realities. *Journal of the National Association of Social Workers,* 1979, *24,* 202–207.

Kalish, R. A., & Visher, E. B. Grandparents of divorce and remarriage. *Journal of Divorce,* in press.

Lewis, J. M., Beavers, W. R., Gossett, J. T., & Phillips, V. A. *No single thread: Psychological health in family systems.* New York: Brunner/Mazel, 1976.

Lutz, P. *Stepfamilies: A descriptive study from the adolescent perspective.* Unpublished doctoral dissertation, West Virginia University, Morgantown, 1980.

Messinger, L. Remarriage between divorced people with children from a previous marriage: A proposal for preparation for remarriage. *Journal of Marriage and Family Counseling,* 1976, *2,* 193–200.

Ransom, W., Schlesinger, S., & Derdeyn, A. P. A stepfamily in formation. *American Journal of Orthopsychiatry,* 1979, *49,* 36–43.

Schulman, G. L. Myths that intrude on the adaptation of the stepfamily. *Social Casework,* 1972, *49,* 131–139.

Simon, A. W. *A stepchild in the family: A view of children in remarriage.* New York: Odyssey Press, 1964.

Sirulnick, C. *Primacy of the couple and stepfamily integration: A case study approach.* Unpublished doctoral dissertation, California School of Professional Psychology, 1980.

Stern, P. N. Stepfather families: Integration around child discipline. *Issues in Mental Health Nursing,* 1978, *1,* 50–56.

Vaillant, G. E. *Adaptation to life.* Boston: Little, Brown, 1977.

Visher, E. B., & Visher, J. S. *Stepfamilies: A guide to working with stepparents and stepchildren.* New York: Brunner/Mazel, 1979.

Wallerstein, J., & Kelly, J. *Surviving the break up.* New York: Basic Books, 1980.

Wilson, K. L., Zurcher, L. A., McAdams, D. C., & Curtis, R. L. Stepfathers and stepchildren: An exploratory analysis from two national surveys. *Journal of Marriage and the Family,* 1975, *37,* 526–536.

# 14

# SEX ROLES AND FAMILY DYNAMICS

## LARRY B. FELDMAN

## INTRODUCTION

"Sex roles" are culturally defined expectations (norms) that delineate a set of "appropriate" (expected or desirable) and "inappropriate" (forbidden or undesirable) attitudes and behaviors for males and females. In this chapter, the characteristics of the male and female roles are described, and the relationship between these roles and marital and family interaction is explored. Following this, the clinical implications of the relationship between sex roles and family dynamics are discussed.

## MALE AND FEMALE ROLES

What are the characteristics of the male and female roles? During the past three decades, a number of research studies have addressed this question. Some of these studies (e.g., Bem, 1974; Broverman, Vogel, Broverman, Clarkson, & Rosenkrantz, 1972; Reece, 1964; Sherriffs & McKee, 1957; Williams & Bennett, 1975) have concentrated on psychological aspects of the male and female roles (personality dimensions), while others (e.g., Nye, 1976; Pleck, 1977; Tomeh, 1978) have concentrated on sociological aspects (obligations and privileges associated with particular social positions). Each of these approaches to the problem is examined here.

### Psychological Aspects

In an effort to develop a conceptual model of the psychological aspects of the female and male roles, the results of five well-designed studies (Bem,

Larry B. Feldman. Center for Family Studies/The Family Institute of Chicago, Institute of Psychiatry, Northwestern Memorial Hospital and Northwestern University Medical School, Chicago, Illinois.

1974; Broverman *et al.*, 1972; Reece, 1964; Sherriffs & McKee; 1957; Williams & Bennett, 1975) were carefully reviewed. Based on this review, a model of the prescriptive characteristics (those that are either expected or allowed) of the female and male roles has been derived (see Table 14-1). The proscriptive characteristics (those that are either forbidden or not expected) of each sex's role generally correspond to the prescriptive characteristics of the other sex's role. In other words, men are not supposed to act like women, and women are not supposed to act like men.

### The Female Role

Characteristics associated with the female role have been grouped into seven categories. The first category encompasses the "woman's place is in the home, taking care of her house and children" aspect of the role. The remaining categories encompass "positive expressive" and "nurturing" behaviors (categories 2 and 3); two groups of "negative expressive" behaviors (categories 4 and 5); and two groups of behaviors delineating the expectations that women will generally behave in ways that can be characterized as weak, submissive, and dependent (categories 6 and 7).

### The Male Role

Characteristics associated with the male role have also been grouped into seven categories. The first of these defines "man's place" as the world of work and prescribes a high degree of ambition and competetiveness in that sphere. The remaining categories include "positive instrumental" behaviors

---

TABLE 14-1. PSYCHOLOGICAL DIMENSIONS OF THE FEMALE AND MALE ROLES

*The female role.* Women are expected to be (or allowed to be) the following:
1. Home-oriented, child(ren)-oriented.
2. Warm, affectionate, gentle, tender.
3. Aware of feelings of others, considerate, tactful, compassionate.
4. Moody, high-strung, temperamental, excitable, emotional, subjective, illogical.
5. Complaining, nagging.
6. Weak, helpless, fragile, easily emotionally hurt.
7. Submissive, yielding, dependent.

*The male role.* Men are expected to be (or allowed to be) the following:
1. Ambitious, competitive, enterprising, worldly.
2. Calm, stable, unemotional, realistic, logical.
3. Strong, tough, powerful.
4. Aggressive, forceful, decisive, dominant.
5. Independent, self-reliant.
6. Harsh, severe, stern, cruel.
7. Autocratic, rigid, arrogant.

(category 2); strength, toughness, and power (category 3); aggressiveness and dominance (category 4); independence and self-reliance (category 5); and two groups of "negative expressive" behaviors (categories 6 and 7).

## Sociological Aspects

From a sociological perspective, sex roles are normative expectations for the allocation of work and family responsibilities between men and women (Pleck, 1977). These responsibilities generally fall into one of three categories: economic providing, housework, and child care. In all three of these areas, sex roles prescribe a rigid differentiation between what is "appropriate" and "inappropriate" for men and for women.

### Economic Providing

With regard to providing for the economic needs of the family, there is a clear expectation that men should assume the major share of this responsibility (Nye, 1976; Pleck, 1977; Tomeh, 1978). Although a great many women are now working outside their homes, there is evidence that in many if not most instances, the woman's work is seen by both spouses as supplementary to rather than primary or equal to the man's (Aldous, 1969; Hartley, 1969; Nye, 1976). Furthermore, most men's sense of self-esteem is based to a high degree on their ability to provide successfully for the economic needs of their families (Yankelovich, 1974), and social disapproval for not working outside the home is much stronger for men than for women—in fact, women are more likely to encounter social disapproval for working outside the home than for not doing so (Nye, 1976).

### Housework

In the area of housework, the norm is clearly that women should assume the major share of the responsibility (Nye, 1976; Pleck, 1977). Even when both spouses are working full-time, women are generally expected (by themselves as well as by their husbands) to assume the major share of the housekeeping responsibilities. A number of time budget studies (Meissner, Humphreys, Meis, & Schew, 1975; Robinson, Juster, & Stafford, 1976; Walker, 1970) have indicated that, on the average, there is little or no difference in the amount of housework that husbands do, whether their wives are employed or not employed. At the same time, Robinson and his colleagues (1976) report that in their national sample, only 23% of the women surveyed answered "yes" to the question, "Do you wish your husband would give you more help with the household chores?"

## *Child Care*

The norm for child care is similar to the norm for housework—child care is considered primarily the wife's responsibility—but to a somewhat lesser degree. For example, in Nye's (1976) study, 62% of the husbands and 44% of the wives answered that the husband and wife should have equal responsibility for child care. However, when the child-care role was broken down into specific tasks, there was considerable expectation for division of responsibility; wives were expected to be primarily responsible for keeping the children clean, fed, and warm, and husbands were expected to be equally (according to the wives) or primarily (according to the husbands) responsible for the physical protection of the children. When actual time spent in child-care activities was examined, wives were found to assume most of the responsibility in all areas except protection from danger and fright, which was usually seen as shared equally. Lopata (1971) reported that even when child-care responsibilities are shared between the husband and wife,

> the fact that so many respondents feel that their husbands "help with the children" is significant, even when stated as a form of praise. It suggests that child care is not part of the role of father and is done as a favor to the wife. (p. 121)

## SEX ROLES AND FAMILY DYNAMICS

What is the relationship between sex roles and family dynamics? While answers to this question are necessarily tentative, I believe that there are sufficient data available to warrant the construction of a middle-range theory about some aspects of this relationship. The theory is presented in the form of a series of hypotheses, along with the research evidence upon which the hypotheses are based. The first three hypotheses focus on the relationship between sex roles and marital interaction. Hypotheses 4, 5, and 6 are concerned with sex roles and parent–child interaction. Hypothesis 7 deals with the role of sanctions in the maintenance of sex-role conformity.

### Marital Interaction

#### *Hypothesis 1*

Sex-role conditioning exerts a negative influence on marital intimacy and marital problem solving by inhibiting the development and/or expression of certain forms of behavior in men and women. For men, the major under-developed or inhibited behaviors are emotional expressiveness, emotional empathy, and mature dependency. For women, there is a corresponding underdevelopment or inhibition of instrumental behavior, assertiveness, and mature independence.

*Husbands*. 1. *Emotional expressiveness*. A number of research investigations of emotional expressiveness have found that on the average, men, in comparison to women, are inhibited in both the verbal (Allen & Haccoun, 1976; Allen & Hamsher, 1974; Balswick & Avertt, 1977; Chelune, 1976; Fuller, 1963; Gitter & Black, 1976; Kopfstein & Kopfstein, 1973; Morgan, 1976; O'Neill, Fein, Velit, & Frank, 1976; Pedersen & Breglio, 1968) and nonverbal (Buck, Caul, & Miller, 1974; Buck, Miller, Savin, & Caul, 1972) expression of emotion. This is particularly true for the emotions of love, joy, fear, and sadness.

Studies of marital interaction (e.g., Cutler & Dyer, 1965; Katz, Goldston, Cohen & Strucker, 1963; Komarovsky, 1964; Levinger & Senn, 1967; Rausch, Barry, Hertel, & Swain, 1974; Wolff, 1976) have revealed that husbands, on the average, are less emotionally expressive with their wives than their wives are with them. This is true across a variety of marital situations, including those times when conflict arises. Studies conducted by Kelley, Cunningham, Grisham, Lefebvre, Sink, and Yablon (1978) and Raush and his colleagues (1974) indicate that men generally do not easily express their feelings about an issue of disagreement.

Direct evidence that men's emotional inexpressiveness is related to sex-role conditioning is provided by Orlofsky and Windle (1978) and Weitz (1976), who found a significant relationship between sex-role orientation and verbal (Orlofsky & Windle) and nonverbal (Weitz) emotional expressiveness. In both studies, men with rigid sex-role orientations were less expressive of their emotions than men with more liberal (androgynous) orientations.

2. *Emotional empathy*. Emotional empathy, defined as "vicarious emotional response to the perceived emotional experiences of others," has been contrasted with cognitive empathy, defined as "recognition of another's feelings" (Mehrabian & Epstein, 1972, p. 525). Most studies of cognitive empathy have found no differences between males and females, while studies of emotional empathy (e.g., Craig & Lowery, 1969; Feshbach & Roe, 1968; Levine & Hoffman, 1975; Mehrabian & Epstein, 1972) have demonstrated such differences, with males consistently being low in emotional empathy. On the basis of these differences in findings, it seems likely that the crucial area of difficulty for men is the vicarious experiencing of emotion, rather than its cognitive recognition. This is consistent with studies of emotional experiencing (e.g., Allen & Haccoun, 1976; Buck *et al*., 1972, 1974; Cooper & Cowen, 1962; Crandall, 1973), which have found that, on the average, both the intensity and frequency of emotional experiencing is lower for men than for women.

3. *Mature dependency.* The ability to seek and be open to receiving emotional, physical, and/or financial support is a characteristic that the male role strongly opposes for men. Research data indicate that the conditioning created by this role expectation has promoted a block to the full development of the capacity for mature dependency in men. Katz and his colleagues (1963) found that husbands discussed their anxieties with their wives far less often than did the latter in return. Likewise, Burke, Weir, and Harrison (1976) reported that the husbands in their study discussed their problems and tensions with their wives less often than their wives did with them. Bartolomé (1972) conducted an intensive interview study with 40 "younger executives" (average age, 37) and their wives and found that a large majority of the men (80%) reported a great reluctance to reveal to their wives feelings of dependence when they experienced them. Some of the reasons given for this reluctance were the following: "Feelings of dependence are identified with weakness or 'untoughness' and our culture doesn't accept these things in men." "You can't express dependence when you feel it, because it's a kind of absolute. . . . You are either dependent or independent; you can't be both."

Another aspect of mature dependency that is affected by male sex-role conditioning is the ability to share power and control on an equal basis with another (especially if the other is a woman). With regard to marriage, men are trained to believe that they should be dominant ("head of the household") and that their wives should be submissive. This conditioning primes men to experience (consciously or unconsciously) the prospect of a truly equal-power marriage as a threat to their self-esteem and internal security.

*Wives.* The female role prescribes emotionality, subjectivity, submissiveness, and dependency for women. There is evidence that conditioning based on these role prescriptions interferes with the development and/or expression by women of certain forms of instrumental problem-solving behavior, assertiveness, and mature independence.

1. *Instrumental problem-solving behavior.* Rubin and Brown (1975), after reviewing approximately 100 studies of bargaining and negotiation, concluded that women often tend to bargain in a reactive, non-task-oriented way that interferes with effective problem solving. Of particular significance is their statement that when the "opponent" behaves in ways that are threatening or provoking, women frequently have difficulty ignoring or overlooking the provocation and often overreact to it. This conclusion is supported by the results of a study of marital conflict conducted by Raush and his colleagues (1974). These investigators found that husbands and wives made approximately the same number of rejecting statements to each other, but that in response to a rejecting statement from the other, husbands used about three times as many resolving and reconciling responses as wives. The husbands seemed to be able to overlook the rejecting behavior of their

spouses in the interest of resolving the conflict. The wives had difficulty doing this.

2. *Assertiveness.* "Assertive behavior" involves standing up for personal rights and expressing thoughts, feelings, and beliefs in direct, honest, and appropriate ways that do not violate another person's rights (Lange & Jakubowski, 1976). Lange and Jakubowski contrast assertive behavior with "deference" (acting in a subservient manner) on the one hand and with "aggression" (humiliating, degrading, belittling, or overpowering other people) on the other. The results of a number of research studies support the hypothesis that female sex-role conditioning inhibits the development and/or expression of assertive behaviors in women, while at the same time promoting the development of deference and certain forms of nonconstructive aggression. (*Note*: Evidence for the hypothesis that female sex-role conditioning encourages the development of certain forms of nonconstructive aggression is presented in the following section under Hypothesis 2.)

Studies of group interaction (e.g., Alkire, Collum, Kaswan, & Love, 1968; Aries, 1974; Strodtbeck, James, & Hawkins, 1957; Wahram & Pugh, 1974) have found that, in general, women tend to be relatively quiet, passive, and nonassertive in groups, particularly in mixed-sex groups. The relationship between lack of assertiveness and sex roles was highlighted by Orlofsky and Windle (1978) who found that sex-typed women were less assertive than non-sex-typed (androgynous) women. With regard to marriage, Scanzoni (1978) reported that women with more traditional sex-role attitudes were less assertive than women with less traditional sex-role attitudes.

3. *Mature independence.* Independent attitudes and behaviors, the ability to think and act in a self-reliant autonomous way, are characteristics that are generally excluded from the female role. There is evidence that this exclusion has exerted an inhibiting effect on the development and expression of mature independence in women.

Reviews of research in this area (e.g., Bardwick, 1971; Frieze, Parsons, Johnson, Ruble, & Zellman, 1978; Maccoby & Jacklin, 1974; O'Leary, 1977) have generally concluded that in early childhood there is no sex difference with regard to independent thinking or behavior, but that in older children and adults there is such a difference. For example, Douvan (1960) reported that the adolescent girls in her study were relatively uninvolved in the development of independent values and standards, tending to maintain a relatively compliant and dependent relationship with their parents. Bart (1971) found that a lack of independent interests and activities contributed to the development of depression in her sample of middle-aged women. A negative relationship between sex roles and autonomy was demonstrated by Bem (1975), who found that sex-typed women behaved less independently than non-sex-typed (androgynous) women in her experimental study of compliance.

With regard to the power and control aspect of mature independence, women have been trained to believe that they should be submissive and that their husbands should be dominant. This training interferes with the development of truly equal-power relationships and promotes the development of dysfunctional forms of control. For example, a woman who feels powerless in her marriage may resort to indirect manipulation or to self-denying, martyrlike behavior.

### Hypothesis 2

Sex-role conditioning promotes the development and expression of certain dysfunctional attitudes and behaviors in men and women, and these have negative effects on marital intimacy and marital problem solving. For women, the main behaviors in this category are nagging and pressuring. For men, passive–aggressive behavior and physical violence are of greatest significance.

*Wives.* There is clear evidence that, on the average, wives complain much more about their husbands' behavior than vice versa (Cutler & Dyer, 1965; Douvan & Kulka, 1979; Komarovsky, 1962; Levinger, 1966). In part, this difference is a result of husbands' inexpressiveness, as described earlier. However, that is only half the story. The other half is that female sex-role conditioning and its consequences (e.g., inhibition of assertiveness and independence) promote the development of excessive complaining ("nagging"). Meade (1975) suggests that such behavior serves two purposes: the expression of serious grievances, and the undermining of the husband's sense of self-esteem ("cutting him down to size"). She goes on to suggest that the impetus for such attacks can be traced to chronic dissatisfaction with the rigidly defined limitations of the female role and to the absence of more constructive channels for self-assertion.

In addition to promoting the development of nagging behavior, female sex-role conditioning also promotes the development of excessive pressuring behavior. In the previously cited study of marital conflict resolution conducted by Raush and his colleagues (1974), wives were found to exert more emotional pressure than their husbands did and to resist husbands' efforts at conciliation. There appeared to be a quality of drivenness to the wives' behavior that made it difficult or impossible for them to approach the conflict in a goal-oriented way or to be constructively responsive to their husbands' efforts to resolve the conflict. Again, it is likely that part of the explanation for these observations is that the husbands were trying to avoid discussing the problem and that the wives were reacting to this avoidance. However, it is also likely that many of the wives were unable to turn off their emotional pressure, even in the face of a genuine offer to discuss the problem constructively.

*Husbands.* Passive–aggressive behavior, particularly procrastination and inconsiderate forgetting (e.g., of birthdays or anniversaries), are behaviors that reflect certain attitudes derived from male sex-role conditioning. The first of these is that a man's major responsibility is to work and earn money, and that everything else is of lesser importance. Secondly, men are taught that they are entitled to be in a superior position vis-à-vis their wives, and, therefore, that they can expect to be the boss (or king). This, in turn, leads to the following expectations: (1) "Since I am the head of the household, I don't have to follow through on commitments if I don't want to." (2) "Since my wife is subservient to me, she won't object if I don't follow through on my commitments." In reality, however, wives do object, vigorously and often. For example, Scanzoni (1978) reports that many of the wives in his sample complained about their husbands' procrastination or neglect of responsibilities. Typical comments were: "He puts off too much . . . in football season, it's football first"; "If I weren't pregnant, I'd get out and do it myself"; "[I wish he would do] his chores without being nagged by me" (p. 95).

In addition to promoting passive–aggressive behavior, the male role also promotes physically violent behavior. As Straus (1976) points out, husband-to-wife violence is legitimated by cultural (sex-role) norms. One way in which this is apparent is the reaction of the legal system. In many jurisdictions, the doctrine of "spousal immunity" prevents a wife from suing her husband for assault and battery. In those jurisdictions where wives are able to sue, little is gained because of the attitudes and behavior of the police and prosecutors. The police generally avoid making an arrest for husband–wife violence, and there is evidence that many policemen believe it is legal for a husband to beat his wife (Truninger, 1971). In those rare instances in which an arrest is made, prosecution is extremely unlikely (Field & Field, 1973). An experimental study cited by Pogrebin (1974) sheds further light on the relationship between cultural norms and husband–wife violence. In this experiment, a series of fights was staged in a public place, so that they would be witnessed by passers-by. The researchers found that male witnesses rushed to the aid of men being assaulted by either women or men, and that men helped women being hit by other women. But not one male bystander interfered when a male actor apparently beat up a woman. Straus (1976) suggests that a likely interpretation of these findings is that male bystanders did not come to the aid of the female victim because they assumed that she was the assailant's wife. He notes that this was precisely the reason given by many of the witnesses who failed to intervene while Kitty Genovese (Rosenthal, 1964) was being murdered.

What about the attitudes of men who are physically violent with their wives? Coleman (1980) conducted an intensive investigation with 33 such men. She reports as follows:

> One prominent characteristic of the men evident in interviews and therapy sessions was their belief that to be a man, one must be strong and dominant, superior and successful. Feelings of inadequacy in any of these areas were devastating to the men's self-esteem and self-regard. . . . Violence erupts when the men can no longer defend themselves from a sense of inadequacy. The act of violence assures them that there is at least one place where they have control and power. (p. 211)

Coleman's findings are consistent with Straus's hypothesis that husband-to-wife violence is, to a significant degree, encouraged by male sex-role conditioning.

### Hypothesis 3

In the marital system, male and female sex roles interact in a synergistic and mutually reinforcing way.

Hypotheses 1 and 2 have delineated some of the effects of male and female sex-role conditioning on husbands' and wives' attitudes and behavior. So far, each sex has been considered separately. Hypothesis 3 takes up the question of how male and female role expectations interact with each other in an ongoing marital system. In describing this interaction, the choice of a beginning point is arbitrary, since the pattern is a circular one.

*Sexuality.* One area of marital functioning in which a reciprocal interaction between male and female sex-role conditioning can be found is sexuality. The female role programs women to be passive recipients or active avoiders of male sexual advances (Frieze *et al.*, 1978). Positive, assertive sexuality is seen as unfeminine and therefore as undesirable. On the other hand, the male role programs men to be active, aggressive pursuers of sexual gratification from women (Gross, 1978). There is little or no expectation in the male role that men should make an effort to develop an empathic understanding of a woman's sexual needs and desires. On the contrary, a man who is empathic and concerned about a woman's needs may be seen as "soft" and "unaggressive."

The female role injunction against assertiveness exerts an inhibiting effect on women's impulses to make direct sexual initiatives and to take an active role in sexual experiences. These inhibitions reinforce the male role expectation that women are not interested in their own sexual needs, but are mainly interested in gratifying those of men. This belief inhibits men from developing an empathic understanding of women's sexual feelings and sexual needs, and this, in turn, reinforces women's inhibitions against the direct expression of those needs. Thus, there is a circular pattern of mutual reinforcement that serves to maintain the sex-role-induced *status quo*.

*Independence–Dependence.* A second area of marital interaction in which sex roles exert a mutually reinforcing influence is independence–dependence. As we have seen, women are trained to be emotionally and financially dependent on their husbands, and men are trained to be emotionally and financially independent. As we have also seen, this training inhibits the development of mature dependency in men and of mature independence in women. In the marital system, these two inhibitions reinforce each other. Beginning this time with the husband (again, the beginning point is arbitrary, since the pattern is circular), it may be noted that his inhibitions against mature dependency prevent him from revealing weaknesses or asking for help and cause him to invest a great amount of his self-esteem in being the sole "breadwinner" of the family (Yankelovich, 1974). This behavior reinforces his wife's image of herself as weak and dependent ("If I need help, but he doesn't, I must be weaker than he") and also reinforces the female role injunction against women's sharing equally in the provider role. The wife's dependency, in turn, reinforces the husband's blocked access to the direct expression of his dependency needs ("She wouldn't understand" or "She wouldn't be able to help") and reinforces his investment in "taking care of" his wife and family.

*Marital Conflict.* With regard to marital conflict, sex roles have an impact in two ways: They contribute to the frequency and intensity of certain forms of marital conflict; and they interfere with constructive problem solving around issues of marital conflict.

One of the most common complaints that spouses have about their marriage is "lack of communication" (Komarovsky, 1962; Krupinski, Marshall, & Yule, 1970). When spouses are carefully questioned about this complaint, two very different descriptions emerge (Feldman, 1980). Wives' complaints about communication generally take the form of such complaints as "My husband doesn't talk to me" or "My husband doesn't share his feelings with me." Husbands, on the other hand, complain that their wives are overly critical or complain too much. These two very different definitions of "lack of communication" have clear connections with male and female sex-role conditioning. Men are trained to be underexpressive; women are trained to be overexpressive. In marriage, these two characteristics form a mutually reinforcing system. Husbands' lack of expressiveness triggers wives' over-expressiveness, which, in turn, further inhibits husbands' expressiveness, creating a vicious circle that interferes with marital intimacy and effective marital problem solving.

Interaction around husbands' passive–aggressive behavior (e.g., pro-crastination) is another area in which sex roles have an important impact. It has been seen that the male role promotes the development of attitudes and beliefs (e.g., "I am the king of the castle"; "My wife is subservient to me") that are conducive to passive–aggressive behavior. When husbands behave in these ways, wives frequently respond by nagging, a form of behavior that expresses in part, frustration with the limitations of the female role. Wives' nagging, in turn, reinforces husbands' sense of superiority and control ("I have more important things to worry about").

Lastly, sex-role conditioning interferes with effective problem solving in regard to issues of marital conflict. As noted previously, the male role inhibits emotional expressiveness and emotional empathy and fosters physi-cally violent behavior in men. The female role inhibits constructive assertive-ness and certain forms of instrumental negotiation behavior and fosters emotional pressuring behavior in women. In the course of marital conflict, these characteristics form a mutually reinforcing system. Husbands' lack of expressiveness and lack of empathic understanding frequently stimulate an emotional overreaction in their wives, which interferes with their ability to implement their rational problem-solving skills and leads to emotional pressuring and coercion. This behavior is experienced by husbands as an attack, and their male role conditioning has trained them to respond to an attack with either withdrawal or physical violence. In either case, effective problem solving is blocked, and a cycle of unresolved conflict and, in some cases, destructive violence is produced.

### Parent–Child Interaction

#### Hypothesis 4

Sex-role conditioning exerts a negative influence on parent–child interaction by inhibiting the development and/or expression of certain forms of behavior in mothers and fathers. For mothers, the major underdeveloped or inhibited behaviors are in the area of parental authority and discipline; for fathers, there is a corresponding underdevelopment or inhibition of expressive and nurturing behaviors.

*Mothers.* The female role prescribes weakness and submissiveness for women and proscribes (forbids) decisiveness and strength. Training based on such norms can be predicted to inhibit the development and/or expression of authority and firmness in women's interactions with their children, particularly with regard to discipline. The results of several research studies support this prediction.

Nye (1976) reports that both the husbands and the wives in his sample of 210 couples expected the wives to have less responsibility than the husbands had for disciplining the children and for teaching the children to take responsibility. When actual behavior was examined, the couples reported that the wives assumed more of the responsibility in these areas because they spent much more time with the children than did their husbands. This discrepency between expectations and enactment suggests that many of these mothers may be performing a task for which they do not feel prepared. This inference is supported by the fact that 25% of the mothers in Nye's sample said they worry frequently about how well they are socializing their children, compared to only 16% of the fathers. (Of course, the possibility that some of this difference may be a result of fathers' inhibitions about revealing worries cannot be ruled out as a competing explanation. However, seen in the context of the other results on parent–child interaction, it seems unlikely that this factor explains all or most of this discrepancy.)

In Bartz's study (1978), mothers were described as being significantly less involved in discipline and in teaching values to the children than fathers were. Since the questions in this study were more global than those in the Nye (1976) study, it is possible that this discrepancy is as much a function of how mothers and fathers feel about assuming responsibility in these areas as it is a function of how often they actually do so.

Another aspect of this question is how children experience their parents with regard to discipline. Walters and Stinnett (1971) concluded, on the basis of an extensive "decade review" of the literature, that children generally perceive mothers as being less restrictive and less punitive than fathers. Britton and Britton (1971) found that when children were asked, "Let's make believe you were bad and your mother and father were both home. Who would punish you, your mother or your father?" more than 50% of the children answered "Father," while only 20% answered "Mother" (the rest answered "neither" or "both").

Another component of parental authority, related to but not identical with discipline, is the making of demands. Shepard (1980) found that, on the average, mothers are experienced as less demanding than fathers are.

To summarize, the results of a number of research studies suggest that parental discipline and authority are aspects of parenting in which female sex-role training inhibits the development and/or expression of confident and fully effective functioning in women. A corollary hypothesis, that male sex-role training promotes the development of overly authoritatian, rigid parental behavior in men, is discussed under Hypothesis 5.

*Fathers.* The male role prescribes toughness, aggressiveness, and strength for men and proscribes gentleness and tenderness. In addition, men are taught that taking care of children is "woman's work." Conditioning based on these norms can be predicted to inhibit the development and expression of nurturance in men's interactions with their children. The results of several research studies support this prediction.

In their decade review of the literature on parent–child relationships, Walters and Stinnett (1971) concluded that, on the average, children experience their fathers as colder, less understanding, and less nurturant than they do their mothers. These conclusions are supported by the results of three more recent studies. Slevin and Balswick (1980) found that fathers were experienced by their children as less expressive than their mothers were, with the largest differences being in verbal and physical expressions of love. Shepard (1980) found that fathers were experienced by their children as less loving, less supportive, and less protective than their mothers were. At the same time, fathers were experienced as more neglecting than were mothers. Lamb (1977) found that while fathers held their infant children as frequently as mothers did, the qualitative nature of the holding was quite different. When fathers held the infants, it was usually for the purpose of play. When mothers held the infants, it was usually for the purpose of providing nurturant care (e.g., feeding).

Evidence for a connection between male sex-role training and fathers' nurturing behavior is provided by Nye (1976), who found that fathers were expected to assume much more responsibility for the "masculine" tasks of protecting the children from danger and keeping the children from being frightened than they were for the "feminine" tasks of keeping the children clean, fed, and warm. Experimental support for the hypothesis that male sex-role training inhibits the development and expression of nurturance is provided by Bem (1975), who found that sex-typed (highly masculine) men displayed significantly less nurturant behavior than did men who were able to incorporate both "masculine" and "feminine" characteristics into their personalities ("androgynous" men).

From a sociological perspective, men are trained to view their "place" in the world as being located primarily outside the home, and to view nurturant child care as "woman's work." This training makes it difficult for men to feel comfortable about spending less of their time at work and more of their time at home, engaging in tasks that they have been conditioned to regard as "feminine."

### Hypothesis 5

Sex-role conditioning promotes the development and expression of certain dysfunctional attitudes and behaviors in men and women that interfere with constructive, growth-promoting parenting by fathers and mothers. For fathers, the main behaviors in this category are authoritarianism and rigidity; for mothers, they are overprotectiveness and overcontrol.

*Fathers.* The male role conditions men to be "tough" in all aspects of their lives, including their relationships with their children. Also, men are rewarded (directly or indirectly) for behaving in ways that cause others to be afraid of them, even when the fearful others are their own children.

Walters and Stinnett (1971) concluded in their "decade review" article that children generally perceive their fathers as more fear-arousing and more punitive than they do their mothers. This conclusion is supported by Britton and Britton (1971), who found that children reported being much more frightened of their fathers than they were of their mothers, and by Shepard (1980), who found that the children in his sample experienced their fathers as more rejecting than they did their mothers. In Tallman's study (1965), fathers were found to be relatively rigid and inflexible in their dealings with their children. L'Abate (1975) has discussed the phenomenon of "pathological role rigidity," in which fathers transfer attitudes and behaviors from their work onto their relationships with their children, leading to overly authoritarian and inflexible parenting behavior.

*Mothers.* Female sex-role training conditions women to believe that their primary commitment should be to the roles of wife and (especially) mother.

Even when women work outside the home, they (and their husbands) frequently regard their work as secondary to their maternal roles. In addition, women are conditioned to be submissive in their marriages. When a woman feels powerless in her relationship with her husband, she may exert too much power with her children and become overcontrolling.

Evidence of a connection between female sex-role training and the behaviors of overprotectiveness and overcontrol is provided by Maxwell, Connor, and Walters (1961), who found that mothers nagged their adolescents more frequently than did fathers, and by Stehbens and Carr (1970), who found that the mothers in their sample were frequently perceived by their sons as "overprotective, controlling of behavior, and forcing themselves into the boys' peer relationships" (p. 71). Two studies of families in which children developed behavioral problems give further support to this hypothesis. Reichard and Tillman (1950) found that the most common pattern in the families of the schizophrenic children in their investigation was one in which the mothers were overprotective and overcontrolling. Similarly, Kaffman (1972) reported that maternal overcontrol was the most frequent form of family pathology in his sample of 196 emotionally disturbed children and their families, occurring in 65% of these families. Maternal overprotectiveness was also present in a significant percentage (34%) of these families.

### Hypothesis 6

In the family system, male and female sex roles interact in a synergistic and mutually reinforcing way.

Hypotheses 4 and 5 have delineated some of the effects of male and female sex-role conditioning on mothers' and fathers' attitudes and behaviors. Hypothesis 6 postulates that in the family system, these attitudes and behaviors interact in a mutually reinforcing, circular pattern.

*Parental Authority and Discipline.* As we have seen, female sex-role conditioning inhibits the development of parental authority behavior in women, while male sex-role conditioning promotes the development of rigid and overly authoritarian behavior in men. In the dynamics of the family system, these two patterns are mutually reinforcing. Mothers have been trained to inhibit their own authoritative behavior and to rely on their husbands as "authority figures" for the children. This often leads to the use of such tactics as "When your father gets home, he will punish you for this." Fathers' sex-role conditioning has trained them to expect to be the authority figures in the family and to be stern and tough with their children. Thus, they are trained to accept the role of the "heavy," even when they find it uncomfortable or distasteful. Fathers' acceptance of the "heavy" role encourages mothers to continue to inhibit their own authority and to defer to the fathers, thus completing a circular pattern in which mothers' inhibited authority and fathers' excessive authority reinforce each other.

*Nurturance and Involvement.* The male role trains men to inhibit their involvement and nurturance with their children. The female role trains women to be overinvolved, overprotective, and overcontrolling with their children. Fathers' lack of involvement encourages mothers' overinvolvement, and vice versa. Likewise, fathers' inhibited nurturance encourages the development of excessive nurturance (overprotectiveness and overcontrol) in mothers, while mothers' excessive nurturance encourages fathers' tendency to inhibit their own nurturance and involvement. Thus, parents' sex-role expectations and the behaviors derived from each are mutually reinforcing.

## Sanctions

### Hypothesis 7

Sex-role-congruent attitudes and behaviors are maintained by positive and negative sanctions. Positive sanctions are rewards for role conformity; negative sanctions are penalties for role deviation. Both positive and negative sanctions may be external (generated by others) or internal (generated by the self).

*External Sanctions.* These generally take the form of approval (for role conformity) or disapproval (for role deviation). A number of research studies (e.g., Broverman, Broverman, Clarkson, Rosenkrantz, & Vogel, 1970; Cherry & Deaux, 1978; Derlega & Chaikin, 1976; Feinman, 1974; Zanna & Pack, 1975) have demonstrated that deviations from sex-role norms frequently evoke feelings of disapproval on the part of external observers. When these feelings are communicated (overtly or covertly) to the person engaging in sex-role-incongruent behavior, they serve to discourage the continuation of the behavior. For example, a man who decides to reduce his work commitment in order to spend more time parenting his children risks being viewed by his employer and/or colleagues as insufficiently ambitious or insufficiently competent. A cogent example of this is presented by Bartolomé (1972), who quotes one of the executives in his sample as follows:

> I group my friends in two ways, those who have made it and don't complain, and those who haven't made it. . . . The ones who concentrate more on communicating with their wives and families are those who have realized that they aren't going to make it and therefore they have changed their focus of attention. (p. 64)

Likewise, a woman who decides to reduce her family commitments in order to pursue a career risks being viewed as a "bad" mother who is abandoning her children. While this attitude may be quite overt, it is often communicated more covertly. For example, Levine (1977) quotes the following passage from a speech by a prominent child psychologist (Bronfenbrenner, 1975) about day care:

> I think that day care should include a guiding principle, one of allowing the
> mother a freedom of choice so that she is not forced either to provide no
> care for her children or, in effect, forced to leave the child in a situation
> which she does not regard as acceptable. (Bronfenbrenner, 1975, p. 2)

As Levine points out, the covert assumption in this passage is that child
care is the mother's exclusive responsibility, and that it is up to her to make
sure that her going to work does not have negative effects on her children.
This type of attitude serves to discourage women from attempting to combine motherhood and a career.

In addition to those sanctions that originate outside the family, there
are also those that are generated by family members. For example, a wife
whose husband expresses a desire to spend more time taking care of the
children and less time at work may feel that her "territory" is being invaded,
and she may react in ways that discourage him from taking this step (e.g., by
focusing on the financial problems that such a change would bring). Or, a
husband whose wife expresses a desire to pursue a career may feel that his
role as "breadwinner" is being threatened, and he may react in ways that
discourage her from doing this (e.g., by refusing to take on any additional
housework responsibility). In both of these examples, there is an underlying
fear of change, based on internalized images of what is "appropriate" and
"inappropriate." This fear expresses itself in the form of external sanctions
(negative feedback signals) that discourage sex role deviations.

*Internal Sanctions.* These are intrapsychic reactions (thoughts and feelings)
of either approval (for sex-role conformity) or disapproval (for sex-role
deviation). The importance of internal sanctions for the maintenance of sex-
role-congruent behavior was clearly demonstrated by Bem and Lenney
(1976). These investigators created an experimental situation in which participants were offered an opportunity to engage in activities which were
either sex-role-congruent or sex-role-incongruent. Monetary rewards were
attached to each activity. The results of this study were that sex-typed
individuals preferred sex-role-congruent behavior to sex-role-incongruent
behavior, even when the external reward (money) was greater for the incongruent behavior. In addition, when sex-typed individuals did engage in role-
incongruent behavior, they reported feeling a high degree of psychological
discomfort and negative feelings about themselves.

In marital and family interaction, sex-role training creates a set of
expectations of self and others that have a decided impact on self-esteem. To
the extent that sex roles have been internalized, any deviations (by self or
others) will be experienced as threats to one's sense of self-esteem. This
threat generates "signal anxiety" (Freud, 1926/1959), which stimulates the
reestablishment of sex-role conformity. For example, suppose that a highly
sex-typed woman experiences an impulse to be more initiating of sexual
activity with her husband. Such an impulse is likely to trigger (consciously or

unconsciously) thoughts such as "Good girls don't do things like that" or
"He'll think I'm too aggressive." These thoughts, in turn, trigger anxiety
connected with the maintenance of self-esteem, and the impulse is inhibited.
In this way, the wife (and husband) are deprived of an opportunity to add a
new dimension to their sexual relationship. Now the other side of this
example is, of course, the husband's reaction. To the degree that he has
internalized sex-role norms, he may well be threatened by a sexual advance
from his wife, and he may respond in a way that discourages her from doing
it again. Here, too, the threat is to his sense of self-esteem. For example, he
may tell himself (consciously or unconsciously) that "The man should take
the lead sexually" or "Only a sissy lets his wife lead the way." Such thoughts
trigger self-esteem-related anxiety, and a defensive (deviation-discouraging)
reaction is generated. Again, sex-role rigidity has deprived the couple of an
opportunity to explore a new avenue in their relationship.

In general, the main problem with sex roles is that they promote the
development of rigid and narrow individual, familial, and social systems,
which are severely limited in their capacity to generate novelty and variety
and which fail to promote adaptive changes in the face of changing circumstances. In the following section, an alternative to sex roles—psychological
and sociological androgyny—is considered.

## AN ALTERNATIVE TO SEX ROLES:
## PSYCHOLOGICAL AND SOCIOLOGICAL ANDROGYNY

In recent years, the concept of androgyny as an alternative to sex roles has
received a steadily increasing amount of attention. "Psychological androgyny" describes a state of affairs in which individuals experience the psychological freedom to develop fully both the "masculine" and "feminine" aspects
of their personalities, as well as to engage in whatever forms of behavior
seem most effective, irrespective of their label or stereotype as "masculine"
or "feminine" (Bem, 1975). "Sociological androgyny" describes a state of
affairs in which the allocation of work and family responsibilities is based on
individual preferences and capabilities, regardless of gender. With regard to
marital and family interaction, "androgyny" describes a situation in which
the attitudes and behaviors of husbands and wives, fathers and mothers,
sons and daughters are freed from the influence of rigid sex-role injunctions.
It is important to note that androgyny does not imply uniformity (i.e., that
all men and women or all marital and family relationships should be completely alike). Rather, it is suggested that by freeing individuals, couples, and
families from the rigid constraints of sex-role conditioning, each person will
be more able to develop both the "masculine" and "feminine" aspects of his
or her particular personality, and that this will have positive effects on
marital and family interaction.

## Psychological Androgyny

Research on psychological androgyny has generally shown that androgynous individuals are, on the average, more flexible and adaptive than are sex-typed individuals. For example, androgynous females have been found to resist peer pressure for conformity more effectively (Bem, 1975) and to behave more assertively (Orlofsky & Windle, 1978) than feminine-typed females, and androgynous males have exhibited higher levels of playful, nurturant, and expressive behaviors than have rigidly masculine males (Bem, 1975; Orlofsky & Windle, 1978). Furthermore, androgynous individuals have reported less psychological discomfort than sex-typed individuals when performing traditionally cross-sex behaviors (Bem & Lenney, 1976). While none of these studies has directly investigated the relationship between psychological androgyny and marital/family interaction, the behaviors that have been investigated (independence, assertiveness, expressiveness, nurturance) are ones that are of great importance in marital and family dynamics. In view of the previously described negative effects of sex-role conditioning on these variables, it seems reasonable to postulate that an androgynous orientation would bring about beneficial changes in these aspects of marital and family interaction.

## Sociological Androgyny

Sex-role conditioning prescribes a rigid division of family and work responsibilities, with men assuming the role of provider and women assuming the roles of housekeeper and child caretaker. Sociological androgyny defines a more flexible and open social system, in which the possibility of men and women each participating in both work and family roles is fully available. Again, it is important to note that sociological androgyny does not imply conformity to a new but equally rigid set of norms about what is "appropriate" or "inappropriate" for men and women. Rather, it describes a situation in which more options would be available, thereby broadening each individual's and each family's freedom of choice.

Research data bearing on sociological androgyny come primarily from the literature on dual-career families. These data must be interpreted cautiously, however, because a number of studies (e.g., Epstein, 1970; Holmstrom, 1972) have shown that in many dual-career marriages, sex-role conditioning continues to exert a major impact on husbands' and wives' attitudes and behaviors. (For instance, the attitude that the wife's career is of secondary importance to the husband's and the related attitude that the husband's child-care responsibility is secondary to his wife's are quite common in dual-career couples.) Nonetheless, dual-career couples have taken at least an initial step away from sex-role rigidity, and their experiences can give some indication of the effects of such a change.

Rapoport and Rapoport (1972) postulate that a marital relationship is likely to be strengthened if each partner is economically viable and feels that he or she is achieving a great deal out of both career and family. Support for this position is provided by Safilios-Rothschild (1970), who found that women with a high degree of work commitment reported significantly higher marital satisfaction than did women not working outside the home. Bernard (1974) reviewed a number of studies that indicated that when mothers were not solely responsible for child care, their maternal functioning improved. Burke and Weir (1976) found that members of dual-career families were more self-reliant and self-sufficient than were members of single-career families. Also, working wives were found to be more self-assertive than were nonworking wives, while the husbands of working wives were less concerned with power and authority than were husbands of housewives. The potential benefits for all family members of fathers' assuming more child-care responsibility have been discussed by Bernard (1974), Lips and Colwill (1978), Lynn (1974), and Pleck (1977).

In addition to the benefits of a dual-career family system, there are many stresses and strains (Price-Bonham & Murphy, 1980). With both spouses actively involved in careers, there is less time available for leisure activities, and schedules are often hectic. Also, internal stress (e.g., guilt or shame) is often generated because of lack of conformity to deeply ingrained sex-role expectations. Women who have children and attempt to pursue a career are vulnerable to feelings of guilt and shame with respect to their child-care responsibilities. Husbands who reduce their career commitments to assume housework and child-care responsibilities are vulnerable to feelings of guilt and shame with respect to their career responsibilities. It seems likely that many of these external and internal stresses would be reduced if there were more social supports for this way of living (e.g., paternal as well as maternal leaves of absence; greater availability of part-time work; etc.) and less pressure to conform to traditional sex-role prescriptions.

## CLINICAL IMPLICATIONS

When couples or families seek therapeutic help, they generally present one of three types of problems: marital conflict; a symptomatic spouse; or a symptomatic child. In all three instances, an understanding of the relationship between sex roles and family dynamics can be helpful to therapists in their efforts to assess and treat such families.

### Marital Conflict

Conflictual couples frequently argue about sex-role-related issues. Some of the more common of these are husbands' procrastination, wives' nagging, husbands' lack of self-disclosure, wives' criticality, husbands' lack of involvement with children, and wives' overinvolvement with children. In working with couples about such issues, it is helpful to consider the internal and external sex-role pressures that help to maintain the problematic behaviors, as well as the anxieties that are aroused by efforts to change the pattern. For example, one couple's arguments invariably began when the husband made a unilateral decision affecting the couple without consulting his wife. In discussing these arguments in therapy, the husband said that he understood intellectually that it was wrong of him to do this, but that he didn't feel it in his "gut." After a bit of probing, he realized that he resented the idea of having to consult with his wife, and that the idea of doing so stimulated a feeling of shame about not being the "head of the household." The wife's contribution to their difficulties consisted primarily of emotional over-reactions to minor provocations, along with a lack of positive response to the husband's efforts to be conciliatory. On examination, it became clear that she routinely failed to be constructively assertive with her husband; as a result, she built up a reservoir of resentment, which periodically exploded. In working with this couple, the therapeutic effort was directed to a significant degree toward increasing the husband's capacity for mature dependency—more accurately, for interdependency—and the wife's ability to be more constructively assertive.

### Symptomatic Spouse

Sex roles are not infrequently involved in the genesis and maintenance of spouses' psychological and physical symptoms. This connection is important for understanding the role of the nonsymptomatic as well as that of the symptomatic spouse. For example, a couple came for therapy because of the wife's recurrent depressions. On examination, it became clear that the wife's depressions invariably were related to success at work. The usual sequence was that she would begin a new job, function very effectively for a while, and soon be promoted to a more responsible position. When this happened, she would begin to experience a great deal of anxiety and soon would be unable to go to work. As a result, she would lose her job and go into a prolonged depression. Exploration of the dynamics of this pattern revealed that, to a significant degree, the wife's anxieties were aroused by the thought that she might attain a level of success that exceeded that of her husband, and that if this were to happen, he would abandon her. While some of this anxiety was related to the wife's projections of her own internalized attitudes onto her husband, much of it was an accurate reflection of the husband's real feelings. He was indeed threatened by the idea that his wife might be more successful than he was. In response to his anxiety, he unconsciously undermined his wife's efforts at work and reinforced her helplessness and dependency.

The dynamics of this couple's marriage are an example of some of the problems that can arise as individuals and families attempt to move away from rigid sex roles toward a more androgynous lifestyle. In this case, both husband and wife were consciously committed to the idea of equality, but unconsciously they were both highly threatened by it. In their therapy, each spouse's anxieties were explored and related to their internalized images of what a man and woman "should be."

### Symptomatic Child

Children's symptomatic behavior is often a result of sex-role-related im- balances or inconsistencies in their parents' behavior. For example, a family came for therapy because their 11-year-old daughter was having problems at school (poor grades, lack of responsibility, and lying). In therapy, it became clear that the parents were not able to work out an effective way of dealing with their daughter because of their very different attitudes and feelings about discipline. The father played the role of the "heavy." He became enraged at any hint of misbehavior from his daughter, was highly critical of her, and resisted seeing any positive aspects of her behavior. The mother played the role of "good parent." She attempted to rationalize the most major forms of misbehavior as "normal," and she resisted imposing any punishments. When a punishment was imposed, she undermined its effec- tiveness by unilaterally reducing its severity. In therapy, it became clear that a part of the motivation for the father's behavior was related to feelings about his masculinity. He experienced his daughter's misbehavior as a threat to his leadership of the family and entered into a power struggle with her about "who's boss around here?" The wife, on the other hand, resisted being an effective authority because of anxiety about her "femininity." She felt guilty and ashamed of herself when she did punish her daughter, in part because this violated an unconscious norm about how a "lady" should behave. Exploration of these sex-role-related anxieties proved to be a major part of this couple's therapy.

## CONCLUSION

The research data that have been reviewed provide a firm basis for con- cluding (1) that sex-role conditioning exerts a variety of dysfunctional influences on marital and family relationships; and (2) that male and female sex roles interact in a mutually reinforcing way that inhibits the psycho- logical development of each family member. For the clinician working with marital and family systems, a clear understanding of the relationship be- tween sex roles and family dynamics is essential for effective assessment and intervention.

## ACKNOWLEDGMENTS

I acknowledge the assistance of Eleanore Feldman, Froma Walsh, and Mary Zaglifa.

## REFERENCES

Aldous, J. Occupational characteristics and males' role performance in the family. *Journal of Marriage and the Family*, 1969, *31*, 707–712.

Alkire, A. A., Collum, M. F., Kaswan, J., & Love, L. R. Information exchange and accuracy of verbal communication under social power conditions. *Journal of Personality and Social Psychology*, 1968, *9*, 301–308.

Allen, J. G., & Haccoun, D. M. Sex differences in emotionality: A multidimensional approach. *Human Relations*, 1976, *29*, 711–722.

Allen, J. G., & Hamsher, J. H. The development and validation of a test of emotional styles. *Journal of Consulting and Clinical Psychology*, 1974, *42*, 663–668.

Aries, E. *Interaction patterns and themes of male, female, and mixed groups.* Paper presented at the annual convention of the American Psychological Association, New Orleans, September 1974.

Balswick, J., & Avertt, C. P. Differences in expressiveness: Gender, interpersonal orientation, and perceived parental expressiveness as contributing factors. *Journal of Marriage and the Family*, 1977, *39*, 121–127.

Bardwick, J. M. *Psychology of women.* New York: Harper & Row, 1971.

Bart, P. Depression in middle-aged women. In V. Gornick & B. Moran (Eds.), *Woman in sexist society.* New York: Basic Books, 1971.

Bartolomé, F. Executives as human beings. *Harvard Business Review*, 1972, *50*, 62–69.

Bartz, K. W. Selected childrearing tasks and problems of mothers and fathers. *Family Coordinator*, 1978, *27*, 209–214.

Bem, S. L. The measurement of psychological androgyny. *Journal of Consulting and Clinical Psychology*, 1974, *42*, 155–162.

Bem, S. L. Sex role adaptability: One consequence of psychological androgyny. *Journal of Personality and Social Psychology*, 1975, *31*, 634–643.

Bem, S. L., & Lenney, E. Sex typing and the avoidance of cross-sex behavior. *Journal of Personality and Social Psychology*, 1976, *33*, 48–54.

Bernard, J. *The future of motherhood.* New York: Dial Press, 1974.

Britton, J. J., & Britton, J. O. Comparison of Finnish and American children. *Journal of Marriage and the Family*, 1971, *33*, 214–218.

Bronfenbrenner, U. Public policy and the survival of families. *Voice for Children*, 1975, *8*, 2.

Broverman, I. K., Broverman, D. M., Clarkson, F. E., Rosenkrantz, P. S., & Vogel, S. R. Sex-role stereotypes and clinical judgements of mental health. *Journal of Consulting and Clinical Psychology*, 1970, *34*, 1–7.

Broverman, I. K., Vogel, S. R., Broverman, D. M., Clarkson, F. E., & Rosenkrantz, P. S. Sex-role stereotypes: A current appraisal. *Journal of Social Issues*, 1972, *28*, 59–78.

Buck, R. W. Nonverbal communication of affect in children. *Journal of Personality and Social Psychology*, 1975, *31*, 644–653.

Buck, R. W., Miller, R. E., Savin, V. J., & Caul, W. F. Communication of affect through facial expressions in humans. *Journal of Personality and Social Psychology* 1972, *23*, 362–371.

Buck, R. W., Caul, W. F., & Miller, R. E. Sex, personality, and physiological variables in the communication of affect via facial expression. *Journal of Personality and Social Psychology*, 1974, *30*, 587–596.

Burke, R. J., & Weir, T. Some personality differences between members of one-career and two-career families. *Journal of Marriage and the Family,* 1976, *38,* 453-459.

Burke, R. J., Weir, T., & Harrison, D. Disclosure of problems and tensions experienced by marital partners. *Psychological Reports,* 1976, *38,* 531-542.

Chelune, G. A multidimensional look at sex and target differences in disclosure. *Psychological Reports,* 1976, *39,* 259-263.

Cherry, F., & Deaux, K. Fear of success versus fear of gender-inappropriate behavior. *Sex Roles,* 1978, *4,* 97-101.

Coleman, K. H. Conjugal violence: What 33 men report. *Journal of Marriage and Family Therapy,* 1980, *6,* 207-213.

Cooper, A., & Cowen, E. L. The social desirability of trait descriptive terms: A study of feeling reactions to adjective descriptions. *Journal of Social Psychology,* 1962, *56,* 207-215.

Cozby, P. C. Self-disclosure: A literature review. *Psychological Bulletin,* 1973, *79,* 73-91.

Craig, K. D., & Lowery, H. J. Heart-rate components of conditioned vicarious autonomic responses. *Journal of Personality and Social Psychology,* 1969, *11,* 381-387.

Crandall, J. E. Sex differences in extreme response style: Differences in frequency of use of extreme positive and negative ratings. *Journal of Social Psychology,* 1973, *89,* 281-293.

Cutler, B. R., & Dyer, W. G. Initial adjustment processes in young married couples. *Social Forces,* 1965, *44,* 195-201.

Derlega, V. J., & Chaikin, A. L. Norms affecting self-disclosure in men and women. *Journal of Consulting and Clinical Psychology,* 1976, *44,* 376-380.

Douvan, E. Sex differences in adolescent character processes. *Merrill-Palmer Quarterly,* 1960, *6,* 203-211.

Douvan, E., & Kulka, R. The American family: A twenty-year view. In J. E. Gullahorn (Ed.), *Psychology and women.* Washington, D.C.: Winston, 1979.

Epstein, C. F. *Woman's place: Options and limits in professional careers.* Berkeley: University of California Press, 1970.

Feinman, S. Approval of cross-sex-role behavior. *Psychological Reports,* 1974, *35,* 643-648.

Feldman, L. Husband-wife differences in marital problem identification. Unpublished data, 1980.

Feshbach, N. D., & Roe, K. Empathy in six and seven year-olds. *Child Development,* 1968, *39,* 133-145.

Field, M. H., & Field, H. F. Marital violence and the criminal process: Neither justice or peace. *Social Service Review,* 1973, *47,* 211-240.

Freud, S. *Inhibitions, symptoms and anxiety.* In *Standard edition* (Vol. 21). London: Hogarth Press, 1959. (Originally published, 1926.)

Frieze, I. H., Parsons, J. E., Johnson, P. B., Ruble, D. N., & Zellman, G. L. *Women and sex roles: A social psychological perspective.* New York: Norton, 1978.

Fuller, F. Influence of sex on expression of feeling. *Journal of Counseling Psychology,* 1963, *10,* 34-40.

Gitter, G. A., & Black, H. Is self-disclosure self-revealing? *Journal of Counseling Psychology,* 1976, *23,* 327-332.

Gross, A. E. The male role and hetersexual behavior. *Journal of Social Issues,* 1978, *34,* 87-107.

Hartley, R. E. Some implications of current changes in sex-role patterns. In J. Edwards (Ed.), *The family and change.* New York: Knopf, 1969.

Holmstrom, L. L. *The two-career family.* Cambridge, Mass.: Schenkman, 1972.

Kaffman, M. Family conflict in the psychopathology of the kibbutz child. *Family Process,* 1972, *11,* 171-188.

Katz, I., Goldston, J., Cohen, M., & Stucker, S. Need satisfaction, perception, and cooperative interaction in married couples. *Marriage and Family Living,* 1963, *25,* 209-214.

Kelley, H. H., Cunningham, J. D., Grisham, J. A., Lefebvre, L. M., Sink, C. R., & Yablon, G. Sex differences in comments made during conflict within close heterosexual pairs. *Sex Roles,* 1978, *4,* 473-491.

Komarovsky, M. *Blue-collar marriage.* New York: Random House, 1962.

Kopfstein, J. H., & Kopfstein, D. Correlates of self-disclosure in college students. *Journal of Consulting and Clinical Psychology,* 1973, *41,* 163.

Krupinski, J., Marshall, E., & Yule, V. Patterns of marital problems in marriage-guidance clinics. *Journal of Marriage and the Family,* 1970, *32,* 138–143.

L'Abate, L. Pathogenic role rigidity in fathers: Some observations. *Journal of Marriage and Family Counseling,* 1975, *1,* 69–79.

Lamb, M. Father–infant and mother–infant interaction in the first year of life. *Child Development,* 1977, *48,* 167–181.

Lange, A. J., & Jakubowski, P. *Responsible assertive behavior.* Champaign, Ill.: Research Press, 1976.

Levine, J. A. Redefining the child care "problem"—men as child nurturers. *Childhood Education,* 1977, *54,* 55–61.

Levine, L. E., & Hoffman, M. L. Empathy and cooperation in 4-year-olds. *Developmental Psychology,* 1975, *11,* 533–534.

Levinger, G. Sources of marital dissatisfaction among applicants for divorce. *American Journal of Orthopsychiatry,* 1966, *36,* 803–807.

Levinger, G., & Senn, D. J. Disclosure of feelings in marriage. *Merrill-Palmer Quarterly,* 1967, *13,* 237–249.

Lips, H. M., & Colwill, N. L. *The psychology of sex differences.* Englewood Cliffs, N.J.: Prentice-Hall, 1978.

Lopata, H. Z. *Occupation: Housewife.* New York: Oxford University Press, 1971.

Lynn, D. B. *The father: His role in child development.* Monterey, Calif.: Brooks/Cole, 1974.

Maccoby, E. E., & Jacklin, C. N. *The psychology of sex differences.* Stanford, Calif.: Stanford University Press, 1974.

Maxwell, P. H., Connor, R., & Walters, J. Family member perception of parent role performance. *Merrill-Palmer Quarterly,* 1961, *7,* 31–37.

Meade, M. *Bitching.* New York: Manor Books, 1975.

Mehrabian, A., & Epstein, N. A measure of emotional empathy. *Journal of Personality,* 1972, *40,* 525–543.

Meissner, M., Humphreys, E. Meis. S., & Schew, W. No exit for wives: Sexual division of labor and the cumulation of household demands. *Canadian Review of Sociology and Anthropology,* 1975, *12,* 424–439.

Morgan, B. S. Intimacy of disclosure topics and sex differences in self-disclosure. *Sex Roles,* 1976, *2,* 161–166.

Nye, F. I. *Role structure and analysis of the family.* Beverly Hills, Calif.: Sage, 1976.

O'Leary, V. E. *Toward understanding women.* Monterey, Calif.: Brooks/Cole, 1977.

O'Neill, S. O., Fein, D., Velit, K. M., & Frank, C. Sex differences in preadolescent self-disclosure. *Sex Roles,* 1976, *2,* 85–88.

Orlofsky, J. L., & Windle, M. T. Sex-role orientation, behavioral adaptability, and personal adjustment. *Sex Roles,* 1978, *4,* 801–811.

Pedersen, D. M., & Breglio, V. J. Personality correlates of actual self-disclosure. *Psychological Reports,* 1968, *22,* 495–501.

Pleck, J. H. The work–family role system. *Social Problems,* 1977, *24,* 417–427.

Pogrebin, L. C. Do women make men violent? *Ms.,* November 1974, pp. 49–55, 80.

Price-Bonham, S., & Murphy, D. C. Dual career marriages: Implications for the clinician. *Journal of Marital and Family Therapy,* 1980, *6,* 181–188.

Rapoport, R., & Rapoport, R. *Dual-career families.* London: Penguin, 1971.

Rapoport, R., & Rapoport, R. Men, women, and equity. *The Family Coordinator,* 1975, *24,* 421–432.

Raush, H. L., Barry, W. A., Hertel, R. K., & Swain, M. A. *Communciation, conflict, and marriage.* San Francisco: Jossey-Bass, 1974.

Reece, M. M. Masculinity and femininity: A factor-analytic study. *Psychological Reports,* 1964, *14,* 123–139.

Reichard, S., & Tillman, C. Patterns of parent–child relationships in schizophrenia. *Psychiatry,* 1950. *13,* 247–257.

Rice, D. G. *Dual-career marriage.* New York: Free Press, 1979.

Robinson, J., Juster, T., & Stafford, F. *Americans' use of time.* Ann Arbor, Mich.: Institute for Social Research, 1976.

Rosenthal, A. M. *Thirty-eight witnesses.* New York: McGraw-Hill, 1964.

Rubin, J. Z., & Brown, B. R. *The social psychology of bargaining and negotiation.* New York: Academic Press, 1975.

Safilios-Rothschild, C. The influence of the wife's degree of work commitment upon some aspects of family organization and dynamics. *Journal of Marriage and the Family,* 1970, *32,* 681–691.

Scanzoni, J. *Sex roles, women's work, and marital conflict.* Lexington, Mass.: Lexington Books, 1978.

Shepard, W. Mothers and fathers, sons and daughters: Perceptions of young adults. *Sex Roles,* 1980, *6,* 421–433.

Sherriffs, A. C., & McKee, J. P. Qualitative aspects of beliefs about men and women. *Journal of Personality,* 1957, *25,* 451–464.

Slevin, K. F., & Balswick, J. Childrens' perceptions of parental expressiveness. *Sex Roles,* 1980, *6,* 293-299.

Stehbens, J. A., & Carr, D. L. Perceptions of parental attitudes by students varying in intellectual ability and educational efficiency. *Psychology in the Schools,* 1970, *7,* 67–73.

Straus, M. A. Sexual inequality, cultural norms, and wife-beating. In E. Viano (Ed.), *Victims and society.* Washington, D.C.: Visage Press, 1976.

Strodtbeck, F., James, R., & Hawkins, C. Social status in jury deliberations. *American Sociology Review,* 1957, *22,* 713–719.

Tallman, I. Spousal role differentiation and the socialization of severely retarded children. *Journal of Marriage and the Family,* 1965, *27,* 37–42.

Tomeh, A. Sex-role orientation: An analysis of structural and·attitudinal predictors. *Journal of Marriage and the Family,* 1978, *40,* 341–354.

Truninger, E. Marital violence: The legal solutions. *Hastings Law Journal,* 1971, *23,* 259–276.

Wahrman, R., & Pugh, M. D. Sex, nonconformity, and influence. *Sociometry,* 1974, *37,* 137–147.

Walker, K. Time spent by husbands in household work. *Family Economics Review,* 1970, *4,* 8–11.

Walters, J., & Stinnett, N. Parent–child relations: A decade review of research. *Journal of Marriage and the Family,* 1971, *33,* 70–111.

Weitz, S. Sex differences in nonverbal communication. *Sex Roles,* 1976, *2,* 175–185.

Williams, J. E., & Bennett, S. M. The definition of sex stereotypes via the adjective check list. *Sex Roles,* 1975, *1,* 327–337.

Wolff, L. O. Self-disclosure in the marital dyad. *Dissertation Abstracts International,* 1976, *37,* 2581–2583.

Yankelovich, D. The meaning of work. In J. M. Rosow (Ed.), *The worker and the job.* Englewood Cliffs, N.J.: Prentice-Hall, 1974.

Zanna, M. P., & Pack, S. J. On the self-fulfilling nature of apparent sex differences in behavior. *Journal of Experimental Social Psychology,* 1975, *11,* 583–591.

# V

# NORMAL FAMILIES IN
# SOCIOCULTURAL CONTEXT

# 15

# NORMALITY FROM A
# CROSS-CULTURAL PERSPECTIVE

JOHN SCHWARTZMAN

## INTRODUCTION

"Normality," considered within its cultural context, can be understood to be one of a number of solutions to universal problems of survival for individuals and for the social systems of which they are a part. These solutions, although numerous, are not infinite. A cybernetic approach provides a means of incorporating these various levels of abstraction, including the individual, the social and ecological system, and the culture necessary to understand "normality" within a cross-cultural perspective. Each of these levels can be viewed as a self-maintaining system within its more inclusive context. "Culture," described in cybernetic terms, can be understood as the out-of-awareness basic premises that guide the behavior of groups; these have been found to be successful solutions in the past for understanding and maintaining the relationships between individuals, the social systems of which they are a part, and the material context.

## A CYBERNETIC PERSPECTIVE ON THE INDIVIDUAL, SOCIAL ORGANIZATION, AND CULTURE

A cybernetic perspective suggests that the individual, a social system, and a culture can all be viewed as adaptive, self-correcting systems in that they maintain their (improbable) order at different levels of organization and abstraction. This perspective is well described in the family therapy literature. Weakland (1960, 1974), Hoffman (1971), Bateson (1972), Watzlawick,

John Schwartzman. Center for Family Studies/The Family Institute of Chicago, Institute of Psychiatry, Northwestern Memorial Hospital and Northwestern University Medical School, Chicago, Illinois.

Beavin, and Jackson (1967), and other thinkers in the field of cybernetics assume the psychosocial world to be characterized by a hierarchy of increasingly inclusive, mutually causal processes that are either deviation-amplifying (in which change elicits more change) or self-maintaining, creating patterns at different levels of abstraction and organization that are not reducible to the sum of the elements (individuals) that compose them. Theorists in many fields have argued that these patterns, the organized complexity characteristic of living systems, and the more inclusive social systems composed of living systems, are by necessity arranged into a hierarchy of levels providing the most viable form for any system of even moderate complexity (Simon, 1969). Consequently, an adaptive system, whether an individual or a group, must be able to function within contexts characterized by hierarchy—that is, in terms of levels of organization.

In addition, limits on the amount of information that systems can store and use necessitates an "economics of flexibility" (Bateson, 1972) within the "mind" of the system, whereby certain basic premises about the nature of the system's relationship to context are automatically assumed to be true without critical examination or trial-and-error testing. This allows attention to be directed to more novel, concrete aspects of its context. In other words, learning (in the broadest sense) is a multileveled phenomenon in which the reception of information is always a part of a "nest" of more abstract information. The more abstract level of information includes the contingencies of interaction (i.e., the definition of the relationship of those interacting), and the metacommunicational mode (e.g., "This is a joke."). Bateson formerly termed this level of learning "deutero-learning" and has since referred to it as "Learning II."

The most probable contingencies encountered in early contexts of learning are deutero-learned at some level within the system and become a template (Jackson, 1970), or what Powers (1973) has termed a "reference condition"— that is, the state of the system's relationship to context that demands no response when expectations match the system's actual experience. The maintenance of this state and the implicit validation of its deutero-learned basic premises are goals of any self-maintaining system. The "purposefulness" (Rosenblueth, Weiner, & Bigelow, 1943) that characterizes self-maintaining systems at any level of organization can be understood as the system's attempt to maintain its reference condition and the structure of the system that is necessary to do this. In their attempts to achieve this state, systems create contexts with analogous basic premises and structure to those encountered in the past. As Bateson states: "To act or be one end of a pattern of interaction is to propose the other end. A context is set for a certain class of response" (1972, p. 275). Each interaction validates the system's basic premises about contingencies in general and those of a certain relationship in particular. Consequently, through a cybernetic perspective, the core problem in family therapy is seen as the introduction of novelty about basic premises into self-maintaining systems that function to eliminate this novelty.

In all societies, the most pervasive early context of learning is that of the family, where infants' basic premises about themselves and about their relationship to the context are deutero-learned. Each family is part of a more inclusive cultural system. The culture provides a set of rules for individual behavior in different relationships at various stages in the life cycle. All cultures must produce individuals capable of both surviving in a group and transmitting the cultural tradition—the basic premises of the group—to the next generation. The family, therefore, must be in "synch," having the same basic premises as its cultural context, so that children can function outside the family successfully (i.e., be normal). There is wide variation, but all cultures must be cognizant of one aspect of human biological heritage. The evolutionary development of *Homo sapiens* has resulted in a life cycle whereby infants are born extremely helpless and dependent on a nurturing other, while their potentialities as autonomous self-regulating entities must be reinforced as they become biologically competent. They require an early context of learning—a context whose structure allows for this cycle and whose contingencies they can deutero-learn as basic premises.

Consequently, a cross-cultural core problem for individuals and for the social systems of which they are a part is autonomy and dependence (Sluzki & Veron, 1971). An individual in any society must learn to function both as an autonomous whole, or self, and as a part of the social group for both individual and group to survive. What is "normal" is the cultural "setting" for relative constraints (including acceptable content) in the various relationships in the group. Each culture determines the outlines for rules of behavior among various members of the group. These rules have been at least successful enough to allow the group to survive and to allow group members to pass these rules on to the next generation.

## NORMALITY IN CROSS-CULTURAL PERSPECTIVE

The family must provide a context that teaches at the deutero-learning level a culturally appropriate solution to individuals' dual position of being independent entities as well as members of a social group. This is accomplished by facilitating the individuals' movement from symbiotic ties with nurturing others, necessitated by evolutionary changes that made culture possible (Bowlby, 1969; Count, 1958), to relatively autonomous adult status, (i.e., reproducing and passing the cultural tradition on to the next generation). This transformation has been termed "differentiation" (Bowen, 1960; Werner, 1957; Witkin, Dyk, Paterson, Goodenough, & Karp, 1962). The process, beginning with an extremely constraining relationship between infants and nurturing others, gradually results in the acquisition of a sense of bounded self—a necessary state for functioning as competent adults. (The necessity is more pronounced in the West than it is in non-Western cultures.)

## The Individual versus the Group: Cultural Variations

In any (surviving) society, a necessary goal is to teach its infants that they are entities interdependent with others in their environment but possessed of the personal capabilities and boundaries of self that are appropriate for that society. One crucial aspect of cross-cultural variation is the degree of constraint between individuals and groups, and the process and change in this constraint throughout the life cycle. These factors vary widely, but they must provide a solution to the core issue of dependency and autonomy. The culturally defined relationship between individuals as entities and the "partness" of being interdependent members of groups varies widely. It determines and maintains the normal level of differentiation, that is, the boundedness of the self (Witkin et al., 1962). "Normality" in its cultural context can be defined as a solution to the autonomy–dependency problem if it is defined as appropriate by the groups of which individuals are a part. "Normality" must include all the cross-cultural variations in this relationship, but the culture must define the relationship among the individual, group, and natural contexts successfully enough to ensure a group's survival.

In many societies, the group is emphasized, while the individual qualities of the self are less explicit and deemphasized. There is a wide variation within the "normal" range, from the hyperautonomous self in the industrial West, which minimizes the constraints of the group, to the other extreme, exemplified in the "groupness" of Bali, where the self is almost totally disqualified.

Balinese society is characterized by a ceremonialized style of interaction. Behaving improperly by commiting a *faux pas* is extremely humiliating (Geertz, 1973). The kinship system defines individuals as elements in an unchanging social system, not as individuals in novel social situations. The formalized kinship system leads to a particular interpersonal style that blocks individuality, spontaneity, and emotionality. The result is that "the illuminating paradox of Balinese formalizations of personhood is that they are—in our terms anyway—depersonalizing" (Geertz, 1970, p. 390).

Another basic element of the Balinese social system is that termed "rame" by Mead and Bateson (1942), defined as "noisily crowded." Almost all communal tasks are divided so that each individual does a small part, even when this is not the most efficient means; individuals are almost always parts of groups. Consequently, social interaction is extremely physically constrained by the constant group interaction with formally prescribed rules for behavior; it is also extremely distant and nonintimate in terms of affect because of the concurrent deemphasis on the sense of a bounded self. As can be seen from the Balinese example, there are wide variations in "normal" differentiation, separation, and individualism.

## The Expression of Affect: Cultural Variations

Individualistic, achievement-oriented behavior is not normal in many cultures and subcultures, although it is considered evidence of mental health by many psychotherapists. The Balinese example questions another generally un-questioned sign of "normality" for many middle-class mental health profes-sionals—the clear expression of affect, especially anger. In other societies, such as Bali, this is culturally inappropriate except under specific circum-stances (e.g., during religious rituals; see Levy, 1973). Levine (1973) states that members of many African societies would be characterized as expressing little affect by Western standards. Goldschmidt (1975) describes one society, the Sebei of Uganda, as an extreme example of how low levels of expressed affect might be deutero-learned. This society is characterized by emotionally distant relationships between spouses, demands for compensation from relatives for the performance of any act, little concern for the dead, and lack of expressed empathy for suffering. In addition, Goldschmidt notes the remoteness and disengagement of the mother when carrying or nursing her child and the lack of contact by the father. Consequently, this appears to be a group in which the norm is low expressed affect, and this must be accepted as one variation of "normality."

## Other Cultural Variations

There is yet another generally assumed aspect of "normality" by clinicians that the cross-cultural perspective questions. The Polish anthropologist Malinowski has argued that in many matrilineal societies—that is, those that determine their descent through the maternal side—the most significant male for a child is the mother's brother, the maternal uncle, who is often more involved with the child than is the child's father. Malinowski (1927) noted ambivalent feelings between mother's brothers and sister's sons much like those described by Freud between fathers and sons in the Oedipus complex (see Parsons, 1969). Consequently, the universality of the Oedipus complex is open to question.

The debate in anthropology (see Spiro, 1954) as to the universality of the nuclear family also remains unresolved. What is certainly true is that in many societies in which the nuclear family is embedded in more inclusive kin groups, it is much less significant as an isolated emotional, socializing, and economic institution than it is in Western society. In fact, Levy (1973) presents evidence that the nuclear family is neither the ideal nor a significant unit in many societies (e.g., traditional China). In many lower-class families in the Caribbean, especially in depressed economic conditions, the primary family unit is one or two generations of female kin and their children. The males are not very emotionally involved and drift away to find work (Smith, 1956). Only in the middle class in industrial society does the isolated nuclear family appear to be the adaptive norm (Goode, 1961).

Yet another frequent assumption of "normality" by mental health professionals is the ability to maintain long-term relationships. Only recently has divorce been considered a normal termination of some marriages. However, in some societies (e.g., the Kanuri of northern Nigeria), the rate of divorce is close to 100% (Cohen, 1970), so that this cannot be universally defined as evidence of pathology.

### Universal Constants: Learning to Function in a Sociocultural Context

Whatever its variations, the structure and function of the family must be such that its children deutero-learn basic premises or "habits of thought" (Bateson, 1972) in "synch" with those of the sociocultural context of which the family is a part, so that they can function within it in an appropriate fashion. For example, change is one of the basic characteristics of the sociocultural context of the industrial West. Consequently, flexibility, the ability to adapt to change, is an important attribute of "normality" in the West. The family structure most likely to produce normal individuals could be hypothesized as one that changes and thus implicitly teaches flexibility. This is less emphasized in many traditional non-Western cultures, except in clearly defined ways at certain times in the life cycle (e.g., onset of puberty).

When viewed within an evolutionary perspective, the fact of different sex roles' creating the basis for a parental dyad helps to prevent either parent from maintaining children in an intimate dependent relationship that would interfere with the process of differentiation necessary for culturally appropriate functioning. Validation for the children's increasing potential autonomy is often contingent on or made easier by a complementary parental dyad that enables the children to move, through the life cycle, from very dependent symbiotic relationships with the mother or nurturing others to varied relationships with other family members and then with those outside the family. This necessitates the maintenance of a clear hierarchy in the family structure (Bowen, 1960; Haley, 1973b; Minuchin, 1974). Universal rules for exogamy and the incest taboo are basic to family structure in that they maintain generational boundaries that necessitate finding sexual and marital partners outside the family. In addition, they are another means to insure, at least to some degree, the process of separation and its accompanying differentiation (Schwartzman, 1974). These cultural rules, coupled with the increasing biological maturity of the children, are all aspects of a "deviation-amplifying, mutually causal process" (Maruyama, 1963)—that is, increasing deviation from the original symbiotic tie with the primary nurturer, which ideally results in adults autonomous enough to function as individuals (at least to the degree of a perceived bounded self appropriate for that society) and concurrently as parts of the group prepared to remain within the constraints of that group.

At the same time, the family as part of a cultural context is constrained by a number of other institutions that regulate its functioning to insure that it prepares its children to live in that culture. In many societies, rites of passage (Van Gennep, 1960), or rituals of transition, are performed to enable individuals to alter their status and relationships at particular times during the life cycle. In addition, as has been noted in non-Western kinship studies, as well as those of England (Bott, 1957; Young & Wilmott, 1962), intimacy in marriage is often "regulated" by "pulls" from members of individuals' own families of origin and extended kin against spouses and their family of origin and extended kin. For example, Bott (1957), in her study of normal English working-class families, noted the following:

> The degree of segregation in the role-relationship of husband and wife varies directly with the connectedness of the families' social network. The more connected the network, the greater the degree of segregation between the roles of husband and wife. The less connected the network, the smaller the degree of segregation between the roles of husband and wife. (p. 272)

Clearly, many aspects of the social context converge to function as a homeostat maintaining distance in the marital dyad. Perhaps the most common regulators of marital emotional distance for the American middle class are the degree of investment in work and career by one or both spouses, parenting, and relations with extended kin. Radcliffe-Brown (1950) notes that in many traditional African kinship systems, the most likely sources of conflict are relationships between spouses and families of origin. Vogel and Bell (1968) have argued that, at least in dysfunctional American families of several ethnic groups (Old Yankee, Irish-American, Italian-American), the disequilibrium created by a marriage in the partners' families of origin is not resolved in those families with disturbed members. Instead, this disequilibrium maintains problems in the relationship. Bell discovered that disturbed families had boundaries that were too permeable and thus made them too sensitive to influences from extended kin.

In contrast, normal family processes reflect successful adaptation to the disequilibrium, caused by marriage, to families of origin and extended kin. Napier (1971) suggests that in normal marriages, partners are loyal to their families of origin and, at the same time, wish "to make the emergent family different, more satisfying" (p 375). He states, "The marital choice represents a complex integration of the possibilities for both continuity and discontinuity with their family of origin" (p. 375). If successful, this results in a clearly bounded system; it is, at the same time subject to some contraints by extended kin on whom the partners can rely for support and some services, but not so constraining that they cannot function as a marital unit.

## The Role of "Culture" in Family Variations

Most systems-oriented therapists do not consider systems more inclusive than extended kin. At a more abstract level, however, "culture" can also be viewed as a self-maintaining system. "Culture," as noted, can be understood as the beliefs and values that maintain the patterns of interaction that are part of the social system, as well as the meanings that individuals in the social system give to these. As Geertz (1973) states, "Man is an animal suspended in webs of significance he himself has spun, I take culture to be those webs . . . the socially established structures of meaning" (pp. 5, 13). The social and cultural systems as omnipresent aspects of social reality can only be separated conceptually. Culture, as the "webs of significance"— beliefs and values—functions as a homeostat, maintaining within limits the relationships between individuals in their social context so that the individuals can function within the constraints of the material context. Culture provides solutions that have been successful in the past for relationships among individuals, social systems, and their physical context. Culture is the most abstract system in which individuals operate, so that cultural basic premises are extremely difficult to change but important for any psychotherapist to consider as an agent of change.

A cross-cultural perspective suggests that the family must be viewed within a number of more inclusive and abstract contexts, especially that of its culture. This level of abstraction has generally been ignored by family therapists (see Vogel & Bell, 1968, and Jackson, 1970, for exceptions). Another exception to this is the work of Kluckhohn (1958) and Spiegel (1971), who have developed a number of ways to analyze the "value orientations" of people, which order their patterns of behavior and thought in all areas of activity. These provide the solution to a limited number of universal, abstract human problems that confront all people at all times. They define the five problems crucial for all human groups as the character of innate human nature, the relationship of humanity to nature, the temporal focus of human life, the modality of human activity, and the modality of humans' relationship to other humans. These universal problems and the value orientations that each society adapts to solve them are perhaps useful comparatively as a "grid"; societies and subcultures can be categorized in terms of these core problems.

There are, however, several problems with this schema, especially for the clinician. For one thing, the variations among cultural or subcultural value orientations are too great to make them useful guides for family diagnoses. In contemporary American society alone, the variation is too great to learn the basic premises of even a small number of the ethnic groups[1] that one might encounter in clinical practice. At the same time, groups exhibit a wide range in their basic premises at least partially contingent on their degree of exposure to and assimilation of the dominant American culture. Interethnic intermarriage makes this an even more complex problem, as do the geographic and socioeconomic mobility characteristic of American society. For example, I encountered in clinical practice a couple composed of a Navaho man who was an alcoholic (which in urban Amerindian males is the "normal" state, since its rate approaches 100%). His spouse was a Polish-American woman. The cultural aspects clearly exacerbated an extremely conflictual relationship.

In addition, some values (e.g., those concerning divorce and sexuality) appear to be changing rapidly. However, the most basic problem with the Kluckhohn and Spiegel value-orientation schema is the systemic relationship between culture, family, and the social context. Variation in cultural values is contingent on a large number of variables in a family's social and ideological context, as Bott and others have demonstrated. Just as the individual develops a unique personality, each family integrates its socioculture into a unique family style. Relying on a preconceived typology, therefore, interferes with sensitivity to the nuances of family functioning that make each family a unique culture. Rather than interpreting family functioning in terms of how it conforms to a preconceived notion about a particular group, it is better to form a diagnosis that includes the cultural level in terms of basic premises as revealed in intrafamilial communication, the family's relationship to its immediate social context, and the world view of individual family members. These together create a family ethnography, analogous to that done by an anthropologist on more inclusive social systems. For the clinician, feedback on the diagnosis is immediately available, provided by whether or not the symptomatic behavior can be understood as an attempted solution for the individual and the family in their social context. Attempted interventions by the therapist also provide feedback for the diagnosis in terms of structure and basic premises.

## FAMILY THERAPY AS ETHNOGRAPHY AND INTERVENTION

As stated in the previous sections of this chapter, "normality" can be understood as representing a number of solutions to the universal problem of functioning as an individual and as part of a social group. "Culture," as

---

[1]"Ethnicity" can be defined as self-concept of belonging to a particular group characterized by similar cultural basic premises. In the United States, ethnicity is not always a clearly defined boundary (e.g., middle-class Americans often define themselves just as Americans). In contrast, everybody has "culture," a more abstract concept, by which individuals determine their "webs of significance" and create meaning in their social world.

basic premises, provides the rules for successful solutions in that social group.

A cybernetic approach is perhaps the only paradigm (Kuhn, 1962) able to describe systems at all of these levels—the family, other institutions, the personality, the social system, and the culture. In a family or systems therapy, a most important diagnostic question is this: "What is the meaning of that which is communicated so that recurring patterns or structure at different levels of organization and abstraction are maintained or changed?" More specifically, the problem or symptom and the responses to it are crucial comments on "dissonances" in the structure and basic premises of the system in question (see Haley, 1963, 1976). For dysfunctional systems, more specific diagnostic questions are these: "How does this symptomatic dysfunctional behavior 'make sense' in terms of dissonances in the structure and basic premises of the individual's social context, and those encountered in the past?" and "What are the beliefs of family members about themselves and each other that maintain and are maintained by the structure of the system?"

The therapist must be able to "hear" the family culture and that of its more inclusive sociocultural context at many levels of organization and abstraction in the dysfunctional family member's own cultural categories in order to intervene successfully. The clinician must not try to force the family into categories that the clinician feels should be appropriate for the subculture to which it belongs. This includes the rules and contingencies of interaction that are acted out and communicated in many modes at many levels of organization and abstraction (e.g., verbal and nonverbal communication, dress, etc.).

A good family ethnography/diagnosis will reveal the basic premises of the family—those assumptions or rules for contingencies of interaction that are never questioned or conscious and are so abstract that they are self-validating (Bateson, 1972). They are acted out at the level of the individual and the family and are validated by beliefs and myths about individuals and by more general cultural values; for example, "For middle-class Americans, the marital dyad is an intimate and in many ways an exclusive relationship." This includes patterns of what people say and do about what they say and do (i.e., multiple levels of organization and abstraction) and ways in which the meanings of that which is communicated maintains the structure of a social system or pushes it to change. The therapist must be sensitive to the family's choice of modes, the content of its interactions, and its values and beliefs, all of which compose the "family culture" maintained by myths (Ferreira, 1963) and the ideology of the family.

At a less inclusive level, family members' world views are metaphors for the contingencies between self and social context, learned in their families of origin and acted out and validated in other contexts. The dysfunction, dysphoria, or symptom within this context as described by Haley (1971) can be viewed as a pseudosolution to the dissonances at varying levels in the social systems within which the individual is oriented, in relationship to those within which interaction takes place in the past in terms of deutero-learned basic premises. Cultural dissonances and individual dissonances can be viewed as analogues to each other at different levels of organization and abstraction.

The problem of change in psychotherapy is similar at the levels of the individual, the family, or the more inclusive social system. It is to introduce novelty about self-validating premises into a self-correcting system. Consequently, an important aspect of this process is to allow the system, individual, or family to stay the same and paradoxically to change at the same time. This is contingent on the transformation of the novel into the expected and the expected into the novel at some level. By this transformation, novelty does not trigger self-correction in self-maintaining systems, such as pathogenic families.

What makes psychotherapy such a difficult process is that structure validates basic premises and basic premises validate structure, and at the same time beliefs, values, and myths at many levels of organization, from the values of the family to the most inclusive basic values of the culture, validate each other. For any system, dissonances in basic premises or structure must either be disqualified or cause dysfunction. At the same time, most family therapists do not consider cultural or value systems to be a means to change. This is unfortunate, epecially since culture can be viewed as an abstract code for adaptation, providing unquestioned rules for understanding and living that have (or had) survival value for the group and its relationship to its members. At a more abstract level than is usually considered by family therapists, cultural values and basic premises can be used as stimuli for change rather than as impediments to it. As Milton Erickson (in Haley, 1973) has suggested throughout his work, the best mechanisms for change are the basic premises of the individuals and family members involved, and few things are as basic as culture.

The most readily utilized technique incorporating the cultural level is what Watzlawick, Weakland, and Fisch (1974) have described as "reframing"; this is reinterpretation

> to change the conceptual and/or emotional settings or viewpoint in relation
> to which a situation is experienced and to place it in another frame which
> fits the "facts" or the same concrete situation equally well or even better,
> and thereby, changes its entire meaning. (p. 94)

One useful technique for American psychotherapists is that of "reframing" traditional values and basic premises of family members within the context of contemporary American culture, so that individuals can retain their traditional values and be adaptive in contemporary American culture at the same time. The general "reframing" statement would be of the nature, "These new behaviors are appropriate in your traditional culture," so that values can be applied as a stimulus for behavior more adaptive to the contemporary cultural or subcultural basic premises when such intervention is considered.

An example can be found among the Navaho with obvious implications for change in psychotherapy. A basic cultural premise of the Navaho is the metastatement in *Blessingway,* one of the main oral texts of Navaho culture; it has as an implicit theme the message that "the only permanence is change," so "to be traditional [Navaho] is to believe in change." This can also be seen as the labeling of the new as "traditional" so that change is an attempt to stay the same. In their attempts to maintain these beliefs, Navahos have become more Western-appearing by adopting Western technologies (e.g., pick-up trucks). As a result, they are generally described as having become Westernized. However, as Farella (1980) notes, the Navaho have changed their technology and material culture to maintain their epistemology, so that by using Western goods, they are maintaining their Navaho culture.

A recurring clinical problem in my own experience, for which the traditional can be redefined as "contemporary" to solve dissonances, is one involving families from cultures (e.g., Syrian) that are traditionally characterized by male dominance and female submissiveness. Often, wives in these families were from more "Americanized" families than their husbands were. The wives perceived their husbands as having a constant need to dominate them and keep them submissive. Concurrently, the husbands stated that their wives disobeyed them just for the sake of defiance. They stated that "The way I was brought up was that a husband protects his wife and she obeys him," while the wives stated the same belief but said that their husbands were unreasonable.[2]

In an attempt to utilize traditional values with this type of family, I stated that one of the current problems in American society was the lack of traditional values, and that many Americans struggle to find basic values in which they can believe and that would provide them with rules for living. Both members of the couple were defined as having strong beliefs, the husband in the traditional Syrian culture that was so difficult to maintain in America, and the wife in her flexibility, the potentiality of which was found in her traditional culture, which made it possible for her to adapt so readily to contemporary American culture. Their problem was "reframed" in cultural terms. I stated that to my knowledge in contemporary American society, one sign of a truly self-assured male was that he generally was able to tolerate a complementary relationship with his wife. At the same time, I stated my belief that contemporary American women were not

[2]Sluzki (1979) notes a similar strain between generations in migrant families; the younger generation more readily adapts to the new culture, while the older maintains and attempts to recreate the traditional culture.

totally controlled by their husbands and that they could choose to agree or disagree with them. These ideas were discussed over five sessions along with a number of other issues and were followed by a decrease in the conflict.

I have seen an analogous problem in a number of Italian-American families, still living in Italian neighborhoods, in which the initial complaint was mutual dissatisfaction with the relationship. The wife in such a family would state that "I married my husband because I thought he was a typical, strong Italian man," and the husband would state that he chose his wife because of her traditional (submissive) values of obeying her husband. The behaviors that were found to be unpleasant to each spouse were relabeled as their mutual attempts to become part of contemporary American culture, and from this point more suitable decision making was negotiated over the next several sessions.

## CONCLUSION

"Normality" viewed within a cross-cultural perspective has a number of important implications for the clinician. When doing therapy with non-middle-class American families, there are several aspects of family therapy that are especially difficult for therapists to learn. Most importantly, there is no "cookbook." It is impossible to learn about cultural aspects of family functioning culture by culture, because there are too many cultures and too wide a variation within each for this to be a useful approach. However, if "culture" is understood as a group's basic premises and the behaviors based upon them, then in fact each family is a unique culture. Each family's interaction creates the context for individual family members' own unique solutions to universal problems, and its cultural context provides the broad outlines for that defined as normal.

Another common problem for clinicians centers around cross-cultural standards for "normal" relationships between males and females or between parents and children that are often dissonant with a therapist's own basic premises. This can vary between cultures and subcultures—for example, from equality and complementarity between the sexes to extreme dominant-submissive relationships. The therapist should inquire about the cultural premises of the family, and the degree to which these traditions are observed, if this is not obvious from the family's interaction as the members describe their lives together.

Working with non-middle-class American families forces therapists to confront their own premises about the normal. At the same time, cultural dissonances might interfere in the relationship between a family and a therapist if they are not discussed—for example, if the therapist is a woman meeting with a couple in whose traditional culture males are dominant. This does not mean that therapists must accept the family's values, but they must acknowledge them and work out mutually agreeable goals and rules for working together.

In a cross-cultural perspective, the goal of therapy should be altered to be "What is the most probable means of eliminating the structural dysfunction, especially concerning violations or confusions of hierarchies, to solve the core problem of dependence–autonomy using the traditional beliefs of family members as a means to change?" At times, the dissonances are at the level of belief between the family and its sociocultural context (e.g., beliefs about appropriate behavior in school). Successful intervention must be at this level and is obviously contingent on understanding the family culture. Consequently, a cross-cultural perspective suggests the necessity of viewing individuals and families within more and more inclusive systems, including those institutions and beliefs that are not commonly utilized by therapists such as mental health bureaucracies, extended kin groups, neighborhoods, and religious organizations; this necessity is both an essential aspect of the problem and a potential solution, so that therapy becomes even more complex, perhaps challenging therapists' basic premise that they can affect change. Interacting with families from other cultures, or at least admitting the possibility that normality can be different from that experienced in the therapists' own culture, forces therapists to confront their basic premises; this can often be a startling, upsetting process.

A cross-cultural approach to normality from a cybernetic perspective has important implications for change in psychotherapy only hinted at in this paper. It extends the boundaries of what Haley (1971) termed the "revolution in psychiatry" that redefined the locus of psychopathology as part of a family or as even more of the social system. In addition, these boundaries are, or should be, extended to another level of abstraction to include the basic cultural premises of family members, the family, and its social context. At the same time, this perspective strengthens the link (by culture) between the individual "personality" and the sociocultural context.

# REFERENCES

Bateson, G. *Steps to an ecology of mind.* New York: Ballantine, 1972.

Bott, E. *Family and social network.* London: Tavistock, 1957.

Bowen, M. A family concept of schizophrenia. In D. Jackson (Ed.), *The etiology of schizophrenia.* New York: Basic Books, 1960.

Bowlby, J. *Attachment and loss* (Vol. 1: *Attachment*). New York: Basic Books, 1969.

Cohen, R. Brittle marriage vs. a stable system. In P. Bohannan (Ed.), *Divorce and after.* New York: Doubleday, 1970.

Count, E. The biological basis of human sociality. *American Anthropologist,* 1958, *60,* 1049–1085.

Farella, J. Personal communication, 1980.

Ferreira, A. Family myth and homeostasis. *Archives of General Psychiatry,* 1958, *9,* 457–463.

Geertz, C. *Interpretation of cultures.* New York: Basic Books, 1973.

Goldschmidt, W. Absent eyes and idle hands: Socialization for low affect among the Sebei. *Ethos,* 1975, *3,* 157–164.

Haley, J. *Strategies of psychotherapy.* New York: Grune & Stratton, 1963.

Haley, J. Family therapy: A radical change. In J. Haley (Ed.), *Changing families.* New York: Grune & Stratton, 1971.

Haley, J. Strategic therapy when a child is presented as the problem. *Journal of Child Psychiatry,* 1973, *12,* 649–659. (a)

Haley, J. *Uncommon therapy: The psychiatric techniques of Milton H. Erickson.* New York: Norton, 1973. (b)

Haley, J. *Problem-solving therapy.* San Francisco: Jossey-Bass, 1976.

Hoffman, L. Deviation-amplifying processes in natural groups. In J. Haley (Ed.), *Changing families.* New York: Grune & Stratton, 1971.

Jackson, D. The study of the family. In N. Ackerman (Ed.), *Family process.* New York: Basic Books, 1970.

Kluckhohn, F. Variations in the basic values of family systems. *Social Casework.* 1958, *39,* 63–72.

Kuhn, T. *The structure of scientific revolutions.* Chicago: University of Chicago Press, 1962.

Levine, R. Patterns of personality in Africa. *Ethos,* 1973, *1,* 123–152.

Levy, R. I. *Tahitians.* Chicago: University of Chicago Press, 1973.

Malinowski, B. *Sex and repression in savage society.* London: Routledge & Kegan Paul, 1927.

Maruyama, M. The second cybernetics: Deviation-amplifying mutual causal processes. *American Scientist,* 1963, *51,* 164–179.

Mead, M., & Bateson, G. *Balinese character.* New York: New York Academy of Sciences, 1942.

Minuchin, S. *Families and family therapy.* Cambridge: Harvard University Press, 1974.

Napier, A. The marriage of families: Cross-generational complementarity. *Family Process,* 1971, *10,* 373–396.

Parsons, A. *Belief, magic, and anomie.* New York: Free Press, 1969.

Powers, W. *Behavior: The control of perceptions.* Chicago: Aldine, 1973.

Radcliffe-Brown, A. Introduction. In A. R. Radcliffe-Brown & D. Ford (Eds.), *African systems of kinship and marriage.* London: Oxford University Press, 1950.

Roberts, J. Three Navajo households. In *Peabody Museum of American Archeology and Ethnography.* Cambridge: Harvard University Press, 1951.

Rosenblueth, A., Weiner, N., & Bigelow, J. Behavior, purpose, and teleology. *Philosophy of Science,* 1943, *10,* 18–24.

Schwartzman, J. The individual, incest and exogamy. *Psychiatry,* 1974, *37,* 171–180.

Simon, H. *The sciences of the artificial.* Cambridge: MIT Press, 1969.

Sluzki, C. Migration and family conflict. *Family Process,* 1979, *18,* 379–390.

Sluzki, C., & Veron, E. The double-bind as a universal pathogenic situation. *Family Process,* 1971, *10,* 397–410.

Spiegel, J. *Transactions: The interplay between individual, family and society.* Science House, 1971.

Spiro, M. Is the family universal? *American Anthropologist,* 1954, *56,* 839–846.

Van Gennep, A. *The rites of passage.* Chicago: University of Chicago Press, 1970.

Vogel, E., & Bell, N. The emotionally disturbed child as family scape goat. In N. Bell & E. Vogel (Eds.), *A modern introduction to the family.* New York: Free Press, 1968.

Watzlawick, P., Weakland, J., & Fisch, R. *Change.* New York: Norton, 1974.

Watzlawick, P., Beavin, J., & Jackson, D. *Pragmatics of human communication.* New York: Norton, 1967.

Weakland, J. The double-bind hypothesis of schizophrenia and three-party interaction. In D. Jackson (Ed.), *The etiology of schizophrenia.* New York: Basic Books, 1960.

Weakland, J. The double-bind theory by self-reflexive hindsight. *Family Process,* 1974, *13,* 269–271.

Werner, H. *Comparative psychology of mental development.* (Rev. ed.). New York: International Universities Press, 1957.

Witkin, H. A., Dyk, R. B., Paterson, H. F., Goodenough, D. E., & Karp, S. A. *Psychological differentiation: Studies of development.* New York: Wiley, 1962.

Young, M., & Wilmott, P. *Family and kinship in East London.* Baltimore: Penguin, 1962.

# 16

# NORMAL FAMILIES:
# AN ETHNIC PERSPECTIVE

## MONICA MCGOLDRICK

Human behavior results from the interplay of intrapsychic, interpersonal, familial, socioeconomic, and cultural forces. Of these, the mental health field has paid greatest attention to the intrapsychic influences—the study of factors within the personality that shape life experiences and behavior. The study of cultural influences on the emotional functioning of human beings has been left primarily to anthropologists. And even they have preferred to explore these influences in distant and fragile non-Western cultures, rather than exploring the great ethnic diversity among Americans of assumptions about illness and health, normality, and pathology.

Greeley, commenting on this tendency of our culture, has said:

> I suspect that the historians of the future will be astonished that American sociologists, the product of the gathering of the nations, could stand in the midst of such an astonishing social phenomenon and take it so much for granted that they would not bother to study it. They will find it especially astonishing in light of the fact that ethnic differences, even in the second half of the 20th century, proved far more important than differences in philosophy or economic system. Men who would not die for a premise or a dogma or a division of labor would more or less cheerfully die for a difference rooted in ethnic origins. (Greeley, 1969, p. 5)

## ETHNICITY AND MENTAL HEALTH

When mental health professionals have considered culture, they, too, have been more absorbed in making international cross-cultural comparisons than in studying the ethnic groups in our own culture (Carpenter & Strauss,

Monica McGoldrick. Family Training, College of Medicine and Dentistry of New Jersey–Rutgers Medical School, Community Mental Health Center, Piscataway, New Jersey, and Faculty, Family Institute of Westchester.

1974; Giordano & Giordano, 1977; Kiev, 1972). Only recently are we beginning to consider ethnic differences when developing therapeutic models (McGoldrick, Giordano, & Pearce, in press; Sluzki & Schnitman, in press). (The National Institute of Mental Health has, for instance, established a task force on ethnic and minority groups.) Ethnicity is a relatively new concept. The term refers to characteristics of historically unique subgroups, each of which possesses an autonomous structure within the larger culture. Ethnicity has been defined as a sense of "commonality or community derived from networks of family experiences" (Feinstein, 1974). It is a fundamental determinant of values, perceptions, needs, modes of expression, behavior, and identity. This definition implicitly includes all ethnic and racial groups. From a clinical point of view, however, ethnicity is more than race, religion, and national or geographical origin. (This is not to minimize the significant aspects of race or the special problems of racism.) It involves conscious and unconscious processes that fulfill a deep psychological need for identity and a sense of historical continuity. It is transmitted by an emotional language within the family and reinforced by the surrounding community (Giordano & Giordano, 1977). It is a profound and abiding aspect of human experience.

Ethnicity is a complex and rapidly changing phenomenon in American society. (Unfortunately, we have a difficult time keeping track of this complex factor, since even the United States Census records include ethnic identification only for foreign-born immigrants and their children. Later generations are not designated ethnically.) Ethnic differences obviously diminish through intermarriage and common experiences in this culture. Some values and traditions prove maladaptive, are recognized as such, and are set aside, usually with great difficulty. However, there is increasing evidence that some ethnic values are retained for many generations after immigration (Greeley, 1969, 1978), and play a significant role in family life and personal development (Lieberman, 1974).

The United States has had the greatest ethnic diversity of any nation in history, but the fact that this country is a nation of immigrants has actually hindered Americans' ability to tolerate differences. We have talked about the melting pot and blinded ourselves to its inherent diversity. The desire to obscure cultural variations and develop homogeneous "norms" dominates our culture. This has led to stress and conflict which is always most evident in the cultural group with the least "seniority."

Ethnicity is deeply tied to the family through which it is transmittted. Billingsley has discussed the community and family strengths that have enabled black people to survive in a hostile environment for more than 300 years. He describes the link between ethnicity and family:

> Ethnicity and family life are two concepts which . . . go hand in hand. They are so intertwined that it is very difficult indeed to observe the one or even to reflect it seriously without coming to grips with the other. So when we think of Italians and certain other Southern Europeans, we think of

large families; we think of the English and certain Northern Europeans in compact nuclear families. When we think of Black families we think of strong extended families, and when we think of Chinese families[1] we must encompass aggregations so large that they often encompass whole communities. (Billingsley, 1976, p. 13)

Common sense tells us that human beings experience life on the basis of their own cultural values and assumptions, most of which are outside their awareness. Unless confronted by others whose values differ from our own, we inevitably see the world through our own "cultural filters," often persisting in established views despite clear information to the contrary (Watzlawick, 1976).

It seems natural that an interest in families should lead to an interest in ethnicity, and vice versa, yet this area has been ignored in clinical teaching and research. Just as there is a paucity of material on the impact of ethnicity in individual psychotherapy, very little has appeared in the family therapy literature on the subject. In addition to the comparative value analysis by Spiegel and Papajohn (Spiegel, 1971; Papajohn & Spiegel, 1975) a few articles have appeared on black Americans (Boyd, 1980; Foley, 1975; McAdoo, 1977), Jewish Americans (Zuk, 1978), Irish-Americans (McGoldrick & Pearce, 1981), and Slovak-Americans (Stein, 1978). There are also a few collections in the sociological literature (Glazer & Moynihan, 1975; Mindel & Halberstein, 1976), but, unfortunately, even these sources rarely become part of the knowledge base of family clinicians.

While a few family therapists have recognized the importance of culture, the major models of family therapy make little reference to ethnic differences in the application of their methods. Minuchin, Montalvo, and their co-workers focused on the multiproblem families and developed specific techniques to deal with poor black and Hispanic families (Minuchin, Montalvo, Guerney, Rosman, & Schumer, 1967). But the other major family models (Bowen systems, strategic, communications), while emphasizing the importance of the family context, do not make explicit reference to ethnic differences.

Very few family training programs integrate material on ethnic differences in any systematic way. The most prominent exception is the pioneering work of Spiegel in viewing families in their ethnic context.[2] Spiegel and Papajohn analyzed the cultural values of Mexican-Americans, Puerto Ricans, Greek-Americans, and Italian-Americans in their book *Transactions in Families*

---

[1]In fact, the Chinese consider the family to include all the generations of the family from the beginning of time into the distant future (Shon & Ja, in press).

[2]Spiegel conducts a program in ethnicity training at Cambridge City Hospital in Boston. Recently a few other training programs, including the Family Practice Residency at the University of California in San Francisco and the Psychiatry Residency at Bronx Psychiatric Hospital, have also started to develop seminars on ethnocultural differences.

(1975). Their schema, based on Kluckhohn's work on value orientations (Kluckhohn & Strodtbeck, 1961), provides a comprehensive framework for considering the therapeutic problems of families at various stages of acculturation.

There has been very little systematic integration of material on ethnicity in the training of any mental health professionals (Giordano & Giordano, 1977; Pinto, 1976; Sanua, 1975). In general, the entire education of most mental health professionals contains hardly a reference to ethnicity. Often clinics established to serve ethnic populations have no one on their staff who speaks the client group's native language. Foreign psychiatric residents are trained to do therapy on the most subtle aspects of psychosocial adjustment in our culture without any mention being made of major experiential gaps between themselves and their patients.


## UNDERSTANDING HELP SEEKING IN ITS ETHNIC CONTEXT

Defining "normal" is an extremely difficult task. "Normality" is at best only an approximation of what is acceptable in a given social and historical context. One may err not only by labeling normal behavior of a given ethnic group as "pathology," but by labeling dysfunctional behavior for that group as "normal."

Problems (whether physical or mental) can be neither diagnosed nor treated without some understanding of the frame of reference, the norms of the person seeking help. As Kleinman, a prominent physician–researcher, has observed:

> How we communicate about our health problems, the manner in which we present our symptoms, when and to whom we go for care, how long we remain in care, and how we evaluate that care are all affected by cultural beliefs. Illness behavior is a normative experience governed by cultural rules; we learn "approved" ways of being ill. . . . And doctors' explanations and activities, as those of their patients, are culture-specific. (Kleinman, Eisenberg, & Good, 1978, p. 252)

Culture may even determine whether a symptom is labeled a problem. For example, the absence of stuttering among certain groups of American Indians is associated with their less stringent demands for fluent speech (Eisenberg, 1977). In fact, their language has no word for stuttering. Thus, it appears that the diagnosis may help to create the problem.

Symptoms differ so much among ethnic groups that it brings into question the usefulness of the present diagnostic nomenclature (Fantl & Shiro, 1959; Opler & Singer, 1956; Singer & Opler, 1956).

In addition, patients' "illness" (the experience of being ill) is very different from the course of their "disease" (a physically identifiable dysfunction) (Stoeckle, Zola, & Davidson, 1964) and is strongly influenced by cultural beliefs. Patients vary markedly in their use of the health care system. Although it is estimated that more than 90% of the population experience some physical symptoms of illness at any given time, the vast majority (70% to 80%) of those believing themselves ill manage their problems outside the formal health care system (Zola, 1972). Of those who do seek professional attention, only about 50% are found to have any diagnosable disease (Kleinman et al., 1978).

Until now, the medical model, with its emphasis on "diagnosing" and "curing" disease, has been the major influence on the psychotherapeutic system. This leads to a systematic inattention to "illness"—that is, to the patient's or family's perception of what is wrong, and is partly responsible for noncompliance, dissatisfaction with clinical care, and treatment failure.

While it makes sense to use a systemic, contextual model of helping, taking such a view has been very difficult. The subject of ethnicity often evokes deep feelings, and discussion frequently becomes polarized or judgmental. According to Greeley, using presumed common origin to define "we" and "they" seems to touch on something basic and primordial in the human psyche (Greeley, 1969).

Indeed, there is a common tendency for human beings to fear, and therefore to reject, that which they cannot understand. The ancient Greeks called all non-Greeks "barbarians," considering them to be without culture. And the Russian word for a German is "nemetz," which means "one who is mute"; this reflects the belief that those who cannot be understood cannot speak at all. We tend to label that which is different as "bad" or "crazy." Thus, in more modern usage, the German may label the Italian "hysterical," while the Italian may label the German "obsessive–compulsive."

It is hard for therapists to remain open to this wide range of cultural possibilities. We all seem to find ambiguity threatening and to close down emotionally when confronted with too much of it. Understanding our own ethnic biases is the best insurance against such rigidity. Yet this insight is hard to gain, since it requires stepping beyond our belief systems. The simple fact is that not all cultures place great value on pursuing insight or truth, "getting ahead," or sharing problems and feelings. By exploring our ethnic assumptions, we are led to question our primary therapeutic techniques. It is no wonder we are threatened.

But we need to learn how different the world is from our assumptions about it. For example, seeking help depends a great deal on one's attitude toward the "helper." Italians tend to rely primarily on the family and to turn to an outsider for help only as a last resort (Gambino, 1974; Rotuno & McGoldrick, in press; Zborowski, 1969; Zola, 1966). Black Americans have long mistrusted the help they can receive from traditional middle-class institutions (Hines & Boyd, in press; McAdoo, 1977). Puerto Ricans (Preto, in press) and Chinese (Kleinman, 1975) are likely to somatize when they are under stress and may seek medical rather than mental health services. Norwegians, too, often convert emotional tensions into physical symptoms, which are more acceptable in their culture. As a result, Norwegians are more likely to seek out the help of a surgeon than a psychotherapist (Midelfort & Midelfort, in press). Likewise, Iranians often view medication and vitamins as a necessary part of treating symptoms, regardless of their origin (Jalali, in press). Thus, a substantial minority of potential patients experience troubles and cures somatically, and strongly doubt the value of psychotherapy.

Almost all of us have multiple belief systems to which we turn when in need of help. We use not only the official medical or psychotherapeutic system, but also turn to religion, self-help groups, alcohol, yoga, chiropractors, and so on. We utilize remedies our mothers taught us and those suggested by our friends. Many factors influence our preferred reliance on one system or another at any given time.

While there is little research on the attitudes of different ethnic groups toward family therapy, studies of ethnic differences in response to physical illness have clear implications for family therapy practice (Sanua, 1960; Zborowski, 1969; Zola, 1966).

In Zborowski's classic study (1969) of physically ill Jewish, Italian, Irish, and white Anglo-Saxon Protestant (WASP) patients, the Jewish and Italian patients tended to complain about their pain, while the Irish and WASPs did not. When it came to describing their pain experience, the WASPs and Jews were accurate, while the Irish and Italians were conspicuously inaccurate. The Italian patients dramatized their pain, and the Irish blocked or denied theirs. When the researchers looked at patients' expected solutions, the results again showed striking differences. The Italians worried about the effects of their pain on their immediate situation (work, finances, family), but once the pain was relieved, they easily forgot their suffering. The Italians wanted an immediate remedy to stop the pain, while the Jewish patients found this unacceptable. They feared anything, such as a pill that stopped the pain immediately, because they felt it would not deal with the real source of their problem. They also worried about harmful, long-range effects of drugs on their general health. Instead, they sought a full explanation of the meaning of their pain and of its relief. The Irish patients did not expect a cure for their ailments at all. They were fatalistic and usually did not complain of, or even mention, their pain. Rather, they tended to view pain as the result of their own sinfulness and held themselves responsible. WASP patients, on the other hand, were optimistic, future-oriented, and confident in the ability of science to cure disease. Operating on the "work ethic," they also sought control over their pain by their own efforts.

Emotional expressiveness can lead to problems in American culture, in general, which tends to be less expressive than many minority groups within it. "Americanized" medical personnel in Zborowski's study (1969) distrusted the uninhibited display of suffering exhibited by Jewish and Italian patients, and they saw these patients' reactions as exaggerated. Another researcher found that doctors frequently labeled their Italian patients as having "psychiatric problems," although there was no evidence that psychosocial problems occurred more frequently among them (Zola, 1963). A group whose characteristic response to illness is too different from the dominant culture is likely to be labeled "abnormal." One would suppose that Jewish and Italian medical staff would also have difficulty understanding the silence of Irish and WASP patients.

Differences in style of interaction may be misinterpreted. A high level of interaction is expected in Jewish, Italian, and Greek families. But WASPs, Irish, and Scandinavian families have much less intense interactions and are more likely to deal with problems by distancing. Intermarriage creates obvious difficulties. Therapeutic problems may develop when a therapist from an ethnic group that values distance is confronted by a family with a high level of intense interaction. The therapist may get confused, see the intensity as a problem, and try inappropriately to control it. On the other hand, a therapist from an intensely interacting culture may try to increase the emotional involvement of a family from a reserved culture and may be frustrated by their lack of response.

Therapists with the same background as their clients may also have difficulties and "blind spots." For example, an Italian therapist may be too reluctant to intrude on Italian family "secrets," knowing how strong their family loyalties are. Or an Irish therapist may be hesitant to question an Irish family about issues that are not "proper," because the therapist shares the family's inhibitions and sees their reticence as "normal."

## PROBLEMS WITH AN ETHNIC PERSPECTIVE

Some potential negative consequences of emphasizing ethnicity must also be recognized. Overly strict adherence to a particular way of doing things, under the supposition that the custom has a universal value, can make an ethnic group resist change and thereby impede its own development. In fact, values that were functional in another place and time often become dysfunctional when translated into modern America. Ethnocentrism, clannishness, prejudice, fear, and distrust of outsiders can prevent cooperation, reinforce exclusivity, and deepen intergroup conflicts (Giordano & Giordano, 1977; Kolm, 1973). However, the solution to these problems lies not in eradicating cultural differences but in developing their potential as a source of cultural enrichment.

Every culture generates characteristic problems for itself. These problems are often consequences of cultural traits that are conspicuous strengths in other contexts. For example, WASP optimism leads to confidence and flexibility in taking initiative, an obvious strength when there are opportunities for initiative. But the one-sided preference for cheerfulness also leads to the inability to cope with tragedy or engage in mourning (Magill & Pearce, in press). Historically, WASPs have perhaps had less misfortune than most other peoples. But optimism becomes a vulnerability when they must contend with tragedy. They have few philosophical or expressive ways to deal with situations in which optimism, rationality, and belief in the efficacy of individuality are insufficient. The WASP strengths of independence and individual initiative work weH in some situations, but WASPs may feel lost when dependence on the group is the only way to ensure survival.

Strengthening the sense of positive cultural identity is often an important aspect of therapy. This may require resolving conflicts within the family, between the family and the community, or in the wider context in which the family is imbedded. Families may at times use their ethnic customs or religious values selectively to justify an emotional position within the family or against outsiders (Friedman, 1980). Family members may need coaching to sort out deeply held convictions from values asserted for emotional reasons.

Describing ethnic patterns necessitates using cultural stereotypes or simplified pictures of the culture. There are obvious disadvantages to this approach, and we view these paradigms only as frameworks within which to expand clinical sensitivity and effectiveness. We use our paradigms not as "truths," but rather as maps, which, while they cover only limited aspects of the terrain, may nevertheless provide guidelines to an explorer seeking a path. By no means do we wish to add to any tendency toward negative labeling or stereotyping of people. As Zola has aptly stated, "The danger of training anyone in the details of a particular ethnic group is that it will ultimately squeeze people into unreal categories, and reify their culture as we have rigidified diagnoses" (Zola, 1979, p. 76).

There are those who argue that such generalizations do more harm than good (Stein, 1979). In our view, developing a relatively simple paradigm is the only possible and realistic way to begin expanding one's knowledge. We think the solution to the problem lies in maintaining openness to new experience once one has a framework, rather than in avoiding a framework because it is not altogether accurate or complete. We believe that negative stereotyping is less of a risk than is trivializing or ignoring a subject.

As long as illness is seen as an individual problem and variability as an individual matter, clinicians will seek individual solutions. Appreciation of cultural variability leads to a radically new conceptual model of clinical intervention. This model requires clinicians to struggle consciously with their own subjectivity and to recognize the limitations of any belief system in their work. We do not mean to imply that culture is the only, or even the most important, contextual factor to be considered in assessing problems and behavior. Social class and economic factors are also extremely important. In addition, the impact of gender on personality (Silverstein, 1981), development (Carter & McGoldrick, 1980; Gluck, Dannefer, & Milea, 1980), and illness behavior (Mechanic, 1978), though largely ignored until recently, cannot be overestimated.

It would require many volumes to consider any single ethnic group in depth. Most groups are themselves combinations of a multitude of cultural groups. Puerto Rican culture, for example, is a product of many diverse influences, including Spanish, African, and Caribbean Indian. Shon (1979) has suggested that the differences among Asian cultures are even greater than those among all the more familiar European cultures.

Many factors influence the extent to which traditional ethnic patterns will surface in any particular family:

1. The reasons for immigration—what the family was seeking and what it was leaving behind (religious or political persecution, poverty, wish for adventure, etc.).

2. The length of time since immigration and the impact of generational acculturation conflicts on the family.

3. The family's place of residence—whether or not the family lives or has lived in an ethnic neighborhood.

4. The order of migration—whether one family member migrated alone or whether a large portion of the family, community, or nation came together.

5. The socioeconomic status, education, and upward mobility of family members.

6. The political and religious ties to the ethnic group.

7. The languages spoken by family members.

8. The extent of family intermarriage with or connection to other ethnic groups.

9. The family members' attitudes toward the ethnic group and its values.

All families in this country have experienced the complex stresses of immigration and migration; these may be "buried" or forgotten, but they subtly continue to influence a family's outlook. Also, under the pressure of accommodating to the new situation, many immigrant groups have been forced to abandon much of their ethnic heritage (Greeley, 1979; Hines & Boyd, in press), and thus have lost a part of their identity. The effects of this cutting off on the family may be all the more powerful for being hidden.

If the first generation is older at the time of immigration, or lives in an ethnic neighborhood in this country, its conflicts of acculturation may be postponed. The next generation, particularly in adolescence, is likely to reject the "ethnic" values of their parents and to strive to become "American-ized" (Sluzki, 1979). The third or fourth generations are usually freer to reclaim aspects of their identities that were sacrificed in the previous genera-tions because of the need to assimilate. To understand ethnic norms, one must maintain a developmental perspective on both variations in family life cycle patterns and the impact that immigration has on families over succeeding generations (Carter & McGoldrick, 1980; Falicov, 1980; Sluzki, 1979).

The extensive geographical and class mobility in American culture, while often cutting individuals off from their ethnic heritage, increases their contact with different ethnic groups. The high rate of interethnic marriage means that many Americans will learn about ethnic differences from marriage partners. But, at best, most Americans probably come to understand well only three or four groups in the course of a lifetime. Obviously, no therapist can become an expert on all ethnic groups. Again, what is essential for clinicians is to develop an attitude of openness to cultural variability and to the relativity of their own values.

The following pages highlight some of the differences in family patterns and typical attitudes toward therapy found in several of America's largest ethnic groups. The reader is reminded that the suggestions are meant only as guidelines and not as "truths" about any particular group.

## JEWISH FAMILIES

There are about 5.5 million Jews living in the United States (half of the world's Jewish population). Of these, 35% live in New York City, and another 45% live in nine other major American cities (Goren, 1980). The following comments refer primarily to American Jews of East European background, the largest Jewish group in this country. Obviously German Jews, Sephardic Jews, and other Jewish groups have different characteristics, influenced by the countries in which Jews lived for centuries before migrating to the United States.

Jewish families have a very strong family orientation and will accept a family definition of their problems more readily than many other groups. Marriage and children play a central role in Jewish family life. As Zborowski and Herzog (1952) have stated in their classic study of East European Jews:

> Marriage is both the climax and the threshold. From birth on, every step is directed with an eye to the "Khupa" (marriage canopy), and if that goal is missed, life itself seems to be lost. Once attained, however, marriage is merely the background for the great goal, the great achievement, the great gratification: children. (p. 290)

Parents in Jewish families tend to have democratic relationships with their children (Zuk, 1978) and less rigid generational boundaries than most other groups (Herz & Rosen, in press). They place a high value on verbal explanations and reasoning in child rearing. For a non-Jewish therapist, the parents' desire to reason out issues may seem unnecessary, but within a

Jewish context is is extremely important. Parents take great pride in their children's verbal skill, intelligence, and ability to think things out logically.

Jewish families are more likely than all other ethnic groups to seek and be receptive to psychotherapy in almost any form. They value talk, insight, and the recognition of complex levels of meaning. They value the gaining of wisdom, and have a long tradition of consulting with a wise person, or several wise people, while always remaining the final judge of the opinions they hear. This contrasts markedly with, for example, the Irish, for whom the priest is always the final judge. The development of psychotherapy has been strongly influenced by these Jewish values. The first problem in therapy may come when the patient questions the therapist's credentials. Although the therapist may perceive this as confrontation or criticism, it may instead reflect the high value Jews place on education and success, as well as their need to be sure they are receiving the best care.

Jewish verbal skill and willingness to talk about troubles and feelings are important assets, but can also lead to problems (Herz & Rosen, in press; Zuk, 1978). Families may get so preoccupied with the need to analyze and understand their experience that at times they become immobilized. The Jewish ability to verbalize thoughts and feelings may also lead the therapist to presume that they possess a greater confidence and sophistication than they really experience. Jewish patients frequently wish to appear intellectual and psychologically aware, and this may make their articulation a difficulty as well as a strength in therapy. The need to appear insightful, interesting, and successful, can, in the extreme, make them unable to experience anything without being concerned with what they are accomplishing. The solutions offered by traditional therapy at times compound these problems. In such situations, the therapist needs to find such ways around the tendency to talk or analyze, as structural techniques (Aponte, 1981; Minuchin, 1974) or those of strategic therapy (Selvini Palazzoli, Boscolo, Cecchin, & Prata, 1978; Watzlawick, Weakland, & Fisch, 1974; Weakland, Watzlawick, & Fisch, 1974). However, therapists should be warned against applying solutions that might seem simplistic. Jewish clients will generally prefer more complex, sophisticated interventions. Behavior modification techniques, for example, might be very useful, but may be viewed as superficial, covering up the "real" problem, which, they fear, will resurface elsewhere.

The Jewish tradition of valuing education and learning has a history dating back many centuries and has produced an unprecedented culture in artistic and intellectual achievements. Jews lived so often in situations of oppression that they naturally came to value those strengths that could not be taken from them but that could be transferred from one context to another, if they were forced to flee from their homes.

Jewish families generally show much more concern for their children's emotional, intellectual, and physical well-being throughout all stages of their development than do other groups. The non-Jewish therapist may fail to appreciate the meaning of Jewish concern for children's success and upward mobility (Sanua, 1967; Strodtbeck, 1957). Raising successful children is a major responsibility of the parents, particularly the mother. Underachievement or more serious problems are often felt to reflect not only on the family, but also on the ethnic group as a whole. Parents are expected to make great sacrifices for their children, and when children grow up they are expected to repay their parents in "naches," a special pleasure one gets only from the success and happiness of one's children. Non-Jewish therapists may be puzzled by the extent of parental upset when their children do not provide them with such rewards. An obvious contrasting value can be seen in WASPs, who raise their children to be independent and to leave home. While WASPs expect their children to be productive and a credit to the family, they do not expect to experience personal pleasure in their children's accomplishments.

Jewish mothers, at times a harshly stereotyped group, reflect many positive aspects of Jewish culture. Mothers have been the ones primarily responsible for the education and development of children. Their success in this realm is overwhelming, as generations of successful Jewish doctors, lawyers, artists, businessmen, and other professionals attest. But until recently they were unable to fulfill their dreams for themselves directly. Their intensity was turned primarily toward their children. The recent opportunities for women to succeed have offered a chance for Jewish women, who had already internalized the values of success and education, to flourish in their own right. Their success reveals the potential that until now has been invested in their children, especially their male children.

Jewish families show a strong concern for the ebb and flow of life at all stages. This is indicated by the importance they place on life cycle rituals, which reflects their awareness of the complexity of the transitions at all phases of life. For example, Jewish mourning rituals have several phases. The burial occurs as soon as possible after the death, followed by a week of "sitting shiva," when friends and extended family come to share in the mourning. After a year has passed, family members again gather for the "unveiling," which marks the end of the mourning period, although yearly prayers are still said after this. The emphasis placed on the bar mitzvah, which marks the transition of children into adulthood, reflects the value of the transition to serious adult learning and work experiences in Jewish culture. It is important for the therapist to recognize the underlying power of these transitions for Jewish families, and to help them to refocus their energies on the important underlying values if they get stuck on the more superficial aspects of the rituals (Friedman, 1980).

Another issue that may be particularly misunderstood by non-Jewish therapists is the meaning of suffering in Jewish families. Suffering is viewed as a form of work, even a magical way to deal with adversity. It is a part of their heritage, to be experienced and shared rather than overcome. This attitude contrasts sharply with that of the Irish, who believe they should suffer alone and in silence, and that of WASPs, who believe suffering is to be overcome by personal fortitude, hard work, and good intentions.

Conflicts and hostility are generally expressed directly in Jewish families. In fact, a therapist from a more restrained culture (e.g., WASP, Irish, Scandinavian) may be uncomfortable with the intensity of Jewish criticism and verbal aggression (Herz & Rosen, in press). Conflicts or cutoffs with the extended family often occur over money or loyalty and may at times be extremely bitter. In a fair number of families, a child's marriage to a non-Jew can also precipitate a cutoff. Preservation of the Jewish heritage (not necessarily religious practices) is crucial to their sense of identity. Intermarriage, which occurs frequently, especially among Jewish males, creates a great sadness and pain for parents. There is considerable pressure for Jews to identify with the group, and if a family member rejects his or her cultural background, it may be a serious issue for others in the family. These problems are naturally more prominent in the Northeast than elsewhere in the United States, where the percentage of Jews is much smaller and the patterns less pronounced (Sanua, 1978).

Jewish families have a number of strengths that are important in therapy. One is their humor—their ability to make fun of their own situation—which offers a release and perspective on themselves and their foibles. Generally, they also have an openness to new ideas and new ways (they are foremost among American ethnic groups in their willingness to explore new ideas). Further strengths are their belief in philanthropy and good works for the benefit of others, and their esteem for family and extended family relationships. While Jews may at times be caught up in deeply ambivalent attitudes about their own ethnicity, their cultural ties are a profound part of their heritage and their identity, perhaps more so than for other groups. This may be because of their 4000-year history of living as foreigners in other cultures, always under the threat of expulsion or persecution. Bringing them back in touch with their cultural roots may be a particularly rich experience for them.

## IRISH-AMERICAN FAMILIES

These comments refer primarily to the almost 15 million Americans of Irish-Catholic background, many of whose families have by now been in this country for four or five generations. The culture of this group has remained relatively homogeneous over almost 2000 years. Irish Catholics began to migrate here in large numbers in the 1840s, primarily because of the potato famines and oppressive conditions in Ireland. Irish Protestants, who are a separate group, have been migrating here since before the American Revolution. They do not think of themselves as Irish in any meaningful sense, have the lowest rate of endogamous marriage of any American ethnic group, and have virtually lost their sense of ethnicity (Fallows, 1979).

The Irish tend to assume that anything that goes wrong is the result of their sins. Their basic belief is that problems are private matters between individuals and God. They are, therefore, unlikely to seek or expect help for their problems (McGoldrick, in press-b; McGoldrick & Pearce, 1981; Sanua, 1960; Zborowski, 1969; Zola, 1966). If they do seek help, the Irish are apt to view therapy as similar to Catholic confession—an occasion in which they tell their "sins" and receive a "penance." They are embarrassed to have to come to therapy, and usually only do so at the suggestion of a third party: for example, a school, a hospital, or a court.

While the Irish rarely seek help for neurotic disorders, they have extremely high rates of psychosis and addiction, primarily alcoholism (Malzberg, 1963; McGoldrick, in press-b; McGoldrick & Pearce, 1981; Murphy, 1975; Rabkin & Struening, 1976; Roberts & Myers, 1954). In contrast, Jews, who value therapy as a "solution" to personal problems, are overrepresented in "neurotic disorders" and underrepresented in hospital admissions for all psychoses and addictive disorders (Malzberg, 1973; Rabkin & Struening, 1976; Rinder, 1963; Roberts & Myers, 1954).

While in other areas the Irish have, perhaps, the most highly developed skill with words of any culture, they may be at a loss to describe their own inner feelings, whether of love, sadness, or anger. They differ markedly in this respect from Jews, who enjoy and find meaning in giving expression to all their experiences. Language and poetry have always been highly valued by the Irish and closely associated with their love of dreaming. Perhaps it is no wonder that they placed so much emphasis on fantasy. For many centuries the Irish existed under wretched circumstances, and they used their words to enrich a dismal reality. The poet was always the most highly valued member of their culture, and even today writers are the only members of Irish society exempted from taxes.

Humor is the greatest resource of the Irish for dealing with life's problems, and wit and satire have long been their most powerful means of attack. Hostility and resentments could (and still can) only be dealt with indirectly in the family, through sarcasm or innuendo. As a result, feelings have often built up until finally family members silently cut one another off. Hostility was (and is) only permitted against the outgroup and then only for a just and moral cause, such as religion or politics. These values create many difficulties for the therapist trying to understand Irish family patterns. As is reflected in the mystifying character of much Irish literature, the most important things are usually left unspoken or referred to only by allusion. Within the family, feelings are often so hidden that it is hard for anyone to know exactly what is going on.

The Irish have been shown to have a much greater tolerance for nonrealistic thinking than other groups do (Wylan & Mintz, 1976). In contrast to WASPs and Jews, for example, who value the pursuit of truth, clarification of feelings does not necessarily make the Irish feel better. Thus, therapy aimed at opening up family feelings will often be unsuccessful. As a general rule, structured therapy, focused specifically on the presenting problem, will be the least threatening and most helpful to Irish clients. Suggestions for opening communication that also preserve the bounds of individual privacy, such as Bowen therapy, will be preferable to therapy that brings the entire family drama into the therapy session. The strategic techniques of the Palo Alto and the Milan groups would also be helpful, since they emphasize change without forcing clients to spell out all their feelings or make changes in front of the therapist.

Characteristically, the Irish mother has played a strong central role in the family. She has been seen as morally superior to her husband, traditionally a more shadowy figure, who has generally found his companionship in the pub. She ran things in the home and socialized through the Church. Children were raised to be respectful and well-behaved. Discipline was traditionally strict and enforced with threats such as: "It's a mortal sin; you'll go to hell." Families do not praise their children for fear of giving them a "swelled head." It is considered important to keep up appearances and not to "make a scene."

Church authority was the major unifier for the Irish, to such an extent that the Church came before the family (Italians have had the opposite priorities). Irish Catholics have traditionally viewed most things moralistically, following the rules of the Church without question. This, of course has changed in recent years (Wills, 1971), but the underlying rigidity often remains. It is important in working with the Irish to understand how they feel about religion, since the values of the Church often have strong bearing on their problems. Even those who have left the Church may have intense feelings about religious issues.

In contrast to those of Jewish, Italian, black, and other American ethnic groups, extended family relationships among the Irish are often not close. Families may get together for "duty visits" on holidays and act jovial and "clannish," but family members do not rely on one another as a source of support. The sense of emotional isolation in Irish relationships is frequently a factor in symptom development and has important implications for therapy. For example, while large family sessions that draw on the resources of the whole family may be supportive for some groups, it is usually inadvisable for the Irish, as it raises anxiety to an unhelpful point. It is often more fruitful to meet with smaller subgroups of the family, at least in the initial stages of opening up family communication.

Trying to talk the Irish out of their need to suffer is a futile effort. Unlike Jews, for whom the very experience of sharing suffering is meaningful, the Irish believe they must suffer alone. Certain strategies may help them limit their guilt and suffering, such as prescribing it within restricted time intervals (see McGoldrick, in press-a; McGoldrick & Pearce, 1981). But they are unlikely to give up suffering altogether. In fact, to do so would make them feel vulnerable, because they believe that sooner or later they will have to pay for their sins.

The therapist working with an Irish family must be content with limited changes. The Irish may not wish to move beyond the initial presenting problem, and it is important for the therapist not to pressure them into further work. Attempting to get spouses to deal with marital issues after a child-focused problem 'has been solved, for example, will probably make them feel guilty and incompetent. It is better to reinforce the change that the family members do make and to let them return for therapy later if they wish. Even if the therapist perceives that there are emotional blocks in the family that are still causing pain, it is important not to push. Because of the lack of immediate feedback about therapeutic progress from the family, the therapist may be surprised to learn that their Irish families have continued therapeutic work on their own. Their deep sense of personal responsibility is, in fact, their greatest personal resource in therapy. They often do continue efforts started in therapy, though they may not openly admit either fault or the resolve to remedy it.

## ITALIAN-AMERICAN FAMILIES

Poverty and hopes of a better life led to large scale Italian immigration to the United States in the late 19th and early 20th centuries. By now they are the fifth largest American ethnic group. Since southern Italians compose by far the largst population of Italian-Americans (80%), the comments here will be limited to this group. Northern Italians are a more industrialized and different group culturally (Nelli, 1980).

While all cultures value the family, Italians give it higher priority than other groups do. Family life is their primary orientation. It is seen as one's greatest resource and protection against all troubles. For this reason, family intervention would seem to be the treatment of choice. But Italians tend to distrust outsiders. Gaining acceptance with the family is the first hurdle in dealing with Italians. The therapist must not take their mistrust personally. Everyone outside the family is mistrusted until proven otherwise.

The basic difficulties for Italian families relate to differentiation and/or separation from the family. The family provides such an intense and wide network of support that developing away from it is a major problem. This tendency is in direct contrast to American core values, which emphasize independence, individualism, and personal achievement over affiliation.

Anyone who tries to break the close bonds of an Italian family collides with Italian cultural norms. Therapy with Italian families involves not so much helping them deal with any particular emotional issue as facilitating the renegotiation of system boundaries, which tend to rigidify, but the holding of insiders (family members) in, and outsiders (everyone else) out. Within the family context itself, all emotions are viewed as understandable. Italians do not have the problem with disallowed feelings that some cultural groups do, although there are clear values for right and wrong behavior, based primarily on how such behavior affects the family.

Historically, the family in Italy became the anchor amidst the constant flux of foreigners, changing governments, and natural disasters (floods, volcanos, and famines). Through the centuries, Italians have learned to define themselves not by an association with Italy, but by their association with their families first and by their immediate neighbors, or "paisani," second. Allegiance to the family has come to surpass all other loyalties, and separation from the family is tantamount to spiritual death. Education and occupation are seen as secondary to the security, affection, and sense of relatedness the family has to offer.

Italians have learned to take maximum advantage of the present. They have a tremendous ability for intense enjoyment and experience in eating, celebrating, fighting, and loving. They take great pleasure in festivals and fiestas. Church rituals have always been prized for their pageantry, spectacle, and value in fostering family celebrations and rites of passage.

The relatively low utilization of mental health facilities by Italians reflects their tendency to turn first to the family for support. While the enmeshment of Italian families certainly creates difficulties and conflicts for them, it also provides much that family members from less supportive cultural environments lack. They have one of the strongest informal community networks of any ethnic group (Fitzpatrick, 1975), and are less likely to leave the neighborhood in order to get ahead. When they do break away, it is often very stressful for both the individuals involved and their families. When cut off from the family, Italians are much more likely to become symptomatic (Rotuno & McGoldrick, in press; Stein, 1971). For example, a study of Italian-American patients in Boston revealed that rates of schizophrenia and manic–depressive disorders varied inversely with the number of Italians living in their particular neighborhood (Mintz & Schwartz, 1976).

There is virtually no such thing as a separate nuclear family unit in Italian culture. "La famiglia" includes, first, all blood relatives and all relatives by marriage. Beyond this come the "comparaggio" or godparents, an important kinship network established in conjunction with rites of passage, and then the "gumbares" (old friends and neighbors). Close and intense contacts are maintained with a wide circle of family and friends. It is not unusual for parents to maintain daily contact with their own siblings and parents throughout their lives. Even if they move apart, frequent telephone calls maintain close ties.

It is essential in working with Italian-American families to learn the whereabouts of and level of contact with members of the extended family.

Usually they are in the same neighborhood, if not on the same block or even in the same building. This contrasts sharply with habits of WASPs, who raise their children to be independent and self-sufficient above all else, and who think themselves failures if their children do not leave home on schedule. Italians raise their children to be mutually supportive and to contribute to the family. Separation from the family is not expected.

The father tends to be the undisputed head of the Italian household, and he is often authoritarian and rigid in his rule setting and guidelines for behavior. A kind of benevolent despot, he usually takes his responsibility to provide for his family very seriously. Any situation that erodes his authority is likely to have a pronounced negative impact on the Italian father. Since it is in the nature of adolescents to question parental authority, the adolescence of his children may be particularly difficult for him.

The Italian mother, on the other hand, is the heart of the home. While yielding authority to the father, she traditionally assumes total control of the affective realm of the family. She is the family's emotional sustenance. Her life centers on domestic activities, and she is expected to receive her primary pleasure from nurturing and servicing her family. Her personal needs are expected to take second place to those of her husband. In exchange, she is offered protection and security from all outside pressure or threat. This pattern is not usually perceived as a problem by either partner, although to an outsider it appears to reinforce an extreme degree of dependence. The mutual support and complementarity of roles between husband and wife relate to their obligations to the entire family of at least three generations, and not to marital intimacy.

There is marked role differentiation between sons and daughters in Italian families. Though both are permitted to leave home when they marry, sons are given considerably greater latitude prior to marriage. A bit of acting out is expected, even subtly encouraged, as a measure of manliness. Proficiency in the sexual domain is important, not only to fulfill the masculine image, but also to exemplify a sense of mastery in interpersonal relations, which is a core Italian value. Although social skills are considered important for females as well, their behavior is subject to closer scrutiny. They are much more restricted socially; in particular, they are taught to eschew personal achievement in favor of respect and service to their parents. Traditionally, Italian males have been trained to control themselves emotionally— to be cautious and understated in their emotional reactions, especially with outsiders. This has nothing to do with embarrassment about expressing feelings, as it does with WASP or Irish males. Rather, it reflects the historical need to protect oneself against dangerous exposure to outsiders. Women, on the other hand, are allowed to express their emotions freely, but are kept out of "men's business."

Italians tend to dramatize their experiences. Similarly, they may exaggerate their symptoms (Zborowski, 1969; Zola, 1966), and are characteristically colorful and dramatic in their talk. Their expressiveness may be over-powering to a therapist from a more restrained culture, in which, for example, powerful expressions of hostility would be interpreted literally. For Italians, words give expression to the emotion of the moment and are not taken so seriously. Another difficulty for a non-Italian therapist may be the way to deal with family "secrets." While Italian families may appear to talk openly and engagingly, even in the initial contact, sharing real family secrets is an entirely different matter. The existence of the secret may be puzzling to the therapist, since otherwise the family seems to talk openly about all kinds of issues, including sex, death, hostility, and/or antisocial behavior. Often the content of the secret itself is not important. Secrets may seem to be aimed more at marking and preserving the boundaries of the system—clarifying who is inside and who is not. Therapists must deal delicately with secrets, remembering the sense of betrayal families will feel if their boundaries are crossed.

Therapists may also be frustrated by the Italian family's demand for immediate solutions. If a therapist operates on the assumption that change occurs through long evaluation and discussion of problems, Italian families will be exceedingly difficult to help. If, on the other hand, the therapist focuses on mobilizing the family's own natural supports (as noted, this is the preferred Italian solution) and does not try to replace this orientation with one that stresses the therapy as primary, there is a much better chance of constructive intervention.

## BLACK AMERICAN FAMILIES

There were an estimated 24 million black Americans in the United States in the mid-1970s, making them the largest ethnic group in America (Holt, 1980). It would be a serious mistake to assume that blacks are an ethnic group like any other, or that their problems can be solved like those of other immigrant groups. However degrading the life conditions of early white immigrant groups, they were not brought here as slaves. The combination of the slavery experience and the difference in skin color has put blacks at an extreme disadvantage in acculturating to American society. The ongoing impact of racism and discrimination is a continuing and pervasive aspect of the lives of black families, and it cannot be overestimated in dealing with them therapeutically.[3]

Much has been written about the characteristics of black family struc-ture and the socioeconomic forces behind these family patterns. In our

[3]For a more detailed discussion of black Americans and family therapy, see Hines and Boyd (in press), Boyd (1980), Pinderhughes (in press), Allen (1978a, 1978b), and Staples and Mirande (1980), to name a few of the most important.

opinion, much useless debate has been generated about the "pathological" nature of black families.

Initially, blacks are likely to view therapy within the context of other traditional dealings with white institutions. Since white institutions have been basically "foreign" to blacks, a certain level of mistrust and alienation is taken for granted. In the early stages of therapy, black families may keep their distance, participate in the situations with some reluctance, and offer minimal information. This may at times look like the inarticulateness characteristic of the Irish, who are uncomfortable, embarrassed, and guilt-ridden about their feelings. By contrast, blacks are likely to be realistic, emotionally aware, and comfortable with the full range of their feelings (Sanua, 1960). Their withholding or reticence has more to do with the specific context of therapy than with discomfort about their feelings or about communication in general.

Religion has been the major formal institution in our society available to blacks for support. It is both a social and a personal resource. It has been a major source of status and community support for black families. Most blacks will turn to religion as a solution to their problems before they think of therapy. It is always important to check out the role that religion plays in the family's life, as it may be a powerful spiritual and emotional resource.

While it is true that females head more black families than white families, and that these numbers are increasing, the two-parent family is the norm among black families. In our time of changing family roles, precipitated by the changing status of women, black families may have actually achieved a better balance in sex roles than white families have. There is more role flexibility between black spouses, and there are indications that black fathers may take a bigger part in housekeeping, child-rearing activities, and the nurturing of children, than white fathers (Allen, 1978; Axelson, 1970; Kunkell & Kennard, 1971; Lewis, 1975). Some research suggests that black women are more likely to enjoy sex and to take the initiative sexually, and that they are less likely to find sex a source of marital tension (Allen, 1978a; Lewis, 1975; Rainwater, 1966; Scanzoni, 1971). Much more research needs to be done on these and many other aspects of family patterns to clarify these issues. But it is possible that in spite of the severe disadvantages of black families in our culture, they may be closer to accomplishing certain shifts in male–female characteristics and relationships that many families have been striving for in recent years (Gluck et al., 1980).

Like the Irish, women in black families tend to be strong and independent, and their sphere of activity often goes beyond the home to work situations and community activities. Given the economic and social pressures on their families, they have often had to work to help support the family.

Black families develop strong kinship networks that serve as their major resource in times of trouble. Among lower-class blacks, economic factors often militate against the establishment and maintenance of nuclear family units. These stresses make blacks more vulnerable to illness and death than whites are (e.g. black males have a mortality rate twice that of white males). Often, extended households are the most stable and enduring form of family unit (Allen, 1978b; Stack, 1974). Kinship networks, including both family and close friends, share resources, household tasks, and housing, in a system characterized by mutual obligation (Stack, 1974).

Research shows clearly that blacks are more likely than whites are to have babies out of wedlock (Furstenberg, 1970; Rainwater, 1966). Abortion and formal adoption are less frequent than they are in white families. Blacks rely on family and friends for necessary support (Furstenberg, 1970; Himes, 1964; Pope, 1969) with premarital pregnancies, and children born in these circumstances are generally accepted readily into the system.

Black families consider children extremely important. There are a number of differences in their child-rearing practices. Early studies indicated that black parents were more lenient regarding weaning and feeding children, but more strict in toilet training (Davis & Havighurst, 1946). Recent evidence suggests that over time black and white child-rearing practices have become more similar (Allen, 1978a, 1978b; Radin & Kamii, 1965; Scanzoni, 1971). Black families tend to deemphasize sex differences in their socialization of children. Other adults often readily assume child-care responsibilities if a mother cannot handle them. Extended kin generally take a more active role in the socialization of black children than is true with white children (Aschenbrenner, 1973; Ladner, 1971; Stack, 1974).

Disciplining of children is often strict and direct, a pragmatic practice necessary for survival—sometimes misjudged by therapists not familiar with black culture. Because they rarely have the support of larger social structures, black families have great difficulty protecting their children against prejudice, crime, or drugs. When black adolescents rebel, they are much more likely than whites are to associate with peers who are engaged in serious antisocial behavior. They have fewer nondangerous options for acting out adolescent rebellion, and their families have very few societal supports to protect them from antisocial influences. In therapy, it is essential for the therapist to take into account the realistic pressures on black youths, even when their families have many financial resources.

When social pressures have led to underorganization of the family (Aponte, 1976), children often either prematurely take on adult roles or fail to develop the discipline necessary for adult functioning. In such situations, "talking" therapy is unlikely to be effective or acceptable for black families. Structural therapy to strengthen family organization and add to its flexibility is probably the most effective model (Aponte, 1976, 1981; Minuchin et al., 1967; Minuchin, 1974).

Initially, the therapist needs to help the family deal with the incipient crisis and promote positive links with whatever resources or institutions are, or should be, involved with the family. Beyond this, strengthening the family's sense of ethnic identity and connectedness may be a crucial part of therapy. As Boyd (1980) has pointed out, genograms are an extremely useful tool in getting a picture of black family structure. As Boyd suggests, their genograms are often "sloppy," if they are complete. They should be taken only after trust with the family has been developed, and not in the initial session. Understanding and supporting the family's network may be extremely important in fostering their ability to mobilize resources and feel supported.

## CONCLUSION

It is hoped that the few suggestions offered here of ethnic differences in definitions of "normality" and in responses to therapy will not be taken as rigid stereotypes, but, rather, as pointers for thought and future research. Our best hope is that, by attending to the profound impact of ethnicity on human values, clinicians will become more sophisticated in research and the development of models of family functioning and therapy.

## REFERENCES

Allen, W. R. The search for applicable theories of Black family life. *Journal of Marriage and the Family*, 1978, *40*, 117–127. (a)

Allen, W. R. Black family research in the United States: A review, assessment and extension. *Journal of Comparative Family Studies*, 1978, *9*, 166–188. (b)

Aponte, H. J. Underorganization in the poor family. In P. J. Guerin (Ed.), *Family therapy.* New York: Gardner Press, 1976.

Aponte, H. J. Structural family therapy. In A. Gurman & D. Kniskern (Eds.), *Handbook of family therapy.* New York: Brunner/Mazel, 1981.

Aschenbrenner, J. Extended families among Black Americans. *Journal of Comparative Family Studies*, 1973, *4*, 257–268.

Axelson, L. J. The working wife: Differences in perception among Negro and white males. *Journal of Marriage and the Family,* 1970, *32,* 457–464.

Billingsley, A. *The family and cultural pluralism.* Address at Baltimore Conference on Ethnicity and Social Welfare, January 1976. New York: Institute on Pluralism and Group Identity, 1976.

Boyd, N. Family therapy with Black families. In S. Corchin & E. Jones (Eds.), *Minority mental health.* New York: Holt, Rinehart & Winston, 1980.

Carpenter, W., & Strauss, J. Cross-cultural evaluation of Schneider's first-rank symptoms of schizophrenia: A report from the International Pilot Study of Schizophrenia. *American Journal of Psychiatry*, 1974, *131*, 204–210.

Carter, E. A., & McGoldrick, M. (Eds.). *The family life cycle: A framework for family therapy.* New York: Gardner Press, 1980.

Davis, A., & Havighurst, R. Social class and color differences in child rearing. *American Sociological Review*, 1946, *11*, 698–710.

Eisenberg, L. Psychiatry and society: A sociobiologic synthesis. *New England Journal of Medicine*, 1977, *296*, 903-910.

Falicov, C. Cultural variations in the family life cycle. In E. A. Carter & M. McGoldrick (Eds.), *The family life cycle: A framework for family therapy*. New York: Gardner Press, 1980.

Fallows, M. A. *Irish Americans: Identity and assimilation*. Englewood Cliffs, N.J.: Prentice-Hall, 1979.

Fantl, B., & Shiro, J. Cultural variables in the behavior pattern of symptom formation of 15 Irish and 15 Italian schizophrenics. *International Journal of Social Psychiatry*, 1959, *4*, 245-253.

Feinstein, O. Why ethnicity? In D. Hartman (Ed.), *Immigrants and Migrants: The Detroit ethnic experience*. Detroit: Wayne State University, 1974.

Fitzpatrick, J. *The role of white ethnic communities in the urban adjustment of newcomers*. Working Paper No. 2. New York: Institute on Pluralism and Group Identity, 1975.

Foley, V. C. Family therapy with Black disadvantaged families: Some observations on roles, communication, and technique. *Journal of Marriage and Family Counseling*, 1975, *1*, 57-65.

Friedman, E. Systems and ceremonies. In E. A. Carter & M. McGoldrick (Eds.), *The family life cycle: A framework for family therapy*. New York: Gardner Press, 1980.

Furstenberg, F. Premarital pregnancy among Black teenagers. *Transaction*, 1970, *7*, 52-55.

Gambino, R. *Blood of my blood: The dilemma of Italian-Americans*. Garden City, N.Y.: Doubleday, 1974.

Giordano, J., & Giordano, G. P. *The ethno-cultural factor in mental health: A literature review and bibliography*. New York: Institute on Pluralism and Group Identity, 1977.

Glazer, N., & Moynihan, D. (Eds.). *Ethnicity: Theory and experience*. Cambridge: Harvard University Press, 1975.

Gluck, N. R., Dannefer, E., & Milea, K. Women in families. In E. A. Carter & M. McGoldrick (Eds.), *The family life cycle: A framework for family therapy*. New York: Gardner Press, 1980.

Goren, A. Jews. In S. Thernstrom (Ed.), *Harvard encyclopedia of American ethnic groups*. Cambridge: Harvard University Press, 1980.

Greeley, A. M. *Why can't they be like us?* New York: Institute of Human Relations Press, 1969.

Greeley, A. M. *The American Catholic*. New York: Basic Books, 1978.

Greeley, A. M. Creativity in the Irish family: The cost of immigration. *International Journal of Family Therapy*, 1979, *1*, 295-303.

Herz, F., & Rosen, E. Family therapy with Jewish Americans. In M. McGoldrick, J. Giordano, & J. K. Pearce (Eds.), *Ethnicity and family therapy*. New York: Guilford Press, in press.

Himes, J. Some reactions to a hypothetical premarital pregnancy by 100 Negro college women. *Marriage and Family Living*, 1964, *26*, 344-349.

Hines, P., & Boyd, N. The Black American family. In M. McGoldrick, J. Giordano, & J. K. Pearce (Eds.), *Ethnicity and family therapy*. New York: Guilford Press, in press.

Holt, T. C. Afro-Americans. In S. Thernstrom (Ed.), *Harvard encyclopedia of American ethnic groups*. Cambridge: Harvard University Press, 1980.

Jalali, B. Family therapy with Iranian American families. In M. McGoldrick, J. Giordano, & J. K. Pearce (Eds.), *Ethnicity and family therapy*. New York: Guilford Press, in press.

Kiev, A. *Transcultural psychiatry*. New York: Free Press, 1972.

Kleinman, A. M. Explanatory models in health care relationships. In *Health of the family (National Council for International Health Symposium)*. Washington D.C.: National Council for International Health, 1975.

Kleinman, A. M., Eisenberg, L., & Good, B. Culture, illness, and care: Clinical lessons from anthropologic and cross-cultural research. *Annals of Internal Medicine*, 1978, *88*, 251-258.

Kluckhohn, F. R., & Strodtbeck, F. L. *Variations in value orientations*. New York: Harper & Row, 1961.

Kolm, R. *Ethnicity and society: A theoretical analysis and its implications for the United States.* Rockville, Md.: National Institute of Mental Health, 1973.

Kunkell, P., & Kennard, S. *Spout Spring: A Black community.* Chicago: Rand McNally, 1971.

Ladner, J. *Tomorrow's tomorrow.* Garden City, N.Y.: Doubleday, 1971.

Lewis, D. The Black family: Socialization and sex roles. *Phylon,* 1975, *36,* 221–237.

Lieberman, M. *Adaptational patterns in middle aged and elderly: The role of ethnicity.* Paper presented at the Conference of the Gerontological Society, Portland, Ore., October 1974.

Magill, D., & Pearce, J. K. Family therapy with White Anglo-Saxon Protestant families. In M. McGoldrick, J. Giordano, & J. K. Pearce (Eds.), *Ethnicity and family therapy.* New York: Guilford Press, in press.

Malzberg, B. Mental disease among the Irish-born and native white of Irish parentage in New York State, 1949–1951. *Mental Hygiene,* 1963, *47,* 284–295.

Malzberg, B. Mental disease among Jews in New York State. *Acta Psychiatrica Scandinavica,* 1973, *49,* 245–251.

McAdoo, H. Family therapy in the Black community. *American Journal of Orthopsychiatry,* 1977, *47,* 75–79.

McGoldrick, M. Clinical issues in family therapy with Irish Americans. In C. Sluzki & D. Schnitman (Eds.), *Culture and health care,* in press. (a)

McGoldrick, M. Irish Americans in family therapy. In M. McGoldrick, J. Giordano, & J. K. Pearce (Eds.), *Ethnicity and family therapy.* New York: Guilford Press, in press. (b)

McGoldrick, M., Giordano, J., & Pearce, J. K. (Eds.). *Ethnicity and family therapy.* New York: Guilford Press, in press.

McGoldrick, M., & Pearce, J. K. Family therapy with Irish Americans. *Family Process,* 1981, *20.*

Mechanic, D. Sex, illness, illness behavior and the use of health services. *Social Science and Medicine,* 1978, *12B,* 207–214.

Midelfort, F. C., & Midelfort, C. Family therapy with Norwegian families. In M. McGoldrick, J. Giordano, & J. K. Pearce (Eds.), *Ethnicity and family therapy.* New York: Guilford Press, in press.

Mindel, C., & Halberstein, R. (Eds.). *Ethnic families in America.* New York: Elsevier, 1976.

Mintz, N., & Schwartz, D. Urban ecology and psychosis: Community factors in the incidence of schizophrenia and manic depression among Italians in Greater Boston. *International Journal of Social Psychiatry,* 1976, *10,* 101–118.

Minuchin, S. *Families and family therapy.* Cambridge: Harvard University Press, 1974.

Minuchin, S., Montalvo, B., Guerney, B., Rosman, B., & Schumer, F. *Families of the slums.* New York: Basic Books, 1967.

Murphy, H. B. M. Alcoholism and schizophrenia in the Irish: A review. *Transcultural Psychiatric Research,* 1975, *12,* 116–139.

Nelli, H. S. Italians. In S. Thernstrom (Ed.), *Harvard encyclopedia of American ethnic groups.* Cambridge: Harvard University Press, 1980.

Opler, M. K., & Singer, J. L. Ethnic differences in behavior and psychopathology: Italian and Irish. *International Journal of Social Psychiatry,* 1956, *1,* 11–17.

Papajohn, J., & Spiegel, J. *Transactions in families.* San Francisco: Jossey-Bass, 1975.

Pinderhughes, E. Afro Americans and the victim system. In M. McGoldrick, J. Giordano, & J. K. Pearce (Eds.), *Ethnicity and family therapy.* New York: Guilford Press, in press.

Pinto, T. *Ethnicity and professional education: A survey of curriculum content.* Unpublished manuscript, Institute on Pluralism and Group Identity, 1976.

Pope, H. Negro–white differences in decisions regarding illegitimate children. *Journal of Marriage and the Family,* 1969, *31,* 756–764.

Preto, N. G. Family therapy with Puerto Rican families. In M. McGoldrick, J. Giordano, & J. K. Pearce (Eds.), *Ethnicity and family therapy.* New York: Guildford Press, in press.

Rabkin, J., & Struening, E. *Ethnicity, social class and mental illness in New York City.* New York: Institute on Pluralism and Group Identity, 1976.

Radin, N., & Kamii, C. The child rearing attitudes of disadvantaged Negro mothers and some educational implications. *Journal of Negro Education*, 1965, *34*, 138–146.

Rainwater, L. Some aspects of lower class sexual behavior. *Journal of Social Issues*, 1966, *22*, 96–108.

Rinder, I. Mental health of American Jewish urbanites: A review of the literature and predictions. *International Journal of Social Psychiatry*, 1963, *9*, 214–220.

Roberts, B., & Myers, J. K. Religion, national origin, immigration and mental illness. *American Journal of Psychiatry*, 1954, *110*, 759–764.

Rotuno, M., & McGoldrick, M. Family therapy with Italian Americans. In M. McGoldrick, J. Giordano, & J. K. Pearce (Eds.), *Ethnicity and family therapy*. New York: Guilford Press, in press.

Sanua, V. Sociocultural factors in responses of stressful life situations: The behavior of aged amputees as an example. *Journal of Health and Human Behavior*, 1960, *1*, 17–24.

Sanua, V. Intermarriage and psychological adjustment. In H. Silverman (Ed.), *Marriage counseling: Psychology, ideology, science*. Springfield, Ill.: Charles C Thomas, 1967.

Sanua, V. *Evaluation of psychotherapy with different socioeconomic and ethnic groups: A need for rethinking in the training of therapists*. Paper presented at the Annual Conference of New York Society of Clinical Psychology, New York, April 1975.

Sanua, V. The contemporary Jewish family: A review of the social science literature. In G. Bubis (Ed.), *Serving the Jewish family*. New York: Ktav Press, 1978.

Scanzoni, J. *The Black family in modern society*. Boston: Allyn & Bacon, 1971.

Selvini Palazzoli, M., Boscolo, L., Cecchin, G., & Prata, G. *Paradox and counterparadox*. New York: Jason Aronson, 1978.

Shon, S. *Asian American families*. Paper presented at The World of Family Therapy symposium, San Francisco, November 1979.

Shon, S., & Ja, D. The Asian American family. In M. McGoldrick, J. Giordano, & J. K. Pearce (Eds.), *Ethnicity and family therapy*. New York: Guilford Press, in press.

Silverstein, O. *Fusion*. Paper presented at conference on Mothers and Daughters, New York, February 1981.

Singer, J., & Opler, M. K. Contrasting patterns of fantasy and motility in Irish and Italian schizophrenics. *Journal of Abnormal and Social Psychiatry*, 1956, *53*, 42–47.

Sluzki, C. Migration and family conflict. *Family Process*, 1979, *18* (4), 379–390.

Sluzki, C., & Schnitman, D. (Eds.). *Culture and health care*. in press.

Spiegel, J. *Transactions: The interplay between individual, family, and society* (J. Papajohn, Ed.). New York: Science House, 1971.

Stack, C. *All our kin: Strategies for survival in a Black community*. New York: Harper & Row, 1974.

Staples, R., & Mirande, A. Racial and cultural variations among American families: A decennial review of the literature on minority families. *Journal of Marriage and the Family*, 1980, *42*, 887–903.

Stein, H. F. The Slovak-American "swaddling ethos": Homeostat for family dynamics and cultural persistence. *Family Process*, 1978, *17*, 31–46.

Stein, H. F. The salience of ethno-psychology for medical education and practice. *Social Science and Medicine*, 1979, *13B*, 199–210.

Stein, R. F. *Disturbed youth and ethnic family patterns*. Albany: State University of New York Press, 1971.

Stoeckle, J., Zola, I. K., & Davidson, G. The quantity and significance of psychological distress in medical patients. *Journal of Chronic Disease*, 1964, *17*, 959–970.

Strodtbeck, F. L. Family interaction, values, and achievement. In M. Sklare (Ed.), *The Jews: Social patterns of an American group*. New York: Free Press, 1958.

Watzlawick, P. *How real is real?* New York: Random House, 1976.

Watzlawick, P., Weakland, J., & Fisch, R., *Change: Principles of problem formation and problem resolution*. New York: Norton, 1974.

Weakland, J., Watzlawick, P., & Fisch, R. Brief therapy: Focused problem resolution. *Family Process,* 1974, *13,* 213–220.

Wills, G. *Bare ruined choirs.* Garden City, N.Y.: Doubleday, 1971.

Wylan, L., & Mintz, N. Ethnic differences in family attitudes toward psychotic manifestations with implications for treatment programmes. *International Journal of Social Psychiatry,* 1976, *22,* 86–95.

Zborowski, M. *People in pain.* San Francisco: Jossey-Bass, 1969.

Zborowski, M., & Herzog, E. *Life is with people.* New York: Schocken Books, 1952.

Zola, I. K. Problems of communications, diagnosis and patient care: The interplay of patient, physician and clinic organization. *Journal of Medical Education,* 1963, *38,* 829–838.

Zola, I. K. Culture and symptoms: An analysis of patients' presenting complaints. *American Sociological Review,* 1966, *5,* 141–55.

Zola, I. K. The concept of trouble and sources of medical assistance. *Social Science and Medicine,* 1972, *6,* 673–679.

Zola, I. K. Oh where, oh where has ethnicity gone? In D. E. Gelfand & A. J. Kutzik (Eds.), *Ethnicity and aging.* New York: Springer, 1979.

Zuk, G. H. A therapist's perspective on Jewish family values. *Journal of Marriage and Family Counseling,* 1978, *4,* 101–111.

# 17

# THE COMMUNITY CONNECTION: THE IMPACT OF SOCIAL NETWORKS ON FAMILY AND INDIVIDUAL FUNCTIONING

## CAROL ANDERSON

In a report from the 1980 White House Conference on Families, one reporter concluded that the family is not disintegrating, but rather changing: "It's the systems that do or don't support it that are disintegrating . . . the family is working overtime to survive" (Lewis, 1980).

Friends, extended family, and all the other contacts family members have each day as they work, go to school, or participate in community activities constitute a potentially powerful influence on the way in which a family operates. The family's ability to manage its primary tasks, developmental transitions, inevitable crises, illnesses, and stresses may well relate to the way the family is connected to the larger social context within which it exists. Until recently, little attention has been given to this context. In fact, Wynne (1969) claims that the most serious shortcoming of family studies is the neglect of extrafamilial interactions of members with extended kin, friends, work associates, and personnel of treatment facilities.

Most family therapists and researchers subscribe to some variation of systems theory, which includes the basic thesis that individual conduct or behavior is interdependent with the family environment. Nevertheless, most researchers and clinicians have emphasized the concept of the family as an "independent" source of stress, which, by impinging upon the individual, causes or perpetuates various behaviors. A complete systems perspective, however, would require an expanded focus. Such a focus would include not only an examination of the reciprocal impact of the individual on the family, but also an examination of the context in which the family operates. A

Carol Anderson. Department of Psychiatry, School of Medicine, University of Pittsburgh, Pittsburgh, Pennsylvania.

systems perspective should include the recognition that the family is no more a closed system than is the individual (Leichter & Mitchell, 1967).

A family that functions well and communicates "normally" may do so because its members receive a great deal of support from outside the family. For instance, a young couple may be able to tolerate a serious prolonged physical illness in a child without developing overprotective responses or marital discord as long as they are well connected to an extended family system that provides both practical help and emotional support. This same family may develop serious interactional problems if the husband is promoted to a position that requires a move to another community.

The degree of support, feedback and/or sense of congruence with one's community may determine the level of adaptive family interaction, as well as the level or irrational, intense, and potentially destructive forces activated within the nuclear family. As Hammer suggests, "deviant intrafamilial communication may in part reflect distortions in the social connections of family members with outsiders" (Hammer, Makiesky-Barrow, & Gutwirth, 1978). For instance, if families with mentally ill members are isolated from their communities, they are deprived of support and feedback functions that otherwise could serve to mitigate negative interactions. Without support during the crisis of illness and feedback about the appropriateness of their techniques of handling stress, they are no doubt more likely to develop strange and idiosyncratic transactional styles. These styles may well create further family stress and further alienation from the larger community, thus perpetuating or escalating both disordered behavior and isolated functioning. Therefore, it is extremely important that the investigation of family processes without consideration of family context be avoided. An investigation of the connectedness of the family with its larger context may explain particular family behaviors in a way that direct observation of family processes alone does not.

If family vulnerability to stress relates to community connectedness, it is not surprising that families in modern societies display evidence of disorganization and distress. Characteristics of our culture, in fact, may contribute to the vulnerability of nuclear families by encouraging disconnectedness and diminished support. Our culture involves tremendous geographic and social mobility and occupational specialization. These factors, along with such phenomena as increased divorce rates and smaller family size, all may contribute to the fragmentation or isolation of families.

Primative societies are more tightly knit than our own, with kinship playing a central role. Kin groups are linked by both biological and legal ties, which provide a potential buffer for the impact of external stresses. Such kin groups are usually organized around a strong central authority and subscribe to norms that control occupational systems and prevent differential mobility of members of the clan.

By comparison, a study of the genealogies of 200 female Vassar students indicated minimal kinds of kinship contacts. Ties were found to be localized in the nuclear family and lacking in historical depth or reciprocity (Codere, 1955). Men have also been reported to be isolated from extended family or social contacts. When asked, "Apart from your wife and children, who are the three or four people you often spend your time with?", 15% of the men responding were able to name only one contact, and 20% were unable to name any contact at all (Toomey, 1971).

There is, however, some evidence that the isolating effects of urbanization and mobility are not as great as was once assumed (Litwak, 1959–1960; Litwak & Szeleny, 1969; Sussman, 1953, 1959; Sussman & Burchinal, 1962). Studies have stressed the significance of kin relations. For instance, despite estimates that one in five families move each year, extended families appear to function even in the absence of geographical propinquity and continue to provide affective and instrumental support (Budson & Jolley, 1978; Firth, Hubert, & Forge, 1970; Litwak, 1959–1960; Litwak & Szeleny, 1969). Furthermore, in a study of 161 families with 2063 exended kin, 90% of the respondents felt an obligation to keep in touch with kin (Reiss, 1962).

Nevertheless, it is probably true that the actual context of families is determined less by kinship, traditions, or geography than by the specific social transactions family members have with others (Bott, 1971). Consequently, the social bonds of family members are more likely to be heterogeneous, transient, and organized around specific purposes or functions. These types of social bonds no doubt contribute to the erosion of traditions and social controls. Furthermore, family members are more likely to be thrown into contact with people who have values and behaviors different from their own, people who are less likely to know or care whether they follow the social rules of their heritage. These factors increase the likelihood that families and individuals will be faced with greater instability, more frequent change, increased stress, and vulnerability for illness (Cassel, 1976).

Other factors also contribute to the lessening of the strength and permanency of family ties to a community. Women in the work force, for instance, influence the way in which a family fits with and relates to those outside the family. Traditionally, women have assumed responsibility for maintaining family ties with extended kin. As they enter the work force, more time is spent with individuals outside the kin system; this must diminish not only their kin contacts, but those of the family as well. In other ways, divorce and single parenthood also disrupt traditional support systems and create time schedules that make it nearly impossible for single parents to maintain active extrafamilial lives.

Family-oriented mental health professionals should be prepared to include an appraisal of extrafamilial stresses and resources in their overall assessment of internal family functioning. Disordered family communication may be caused by deficient social contacts. Normal communication processes and normal functioning in the face of excessive stress, on the other hand, may be possible because extensive support systems have been mobilized.

## SOCIAL NETWORKS AS A WAY OF
## STUDYING THE FAMILY-COMMUNITY INTERFACE

One possible way of studying the family's relationship to its context is by investigating personal social networks. As individual's or family's "social network" consists of those people with whom the individual or family maintains contact or has some form of social bond (Adams, 1967; Bott, 1971; Mitchell, 1969). The concept of "social network" is a logical extension of family systems principles; it is potentially more useful than is the concept of "class" or "neighborhood" because it is not a static concept, limited by spatial and temporal relationships. Given the high mobility and other rapid changes characteristic of highly industrialized countries, it is likely that the most relevant bonds between people would be determined by series of actually existing social relationships that allow various people to be mobilized under specific conditions for specific purposes (Pilisuk & Froland, 1978; Radcliffe-Brown, 1952). The concept of "social network" also has methodological advantages. The use of such network variables as size, density, and reciprocity allows systematic, comparable, and replicable studies of individuals in their social contexts. Network concepts are particularly useful because they are not affected by cultural differences in such factors as family composition, family role definitions, and the range of socializing agents.

The application of network methodology to the study of family context, as other methods are used to study family interaction variables, may be valuable for several reasons. It may be possible to gain increased understanding of the differential vulnerability of individuals and families to stress and social disorganization, as well as to attain some measure of the number and quality of social factors that may protect given families and the individuals within them from destructive physiological or psychological events (Kessler, 1979).

Although network concepts and methodologies have only recently begun to be applied to this area of family functioning, some current data are relevant to our exploration of this relationship. This chapter explores three areas in detail: family relationships and networks; individual functioning and networks; and the significance of networks for healthy family functioning.

## FAMILY RELATIONSHIPS AND THE CONTEXT OF THE FAMILY

Most of the studies investigating the relationship between the internal structure of the family and variables within the family's social environment are found within the anthropological or sociological literature, and these focus primarily on marriages rather than on families. Nevertheless, several studies highlight the point that there is a connection between the way in which families operate internally and the way in which they relate to their communities.

## Networks and Conjugal Roles

Perhaps the most important of these studies was conducted by Bott in London over 20 years ago (Bott, 1957, 1971). This landmark study examined the relationship between the organization of marital roles and the social networks of the spouses, both separately and together, in order to "understand how the internal functioning of a group is affected not only by its relationship with the people and organizations of its environment, but also by the relationship among people and organizations" (Bott, 1971, p. 249).

Bott found that the degree of segregation of husband–wife role relationships varied directly with the connectedness of a family's social network (Bott, 1971). Those couples who maintained traditional, separate, complementary marital roles had separate, same-sex, kin-predominant, close-knit social networks. "Close-knit" or "high-density" social networks are those in which most of the members tend to know and have access to one another. Such networks are able to meet many of an individual's needs for companionship and social contact. It is not surprising, therefore, that partners maintaining traditional marital roles or separate tasks within the family had separate contacts with outside people and separate institutions to whom they turned for support and satisfaction. Nontraditional, joint-conjugal-role couples— that is, those with common overlapping tasks within the family—tended to rely more on each other for support and satisfaction and to have "loose-knit" and overlapping social networks. These "loose-knit" networks tended to contain individuals who were less likely to know one another, yet were more likely to be friends the couple had in common.

Bott's work has stimulated a good deal of research over the past 20 years. While some "replication" studies did not actually duplicate Bott's design, and others have only partially confirmed her hypothesis, these studies generally tend to support the view that differences in internal family behaviors are associated with the manner in which family members relate to the outside world (Aldous & Straus, 1966; Chatterjee, 1977; Ginsberg, 1975; Harris, 1969; Nelson, 1966; Turner, 1967; Udry & Hall, 1965; Wimberly, 1973).

A number of other studies have related network variables to the psychological and marital well-being of spouses and families. Some suggest that tightly knit neighborhoods with high couple interaction are associated with marital solidarity (Whyte, 1957). Others have found that the more characteristics a husband and wife have in common with close friends, the less likely they are to divorce (Zimmerman, 1956). Of course a point could be made that these marriages are less likely to be companionate and more likely to involve lower expectations on the part of the spouses, since both partners meet their needs elsewhere. It is probably safe to assume that there is a curvilinear relationship between closeness to kin and measures of marital solidarity (Blood, 1969), as too much closeness can be as great a problem as too little. Others have suggested that the pressure for lower- and working-class men to participate in male cliques rather than associate with women persists even after marriage (Komarovsky, 1962). The families of these same men are likely to live geographically closer to relatives, perhaps providing additional resources to both partners and encouraging the lack of emphasis on mutuality in marriage (Adams, 1968).

## Networks, Power, and Solidarity

There is some evidence that those spouses who participate actively with kin, in the community, or in community organizations have more power in relationship to their marital partners than do those who are not active in this way (Blood & Wolfe, 1960; Farber, 1966; Komarovsky, 1962; Rogers, 1975). For instance, if a couple was found to have more interaction with the kin of one spouse than with the kin of the other, the spouse with whose kin the couple was more connected had more power in the marital relationship (Farber, 1966). Wives who participate in community or organizations outside the home have been found to have more power within the home (Blood & Wolfe, 1960; Komarovsky, 1962; Rogers, 1975). Furthermore, high frequency of contact with individuals external to the nuclear family appears to contribute to marital solidarity (Adams, 1968; Blood, 1969; Whyte, 1957).

## Networks and Mobility

If networks are indeed important to conjugal roles and marital relationships, particularly for traditional couples, it would follow that such couples should be particularly vulnerable to external disruptions such as geographic relocation, which affect the family's relationship to the community, decrease the support received from the network, and increase the pressures on the conjugal relationship. Joint-conjugal-role couples, on the other hand, would be more likely to be vulnerable to stresses internal to the nuclear family, such as an illness that affects a spouse's ability to perform his or her roles. There is evidence for at least the first part of this hypothesis. Several studies have emphasized that geographic mobility results in such events as the breakup of close-knit networks, increased marital tension, and at least temporary increased joint performance of marital roles (Bott, 1971; Rainwater & Handel, 1964; Handel & Rainwater, 1964). Comparing couples recently relocated in the suburbs with those who continued to live in the central city, Tallman (1969) found the move to the suburbs to be a disruptive, disintegrative force on the network of social relationships that served to integrate these families' lives, particularly for working-class women, who were more likely to have been closely tied to close-knit networks of childhood friends and relatives. Working-class women who moved were more isolated and had more marital conflict than middle-class women, who were more likely to have resources available to facilitate adaptation to change.

In addition to loosening network ties, mobility also appears to influence the health of the individuals involved. Residents of a new housing project in a suburban area were found to have higher rates of mental hospital admissions, general practitioner consultations, and self-reports of symptoms (Martin, Brotherston, & Chave, 1957).

### Family Insularity

A number of studies have explored the issue of family isolation or insularity and its relationship to psychological adjustment; they have generally demonstrated more insularity in troubled families. Families who are troubled, or who have troubled members, do not have as much contact with a social support system. For instance, troubled families possessing high-risk characteristics (poverty, single parenthood, poor education, etc.) have been found to have fewer social contacts than those who were at low risk. Low-risk mothers averaged ten daily social contacts, while high-risk mothers reported less than half this number. Furthermore, low-risk mothers showed more initiative in generating contacts and were more likely to use friends, not just relatives, as a source of help (Wahler, Leake, & Rogers, 1977).

Married patients classified as neurotic also appear to be more isolated from the outside world. Nelson, Collins, Kreitman, and Troop (1970) found that neurotic husbands and their wives had more face-to-face contact with each other, and yet that they spent less time as a couple in social interaction and had less social activity independent of one another. Clearly, this type of insularity has the potential for placing additional burdens and stresses on the marital relationship, since spouses are more dependent on each other for meeting all of their needs for companionship, are less likely to get feedback about unrealistic expectations or inappropriate behaviors, and are less likely to be supported in their identity as a couple.

The level of insularity of family members has also been associated with various states of physical illness and responses to treatment. Finlayson (1976) investigated the lay help given to wives of myocardial infarction patients and found recovery levels of their husbands to be associated with levels of contact of these wives with different categories of network members. In a similar study, Walker reported that men with heart attacks had a more successful outcome when their wives utilized a larger number of sources of help (Walker, MacBride, & Vachon, 1977). The cause of this correction is not known, although one might speculate that an extensive use of a variety of resources would diffuse stress rather than contain it within a family and thus would have a positive effect on the course of a patient's illness.

## INDIVIDUAL DISORDERS AND THE CONTEXT OF THE FAMILY

In general, studies of individual personal social networks assume that the immediate family is part of the network without examining the family and its relationship to larger networks as separate variables. Nevertheless, much of this literature is of interest because it suggests that the size, congruence, and density of an individual's network relates to a number of measures of health and well-being.

### Size

It has been estimated that an average individual in the United States is embedded in a series of social relationships that includes direct or indirect connections with 1000 to 1500 people (Boissevan, 1974; Lee, 1969; Pool, 1973). These people are linked in a variety of ways, such as by kin networks or work networks, all of which together constitute the original individual's social community (Westermeyer & Pattison, 1979). The average urban individual's intimate network (that with which he or she is in direct and regular contact) appears to contain about 30 people of whom 6 to 10 are intimately known, though estimates of the size of these networks range from 18 to 40 (Fischer & Phillips, 1979; Hammer et al., 1978; Killworth & Bernard, 1974; Mitchell, 1974; Pattison, Defrancisco, Wood, Frazier, & Crowder, 1975). These individuals appear to exist in five- to six-person clusters in each of the areas of family, relatives, friends, neighbors, and social/work associates (Pattison et al., 1975); some of these persons know one another, and some of them do not. There is some disagreement as to the degree of interconnectedness of these primary ties, with esimates ranging from 20%–60% (Hammer et al., 1978; Pattison et al., 1975).

While, as stated earlier, there is probably no such thing as a network that is universally beneficial to individuals and families, there appears to be little doubt that the networks of normal individuals and those of individuals with psychiatric problems differ in a number of important ways. Normal individuals' networks are larger than those of neurotic and psychotic individuals. In comparison with the estimate of 30 contacts for normal individuals, neurotic individuals tend to have networks of about 10 to 12 individuals, with greater reliance on the nuclear family and lower density or fewer interconnections among network members. Psychotic individuals tend to have networks of four to five people (usually family) that are highly interconnected, but with interpersonal ratings that are nonreciprocal and ambivalent (Pattison *et al.*, 1975).

Even within normal populations, sheer size of networks and/or frequency of contact with others appears to contribute to well-being (Fischer & Phillips, 1979; Phillips, 1967). For the elderly, for instance, frequency of contact with others and participation in more than one social role (worker, spouse, etc.) predicted higher ratings of life satisfaction (Tobin & Neugarten, 1961). In addition to size, comparisons of psychiatric and family-practice outpatients revealed that psychiatric patients average and spend markedly less time with their relationship contacts, and have fewer network contacts per week (Silberfeld, 1978).

Other studies have stressed the significance of the provisions of the network—in particular, that of social support. A minimum level and quality of social interaction is thought to be necessary to maintain a reasonable amount of affective comfort and ability to operate effectively in adversity (Henderson, 1977; Henderson & Bostock, 1977).

The availability of support from relatives, friends and neighbors in adversity has been associated with higher rates of general well-being and lower rates of physical illness and psychiatric impairment (Andrews, Tennant, Hewson, & Vaillant, 1978). Specifically, college students who had personal networks with higher proportions of persons providing encouragement and support were found to have lower reports of feelings of inadequacy and depression (Liem & Liem, 1976).

The level of support may enhance or reduce susceptibility to physical and mental problems. In a study of psychological assets, life crises, and the prognosis of pregnancy, women with high life-change scores were far more likely to have complications with their pregnancies if they did not have significant "psychosocial assets" (Nuckolls, Cassel, & Kaplan, 1971). Men who had little or no support during periods of unemployment experienced more symptoms of physical illness and negative affect (Gore, 1978).

### Congruence

While the size or range of a personal network is significant in and of itself, some suggest that the social heterogeneity of the involved individuals is at least as crucial. Network homogeneity or congruence is inversely correlated with rates of mental illness, depression, anxiety, low self-esteem, and divorce. Mintz and Schwartz (1964) reported that Italian-Americans living in high-density Italian-American communities had fewer hospital admissions for schizophrenia than did those living in communities with fewer Italian-Americans. Similar results have also been found for blacks living in predominantly white areas, whites in black areas, and Puerto Ricans in non-Puerto Rican areas (Rabkin, 1979; Wechsler & Pugh, 1967). The significance of congruence with one's community, however, extends beyond racial or ethnic affiliation. Those raised in a dissonant religious context are more likely to have low self-esteem, psychosomatic symptomatology, and depressive affect (Rosenberg, 1962). Hammer suggests that lack of congruence with one's neighbors is important because it restricts the range of possible social contacts (Hammer et al., 1978) and thus leads to smaller networks. It could also be that minority status in one's community affects self-concept and a sense of security and belonging, and also promotes increased rates of negative feedback and stress due to prejudice.

## Density

Networks have varying degrees of density. "Density," or the connectedness or completeness of a network, refers to the extent to which everyone has contact with or knows everyone else (Mitchell, 1969). This can be estimated by the ratio between the potential links in a community (the maximum number of links that could possibly exist) and the number of links that actually exist (Mitchell, 1969).

The relationship between network density and emotional health and illness is a complicated one. Dense networks, particularly homogeneous ones, are more likely to share ethnic, religious and political identities, as well as to involve greater intimacy and emotion (Walker et al., 1977). When "close-knit" networks exist, the behavior of all members appears to be influenced by the wishes and expectations of the group of friends as a whole (Harris, 1969; Mitchell, 1969), which would seem to account for the stability of behaviors and traditions in such communities. For instance, gang membership has been shown to relate to age of marriage (Miller, 1963; Rosenberg & Bensman, 1968). In a study of Appalachian migrants to Chicago, considerable pressure was found to be placed on gang members to maintain a primary loyalty to the gang, thus delaying marriage. In fact, at least one study suggests that some young men used "inadvertent" pregnancies (an acceptable excuse for marriage) to counteract the gang pressure to remain single (Miller, 1963).

Dense networks appear to be a positive force in maintaining a consistent identity, role behaviors, morale, and aid in emergencies (Barton, 1962; Brown, Davidson, Harris, Maclean, Pollack, & Prudo, 1977). For instance, college students with high-density social networks have been found to receive significantly more social and emotional support than have those students with low density social networks (Hirsch, 1979). Women who are densely connected and integrated into their community show lower rates of depression than do less connected women (Brown et al., 1977). This last study, however, which investigated 154 women living on an isolated island off the coast of Scotland, would also seem to indicate that high density is not an unmixed blessing. Although they were less depressed, well-integrated women experienced higher rates of anxiety than their less well connected counterparts. While, as Brown concludes, community support may reduce vulnerability to depression by giving meaning to life and a place in the system, it may be that this same integration promotes more closeness and social control than is desired and thus increases susceptibility to anxiety. For these reasons, dense networks may have a more negative impact on peripheral members and on members experiencing events or changes that are unusual or unfamiliar to the membership in general.

Members of loose-knit groups appear to be more able to behave inconsistently from time to time or even to make permanent life and role changes without network disruption. In fact, if an individual has experiences that are unusual, loose-knit networks may be better able to provide support than dense ones may be, since there is a greater likelihood of encountering members with similar experiences (Walker *et al.,* 1977). Furthermore, since dense networks tend to support the *status quo,* individuals experiencing desired or inevitable life changes may find a dispersed network more tolerant and adaptable, as such a network is more likely to provide new information and new social contacts and to discourage the spread of emotional upset among network members. For instance, low-density and multidimensional relationships were associated with better support and mental health for women undergoing major life transitions (mature women returning to college and recent widows). Those women undergoing transitions who had dense support systems, on the other hand, were found to have lower levels of socializing, reinforcement, emotional support, and cognitive guidance, as well as lower mood and lower self-esteem.

Thus, in low-density networks, conformity may be less essential to network maintenance; there may also be greater likelihood of finding someone to support to satisfy one's changing needs (Hirsch, 1979) in obtaining new information or making new social contacts, and there may be less contagion of emotional upset and stress. In fact, low density (low levels of contact between portions of the network) may allow one part of a network to serve as a source of support against stresses in other network parts or segments.

It would appear, then, that "closed" networks may operate both for and against a family's or individual's well-being. There appears to be at least some cause for concern about the health care of individuals in dense social networks. It has been shown that individuals belonging to "parochial" networks (those with ethnic exclusivity, friendship solidarity, and traditional family form—in other words, high density), are more likely to have a popular health orientation (i.e., to depend on home remedies, etc.), to rely less on the medical profession, and to display poorer preventive behaviors (Langlie, 1977). Individuals with a smaller proportion of kin or larger "friend networks" have been found to have less delay in the utilization of health services, while those with larger family networks have longer delays

(Salloway & Dillon, 1973). This may be true because friend networks more readily share current information about health services, while family-dominated networks operate more as role-support systems.

As might be expected, similar findings have been obtained regarding the use of psychiatric services. In a study of psychiatric patients, the structure of kinship and friendship networks was better able to predict the path into psychiatric treatment than was social class. Closed networks (high kin density) tended to encapsulate patients within their primary groups, thus delaying the initiation of psychiatric treatment (Freidson, 1960; Horwitz, 1977; McKinley, 1972). Open networks were more conducive to the use of psychiatric resources. Individuals with few social supports had high rates of utilization of a community mental health center (Tischler, Henisz, Myers, & Boswell, 1975). Those seeking help had fewer friendships with relatives, fewer relatives living close by, and even fewer family memberships in organizations.

The ability to encapsulate and support individuals within primary groups may decrease the need for professional help and may even make psychiatric treatment unnecessary. While such community care may be a desirable alternative to institutionalization, this same process of encapsulation may prevent individuals and families from getting new information or helpful services and from developing newer and healthier family roles. In other words, there is a price for the support of one's connections. This price may include pressures to conform to expectations in one's opinions and life style, as well as decreased opportunities for new experiences and new information. The increased anxiety noted by Brown (Brown *et al.,* 1977) may be one of the least problematic results for individuals who do not feel completely in tune with those to whom they are close or who are providing for their needs (Hammer, 1979). These individuals may even be required to define themselves as deviant or disturbed when such labels would not be required by a less close-knit, homogeneous, or parochial group.

### Proportion of Kin

The proportion of kin in an individual's network relates to the concept of density, since kin are more likely to know one another and to have relatively permanent relationships (Bott, 1971). It is not surprising therefore that the proportion of kin in one's network also relates to individual mental health and illness. Silberfeld, comparing family practice and psychiatric outpatients (1978), found that psychiatric patients have lower proportions of close relationships with relatives other than their spouses or children, as well as lower proportions of ties associated with work or societal institutions.

The need for and desirability of kin as a resource for help during crises or emergencies has been shown repeatedly. Yet, adequate representation of nonkin in the network appears to have a significant correlation with morale, at least in studies of aging populations. If the network has a large family component, the individual is more likely to report lower morale (Arling, 1976; Blau, 1961; Wood & Robertson, 1978). In fact, Blau contends that an older person with a single good friend is better able to cope with old age than one with a dozen grandchildren and no friends (Blau, 1961). It may be that the size and type of network needed and maintained differ for various family members and are dependent on such factors as sex, age, and/or changes in the family life cycle.

For instance, epidemiologic studies have demonstrated higher rates of neurosis in women than in men (see Dohrenwend & Dohrenwend, 1969, for a review of 21 epidemiological studies of neurosis). While these differences may be due to differing biological vulnerabilities or greater requirements for support by women, the fact remains that, while women tend to have more kin members in their networks than men, many women automatically have fewer network contacts available to them by virtue of their "in-home" role. The networks' contribution to the ill health of women would tend to be supported by the fact that full- or part-time employment increases a woman's well-being (Brown, Bhrolchain, & Harris, 1975; Gove & Geerken, 1977). Married women who work report higher levels of well-being than housewives (Gove & Geerken, 1977) and appear to have some protection against depression (Brown *et al.,* 1975), perhaps because holding a job links women to a second major support system, thus increasing size and decreasing density of networks. Since the pressure of young children is associated with higher levels of psychiatric symptoms for women, a second, work-related network may be particularly important for mothers, increasing the likelihood of rewards in one arena when the other becomes frustrating. Work for women may provide a relief not only from boredom but from isolation, and may enhance their self-esteem sufficiently to cause increased initiative in interpersonal activity.

## CONCLUSIONS

The link between families and networks is only just beginning to be explored, particularly as it relates to the details of family interaction and family functioning. Nevertheless, from the data reviewed here, it can be concluded that networks appear to supply a number of vital provisions for the family and its members.

Social networks address functional needs for information, concrete services, support, and companionship. They appear to promote a sense of security, connectedness, and belonging. Most mental health professionals stress the universal need for connectedness and attachment, which appears to be central to an individual's security and self-worth (Henderson, 1977). Bowlby, for instance, suggests that we are all most content and effective when we are certain that there are people whom we can count on and trust

(Bowlby, 1973). Yet very little research has been conducted that addresses the issue of how and by whom these needs are met. Although the most crucial people giving a sense of connectedness are likely to be members of one's immediate nuclear family, the family alone may or may not meet all of these needs. Some family members may be temporarily or even permanently unable to be responsive to some or all of an individual's requirements. Furthermore, the family as a whole may have more difficulty meeting these needs of its members if it is not receiving input and support from a larger network. Clearly, an "adequate" or "healthy" network is relevant to family functioning.

The literature just reviewed provides some clues as to what constitutes a healthy network. Current research would suggest that variables of relevance would include such factors as size, congruence, density, and proportion of kin. Other variables, and more complex ones, are likely to be defined as these connections are studied in more detail. It will be important to learn more about "normal" and "pathological" networks to determine whether there is something about normal networks that is protective and stress-reducing and something about neurotic or psychotic networks that maintains or exacerbates stress. Although it may be possible to define those network variables that are likely to facilitate family tasks, or to correlate with certain types of communication and boundary maintenance (Reiss, 1971), it is unlikely that we will discover one "normal" or "best" type of network that works for all families and individuals in all circumstances.

As Walker and his colleagues state, "to suggest that one specific type of network is unusually most supportive in a crisis situation is to ignore the diversity of needs that can be experienced by an individual under stress" (Walker *et al.*, 1977, p. 37). These authors stress that three characteristics influence the type of network most suitable to meet the needs of individuals: the nature of the crisis (temporary inability or major role change); the time (needs may change at various stages of the crisis); and the external and internal resources of the individual (personality and the ability to use the network). Other factors may be important in determining the usefulness of various networks to families. The patterns of network needs for individuals and families at various stages of the family life cycle must be determined. We might hypothesize, for instance, that dense kin-oriented networks that offer practical assistance would be most useful during the child-rearing years, while more loose-knit networks would be most useful during times of family transitions (children's emancipations, husbands' promotions, wives' returning to the work world). Alternatively, one could hypothesize that the networks in general are more significant during early marriage (when roles are being learned) and late marriage, (when illness is more common), and less important during child-rearing years (when time and energy tends to be concentrated in the nuclear family). In any case, we must investigate the fit between the social and psychological needs of the individual at a given time and the individual's social support network (Walker *et al.*, 1977). For instance, we need more data about the optimal level of density that would promote adjustment in a given situation. We need to understand what is supportive about some networks and not about others.

This entire area of research, however, is plagued to some extent by conceptual and methodological problems. Most current studies are correlational in nature; thus, while preliminary findings suggest relationships between network variables and family functioning or individual health, it is not known whether this is a causal connection. Certain types of networks could contribute to the development of particular types of personalities: for example, one type—competitive, hard-driving, work-oriented—may be incompatible with highly social, cooperative, and mutually supportive network relationships. Indeed, there is some evidence that communal networks are associated with *more* commitment, loyalty and cohesion, but with *less* individual achievement, career orientation and self-reliance (Radecki, 1978).

Similarly, while we know that disturbed families have smaller networks, it is unclear whether they choose to have smaller networks, whether they were rejected by network members because of their unusual behaviors, or whether smaller networks caused them to become *more* disturbed. In the first case, individuals under stress may not be comfortable with others, or they may voluntarily restrict their extrafamilial contacts so as not to risk rejection or to expend the energy necessary to establish and/or maintain a large, complex network. The networks of neurotics and psychotics may also be smaller because they have diminished their social contacts as they became overwhelmed with depressive or psychotic processes. On the other hand, previously small networks may have provided less support and less feedback about inappropriate behaviors, thus precipitating or exacerbating disturbed behaviors.

Even if these cause–effect issues could be resolved by sophisticated longitudinal studies, we are left with many methodological problems. For example, the validity of self-report data about networks is a serious issue. In studies of the "provisions" of networks, we may find that subjects who receive the most help may feel they receive the least. Underreporting of network members due to depressed perceptions, denial of events, distortions of recall, or selective memory all influence the data obtained from self-report studies. For instance, Liem and Liem (1978) found that the amount of actual help received from network members is not always closely related to perceptions of being supported. In another study (Finlayson, 1976), individuals studied during a crisis and again a year later consistently underestimated the amount of support they had received, tending to remember sustained support and to forget support that was significant but temporary. Furthermore, Gore (1978) found a difference between respondents' overall impressions of support and their reports of specific forms of help received. To compound the issue of the subjectivity of self-report ratings, we do not even know whether it is crucial to determine the actual amount of support received. The belief that people are standing by may be more important than their actual availability is. Conversely, large numbers of available ties may be irrelevant if the focal individual does not perceive or use them as members of his or her network.

Nevertheless, even before all the questions are answered and all the data are in, existing network data could have some practical significance for family clinicians and researchers. Data about social networks could be valuable in the assessment and treatment of individuals and families. Minimally, a simple awareness of the significance of the quality of network connectedness may help clinicians to begin to ask about extrafamilial contacts. Additionally, knowledge of the approximate range of "normal" network characteristics may provide the clinician with a yardstick against which to compare families that seem unusually isolated or unusually connected.

A general awareness of these network phenomena may stimulate the clinician to ask questions about the network connectedness of a specific family. The answers to such questions may help to explain the family's level of stress. For instance, in a family that recently presented with a 9-year-old child who had suddenly developed a school phobia, the mother appeared to be extremely anxious and overinvolved, yet subtly encouraging of the child's school refusal. An assessment of the family's network connections revealed three major network changes within the past year. The mother's parents, with whom she had always been close, had retired to Florida. The mother's neighbor and best friend had returned to college, thus becoming much less available. The mother's sister, a favorite confidant, was having marital problems that made her preoccupied and emotionally unresponsive. These factors combined to increase the anxiety of a woman who described herself as always having been "dependent and nervous." The process of identifying these network losses began to refocus family energies to help the mother reestablish a support system, at which point the child's school phobia began to dissolve.

Awareness of the impact of changes in networks may also prevent misassessments or overreactions to symptoms of family dysfunction. Since increased marital conflict may well bring a family to treatment, and since increased marital conflict is often a temporary response to the loss of network members during relocation, it would be important to include questions about network changes in the assessment of any family in trouble. Families that appear quite conflictual may be experiencing nothing more than a temporary reaction to dislocation. On the other hand, network data also suggest that geographic relocation has a differential impact on various individuals. Such knowledge should increase the sensitivity of the clinician to the specific needs of family members at such a time. For instance, if the wife/mother is lower-middle-class, if she is unemployed, and if she had been well connected to a same-sex social group from which she is now isolated, relocation may present a serious problem for her and her family. In such cases, however, it may be more important to attend to and aid her efforts to establish new connections than to deal with the marital discord directly.

An assessment of network issues should not be limited to the discovery of potential stresses and disruptions. At times, hidden resources and additional supports might also be revealed. In addition to people available to be confidants and/or to provide emotional support, sources of practical help, such as baby-sitting, transportation, or information, can be discovered in the ranks of extended kin, friends, and neighbors.

In some cases, clinicians may find it helpful to facilitate the mobilization of current networks or to encourage the formation of new network ties in order to increase the effectiveness of family functioning without directly challenging established internal family patterns that are difficult to alter. In other cases, it may be necessary to create artificial networks to serve a particular purpose. For instance, families with a psychotic family member are likely to be isolated from a support system, particularly if the patient has been ill for an extended period of time. Misunderstandings about mental illness, fears of stigmatization, sensitivity to issues of confidentiality, or just plain exhaustion may prevent the mobilization of current network members or the development of new contacts. Despite needs for support, many families are reluctant to talk to network members about a relative's illness. They fear, sometimes legitimately, that those who have not had such an experience will not understand the problems of living with someone who is mentally ill. One father reported responding to all who questioned him about his son's illness with the phrase, "He's coming along." This, he felt, saved him from having to explain situations others did not understand, and it cut off what he viewed as unhelpful and unsolicited advice. When people experience unusual and chronic stress, such as a chronic and serious illness, the creation of new networks in the form of multiple family groups or self-help organizations may be the most effective strategy of intervention (Anderson, Meisel, & Houpt, 1975; Lamb & Oliphant, 1978; Strelnick, 1977; Wechsler, 1960). In such groups the isolated are more likely to meet others who truly understand the pain they are experiencing and the specific problems they have encountered in attempting to cope with it. In rare instances, they find that others have developed some hard-won solutions that are applicable to their own circumstances. Such artificial networks, since they are organized around a specific purpose, may only operate for certain needs and during specific time periods. Nevertheless, they may be extremely useful in meeting needs that cannot be met elsewhere.

Finally, an assessment of the attitude of network members towards treatment adds an important dimension to both the immediate and long-term management of cases, and it may provide further insight about "treatment resistance" (Kadushin, 1966). The family's level of connectedness and style of handling extrafamilial connections could be used to predict responses to therapeutic interventions and receptivity to external information. If a family has a highly dense network, composed mainly of kin, they are less likely to turn to professionals and to accept treatment interventions. These families may be less resistant if the choice between receiving help from kin and receiving help from professionals is less polarized. It may be helpful, therefore, to inquire about the attitudes and opinions of network members. Once these factors are known, a range of interventions can be initiated. Minimally, treatment interventions can be kept congruent with the values and style of the network to prevent therapy dropouts or treatment sabotage. More ambitiously, the clinician can move to involve network members in the process of treatment. This can be accomplished by inviting extended family or significant others to attend family sessions, or even by instituting network therapy.

# REFERENCES

Adams, B. N. Interaction theory and the social network. *Sociometry,* 1967, *30,* 64–78.

Adams, B. N. *Kinship in an urban setting.* Chicago: Markham Press, 1968.

Aldous, J., & Straus, M. A. Social networks and conjugal roles: A test of Botts' hypothesis. *Social Forces,* 1966, *44,* 576–580.

Anderson, C., Meisel, S., & Houpt, J. Training former patients as task group leaders. *International Journal of Group Psychotherapy,* 1975, *25,* 32–43.

Andrews, G., Tennant, C., Hewson, D. M., & Vaillant, G. Life event stress, social support, coping style, and risk of psychological impairment. *Journal of Nervous and Mental Disease,* 1978, *166,* 307–316.

Arling, G. The elderly widow and her family, neighbors, and friends. *Journal of Marriage and the Family,* 1976, 757–768.

Barton, A. The emergency social system. In G. W. Baker & D. W. Chapman (Eds.), *Man and society in disaster.* New York: Basic Books, 1962.

Blau, Z. S. Structural constraints on friendships in old age. *American Sociological Review,* 1961, *26,* 429–439.

Blood, R. O. Kinship interaction and marital solidarity. *Merrill-Palmer Quarterly,* 1969, *15,* 171–184.

Blood, R. O., & Wolfe, D. M. *Husbands and wives: The dynamics of married living.* New York: Free Press, 1960.

Boissevan, J. *Friends of friends: Networks, manipulators and coalitions.* New York: St. Martins, 1974.

Bott, E. *Family and social network* (2nd ed.). New York: Free Press, 1971.

Bowlby, J. *Attachment and loss* (Vol. 2: *Separation: anxiety and anger*). New York: Basic Books, 1973.

Brown, G. W., Bhrolchain, M. W., & Harris, T. Social class and psychiatric disturbance among women in an urban population. *Sociology,* 1975, *9,* 223–254.

Brown, G. W., Davidson, S., Harris, T., Maclean, U., Pollack, S., & Prudo, R. Psychiatric disorder in London and North Uist. *Social Science and Medicine,* 1977, *11,* 367–377.

Budson, R. D., & Jolley, R. E. A crucial factor in community program success: The extended psychosocial kinship system. *Schizophrenia Bulletin,* 1978, *4,* 609–621.

Cassel, J. The contribution of social environment to host resistance. *American Journal of Epidemiology,* 1976, *104,* 107–123.

Chatterjee, M. Conjugal roles and social networks in an Indian urban sweeper locality. *Journal of Marriage and the Family*, 1977, *39*, 193–202.

Codere, H. A genealogical study of kinship in the United States. *Psychiatry*, 1955, *18*, 65–79.

Dohrenwend, B. P., & Dohrenwend, B. S. *Social status and psychological disorder.* New York: Wiley, 1969.

Farber, B. *Kinship and family organization.* New York: Wiley, 1966.

Finlayson, A. Social networks as coping resources: Lay help and consultation patterns used by women in husband's post infarction career. *Social Science and Medicine*, 1976, *10*, 97–103.

Firth, R., Hubert, J., & Forge, A. *Families and their relatives: Kinship in a middle-class sector of London.* London: Routledge & Kegan Paul, 1970.

Fischer, C. S., & Phillips, S. L. *Who is alone: Social characteristics of people with small networks.* Paper presented at the University of California at Los Angeles Research Conference on Loneliness, May 1979.

Freidson, E. Client control and medical practice. *American Journal of Sociology*, 1960, *65*, 374–382.

Ginsberg, Y. Joint leisure activities and social networks in two neighborhoods in Tel Aviv. *Journal of Marriage and the Family*, 1975, *37*, 668–676.

Gore, S. The effect of social support in moderating the wealth consequences of unemployment. *Journal of Health and Social Behavior*, 1978, *19*, 157–165.

Gove, W., & Geerken, M. The effect of children and employment on the mental health of married men and women. *Social Forces*, 1977, *56*, 66–76.

Handel, G., & Rainwater, L. Persistence and chance in working class life style. In A. B. Shostak & W. Gomberg (Eds.), *Blue collar world.* Englewood Cliffs, N.J.: Prentice-Hall, 1964.

Hammer, M. *Social supports, social networks, and schizophrenia.* Paper presented at the Vermont Conference on Stress, Social Support, and Schizophrenia, September 1979.

Hammer, M., Makiesky-Barrow, S., & Gutwirth, L. Social networks and schizophrenia. *Schizophrenia Bulletin*, 1978, *4*, 522–545.

Harris, C. C. *The family.* London: Allen & Unwin, 1969.

Henderson, S. The social network, support and neurosis: The function of attachment in adult life. *British Journal of Psychiatry*, 1977, *131*, 185–191.

Henderson, S., & Bostock, T. Coping behavior after shipwreck. *British Journal of Psychiatry*, 1977, *131*, 15–20.

Hirsch, B. J. Psychological dimensions of social networks: A multimethod analysis. *American Journal of Community Psychology*, 1979, *7*, 263–277.

Horwitz, A. Social networks and pathways to psychiatric treatment. *Social Forces*, 1977, *56*, 86–105.

Kadushin, C. The friends and supporters of psychotherapy: On social circles in urban life. *American Sociological Review*, 1966, *31*, 786–802.

Kessler, R. C. A strategy for studying differential vulnerability to the psychological consequences of stress. *Journal of Health and Social Behavior*, 1979, *20*, 100–108.

Killworth, P., & Bernard, H. R. Catij: A new sociometric and its application to a prison living unit. *Human Organization*, 1974, *33*, 335–350.

Komarovsky, M. *Blue-collar marriage.* New York: Random House, 1962.

Lamb, H. R., & Oliphant, E. Schizophrenia through the eyes of families. *Hospital and Community Psychiatry*, 1978, *29*, 803–806.

Langlie, J. K. Social networks, health beliefs, and preventive health behavior. *Journal of Health and Social Behavior*, 1977, *18*, 244–260.

Lee, N. H. *The search for an abortionist.* Chicago: University of Chicago Press, 1969.

Leichter, H. J., & Mitchell, W. E. *Kinship and casework.* New York: Russell Sage Foundation, 1967.

Lewis, P. Family working overtime to survive. *Report from the White House Conference on Families,* 1980, *1,* 5–6.

Liem, J. H., & Liem, R. *Life events, social supports, and physical and psychological well-being.* Paper presented at the annual meeting of the American Psychological Association, Washington, D.C., 1976.

Liem, R., & Liem, J. Social class and mental illness reconsidered: The role of economic stress and social support. *Journal of Health and Social Behavior,* 1978, *19,* 139–156.

Litwak, E. The use of extended family groups in the achievement of social goals: Some policy implications. *Social Problems,* 1959–1960, *7,* 177–187.

Litwak, E., & Szeleny, I. Primary group structures and their functions: Kin, neighbors, and friends. *American Sociological Review,* 1969, *34,* 465–481.

Martin, F. M., Brotherston, J. H. F., & Chave, S. P. W. Incidence of neurosis in a new housing estate. *British Journal of Preventive and Social Medicine,* 1957, *11,* 196–202.

McKinley, J. B. Some approaches and problems in the study of the use of services: An overview. *Journal of Health and Social Behavior,* 1972, *13,* 115–152.

Miller, W. B. The corner gang boys get married. *Transaction,* 1963, *1,* 10–12.

Mintz, N., & Schwartz, D. Urban ecology and psychosis: Community factors in the incidence of schizophrenia and manic–depression among Italians in greater Boston. *International Journal of Social Psychiatry,* 1964, *10,* 101–118.

Mitchell, J. C. The concept and use of social networks. In J. C. Mitchell (Ed.), *Social networks in urban situations.* Manchester, England: Manchester University Press, 1969.

Mitchell, J. C. (Ed.). *Social networks in urban situations.* Manchester, England: Manchester University Press, 1969.

Mitchell, J. C. Social networks. In P. J. Siegel, A. R. Beals, & S. A. Tyler (Eds.), *Annual review of anthropology.* Palo Alto: Annual Reviews, 1974.

Nelson, J. I. Clique contacts and family orientations. *American Sociological Review,* 1966, *31,* 663–71.

Nelson, B., Collins, J., Kreitman, N., & Troop, J. Neuroses and marital interaction: II. Time sharing and social activity. *British Journal of Psychiatry,* 1970, *117,* 47–58.

Nuckolls, K. B., Cassel, J., & Kaplan, B. H. Psychosocial assets, life crises and the prognosis of pregnancy. *American Journal of Epidemiology,* 1971, *25,* 431–442.

Pattison, E. M., Defrancisco, D., Wood, P., Frazier, H., & Crowder, J. A psychosocial kinship model for family therapy. *American Journal of Psychiatry,* 1975, *132,* 1246–1256.

Phillips, D. Social participation and happiness. *American Journal of Sociology,* 1967, *72,* 479–488.

Pilisuk, M., & Froland, C. Kinship, social networks, social support and health. *Social Science and Medicine,* 1978, *12B,* 273–280.

Pool, I. de S. Communication systems. In I. de S. Pool & W. Schramm (Eds.), *Handbook of communication.* Chicago: Rand McNally, 1973.

Rabkin, J. G. Ethnic density and psychiatric hospitalization: Hazards of minority status. *American Journal of Psychiatry,* 1979, *136,* 1562–1566.

Radcliffe-Brown, A. R. *Structure and function in primitive society: Essays and addresses.* London: Cohen & West, 1952.

Radecki, S. Social networks and occupational careers. *Connections,* 1978, *1,* 43–45.

Rainwater, L., & Handel, G. Changing family roles in the working class. In A. B. Shostak & W. Gomberg (Eds.), *Blue collar world.* Englewood Cliffs, N.J.: Prentice-Hall, 1964, 70–76.

Reiss, D. Varieties of consensual experience: III. Contrasts between families of normals, character disorders, and schizophrenics. *Journal of Nervous and Mental Disease,* 1971, *152,* 73–95.

Reiss, P. J. The extended family system: correlates of and attitudes on frequency of interaction. *Marriage and Family Living,* 1962, *24,* 333–339.

Rogers, S. C. Female forms of power and the myth of male dominance: A model of female/male interaction in peasant society. *American Ethnologist,* 1975, *2,* 727–756.

Rosenberg, M. The dissonant religious context and emotional disturbance. *American Journal of Sociology*, 1962, *68*, 1–10.

Rosenberg, B., & Bensman, J. Sexual patterns in three ethnic subcultures of an American underclass. *Annals of the American Academy of Political and Social Science*, 1968, *376*, 61–75.

Salloway, J. C., & Dillon, P. B. A comparison of family network and friend network in health care utilization. *Journal of Comparative Family Studies*, 1973, *4*, 131–142.

Silberfeld, M. The economy of time applied to interpersonal relationships. *Perceptual and Motor Skills*, 1973, *43*, 585–586.

Silberfeld, M. Psychological symptoms and social supports. *Social Psychiatry*, 1978, *13*, 11–17.

Strelnick, A. H. Multiple family group therapy: A review of the literature. *Family Process*, 1977, *16*, 307–326.

Sussman, M. B. The help pattern in the middle-class family. *American Sociological Review*, 1953, *18*, 22–28.

Sussman, M. B. The isolated nuclear family: Fact or fiction? *Social Problems*, 1959, *6*, 333–340.

Sussman, M. B., & Burchinal, L. Kin family network: Unheralded structure in current conceptualizations of family functioning. *Marriage and Family Living*, 1962, *24*, 231–240.

Tallman, I. Working-class wives in suburbia: Fulfillment or crisis? *Journal of Marriage and the Family*, 1969, *31*, 65–72.

Tischler, G. L., Henisz, J. E., Myers, J. K., & Boswell, P. C. Utilization of mental health services. *Archives of General Psychiatry*, 1975, *32*, 411–415.

Tobin, S., & Neugarten, B. Life satisfaction and social interaction in the dying. *Journal of Gerontology*, 1961, *26*, 344–346.

Toomey, D. M. Conjugal roles and social networks in an urban working-class sample. *Human Relations*, 1971, *24*, 417–431.

Turner, C. Conjugal roles and social networks: Reexamination of a hypothesis. *Human Relations*, 1967, *20*, 121–130.

Udry, J. R., & Hall, M. Marital role segregation and social networks in middle-class, middle-aged couples. *Journal of Marriage and Family Living*, 1965, *27*, 392–395.

Wahler, R. G., Leake, G., & Rogers, E. S. *The insular family: A deviance support system for oppositional children.* Paper presented at the International Conference on Behavior Modification, Banff, Alberta, March 1977.

Walker, K. N., MacBride, A., & Vachon, M. L. S. Social support and the crisis of bereavement. *Social Science and Medicine*, 1977, *11*, 35–41.

Wechsler, H. The ex-patient organization: A survey. *Journal of Social Issues*, 1960, *16*, 47–53.

Wechsler, H., & Pugh, T. Fit of individual and community characteristics and roles of psychiatric hospitalization. *American Journal of Sociology*, 1967, *73*, 331–338.

Westermeyer, J., & Pattison, E. M. *Social networks and psychosis in a peasant society.* Paper presented at the annual meeting of the American Psychiatric Association, Chicago, 1979.

Whyte, W. J., Jr. *The organization man.* Garden City, N.Y.: Doubleday–Anchor, 1957.

Wimberly, H. Conjugal-role organization and social networks in Japan and England. *Journal of Marriage and the Family*, 1973, *35*, 125–131.

Wood, V., & Robertson, J. F. Friendship and kinship interaction: Differential effect on the morale of the family. *Journal of Marriage and the Family*, 1978, *40*, 367–378.

Wynne, L. The family as a strategic focus in cross-cultural psychiatric studies. In W. Caudill & T. Lynn (Eds.), *Mental health research in Asia and the Pacific.* Honolulu: East–West Center Press, 1969.

Zimmerman, C. The present crisis. In C. Zimmerman & L. F. Cervantes (Eds.), *Marriage and the family.* Chicago: Henry Regnery, 1956.

# 18

# AMERICAN FAMILIES
# IN TRANSITION: HISTORICAL
# PERSPECTIVES ON CHANGE

TAMARA K. HAREVEN

## INTRODUCTION: MYTHS ABOUT THE PAST

The American family has recently been the subject of much concern. Anxiety over its future has escalated over the past decade; the youth movement of the 1960s, and subsequently the women's movement, have brought it under scrutiny and attack. Policy debates over governmental family welfare programs have also directed attention to it. More recently, the emergence of the elderly in American society as a significant group with its own problems has led to a further examination of inadequacies of the family that contribute to the isolation of older people in modern America.

The consequences of all these developments, combined with the impact of increasing divorce rates and declining birth rates and the increase in the proportion of single-parent families, have given rise to the fear that the family might be breaking down or going out of existence. Anxiety over family breakdown is not unique to our times. It appears that since the time of the Founding Fathers every generation has expressed its doubts about the stability and continuity of the family. This very intense concern over the fate of the family both in the past and today points to the crucial place that the family holds in American culture. Yet the question still needs to be asked: Is the family in crisis, or is it simply undergoing some important changes? What can we learn from the past about the transitions the family life is undergoing and the directions in which it is heading?

Through much of American history, the family has been seen as the linchpin of the social order and the basis for stable governance. Even though changes appear more gradually in the family than they do in other institutions,

Tamara K. Hareven. Department of History, Clark University, Worcester, Massachusetts, and Center for Population Studies, Harvard University, Cambridge, Massachusetts.

educators, moralists, and social planners frequently express fear of family breakdown under the pressures of social changes. Every generation has thought itself to be witnessing the breakdown of the "traditional" family. In the era of the American Revolution, much anxiety was expressed about the possible disappearance of the American family, and during the Civil War the nation's crisis was projected onto the fate of the family itself. More than any other developments, however, industrialization and urbanization have been viewed as the major threats to traditional family life over the past decade and a half.

Family disorganization has been identified as a major characteristic of industrial society and has been associated with the loss of a Utopian pre-industrial past. Even the adaptation of functions of and within the family that developed in response to social change were frequently interpreted as manifestations of breakdown.

Perceptions of American family life today are governed by commonly held myths about American family life in the past. Such myths maintain that there once was a golden age of family relations, when three generations lived together happily in the same household. This belief in a lost golden age has led people to depict the present as a period of decline and family breakdown. Nostalgia for a mythical past has resulted in the idealization of such families as the Waltons of TV and the world that supposedly produced them.

In order to come to grips with the problems of the present, it is essential to examine changes in family life over the past two centuries. A historical consideration of the family places some of the changes in their proper context. Looking at developments over time enables us better to assess the uniqueness of present conditions, and it also helps us to distinguish between long-term trends and temporary developments. To what extent are some of these changes part of a continuing historical process, and to what extent are they new departures? Most importantly, a historical consideration enables us to distinguish between passing fads and critical changes, and it can even offer some precedents from the past that could be revived and applied to present conditions.

In the ensuing discussion, I first examine major historical changes in the American family in relation to the current, seemingly "dramatic" transitions. I discuss changes in the following areas: organization of the family and kin; family functions and values; and changes in the life course.

## CHANGE AND CONTINUITY IN FAMILY STRUCTURE

Recent research on the family in preindustrial American society has dispelled the myths about the existence of ideal three-generational families in the American past (Demos, 1970; Goode, 1963; Greven, 1970; Laslett, 1965;

Laslett & Wall, 1972).[1] There has never been in American society an era when three generations were coresiding in the same household. The "great extended families" that have become part of the folklore of modern industrial society were rarely actually in existence. Households and families were simple in their structure and not drastically different in their organization from contemporary families. Nuclear households, consisting of parents and their children, were characteristic residential units (although, as will be suggested later, they often contained strangers in addition to nuclear family members). Three generations rarely lived together in the same household. Given the high mortality rate in preindustrial societies, most parents could not have expected to live with their grandchildren (Davis, 1972; Glick, 1947, 1957). (On the changing life cycles of American women in particular, see Uhlenberg, 1969.) It would thus be futile to argue that industrialization destroyed the great extended family of the past, since such a family type rarely existed. And, as will be shown below, the process of industrialization had actually contributed in many ways to strengthening family ties and to increasing the chances of family members to stay together in the same place for longer time periods.

Contrary to popular assumption, preindustrial households were thus not filled by large numbers of extended kin. These households did contain strangers, however, who lived in the home as boarders, lodgers, apprentices, or servants. In this respect, the composition of the household in the pre-industrial and early industrial period was significantly different from that in contemporary society. The tendency of families to include strangers in the household was connected with an entirely different concept of family life. In contrast to the current emphasis on the family as a private retreat, the household of the past was the site of a broad array of functions and activities that transcended the more restricted circle of the nuclear family. This fact had especially important implications for the role of women: it meant that women were involved in a variety of domestic management tasks beyond the care of their immediate family members. They took care of apprentices, boarders, and possibly other strangers who were placed with the family because they were delinquent youth, orphaned children, or abandoned old men or women.

The household then, was not the exclusive abode of the nuclear family. It did not include relatives other than nuclear family members, but it did

---

[1]Historians have frequently confused "family" with "household." This distinction must be made clear, however, if changes in the family are to be put in proper perspective. The "household" is the residential unit, which has also been recorded in the population censuses. The "family" can contain kin living inside the household, as well as relatives outside the household. It is now clear that preindustrial households were not extended. But this does not mean that the family was nuclear and isolated. Although several relatives did not reside in the same household, they were still interactive (see Hareven, 1971, 1974).

include strangers. The presence of strangers in the household continued in different forms throughout the 19th and into the early 20th century. Although apprentices virtually disappeared from households by the middle of the 19th century, and dependent, delinquent, and sick people were being placed in institutions, the practice of taking strangers into the household persisted—primarily through boarding and lodging. Throughout the 19th and early 20th centuries, about one-fourth to one-third of the population either had lived in someone's household as a boarder or had taken in boarders or lodgers at some point in their lives (Modell & Hareven, 1973). Boarding and lodging fulfilled the function of what Taeuber has referred to as "the social equalization of the family" (1969, p. 5). Young men and women in their late teens and 20s who had left their own parents' households, or who had migrated from other communities, lived as boarders in the households of older people whose own children had left home. This practice thus enabled young people to stay in surrogate family arrangements, while at the same time it provided old people with the opportunity to continue heading their own households without being isolated.

The practice of taking in boarders and lodgers was extremely valuable in providing continuity in urban life and in allowing new migrants and immigrants to adapt to urban living. Its existence suggests the great flexibility in families and households, a flexibility that has been lost over the past half century. Increasing availability in housing and the spread of the values of privacy in family life have led to the phasing out of this practice. The practice has survived to some extent among black families, but it has almost virtually disappeared from the larger society. With its disappearance, the family has lost some of its major sources of resilience and adaptability to urban living. Thus, the most important change in American family life has not been the breakdown of a three-generational family pattern, but, rather, the loss of flexibility in regard to taking strangers into the household.

The practice of boarding and lodging has been replaced since the 1920s by solitary living. The increase in the rates of "primary individual" households, as the Census Bureau refers to the households of individuals residing alone, is a spreading phenomenon. While in the 19th century solitary residence was almost unheard of, now a major portion of the population resides alone. The disquieting aspect of this pattern is in the high percentage of aging widows living alone. Thus, solitary residence for a major portion of the population is not a matter of free choice, but rather an unavoidable and often unbearable arrangement. Again, what has been lost is not a great extended family of the past, but the flexibility of the family that enabled households to expand when necessary and to take people in to live in surrogate family settings rather than in isolation (Kobrin, 1976).

Another pervasive myth about family life in the past has been the assumption that industrialization broke up traditional kinship ties and destroyed organic interdependence between the family and the community.

Once again, historical research has shown that industrialization led to the redefinition of the family's roles and functions, but by no means broke up traditional family patterns. In industrial communities, the family continued to function as a work unit. Relatives acted as recruitment, migration, and housing agents for industrial laborers, helping each other to shift from rural to industrial work. Preindustrial family patterns and values were carried over into the industrial system, providing important continuities between rural and urban industrial life (Anderson, 1971; Hareven, 1978, 1982 forthcoming). Rather than being a passive victim, the family was an active agent in the process of industrialization. Families migrated in groups to industrial centers, recruiting workers into the factory system, and often several family members continued to work in the same place. Migration to industrial communities did not break up traditional kinship ties. Rather, families used these ties to facilitate their own transitions into industrial life.

Despite changes wrought under the impact of industrialization, reliance on kin as the most basic resource for assistance persisted. Throughout the 19th and 20th centuries, kin in rural and urban areas continued to engage in mutual assistance and in reciprocal services. Kin performed a crucial role in initiating and organizing migration from rural areas to factory towns locally and from rural communities abroad to American factories. While rural/urban or overseas migration temporarily depleted kinship groups, networks were gradually reconstructed in the new location through chain migration. Thus, although people did not share the same household with relatives outside the nuclear family, they were still enmeshed in close ties with their kin outside the household.

In 19th-century American cities, chain migration facilitated transition and settlement, assured a continuity in kin contacts, and made mutual assistance in personal and family crises an important factor in the adjustment of immigrants to the urban environment. Even in the later part of the last century and in the early parts of this one, workers who migrated from rural areas to cities in most industrializing communities carried major parts of their kinship ties and family traditions into new settings. Young unmarried sons and daughters of working age, or young married couples without their children, tended to migrate first. After they found jobs and housing, they would send for their relations. Chain migration thus helped maintain ties and continuities between family members in their new communities of settlement. In factories or other places of employment, newly arrived workers utilized the good offices of their relatives who were already working in the establishment to facilitate the hiring of their newly arrived kin.

Hiring and placement through kin often continued even in large-scale modern factories. Kinship networks were able to permeate and infiltrate formal, bureaucratized industrial cooperatives and to cluster within them.

Even where they worked in different locales, kin made collective decisions about the work careers of their members. Workers migrated in kin groups and carried with them traditional patterns of kin assistance, but adapted these to the requirements of modern industrial organizations. Immigrants successfully adapted their traditional kinship patterns to modern modes of production and the organization of work, which required familiarity with bureaucratic structures and organizations, adherence to modern work schedules, responsiveness to the rhythms of industrial employment, and specialization in technological skill (Anderson, 1971; Hareven, 1978, 1982 forthcoming).

## CHANGING FAMILY FUNCTIONS AND VALUES

Industrialization, however, did affect major changes in family functions. Through a process of differentiation, the family gradually surrendered functions previously concentrated within it to other social institutions. During the preindustrial period, the family not only reared children, but also served as a workshop, a school, a church, and an asylum. Preindustrial families meshed closely with the community and carried a variety of public responsibilities within the larger society. "Family and community," writes Demos, "private and public life, formed part of the same moral equation. The one supported the other and they became in a sense indistinguishable" (1970, p. 186).

In preindustrial society, most of the work took place in the household. Reproductive roles were therefore congruent with social and economic roles. Children were considered members of the work force and were seen as economic assets. Childhood was a brief preparatory period terminated by apprenticeship and the commencement of work, generally before puberty. Adolescence was virtually unknown as a distinct stage of life. Such a social system encouraged the integration of family members into common economic activities. The segregation along sex and age lines that characterizes middle-class family life in modern society had not yet appeared.

As long as the household functioned as a workshop as well as a family home, there was no clear separation between family life and work life. Even though preindustrial families contained large numbers of children, women invested relatively less time in motherhood than their successors in the 19th century and in our time did and still do. The integration of family and work allowed for an intensive sharing of labor between husbands and wives and between parents and children that would not exist in industrial society.

Even though households were nuclear, family members were not totally isolated from kin who were residing in the neighborhood. Consequently, the tasks of child rearing did not fall exclusively on mothers; other relatives living nearby also participated in this function. As long as the family was a production unit, housework was inseparable from domestic industries or agricultural work, and it was valued, therefore, for its economic contribution. Since children constituted a viable part of the labor force, motherhood, too, was valued for its economic contributions, and not only for its nurturing qualities.

Under the impact of industrialization, many of these functions were transferred to agencies and institutions outside the family. The work place was separated from the home, and functions of social welfare were transferred from the family to asylums and reformatories. "The family has become a *more specialized agency* than before," note Parsons and Bales, "probably more specialized than in any previous known society . . . but not in any general sense less important, because the society is dependent *more* exclusively on it for the performance of *certain* of its vital functions" (1955, pp. 9–10). These vital functions included (and include) childbearing, child rearing, and socialization. The family ceased to be a work unit and limited its economic activities primarily to consumption and child care.

The transformation of the household from a busy work place and social center to a private family abode involved the withdrawal of strangers, such as business associates, partners, journeymen, apprentices, and boarders and lodgers, from the household; it also involved a more rigorous segregation in the tasks and the work responsibilities of different family members. New systemized work schedules led to the segregation of husbands from wives and fathers from children in the course of the work day. In middle-class families, housework lost its economic and productive value. Since it was not paid for, and since it no longer led to the production of visible goods, it had no place in the occupational hierarchy.

Differentiation and specialization in work schedules significantly altered the daily lives of men and women who worked outside the home. Housework, on the other hand, continued to be governed by traditional time schedules, remaining throughout the nineteenth century a nonindustrial occupation. This is another reason (in addition to economic ones) why housework has been devalued in modern society, where achievement is measured not only by products but also by systematic time and production schedules. This may also explain why, since the 19th century, the home economics movement has been so intent on introducing efficient management and industrial time schedules into the home. For several decades, reformers maintained the illusion that if housework were more systematically engineered, it would become more respectable.

In trying to assess the significance of the changes in family life brought about by industrialization, we must recognize the fact that these changes were gradual, and that they varied significantly from class to class as well as among different ethnic groups. While historians have sometimes generalized for an entire society on the basis of middle-class experience, it is now becoming clear that preindustrial family patterns persisted over longer time periods in rural and in urban working-class families. Since the process of industrialization was gradual, domestic industries and a variety of small family enterprises carried over into the industrial system. In New England, for example, during the first half of the 19th century, rural families were sending their daughters to work in factories while the farm continued to be the family's economic base (Dublin, 1979). In most working-class families, work continued to be considered a family enterprise, even if it did not take place in the home. In such families, the work of wives, sons, and daughters was carefully regulated by the collective strategies of the family unit. Many of what we perceive today as individual work careers were actually part of a collective family effort.

Even though the process of industrialization offered women opportunities for independent work outside their homes, women continued to function as an integral part of the productive effort of the family unit, even when they worked in factories. Working women were bound by family obligations and contributed most of their earnings to their parents—a woman's work was considered part of the family's work, not an independent career. Even during periods of large-scale industrial development, families continued to function as collective economic units, in which husbands, wives, and children were all responsible for the well-being of the family unit. This continuity in the function of the family economy as a corporate enterprise is significant for understanding the limited changes in working-class gender roles under the impact of the industrial revolution. Industrialization changed the nature and the pace of the work, but these families survived as collective economic units for a long time to come (Hareven, 1982 forthcoming).

Industrialization, however, had a more dramatic effect on the experience of the middle class. The separation between the home and the work place that followed in the wake of industrialization led to the glorification of the home as a domestic retreat from the outside world. The new ideology of domesticity that developed in the first half of the 19th century relegated women to the home and glorified their domestic role. (On the cult of domesticity, see Jeffrey, 1972; Sennett, 1971; Welter, 1966; Young & Wilmott, 1973.)

These changes were closely connected with the decline in the number of children a woman had and with the new attitudes toward childhood. The discovery of childhood as a distinct stage of life was intimately tied to the emergence of the middle-class family in Europe and in the United States in the early 19th century. Stripped of the multiplicity of functions that had been previously concentrated in the household, these families developed into private, domestic, and child-centered retreats. Children were no longer expected to join the work force until their late teens, a major indication of the growing recognition of childhood as a distinct stage of development. Instead of considering children as potential working members of the family group, parents perceived them as dependent subjects of tender nurture and protection. This was the emergence of the domestic middle-class family as we know it today (Aries, 1962; Bremner, Barnard, Hareven, & Mennel, 1970–1974; Demos, 1970; Greven, 1970; Kett, 1971).

The glorification of motherhood as a full-time career served both to enshrine the family as a domestic retreat from the world of work and to make families child-centered. The gradual separation of the home from the work place that had started with industrialization reached its peak in the designation of the home as a therapeutic refuge from the outside world. As custodians of this retreat, women were expected to have attributes distinctly different from those of the working wife who had been an economic partner in the family. Tenderness, gentleness, affection, sweetness, and a comforting demeanor were all considered ideal characteristics for the domestic wife. Sentiment began to replace instrumental relationship. (On family sentiment, see Aries, 1962, 1981.)

The ideology of domesticity and the new view of childhood combined to revise expectations of parenthood. The roles of husbands and wives became gradually segregated; a clear division of labor replaced the old economic partnership, with the husband now responsible for economic support and the wife's efforts directed toward homemaking and child rearing. With men leaving the home to work elsewhere, time invested in fatherhood occurred primarily during leisure hours. Thus, the separation of husbands from wives and parents from children for major parts of the day came about. The cult of domesticity emerged as a major part of the ideology of family life in American society. One of its central assumptions was the role of women as custodians of the domestic retreat and as full-time mothers. The very notion has dominated perceptions of women's roles in American society until very recently and has shaped the prevailing assumptions governing family life. One of its major consequences was the insistence that women confine their main activities to the domestic sphere, and that women's work in the labor market would be harmful to the family and to society (Lerner, 1969; Scott, 1970; Welter, 1966).

Ironically, this ideology was adopted by middle-class families just at the point in time when rural and immigrant women were recruited into the newly established giant textile centers. Even though the ideology of domesticity originated in urban middle-class families, it emerged as part of the ideology of American family life in the larger society. Second- and third-generation immigrant families embraced this outlook as part of their "Americanization" process. The ideals of urban middle-class life emerged as the ideology of the larger society and subsequently handicapped the role of women as workers outside the home as well.

The impact of the ideology of domesticity became apparent in patterns of women's labor force participation. In the late 19th century, despite the convergence of many factors that could actually have facilitated women's work outside the home, very few women actually took advantage of the opportunity. Demographic changes, combined with technological advances, offered advantageous conditions for the entry of married women into the labor force. By the late 19th century the birth rate had declined, particularly among native-born families. Women had fewer children and at the same time benefited from new labor-saving appliances, which should have freed up their time considerably. Expanded industrial and commercial facilities, made easily accessible by new transportation systems, provided increased employment opportunities for women. But despite all this, 97% of all married women did not assume gainful employment, because ideological barriers placed women's domestic and work roles in conflict (Kenniston & Kenniston, 1964; Smuts, 1959; Sweet, 1973; Tilly & Scott, 1978).

The ideology of domesticity also began to influence working-class and immigrant families during the early part of the 20th century. As immigrants became "Americanized," particularly in the second generation, they internalized the values of domesticity and began to view women's work outside the home as demeaning, as having low status, or as compromising for the husband and dangerous for the children. Consequently, married women entered the labor force only when driven by economic necessity.

It is important to realize, however, that despite its threat in the larger society, and despite its adoption as the dominant ideology in "American culture," a majority of working-class and ethnic families continued to adhere to the earlier way of life; most importantly, they maintained a collective view of the family and its economy. In contrast to the values of individualism that govern much of family life today, the traditional values of family collectivity persisted at this level of American society.

With the growth of industrial child labor in the 19th century, working-class families continued to recognize the economic value of motherhood, as they had in rural society. Segregation along age groups within working-class families was almost nonexistent. Children were socialized for industrial work from an early age and began to contribute to the family's work effort at a lower age than specified by law. They were considered an asset, both for their contribution to the family's eocnomy during their youth and for the prospect of their support during their parents' old age. Parents viewed their efforts in child rearing as investments in future social security.

The relationships between husbands and wives, parents and children, and other kin were based upon reciprocal services, support, and assistance. Such exchange relationships, often defined as "instrumental," were based on the assumption that family members were all engaged in mutual obligations and in reciprocal relationships. Although such obligations were not specifically defined by contract, they rested on the accepted social norms of what family members owed to each other. In the period preceding the welfare state and public assistance, instrumental relationships provided important supports to individuals and families, particularly during critical life situations (Anderson, 1971; Hareven, 1978).

A collective view of familial obligations was the very basis of survival. From such a perspective, marriage and parenthood were not merely love relationships, but partnerships governed by family economic and social needs. In this respect, the experience of 19th-century working-class families and of ethnic families in the more recent past was drastically different from that of middle-class ones, in which sentimentality emerged as the dominant base of family relationships. This is not to argue that husbands and wives in the past did not love each other or that parents harbored no sentiment for their children. It suggests, rather, that sentiment was secondary to family needs and survival strategies. Under such conditions, childbearing and work were not governed by individual decisions. Mate selection and the timing of marriage were regulated in accordance with collective family considerations, rather than directed by strictly individual whim. The transfer of property and work partnerships were important considerations in the selection of partners. At times, such collective family "plans" took priority over individual preferences. Parents tried to delay the marriage of the last child in the household— commonly that of a daughter—in order to secure continued economic support, especially in later life when they were withdrawing from the labor force.

The major historical change in family values has been a change from a collective view of the family to one of individualism and sentiment. These have led to an increasing emphasis on individual priorities and preferences over collective family needs. They have also led to an exaggerated emphasis on emotional nurture, intimacy, and privacy as the major justification for family relations. This shift in values has contributed considerably to the "liberation of individuals," but it has also eroded the resilience of the family and its ability to handle crises. Moreover, it has contributed to a greater separation among family members and especially to the isolation of older people.

## CHANGES IN THE LIFE COURSE

The full impact of changes in family values and functions on the condition of the family today can be best understood in the context of demographic changes affecting the time of life transitions, such as marriage, parenthood, the "empty nest," and widowhood. Since the end of the 19th century, important changes have occurred in the family cycle that have affected age configurations within the family and generational relations (Hareven, 1977).

Beginning in the early 19th century, the American population has experienced a steady decline in the birth rate. Over the 19th and early 20th centuries, the birth rate of the American population went down steadily; it declined from an average of 7.04 children per family in 1800 to 3.56 children per family in 1900. This decline and the subsequent decline since 1900 have had a profound impact on the cycle of family life, especially on the timing of marriage, the birth of the first child and of subsequent children, and the spacing of children. They have also considerably affected the meaning of marriage and of parenthood. In traditional society, little time elapsed between marriage and parenthood, since procreation was the major goal of marriage. In modern society, contraception has permitted a gap between these two stages of the family cycle. Marriage has become recognized as important in its own right, rather than merely as a transition to parenthood (Smith, 1974; Wells, 1971; Yasuba, 1961).

One widely held myth about the past is that the timing of family transitions was once more orderly and stable than it is today. The complexity that governs family life today and the variations in family roles and in transitions into them are frequently contrasted to this more placid past. The historical record, however, frequently reveals precisely the opposite condition: patterns of family timing in the past were often more complex, more diverse, and less orderly than they are today. Voluntary and involuntary demographic changes that have come about since the late 19th century have in fact paradoxically resulted in greater uniformity in the timing of transitions along the life course, despite greater societal complexity. The growing uniformity in timing has been accompanied by a shift from involuntary to voluntary factors affecting the timing of family events. The increase in life expectancy, the decline in fertility, and the earlier marriage age have, for example, greatly increased the chances for temporal overlap in the lives of family members. Families are now able to go through a life course much less subject to sudden change than that experienced by the majority of the population in the 19th century.

The "typical" family cycle of modern American families includes early marriage and early commencement of childbearing, but a small number of children. Families following this type of family cycle experience a compact period of parenthood in the middle years of life; then an extended period, encompassing one-third of their adult life, without children; and finally, often, a period of solitary living following the death of a spouse, most frequently that of the husband (Glick, 1955, 1977; Glick & Parke, 1965).

This type of cycle has important implications for the composition of the family and for relationships within it in current society: husbands and wives are spending a relatively longer lifetime together; they invest a shorter segment of their lives in childrearing; and they more commonly survive to grandparenthood. This sequence has been uniform for the majority of the popu-

NORMAL FAMILIES IN SOCIOCULTURAL CONTEXT

lation since the beginning of the 20th century. In contrast to past times, most families see their children through to adulthood with both parents still alive. As Uhlenberg (1974) points out, the normal family cycle for women—a sequence of leaving home, marriage, family formation, child rearing, launching, and survival at age 50 with the first marriage still intact—unless broken by divorce, has not been the dominant pattern of family timing before the early 20th century. Prior to 1900, only about 40% of the female population in the United States experienced this ideal family cycle. The remainder either never married, never reached marriageable age, died before childbirth, or were widowed while their offspring were still young children.

In the 19th century, the combination of a later age at marriage and higher fertility provided little opportunity for a family to experience an "empty nest" stage. Prior to the decline in mortality among the young at the beginning of the 20th century, marriage was frequently broken by the death of a spouse before the end of the child-rearing period. Even when fathers survived the child-rearing years, they rarely lived beyond the marriage of their second child. As a result of higher fertility, children were spread over a wider age range; frequently, the youngest child was just entering school as the oldest was preparing for marriage. The combination of later marriage, higher fertility, and widely spaced childbearing resulted in a different timing of family transitions. Individuals became parents later, but carried child-rearing responsibilities almost until the end of their lives. Consequently, the lives of parents overlapped with those of their children for shorter periods than they do currently.

Under the demographic conditions of the 19th century—higher mortality and higher fertility—functions within the family were less specifically tied to age, and members of different age groups were consequently not so completely segregated by the tasks they were required to fulfill. The spread of children over a larger age spectrum within the family had important implications for family relationships, as well as for their preparations for adult roles. Children were accustomed to growing up with larger numbers of siblings and were exposed to a greater variety of models from which to choose than they would have been in a small nuclear family. Older children often took charge of their younger siblings. Sisters, in particular, carried a major share of the responsibility for raising the youngest siblings, and they frequently acted as surrogate mothers if the mother worked outside the home or had died. The smaller age overlap between children and their parents was also significant: the oldest child was the one most likely to overlap with its father in adulthood, and the youngest child was the least likely to do so.

The oldest child would have been most likely to embark on an independent career before the parents reached old-age dependency; the youngest children were most likely to carry responsibilities for parental support and to overlap in adulthood with a widowed mother. The oldest child had the greatest chance to overlap with grandparents, the youngest child the least. Late-marrying children were most likely to be responsible for the support of a widowed mother, while early-marrying children depended on their parents' household space after marriage. One can better grasp the implications of these differences in age at marriage, number of children, assigned tasks, and generational overlap when one takes into consideration the uncertainties and the economic precariousness that characterized the period. These made the orderly sequence of progression along stages of the family cycle, which sociologists have observed in the contemporary American population, impossible for the 19th-century family.

Another comparison between what is considered the "normal" family cycle today and its many variants in the 19th century reverses one more stereotype about the past—namely, that American society has been experiencing breakdown and diversification in family organization. In reality, the major transitions in family roles have been characterized by greater stability and conformity because of the greater opportunity for generational continuities. The opportunity for a meaningful period of overlap in the lives of grandparents and grandchildren is a 20th-century phenomenon, a surprising fact that runs counter to the popular myth of a family solidarity in the past that was based on three-generational ties.

The relative significance of transition into family roles also differed in the 19th century. In the 19th century, when conception was likely to take place very shortly after marriage, the major transition in a woman's life was represented by marriage itself. But, as the interval between marriage and first pregnancy has increased in modern society, the transition to parenthood has become more significant than the transition to marriage. Family limitation has also had an impact on the timing of marriage. Since marriage no longer inevitably leads to parenthood, postponing marriage is no longer needed to delay it. On the other end of the life course, transitions into the "empty nest" roles are much more critical today than they were in the past, when parental or surrogate-parental roles encompassed practically the entire adult life span. Completion of parental roles today involves changes in residence, changes in work, and, perhaps, eventual removal into institutions or retirement communities (Chudacoff & Hareven, 1978).

The overall historical pattern of family behavior has thus been marked by a shift from involuntary to voluntary forces conrolling the timing of family events. It has also been characterized by greater rigidity and uniformity in the timing of the passage from one family role to another. In their comparison of such transitions in 19th-century Philadelphia with those of the present, Modell, Furstenberg, and Hershberg (1976) conclude that transitions into adult roles (departure from the family of origin, marriage, and the establishment of a household) follow a more ordered sequence and are accomplished over a shorter time period in a young person's life today than they were in the 19th century. Such transitions to familial roles also coincide today with transitions into occupational roles: "Transitions are today more contingent, more integrated because they are constrained by a set of formal institutions. 'Timely' action to nineteenth-century families consisted of helpful response in times of trouble; in the twentieth century, timeliness connotes adherence to a schedule" (Modell, Furstenberg, & Hershberg, 1976, p. 30).

The demographic changes that have led to this isolation, continued with the decline in "instrumental" relations in the family discussed earlier, have caused isolation of older people in American society—a problem that is much more severe and immediate than the issue of "family breakdown." While the major historical changes in family functions occurred in the 19th and early 20th centuries, changes in the timing of family transitions are much more strictly 20th-century phenomena and particularly affect the family in our times. Changes in the family cycle, such as the emergence of the "empty nest," extensions of the period of widowhood, and increasing age segregation in the family and the larger society, reflect major discontinuities that have resulted in increasing problems in the middle and later years of life. It is precisely in this area that one needs to be concerned with future changes in the family.

## IMPLICATIONS OF CHANGE

One of the major causes of the anxiety about the future of the family is rooted not so much in reality as in the tension between the idealized expectation in the culture and the reality itself. Nostalgia for a lost family tradition that in fact never existed has prejudiced our understanding of the conditions of families in contemporary society. Thus, the current anxiety over the fate of the family reflects not merely problems in the family, but a variety of fears about other social problems that are eventually projected onto the family.

The real problems that the American family is facing today are not symptoms of breakdown, as is often suggested. Rather, they reflect the difficulties that the family faces in its adaptation to recent social changes, particularly in the loss of diversity in household membership it had in the past, the reduction of the variety of its functions, and, to some extent, the weakening of its adaptability. The idealization of the family as a refuge from the world and the myth that the work of mothers is harmful have added considerable strain. The continuous emphasis on the family as a universal private retreat and as an emotional haven is misguided in light of the historical experience. In the past, the family fulfilled a broad array of functions, not merely emotional ones. Most of its functions in the past were intertwined with the larger community. Rather than being the custodian of privacy, the family prepared its members for interaction with the larger society. Family relationships were valued not merely for their emotional contents, but for a wide array of services and contributions to the collective family unit. By contrast, one of the major sources of the crisis of nuclear families today is its difficulty in adapting to the emotional functions thrust upon it and to the expectations of romantic love that accompany marriage, precisely because these functions and expectations represent an artificial boundary between individuals and the larger society.

Concentration on the emotional functions of the family has grown at the expense of another of its much-needed roles in industrial society; namely, the preparation of its members for their interaction with bureaucratic institutions. In American society, the education and welfare systems have made dramatic inroads into areas that had previously been the private preserve of the family. At the same time, however, the tendency of the family to shelter its members from other social institutions has weakened its ability to affect the structure of or to influence the programs and legislation that public agencies have directed at the family.

Attitudes towards family life in American society have been governed by the stereotype of the "ideal family," which is based on the middle-class nuclear family. In reality, American society has contained within it great diversities in family types and family behavior that were associated with the recurring entrance of new immigrant groups into American society. Ethnic, racial, cultural, and class differences have also resulted in diversity in family behavior. The tensions between family behavior in the dominant culture and the traditional patterns of the black family and of immigrant families has been a continuing pattern in American life (Hareven & Modell, 1980).

There has been a tendency toward homogenization of American culture, through the absorption of ethnic traditions on the one hand, and immigrant acceptance of the dominant cultural models on the other. Immigrants, primarily in the second generation, adopted "American" family behavior, and this adoption has been reflected in several areas: a decline in fertility, earlier marriage, growing privatization of the family, withdrawal of women and children from the labor force, and changing patterns of consumption and tastes. However, this ongoing process did not result in total assimilation of family ways and traditional customs, because the influx of new immigrants kept introducing new cultural variety. The result has been continuing diversity in family patterns. Contrary to the official creed of the "melting pot," a great many varieties of ethnic family behavior have survived in American society, and new patterns are still being introduced through recent migration. It is therefore unrealistic to talk simply about *the* American family.

For over a century, until very recently, the stereotype of the private nuclear family as the ideal family in American society has been dominant.

Alternative forms of family organization, such as those of the black family or of other ethnic families, were misinterpreted as "family disorganization" simply because they did not conform to the official stereotype. But actually, over the past decade, the strength and resilience of ethnic and black family ways has been recognized. These traditional resources of family and kinship among black and ethnic families have been rediscovered as the middle-class nuclear family, besieged by its own isolation, has proven its limitations in coping with stress.

One of the most unique features of American families today is their cultural and ethnic diversity; this diversity, which is in itself a continuation of a historical pattern, is now being valued as a source of strength and continuity, rather than, as in the past, being decried as a manifestation of deviance. One of the challenges today faced by individuals and policy makers is the creative use of these family patterns in coping with contemporary problems.

An understanding of the historical changes over the past century provides a different perspective on family life today. There is no question that American families have been undergoing important transitions over the past century. But the main question is that of whether these changes represent family breakdown and whether they threaten the disappearance of the family. Some of these transitions represent the continuation of a long historical process: the decline in the birth rate, the earlier marriage rate, and changes in the timing of life transitions are all the result of a continuing process of change over the past century and a half. Similarly, the moratorium from adult responsibilities that teenagers now experience and the increasing isolation of older people on the other end of the cycle, are both the results of long-term historical changes.

On the other hand, the increase in divorce rates and the concomitant increase in single-parent households represent a much more dramatic transition in our times. But the rise in divorce as such, which has been often cited as a symptom of family breakdown, should not be necessarily misconstrued. In the 19th century people did not resort to divorce as frequently as they do now, because divorce was considered socially unacceptable. This does not mean, however, that families were living happily and in harmony. A high rate of desertion and separation of couples replaced legal divorce. And incompatible couples who did not resort to divorce or separation lived together as strangers or in deep conflict. Thus, the increase in divorce statistics as such is no proof of family breakdown. In some respects, it is proof that people care enough about the contents and quality of family life and marriage to be willing to dissolve an unsatisfactory marriage (and commonly to replace it with a more successful one).

Much anxiety has also been expressed over the increase in the proportion of couples living together unmarried, over homosexual partners or parents, and over a whole variety of alternative family forms and life styles. What we are witnessing in all these varieties of life styles are not necessarily new inventions. Many different forms have been in existence all along, but they have been less visible. The more recent forms of alternative life styles have now become part of the official fiber of society, because they are now being tolerated much more than in the past. In short, what we are witnessing is not a fragmentation of traditional family patterns, but, rather, the emergence of a pluralism in family ways.

Thus, from a long-range perspective, the greatest concerns over family life in America need not be divorce, the declining birth rate, or alternative life styles. Of much greater concern for the future, and especially for policy, should be the problem of the isolation of the elderly and the inability of families in all ages to cope with inflation and with diminishing resources.

The historical lesson is valuable in demonstrating the extent to which a variety of traditional family ways and continuities with the past are still surviving in American society today. It is particularly helpful in revealing the salient role of surrogate families (taking in boarders and lodgers), as well as in emphasizing the effectiveness of kinship ties in coping with migration, economic insecurity, and personal family crises. The persistence of kinship ties as a major source of support has been a source of resilience and strength in urban neighborhoods. This rediscovery of the strength of kin should not lead us, however, to a new myth of self-reliance. It would be a mistake to assume that the fact that family members are helping each other in times of crisis means that families should be left to take care of their own. The historical experience also suggests the high price that family members had to pay in order to support their kin and help aging parents. The pressures on the nuclear family today, combined with economic and technological stresses, would make it difficult if not impossible for families to sustain continued assistance and support for their kin, especially for aging relatives.

A creative and constructive family policy will have to take into consideration, therefore, both the survival of support networks among kin and the escalating pressures on individuals and families. Such a policy, by necessity, will have to provide public programs and assistance where informal support networks fall short. It will also need to strengthen kinship and neighborhood support networks without bureaucratizing them.

## ACKNOWLEDGMENTS

An earlier version of this chapter was prepared for the Research Forum on Family Issues, White House Conference on Families, April 1980.

I am grateful to Kathleen Adams for her editorial help.

# REFERENCES

Anderson, M. *Family structure in nineteenth-century Lancashire.* Cambridge, England: Cambridge University Press, 1971.

Aries, P. [*Centuries of childhood*] (R. Baldick, trans.). New York: Knopf, 1962.

Aries, P. [*The hour of our death*] (H. Weaver, trans.). New York: Knopf, 1981.

Bremner, R. H., Barnard, J., Hareven, T. K., & Mennel, R. M. (Eds.). *Children and youth in America* (3 vols.). Cambridge: Harvard University Press, 1970-1974.

Chudacoff, H. P., & Hareven, T. K. The later years of life and the family cycle. In T. K. Hareven (Ed.), *Transitions: The family and the life course in historical perspective.* New York: Academic Press, 1978.

Davis, K. The American family in relation to demographic change. In C. F. Westoff & R. Parke, Jr. (Eds.), *Demographic and social aspects of population growth.* Washington, D.C.: U.S. Government Printing Office, 1972.

Demos, J. *A little commonwealth: Family life in Plymouth Colony.* New York: Oxford University Press, 1970.

Dublin, T. *Women at work: The transformation of work and community in Lowell, Massachusetts, 1826-1860.* New York: Columbia University Press, 1979.

Glick, P. C. The family cycle. *American Sociological Review,* 1947, *12,* 164-174.

Glick, P. C. The life cycle of the family. *Marriage and Family Living,* 1955, *18,* 3-9.

Glick, P. C. *American families.* New York: Wiley, 1957.

Glick, P. C. Updating the life cycle of the family. *Journal of Marriage and the Family,* 1977, *39,* 5-13.

Glick, P. C., & Parke, R., Jr. New approaches in studying the life cycle of the family. *Demography,* 1965, *2,* 187-212.

Goode, W. J. *World revolution and family patterns.* New York: Macmillan, Free Press, 1969.

Greven, P. *Four generations: Population, land, and family in colonial Andover, Massachusetts.* Ithaca, N.Y.: Cornell University Press, 1970.

Hareven, T. K. The history of the family as an interdisciplinary field. *Journal of Interdisciplinary History,* 1971, *2,* 399-414.

Hareven, T. K. The family as process: The historical study of the family cycle. *Journal of Social History,* 1974, *7,* 322-329.

Hareven, T. K. Family time and historical time. *Daedalus,* Spring 1977, pp. 57-70.

Hareven, T. K. The dynamics of kin in an industrial community. In J. Demos & S. Boocock (Eds.), *Turning points.* Supplement to *American Journal of Sociology,* 1978, *84.*

Hareven, T. K. *Family time and industrial time.* New York: Cambridge University Press, 1982 forthcoming.

Hareven, T. K., & Modell, J. Ethnic families. In S. Thernstrom (Ed.), *Harvard encyclopedia of American ethnic groups.* Cambridge: Harvard University Press, 1980.

Jeffrey, K. The family as Utopian retreat from the city: The nineteenth-century contribution. In S. TeSelle (Ed.), *The family, communes, and Utopian societies.* New York: Harper & Row, 1972.

Kenniston, E., & Kenniston, K. An American anachronism: The image of women and work. *American Scholar,* 1964, *33,* 353-375.

Kett, J. H. Growing up in rural New England, 1800-1840. In T. K. Hareven (Ed.), *Anonymous Americans: Explorations in nineteenth century social history.* Englewood Cliffs, N.J.: Prentice-Hall, 1971.

Kobrin, F. The fall in household size and the rise in the primary individual in the United States. *Demography,* 1976, *13,* 127-138.

Laslett, P. *The world we have lost.* London: Methuen, 1965.

Laslett, P., & Wall, R. (Eds.). *Household and family in past time.* Cambridge, England: Cambridge University Press, 1972.

Lerner, G. The lady and the mill girl. *Mid-Continent American Studies Journal,* 1969, *10,* 5-14.

Modell, J., Furstenberg, F., & Hershberg, T. Social change and transitions to adulthood in historical perspective. *Journal of Family History,* 1976, *1,* 7-32.

Modell, J., & Hareven, T. K. Urbanization and the malleable household: An examination of boarding and lodging in American families. *Journal of Marriage and the Family,* 1973, *35,* 467-478.

Parsons, T., & Bales, R. F. *Family socialization and interaction process.* Glencoe, Ill.: Free Press, 1955.

Scott, A. F. *The Southern lady: From pedestal to politics, 1830-1930.* Chicago: University of Chicago Press, 1970.

Sennett, R. *Families against the city: Middle-class homes of industrial Chicago, 1872-1890.* Cambridge: Harvard University Press, 1971.

Smith, D. S. Family limitation, sexual control, and domestic feminism in Victorian America. In M. S. Hartman & L. Banner (Eds.), *Clio's consciousness raised: New perspectives on the history of women.* New York: Harper & Row, 1974.

Smuts, R. W. *Women and work in America.* New York: Columbia University Press, 1959.

Sweet, J. *Women in the labor force.* New York: Academic Press, 1973.

Taeuber, I. B. Change and transition in family structures. In *The family in transition* (Fogarty International Center Proceedings). Washington, D.C.: U.S. Government Printing Office, 1969.

Tilly, L., & Scott, J. *Women, work, and family.* New York: Holt, Rinehart & Winston, 1978.

Uhlenberg, P. R. A study of cohort life cycles: Cohorts of native-born Massachusetts women, 1830-1920. *Population Studies,* 1969, *23,* 407-420.

Uhlenberg, P. R. Cohort variations in family life cycle experiences of United States females. *Journal of Marriage and the Family,* 1974, *36,* 284-292.

Wells, R. V. Demographic change and the life cycle of American families. *Journal of Interdisciplinary History,* 1971, *2,* 273-282.

Welter, B. The cult of true womanhood, 1820-1860. *American Quarterly,* 1966, *18,* 151-174.

Yasuba, Y. *Birth rates of the white population in the United States, 1800-1860.* Baltimore: Johns Hopkins University Press, 1961.

Young, M. D., & Wilmott, P. *The symmetrical family: A study of work and leisure in the London region.* London: Routledge & Kegan Paul, 1973.

# AUTHOR INDEX

# SUBJECT INDEX